ETHICAL ISSUES
IN BUSINESS

ETHICAL ISSUES IN BUSINESS

MICHAEL BOYLAN

Marymount University

HARCOURT BRACE COLLEGE PUBLISHERS

FORT WORTH   PHILADELPHIA   SAN DIEGO   NEW YORK   ORLANDO   AUSTIN   SAN ANTONIO
TORONTO   MONTREAL   LONDON   SYDNEY   TOKYO

Publisher	TED BUCHHOLZ
Senior Acquisitions Editor	DAVID TATOM
Developmental Editor	J. CLAIRE BRANTLEY
Project Editors	KAREN ANDERSON/ANGELA WILLIAMS
Senior Production Manager	TAD GAITHER
Art Director	BURL SLOAN

Address for Editorial Correspondence
Harcourt Brace College Publishers
301 Commerce Street, Suite 3700
Fort Worth, Texas 76102

Address for Orders
Harcourt Brace and Company
6277 Sea Harbor Drive
Orlando, FL 32887
1-800-782-4479, or
1-800-433-0001 (in Florida)

ISBN: 0-15-501442-0

Library of Congress Catalogue Number: 94-76727

Printed in the United States of America

4 5 6 7 8 9 0 1 2 3   016   9 8 7 6 5 4 3 2 1

PREFACE

Business ethics is a relatively new area of academic analysis. It links two rather disparate subjects—philosophy and business. They are odd partners because philosophy emphasizes theoretical speculation about principles and business tends to focus on the most efficient way to bring about some action. The tension between theory and practice is older than Aristotle, and the study of business ethics must avoid leaning toward either extreme. *Ethical Issues in Business* stays within the developing business ethics tradition but suggests new directions for its further growth. The book's five parts, divided into sixteen chapters, address the major concerns in a useful format for the college classroom.

Ethical Issues in Business has several goals. First, it offers a sample of outstanding contemporary readings on business ethics. It aims to combine readings that are particularly strong in either business or philosophy with readings that successfully address both concerns. The choice of selections is meant to stimulate the reader to think about some of the important problems of business in a balanced way, recognizing the demands of both theory and practice. This book includes articles from academic journals, both ethics and business, as well as from the popular press. This mix is intended to provide a perspective that balances scholarly approaches and the general population's attitudes toward the crucial issues in business ethics.

Second, *Ethical Issues in Business* presents a new approach to "case studies" and a pedagogical apparatus for integrating the theoretical and practical issues that concern typical corporate employees. Case studies in business schools typically work through business management decisions. To this end, there is an emphasis on simulating all of the economic and market factors present when a crucial decision was made.

Ethical case studies are different: Mastery of the prescriptive scenario is of more importance than mastery of the descriptive. This important difference requires that the ethical case study be targeted at a single individual in the given situation, allowing the reader to see the problem from a single perspective. This book also offers a series of essays directing students to respond to the case studies. These essays assist students step-by-step in (a) analyzing the problem into the practical and ethical components, (b) weighing the competing factors, (c) finding an ethical position, (d) applying the position, (e) coming up with a solution, and (f) expressing that solution in the form of a written report.

Third, this book offers two levels of case studies; half are written for analysis at the macro level of the CEO and half at the micro level of a mid-level manager or line employee. Traditionally, case studies have focused on heads of corporations. These important perspectives are represented in the macro case studies. However, most students will find themselves in the position of the ordinary employee one day. And, because important ethical dilemmas occur at this level as well, these issues are addressed in the micro level cases.

Ethical Issues in Business also offers a real-world dimension to business ethics through original interviews with prominent figures who offer insights into the interplay between business and ethics. These interviews demonstrate that the theoretical concerns of scholars are important to the real, corporate world.

Fourth, the theoretical section of this textbook goes beyond the great thinkers to provide a feedback mechanism to aid students in applying the salient features of the important ethical theories. Part 1 of *Ethical Issues in Business* presents readings from both the business world and the world of philosophy on the traditional ethical systems: Virtue Ethics, Intuitionism, Utilitarianism, and Deontology. Other business ethics books do not generally supply help to students who lack a background in the analysis of difficult theoretical material. Students often have problems translating the theories into action.

This book provides ethical checklists to answer this problem. The checklists help students make the transition from an abstract set of problems to a plan for action to use in the case studies and in their daily lives.

Finally, *Ethical Issues in Business* places a greater emphasis on perspectives from outside the Western tradition and perspectives from women. All segments of our society are potentially affected by problems in the workplace. One could write an entire book addressing business problems related to gender and race. *Ethical Issues in Business* takes a modest step in the direction of highlighting some of these issues within the larger context. Multicultural perspectives are increasingly important as the corporate world becomes a global marketplace; this book emphasizes topics that will stimulate discussion in this direction.

Every new book requires the work of not only the author but a great many others, and I would like to acknowledge their help. I would like to thank my students at Loyola, Marquette, Georgetown, and Marymount. Their reactions to my classes in ethical theory and applied ethics (including business ethics) have shaped my ideas on what works in the classroom. I would also like to thank those who contributed original material to this book: Roderick DeArment, Richard Grant, Linda Chavez, and S. Janakiram appear as subjects of the interview sections; Jane Ubelhoer and Thomas Donaldson prepared readings especially for *Ethical Issues in Business.*

A word of thanks is also due to the reviewers: John B. Dilworth, Western Michigan University; Harold Greenstein, State University of New York at Brockport; Joan Whitman Hoff, Lock Haven University; Lisa Newton, Fairfield University; Thomas Oberdan, Clemson University; and Robert M. Stewart, California State University at Chico.

I also appreciate the assistance I received from Harcourt Brace College Publishers—David Tatom, Claire Brantley, Karen Anderson, Burl Sloan, and Tad Gaither have all made this a better textbook.

Finally, I thank my family: my wife Rebecca and my children Arianne, Seán, and Éamon. Their patience, love, and support nourishes everything I do.

To my mother and father—
my first teachers in ethics

ONTENTS

PART 4 GOVERNMENT ISSUES   **427**

CHAPTER 13 REGULATION   **428**

CHAPTER 14 THE GOVERNMENT'S ROLE IN ECONOMIC
JUSTICE   **456**

PART 5 INTERNATIONAL ISSUES   503

ETHICAL ISSUES
IN BUSINESS

Ethical Theory

▶ **Virtue Ethics**
▶ **Intuitionism**
▶ **Utilitarianism**
▶ **Deontology**

$\mathcal{E}$THICAL THEORY: AN OVERVIEW

This first section of the reader deals with Ethical Theory. The reason why ethical theory needs to be studied in an applied ethics text is because it is the tool that allows you, the student, to make a reasoned judgment about ethical situations.* An ethical theory is an account of *what* is right and wrong in human action and *why*.†

The *what* requires a decision making process whereby the adherent can: 1. Analyze a situation into its elements; 2. Assess which elements are most important; 3. Calculate the moral dimensions of the important elements so that a determinate outcome is reached; 4. Re-apply the conclusions of #3 back into the case so that a judgment is reached and the resultant action carried out.

The mechanics of 1–4 above are dealt with in the "Writing the Report" essays found near the end of each section. What concerns us here is obtaining facility with each of the ethical theories presented: virtue ethics, intuitionism, utilitarianism, and deontology. This facility will allow you to understand how each theory can be applied to actual cases.

Each theory is different in the way that it categorizes the right and wrong in human action. Some of this distinctive character can be seen in the *why* or justification of each. Justification refers to those principles to which we appeal for acceptance of the theory. When we study an ethical theory, part of our understanding is the rationale for accepting it in the first place. You must decide which justification is most plausible. It is important to reason in this way because you must make choices among competing theories. Different theories will often suggest different actions or at least different reasons for why one outcome was chosen over another.

When writing a case assessment report you must take the point of view of a single ethical theory (or some combination that remains internally consistent) and use the tenets of this theory to support your outcomes recommendation.

Some students ask whether the fact that there are several varieties of ethical theory means that there are no universally correct theories. Such a

---

*This text, whilve generally concerned with *practice* is also concerned with the rules which underlie the "action-oriented"—i.e., practical, prescriptions. As Aristotle says in the *Posterior Analytics* I.1 there must be a stopping place for demonstration. The discussion of the "stopping place" is the subject matter of this section of text.

†It should be noted that there are many ways to parce the realm of *ta ethica*. Some readers may wish to adhere to the traditional distinction of *normative* vrs. *meta* ethics. This has been an important distinction throughout this century [and, by extension, a distinction that has always existed—whether recognized or not]. In brief, since this is an introductory text, this distinction is not highlighted in all the detail that a text on ethical theory would demand. However, let it suffice to students of this text, that "normative ethics" or that which is proximately concerned with the "ought" should stand separate from "meta-ethics" which is concerned with the procedure by which one determines the correctness of various methodological procedures of discussing ethical questions. This is similar to the distinction between philosophy of science and the actual practice of science.

relativistic view suggests either: (a) all theories are flawed, ergo; no theory is correct; or (b) since there are many theories, each is equally correct and the choice among them is merely random or accidental.

Most proponents of a particular ethical theory would reject both (a) and (b). Their argument against (a) is often an apology for their own theory. They believe the attackers to be wrong. By creating a counterattack, it is thought that no damage is done. It is sometimes pointed out that any process which "grows" through the critical process of philosophical examination is stronger and probably closer to Truth than it would have been without the searching criticism. Thus, the existence of arguments against any particular theory portends nothing more than that the theory has garnered critical attention. This attention, in and of itself, does not make the theory any more or less true. A judgment of this sort must be made by students of the debates who decide for themselves which is the better theory.

Likewise, in (b) it could be argued that the fact that there is variation among competing theories does not in and of itself imply that any one of the theories is right or wrong. There may be a single "correct" ethical theory. Whether there is or isn't, is determined via the theory's justification. If a theory is logically sound, and if we seek to be ruled by reason, then we are compelled to follow the action guiding conclusions of our chosen theory.

In the readings within this section of the book you will see three sorts of input that may help you with your decision. The first is a group of philosophical reflections by authors who have made significant contributions to that type of ethical theory. Second, is input from the perspective of business ethics. This second level is not as theoretical as the first, but does address some problems in the application of theories consistent with those presented in the section to business problems. Third, is a checklist that can make it easier to see just how one might apply the given theory to actual problems. This checklist can be used in conjunction with the "Writing the Report" essays as a guide for your own essays that you will have to write during the term.

One final note—though the various ethical theories are separated very distinctly in their presentation within this text, it still should be noted that some mixing of theories can and does go on. For example, though Ross employs an intuitionistic justification for his theory, he also emphasizes the role of duty in ethics. This makes him a deontologist as well. This overlap does not create internal inconsistency so that it is permitted. What would not be permitted would be mixing inconsistent tenets. For example, if one were a utilitarian who believed that the right action was the one which produced the highest aggregate happiness, then one could not mix this with a theory which disregards consequences or "aggregation of happiness."

CHAPTER 1

Virtue Ethics

▼ The Philosophical Perspective

Nicomachean Ethics

Aristotle

Book I

Every art and every inquiry, and similarly every action and pursuit, is thought to aim at some good; and for this reason the good has rightly been declared to be that at which all things aim. But a certain difference is found among ends; some are activities, others are products apart from the activities that produce them. Where there are ends apart from the actions, it is the nature of the products to be better than the activities. Now, as there are many actions, arts, and sciences, their ends also are many; the end of the medical art is health, that of shipbuilding a vessel, that of strategy victory, that of economics wealth. But where such arts fall under a single capacity—as bridle-making and the other arts concerned with the equipment of horses fall under the art of riding, and this and every military action under strategy, in the same way other arts fall under yet others—in all of these the ends of the master arts are to be preferred to all the subordinate ends; for it is for the sake of the former that the latter are pursued. It makes no difference whether the

Aristotle, *Ethica Nicomachea* tr. W.D. Ross. (Oxford: Ox University Press). 1094^{a}1–16; 1097^{a}15–1098^b, 1106^{a}15–1108^{b}10.

activities themselves are the ends of the actions, or something else apart from the activities, as in the case of the sciences just mentioned.

*   *   *

Let us again return to the good we are seeking, and ask what it can be. It seems different in different actions and arts; it is different in medicine, in strategy, and in the other arts likewise. What then is the good of each? Surely that for whose sake everything else is done. In medicine this is health, in strategy victory, in architecture a house, in any other sphere something else, and in every action and pursuit the end; for it is for the sake of this that all men do whatever else they do. Therefore, if there is an end for all that we do, this will be the good achievable by action, and if there are more than one, these will be the goods achievable by action.

So the argument has by a different course reached the same point; but we must try to state this even more clearly. Since there are evidently more than one end, and we choose some of these (e.g. wealth, flutes, and in general instruments) for the sake of something else, clearly not all ends are final ends; but the chief good is evidently something final. Therefore, if there is only one final end, this will be what we are seeking, and if there are more than one, the most final of these will be what we are seeking. Now we call that which is in itself worthy of pursuit more final than that which is worthy of pursuit for the sake of something else, and that which is never desirable for the sake of something else more final than the things that are desirable both in themselves and for the sake of that other thing, and therefore we call final without qualification that which is always desirable in itself and never for the sake of something else.

Now such a thing happiness, above all else, is held to be; for this we choose always for itself and never for the sake of something else, but honour, pleasure, reason, and every virtue we choose indeed for themselves (for if nothing resulted from them we should still choose each of them), but we choose them also for the sake of happiness, judging that by means of them we shall be happy. Happiness, on the other hand, no one chooses for the sake of these, nor, in general, for anything other than itself.

From the point of view of self-sufficiency the same result seems to follow; for the final good is thought to be self-sufficient. Now by self-sufficient we do not mean that which is sufficient for a man by himself, for one who lives a solitary life, but also for parents, children, wife, and in general for his friends and fellow citizens, since man is born for citizenship. But some limit must be set to this; for if we extend our requirement to ancestors and descendants and friends' friends we are in for an infinite series. Let us examine this question, however, on another occasion,[1] the self-sufficient we now define as that which when isolated makes life desirable and lacking in nothing; and such we think happiness to be; and further we think it most desirable of all things, without being counted as one good thing among others—if it were so counted it would clearly be made more desirable by the addition of even the least of goods; for that which is added becomes an excess of goods, and of goods the greater is always more desirable. Happiness, then, is something final and self-sufficient, and is the end of action.

Presumably, however, to say that happiness is the chief good seems a platitude, and a clearer account of what it is is still desired. This might perhaps be given, if we could first ascertain the function of man. For just as for a flute-player, a sculptor, or any artist, and, in general, for all things that have a function or activity, the good and the 'well' is thought to reside in the function, so would it seem to be for man, if he has a function. Have the carpenter, then, and the tanner certain functions or activities, and has man none? Is he born without a function? Or as eye, hand, foot, and in general each of the parts evidently has a function, may one lay it down that man similarly has a function apart from all these? What then can this be? Life seems to be common even to plants, but we are seeking what is peculiar to man. Let us exclude, therefore, the life of nutrition and growth. Next there would be a life of perception, but *it* also seems to be common even to the horse, the ox, and every animal. There remains, then, an active life of the element that has a rational principle; of this, one part has such a principle in the sense of being obedient to one, the other in the sense of possessing one and exercising thought. And, as 'life of the rational element' also has two meanings, we must state that life in the sense of activity is what we mean; for this seems to be the more proper sense of the term. Now if the function of man is an activity of soul which follows or implies a rational principle, and if we say 'a so-and-so' and 'a good so-and-so' have a function which is the same in kind, e.g. a lyre-player and a good lyre-player, and so without qualification in all cases, eminence in respect of goodness being added to the name of the function (for the function of a lyre-player is to play the lyre, and that of a good lyre-player is to do so well): if this is the case, [and we state the function of man to be a certain kind of life, and this to be an activity or actions of the soul implying a rational principle, and the function of a good man to be the good and noble performance of these, and if any action is well performed when it is performed in accordance with the appropriate excellence: if this is the case,] human good turns out to be activity of soul in accordance with virtue, and if there are more than one virtue, in accordance with the best and most complete.

But we must add 'in a complete life'. For one swallow does not make a summer, nor does one day; and so too one day, or a short time, does not make a man blessed and happy.

Let this serve as an outline of the good; for we must presumably first sketch it roughly, and then later fill in the details. But it would seem that any one is capable of carrying on and articulating what has once been well outlined, and that time is a good discoverer or partner in such a work; to which facts the advances of the arts are due; for any one can add what is lacking. And we must also remember what has been said before,[2] and not look for precision in all things alike, but in each class of things such precision as accords with the subject-matter, and so much as is appropriate to the inquiry. For a carpenter and a geometer investigate the right angle in different ways; the former does so in so far as the right angle is useful for his work, while the latter inquires what it is or what sort of thing it is; for he is a spectator of the truth. We must act in the same way, then, in all other matters as well, that our main task may not be subordinated to minor questions. Nor must we demand the cause in all matters alike; it is enough in some cases that the *fact* be well established, as in the case of the first principles; the fact is the primary thing or first principle. Now of first principles we see some by induction, some by perception, some by a certain habituation, and others too in other ways. But each set of principles we must try to investigate in the natural way, and we must take pains to state them definitely, since they have a great influence on what follows. For the beginning is thought to be more than half of the whole, and many of the questions we ask are cleared up by it.

Book II

Next we must consider what virtue is. Since things that are found in the soul are of three kinds—passions, faculties, states of character, virtue must be one of these. By passions I mean appetite, anger, fear, confidence, envy, joy, friendly feeling, hatred, longing, emulation, pity, and in general the feelings that are accompanied by pleasure or pain; by faculties the things in virtue of which we are said to be capable of feeling these, e.g. of becoming angry or being pained or feeling pity; by states of character the things in virtue of which we stand well or badly with reference to the passions, e.g. with reference to anger we stand badly if we feel it violently or too weakly, and well if we feel it moderately; and similarly with reference to the other passions.

Now neither the virtues nor the vices are *passions,* because we are not called good or bad on the ground of our passions, but are so called on the ground of our virtues and our vices, and because we are neither praised nor blamed for our passions (for the man who feels fear or anger is not praised, nor is the man who simply feels anger blamed, but the man who feels it in a certain way), but for our virtues and our vices we *are* praised or blamed.

Again, we feel anger and fear without choice, but the virtues are modes of choice or involve choice. Further, in respect of the passions we are said to be moved, but in respect of the virtues and the vices we are said not to be moved but to be disposed in a particular way.

For these reasons also they are not *faculties;* for we are neither called good nor bad, nor praised nor blamed, for the simple capacity of feeling the passions; again, we have the faculties by nature, but we are not made good or bad by nature; we have spoken of this before.[3]

If, then, the virtues are neither passions nor faculties, all that remains is that they should be *states of character.*

Thus we have stated what virtue is in respect of its genus.

We must, however, not only describe virtue as a state of character, but also say what sort of state it is. We may remark, then, that every virtue or excellence both brings into good condition the thing of which it is the excellence and makes the work of that thing be done well; e.g. the excellence of the eye makes both the eye and its work good; for it is by the excellence of the eye that we see well. Similarly the excellence of the horse makes a horse both good in itself and good at running and at carrying its rider and at awaiting the attack of the enemy. Therefore, if this is true in every case, the virtue of man also will be the state of character which makes a man good and which makes him do his own work well.

How this is to happen we have stated already,[4] but it will be made plain also by the following consideration of the specific nature of virtue. In everything that is continuous and divisible it is possible to take more, less, or an equal amount, and that either in terms of the thing itself or relatively to us; and the equal is an intermediate between excess and defect. By the intermediate in the object I mean that which is equidistant from each of the extremes, which is one and the same for all men; by the intermediate relatively to us that which is neither too much nor too little—and this is not one, nor the same for all. For instance, if ten is many and two is few, six is the intermediate, taken in terms of the object; for it exceeds and is exceeded by an equal amount; this is intermediate according to arithmetical proportion. But the intermediate relatively to us is not to be taken so; if ten pounds are too much for a particular person to eat and two too little, it does not follow that the trainer will order six pounds; for this also is perhaps too much for the person who is to take it, or too little—too little for Milo,[5] too much for the beginner in athletic exercises. The same is true of running and wrestling. Thus a master of any art avoids excess and defect, but seeks the intermediate and chooses this—the intermediate not in the object but relatively to us.

If it is thus, then, that every art does its work well—by looking to the intermediate and judging its works by this standard (so that we often say of good works of art that it is not possible either to take away or to add anything, implying that excess and defect destroy the goodness of works of art, while the mean preserves it; and good artists, as we say, look to this in their work), and if, further, virtue is more exact and better than any art, as nature also is, then virtue must have the quality of aiming at the intermediate. I mean moral virtue; for it is this that is concerned with passions and actions, and in these there is excess, defect, and the intermediate. For instance, both fear and confidence and appetite and anger and pity and in general pleasure and pain may be felt both too much and too little, and in both cases not well; but to feel them at the right times, with reference to the right objects, towards the right people, with the right motive, and in the right way, is what is both intermediate and best, and this is characteristic of virtue. Similarly with regard to actions also there is excess, defect, and the intermediate. Now virtue is concerned with passions and actions, in which excess is a form of failure, and so is defect, while the intermediate is praised and is a form of success; and being praised and being successful are both characteristics of virtue. Therefore virtue is a kind of mean, since, as we have seen, it aims at what is intermediate.

Again, it is possible to fail in many ways (for evil belongs to the class of the unlimited, as the Pythagoreans conjectured, and good to that of the limited), while to succeed is possible only in one way (for which reason also one is easy and the other difficult—to miss the mark easy, to hit it difficult); for these reasons also, then, excess and defect are characteristic of vice, and the mean of virtue;

For men are good in but one way, but bad in many.

Virtue, then, is a state of character concerned with choice, lying in a mean, i.e. the mean relative to us, this being determined by a rational principle, and by that principle by which the man of practical wisdom would determine it. Now it is a mean between two vices, that which depends on excess and that which depends on defect; and again it is a mean because the vices respectively fall short of or exceed what is right in both passions and actions, while virtue both finds and chooses that which is intermediate. Hence in respect of its substance and the definition which states its essence virtue is a mean, with regard to what is best and right an extreme.

But not every action nor every passion admits of a mean; for some have names that already imply badness, e.g. spite, shamelessness, envy, and in the case of actions adultery, theft, murder; for all of these and suchlike things imply by their names that they are themselves bad, and not the excesses or deficiencies of them. It is not possible, then, ever to be right with regard to them; one must always be wrong. Nor does goodness or badness with regard to such things depend on committing adultery with the right woman, at the right time, and in the right way, but simply to do any of them is to go wrong. It would be equally absurd, then, to expect that in unjust, cowardly, and voluptuous action there should be a mean, an excess, and a deficiency; for at that rate there would be a mean of excess and of deficiency, an excess of excess, and a deficiency of deficiency. But as there is no excess and deficiency of temperance and courage because what is intermediate is in a sense an extreme, so too of the actions we have mentioned there is no mean nor any excess and deficiency, but however they are done they are wrong; for in general there is neither a mean of excess and deficiency, nor excess and deficiency of a mean.

We must, however, not only make this general statement, but also apply it to the individual facts. For among statements about conduct those which are general apply more widely, but those which are particular are more genuine, since conduct has to do with individual cases, and our statements must harmonize with the facts in these cases. We may take these cases from our table. With regard to feelings of fear and confidence courage is the mean; of the people who exceed, he who exceeds in fearlessness has no name (many of the states have no name), while the man who exceeds in confidence is rash, and he who exceeds in fear and falls short in confidence is a coward. With regard to pleasures and pains—not all of them, and not so much with regard to the pains—the mean is temperance, the excess self-indulgence. Persons deficient with regard to the pleasures are not often found; hence such persons also have received no name. But let us call them 'insensible'.

With regard to giving and taking of money the mean is liberality, the excess and the defect prodigality and meanness. In these actions people exceed and fall short in contrary ways; the prodigal exceeds in spending and falls short in taking, while the mean man exceeds in taking and falls short in spending. (At present we are giving a mere outline or summary, and are satisfied with this; later these states will be more exactly determined.[6]) With regard to money there are also other dispositions—a mean, magnificence (for the magnificent man differs from the liberal man; the former deals with large sums, the latter with small ones), an excess, tastelessness and vulgarity, and a deficiency, niggardliness; these differ from the states opposed to liberality, and the mode of their difference will be stated later.[7]

With regard to honour and dishonour the mean is proper pride, the excess is known as a sort of 'empty vanity', and the deficiency is undue humility; and as we said[8] liberality was related to magnificence, differing from it by dealing with small sums, so there is a state similarly related to proper pride, being concerned with small honours while that is concerned with great. For it is possible to desire honour as one ought, and more than one ought, and less, and the man who exceeds in his desires is called ambitious, the man who falls short unambitious, while the intermediate person has no name. The dispositions also are nameless, except that that of the ambitious man is called ambition. Hence the people who are at the extremes lay claim to the middle place; and we ourselves sometimes call the intermediate person ambitious and sometimes unambitious, and sometimes praise the ambitious man and sometimes the unambitious. The reason of our doing this will be stated in what follows;[9] but now let us speak of the remaining states according to the method which has been indicated.

With regard to anger also there is an excess, a deficiency, and a mean. Although they can scarcely be said to have names, yet since we call the intermediate person good-tempered let us call the mean good temper; of the persons at the extremes let the one who exceeds be called irascible, and his vice irascibility, and the man who falls short an inirascible sort of person, and the deficiency inirascibility.

There are also three other means, which have a certain likeness to one another, but differ from one another: for they are all concerned with intercourse in words and actions, but differ in that one is concerned with truth in this sphere, the other two with pleasantness; and of this one kind is exhibited in giving amusement, the other in all the circumstances of life. We must therefore speak of these too, that we may the better see that in all things the mean is praiseworthy, and the extremes neither praiseworthy nor right, but worthy of blame. Now most of these states also have no names, but we must try, as in the other cases, to invent names ourselves so that we may be clear and easy to follow. With regard to truth, then, the intermediate is a truthful sort of person and the mean may be called truthfulness, while the pretence which exaggerates is boastfulness and the person characterized by it a boaster, and that which understates is mock modesty and the person characterized by it mock-modest. With regard to pleasantness in the giving of amusement the intermediate person is ready-witted and the disposition ready wit, the excess is buffoonery and the person characterized by it a buffoon, while the man who falls short is a sort of boor and his state is boorishness. With regard to the remaining kind of pleasantness, that which is exhibited in life in general, the man who is pleasant in the right way is friendly and the mean is friendliness, while the man who exceeds is an obsequious person if he has no end in view, a flatterer if he is aiming at his own advantage, and the man who falls short and is unpleasant in all circumstances is a quarrelsome and surly sort of person.

There are also means in the passions and concerned with the passions; since shame is not a virtue, and yet praise is extended to the modest man. For even in these matters one man is said to be intermediate, and another to exceed, as for instance the bashful man who is ashamed of everything; while he who falls short or is not ashamed of anything at all is shameless, and the intermediate person is modest. Righteous indignation is a mean between envy and spite, and these states are concerned with the pain and pleasures that are felt at the fortunes of our neighbours; the man who is characterized by righteous indignation is pained at undeserved good fortune, the envious man, going beyond him, is pained at all good fortune, and the spiteful man falls so far short of being pained that he even rejoices. But these states there will be an opportunity of describing elsewhere;[10] with regard to justice, since it has not one simple meaning, we shall, after describing the other states, distinguish its two kinds and say how each of them is a mean;[11] and similarly we shall treat also of the rational virtues.[12]

Notes

1. i. 10, 11, ix. 10.
2. 1094^b 11–27.
3. 1103^a 18-^{b} 2.
4. 1104^a 11–27.
5. A famous wrestler.
6. iv. 1.
7. 1122^a 20–9,^{b} 10–18.
8. ll. 17–19.
9. ^{b}11–26, 1125^b 14–18.
10. The reference may be to the whole treatment of the moral virtues in iii. 6-iv. 9, or to the discussion of shame in iv. 9 and an intended corresponding discussion of righteous indignation, or to the discussion of these two states in *Rhet*. ii. 6, 9, 10.
11. 1129^a 26-^{b}1; 1130^{a}14-^{b}5; 1131^b 9–15; Bk vi.
12. 1132^a 24–30; 1133^{b}30–1134^{a}1.

Summa Theologica

St. Thomas Aquinas

Question LV

On the Virtues, as to Their Essence

(In Four Articles)

We come now to a particular consideration of habits. And since habits, as we have said, are divided into good and bad,[1] we must speak in the first place of good habits, which are virtues, and of other matters connected with them, namely, the Gifts, Beatitudes and Fruits,[2] in the second place, of bad habits, namely, of vices and sins.[3] Now five things must be considered about virtues: (1) the essence of virtue; (2) its subject;[4] (3) the division of the virtues;[5] (4) the cause of virtue;[6] (5) certain properties of virtue.[7]

Under the first head, there are four points of inquiry: (1) Whether human virtue is a habit? (2) Whether it is an operative habit? (3) Whether it is a good habit? (4) The definition of virtue.

First Article

Whether Human Virtue Is a Habit?

We proceed thus to the First Article:—

Objection 1. It would seem that human virtue is not a habit. For virtue is *the peak of power*.[8] But the peak of anything is reducible to the genus of that of which it is the peak, as a point is reducible to the genus of line. Therefore virtue is reducible to the genus of power, and not to the genus of habit.

Obj. 2. Further, Augustine says that *virtue is good use of free choice*.[9] But use of free choice is an act. Therefore virtue is not a habit, but an act.

Obj. 3. Further, we do not merit by our habits, but by our actions, or otherwise a man would merit continually, even while asleep. But we do merit by our virtues. Therefore virtues are not habits, but acts.

Obj. 4. Further, Augustine says that *virtue is the order of love*,[10] and that *the ordering which is called virtue consists in enjoying what we ought to enjoy, and using what we ought to use*.[11] Now order, or ordering, denominates either an action or a relation. Therefore virtue is not a habit, but an action or a relation.

Obj. 5. Further, just as there are human virtues, so there are natural virtues. But natural virtues are not habits, but powers. Neither therefore are human virtues habits.

St. Thomas Aquinas. *Summa Theologica.* II–1 QLV, a1; QLVIII a1-a2; QLXI, a2 in *Basic Writings of St. Thomas Aquinas* vol 1 ed by Anton C. Pegis (N.Y.: Random House, 1945), pp. 560–62, 579, 581–2, 588–9.

On the contrary, The Philosopher says that *science and virtue are habits.*[12]

I answer that, Virtue denotes a certain perfection of a power. Now a thing's perfection is considered chiefly in relation to its end. But the end of power is act. Therefore power is said to be perfect according as it is determined to its act. Now there are some powers which of themselves are determined to their acts, for instance, the active natural powers. And therefore these natural powers are in themselves called virtues. But the rational powers, which are proper to man, are not determined to one particular action, but are inclined indifferently to many; but they are determined to acts by means of habits, as is clear from what we have said above.[13] Therefore human virtues are habits.

Reply Obj. 1. Sometimes we give the name of a virtue to that to which the virtue is directed, namely, either to its object or to its act. For instance, we give the name faith to that which we believe, or to the act of believing, as also to the habit by which we believe. When therefore we say that *virtue is the peak of power,* virtue is taken for the object of virtue. For the highest point to which a power can reach is said to be its virtue: for instance, if a man can carry a hundredweight and not more, his virtue [*i.e.,* his strength] is put at a hundredweight, and not at sixty. But the objection takes virtue as being essentially the peak of power.

Reply Obj. 2. Good use of free choice is said to be a virtue in the same sense as above, that is to say, because it is that to which virtue is directed as to its proper act. For an act of virtue is nothing else than the good use of free choice.

Reply Obj. 3. We are said to merit by something in two ways. First, as by merit itself, just as we are said to run by running; and thus we merit by acts. Secondly, we are said to merit by something as by the principle whereby we merit, as we are said to run by the power of locomotion; and thus are we said to merit by virtues and habits.

Reply Obj. 4. When we say that virtue is the order or ordering of love, we refer to the end to which virtue is ordered; because in us love is set in order by virtue.

Reply Obj. 5. Natural powers are of themselves determined to one act; not so the rational powers. Hence there is no comparison, as we have said.

Question LVIII

First Article

Distinction of Virtues

. . . The Philosopher says: *When we speak of a man's morals, we do not say that he is wise or intelligent, but that he is gentle or sober.* Accordingly, then, wisdom and understanding are not moral virtues; and yet they are virtues, as was stated above. Therefore, not every virtue is a moral virtue.

I answer that, In order to answer this question clearly, we must consider the meaning of the Latin word *mos,* for thus we shall be able to discover what *moral* virtue is. Now *mos* has a twofold meaning. For sometimes it means custom, in which sense we read (*Acts* xv. 1): *Except you be circumcised after the manner [morem] of Moses, you cannot be saved;* sometimes it means a natural or quasi-natural inclination to do some particular action, in which sense the word is applied to brute animals. Thus we read (2 *Macc.* xi. 11) that *rushing violently upon the enemy, like lions [leonum more], they slew them.* The word is used in the same sense is *Ps.* lxvii. 7, where we read: *Who maketh men of one manner [moris] to dwell in a house.* For both these significations there is but one word in Latin; but in Greek there is a distinct word for each, for the word *ethos,* which signifies the same as the Latin *mos,* is written sometimes with a long *e,* and is written η, and sometimes with a short *e,* and is written ε.

Now *moral* virtue is so called from *mos* in the sense of a natural or quasi-natural inclination to do some particular action. And the other meaning of *mos, i.e.,* custom, is akin to this, because custom somehow becomes a nature, and produces an inclination similar to a natural one. But it is evident that inclination to an action belongs properly to the appetitive power, whose function it is to move all the powers to their acts, as was explained above. Therefore not every virtue is a moral virtue, but only those that are in the appetitive power.

*   *   *

Second Article

Reason is the first principle of all human acts, and whatever other principles of human acts may be found, they obey reason in some way, but diversely. For some obey reason instantaneously and without any contradiction whatever. Such are the members of the body, provided they be in a healthy condition, for as soon as reason commands, the hand or the foot proceeds to action. Hence the Philosopher says that *the soul rules the body with a despotic rule,*[14] *i.e.,* as a master rules his slave, who has no right to rebel. Accordingly, some held that all the active principles in man are subordinate to reason in this way. If this were true, for a man to act well it would suffice that his reason be perfect. Consequently, since virtue is a habit perfecting man in view of his doing good actions, it would follow that virtue existed only in the reason, so that there would be none but intellectual virtues. This was the opinion of Socrates, who said *every virtue is a kind of prudence,* as is stated in *Ethics* vi.[15] Hence he maintained that as long as a man was in possession of knowledge, he could not sin, and that every one who sinned did so through ignorance.[16]

Now this is based on a false supposition. For the appetitive part obeys the reason, not instantaneously, but with a certain power of opposition; and so the Philosopher says that *reason commands the appetitive part by a political rule,*[17] whereby a man rules over subjects that are free, having a certain right of opposition. Hence Augustine says on *Ps.* cxviii. that *sometimes the intellect marks the way, while desire lags, or follows not at all,* so much so, that sometimes the habits or passions of the appetitive part cause the use of reason to be impeded in some particular action. And in this way, there is some truth in the saying of Socrates that so long as a man is in possession of knowledge he does not sin: provided, however, that this knowledge is made to include the use of reason in this individual act of choice.

Accordingly, for a man to do a good deed, it is requisite not only that his reason be well disposed by means of a habit of intellectual virtue, but also that his appetite be well disposed by means of a habit of moral virtue. And so moral differs from intellectual virtue, even as the appetite differs from the reason. Hence, just as the appetite is the principle of human acts, in so far as it partakes of reason, so moral habits are to be considered human virtues in so far as they are in conformity with reason.

*   *   *

Question LXI

Second Article

Whether There Are Four Cardinal Virtues?

We proceed thus to the Second Article:—

Objection 1. It would seem that there are not four cardinal virtues. For prudence is the directing principle of the other moral virtues, as is clear from what has been said above.[18] But that which directs others ranks before them. Therefore prudence alone is a principal virtue.

Obj. 2. Further, the principal virtues are, in a way, moral virtues. Now we are directed to moral works both by the practical reason and by a right appetite, as is stated in *Ethics* vi.[19] Therefore there are only two cardinal virtues.

Obj. 3. Further, even among the other virtues one ranks higher than another. But in order that a virtue be principal, it need not rank above all the others, but above some. Therefore it seems that there are many more principal virtues.

On the contrary, Gregory says: *The entire structure of good works is built on four virtues.*[20]

I answer that, Things may be numbered either in respect of their formal principles, or according to the subjects in which they are; and in either way we find that there are four cardinal virtues.

For the formal principle of the virtue of which we speak now is the good as defined by reason. This good can be considered in two ways. First, as existing in the consideration itself of reason, and thus we have one principal virtue called *prudence.*—Secondly, according as the reason puts its order into something else, and this either into operations, and then we have *justice,* or into passions, and then we need two virtues. For the need of putting the order of reason into the passions is due to their thwarting reason; and this occurs in two ways. First, when the passions incite to something against reason, and then they need a curb, which we thus call *temperance;* secondly, when the passions withdraw us from following the dictate of reason, *e.g.,* through fear of danger or toil, and then man needs to be strengthened for that which reason dictates, lest he turn back, and to this end there is *fortitude*.

In like manner, we find the same number if we consider the subjects of virtue. For there are four subjects of the virtue of which we now speak, viz., the power which is rational in its essence, and this is perfected by *prudence;* and that which is rational by participation, and is threefold, the will, subject of *justice,* the concupiscible power, subject of *temperance,* and the irascible power, subject of *fortitude.*

Reply Obj. 1. Prudence is absolutely the principal of all the virtues. The others are principal, each in its own genus.

Reply Obj. 2. That part of the soul which is rational by participation is threefold, as was stated above.

Reply Obj. 3. All the other virtues, among which one ranks before another, are reducible to the above four, both as to the subject and as to the formal principles.

Notes
1. Q. 54, a. 3.
2. Q. 68.
3. Q. 71.
4. Q. 56.
5. Q. 57.
6. Q. 63.
7. Q. 64.
8. Aristotle, *De Caelo,* I, 11 (281a 14; a 18).—Cf. St. Thomas, *In De Caelo,* I, lect. 25.
9. *De Lib. Arb.,* II, 19 (PL 32, 1268); *Retract.,* I, 9 (PL 32, 598).
10. *De Mor. Eccl.,* I, 15 (PL 32, 1322).
11. *Lib. 83 Quaest.,* q. 30 (PL 40, 19).
12. *Cat.,* VIII (8b 29).
13. Q. 49, a. 4.
14. *Polit.,* I, 2 (1254b 4).
15. Aristotle, *Eth.,* VI, 13 (1144b 19).
16. Cf. *op. cit.,* VII, 2 (1145b 23).—Cf. also Plato, *Protag.* (pp. 352B; 355A; 357B).
17. *Polit.,* I, 5 (1254b 4).
18. Q. 58, a. 4.
19. Aristotle, *Eth.,* VI, 2 (1139a 24).
20. *Moral.,* II, 49 (PL 75, 592).

After Virtue

Alasdair MacIntyre

Every activity, every enquiry, every practice aims at some good; for by 'the good' or 'a good' we mean that at which human beings characteristically aim.[1]

Alasdair MacIntyre, *After Virtue: A Study in Moral Theory* 2nd ed. (London: Duckworth, 1985), pp. 148–152.

It is important that Aristotle's initial arguments in the *Ethics* presuppose that what G.E. Moore was to call the 'naturalistic fallacy' is not a fallacy at all and that statements about what is good—and what is just or courageous or excellent in other ways—just are a kind of factual statement.[2] Human beings, like the members of all other species, have a specific nature; and that nature is such that they have certain aims and goals, such that they move by nature towards a specific *telos*. The good is defined in terms of their specific characteristics. Hence Aristotle's ethics, expounded as he expounds it, presupposes his metaphysical biology. Aristotle thus sets himself the task of giving an account of the good which is at once local and particular—located in and partially defined by the characteristics of the *polis*—and yet also cosmic and universal. The tension between these poles is felt throughout the argument of the *Ethics*.

What then does the good for man turn out to be? Aristotle has cogent arguments against identifying that good with money, with honor or with pleasure. He gives to it the name of *eudaimonia*—as so often there is a difficulty in translation: blessedness, happiness, prosperity. It is the state of being well and doing well in being well, of a man's being well-favored himself and in relation to the divine. But when Aristotle first gives this name to the good for man, he leaves the question of the content of *eudaimonia* largely open.

The virtues are precisely those qualities the possession of which will enable an individual to achieve *eudaimonia* and the lack of which will frustrate his movement toward that *telos*. But although it would not be incorrect to describe the exercise of virtues as a means to the end of achieving the good for man, that description is ambiguous. Aristotle does not in his writings explicitly distinguish between two different types of means-end relationship. When we speak of any happening or state or activity as a means to some other, we may on the one hand mean that the world is as a matter of contingent fact so ordered that if you are able to bring about a happening or state or activity of the first kind, an event or state or activity of the second kind will ensue. The means and the end can each be adequately characterized without reference to the other; and a number of quite different means may be employed to achieve one and the same end. But the exercise of the virtues is not in this sense *a* means to the end of the good for man. For what constitutes the good for man is a complete human life lived at its best, and the exercise of the virtues is a necessary and central part of such a life, not a mere preparatory exercise to secure such a life. We thus cannot characterize the good for man adequately without already having made reference to the virtues. And within an Aristotelian framework the suggestion therefore that there might be some means to achieve the good for man without the exercise of the virtues makes no sense.

The immediate outcome of the exercise of a virtue is a choice which issues in right action: 'It is the correctness of the end of the purposive choice of which virtue is the cause' (1228a1, Kenny's translation, Kenny 1978) wrote Aristotle in the *Eudemian Ethics*. It does not of course follow that in the absence of the relevant virtue a right action may not be done. To understand why, consider Aristotle's answer to the question: what would someone be like who lacked to some large degree an adequate training in the virtues of character? In part this would depend on his natural traits and talents; some individuals have an inherited natural disposition to do on occasion what a particular virtue requires. But this happy gift of fortune is not to be confused with the possession of the corresponding virtue; for just because it is not informed by systematic training and by principle even such fortunate individuals will be the prey of their own emotions and desires. This victimization by one's own emotions and desires would be of more than one kind. On the one hand one would lack any means of ordering one's emotions and desires, of deciding rationally which to cultivate and encourage, which to inhibit and reduce; on the other hand on particular occasions one would lack those dispositions which enable a desire for something other than what is actually one's good to be held in check. Virtues are dispositions not only to act in particular ways, but also to feel in particular ways. To act virtuously is not, as Kant was later to think, to act against inclination; it is to act from inclination formed by the cultivation of the virtues. Moral education is an 'education sentimentale'.

The educated moral agent must of course know what he is doing when he judges or acts virtuously. Thus he does what is virtuous *because* it is virtuous. It is this fact that distinguishes the exercise of the virtues from the exercise of certain qualities which are not virtues, but rather simulacra of virtues. The well-trained soldier, for instance, may do what courage would have demanded in a particular situation, but not because he is courageous but because he is well-trained or perhaps—to go beyond Aristotle's example by remembering Frederick the Great's maxim—because he is more frightened of his own officers than he is of the enemy. The genuinely virtuous agent however acts on the basis of a true and rational judgment.

An Aristotelian theory of the virtues does therefore presuppose a crucial distinction between what any particular individual at any particular time takes to be good for him and what is really good for him as a man. It is for the sake of achieving this latter good that we practice the virtues and we do so by making choices about means to achieve that end, means in both senses characterized earlier. Such choices demand judgment and the exercise of the virtues requires therefore a capacity to judge and to do the right thing in the right place at the right time in the right way. The exercise of such judgment is not a routinizable application of rules. Hence perhaps the most obvious and astonishing absence from Aristotle's thought for any modern reader: there is relatively little mention of rules anywhere in the *Ethics*. Moreover Aristotle takes that part of morality which is obedience to rules to be obedience to laws enacted by the city-state—if and when the city-state enacts as it ought. Such law prescribes and prohibits certain types of action absolutely and such actions are among those which a virtuous man would do or refrain from doing.

Hence it is a crucial part of Aristotle's view that certain types of action are absolutely prohibited or enjoined irrespective of circumstances or consequences. Aristotle's view is teleological, but it is not consequentialist. Moreover the examples Aristotle gives of what is absolutely prohibited resemble the precepts of what is at first sight a completely different kind of moral system, that of the Jewish law. What he says about the law is very brief, although he does insist that there are natural and universal as well as conventional and local rules of justice. It seems likely that he means to insist that natural and universal justice absolutely prohibits certain types of act; but that which penalties are assigned to which offence may vary from city to city. Nonetheless what he says on this topic is so brief as to be cryptic. It therefore seems worth asking in a more general way—rather than imputing to Aristotle views that would go too far beyond what is in the text—how it might be that views such as Aristotle's on the place of the virtues in human life should require some reference to the absolute prohibitions of natural justice. And in asking this question it is worth remembering Aristotle's insistence that the virtues find their place not just in the life of the individual, but in the life of the city and that the individual is indeed intelligible only as a *politikon zôon*.

This last remark suggests that one way to elucidate the relationship between virtues on the one hand and a morality of laws on the other is to consider what would be involved in any age in founding a community to achieve a common project, to bring about some good recognized as their shared good by all those engaging in the project. As modern examples of such a project we might consider the founding and carrying forward of a school, a hospital or an art gallery; in the ancient world the characteristic examples would have been those of a religious cult or of an expedition or of a city. Those who participated in such a project would need to develop two quite different types of evaluative practice. On the one hand they would need to value—to praise as excellences—those qualities of mind and character which would contribute to the realization of their common good or goods. That is, they would need to recognize a certain set of qualities as virtues and the corresponding set of defects as vices. They would also need however to identify certain types of action as the doing or the production of harm of such an order that they destroy the bonds of community is such a way as to render the doing or achieving of good impossible in some respect at least for some time. Examples of such offences would characteristically be the taking of innocent life, theft and perjury and betrayal. The table of the virtues promulgated in such a community would teach its citizens what kinds of actions would gain them merit and honor; the table of legal offences would teach them what kinds of actions would be regarded not simply as bad, but as intolerable.

The response to such offences would have to be that of taking the person who committed them to have thereby excluded himself or herself from the community. A violation of the bonds of community by the offender has to be recognized for what it is by the community, if the community is not itself to fail. Hence the offender in one crucial sense has excluded him or herself, has by his or her own action invited punishment. Whether the exclusion were permanent—by way of execution or irrevocable exile—or temporary—by way of imprisonment or exile for a term—would depend upon the gravity of the particular offence. A broad measure of agreement on a scale of gravity of offences would be partially constitutive of such a community as would a similar broad measure of agreement on the nature and importances of the various virtues.

The need for *both* these types of practice arises from the fact that an individual member of such a community could fail in his role as a member of that community in two quite different ways. He could on the one hand simply fail to be good enough; that is he could be deficient in the virtues to such an extent as to render his contribution to the achievement of the community's common good negligible. But someone could fail in this way without committing any of the particular offences specified in the community's laws; indeed it might be precisely because of his vices that someone abstained from committing offences. Cowardice can be someone's reason for not committing murder; vanity and boastfulness can on occasion lead someone to tell the truth.

Conversely to fail the community by committing an offence against the law is *not* simply to fail by not being good enough. It is to fail in a quite different way. Indeed although someone who possesses the virtues to a high degree will be far less apt than others to commit grave offences, a brave and modest man may on occasion commit murder and his offence is no less and no more than the offence of a coward or a braggart. To do positive wrong is not the same as to be defective in doing or being good. Nonetheless the two kinds of failure are intimately related. For both injure the community to some degree and make its shared project less likely to be successful. An offence against the laws destroys those relationships which make common pursuit of the good possible; defective character, while it may also render someone more liable to commit offences, makes one unable to contribute to the achievement of that good without which the community's common life has no point. Both are bad because deprivations of good, but deprivations of very different kinds. So that an account of the virtues while an essential part of an account of the moral life of such a community could never be complete by itself. And Aristotle, as we have seen, recognizes that his account of the virtues has to be supplemented by some account, even if a brief one, of those types of action which are absolutely prohibited.

Notes
1. Compare to Aristotle EN 1094ª1, p. 4.
2. Compare to Moore, pp. 31–33.

▼ **The Business Perspective**

A Different Look at Codes of Ethics

Donald Robin, Michael Giallourakis, Fred R. David, and Thomas E. Moritz

Organizational codes of ethics are: 1. very different; 2. often similar; 3. not connected with ethics; 4. perceived as an important tool for fostering ethical conduct; and 5. not very effective in a broad ethical sense. A welter of contradictions? Indeed, all of the above statements are true—and this fact makes an analysis of ethical codes extremely difficult. However, in order to understand why codes are not very effective (point five), we must be able to analyze them. And in order to perform any kind of analysis, we must deal with points one through four.

Point one frustrates the analysis of ethical codes because the differences seem to prevent us from classifying the items found in them. We are then faced with the problem of analyzing codes one at a time, which reduces our ability to offer any general means of improvement. Point two, however, offers some hope. If there are any important similarities, they can form a basis for our grouping activities. With clusters of code items to analyze, we can: make statements about their ethical content (point three); attempt to determine why they haven't been very effective (point five); and suggest what might be done to improve them. If codes were not used by organizations as important tools for fostering ethical conduct (point four), none of this discussion would be interesting or important. But businesses do seem to perceive them in that way.

One of the similarities among the codes is their tendency to be legalistic. The first title in Motorola's summary of their "Code of Conduct" is "Improper Use of Company Funds and Assets," with the following two entries:

1. The funds and assets of Motorola may not be used for influential gifts, illegal payments of any kind or political contributions whether legal or illegal.
2. The funds and assets of Motorola must be properly and accurately recorded on the books and records of Motorola.

Under "Dealings with Distributors or Agents," one finds, "Motorola shall not enter into any agreements with dealers, distributors, agents or consultants which are not in compliance with U.S. laws and the laws of any other

country that may be involved; or which provide for the payment of a com-
mission or fee that is not commensurate with the services to be rendered."
The other two titles, "Customer/Supplier/Government Relationships" and
"Conflict of Interest," contain similar legalistic statements, all of the form
"Thou shall . . ." or "Thou shall not . . ." Motorola's approach is far from
unique. It appears in almost every code that we studied.

The headings in the code of the Coca-Cola Company are also narrow
and legalistic, but they can be compared to Motorola's code as an example of
the *differences* that occur between code items from various companies. The
Coca-Cola "Code of Business Conduct" contains nine, rather than Motorola's
four, major headings. These titles include, among others: "General," which begins: "The Company, its employees and agents shall comply with all applicable legal requirements . . ."; "Political Campaign Contributions"; "Payments,
Gifts and Entertainment Involving Customers and Suppliers"; "Accuracy and
Completeness of Company Books and Records"; and "Business Conduct Inquiries." While Coca-Cola's code is different from Motorola's in important
ways, there are several similarities in the *content* of these two codes. For example, the use and recording of company funds and dealings with persons outside the firm appear in both codes. Thus, although substantive differences
existed between codes, important similarities in their character and content
also could be discerned.

In order to use the similarities in the codes as the basis for analysis, some
form of classification was necessary. Classification involves the division of
items into groups that are homogeneous with respect to some criteria. There
are two approaches to classification, both of which are used in this study.
With groups established, it becomes possible to suggest what characteristics
of codes aren't working, why they aren't working, and what might be done to
improve them.

Organization of Code by Category

In a survey of the organizations appearing in the *Business Week* 1000, firms
were asked for a copy of their code of ethics, if one existed. They returned 84
codes, while 168 responses to a separate and additional questionnaire were
also received. The difference in the two figures is due to either the nonexis-
tence of a code or the company's unwillingness to send one to the authors. The
84 codes came from some of the largest service and manufacturing organizations in the United States.

A two-step process was developed to provide an initial grouping of the
code items. The first step used the personal judgment of two reviewers to
evaluate the items listed and group them under broader, more descriptive
headings where appropriate. The second step involved a third reviewer to test
the results of the first two. The lists generated by these reviewers were then
compared and titles composed for the groupings. The final list contains 30
categories.

It was also desirable to statistically group the 30 categories based on their usage by the different companies. Three clusters of items from codes of ethics resulted from this analysis, accounting for 24 of the 30 categories. **Table 1** (pp. 24–25) is a presentation of all 30 categories with suggested labels for the clusters.

Ethical Tools to Evaluate Clusters

To assess the clusters, we must first define the tools of evaluation. The most important of these tools is philosophical ethics. Philosophers have been struggling for centuries to provide us with approaches for defining right and wrong. Unfortunately, philosophical ethics is often viewed as nonspecific in character by people who aren't familiar with it. However, the discipline actually offers very specific advice about how to behave ethically. The study of ethics existed long before the business disciplines were formally developed; over that time period it has generated several philosophies that can be used to direct our behavior. These philosophies are similar to those in economics in that they sometimes disagree over the approach that should be used to solve a problem. Nevertheless, like the economic philosophies, the ethical philosophies can provide us with considerable guidance.

Evaluation of Clusters[1]

In the current study of codes of ethics, one cluster was labeled, "Be a dependable organizational citizen" (**Table 1**). The categories included in this cluster all direct the employee to be a nice, dependable person. Such dictates may or may not describe desirable outcomes for the organization, but they have very little to do with ethical conduct. Deontology and utilitarianism have little or nothing to say about these dictates, and their appearance in a code of ethics suggests a lack of understanding or a mislabeling on the part of those organizations that use them. Furthermore, these rules are very specific, providing only limited direction for employees. Service organizations such as banks and utilities were heavy users of categories in this cluster. . . .

Another cluster is entitled, "Don't do anything unlawful or improper that will harm the organization." This cluster contained the largest number of categories and was by far the group most subscribed to. Over fifty companies included some of these categories in their codes of ethics. The legalistic character of the items in this cluster make it a set of rules designed to protect the organization, rather than a set of values to guide behavior. . . .

The ethics literature does deal with some of the issues raised in the second cluster, but in the context of ethics, these issues lead to reasoned and rational decisions based on certain central values. For example, two of the categories in this cluster deal with bribery. Within the context of this cluster, the issue seems to be one of prohibiting bribery because it is against the law, and the organization could get into trouble if bribes are given or taken. The

Table 1.   Clusters of Categories Found in Corporate Codes of Ethics

Cluster 1
"Be a dependable organization citizen."

1. Demonstrate courtesy, respect, honesty, and fairness in relationships with customers, suppliers, competitors, and other employees.
2. Comply with safety, health, and security regulations.
3. Do not use abusive language or actions.
4. Dress in business-like attire.
5. Possession of firearms on company premises is prohibited.
6. Use of illegal drugs or alcohol on company premises is prohibited.
7. Follow directives from supervisors.
8. Be reliable in attendance and punctuality.
9. Manage personal finances in a manner consistent with employment by a fiduciary institution.

Cluster 2
"Don't do anything unlawful or improper that will harm the organization."

1. Maintain confidentiality of customer, employee, and corporate records and information.
2. Avoid outside activities which conflict with or impair the performance of duties.
3. Make decisions objectively without regard to friendship or personal gain.
4. The acceptance of any form of bribe is prohibited.
5. Payment to any person, business, political organization, or public official for unlawful or unauthorized purposes is prohibited.
6. Conduct personal and business dealings in compliance with all relevant laws, regulations, and policies.
7. Comply fully with antitrust laws and trade regulations.
8. Comply fully with accepted accounting rules and controls.
9. Do not provide false or misleading information to the corporation, its auditors, or a government agency.
10. Do not use company property or resources for personal benefit or any other improper purpose.
11. Each employee is personally accountable for company funds over which he or she has control.
12. Staff members should not have any interest in any competitor or supplier of the company unless such interest has been fully disclosed to the company.

Cluster 3
"Be good to our customers."

1. Strive to provide products and services of the highest quality.
2. Perform assigned duties to the best of your ability and in the best interest of the corporation, its shareholders, and its customers.
3. Convey true claims for products.

Table 1.   (*Continued*)

Unclustered Items

1. Exhibit standards of personal integrity and professional conduct.
2. Racial, ethnic, religious, or sexual harassment is prohibited.
3. Report questionable, unethical, or illegal activities to your manager.
4. Seek opportunities to participate in community services and political activities.
5. Conserve resources and protect the quality of the environment in areas where the company operates.
6. Members of the corporation are not to recommend attorneys, accountants, insurance agents, stockbrokers, real estate agents or similar individuals to customers.

message is actually "Don't break the law." This message, while certainly desirable, is substantially different from a deontological value that might, for example, state: "Always act in such a manner that you would be willing to live and work in a world where everyone acted as you do." This latter statement effectively prohibits bribery just as well as the rules that are part of this cluster, but it does many other things as well.

The final cluster was entitled "Be good to our customers."[2] It contained only three categories, which roughly dealt with ways in which the behavior of employees could satisfy customers. While these three categories lack the breadth of, say, Peters and Waterman's "Close to the Customer" from *In Search of Excellence*,[3] the intent is somewhat broader than in the other clusters. The first item from this cluster in Table 1 was adopted by only 10 companies, item two by 15, and item three by 24 out of the 84 companies represented in the study. There was no obvious tendency toward one or more particular industries.

The six unclustered items also appear in Table 1. Item one of this group was adopted by 31 companies. It is not an ethical dictate and could be confusing to individuals attempting to apply it, since personal integrity and professional conduct can mean different things to different people. The second item, dealing with harassment, could be the result of an ethical analysis, or it could simply be a reaction to societal concerns. Of the 84 codes that were analyzed, this item appeared in 19.

Item three also appeared in 19 codes, but it simply supplies directions on how to deal with perceived unethical occurrences. Directions about reporting such occurrences ought to be in every code, but they probably should not be part of the ethical statements in the code itself. The most popular of these six unclustered items was number four, dealing with community and political service, which was adopted by 46 companies. It would be difficult to fit this item into any of the most popular moral philosophies, but it does have social responsibility connotations.

Item five, conservation of the environment, again reflects social responsibility issues rather than ethics, but it could be the result of an ethical analysis. Only 12 companies used this category in their codes. Finally, item six lacks both ethical and social responsibility ties. It was adopted by three financial institutions and was the only one of the six that suggested any specific usage.

Before moving to the second grouping effort, we need to examine the expectations for, and effectiveness of, codes of ethics. The following discussion sets the stage for selection of appropriate categories in the second grouping and for evaluation of the results.

Management Expectations for Codes of Ethics

It was argued in the preceding sections that current codes were for the most part not ethical statements, but dictates or rules that either prohibited or demanded specific behaviors. It is suggested in this section that despite the fact that codes are currently not very effective, business has high expectations for them.

A considerable amount of work has been spent in analyzing codes of ethics. However, two relatively recent articles summarize the general feeling by many (not all) researchers that codes lack much impact. Cressey and Moore, in an elaborate analysis of corporate codes of ethics, are convinced "that any improvements in business ethics taking place in the last decade are not a consequence of business leaders' calls for ethics or of the codes themselves. We believe that, instead, any changes have stemmed from conditions imposed by outsiders."[4] Further, an empirical study by Chonko and Hunt involving marketing managers found that "the existence of corporate or industry codes of ethics seems to be unrelated to the extent of ethical problems in marketing management."[5]

Both results suggest that codes of ethics are not a major factor in important decisions involving ethical questions. Codes may communicate the specific rules suggested by the three clusters in the last section, but they have little impact on what might be considered the *important* problems of business. Unfortunately, corporate management seems to expect more from them. The Center of Business Ethics at Bentley College published the results of a study in which they inquired whether the respondent's company had been "taking steps to incorporate ethical values and concerns into the daily operations of [its] organization" and, if they had, what they hoped to achieve by doing so. About 80 percent of the 279 respondents said that they had taken such steps, with five major objectives. In order of perceived importance they were: "to be a socially responsible corporation"; "to provide guidelines for employees' behavior"; "to improve management"; "to comply with local, state, or federal guidelines"; and "to establish a better corporate culture." The first two were substantially more important, while the last three were seen as about equal in importance. Codes of conduct were used by 93 percent of the respondents to achieve these objectives. The next most popular approach, employee training in ethics, was used by only 44 percent of the respondents.[6]

In a study published in January 1988 by Touche Ross, respondents again cited the adoption of business codes of ethics as "the most effective measure for encouraging ethical business behavior." In this study, 39 percent of the respondents selected codes of ethics as most effective, 30 percent selected a "more humanistic curriculum in business education," and 20 percent selected "legislation." Interestingly, 55 percent selected "legislation" as *least* effective.[7] Thus, codes are still seen by managers as the most viable approach for dealing with ethical problems.

However, there is a gap between what managers hope to accomplish with corporate codes and what is actually accomplished. Compliance with local, state, or federal guidelines might be achieved based on the categories in cluster one. Also, *very specific* guidelines for employees' behavior might be set based on the character of the categories, but broad guidelines and other objectives seem to be beyond what is currently attainable. To the degree the codes analyzed in this article are representative, their content and apparent intent lack the ability to truly aid in ethical decision making.

Cressey and Moore, in their analysis of corporate codes of ethics, believe that these documents "tend to imitate the criminal law and thus contain few innovative ideas about how the ethical standards of a firm, let alone of business in general, can be improved."[8] A quick review of the 30 categories listed in Table 1 and the examples presented throughout this article should verify that our findings confirm this belief. Rule-based statements dominate, while broad, shared values are almost absent.

Logical Partition of Codes by Dimension of Guidance

Many of the early attempts at developing codes of ethics were broad value-based statements of the "Be good!" type. They tended to be altruistic and unattainable, to confuse rather than aid understanding. The problems that occur with these statements revolve around whose values are used in describing "personal integrity" or determining "quality" and what is meant by these broad, ill-defined value statements.

Historically, the critic's reaction to ineffective statements is a call for more specificity. In all this call for specificity accounts for 27 of the 30 items. However, since rules are supposed to provide very specific guidance, and since the item labels were composites created by the authors, the companies using them have been given the benefit of the doubt. It is the *intent* of the companies in creating the code items that is important in this article, and the intent seems to have been the creation of highly specific guidance directives.

Creating rule-type statements to deal with all of the important issues from the organization's environment is simply too massive an undertaking to be handled effectively. However, if core values could be created to direct organizational behavior—values felt and understood by everyone in the organization—they could be the basis of a very effective code of ethics. This approach seems to call for the study and development of a specific corporate culture. The principal determinant of any culture is its values or guides to behavior. If such values were established as part of a corporate culture to guide the ethical behavior of an organization, many unforeseen events could be dealt with ethically.

What would highly specific guidelines that were value based look like? What role would they play in directing corporate behavior? Such a code of ethics would be a statement of the company's ethical and socially responsible values. It would be a document that is open to all of the organization's publics and a constant reminder to employees about the expected approach for conducting all activities. Such a code would be a tool in the training program for new employees and part of the broad effort to enculturate all employees. Eventually, it would become an aid in spreading the folklore of the organization, providing the themes around which corporate myths and heros are created. However, only if the code is used in conjunction with strong enculturation efforts would it reach the high level of guidance that is part of cell four.

Some progress in this direction seems to be occurring. A February 1988 document by The Business Roundtable made the following observation:

> In the growing movement among major U.S. corporations to develop and refine mechanisms to make their ethics effective, there are two interrelated purposes:
>
> —First, there is the aim to ensure compliance with company standards of conduct. At work in the realization that human consciences are fragile and need the support of institutions.
>
> —Second, there is the growing conviction that strong corporate culture and ethics are a vital strategic key to survival and profitability in a highly competitive era.[9]

We believe that the most effective results will occur when these two purposes are combined. When standards of conduct become ethically determined values and are integrated into a strong corporate culture, then corporate behavior will become more ethical.

Notes

1. The use of cluster concepts of various moral maxims is typical of virtue ethics. The advocate states that "everyone knows" that such and such behavior is a virtue. Thus the acquisition of these will make you better. Compare to the calculations involved in utilitarianism and deontology. Compare also to the epistemological position of intuitionism that these are grasped directly instead of being empirically available—as virtue ethics asserts.
2. Compare the use of "good" by Aristotle, p. 4 to Moore, p. 33. Both assume we all know what this is but Aristotle gives us a prescription for discovering the definition, viz., an empirical investigation of common opinion. Moore believes we know this "directly."
3. Thomas J. Peters and Robert H. Waterman, Jr., *In Search of Excellence* (NY: Harper & Row, Publishers, 1982).
4. Donald R. Cressey and Charles A. Moore, "Managerial Values and Corporate Codes of Ethics," *California Management Review,* Summer 1983, pp. 73–4.

5. Lawrence B. Chonko and Shelby D. Hunt, "Ethics and Marketing Management: An Empirical Analysis," *Journal of Business Research,* August 1985, p. 356.

6. Center for Business Ethics, "Are Corporations Institutionalizing Ethics?" *Journal of Business Ethics,* October 1986, p. 86.

7. Touche Ross, *Ethics in American Business* (Detroit: Touche Ross, January 1988).

8. Cressey and Moore (see note 4), p. 73.

9. The Business Roundtable, *Corporate Ethics: A Prime Business Asset* (NY: The Business Roundtable, February 1988), p. 6.

 ## *CHECKLIST* for Virtue Ethics

The ethical checklists are short summaries meant to help students apply the theories they have been studying in the preceding section. They are not meant to stand alone nor are they meant to supplant deeper reading into primary sources of each ethical theory.

It also should be noted that **there is no single application of any theory that everyone will accept.** Therefore, the checklist below is just one version of the ethical theory presented. It is set down in this succinct format as a pedagogical aid for applying ethical theories that will be used in the Case Studies Reports.

Directions: Read the short epitome on virtue ethics and then go through the steps outlined below. When you have finished the assignment, your list will include your own checklist for virtue ethics.

Virtue Ethics

Epitome:

Virtue Ethics works from an established list of accepted character traits called virtues. These traits are acquired by habit and guide the practitioner in making moral decision. Aristotle described these character traits as being a mean between extremes. The good man so habituates his behavior to these virtues that he will carry out the good actions over and over again throughout his life.

Application:

Step One: Set out a list of traits you believe to be virtues. Make sure you have at least three virtues and no more than ten.

Step Two: Establish the mean by outlining how the virtues in step one are really somewhere in the middle of two extremes.

Step Three: Describe how one might ingrain this trait into his or her character. What consequences would it have?

Step Four: Create a moral situation of your own and show how the individual guided by virtue ethics would resolve it. How does virtue ethics make a difference in this situation?

CHAPTER 2

Intuitionism

▼
The Philosophical Perspective

"The Naturalistic Fallacy"

G. E. Moore

12. Suppose a man says 'I am pleased'; and suppose that is not a lie or a mistake but the truth. Well, if it is true, what does that mean? It means that his mind, a certain definite mind, distinguished by certain definite marks from all others, has at this moment a certain definite feeling called pleasure. "Pleased" *means* nothing but having pleasure, and though we may be more pleased or less pleased, and even, we may admit for the present, have one or another kind of pleasure; yet in so far as it is pleasure we have, whether there be more or less of it, and whether it be of one kind or another, what we have is one definite thing, absolutely indefinable, some one thing that is the same in all the various degrees and in all the various kinds of it that there may be. We may be able to say how it is related to other things: that, for example, it is in the mind, that it causes desire, that we are conscious of it, etc., etc. We can, I say, describe its relations to other things, but define it we can *not*. And if anybody tried to define pleasure for us as being any other natural object; if anybody were to say, for instance, that pleasure *means* the sensation of red, and were to proceed to

G. E. Moore, *Principia Ethica* (Cambridge: Cambridge University Press; 1903), pp. 12–27.

deduce from that that pleasure is a colour, we should be entitled to laugh at him and to distrust his future statements about pleasure. Well, that would be the same fallacy which I have called the naturalistic fallacy. That 'pleased' does not mean 'having the sensation of red,' or anything else whatever, does not prevent us from understanding what it does mean. It is enough for us to know that 'pleased' does mean 'having the sensation of pleasure,' and though pleasure is absolutely indefinable, though pleasure is pleasure and nothing else whatever, yet we feel no difficulty in saying that we are pleased. The reason is, of course, that when I say 'I am pleased,' I do *not* mean that 'I' am the same thing as 'having pleasure.' And similarly no difficulty need be found in my saying that 'pleasure is good' and yet not meaning that 'pleasure' is the same thing as 'good,' that pleasure *means* good, and that good *means* pleasure. If I were to imagine that when I said 'I am pleased,' I meant that I was exactly the same thing as 'pleased,' I should not indeed call that a naturalistic fallacy, although it would be the same fallacy as I have called naturalistic with reference to Ethics. The reason of this is obvious enough. When a man confuses two natural objects with one another, defining the one by the other, if for instance, he confuses himself, who is one natural object, with 'pleased' or with 'pleasure' which are others, then there is no reason to call the fallacy naturalistic. But if he confuses 'good,' which is not in the same sense a natural object, with any natural object whatever, then there is a reason for calling that a naturalistic fallacy; its being made with regard to 'good' marks it as something quite specific, and this specific mistake deserves a name because it is so common. As for the reasons why good is not to be considered a natural object, they may be reserved for discussion in another place. But, for the present, it is sufficient to notice this: Even if it were a natural object, that would not alter the nature of the fallacy nor diminish its importance one whit. All that I have said about it would remain quite equally true: only the name which I have called it would not be so appropriate as I think it is. And I do not care about the name: what I do care about is the fallacy. It does not matter what we call it, provided we recognise it when we meet with it. It is to be met with in almost every book on Ethics; and yet it is not recognised: and that is why it is necessary to multiply illustrations of it, and convenient to give it a name. It is a very simple fallacy indeed. When we say that an orange is yellow, we do not think our statement binds us to hold that 'orange' means nothing else than 'yellow,' or that nothing can be yellow but an orange. Supposing the orange is also sweet! Does that bind us to say that 'sweet' is exactly the same thing as 'yellow,' that 'sweet' must be defined as 'yellow'? And supposing it be recognised that 'yellow' just means 'yellow' and nothing else whatever, does that make it any more difficult to hold that oranges are yellow? Most certainly it does not: on the contrary, it would be absolutely meaningless to say that oranges were yellow, unless yellow did in the end mean just 'yellow' and nothing else whatever—unless it was absolutely indefinable. We should not get any very clear notion about things, which are yellow—we should not get very far with our science, if we were bound to hold that everything which was yellow, *meant* exactly the same thing as yellow. We should find we had to hold that an orange was exactly the same thing as a stool, a piece of paper, a lemon, anything you like. We could prove any number of absurdities; but should we be the nearer to the truth? Why, then, should it be different with 'good'? Why, if good is good and indefinable, should I be held to deny that pleasure is good? Is there any difficulty in holding both to be true at once? On the contrary, there is no meaning in saying that pleasure is good, unless good is something different from pleasure. It is absolutely useless, so far as Ethics is concerned, to prove, as Mr Spencer tries to do, that increase of pleasure coincides with increase of life, unless good *means* something different from either life or pleasure. He might just as well try to prove that an orange is yellow by shewing that it always is wrapped up in paper.

13. In fact, if it is not the case that 'good' denotes something simple and indefinable, only two alternatives are possible: either it is a complex, a given whole, about the correct analysis of which there may be disagreement; or else it means nothing at all, and there is no such subject as Ethics. In general, however, ethical philosophers have attempted to define good, without recognising what such an attempt must mean. We are, therefore, justified in concluding that the attempt to define good is chiefly due to want of clearness as to the possible nature of definition. There are, in fact, only two serious alternatives to be considered, in order to establish the conclusion that 'good' does denote a simple and indefinable notion. It might possibly denote a complex, as 'horse' does; or it might have no meaning at all. Neither of these possibilities has, however, been clearly conceived and seriously maintained, as such, by those who presume to define good; and both may be dismissed by a simple appeal to facts.

(1) The hypothesis that disagreement about the meaning of good is disagreement with regard to the correct analysis of a given whole, may be most plainly seen to be incorrect by consideration of the fact that, whatever definition be offered, it may be always asked, with significance, of the complex so defined, whether it is itself good. To take, for instance, one of the more plausible, because one of the more complicated, of such proposed definitions, it may easily be thought, at first sight, that to be good may mean to be that which we desire to desire. Thus if we apply this definition to a particular instance and say 'When we think that A is good, we are thinking that A is one of the things which we desire to desire,' our proposition may seem quite plausible. But, if we carry the investigation further, and ask ourselves 'Is it good to desire to desire A?' it is apparent, on a little reflection, that this question is itself as intelligible, as the original question 'Is A good?'—that we are, in fact, now asking for exactly the same information about the desire to desire A, for which we formerly asked with regard to A itself. But it is also apparent that the meaning of this second question cannot be correctly analysed into 'Is the desire to desire A one of the things which we desire to desire?': we have not before our minds anything so complicated as the question 'Do we desire to desire to desire to desire A?' Moreover any one can easily convince himself by inspection that the predicate of this proposition—'good'—is positively different from the notion of 'desiring to desire' which enters into its subject:

'That we should desire to desire A is good' is *not* merely equivalent to 'That A should be good is good.' It may indeed be true that what we desire to desire is always also good; perhaps, even the converse may be true: but it is very doubtful whether this is the case, and the mere fact that we understand very well what is meant by doubting it, shews clearly that we have two different notions before our minds.

(2) And the same consideration is sufficient to dismiss the hypothesis that 'good' has no meaning whatsoever. It is very natural to make the mistake of supposing that what is universally true is of such a nature that its negation would be self-contradictory: the importance which has been assigned to analytic propositions in the history of philosophy shews how easy such a mistake is. And thus it is very easy to conclude that what seems to be a universal ethical principle is in fact an identical proposition; that, if, for example, whatever is called 'good' seems to be pleasant, the proposition 'Pleasure is the good' does not assert a connection between two different notions, but involves only one, that of pleasure, which is easily recognised as a distinct entity. But whoever will attentively consider with himself what is actually before his mind when he asks the question 'Is pleasure (or whatever it may be) after all good?' can easily satisfy himself that he is not merely wondering whether pleasure is pleasant. And if he will try this experiment with each suggested definition in succession, he may become expert enough to recognise that in every case he has before his mind a unique object, with regard to the connection of which with any other object, a distinct question may be asked. Every one does in fact understand the question 'Is this good?' When he thinks of it, his state of mind is different from what it would be, were he asked 'Is this pleasant, or desired, or approved?' It has a distinct meaning for him, even though he may not recognise in what respect it is distinct. Whenever he thinks of 'intrinsic value,' or 'intrinsic worth,' or says that a thing 'ought to exist,' he has before his mind the unique object—the unique property of things—which I mean by 'good.' Everybody is constantly aware of this notion, although he may never become aware at all that it is different from other notions of which he is also aware. But, for correct ethical reasoning, it is extremely important that he should become aware of this fact; and, as soon as the nature of the problem is clearly understood, there should be little difficulty in advancing so far in analysis.

14. 'Good,' then, is indefinable; and yet, so far as I know, there is only one ethical writer, Prof. Henry Sidgwick, who has clearly recognised and stated this fact. We shall see, indeed, how far many of the most reputed ethical systems fall short of drawing the conclusions which follow from such a recognition. At present I will only quote one instance, which will serve to illustrate the meaning and importance of this principle that 'good' is indefinable, or, as Prof. Sidgwick says, an 'unanalysable notion.' It is an instance to which Prof. Sidgwick himself refers in a note on the passage, in which he argues that 'ought' is unanalysable.[1]

'Bentham,' says Sidgwick, 'explains that his fundamental principle "states the greatest happiness of all those whose interest is in question as being the right and proper end of human action"'; and yet 'his language in other passages of the same chapter would seem to imply' that he *means* by the word "right" "conducive to the general happiness." Prof. Sidgwick sees that, if you take these two statements together, you get the absurd result that 'greatest happiness is the end of human action, which is conducive to the general happiness'; and so absurd does it seem to him to call this result, as Bentham calls it, 'the fundamental principle of a moral system,' that he suggests that Bentham cannot have meant it. Yet Prof. Sidgwick himself states elsewhere[2] that Psychological Hedonism is 'not seldom confounded with Egoistic Hedonism'; and that confusion, as we shall see, rests chiefly on that same fallacy, the naturalistic fallacy, which is implied in Bentham's statements. Prof. Sidgwick admits therefore that this fallacy is sometimes committed, absurd as it is; and I am inclined to think that Bentham may really have been one of those who committed it. Mill, as we shall see, certainly did commit it. In any case, whether Bentham committed it or not, his doctrine, as above quoted, will serve as a very good illustration of this fallacy, and of the importance of the contrary proposition that good is indefinable.

Let us consider this doctrine. Bentham seems to imply, so Prof. Sidgwick says, that the word 'right' *means* 'conducive to general happiness.' Now this, by itself, need not necessarily involve the naturalistic fallacy. For the word 'right' is very commonly appropriated to actions which lead to the attainment of what is good; which are regarded as *means* to the ideal and not as ends-in-themselves. This use of 'right,' as denoting what is good as a means, whether or not it be also good as an end, is indeed the use to which I shall confine the word. Had Bentham been using 'right' in this sense, it might be perfectly consistent for him to *define* right as 'conducive to the general happiness,' *provided only* (and notice this proviso) he had already proved, or laid down as an axiom, that general happiness was *the* good, or (what is equivalent to this) that general happiness alone was good. For in that case he would have already defined *the* good as general happiness (a position perfectly consistent, as we have seen, with the contention that 'good' is indefinable), and, since right was to be defined as 'conducive to *the* good,' it would actually *mean* 'conducive to general happiness.' But this method of escape from the charge of having committed the naturalistic fallacy has been closed by Bentham himself. For his fundamental principle is, we see, that the greatest happiness of all concerned is the *right* and proper *end* of human action. He applies the word 'right,' therefore, to the end, as such, not only to the means which are conducive to it; and, that being so, right can no longer be defined as 'conducive to the general happiness,' without involving the fallacy in question. For now it is obvious that the definition of right as conducive to general happiness can be used by him in support of the fundamental principle that general happiness is the right end; instead of being itself derived from that principle. If right, by definition, means conducive to general happiness, then it is obvious that general happiness is the right end. It is not necessary now first to prove or assert that general happiness is the right end, before right is defined as conducive to general happiness—a perfectly valid procedure; but on the contrary the definition of right as conducive to general happiness proves general happiness to be the right end—a perfectly invalid procedure, since in this case the statement that 'general happiness is the right end of human action' is not an ethical principle at all, but either, as we have seen, a proposition about the meaning of words, or else a proposition about the *nature* of general happiness, not about its rightness or goodness.

Now, I do not wish the importance I assign to this fallacy to be misunderstood. The discovery of it does not at all refute Bentham's contention that greatest happiness is the proper end of human action, if that be understood as an ethical proposition, as he undoubtedly intended it. That principle may be true all the same; we shall consider whether it is so in succeeding chapters. Bentham might have maintained it, as Prof. Sidgwick does, even if the fallacy had been pointed out to him. What I am maintaining is that the *reasons* which he actually gives for his ethical proposition are fallacious ones so far as they consist in a definition of right. What I suggest is that he did not perceive them to be fallacious; that, if he had done so, he would have been led to seek for other reasons in support of his Utilitarianism; and that, had he sought for other reasons, he *might* have found none which he thought to be sufficient. In that case he would have changed his whole system—a most important consequence. It is undoubtedly also possible that he would have thought other reasons to be sufficient, and in that case his ethical system, in its main results, would still have stood. But, even in this latter case, his use of the fallacy would be a serious objection to him as an ethical philosopher. For it is the business of Ethics, I must insist, not only to obtain true results, but also to find valid reasons for them. The direct object of Ethics is knowledge and not practice; and any one who uses the naturalistic fallacy has certainly not fulfilled this first object, however correct his practical principles may be.

My objections to Naturalism are then, in the first place, that it offers no reason at all, far less any valid reason, for any ethical principle whatever; and in this it already fails to satisfy the requirements of Ethics, as a scientific study. But in the second place I contend that, though it gives a reason for no ethical principle, it is a *cause* of the acceptance of false principles—it deludes the mind into accepting ethical principles, which are false; and in this it is contrary to every aim of Ethics. It is easy to see that if we start with a definition of right conduct as conduct conducive to general happiness; then, knowing that right conduct is universally conduct conducive to the good, we very easily arrive at the result that the good is general happiness. If, on the other hand, we once recognise that we must start our Ethics without a definition, we shall be much more apt to look about us, before we adopt any ethical principle whatever; and the more we look about us, the less likely are we to adopt a false one. It may be replied to this: Yes, but we shall look about us just as much, before we settle on our definition, and are therefore just as likely to be right. But I will try to shew that this is not the case. If we start with the conviction that a definition of good can be found, we start with the conviction that good *can mean* nothing else than some one property of things; and our only business will then be to discover what that property is. But if we recognise that, so far as the meaning of good goes, anything whatever may be good, we start with a much more open mind. Moreover, apart from the fact that, when we think we have a definition, we cannot logically defend our ethical principles in any way whatever, we shall also be much less apt to defend them well, even if illogically. For we shall start with the conviction that good must mean so and so, and shall therefore be inclined either to misunderstand our opponent's arguments or to cut them short with the reply, 'This is not an open question: the very meaning of the word decides it; no one can think otherwise except through confusion.'

15. Our first conclusion as to the subject-matter of Ethics is, then, that there is a simple, indefinable, unanalysable object of thought by reference to which it must be defined. By what name we call this unique object is a matter of indifference, so long as we clearly recognise what it is and that it does differ from other objects.

*   *   *

17. Ethics has always been predominantly concerned with the investigation of a limited class of actions. With regard to these we may ask *both* how far they are good in themselves *and* how far they have a general tendency to produce good results. And the arguments brought forward in ethical discussion have always been of both classes—both such as would prove the conduct in question to be good in itself and such as would prove it to be good as a means. But that these are the only questions which any ethical discussion can have to settle, and that to settle the one is *not* the same thing as to settle the other—these two fundamental facts have in general escaped the notice of ethical philosophers. Ethical questions are commonly asked in an ambiguous form. It is asked 'What is a man's duty under these circumstances?' or 'Is it right to act in this way?' or 'What ought we to aim at securing?' But all these questions are capable of further analysis; a correct answer to any of them involves both judgments of what is good in itself and causal judgments. This is implied even by those who maintain that we have a direct and immediate judgment of absolute rights and duties. Such a judgment can only mean that the course of action in question is *the* best thing to do; that, by acting so, every good that *can* be secured will have been secured. Now we are not concerned with the question whether such a judgment will ever be true. The question is: What does it imply, if it is true? And the only possible answer is that, whether true or false, it implies both a proposition as to the degree of goodness of the action in question, as compared with other things, and a number of causal propositions. For it cannot be denied that the action will have consequences: and to deny that the consequences matter is to make a judgment of their intrinsic value, as compared with the action itself. In asserting that the action is *the* best thing to do, we assert that it together with its consequences presents a greater sum of intrinsic value than any possible alternative. And this condition may be realised by any of the three cases:—*(a)* If the action itself

has greater intrinsic value than any alternative, whereas both its consequences and those of the alternatives are absolutely devoid either of intrinsic merit or intrinsic demerit; or *(b)* if, though its consequences are intrinsically bad, the balance of intrinsic value is greater than would be produced by any alternative; or *(c)* if, its consequences being intrinsically good, the degree of value belonging to them and it conjointly is greater than that of any alternative series. In short, to assert that a certain line of conduct is, at a given time, absolutely right or obligatory, is obviously to assert that more good or less evil will exist in the world, if it be adopted than if anything else be done instead. But this implies a judgment as to the value both of its own consequences and of those of any possible alternative. And that an action will have such and such consequences involves a number of causal judgments.

Similarly, in answering the question 'What ought we to aim at securing?' causal judgments are again involved, but in a somewhat different way. We are liable to forget, because it is so obvious, that this question can never be answered correctly except by naming something which *can* be secured. Not everything can be secured; and, even if we judge that nothing which cannot be obtained would be of equal value with that which can, the possibility of the latter, as well as its value is essential to its being a proper end of action. Accordingly neither our judgments as to what actions we ought to perform, nor even our judgments as to the ends which they ought to produce, are pure judgments of intrinsic value. With regard to the former, an action which is absolutely obligatory *may* have no intrinsic value whatsoever; that it is perfectly virtuous may mean merely that it causes the best possible effects. And with regard to the latter, these best possible results which justify our action can, in any case, have only so much of intrinsic value as the laws of nature allow us to secure; and they in their turn *may* have no intrinsic value whatsoever, but may merely be a means to the attainment (in a still further future) of something that has such value. Whenever, therefore, we ask 'What ought we to do?' or 'What ought we to try to get?' we are asking questions which involve a correct answer to two others, completely different in kind from one another. We must know *both* what degree of intrinsic value different things have, *and* how these different things may be obtained. But the vast majority of questions which have actually been discussed in Ethics—*all* practical questions, indeed—involve this double knowledge; and they have been discussed without any clear separation of the two distinct questions involved. A great part of the vast disagreements prevalent in Ethics is to be attributed to this failure in analysis. By the use of conceptions which involve both that of intrinsic value and that of causal relation, as if they involved intrinsic value only, two different errors have been rendered almost universal. Either it is assumed that nothing has intrinsic value which is not possible or else it is assumed that what is necessary must have intrinsic value. Hence the primary and peculiar business of Ethics, the determination what things have intrinsic value and in what degrees, has received no adequate treatment at all. And on the other hand a *thorough* discussion of means has been also largely neglected, owing to an obscure perception of the truth that it is perfectly irrelevant to the question of intrinsic values. But however this may be, and however strongly any particular reader may be convinced that some one of the mutually contradictory systems which hold the field has given a correct answer either to the question what has intrinsic value, or to the question what we ought to do, or to both, it must at least be admitted that the questions what is best in itself and what will bring about the best possible, are utterly distinct; that both belong to the actual subject-matter of Ethics; and that the more clearly distinct questions are distinguished, the better is our chance of answering both correctly.

Notes

1. *Methods of Ethics,* Bk. 1, Chap. iii, §1 (6th edition).
2. *Methods of Ethics,* Bk. 1, Chap. iv, §1.

Prima Facie Duty

W. D. Ross

When a plain man fulfills a promise because he thinks he ought to do so, it seems clear that he does so with no thought of its total consequences, still less with any opinion that these are likely to be the best possible. He thinks in fact much more of the past than of the future. What makes him think it right to act in a certain way is the fact that he has promised to do so—that and, usually, nothing more. That his act will produce the best possible consequences is not his reason for calling it right. What lends color to the theory we are examining, then, is not the actions (which form probably a great majority of our actions) in which some such reflection as "I have promised" is the only reason we give ourselves for thinking a certain action right, but the exceptional cases in which the consequences of fulfilling a promise (for instance) would be so disastrous to others that we judge it right not to do so. It must of course be admitted that such cases exist. If I have promised to meet a friend at a particular time for some trivial purpose, I should certainly think myself justified in breaking my engagement if by doing so I could prevent a serious accident or bring relief of the victims of one. And the supporters of the view we are examining hold that my thinking so is due to my thinking that I shall bring more good into existence by the one action than by the other. A different account may, however, be given of the matter, an account which will, I believe, show itself to be the true one. It may be said that besides the duty of fulfilling promises I have and recognize a duty of relieving distress, and that when I think it right to do the latter at the cost of not doing the former, it is

W. D. Ross, *The Right & the Good* (N.Y.: Oxford U. Press, 1930), pp. 17–22, 24–28, 29–30, 32–34.

not because I think I shall produce more good thereby but because I think it the duty which is in the circumstances more of a duty. This account surely corresponds much more closely with what we really think in such a situation. If, so far as I can see, I could bring equal amounts of good into being by fulfilling my promise and by helping someone to whom I had made no promise, I should not hesitate to regard the former as my duty. Yet on the view that what is right is right because it is productive of the most good I should not so regard it. . . .

In fact the theory of "ideal utilitarianism" . . . seems to simplify unduly our relations to our fellows. It says, in effect, that the only morally significant relation in which my neighbors stand to me is that of being possible beneficiaries by my action. They do stand in this relation to me, and this relation is morally significant. But they may also stand to me in the relation of promisee to promiser, of creditor to debtor, of wife to husband, of child to parent, of friend to friend, of fellow countryman to fellow countryman, and the like; and each of these relations is the foundation of a *prima facie* duty, which is more or less incumbent on me according to the circumstances of the case. When I am in a situation, as perhaps I always am, in which more than one of these *prima facie* duties is incumbent on me, what I have to do is to study the situation as fully as I can until I form the considered opinion (it is never more) that in the circumstances one of them is more incumbent than any other; then I am bound to think that to do this *prima facie* duty is my duty *sans phrase* in the situation. . . .

I suggest "*prima facie* duty" or "conditional duty" as a brief way of referring to the characteristic (quite distinct from that of being a duty proper) which an act has, in virtue of being of a certain kind (e.g., the keeping of a promise), of being an act which would be a duty proper if it were not at the same time of another kind which is morally significant. Whether an act is a duty proper or actual duty depends on *all* the morally significant kinds it is an instance of. . . .

There is nothing arbitrary about these *prima facie* duties. Each rests on a definite circumstance which cannot seriously be held to be without moral significance. Of *prima facie* duties I suggest, without claiming completeness or finality for it, the following division.

(1) Some duties rest on previous acts of my own. These duties seem to include two kinds, (a) those resting on a promise or what may fairly be called an implicit promise, such as the implicit undertaking not to tell lies which seems to be implied in the act of entering into conversation (at any rate by civilized men), or of writing books that purport to be history and not fiction. These may be called the duties of fidelity. (b) Those resting on a previous wrongful act. These may be called the duties of reparation. (2) Some rest on previous acts of other men, i.e., services done by them to me. These may be loosely described as the duties of gratitude. (3) Some rest on the fact or possibility of a distribution of pleasure or happiness (or of the means thereto) which is not in accordance with the merit of the persons concerned; in such cases there arises a

duty to upset or prevent such a distribution. These are the duties of justice. (4) Some rest on the mere fact that there are other beings in the world whose condition we can make better in respect of virtue, or of intelligence, or of pleasure. These are the duties of beneficence. (5) Some rest on the fact that we can improve our own condition in respect of virtue or of intelligence. These are the duties of self-improvement. (6) I think that we should distinguish from (4) the duties that may be summed up under the title of "not injuring others." No doubt to injure others is incidentally to fail to do them good; but it seems to me clear that nonmaleficence is apprehended as a duty distinct from that of beneficence, and as a duty of a more stringent character. It will be noticed that this alone among the types of duty has been stated in a negative way. An attempt might no doubt be made to state this duty, like the others, in a positive way. It might be said that it is really the duty to prevent ourselves from acting either from an inclination to harm others or from an inclination to seek our own pleasure, in doing which we should incidentally harm them. But on reflection it seems clear that the primary duty here is the duty not to harm others, this being a duty whether or not we have an inclination that if followed would lead to our harming them; and that when we have such an inclination the primary duty not to harm others gives rise to a consequential duty to resist the inclination. The recognition of this duty of nonmaleficence is the first step on the way to the recognition of the duty of beneficence; and that accounts for the prominence of the commands, "thou shalt not kill," "thou shalt not commit adultery," "thou shalt not steal," "thou shalt not bear false witness," in so early a code as the Decalogue. But even when we have come to recognize the duty of beneficence, it appears to me that the duty of nonmaleficence is recognized as a distinct one, as *prima facie* more binding. We should not in general consider it justifiable to kill one person in order to keep another alive, or to steal from one in order to give alms to another.

The essential defect of the "ideal utilitarian" theory is that it ignores, or at least does not do full justice to, the highly personal character of duty. If the only duty is to produce the maximum of good, the question who is to have the good—whether it is myself, or my benefactor, or a person to whom I have made a promise to confer that good on him, or a mere fellow man to whom I stand in no such special relation—should make no difference to my having a duty to produce that good. But we are in fact sure that it makes a vast difference. . . .

I would contend that in principle there is no reason to anticipate that every act that is our duty is so for one and the same reason. Why should two sets of circumstances, or one set of circumstances, *not* possess different characteristics, any one of which makes a certain act our *prima facie* duty? When I ask what it is that makes me in certain cases sure that I have a *prima facie* duty to do so and so, I find that it lies in the fact that I have made a promise; when I ask the same question in another case, I find the answer lies in the fact that I have done a wrong. And if on reflection I find (as I think I do) that neither of these reasons is reducible to the other, I must not on any *a priori* ground assume that such a reduction is possible.

It is necessary to say something by way of clearing up the relation between *prima facie* duties and the actual or absolute duty to do one particular act in particular circumstances. If as almost all moralists except Kant are agreed, and as most plain men think, it is sometimes right to tell a lie or to break a promise, it must be maintained that there is a difference between *prima facie* duty and actual or absolute duty. When we think ourselves justified in breaking, and indeed morally obligated to break, a promise in order to relieve someone's distress, we do not for a moment cease to recognize a *prima facie* duty to keep our promise, and this leads us to feel, not indeed shame or repentance, but certainly compunction, for behaving as we do; we recognize, further, that it is our duty to make up somehow to the promisee for the breaking of the promise. We have to distinguish from the characteristic of being our duty that of tending to be our duty. Any act that we do contains various elements in virtue of which it falls under various categories. In virtue of being the breaking of a promise, for instance, it tends to be wrong; in virtue of being an instance of relieving distress it tends to be right. Tendency to be one's duty may be called a parti-resultant attribute, i.e., one which belongs to an act in virtue of some one component in its nature. *Being* one's duty is a toti-resultant attribute, one which belongs to an act in virtue of its whole nature and of nothing less than this.

*   *   *

Something should be said of the relation between our apprehension of the *prima facie* rightness of certain types of act and our mental attitude towards particular acts. It is proper to use the word "apprehension" in the former case and not in the latter. That an act, *qua* fulfilling a promise, or *qua* effecting a just distribution of good, or *qua* returning services rendered, or *qua* promoting the good of others, or *qua* promoting the virtue or insight of the agent, is *prima facie* right, is self-evident; not in the sense that it is evident from the beginning of our lives, or as soon as we attend to the proposition for the first time, but in the sense that when we have reached sufficient mental maturity and have given sufficient attention to the proposition it is evident without any need of proof, or of evidence beyond itself. It is self-evident just as a mathematical axiom, or the validity of a form of inference, is evident. The moral order expressed in these propositions is just as much part of the fundamental nature of the universe (and, we may add, of any possible universe in which there were moral agents at all) as is the spatial or numerical structure expressed in the axioms of geometry or arithmetic. In our confidence that these propositions are true there is involved the same trust in our reason that is involved in our confidence in mathematics; and we should have no justification for trusting it in the latter sphere and distrusting it in the former. In both cases we are dealing with propositions that cannot be proved, but that just as certainly need no proof. . . .

Our judgments about our actual duty in concrete situations have none of the certainty that attaches to our recognition of the general principles of duty. A statement is certain, i.e., is an expression of knowledge, only in one or other of two cases: when it is either self-evident, or a valid conclusion from self-evident premises. And our judgments about our particular duties have neither of these characters. (1) They are not self-evident. Where a possible act is seen to have two characteristics, in virtue of one of which it is *prima facie* right, and in virtue of the other *prima facie* wrong, we are (I think) well aware that we are not certain whether we ought or ought not to do it; that whether we do it or not, we are taking a moral risk. We come in the long run, after consideration, to think one duty more pressing than the other, but we do not feel certain that it is so. And though we do not always recognize that a possible act has two such characteristics, and though there *may* be cases in which it has not, we are never certain that any particular possible act has not, and therefore never certain that it is right, nor certain that it is wrong. For, to go no further in the analysis, it is enough to point out that any particular act will in all probability in the course of time contribute to the bringing about of good or of evil for many human beings, and thus have a *prima facie* rightness or wrongness of which we know nothing. (2) Again, our judgments about our particular duties are not logical conclusions from self-evident premises. The only possible premises would be the general principles stating their *prima facie* rightness or wrongness *qua* having the different characteristics they do have; and even if we could (as we cannot) apprehend the extent to which an act will tend on the one hand, for example, to bring about advantages for our benefactors and on the other hand to bring about disadvantages for fellow men who are not our benefactors, there is no principle by which we can draw the conclusion that is on the whole right or on the whole wrong. In this respect the judgment as to the rightness of a particular act is just like the judgment as to the beauty of a particular natural object or work of art. A poem is, for instance, in respect of certain qualities beautiful and in respect of certain others not beautiful; and our judgment as to the degree of beauty it possesses on the whole is never reached by logical reasoning from the apprehension of its particular beauties or particular defects. Both in this and in the moral case we have more or less probable opinions which are not logically justified conclusions from the general principles that are recognized as self-evident. . . .

The general principles of duty are obviously not self-evident from the beginning of our lives. How do they come to be so? The answer is, that they come to be self-evident to us just as mathematical axioms do. We find by experience that this couple of matches and that couple makes four matches, that this couple of balls on a wire and that couple make four balls; and by reflection on these and similar discoveries we come to see that it is of the nature of two and two to make four. In a precisely similar way, we see the *prima facie* rightness of an act which would be the fulfillment of a particular promise, and of another which would be the fulfillment of another promise, and when we have reached sufficient maturity to think in general terms, we apprehend *prima facie* rightness to belong to the nature of any fulfillment of promise. What comes first in time is the apprehension of the self-evident *prima facie* rightness of an individual act of a particular type. From this we come by reflection to apprehend the self-evident general principle of *prima facie* duty. From this, too, perhaps along with the apprehension of the self-evident *prima facie* rightness of the same act in virtue of its having another characteristic as well, and perhaps in spite of the apprehension of its *prima facie* wrongness in virtue of its having some third characteristic, we come to believe something not self-evident at all, but an object of probable opinion, viz., that this particular act is (not *prima facie* but) actually right.

In this respect there is an important difference between rightness and mathematical properties. A triangle which is isosceles necessarily has two of its angles equal, whatever other characteristics the triangle may have—whatever, for instance, be its area, or the size of its third angle. The equality of the two angles is a parti-resultant attribute. And the same is true of all mathematical attributes. It is true, I may add, of *prima facie* rightness. But no act is ever, in virtue of falling under some general description, necessarily actually right; its rightness depends on its whole nature and not on any element in it. The reason is that no mathematical object (no figure, for instance, or angle) ever has two characteristics that tend to give it opposite resultant characteristics, while moral acts often (as everyone knows) and indeed always (as on reflection we must admit) have different characteristics that tend to make them at the same time *prima facie* right and *prima facie* wrong; there is probably no act, for instance, which does good to anyone without doing harm to someone else, and vice versa.

Intuitionism

John Rawls

I shall think of intuitionism in a more general way than is customary: namely, as the doctrine that there is an irreducible family of first principles which have to be weighed against one another by asking ourselves which balance, in our considered judgment, is the most just. Once we reach a certain level of generality, the intuitionist maintains that there exist no higher-order constructive criteria for determining the proper emphasis for the competing principles of justice. While the complexity of the moral facts requires a number of distinct principles, there is no single standard that accounts for them or assigns them their weights. Intuitionist theories, then, have two features: first, they consist

John Rawls, *A Theory of Justice* (Cambridge, Mass: Harvard University Press, 1971), pp. 34–41.

of a plurality of first principles which may conflict to give contrary directives in particular types of cases; and second, they include no explicit method, no priority rules, for weighing these principles against one another: we are simply to strike a balance by intuition, by what seems to us most nearly right. Or if there are priority rules, these are thought to be more or less trivial and of no substantial assistance in reaching a judgment.[1]

Various other contentions are commonly associated with intuitionism, for example, that the concepts of the right and the good are unanalyzable, that moral principles when suitably formulated express self-evident propositions about legitimate moral claims, and so on. But I shall leave these matters aside. These characteristic epistemological doctrines are not a necessary part of intuitionism as I understand it. Perhaps it would be better if we were to speak of intuitionism in this broad sense as pluralism. Still, a conception of justice can be pluralistic without requiring us to weigh its principles by intuition. It may contain the requisite priority rules. To emphasize the direct appeal to our considered judgment in the balancing of principles, it seems appropriate to think of intuitionism in this more general fashion. How far such a view is committed to certain epistemological theories is a separate question.

Now so understood, there are many kinds of intuitionism. Not only are our everyday notions of this type but so perhaps are most philosophical doctrines. One way of distinguishing between intuitionist views is by the level of generality of their principles. Common sense intuitionism takes the form of groups of rather specific precepts, each group applying to a particular problem of justice. There is a group of precepts which applies to the question of fair wages, another to that of taxation, still another to punishment, and so on. In arriving at the notion of a fair wage, say, we are to balance somehow various competing criteria, for example, the claims of skill, training, effort, responsibility, and the hazards of the job, as well as to make some allowance for need. No one presumably would decide by any one of these precepts alone, and some compromise between them must be struck. The determination of wages by existing institutions also represents, in effect, a particular weighting of these claims. This weighting, however, is normally influenced by the demands of different social interests and so by relative positions of power and influence. It may not, therefore, conform to any one's conception of a fair wage. This is particularly likely to be true since persons with different interests are likely to stress the criteria which advance their ends. Those with more ability and education are prone to emphasize the claims of skill and training, whereas those lacking these advantages urge the claim of need. But not only are our everyday ideas of justice influenced by our own situation, they are also strongly colored by custom and current expectations. And by what criteria are we to judge the justice of custom itself and the legitimacy of these expectations? To reach some measure of understanding and agreement which goes beyond a mere de facto resolution of competing interests and a reliance on existing conventions and established expectations, it is necessary to move to a more general scheme for determining the balance of precepts, or at least for confining it within narrower limits.

Thus we can consider the problems of justice by reference to certain ends of social policy. Yet this approach also is likely to rely on intuition, since it normally takes the form of balancing various economic and social objectives. For example, suppose that allocative efficiency, full employment, a larger national income, and its more equal distribution are accepted as social ends. Then, given the desired weighting of these aims, and the existing institutional setup, the precepts of fair wages, just taxation, and so on will receive their due emphasis. In order to achieve greater efficiency and equity, one may follow a policy which has the effect of stressing skill and effort in the payment of wages, leaving the precept of need to be handled in some other fashion, perhaps by welfare transfers. An intuitionism of social ends provides a basis for deciding whether the determination of fair wages makes sense in view of the taxes to be imposed. How we weigh the precepts in one group is adjusted to how we weigh them in another. In this way we have managed to introduce a certain coherence into our judgments of justice; we have moved beyond the narrow de facto compromise of interests to a wider view. Of course we are still left with an appeal to intuition in the balancing of the higher-order ends of policy themselves. Different weightings for these are not by any means trivial variations but often correspond to profoundly opposed political convictions.

The principles of philosophical conceptions are of the most general kind. Not only are they intended to account for the ends of social policy, but the emphasis assigned to these principles should correspondingly determine the balance of these ends. For purposes of illustration, let us discuss a rather simple yet familiar conception based on the aggregative-distributive dichotomy. It has two principles: the basic structure of society is to be designed first to produce the most good in the sense of the greatest net balance of satisfaction, and second to distribute satisfactions equally. Both principles have, of course, *ceteris paribus* clauses. The first principle, the principle of utility, acts in this case as a standard of efficiency, urging us to produce as large a total as we can, other things equal; whereas the second principle serves as a standard of justice constraining the pursuit of aggregate well-being and evening out of the distribution of advantages.

This conception is intuitionist because no priority rule is provided for determining how these two principles are to be balanced against each other. Widely different weights are consistent with accepting these principles. No doubt it is natural to make certain assumptions about how most people would in fact balance them. For one thing, at different combinations of total satisfaction and degrees of equality, we presumably would give these principles different weights. For example, if there is a large total satisfaction but it is unequally distributed, we would probably think it more urgent to increase equality than if the large aggregate well-being were already rather evenly shared.

*   *   *

Now there is nothing intrinsically irrational about this intuitionist doctrine. Indeed, it may be true. We cannot take for granted that there must be a complete derivation of our judgments of social justice from recognizably ethical principles. The intuitionist believes to the contrary that the complexity of the moral facts defies our efforts to give a full account of our judgments and necessitates a plurality of competing principles. He contends that attempts to go beyond these principles either reduce to triviality, as when it is said that social justice is to give every man his due, or else lead to falsehood and oversimplification, as when one settles everything by the principle of utility. The only way therefore to dispute intuitionism is to set forth the recognizably ethical criteria that account for the weights which, in our considered judgments, we think appropriate to give to the plurality of principles. A refutation of intuitionism consists in presenting the sort of constructive criteria that are said not to exist. To be sure, the notion of a recognizably ethical principle is vague, although it is easy to give many examples drawn from tradition and common sense. But it is pointless to discuss this matter in the abstract. The intuitionist and his critic will have to settle this question once the latter has put forward his more systematic account.

It may be asked whether intuitionistic theories are teleological or deontological. They may be of either kind, and any ethical view is bound to rely on intuition to some degree at many points. For example, one could maintain, as Moore did, that personal affection and human understanding, the creation and the contemplation of beauty, and the gaining and appreciation of knowledge are the chief good things, along with pleasure.[2] And one might also maintain (as Moore did not) that these are the sole intrinsic goods. Since these values are specified independently from the right, we have a teleological theory of a perfectionist type if the right is defined as maximizing the good. Yet in estimating what yields the most good, the theory may hold that these values have to be balanced against each other by intuition: it may say that there are no substantive criteria for guidance here. Often, however, intuitionist theories are deontological. In the definitive presentation of Ross, the distribution of good things according to moral worth (distributive justice) is included among the goods to be advanced; and while the principle to produce the most good ranks as a first principle, it is but one such principle which must be balanced by intuition against the claims of the other prima facie principles.[3] The distinctive feature, then, of intuitionistic views is not their being teleological or deontological, but the especially prominent place that they give to the appeal to our intuitive capacities unguided by constructive and recognizably ethical criteria. Intuitionism denies that there exists any useful and explicit solution to the priority problem. I now turn to a brief discussion of this topic.

The Priority Problem

We have seen that intuitionism raises the question of the extent to which it is possible to give a systematic account of our considered judgments of the just and the unjust. In particular, it holds that no constructive answer can be given to the problem of assigning weights to competing principles of justice. Here at least we must rely on our intuitive capacities. Classical utilitarianism tries, of course, to avoid the appeal to intuition altogether. It is a single-principle conception with one ultimate standard; the adjustment of weights is, in theory anyway, settled by reference to the principle of utility. Mill thought that there must be but one such standard, otherwise there would be no umpire between competing criteria, and Sidgwick argues at length that the utilitarian principle is the only one which can assume this role. They maintain that our moral judgments are implicitly utilitarian in the sense that when confronted with a clash of precepts, or with notions which are vague and imprecise, we have no alternative except to adopt utilitarianism. Mill and Sidgwick believe that at some point we must have a single principle to straighten out and to systematize our judgments.[4] Undeniably one of the great attractions of the classical doctrine is the way it faces the priority problem and tries to avoid relying on intuition.

As I have already remarked, there is nothing necessarily irrational in the appeal to intuition to settle questions of priority. We must recognize the possibility that there is no way to get beyond a plurality of principles. No doubt any conception of justice will have to rely on intuition to some degree. Nevertheless, we should do what we can to reduce the direct appeal to our considered judgments. For if men balance final principles differently, as presumably they often do, then their conceptions of justice are different. The assignment of weights is an essential and not a minor part of a conception of justice. If we cannot explain how these weights are to be determined by reasonable ethical criteria, the means of rational discussion have come to an end. An intuitionist conception of justice is, one might say, but half a conception. We should do what we can to formulate explicit principles for the priority problem, even though the dependence on intuition cannot be eliminated entirely.

Notes

1. Intuitionist theories of this type are found in Brian Barry, *Political Argument* (London, Routledge and Kegan Paul, 1965), see esp. pp. 4–8, 286f; R. B. Brandt, *Ethical Theory* (Englewood Cliffs, N.J., Prentice-Hall, Inc. 1959), pp. 404, 426, 429f, where the principle of utility is combined with a principle of equality; and Nicholas Rescher, *Distributive Justice* (New York, Bobbs-Merrill, 1966), pp. 35–41, 115–121, where analogous restrictions are introduced by the concept of the effective average. Robert Nozick discusses some of the problems in developing this kind of intuitionism in "Moral Complications and Moral Structures," *Natural Law Forum,* vol. 13 (1968).

   Intuitionism in the traditional sense includes certain epistemological theses, for example, those concerning the self-evidence and necessity of moral principles. Here representative works are G. E. Moore, *Principia Ethica* (Cambridge, The University Press, 1903), esp. chs. I and VI; H. A. Prichard's essays and lectures in *Moral Obligation* (Oxford, The Clarendon Press, 1949), especially the first essay, "Does Moral Philosophy Rest on a Mistake?" (1912); W. D. Ross, *The Right and the Good* (Oxford, The Clarendon Press, 1930), especially chs. I and II, and *The Foundations of Ethics* (Oxford, The Clarendon Press, 1939). See also the eighteenth century treatise by Richard Price, *A Review of the Principal Questions of Morals,* 3rd ed., 1787, ed. D. D. Raphael (Oxford, The Clarendon Press, 1948). For a recent discussion of this classical form of intuitionism, see H. J. McCloskey, *Meta-Ethics and Normative Ethics* (The Hague, Martinus Nijhoff, 1969).

2. See *Principia Ethica,* ch. VI. The intuitionist nature of Moore's doctrine is assured by his principle of organic unity, pp. 27–31.
3. See W. D. Ross, *The Right and the Good,* pp. 21–27.
4. For Mill, see *A System of Logic,* Book 6, Chapter 12, Sec. 7; *Utilitarianism,* Chapter 5, Parts 26 and 31 where this argument is made in connection with common sense precepts of justice. For Sidgwick, see *Methods of Ethics,* for example Book 4, Chapters 2 and 3.

▼ ## The Business Perspective

Is Business Bluffing Ethical?[1]

Albert Carr

> A respected businessman with whom I discussed the theme of this article remarked with some heat, "You mean to say you're going to encourage men to bluff? Why, bluffing is nothing more than a form of lying! You're advising them to lie!"

I agreed that the basis of private morality is a respect for truth and that the closer a businessman comes to the truth, the more he deserves respect. At the same time, I suggested that most bluffing in business might be regarded simply as game strategy—much like bluffing in poker, which does not reflect on the morality of the bluffer.

I quoted Henry Taylor, the British statesman who pointed out that "falsehood ceases to be falsehood when it is understood on all sides that the truth is not expected to be spoken"—an exact description of bluffing in poker, diplomacy, and business. I cited the analogy of the criminal court, where the criminal is not expected to tell the truth when he pleads "not guilty." Everyone from the judge down takes it for granted that the job of the defendant's attorney is to get his client off, not to reveal the truth; and this is considered ethical practice. I mentioned Representative Omar Burleson, the Democrat from Texas, who was quoted as saying, in regard to the ethics of Congress, "Ethics is a barrel of worms"[2]—a pungent summing up of the problem of deciding who is ethical in politics.

I reminded my friend that millions of businessmen feel constrained every day to say *yes* to their bosses when they secretly believe *no* and that this is generally accepted as permissible strategy when the alternative might be the loss of a job. The essential point, I said, is that the ethics of business are game ethics, different from the ethics of religion.

He remained unconvinced. Referring to the company of which he is president, he declared: "Maybe that's good enough for some businessmen, but I can tell you that we pride ourselves on our ethics. In 30 years not one customer has ever questioned my word or asked to check our figures. We're loyal to our customers and fair to our suppliers. I regard my handshake on a deal as a contract. I've never entered into price-fixing schemes with my competitors. I've never allowed my salesmen to spread injurious rumors about other companies. Our union contract is the best in our industry. And, if I do say so myself, our ethical standards are of the highest!"

He really was saying, without realizing it, that he was living up to the ethical standards of the business game—which are a far cry from those of private life. Like a gentlemanly poker player, he did not play in cahoots with others at the table, try to smear their reputations, or hold back chips he owed them.

But this same fine man, at that very time, was allowing one of his products to be advertised in a way that made it sound a great deal better that it actually was. Another item in his product line was notorious among dealers for its "built-in obsolescence." He was holding back from the market a much-improved product because he did not want to interfere with sales of the inferior item it would have replaced. He had joined with certain of his competitors in hiring a lobbyist to push a state legislature, by methods that he preferred not to know too much about, into amending a bill then being enacted.

In his view these things had nothing to do with ethics; they were merely normal business practice. He himself undoubtedly avoided outright falsehoods—never lied in so many words. But the entire organization that he ruled was deeply involved in numerous strategies of deception.

Pressure to Deceive

Most executives from time to time are almost compelled, in the interests of their companies or themselves, to practice some form of deception when negotiating with customers, dealers, labor unions, government officials, or even other departments of their companies. By conscious misstatements, concealment of pertinent facts, or exaggeration—in short, by bluffing—they seek to persuade others to agree with them. I think it is fair to say that if the individual executive refuses to bluff from time to time—if he feels obligated to tell the truth, the whole truth, and nothing but the truth—he is ignoring opportunities permitted under the rules and is at a heavy disadvantage in his business dealings.

But here and there a businessman is unable to reconcile himself to the bluff in which he plays a part. His conscience, perhaps spurred by religious idealism, troubles him. He feels guilty; he may develop an ulcer or a nervous tic. Before any executive can make profitable use of the strategy of the bluff, he needs to make sure that in bluffing he will not lose self-respect or become emotionally disturbed. If he is to reconcile personal integrity and high standards of honesty with the practical requirements of business, he must feel that his bluffs are ethically justified. The justification rests on the fact that business, as practiced by individuals as well as by corporations, has the impersonal character of a game—a game that demands both special strategy and an understanding of its special ethics.

The game is played at all levels of corporate life, from the highest to the lowest. At the very instant that a man decides to enter business, he may be forced into a game situation, as is shown by the recent experience of a Cornell honor graduate who applied for a job with a large company:

- This applicant was given a psychological test which included the statement, "Of the following magazines, check any that you have read either regularly or from time to time, and double-check those which interest you most. *Reader's Digest, Time, Fortune, Saturday Evening Post, The New Republic, Life, Look, Ramparts, Newsweek, Business Week, U.S. News & World Report, The Nation, Playboy, Esquire, Harper's, Sports Illustrated.*"

  His tastes in reading were broad, and at one time or another he had read almost all of these magazines. He was a subscriber to *The New Republic,* an enthusiast for *Ramparts,* and an avid student of the pictures in *Playboy.* He was not sure whether his interest in *Playboy* would be held against him, but he had a shrewd suspicion that if he confessed to an interest in *Ramparts* and *The New Republic,* he would be thought a liberal, a radical, or at least an intellectual, and his chances of getting the job, which he needed, would greatly diminish. He therefore checked five of the more conservative magazines. Apparently it was a sound decision, for he got the job.

  He had made a game player's decision, consistent with business ethics.

A similar case is that of a magazine space salesman who, owing to a merger, suddenly found himself out of a job:

- This man was 58, and, in spite of a good record, his chances of getting a job elsewhere in a business where youth is favored in hiring practice was not good. He was a vigorous, healthy man, and only a considerable amount of gray in his hair suggested his age. Before beginning his job search he touched up his hair with a black dye to confine the gray to his temples. He knew that the truth about his age might well come out in time, but he calculated that he could deal with that situation when it arose. He and his wife decided that he could easily pass for 45, and he so stated his age on his résumé.

  This was a lie; yet within the accepted rules of the business game, no moral culpability attaches to it.

The Poker Analogy

We can learn a good deal about the nature of business by comparing it with poker. While both have a large element of chance, in the long run the winner is the man who plays with steady skill. In both games ultimate victory requires intimate knowledge of the rules, insight into the psychology of the other players, a bold front, a considerable amount of self-discipline, and the ability to respond swiftly and effectively to opportunities provided by chance.

No one expects poker to be played on the ethical principles preached in churches. In poker it is right and proper to bluff a friend out of the rewards of being dealt a good hand. A player feels no more than a slight twinge of sympathy, if that, when—with nothing better than a single ace in his hand— he strips a heavy loser, who holds a pair, of the rest of his chips. It was up to the other fellow to protect himself. In the words of an excellent poker player, former President Harry Truman, "If you can't stand the heat, stay out of the kitchen." If one shows mercy to a loser in poker, it is a personal gesture, divorced from the rules of the game.

Poker has its special ethics, and here I am not referring to rules against cheating. The man who keeps an ace up his sleeve or who marks the cards is more than unethical; he is a crook, and can be punished as such—kicked out of the game or, in the Old West, shot.

In contrast to the cheat, the unethical poker player is one who, while abiding by the letter of the rules, finds ways to put the other players at an unfair disadvantage. Perhaps he unnerves them with loud talk. Or he tries to get them drunk. Or he plays in cahoots with someone else at the table. Ethical poker players frown on such tactics.

Poker's own brand of ethics is different from the ethical ideals of civilized human relationships. The game calls for distrust of the other fellow. It ignores the claim of friendship. Cunning deception and concealment of one's strength and intentions, not kindness and openheartedness, are vital in poker. No one thinks any the worse of poker on that account. And no one should think any the worse of the game of business because its standards of right and wrong differ from the prevailing traditions of morality in our society. . . .

We Don't Make the Laws

Wherever we turn in business, we can perceive the sharp distinction between its ethical standards and those of the churches. Newspapers abound with sensational stories growing out of this distinction:

- We read one day that Senator Philip A. Hart of Michigan has attacked food processors for deceptive packaging of numerous products.[3]
- The next day there is a Congressional to-do over Ralph Nader's book, *Unsafe At Any Speed,* which demonstrates that automobile companies for years have neglected the safety of car-owning families.[4]
- Then another Senator, Lee Metcalf of Montana, and journalist Vic Reinemer show in their book, *Overcharge,* the methods by which utility companies elude regulating government bodies to extract unduly large payments from users of electricity.[5]

These are merely dramatic instances of a prevailing condition; there is hardly a major industry at which a similar attack could not be aimed. Critics of business regard such behavior as unethical, but the companies concerned know that they are merely playing the business game.

Among the most respected of our business institutions are the insurance companies. A group of insurance executives meeting recently in New England was startled when their guest speaker, social critic Daniel Patrick Moynihan, roundly berated them for "unethical" practices. They had been guilty, Moynihan alleged, of using outdated actuarial tables to obtain unfairly high premiums. They habitually delayed the hearings of lawsuits against them in order to tire out the plaintiffs and win cheap settlements. In their employment policies they used ingenious devices to discriminate against certain minority groups.[6]

It was difficult for the audience to deny the validity of these charges. But these men were business game players. Their reaction to Moynihan's attack was much the same as that of the automobile manufacturers to Nader, of the utilities to Senator Metcalf, and of the food processors to Senator Hart. If the laws governing their business change, or if public opinion becomes clamorous, they will make the necessary adjustments. But morally they have in their view done nothing wrong. As long as they comply with the letter of the law, they are within their rights to operate their businesses as they see fit.

The small business is in the same position as the great corporation in this respect. For example:

- In 1967 a key manufacturer was accused of providing master keys for automobiles to mail-order customers, although it was obvious that some of the purchasers might be automobile thieves. His defense was plain and straightforward. If there was nothing in the law to prevent him from selling his keys to anyone who ordered them, it was not up to him to inquire as to his customers' motives. Why was it any worse, he insisted, for him to sell car keys by mail, than for mail-order houses to sell guns that might be used for murder? Until the law was changed, the key manufacturer could regard himself as being just as ethical as any other businessman by the rules of the business game.[7]

Violations of the ethical ideals of society are common in business, but they are not necessarily violations of business practices. Each year the Federal Trade Commission orders hundreds of companies, many of them of the first magnitude, to "cease and desist" from practices which, judged by ordinary standards, are of questionable morality but which are stoutly defended by the companies concerned.

In one case, a firm manufacturing a well-known mouthwash was accused of using a cheap form of alcohol possibly deleterious to health. The company's chief executive, after testifying in Washington, made this comment privately:

> We broke no law. We're in a highly competitive industry. If we're going to stay in business, we have to look for profit wherever the law permits. We

don't make the laws. We obey them. Then why do we have to put up with this 'holier than thou' talk about ethics? It's sheer hypocrisy. We're not in business to promote ethics. Look at the cigarette companies, for God's sake! If the ethics aren't embodied in the laws by the men who made them, you can't expect businessmen to fill the lack. Why, a sudden submission to Christian ethics by businessmen would bring about the greatest economic upheaval in history!

It may be noted that the government failed to prove its case against him.

Last Illusions Aside

Talk about ethics by businessmen is often a thin decorative coating over the hard realities of the game:

• Once I listened to a speech by a young executive who pointed to a new industry code as proof that his company and its competitors were deeply aware of their responsibilities to society. It was a code of ethics, he said. The industry was going to police itself, to dissuade constituent companies from wrongdoing. His eyes shone with conviction and enthusiasm.

The same day there was a meeting in a hotel room where the industry's top executives met with the "czar" who was to administer the new code, a man of high repute. No one who was present could doubt their common attitude. In their eyes the code was designed primarily to forestall a move by the federal government to impose stern restrictions on the industry. They felt that the code would hamper them a good deal less than new federal laws would. It was, in other words, conceived as a protection for the industry, not for the public.

The young executive accepted the surface explanation of the code; these leaders, all experienced game players, did not deceive themselves for a moment about its purpose.

The illusion that business can afford to be guided by ethics as conceived in private life is often fostered by speeches and articles containing such phrases as, "It pays to be ethical," or, "Sound ethics is good business." Actually this is not an ethical position at all; it is a self-serving calculation in disguise. The speaker is really saying that in the long run a company can make more money if it does not antagonize competitors, suppliers, employees, and customers by squeezing them too hard. He is saying that oversharp policies reduce ultimate gains. That is true, but it has nothing to do with ethics. The underlying attitude is much like that in the familiar story of the shopkeeper who finds an extra $20 bill in the cash register, debates with himself the ethical problem—should he tell his partner?—and finally decides to share the money because the gesture will give him an edge over the s.o.b. the next time they quarrel.

I think it is fair to sum up the prevailing attitude of businessmen on ethics as follows:

We live in what is probably the most competitive of the world's civilized societies. Our customs encourage a high degree of aggression in the individual's striving for success. Business is our main area of competition, and it has been ritualized into a game of strategy. The basic rules of the game have been set by the government, which attempts to detect and punish business frauds. But as long as a company does not transgress the rules of the game set by law, it has the legal right to shape its strategy without reference to anything but its profits. If it takes a long-term view of its profits, it will preserve amicable relations, so far as possible, with those with whom it deals. A wise businessman will not seek advantage to the point where he generates dangerous hostility among employees, competitors, customers, government, or the public at large. But decisions in this area are, in the final test, decisions of strategy, not of ethics.

. . . If a man plans to make a seat in the business game, he owes it to himself to master the principles by which the game is played, including its special ethical outlook. He can then hardly fail to recognize that an occasional bluff may well be justified in terms of the game's ethics and warranted in terms of economic necessity. Once he clears his mind on this point, he is in a good position to match his strategy against that of the other players. He can then determine objectively whether a bluff in a given situation has a good chance of succeeding and can decide when and how to bluff, without a feeling of ethical transgression.

To be a winner, a man must play to win. This does not mean that he must be ruthless, cruel, harsh, or treacherous. On the contrary, the better his reputation for integrity, honesty, and decency, the better his chances of victory will be in the long run. But from time to time every businessman, like every poker player, is offered a choice between certain loss or bluffing within the legal rules of the game. If he is not resigned to losing, if he wants to rise in his company and industry, then in such a crisis he will bluff—and bluff hard.

Every now and then one meets a successful businessman who has conveniently forgotten the small or large deceptions that he practiced on his way to fortune. "God gave me my money," old John D. Rockefeller once piously told a Sunday school class. It would be a rare tycoon in our time who would risk the horse laugh with which such a remark would be greeted.

In the last third of the twentieth century even children are aware that if a man has become prosperous in business, he has sometimes departed from the strict truth in order to overcome obstacles or has practiced the more subtle deceptions of the half-truth or the misleading omission. Whatever the form of the bluff, it is an integral part of the game, and the executive who does not master its techniques is not likely to accumulate much money or power.

Notes

1. Some have wondered at the role of "intuitionism" in business decisions. To me it is ever present. This is the facet that "ethical intuitionism" brings to business decisions. If all business decisions have this element (some would say the *determining* element), then it is important to focus on this in the "gamesmanship" aspect of business. In games people

operate on immediate reactions. This fits the description of intuitionism. Thus, the immediate-reaction-element that exists in gamesmanship sets this article off as employing ethical intuitionism.—Ed.

2. *The New York Times,* March 9, 1967.
3. *The New York Times,* November 21, 1966.
4. New York, Grossman Publishers, Inc., 1965.
5. New York, David McKay Company, Inc., 1967.
6. *The New York Times,* January 17, 1967.
7. Cited by Ralph Nader in "Business Crime," *The New Republic,* July 1, 1967, p. 7.

CHECKLIST for Intuitionism

The ethical checklists are short summaries meant to help students apply the theories they have been studying in the preceding section. They are not meant to stand alone nor are they meant to supplant deeper reading into primary sources of each ethical theory.

It also should be noted that **there is no single application of any theory that everyone will accept.** Therefore, the checklist below is just one version of the ethical theory presented. It is set down in this succinct format as a pedagogical aid for applying ethical theories that will be used in the Case Studies Reports.

Directions: Read the short epitome on Intuitionism and then go through the steps outlined below. When you have finished the assignment, you will have constructed your own checklist for intuitionism.

Intuitionism

Epitome:
Intuitionism works from an established list of moral maxims which have no other justification other than they are immediately perceived to be true. In any given moral situation the practitioner picks the moral maxim that applies in the given situation and follows that. Sometimes you may have two moral maxims which contradict each other, e.g., "Turn the other cheek" and "Defend your rights against those who wish to take them away." In cases such as this, the practitioner will immediately perceive which maxim takes priority in the given situation. Thus intuitionism is involved in two parts of the process: (a) in picking the moral maxims for which you have a prima facie duty to obey; and (b) in applying the moral maxims and in creating priorities among competing maxims.

Application:

Step One: Set out a list of moral maxims that are general and which you believe will cover most moral situations (e.g., "Don't lie"). Choose at least three and no more than ten. [You may wish to use Moore's "open question" test to determine the character of your choices.]

Step Two: Establish a hierarchy among your maxims that will apply "for the most part."

Step Three: Create a moral situation of your own which involves at least two moral maxims from your list. Set out which moral maxim best applies in the situation. State the reasons for your choice. How would you respond to someone else who might disagree with your choice?

CHAPTER 3

Utilitarianism

▼
The Philosophical Perspective

What Utilitarianism Is

John Stuart Mill

A passing remark is all that needs be given to the ignorant blunder of supposing that those who stand up for utility as the test of right and wrong, use the term in that restricted and merely colloquial sense in which utility is opposed to pleasure. An apology is due to the philosophical opponents of utilitarianism, for even the momentary appearance of confounding them with any one capable of so absurd a misconception; which is the more extraordinary, inasmuch as the contrary accusation, of referring everything to pleasure, and that too in its grossest form, is another of the common charges against utilitarianism: and, as has been pointedly remarked by an able writer, the same sort of persons, and often the very same persons, denounce the theory "as impracticably dry when the word utility precedes the word pleasure, and as too practicably voluptuous when the word pleasure precedes the word utility." Those who know anything about the matter are aware that every writer, from Epicurus to Bentham, who maintained the theory of utility, meant by it, not something to be contradistinguished from pleasure, but pleasure itself, together with exemption from pain; and instead of opposing the useful to the

John Stuart Mill, *Utilitarianism* (London, Parker, Son and Bourn; 1863).

agreeable or the ornamental, have always declared that the useful means these, among other things. Yet the common herd, including the herd of writers, not only in newspapers and periodicals, but in books of weight and pretension, are perpetually falling into this shallow mistake. Having caught up the word utilitarian, while knowing nothing whatever about it but its sound, they habitually express by it the rejection, or the neglect, of pleasure in some of its forms; of beauty, of ornament, or of amusement. Nor is the term thus ignorantly misapplied solely in disparagement, but occasionally in compliment; as though it implied superiority to frivolity and the mere pleasures of the moment. And this perverted use is the only one in which the word is popularly known, and the one from which the new generation are acquiring their sole notion of its meaning. Those who introduced the word, but who had for many years discontinued it as a distinctive appellation, may well feel themselves called to resume it, if by doing so they can hope to contribute anything towards rescuing it from this utter degradation.[1]

The creed which accepts as the foundation of morals, Utility, or the Greatest Happiness Principle, holds that actions are right in proportion as they tend to promote happiness, wrong as they tend to produce the reverse of happiness. By happiness is intended pleasure, and the absence of pain; by unhappiness, pain, and the privation of pleasure. To give a clear view of the moral standard set up by the theory, much more requires to be said; in particular, what things it includes in the ideas of pain and pleasure; and to what extent this is left an open question. But these supplementary explanations do not affect the theory of life on which this theory of morality is grounded—namely, that pleasure, and freedom from pain, are the only things desirable as ends; and that all desirable things (which are as numerous in the utilitarian as in any other scheme) are desirable either for the pleasure inherent in themselves, or as means to the promotion of pleasure and the prevention of pain.

Now, such a theory of life excites in many minds, and among them in some of the most estimable in feeling and purpose, inveterate dislike. To suppose that life has (as they express it) no higher end than pleasure—no better and nobler object of desire and pursuit—they designate as utterly mean and grovelling; as a doctrine worthy only of swine, to whom the followers of Epicurus were, at a very early period, contemptuously likened; and modern holders of the doctrine are occasionally made the subject of equally polite comparisons by its German, French, and English assailants.

When thus attacked, the Epicureans have always answered, that it is not they, but their accusers, who represent human nature in a degrading light; since the accusation supposes human beings to be capable of no pleasures except those of which swine are capable. If this supposition were true, the charge could not be gainsaid, but would then be no longer an imputation; for if the sources of pleasure were precisely the same to human beings and to swine, the rule of life which is good enough for the one would be good enough for the other. The comparison of the Epicurean life to that of beasts is felt as degrading, precisely because a beast's pleasures do not satisfy a human being's conception of happiness. Human beings have faculties more el-evated than the animal appetites, and when once made conscious of them, do not regard anything as happiness which does not include their gratifica-tion. I do not, indeed, consider the Epicureans to have been by any means faultless in drawing out their scheme of consequences from the utilitarian principle. To do this in any sufficient manner, many Stoic, as well as Christ-ian elements require to be included. But there is no known Epicurean theory of life which does not assign to the pleasures of the intellect, of the feelings and imagination, and of the moral sentiments, a much higher value as plea-sures than to those of mere sensation. It must be admitted, however, that utilitarian writers in general have placed the superiority of mental over bod-ily pleasures chiefly in the greater permanency, safety, uncostliness, etc., of the former—that is, in their circumstantial advantages rather than in their intrinsic nature. And on all these points utilitarians have fully proved their case; but they might have taken the other, and, as it may be called, higher ground, with entire consistency. It is quite compatible with the principle of utility to recognise the fact, that some *kinds* of pleasure are more desirable and more valuable than others. It would be absurd that while, in estimating all other things, quality is considered as well as quantity, the estimation of pleasures should be supposed to depend on quantity alone.

If I am asked, what I mean by difference of quality in pleasures, or what makes one pleasure more valuable than another, merely as a pleasure, except its being greater in amount, there is but one possible answer. Of two plea-sures, if there be one to which all or almost all who have experience of both give a decided preference, irrespective of any feeling of moral obligation to prefer it, that is the more desirable pleasure. If one of the two is, by those who are competently acquainted with both, placed so far above the other that they prefer it, even though knowing it to be attended with a greater amount of discontent, and would not resign it for any quantity of the other pleasure which their nature is capable of, we are justified in ascribing to the preferred enjoyment a superiority in quality, so far out-weighing quantity as to render it, in comparison, of small account.

Now it is an unquestionable fact that those who are equally acquainted with, and equally capable of appreciating and enjoying, both, do give a most marked preference to the manner of existence which employs their higher fac-ulties. Few human creatures would consent to be changed into any of the lower animals, for a promise of the fullest allowance of a beast's pleasures; no intel-ligent human being would consent to be a fool, no instructed person would be an ignoramus, no person of feeling and conscience would be selfish and base, even though they should be persuaded that the fool, the dunce, or the rascal is better satisfied with his lot than they are with theirs. They would not re-sign what they possess more than he for the most complete satisfaction of all the desires which they have in common with him. If they ever fancy they would, it is only in cases of unhappiness so extreme, that to escape from it they would exchange their lot for almost any other, however undesirable in their own eyes. A being of higher faculties requires more to make him happy, is capable probably of more acute suffering, and certainly accessible to it at more points, than one of an inferior type; but in spite of these liabilities, he can never really wish to sink into what he feels to be a lower grade of existence. We may give what explanation we please of this unwillingness; we may attribute it to pride, a name which is given indiscriminately to some of the most and to some of the least estimable feelings of which mankind are capable: we may refer it to the love of liberty and personal independence, an appeal to which was with the Stoics one of the most effective means for the inculcation of it; to the love of power, or to the love of excitement, both of which do really enter into and contribute to it: but its most appropriate appellation is a sense of dignity, which all human beings possess in one form or another, and in some, though by no means in exact, proportion to their higher faculties, and which is so essential a part of the happiness of those in whom it is strong, that nothing which conflicts with it could be, otherwise than momentarily, an object of desire to them. Whoever supposes that this preference takes place at a sacrifice of happiness—that the superior being, in anything like equal circumstances, is not happier than the inferior—confounds the two very different ideas, of happiness, and content. It is indisputable that the being whose capacities of enjoyment are low, has the greatest chance of having them fully satisfied; and a highly endowed being will always feel that any happiness which he can look for, as the world is constituted, is imperfect. But he can learn to bear its imperfections, if they are at all bearable; and they will not make him envy the being who is indeed unconscious of the imperfections, but only because he feels not at all the good which those imperfections qualify. It is better to be a human being dissatisfied than a pig satisfied; better to be Socrates dissatisfied than a fool satisfied. And if the fool, or the pig, are of a different opinion, it is because they only know their own side of the question. The other party to the comparison knows both sides.

It may be objected, that many who are capable of the higher pleasures, occasionally, under the influence of temptation, postpone them to the lower. But this is quite compatible with a full appreciation of the intrinsic superiority of the higher. Men often, from infirmity of character, make their election for the nearer good, though they know it to be the less valuable; and this no less when the choice is between two bodily pleasures, than when it is between bodily and mental. They pursue sensual indulgences to the injury of health, though perfectly aware that health is the greater good. It may be further objected, that many who begin with youthful enthusiasm for everything noble, as they advance in years sink into indolence and selfishness. But I do not believe that those who undergo this very common change, voluntarily choose the lower description of pleasures in preference to the higher. I believe that before they devote themselves exclusively to the one, they have already become incapable of the other. Capacity for the nobler feelings is in most natures a very tender plant, easily killed, not only by hostile influences, but by mere want of sustenance; and in the majority of young persons it speedily dies away if the occupations to which their position in life has devoted them, and the society into which it has thrown them, are not favourable to keeping that higher capacity in exercise. Men lose their high aspirations as they lose their intellectual tastes, because they have not time or opportunity for indulging them; and they addict themselves to inferior pleasures, not because they deliberately prefer them, but because they are either the only ones to which they have access, or the only ones which they are any longer capable of enjoying. It may be questioned whether any one who has remained equally susceptible to both classes of pleasures, ever knowingly and calmly preferred the lower; though many, in all ages, have broken down in an ineffectual attempt to combine both.

From this verdict of the only competent judges, I apprehend there can be no appeal. On a question which is the best worth having of two pleasures, or which of two modes of existence is the most grateful to the feelings, apart from its moral attributes and from its consequences, the judgment of those who are qualified by knowledge of both, or, if they differ, that of the majority among them, must be admitted as final. And there needs be the less hesitation to accept this judgment respecting the quality of pleasures, since there is no other tribunal to be referred to even on the question of quantity. What means are there of determining which is the acutest of two pains, of the intensest of two pleasurable sensations, except the general suffrage of those who are familiar with both? Neither pains nor pleasures are homogeneous, and pain is always heterogeneous with pleasure. What is there to decide whether a particular pleasure is worth purchasing at the cost of a particular pain, except the feeling and judgment of the experienced? When, therefore, those feelings and judgments declare the pleasures derived from the higher faculties to be preferable *in kind,* apart from the question of intensity, to those of which the animal nature, disjoined from the higher faculties, is susceptible, they are entitled on this subject to the same regard.

I have dwelt on this point, as being a necessary part of a perfectly just conception of Utility or Happiness, considered as the directive rule of human conduct. But it is by no means an indispensable condition to the acceptance of the utilitarian standard; for that standard is not the agent's own greatest happiness, but the greatest amount of happiness altogether; and if it may possibly be doubted whether a noble character is always the happier for its nobleness, there can be no doubt that it makes other people happier, and that the world in general is immensely a gainer by it. Utilitarianism, therefore, could only attain its end by the general cultivation of nobleness of character, even if each individual were only benefited by the nobleness of others, and his own, so far as happiness is concerned, were a sheer deduction from the benefit. But the bare enunciation of such an absurdity as this last, renders refutation superfluous.

Notes

1. The author of this essay has reason for believing himself to be the first person who brought the word utilitarian into use. He did not invent it, but adopted it from a passing expression in Mr. Galt's *Annals of the Parish.* After using it as a designation for several

years, he and others abandoned it from a growing dislike to anything resembling a badge or watchword of sectarian distinction. But as a name for one single opinion, not a set of opinions—to denote the recognition of utility as a standard, not any particular way of applying it—the term supplies a want in the language, and offers, in many cases, a convenient mode of avoiding tiresome circumlocution.

The Interpretation of the Moral Philosophy of J. S. Mill[1]

J. O. Urmson

It is a matter which should be of great interest to those who study the psychology of philosophers that the theories of some great philosophers of the past are studied with the most patient and accurate scholarship, while those of others are so burlesqued and travestied by critics and commentators that it is hard to believe that their works are ever seriously read with a sympathetic interest, or even that they are read at all. Amongst those who suffer most in this way John Stuart Mill is an outstanding example. With the exception of a short book by Reginald Jackson,[2] there is no remotely accurate account of his views on deductive logic, so that, for example, the absurd view that the syllogism involves *petitio principii* is almost invariably fathered on him; and, as Von Wright says, 'A good systematic and critical monograph on Mill's Logic of Induction still remains to be written'.[3] But even more perplexing is the almost universal misconstruction placed upon Mill's ethical doctrines; for his *Utilitarianism* is a work which every undergraduate is set to read and which one would therefore expect Mill's critics to have read at least once. But this, apparently, is not so; and instead of Mill's own doctrines a travesty is discussed, so that the most common criticisms of him are simply irrelevant. It will not be the thesis of this paper that Mill's views are immune to criticism, or that they are of impeccable clarity and verbal consistency; it will be maintained that, if interpreted with, say, half the sympathy automatically accorded to Plato, Leibniz, and Kant, an essentially consistent thesis can be discovered which is very superior to that usually attributed to Mill and immune to the common run of criticisms.

One further note must be made on the scope of this paper. Mill in his *Utilitarianism* attempts to do two things; first, he attempts to state the place of the conception of a *summum bonum* in ethics, secondly, he attempts to give an account of the nature of this ultimate end. We shall be concerned only with the first of these two parts of Mill's ethical theory; we shall not ask what Mill thought the ultimate end was, and how he thought that his view on this point could be substantiated, but only what part Mill considered that the notion of an ultimate end, whatever it be, must play in a sound ethical theory. This part of Mill's doctrine is logically independent of his account of happiness.

Philosophical Quarterly, Vol. 3 (1953), pp. 33–39. Reprinted by permission of the author and the *Philosophical Quarterly*.

Two Mistaken Interpretations of Mill

Some of Mill's expositors and critics have thought that Mill was attempting to analyse or define the notion of right in terms of the *summum bonum*. Thus Mill is commonly adduced as an example of an ethical naturalist by those who interpret his account of happiness naturalistically, as being one who defined rightness in terms of the natural consequences of actions. Moore, for example, while criticising Mill's account of the ultimate end says: 'In thus insisting that what is right must mean what produces the best possible results Utilitarianism is fully justified.'[4] Others have been less favourable in their estimation of this alleged view of Mill's. But right or wrong, it seems clear to me that Mill did not hold it. In Mill's only reference to this analytic problem, (of the Everyman edition, to which all references will be made), he refers to a person 'who sees in moral obligation a transcendent fact, an objective reality belonging to the province of "Things in themselves"', and goes on to speak of this view as an irrelevant opinion 'on this point of Ontology', as though the analysis of ethical terms was not part of ethical philosophy at all as he conceived it, but part of ontology. It seems clear that when Mill speaks of his quest being for the 'criterion of right and wrong', 'concerning the foundation of morality' for a 'test of right and wrong', he is looking for a 'means of ascertaining what is right or wrong', not for a definition of these terms. We shall not, therefore, deal further with this interpretation of Mill; if a further refutation of it is required it should be sought in the agreement of the text with the alternative exposition shortly to be given.

The other mistaken view avoids the error of this first view, and indeed is incompatible with it. It is, probably, the received view. On this interpretation Mill is looking for a test of right or wrong as the ultimate test by which one can justify the ascription of rightness or wrongness to courses of action, rightness and wrongness being taken to be words which we understand. This test is taken to be whether the course of action does or does not tend to promote the ultimate end (which Mill no doubt says is the general happiness). So far there is no cause to quarrel with the received view, for it is surely correct. But in detail the view is wrong. For it is further suggested that for Mill this ultimate test is also the immediate test; the rightness or wrongness of any particular action is to be decided by considering whether it promotes the ultimate end. We may, it might be admitted, on Mill's view sometimes act, by rule of thumb or in a hurry, without actually raising this question; but the actual justification, if there is one, must be directly in terms of consequences, including the consequences of the example that we have set. On this view, then, Mill holds that an action, a particular action, is right if it promotes the ultimate end better than any alternative, and otherwise it is wrong. However we in fact make up our minds in moral situations, so far as justification goes no other factor enters into the matter. It is clear that on this interpretation Mill is immediately open to two shattering objections; first, it is obviously and correctly urged, if one has, for example, promised to do something it is one's duty to do it at least partly because one has promised to do it and not merely because of consequences, even if these consequences are taken to include one's example in promise-breaking. Secondly, it is correctly pointed out that on this view a man who, *ceteris paribus,* chooses the inferior of two musical comedies for an evening's entertainment has done a moral wrong, and this is preposterous.[5] If this were in fact the view of Mill, he would indeed be fit for little more than the halting eristic of philosophical infants.

A Revised Interpretation of Mill

I shall now set out in a set of propositions what I take to be in fact Mill's view and substantiate them afterwards from the text. This will obscure the subtleties but will make clearer the main lines of interpretation.

A. A particular action is justified as being right by showing that it is in accord with some moral rule. It is shown to be wrong by showing that it transgresses some moral rule.

B. A moral rule is shown to be correct by showing that the recognition of that rule promotes the ultimate end.

C. Moral rules can be justified only in regard to matters in which the general welfare is more than negligibly affected.

D. Where no moral rule is applicable the question of the rightness or wrongness of particular acts does not arise, though the worth of the actions can be estimated in other ways.

As a terminological point it should be mentioned that where the phrase 'moral rule' occurs above Mill uses the phrase 'secondary principle' more generally, though he sometimes says 'moral law'. By these terms, whichever is preferred, Mill is referring to such precepts as 'Keep promises', 'Do no murder', or 'Tell no lies'. A list of which Mill approves is to be found in *On Liberty.*

   There is, no doubt, need of further explanation of these propositions; but that, and some caveats, can best be given in the process of establishing that these are in fact Mill's views. First, then, to establish from the text that in Mill's view particular actions are shown to be right or wrong by showing that they are or are not in accord with some moral rule. (i) He says with evident approbation: 'The intuitive, no less than what may be termed the inductive, school of ethics, insists on the necessity of general laws. They both agree that the morality of an individual action is not a question of direct perception, but of the application of a law to an individual case. They recognise also, to a great extent, the same moral laws'. Mill reproaches these schools only with being unable to give a unifying rationale of these laws (as he will do in proposition B). (ii) 'But to consider the rules of morality as improvable is one thing; to pass over the intermediate generalisations entirely, and endeavour to test each individual action directly by the first principle, is another. It is a strange notion that the acknowledgement of a first principle is inconsistent with the admission of secondary ones'. He adds, with feeling: 'Men really ought to leave off talking a kind of nonsense on this subject which they would neither talk nor listen to on other matters of practical concernment'. (iii) Having admitted that 'rules of conduct cannot be so framed as to require no exceptions', he adds 'We must remember that only in these cases of conflict between secondary principles is it requisite that first principles should be appealed to. There is no case of moral obligation in which some secondary principle is not involved; and if only one, there can seldom be any real doubt which one it is, in the mind of any person by whom the principle itself is recognised'. This quotation supports both propositions A and D. It shows that for Mill moral rules are not merely rules of thumb which aid the unreflective man in making up his mind, but an essential part of moral reasoning. The relevance of a moral rule is the criterion of whether we are dealing with a case of right or wrong or some other moral or prudential situation. (iv) The last passage which we shall select to establish this interpretation of Mill (it would be easy to find more) is also a joint confirmation of propositions A and D, showing that our last was not an *obiter dictum* on which we have placed too much weight. In the chapter entitled 'On the connection between justice and utility', Mill has maintained that it is a distinguishing mark of a just act that it is one required by a specific rule or law, positive or moral, carrying also liability to penal sanctions. He then writes this important paragraph, which in view of its importance and the neglect that it has suffered must be quoted at length: 'The above is, I think, a true account, as far as it goes, of the origin and progressive growth of the idea of justice. But we must observe, that it contains, as yet, nothing to distinguish that obligation from moral obligation in general. For the truth is, that the idea of penal sanction, which is the essence of law, enters not only into the conception of injustice, but into that of any kind of wrong. We do not call anything wrong, unless we mean to imply that a person ought to be punished in some way or other for doing it; if not by law, by the opinion of his fellow-creatures; if not by opinion, by the reproaches of his own conscience. This seems to be the real turning point of the distinction between morality and simple expediency. It is a part of the notion of Duty in every one of its forms, that a person may rightfully be compelled to fulfil it. Duty is a thing which may be exacted from a person, as one exacts a debt. Unless we think that it may be exacted from him, we do not call it his duty. . . . There are other things, on the contrary, which we wish that people should do, which we like or admire them for doing, perhaps dislike or despise them for not doing, but yet admit that they are not bound to do; it is not a case of moral obligation; we do not blame them, that is, we do not think that they are proper objects of punishment. . . . I think there is no doubt that this distinction lies at the bottom of the notions of right and wrong; that we call any conduct wrong, or employ, instead, some other term of dislike or disparagement, according as we think that the person ought, or ought not, to be punished for it; and we say, it would be right to do so and so, or merely that it would be desirable or laudable, according as we would wish to see the person whom it concerns, compelled, or only persuaded and exhorted, to act in that manner'. How supporters of the received view have squared it with this passage I do not know; they do not mention it. If they have noticed it at all it is, presumably, regarded as an example of Mill's inconsistent eclecticism. Mill here makes it quite clear that in his view right and wrong are derived from moral rules; in other cases where the ultimate end is no doubt affected appraisal of conduct must be made in other ways. For example, if one's own participation in the ultimate end is impaired without breach of moral law, it is imprudence or lack of self respect, it is not wrong-doing. So much for the establishment of this interpretation of Mill, in a positive way, as regards points A and D. We must now ask whether there is anything in Mill which is inconsistent with it and in favour of the received view.

It is impossible to show positively that there is nothing in Mill which favours the received view against the interpretation here given, for it would require a complete review of everything that Mill says. We shall have to be content with examining two points which might be thought to tell in favour of the received view.

(*a*) Mill says: 'The creed which accepts as the foundation of morals, Utility, or the Greatest Happiness Principle, holds that actions are right in proportion as they tend to promote happiness, wrong as they tend to promote the reverse of Happiness'. This seems to be the well-known sentence which is at the bottom of the received interpretation. Of course, it could be taken as a loose and inaccurate statement of the received view, if the general argument required it. But note that strictly one can say that a certain action tends to produce a certain result only if one is speaking of type- rather than token-actions. Drinking alcohol may tend to promote exhilaration, but my drinking this particular glass either does or does not produce it. It seems, then, that Mill can well be interpreted here as regarding moral rules as forbidding or enjoining types of action, in fact as making the point that the right moral rules are the ones which promote the ultimate end (my proposition B), not as saying something contrary to proposition A. And this, or something like it, is the interpretation which consistency requires. Mill's reference to 'tendencies of actions' supports the stress here laid on the word 'tend', and that context should be examined by those who require further conviction.

(*b*) Mill sometimes refers to moral rules as 'intermediate generalisations' from the supreme principle, or as 'corollaries' of it. These are probably the sort of phrases which lead people to think that they play a purely heuristic role in ethical thinking for Mill. As for the expression 'intermediate generalisation', Mill undoubtedly thinks that we should, and to some extent do, arrive at and improve our moral rules by such methods as observing that a certain type of action has had bad results of a social kind in such an overwhelming majority of cases that it ought to be banned. (But this is an oversimplification.) But this account of the genesis of moral rules does not require us to interpret them as being anything but rules when once made. It really seems unnecessary to say much of the expression 'corollary'; Mill obviously cannot wish it to be taken literally; in fact it is hard to state the relation of moral rules to a justifying principle with exactitude and Mill, in a popular article in *Fraser*, did not try very hard to do so.

Moral Rules and the Ultimate End

We have already been led in our examination of possible objections to proposition A to say something in defence of the view that Mill thought that a moral rule is shown to be correct by showing that the recognition of that rule promotes the ultimate end (proposition B). A little more may be added on this point, though it seems fairly obvious that if we are right in saying that the supreme principle is not to be evoked, in Mill's view, in the direct justification of particular right acts, it must thus come in an indirect way in view of the importance that Mill attached to it. And it is hard to think what the indirect way is if not this. (i) Mill reproaches other moral philosophers with not giving a satisfactory account of moral rules in terms of a fundamental principle, though they have correctly placed moral rules as governing particular actions. It would be indeed the mark of an inconsistent philosopher if he did not try to repair the one serious omission which he ascribes to others. (ii) Mill ascribes to Kant the use of utilitarian arguments because, Mill alleges, he in fact supports the rules of morality by showing the evil consequences of not adopting them or adopting alternatives. Thus Mill is here regarding as distinctively utilitarian the justification or rejection of moral rules on the ground of consequences. He could hardly have wished to suggest that Kant would directly justify, even inadvertently, particular actions on such grounds. But it is perhaps not to the point to argue this matter more elaborately. If anyone has been convinced by what has gone before, he will not need much argument on this point; with others it is superfluous to make the attempt.

In What Fields Are Moral Rules of Right and Wrong Applicable?

The applicability of moral rules is, says Mill, 'the characteristic difference which marks off, not justice, but morality in general, from the remaining provinces of Expediency and Worthiness'. Mill says little or nothing in *Utilitarianism* about the boundary between morality and worthiness (surely it would be better to have said the boundary between right and wrong on the one hand and other forms of both moral and non-moral appraisal on the other?). It seems reasonable to suppose that he would have recognised that the use of moral rules must be confined to matters in which the kind of consequence is sufficiently invariable for there not to be too many exceptions. But this is a pragmatic limitation; Mill does have something to say about a limitation in principle in *Liberty* which I have crudely summarised in my proposition C—moral rules can be justifiably maintained in regard only to matters in which the general welfare is more than negligibly affected.

It is important to note that Mill in *Liberty* is concerned with freedom from moral sanctions as well as the sanctions of positive law. The distinction between self-regarding and other actions is regarded by him as relevant to moral as well as to political philosophy. Here he mentions such things as

encroachment on the rights of others as being 'fit objects of moral reproba-
tion, and, in grave cases, of moral retribution and punishment'. But self-
regarding faults (low tastes and the like) are 'not properly immoralities and
to whatever pitch they are carried, do not constitute wickedness . . . The
term duty to oneself, when it means anything more than prudence, means
self-respect or self-development'. Self-regarding faults render the culprit 'necessarily and properly a subject of distaste, or, in extreme cases, even of con-
tempt', but this is in the sphere of worthiness not of right and wrong.

So much then for Mill's account of the logic of moral reasoning. It must
be emphasised that no more has been attempted than a skeleton plan of Mill's
answer, and that Mill puts the matter more richly and more subtly in his book.
Even on the question of general interpretation more store must be laid on the
effect of a continuous reading in the light of the skeleton plan than on the effect of the few leading quotations introduced in this paper. It is emphatically
not the contention of this paper that Mill has given a finally correct account of
these matters which is immune to all criticism; an attempt has been made only
to give a sympathetic account without any criticism favourable or unfavourable.
But I certainly do maintain that the current interpretations of Mill's *Utilitarianism* are so unsympathetic and so incorrect that the majority of criticisms
which have in fact been based on them are irrelevant and worthless.

Notes

1. This article is discussed by H. J. McCloskey in 'An Examination of Restricted Utilitarianism', *Philosophical Review*, (1957).—Ed.
2. *An Examination of the Deductive Logic of J. S. Mill* (1941).
3. *A Treatise on Induction and Probability* (1951), p. 164.
4. *Principia Ethica*, reprinted 1948, p. 106.
5. For one example of this interpretation of Mill and the first and more important objection,
see Carritt, *The Theory of Morals*, ch. iv.

Extreme and Restricted Utilitarianism[1]

J. J. C. Smart

I

Utilitarianism is the doctrine that the rightness of actions is to be judged by
their consequences. What do we mean by 'actions' here? Do we mean particular actions or do we mean classes of actions? According to which way we interpret the word 'actions' we get two different theories, both of which merit
the appellation 'utilitarian'.

(1) If by 'actions' we mean particular individual actions we get the sort
of doctrine held by Bentham, Sidgwick, and Moore. According to this doctrine

Philosophical Quarterly, Vol. 6 (1956), pp. 344–54. Reprinted, with emendation, by permission of the author and the *Philosophical Quarterly*.

we test individual actions by their consequences, and general rules, like 'keep promises', are mere rules of thumb which we use only to avoid the necessity of estimating the probable consequences of our actions at every step. The rightness or wrongness of keeping a promise on a particular occasion depends only on the goodness or badness of the consequences of keeping or of breaking the promise on that particular occasion. Of course part of the consequences of breaking the promise, and a part to which we will normally ascribe decisive importance, will be the weakening of faith in the institution of promising. However, if the goodness of the consequences of breaking the rule is *in toto* greater than the goodness of the consequences of keeping it, then we must break the rule, irrespective of whether the goodness of the consequences of *everybody's* obeying the rule is or is not greater than the consequences of *everybody's* breaking it. To put it shortly, rules do not matter, save *per accidens* as rules of thumb and as *de facto* social institutions with which the utilitarian has to reckon when estimating consequences. I shall call this doctrine 'extreme utilitarianism'.

(2) A more modest form of utilitarianism has recently become fashionable. The doctrine is to be found in Toulmin's book *The Place of Reason in Ethics,* in Nowell-Smith's *Ethics* (though I think Nowell-Smith has qualms), in John Austin's *Lectures on Jurisprudence* (Lecture II), and even in J. S. Mill, if Urmson's interpretation of him is correct (*Philosophical Quarterly,* Vol. 3, pp. 33–39, 1953). Part of its charm is that it appears to resolve the dispute in moral philosophy between intuitionists and utilitarians in a way which is very neat. The above philosophers hold, or seem to hold, that moral rules are more than rules of thumb. In general the rightness of an action is *not* to be tested by evaluating its consequences but only by considering whether or not it falls under a certain rule. Whether the rule is to be considered an acceptable moral rule, is, however, to be decided by considering the consequences of adopting the rule. Broadly, then, actions are to be tested by rules and rules by consequences. The only cases in which we must test an individual action directly by its consequences are (*a*) when the action comes under two different rules, one of which enjoins it and one of which forbids it, and (*b*) when there is no rule whatever that governs the given case. I shall call this doctrine 'restricted utilitarianism'.

*   *   *

How are we to decide the issue between extreme and restricted utilitarianism? I wish to repudiate at the outset that milk and water approach which describes itself sometimes as 'investigating what is implicit in the common moral consciousness' and sometimes as 'investigating how people ordinarily talk about morality'. We have only to read the newspaper correspondence about capital punishment or about what should be done with Formosa to realize that the common moral consciousness is in part made up of superstitious elements, of morally bad elements, and of logically confused elements. I address myself to good hearted and benevolent people and so I hope that if we rid ourselves of the logical confusion the superstitious and morally bad elements will largely fall away. For even among good hearted and benevolent people it is possible to find superstitious and morally bad reasons for moral beliefs. These superstitious and morally bad reasons hide behind the protective screen of logical confusion. With people who are not logically confused but who are openly superstitious or morally bad I can of course do nothing. That is, our ultimate pro-attitudes may be different. Nevertheless I propose to rely on *my own* moral consciousness and to appeal to *your* moral consciousness and to forget about what people ordinarily say. 'The obligation to obey a rule', says Nowell-Smith (*Ethics,* p. 239), 'does not, *in the opinion of ordinary men',* (my italics), 'rest on the beneficial consequences of obeying it in a particular case'. What does this prove? Surely it is more than likely that ordinary men are confused here. Philosophers should be able to examine the question more rationally.

II

For an extreme utilitarian moral rules are rules of thumb. In practice the extreme utilitarian will mostly guide his conduct by appealing to the rules ('do not lie', 'do not break promises', etc.) of common sense morality. This is not because there is anything sacrosanct in the rules themselves but because he can argue that probably he will most often act in an extreme utilitarian way if he does not think as a utilitarian. For one thing, actions have frequently to be done in a hurry. Imagine a man seeing a person drowning. He jumps in and rescues him. There is no time to reason the matter out, but usually this will be the course of action which an extreme utilitarian would recommend if he did reason the matter out. If, however, the man drowning had been drowning in a river near Berchtesgaden in 1938, and if he had had the well known black forelock and moustache of Adolf Hitler, an extreme utilitarian would, if he had time, work out the probability of the man's being the villainous dictator, and if the probability were high enough he would, on extreme utilitarian grounds, leave him to drown. The rescuer, however, has not time. He trusts to his instincts and dives in and rescues the man. And this trusting to instincts and to moral rules can be justified on extreme utilitarian grounds. Furthermore, an extreme utilitarian who knew that the drowning man was Hitler would nevertheless praise the rescuer, not condemn him. For by praising the man he is strengthening a courageous and benevolent disposition of mind, and in general this disposition has great positive utility. (Next time, perhaps, it will be Winston Churchill that the man saves!) We must never forget that an extreme utilitarian may praise actions which he knows to be wrong. Saving Hitler was wrong, but it was a member of a class of actions which are generally right, and the motive to do actions of this class is in general an optimific one. In considering questions of praise and blame it is not the expediency of the praised or blamed action that is at issue, but the expediency of the praise. It can be expedient to praise an inexpedient action and inexpedient to praise an expedient one.

Lack of time is not the only reason why an extreme utilitarian may, on extreme utilitarian principles, trust to rules of common sense morality. He knows that in particular cases where his own interests are involved his calculations are likely to be biased in his own favour. Suppose that he is unhappily married and is deciding whether to get divorced. He will in all probability greatly exaggerate his own unhappiness (and possibly his wife's) and greatly underestimate the harm done to his children by the break up of the family. He will probably also underestimate the likely harm done by the weakening of the general faith in marriage vows. So probably he will come to the correct extreme utilitarian conclusion if he does not in this instance think as an extreme utilitarian but trusts to common sense morality.

*   *   *

The extreme utilitarian, then, regards moral rules as rules of thumb and as sociological facts that have to be taken into account when deciding what to do, just as facts of any other sort have to be taken into account. But in themselves they do not justify any action.

III

The restricted utilitarian regards moral rules as more than rules of thumb for short-circuiting calculations of consequences. Generally, he argues, consequences are not relevant at all when we are deciding what to do in a particular case. In general, they are relevant only to deciding what rules are good reasons for acting in a certain way in particular cases. This doctrine is possibly a good account of how the modern unreflective twentieth century Englishman often thinks about morality, but surely it is monstrous as an account of how it is most rational to think about morality. Suppose that there is a rule R and that in 99 percent of cases the best possible results are obtained by acting in accordance with R. Then clearly R is a useful rule of thumb; if we have not time or are not impartial enough to assess the consequences of an action it is an extremely good bet that the thing to do is to act in accordance with R. But is it not monstrous to suppose that if we *have* worked out the consequences and if we have perfect faith in the impartiality of our calculations, and if we *know* that in this instance to break R will have better results than to keep it, we should nevertheless obey the rule? Is it not to erect R into a sort of idol if we keep it when breaking it will prevent, say, some avoidable misery? Is not this a form of superstitious rule-worship (easily explicable psychologically) and not the rational thought of a philosopher?

The point may be made more clearly if we consider Mill's comparison of moral rules to the tables in the nautical almanack. This comparison of Mill's is adduced by Urmson as evidence that Mill was a restricted utilitarian, but I do not think that it will bear this interpretation at all. (Though I quite agree with Urmson that many other things said by Mill are in harmony with restricted rather than extreme utilitarianism. Probably Mill had never thought very much about the distinction and was arguing for utilitarianism, restricted or extreme, against other and quite non-utilitarian forms of moral argument.) Mill says: 'Nobody argues that the art of navigation is not founded on astronomy, because sailors cannot wait to calculate the Nautical Almanack. Being rational creatures, they go out upon the sea of life with their minds made up on the common questions of right and wrong, as well as on many of the far more difficult questions of wise and foolish . . . . Whatever we adopt as the fundamental principle of morality, we require subordinate principles to apply it by'. Notice that this is, as it stands, only an argument for subordinate principles as rules of thumb. The example of the nautical almanack is misleading because the information given in the almanack is in all cases the same as the information one would get if one made a long and laborious calculation from the original astronomical data on which the almanack is founded. Suppose, however, that astronomy were different. Suppose that the behaviour of the sun, moon and planets was very nearly as it is now, but that on rare occasions there were peculiar irregularities and discontinuities, so that the almanack gave us rules of the form 'in 99 percent of cases where the observations are such and such you can deduce that your position is so and so'. Furthermore, let us suppose that there were methods which enabled us, by direct and laborious calculation from the original astronomical data, not using the rough and ready tables of the almanack, to get our correct position in 100 percent of cases. Seafarers might use the almanack because they never had time for the long calculations and they were content with a 99 percent chance of success in calculating their positions. Would it not be absurd, however, if they *did* make the direct calculation, and finding that it disagreed with the almanack calculation, nevertheless they ignored it and stuck to the almanack conclusion?

*   *   *

We could quite well imagine a race of sailors who acquired a superstitious reverence for their almanack, even though it was only right in 99 percent of cases, and who indignantly threw overboard any man who mentioned the possibility of a direct calculation. But would this behaviour of the sailors be rational?

Let us consider a much discussed sort of case in which the extreme utilitarian might go against the conventional moral rule. I have promised to a friend, dying on a desert island from which I am subsequently rescued, that I will see that his fortune (over which I have control) is given to a jockey club. However, when I am rescued I decide that it would be better to give the money to a hospital, which can do more good with it. It may be argued that I am wrong to give the money to the hospital. But why? (a) The hospital can do more good with the money than the jockey club can. (b) The present case is unlike most cases of promising in that no one except me knows about the promise. In breaking the promise I am doing so with complete secrecy and am doing nothing to weaken the general faith in promises. That is, a factor, which would normally keep the extreme utilitarian from promise breaking even in otherwise unoptimific cases, does not at present operate. (c) There is no doubt a slight weakening in my own character as an habitual promise keeper, and moreover psychological tensions will be set up in me every time I am asked what the man made me promise him to do. For clearly I shall have to say that he made me promise to give the money to the hospital, and, since I am an habitual truth teller, this will go very much against the grain with me. Indeed I am pretty sure that in practice I myself would keep the promise. But we are not discussing what my moral habits would probably make me do; we are discussing what I ought to do. Moreover, we must not forget that even if it would be most rational of me to give the money to the hospital it would also be most rational of you to punish or condemn me if you did, most improbably, find out the truth (e.g. by finding a note washed ashore in a bottle). Furthermore, I would agree that though it was most rational of me to give the money to the hospital it would be most rational of you to condemn me for it.

*   *   *

So far I have been considering the duty of an extreme utilitarian in a predominantly non-utilitarian society. The case is altered if we consider the extreme utilitarian who lives in a society every member, or most members, of which can be expected to reason as he does. Should he water his flowers now? (Granting, what is doubtful, that in the case already considered he would have been right to water his flowers.) As a first approximation, the answer is that he should not do so. For since the situation is a completely symmetrical one, what is rational for him is rational for others. Hence, by a *reductio ad absurdum* argument, it would seem that watering his garden would be rational for none. Nevertheless, a more refined analysis shows that the above argument is not quite correct, though it is correct enough for practical purposes. The argument considers each person as confronted with the choice either of watering his garden or of not watering it. However there is a third possibility, which is that each person should, with the aid of a suitable randomizing device, such as throwing dice, give himself a certain probability of watering his garden. This would be to adopt what in the theory of games is called 'a mixed strategy'. If we could give numerical values to the private benefit of garden watering and to the public harm done by 1, 2, 3, etc., persons using the water in this way, we could work out a value of the probability of watering his garden that each extreme utilitarian should give himself. Let a be the value which each extreme utilitarian gets from watering his garden, and let $f(1)$, $f(2)$, $f(3)$, etc., be the public harm done by exactly 1, 2, 3, etc., persons respectively watering their gardens. Suppose that p is the probability that each person gives himself of watering his garden. Then we can easily calculate, as functions of p, the probabilities that exactly 1, 2, 3, etc., persons will water their gardens. Let these probabilities be $p_1, p_2, \ldots p_n$. Then the total net probable benefit can be expressed as

$$V = p_1\,(a - f(1)) + p_2\,(2a - f(2)) + \ldots p_n\,(na - f(n))$$

Then if we know the function $f(x)$ we can calculate the value of p for which $(dV/dp)=0$. This gives the value of p which it would be rational for each extreme utilitarian to adopt. The present argument does not of course depend on a perhaps unjustified assumption that the values in question are measurable, and in a practical case such as that of the garden watering we can doubtless assume that p will be so small that we can take it near enough as equal to zero. However the argument is of interest for the theoretical underpinning of extreme utilitarianism, since the possibility of a mixed strategy is usually neglected by critics of utilitarianism, who wrongly assume that the only relevant and symmetrical alternatives are of the form 'everybody does X' and 'nobody does X'.[2]

I now pass on to a type of case which may be thought to be the trump card of restricted utilitarianism. Consider the rule of the road. It may be said that since all that matters is that everyone should do the same it is indifferent which rule we have, 'go on the left hand side' or 'go on the right hand side'. Hence the only *reason* for going on the left hand side in British countries is that this is the rule. Here the rule does seem to be a reason, in itself, for acting in a certain way. I wish to argue against this. The rule in itself is not a reason for our actions. We would be perfectly justified in going on the right hand side if (*a*) we knew that the rule was to go on the left hand side, and (*b*) we were in a country peopled by super-anarchists who always on principle did the opposite of what they were told. This shows that the rule does not give us a reason for acting so much as an indication of the probable actions of others, which helps us to find out what would be our own most rational course of action. If we are in a country not peopled by anarchists, but by non-anarchist extreme Utilitarians, we expect, other things being equal, that they will keep rules laid down for them. Knowledge of the rule enables us to predict their behaviour and to harmonize our own actions with theirs. The rule 'keep to the left hand side', then, is not a logical *reason* for action but an anthropological *datum* for planning actions.

I conclude that in every case if there is a rule R the keeping of which is in general optimific, but such that in a special sort of circumstances the optimific behaviour is to break R, then in these circumstances we should break R. Of course we must consider all the less obvious effects of breaking R, such as reducing people's faith in the moral order, before coming to the conclusion that to break R is right: in fact we shall rarely come to such a conclusion. Moral rules, on the extreme utilitarian view, are rules of thumb only, but they are not bad rules of thumb. But if we *do* come to the conclusion that we should break the rule and if we have weighed in the balance our own fallibility and liability to personal bias, what good reason remains for keeping the rule? I can understand 'it is optimific' as a reason for action, but why should 'it is a member of a class of actions which are usually optimific' or 'it is a member of a class of actions which as a class are more optimific than any alternative general class' be a good reason? You might as well say that a person ought to be picked to play for Australia just because all his brothers have been, or that the Australian team should be composed entirely of the Harvey family because this would be better than composing it entirely of any other family. The extreme utilitarian does not appeal to artificial feelings, but only to our feelings of benevolence, and what better feelings can there be to appeal to? Admittedly we can have a pro-attitude to anything, even to rules, but such artificially begotten pro-attitudes smack of superstition. Let us get down to realities, human happiness and misery, and make these the objects of our pro-attitudes and anti-attitudes.

The restricted utilitarian might say that he is talking only of *morality*, not of such things as rules of the road. I am not sure how far this objection, if valid, would affect my argument, but in any case I would reply that as a philosopher I conceive of ethics as the study of how it would be *most rational* to act. If my opponent wishes to restrict the word 'morality' to a narrower use he can have the word. The fundamental question is the question of rationality of action *in general*. Similarly if the restricted utilitarian were to appeal to ordinary usage and say 'it might be most rational to leave Hitler to drown but it would surely not be *wrong* to rescue him', I should again let him have the words 'right' and 'wrong' and should stick to 'rational' and 'irrational'. We already saw that it would be rational to praise Hitler's rescuer, even though it would have been most rational not to have rescued Hitler. In ordinary language, no doubt, 'right' and 'wrong' have not only the meaning 'most rational to do' and 'not most rational to do' but also have the meaning 'praiseworthy' and 'not praiseworthy'. Usually to the utility of an action corresponds utility of praise of it, but as we saw, this is not always so. Moral language could thus do with tidying up, for example by reserving 'right' for 'most rational' and 'good' as an epithet of praise for the motive from which the action sprang. It would be more becoming in a philosopher to try to iron out illogicalities in moral language and to make suggestions for its reform than to use it as a court of appeal whereby to perpetuate confusions.

One last defence of restricted utilitarianism might be as follows. 'Act optimifically' might be regarded as itself one of the rules of our system (though it would be odd to say that this rule was justified by its optimificality). According to Toulmin (*The Place of Reason in Ethics*, pp. 146–8) if 'keep promises', say, conflicts with another rule we are allowed to argue the case on its merits, as if we were extreme utilitarians. If 'act optimifically' is itself one of our rules then there will always be a conflict of rules whenever to keep a rule is not itself optimific. If this is so, restricted utilitarianism collapses into extreme utilitarianism. And no one could read Toulmin's book or Urmson's article on Mill without thinking that Toulmin and Urmson are of the opinion that they have thought of a doctrine which does *not* collapse into extreme utilitarianism, but which is, on the contrary, an improvement on it.

Notes

1. Based on a paper read to the Victorian Branch of the Australasian Association of Psychology and Philosophy, October 1955. [The article is discussed in H. J. McCloskey, 'An Examination of Restricted Utilitarianism' *Philosophical Review* (1957); also by D. Lyons, *Forms and Limits of Utilitarianism* (Clarendon Press, Oxford, 1965).—Ed.]
2. This paragraph has been substantially emended by the author.—Ed.

▼   ## The Business Perspective

The Social Responsibility of Business Is to Increase Its Profits

Milton Friedman

For the Nobel Prize-winning economist Milton Friedman, the doctrine of corporate social responsibility is a well-disguised bit of managerial irresponsibility. His argument against business spending corporate funds for social ends is relatively straightforward. According to Friedman, the managers of a corporation are hired by the owners of a firm—the shareholders—for only one solitary purpose: to increase the profits of the firm so that the owners can achieve a fair return on their investment. Since corporate expenditures earmarked for alleviating society's ills will cut into profit and thereby into return on investment, managers who undertake such expenditures are not fulfilling their fiduciary responsibility to the owners and are acting contrary to their contractual obligations. Such actions are inherently irresponsible. Furthermore corporate expenditures for social causes function as a form of taxation without representation. The task of alleviating social problems is not within the purview of business; rather, it is the prerogative and obligation of government. When management spends funds for social ends, they are acting like governmental decision makers but without the legitimizing feature of having been elected. Consequently, the doctrine of corporate social responsibility is ultimately a "subversive doctrine" for the conservative-minded Friedman.

When I hear businessmen speak eloquently about the "social responsibilities of business in a free-enterprise system," I am reminded of the wonderful line about the Frenchman who discovered at the age of 70 that he had been speaking prose all his life. The businessmen believe that they are defending free enterprise when they declaim that business is not concerned "merely" with profit but also with promoting desirable "social" ends; that business has a "social conscience" and takes seriously its responsibilities for providing employment, eliminating discrimination, avoiding pollution and whatever else may be the catchwords of the contemporary crop of reformers. In fact they are—or would be if they or anyone else took them seriously—preaching pure and unadulterated socialism. Businessmen who talk this way are unwitting puppets of the intellectual forces that have been undermining the basis of a free society these past decades.

The discussions of the "social responsibilities of business" are notable for their analytical looseness and lack of rigor. What does it mean to say that "business" has responsibilities? Only people can have responsibilities. A corporation is an artificial person and in this sense may have artificial responsibilities, but "business" as a whole cannot be said to have responsibilities, even in this vague sense. The first step toward clarity in examining the doctrine of the social responsibility of business is to ask precisely what it implies for whom.

Presumably, the individuals who are to be responsible are businessmen, which means individual proprietors or corporate executives. Most of the discussion of social responsibility is directed at corporations, so in what follows I shall mostly neglect the individual proprietor and speak of corporate executives.

In a free-enterprise, private-property system, a corporate executive is an employee of the owners of the business. He has direct responsibility to his employers. That responsibility is to conduct the business in accordance with their desires, which generally will be to make as much money as possible while conforming to the basic rules of the society, both those embodied in law and those embodied in ethical custom. Of course, in some cases his employers may have a different objective. A group of persons might establish a corporation for an eleemosynary purpose—for example, a hospital or a school. The manager of such a corporation will not have money profit as his objective but the rendering of certain services.

In either case, the key point is that, in his capacity as a corporate executive, the manager is the agent of the individuals who own the corporation or establish the eleemosynary institution, and his primary responsibility is to them.

Needless to say, this does not mean that it is easy to judge how well he is performing his task. But at least the criterion of performance is straightforward, and the persons among whom a voluntary contractual arrangement exists are clearly defined.

Of course, the corporate executive is also a person in his own right. As a person, he may have many other responsibilities that he recognizes or assumes voluntarily—to his family, his conscience, his feelings of charity, his church, his clubs, his city, his country. He may feel impelled by these responsibilities to devote part of his income to causes he regards as worthy, to refuse to work for particular corporations, even to leave his job, for example, to join his country's armed forces. If we wish, we may refer to some of these responsibilities as "social responsibilities." But in these respects he is acting as a principal, not an agent; he is spending his own money or time or energy, not the money of his employers or the time or energy he has contracted to devote to their purposes. If these are "social responsibilities," they are the social responsibilities of individuals, not of business.

What does it mean to say that the corporate executive has a "social responsibility" in his capacity as businessman? If this statement is not pure rhetoric, it must mean that he is to act in some way that is not in the interest of his employers. For example, that he is to refrain from increasing the price of the product in order to contribute to the social objective of preventing inflation, even though a price increase would be in the best interests of the corporation. Or that he is to make expenditures on reducing pollution beyond the amount that is in the best interests of the corporation or that is required by law in order to contribute to the social objective of improving the environment. Or that, at the expense of corporate profits, he is to hire "hard-core" unemployed instead of better-qualified available workmen to contribute to the social objective of reducing poverty.

In each of these cases, the corporate executive would be spending someone else's money for a general social interest. Insofar as his actions in accord with his "social responsibility" reduce returns to stockholders, he is spending their money. Insofar as his actions raise the price to customers, he is spending the customers' money. Insofar as his actions lower the wages of some employees, he is spending their money.

The stockholders or the customers or the employees could separately spend their own money on the particular action if they wished to do so. The executive is exercising a distinct "social responsibility," rather than serving as an agent of the stockholders or the customers or the employees, only if he spends the money in a different way than they would have spent it.

But if he does this, he is in effect imposing taxes, on the one hand, and deciding how the tax proceeds shall be spent, on the other.

This process raises political questions on two levels: principle and consequences. On the level of political principle, the imposition of taxes and the expenditure of tax proceeds are governmental functions. We have established elaborate constitutional, parliamentary and judicial provisions to control these functions, to assure that taxes are imposed so far as possible in accordance with the preferences and desires of the public—after all, "taxation without representation" was one of the battle cries of the American Revolution. We have a system of checks and balances to separate the legislative function of imposing taxes and enacting expenditures from the executive function of collecting taxes and administering expenditure programs and from the judicial function of mediating disputes and interpreting the law.

Here the businessman—self-selected or appointed directly or indirectly by stockholders—is to be simultaneously legislator, executive and jurist. He is to decide whom to tax by how much and for what purpose, and he is to spend the proceeds—all this guided only by general exhortations from on high to restrain inflation, improve the environment, fight poverty and so on and on.

The whole justification for permitting the corporate executive to be selected by the stockholders is that the executive is an agent serving the interests of his principal. This justification disappears when the corporate executive imposes taxes and spends the proceeds for "social" purposes. He becomes in effect a public employee, a civil servant, even though he remains in name an employee of a private enterprise. On grounds of political principle, it is intolerable that such civil servants—insofar as their actions in the name of social responsibility are real and not just window-dressing—should be selected as they are now. If they are to be civil servants, then they must be selected through a political process. If they are to impose taxes and make expenditures to foster "social" objectives, then political machinery must be set up to guide the assessment of taxes and to determine through a political process the objectives to be served.

This is the basic reason why the doctrine of "social responsibility" involves the acceptance of the socialist view that political mechanisms, not market mechanisms, are the appropriate way to determine the allocation of scarce resources to alternative uses.

On the grounds of consequences, can the corporate executive in fact discharge his alleged "social responsibilities"? On the one hand, suppose he could get away with spending the stockholders' or customers' or employees' money. How is he to know how to spend it? He is told that he must contribute to fighting inflation. How is he to know what action of his will contribute to that end? He is presumably an expert in running his company—in producing a product or selling it or financing it. But nothing about his selection makes him an expert on inflation. Will his holding down the price of his product reduce inflationary pressure? Or, by leaving more spending power in the hands of his customers, simply divert it elsewhere? Or, by forcing him to produce less because of the lower price, will it simply contribute to shortages? Even if he could answer these questions, how much cost is he justified in imposing on his stockholders, customers and employees for this social purpose? What is his appropriate share and what is the appropriate share of others?

And, whether he wants to or not, can he get away with spending his stockholders', customers' or employees' money? Will not the stockholders fire him? (Either the present ones or those who take over when his actions in the name of social responsibility have reduced the corporation's profits and the price of its stock.) His customers and his employees can desert him for other producers and employers less scrupulous in exercising their social responsibilities.

This facet of "social responsibility" doctrine is brought into sharp relief when the doctrine is used to justify wage restraint by trade unions. The conflict of interest is naked and clear when union officials are asked to subordinate the interest of their members to some more general social purpose. If the union officials try to enforce wage restraint, the consequence is likely to be wildcat strikes, rank-and-file revolts and the emergence of strong competitors for their jobs. We thus have the ironic phenomenon that union leaders—at least in the U.S.—have objected to government interference with the market far more consistently and courageously than have business leaders.

The difficulty of exercising "social responsibility" illustrates, of course, the great virtue of private competitive enterprise—it forces people to be responsible for their own actions and makes it difficult for them to "exploit" other people for either selfish or unselfish purposes. They can do good—but only at their own expense.

Many a reader who has followed the argument this far may be tempted to remonstrate that it is all well and good to speak of government's having the responsibility to impose taxes and determine expenditures for such "social" purposes as controlling pollution or training the hard-core unemployed, but that the problems are too urgent to wait on the slow course of political processes, that the exercise of social responsibility by businessmen is a quicker and surer way to solve pressing current problems.

Aside from the question of fact—I share Adam Smith's skepticism about the benefits that can be expected from "those who affected to trade for the public good"—this argument must be rejected on grounds of principle. What it amounts to is an assertion that those who favor the taxes and expenditures in question have failed to persuade a majority of their fellow citizens to be of like mind and that they are seeking to attain by undemocratic procedures what they cannot attain by democratic procedures. In a free society, it is hard for "good" people to do "good," but that is a small price to pay for making it hard for "evil" people to do "evil," especially since one man's good is another's evil.

I have, for simplicity, concentrated on the special case of the corporate executive, except only for the brief digression on trade unions. But precisely the same argument applies to the newer phenomenon of calling upon stockholders to require corporations to exercise social responsibility (the recent GM crusade, for example). In most of these cases, what is in effect involved is some stockholders trying to get other stockholders (or customers or employees) to contribute against their will to "social" causes favored by the activists. Insofar as they succeed, they are again imposing taxes and spending the proceeds.

The situation of the individual proprietor is somewhat different. If he acts to reduce the returns of his enterprise in order to exercise his "social responsibility," he is spending his own money, not someone else's. If he wishes to spend his money on such purposes, that is his right, and I cannot see that there is any objection to his doing so. In the process, he, too, may impose costs on employees and customers. However, because he is far less likely than a large corporation or union to have monopolistic power, any such side effects will tend to be minor.

Of course, in practice the doctrine of social responsibility is frequently a cloak for actions that are justified on other grounds rather than a reason for those actions.

To illustrate, it may well be in the long-run interest of a corporation that is a major employer in a small community to devote resources to providing amenities to that community or to improving its government. That may make it easier to attract desirable employees, it may reduce the wage bill or lessen losses from pilferage and sabotage or have other worthwhile effects. Or it may be that, given the laws about the deductibility of corporate charitable contributions, the stockholders can contribute more to charities they favor by having the corporation make the gift than by doing it themselves, since they can in that way contribute an amount that would otherwise have been paid as corporate taxes.

In each of these—and many similar—cases, there is a strong temptation to rationalize these actions as an exercise of "social responsibility." In the present climate of opinion, with its widespread aversion to "capitalism," "profits," the "soulless corporation" and so on, this is one way for a corporation to generate goodwill as a by-product of expenditures that are entirely justified in its own self-interest.

It would be inconsistent of me to call on corporate executives to refrain from this hypocritical window-dressing because it harms the foundations of a free society. That would be to call on them to exercise a "social responsibility"! If our institutions, and the attitudes of the public, make it in their self-interest to cloak their actions in this way, I cannot summon much indignation to denounce them. At the same time, I can express admiration for those individual proprietors or owners of closely held corporations or stockholders of more broadly held corporations who disdain such tactics as approaching fraud.

Whether blameworthy or not, the use of the cloak of social responsibility, and the nonsense spoken in its name by influential and prestigious businessmen, does clearly harm the foundations of a free society. I have been impressed time and again by the schizophrenic character of many businessmen. They are capable of being extremely far-sighted and clear-headed in matters that are internal to their businesses. They are incredibly short-sighted and muddle-headed in matters that are outside their businesses but affect the possible survival of business in general. This short-sightedness is strikingly exemplified in the calls from many businessmen for wage and price guidelines or controls or incomes policies. There is nothing that could do more in a brief period to destroy a market system and replace it by a centrally controlled system than effective governmental control of prices and wages.

The short-sightedness is also exemplified in speeches by businessmen on social responsibility. This may gain them kudos in the short run. But it helps to strengthen the already too prevalent view that the pursuit of profits is wicked and immoral and must be curbed and controlled by external forces. Once this view is adopted, the external forces that curb the market will not be the social consciences, however highly developed, of the pontificating executives; it will be the iron fist of government bureaucrats. Here, as with price and wage controls, businessmen seem to me to reveal a suicidal impulse.

The political principle that underlies the market mechanism is unanimity. In an ideal free market resting on private property, no individual can coerce any other, all cooperation is voluntary, all parties to such cooperation benefit or they need not participate. There are no "social" values, no "social" responsibilities in any sense other than the shared values and responsibilities of individuals. Society is a collection of individuals and of the various groups they voluntarily form.

The political principle that underlies the political mechanism is conformity. The individual must serve a more general social interest—whether that be determined by a church or a dictator or a majority. The individual may have a vote and a say in what is to be done, but if he is overruled, he must conform. It is appropriate for some to require others to contribute to a general social purpose whether they wish to or not.

Unfortunately, unanimity is not always feasible. There are some respects in which conformity appears unavoidable, so I do not see how one can avoid the use of the political mechanism altogether.

But the doctrine of "social responsibility" taken seriously would extend the scope of the political mechanism to every human activity. It does not differ in philosophy from the most explicitly collectivist doctrine. It differs only by professing to believe that collectivist ends can be attained without collectivist means. That is why, in my book *Capitalism and Freedom,* I have called it a "fundamentally subversive doctrine" in a free society, and have said that in such a society, "there is one and only one social responsibility of business—to use its resources and engage in activities designed to increase its profits so long as it stays within the rules of the game, which is to say, engages in open and free competition without deception or fraud."

CHECKLIST for Utilitarianism

The ethical checklists are short summaries meant to help students apply the theories they have been studying in the preceding section. They are not meant to stand alone nor are they meant to supplant deeper reading into primary sources of each ethical theory.

It also should be noted that **there is no single application of any theory that everyone will accept.** Therefore, the checklist below is just one version of the ethical theory presented. It is set down in this succinct format as a pedagogical aid for applying ethical theories that will be used in the Case Studies Reports.

Directions: Read the short epitome on Utilitarianism and then go through the steps outlined below. When you have finished the assignment, you will have constructed your own checklist for utilitarianism.

▼ Utilitarianism

Epitome:
Utilitarianism is a theory which states that the moral choice which produces the greatest happiness for the greatest number of people is the moral choice. Thus, under this system we have to have a mechanism for determining: (a) the alternatives involved; (b) a list of possible outcomes of the alternatives; (c) a clear definition of the population sample to be affected by the alternatives; (d) a way to measure the possible impact that each alternative would have on the population sample so that it will become clear which alternative will yield the most pleasure.

It should also be noted that the test you choose must be one that can be carried out and have relatively uncontroversial units by which the happiness/benefits-impact can be measured and examined.

Application:

Step One: Create a moral situation of your own which seems to involve a difficult choice of alternative actions. [Cases which pit the majority interests against rights of the minority are often good for this exercise.]

Step Two: Set out the possible alternatives along with their projected outcomes.

Step Three: Define the population that is affected by your case.

Step Four: Propose a way to measure the happiness of the parties involved. Be sure that your measuring system can be quantified. What sorts of attacks could people make against your test? How would you defend it?

Step Five: Run your test on your sample population and give the actual numbers of the happiness coefficients that each group will possess according to each alternative.

Step Six: Justify your choice from step five against possible attacks.

CHAPTER 4

Deontology

▼ ## The Philosophical Perspective

The Categorical Imperative

Immanuel Kant

[Imperatives in General.]

Everything in nature works in accordance with laws. Only a rational being has the power to act *in accordance with his idea* of laws—that is, in accordance with principles—and only so has he *a will*. Since *reason* is required in order to derive actions from laws, the will is nothing but practical reason.

*   *   *

The conception of an objective principle so far as this principle is necessitating for a will is called a command (of reason), and the formula of this command is called an *Imperative*.

All imperatives are expressed by an *'ought'* (*Sollen*). By this they mark the relation of an objective law of reason to a will which is not necessarily determined by this law in virtue of its subjective constitution (the relation of necessitation). They say that something would be good to do or to leave undone; only they say it to a will which does not always do a thing because it has been

I. Kant, *Groundwork of the Metaphysics of Morals*. Trans. H. J. Paton (NY: Harper Row, 1948), pp. 80–91, 95, 96, 100–103.

informed that this is a good thing to do. The practically *good* is that which determines the will by concepts of reason, and therefore not by subjective causes, but objectively—that is, on grounds valid in every rational being as such. It is distinguished from the *pleasant* as that which influences the will, not as a principle of reason valid for every one, but solely through the medium of sensation by purely subjective causes valid only for the senses of this person or that.

A perfectly good will would thus stand quite as much under objective laws (laws of the good), but it could not on this account be conceived as *necessitated* to act in conformity with law, since of itself, in accordance with its subjective constitution, it can be determined only by the concept of the good. Hence for the *divine* will, and in general for a *holy* will, there are no imperatives: *'I ought'* is here out of place, because *'I will'* is already of itself necessarily in harmony with the law. Imperatives are in consequence only formulae for expressing the relation of objective laws of willing to the subjective imperfection of the will of this or that rational being—for example, of the human will.

[Classification of Imperatives.]

All *imperatives* command either *hypothetically* or *categorically*. Hypothetical imperatives declare a possible action to be practically necessary as a means to the attainment of something else that one wills (or that one may will). A categorical imperative would be one which represented an action as objectively necessary in itself apart from its relation to a further end.

Every practical law represents a possible action as good and therefore as necessary for a subject whose actions are determined by reason. Hence all imperatives are formulae for determining an action which is necessary in accordance with the principle of a will in some sense good. If the action would be good solely as a means *to something else,* the imperative is *hypothetical;* if the action is represented as good *in itself* and therefore as necessary, in virtue of its principle, for a will which of itself accords with reason, then the imperative is *categorical.*

An imperative therefore tells me which of my possible actions would be good; and it formulates a practical rule for a will that does not perform an action straight away because the action is good—whether because the subject does not always know that it is good or because, even if he did know this, he might still act on maxims contrary to the objective principles of practical reason.

A hypothetical imperative thus says only that an action is good for some purpose or other, either *possible* or *actual*. In the first case it is a *problematic* practical principle; in the second case an *assertoric* practical principle. A categorical imperative, which declares an action to be objectively necessary in itself without reference to some purpose—that is, even without any further end—ranks as an *apodeictic* practical principle.

Everything that is possible only through the efforts of some rational being can be conceived as a possible purpose of some will; and consequently there are in fact innumerable principles of action so far as action is thought necessary in order to achieve some possible purpose which can be effected by it. All sciences have a practical part consisting of problems which suppose that some end is possible for us and of imperatives which tell us how it is to be attained. Hence the latter can in general be called imperatives of *skill*. Here there is absolutely no question about the rationality or goodness of the end, but only about what must be done to attain it. A prescription required by a doctor in order to cure his man completely and one required by a poisoner in order to make sure of killing him are of equal value so far as each serves to effect its purpose perfectly. Since in early youth we do not know what ends may present themselves to us in the course of life, parents seek above all to make their children learn things *of many kinds;* they provide carefully for *skill* in the use of means to all sorts of *arbitrary* ends, of none of which can they be certain that it could not in the future become an actual purpose of their ward, while it is always *possible* that he might adopt it. Their care in this matter is so great that they commonly neglect on this account to form and correct the judgement of their children about the worth of the things which they might possibly adopt as ends.

There is, however, *one* end that can be presupposed as actual in all rational beings (so far as they are dependent beings to whom imperatives apply); and thus there is one purpose which they not only *can* have, but which we can assume with certainty that they all *do* have by a natural necessity—the purpose, namely, of *happiness*. A hypothetical imperative which affirms the practical necessity of an action as a means to the furtherance of happiness is *assertoric*. We may represent it, not simply as necessary to an uncertain, merely possible purpose, but as necessary to a purpose which we can presuppose *a priori* and with certainty to be present in every man because it belongs to his very being. Now skill in the choice of means to one's own greatest well-being can be called *prudence*[1] in the narrowest sense. Thus an imperative concerned with the choice of means to one's own happiness—that is, a precept of prudence—still remains *hypothetical:* an action is commanded, not absolutely, but only as a means to a further purpose.

Finally, there is an imperative which, without being based on, and conditioned by, any further purpose to be attained by a certain line of conduct, enjoins this conduct immediately. This imperative is *categorical*. It is concerned, not with the matter of the action and its presumed results, but with its form and with the principle from which it follows; and what is essentially good in the action consists in the mental disposition, let the consequences be what they may. This imperative may be called the imperative of *morality*.

How Are Moral Imperatives Possible?

Beyond all doubt, the question 'How is the imperative of *morality* possible?' is the only one in need of a solution; for it is in no way hypothetical, and consequently we cannot base the objective necessity which it affirms on any presupposition, as we can with hypothetical imperatives. Only we must never forget here that it is impossible to settle *by an example,* and so empirically, whether there is any imperative of this kind at all: we must rather suspect that all imperatives which seem to be categorical may nonetheless be covertly hypothetical. Take, for example, the saying 'Thou shalt make no false promises'. Let us assume that the necessity for this abstention is no mere advice for the avoidance of some further evil—as it might be said 'You ought not to make a lying promise lest, when this comes to light, you destroy your credit'. Let us hold, on the contrary, that an action of this kind must be considered as bad in itself, and that the imperative of prohibition is therefore categorical. Even so, we cannot with any certainty show by an example that the will is determined here solely by the law without any further motive, although it may appear to be so; for it is always possible that fear of disgrace, perhaps also hidden dread of other risks, may unconsciously influence the will. Who can prove by experience that a cause is not present? Experience shows only that it is not perceived. In such a case, however, the so-called moral imperative, which as such appears to be categorical and unconditioned, would in fact be only a pragmatic prescription calling attention to our advantage and merely bidding us take this into account.

We shall thus have to investigate the possibility of a *categorical* imperative entirely *a priori,* since here we do not enjoy the advantage of having its reality given in experience and so of being obliged merely to explain, and not to establish, its possibility. So much, however, can be seen provisionally—that the categorical imperative alone purports to be a practical *law,* while all the rest may be called *principles* of the will but not laws; for an action necessary merely in order to achieve an arbitrary purpose can be considered as in itself contingent, and we can always escape from the precept if we abandon the purpose; whereas an unconditioned command does not leave it open to the will to do the opposite at its discretion and therefore alone carries with it that necessity which we demand from a law.

In the second place, with this categorical imperative or law of morality the reason for our difficulty (in comprehending its possibility) is a very serious one. We have here a synthetic *a priori* practical proposition;[2] and since in theoretical knowledge there is so much difficulty in comprehending the possibility of propositions of this kind, it may readily be gathered that in practical knowledge the difficulty will be no less.

[The Formula of Universal Law.]

In this task we wish first to enquire whether perhaps the mere concept of a categorical imperative may not also provide us with the formula containing the only proposition that can be a categorical imperative; for even when we know the purport of such an absolute command, the question of its possibility will still require a special and troublesome effort, which we postpone to the final chapter.

When I conceive a *hypothetical* imperative in general, I do not know beforehand what it will contain—until its condition is given. But if I conceive a *categorical* imperative, I know at once what it contains. For since besides the law this imperative contains only the necessity that our maxim[3] should conform to this law, while the law, as we have seen, contains no condition to limit it, there remains nothing over to which the maxim has to conform except the universality of a law as such; and it is this conformity alone that the imperative properly asserts to be necessary.

There is therefore only a single categorical imperative and it is this: *'Act only on that maxim through which you can at the same time will that it should become a universal law'*.

Now if all imperatives of duty can be derived from this one imperative as their principle, then even although we leave it unsettled whether what we call duty may not be an empty concept, we shall still be able to show at least what we understand by it and what the concept means.

[The Formula of the Law of Nature.]

Since the universality of the law governing the production of effects constitutes what is properly called *nature* in its most general sense (nature as regards its form)—that is, the existence of things so far as determined by universal laws—the universal imperative of duty may also run as follows: *'Act as if the maxim of your action were to become through your will a universal law of nature.'*

[Illustrations.]

We will now enumerate a few duties, following their customary division into duties towards self and duties towards others and into perfect and imperfect duties.[4]

1. A man feels sick of life as the result of a series of misfortunes that has mounted to the point of despair, but he is still so far in possession of his reason as to ask himself whether taking his own life may not be contrary to his duty to himself. He now applies the test 'Can the maxim of my action really become a universal law of nature?' His maxim is 'From self-love I make it my principle to shorten my life if its continuance threatens more evil than it promises pleasure'. The only further question to ask is whether this principle of self-love can become a universal law of nature. It is then seen at once that a system of nature by whose law the very same feeling whose function (*Bestimmung*) is to stimulate the furtherance of life should actually destroy life would contradict itself and consequently could not subsist as a system of nature. Hence this maxim cannot possibly hold as a universal law of nature and is therefore entirely opposed to the supreme principle of all duty.

2. Another finds himself driven to borrowing money because of need. He well knows that he will not be able to pay it back; but he sees too that he will get no loan unless he gives a firm promise to pay it back within a fixed time. He is inclined to make such a promise; but he has still enough conscience to ask 'Is it not unlawful and contrary to duty to get out of difficulties in this way?' Supposing, however, he did resolve to do so, the maxim of his action

would run thus: 'Whenever I believe myself short of money, I will borrow money and promise to pay it back, though I know that this will never be done'. Now this principle of self-love or personal advantage is perhaps quite compatible with my own entire future welfare; only there remains the question 'Is it right?' I therefore transform the demand of self-love into a universal law and frame my question thus: 'How would things stand if my maxim became a universal law?' I then see straight away that this maxim can never rank as a universal law of nature and be self-consistent, but must necessarily contradict itself. For the universality of a law that every one believing himself to be in need can make any promise he pleases with the intention not to keep it would make promising, and the very purpose of promising, itself impossible, since no one would believe he was being promised anything, but would laugh at utterances of this kind as empty shams.

3. A third finds in himself a talent whose cultivation would make him a useful man for all sorts of purposes. But he sees himself in comfortable circumstances, and he prefers to give himself up to pleasure rather than to bother about increasing and improving his fortunate natural aptitudes. Yet he asks himself further 'Does my maxim of neglecting my natural gifts, besides agreeing in itself with my tendency to indulgence, agree also with what is called duty?' He then sees that a system of nature could indeed always subsist under such a universal law, although (like the South Sea Islanders) every man should let his talents rust and should be bent on devoting his life solely to idleness, indulgence, procreation, and, in a word, to enjoyment. Only he cannot possibly *will* that this should become a universal law of nature or should be implanted in us as such a law by a natural instinct. For as a rational being he necessarily wills that all his powers should be developed, since they serve him, and are given him, for all sorts of possible ends.

4. Yet a *fourth* is himself flourishing, but he sees others who have to struggle with great hardships (and whom he could easily help); and he thinks 'What does it matter to me? Let every one be as happy as Heaven wills or as he can make himself; I won't deprive him of anything; I won't even envy him; only I have no wish to contribute anything to his well-being or to his support in distress!' Now admittedly if such an attitude were a universal law of nature, mankind could get on perfectly well—better no doubt than if everybody prates about sympathy and goodwill, and even takes pains, on occasion, to practise them, but on the other hand cheats where he can, traffics in human rights, or violates them in other ways. But although it is possible that a universal law of nature could subsist in harmony with this maxim, yet it is impossible to *will* that such a principle should hold everywhere as a law of nature. For a will which decided in this way would be in conflict with itself, since many a situation might arise in which the man needed love and sympathy from others and in which, by such a law of nature sprung from his own will, he would rob himself of all hope of the help he wants for himself.

*   *   *

[The Formula of the End in Itself.]

The will is conceived as a power of determining oneself to action *in accordance with the idea of certain laws*. And such a power can be found only in rational beings. Now what serves the will as a subjective ground of its self-determination is an *end;* and this, if it is given by reason alone, must be equally valid for all rational beings. What, on the other hand, contains merely the ground of the possibility of an action whose effect is an end is called a *means*. The subjective ground of a desire is an *impulsion (Triebfeder);* the objective ground of a volition is a *motive (Bewegungsgrund)*. Hence the difference between subjective ends, which are based on impulsions, and objective ends, which depend on motives valid for every rational being. Practical principles are *formal* if they abstract from all subjective ends; they are *material,* on the other hand, if they are based on such ends and consequently on certain impulsions. Ends that a rational being adopts arbitrarily as *effects* of his action (material ends) are in every case only relative; for it is solely their relation to special characteristics in the subject's power of appetition which gives them their value. Hence this value can provide no universal principles, no principles valid and necessary for all rational beings and also for every volition—that is, no practical laws. Consequently all these relative ends can be the ground only of hypothetical imperatives.

Suppose, however, there were something *whose existence* has *in itself* an absolute value, something which as *an end in itself* could be a ground of determinate laws; then in it, and in it alone, would there be the ground of a possible categorical imperative—that is, of a practical law.

Now I say that man, and in general every rational being, *exists* as an end in himself, *not merely as a means* for arbitrary use by this or that will: he must in all his actions, whether they are directed to himself or to other rational beings, always be viewed *at the same time as an end*. All the objects of inclination have only a conditioned value; for if there were not these inclinations and the needs grounded on them, their object would be valueless. Inclinations themselves, as sources of needs, are so far from having an absolute value to make them desirable for their own sake that it must rather be the universal wish of every rational being to be wholly free from them. Thus the value of all objects that can *be produced* by our action is always conditioned. Beings whose existence depends, not on our will, but on nature, have nonetheless, if they are non-rational beings, only a relative value as means and are consequently called *things*. Rational beings, on the other hand, are called *persons* because their nature already marks them out as ends in themselves—that is, as something which ought not to be used merely as a means—and consequently imposes to that extent a limit on all arbitrary treatment of them (and is an object of reverence). Persons, therefore, are not merely subjective ends whose existence as an object of our actions has a value *for us:* they are *objective ends*—that is, things whose existence is in itself an end, and indeed an end such that in its place we can put no other end to which they should serve *simply* as means; for unless this is so, nothing at all of *absolute* value would be found anywhere. But if all value were conditioned—that is, contingent—then no supreme principle could be found for reason at all.

If then there is to be a supreme practical principle and—so far as the human will is concerned—a categorical imperative, it must be such that from the idea of something which is necessarily an end for every one because it is an *end in itself* it forms an *objective* principle of the will and consequently can serve as a practical law. The ground of this principle is: *Rational nature* exists as an end in *itself*. This is the way in which a man necessarily conceives his own existence: it is therefore so far a *subjective* principle of human actions. But it is also the way in which every other rational being conceives his existence on the same rational ground which is valid also for me; hence it is at the same time an *objective* principle, from which, as a supreme practical ground, it must be possible to derive all laws for the will. The practical imperative will therefore be as follows: *Act in such a way that you always treat humanity, whether in your own person or in the person of any other, never simply as a means, but always at the same time as an end*.

*   *   *

Notes

1. The word 'prudence' (*Klugheit*) is used in a double sense: in one sense it can have the name of 'worldly wisdom' (*Weltklugheit*); in a second sense that of 'personal wisdom' (*Privatklugheit*). The first is the skill of a man in influencing others in order to use them for his own ends. The second is sagacity in combining all these ends to his own lasting advantage. The latter is properly that to which the value of the former can itself be traced; and of him who is prudent in the first sense, but not in the second, we might better say that he is clever and astute, but on the whole imprudent.

2. Without presupposing a condition taken from some inclination I connect an action with the will *a priori* and therefore necessarily (although only objectively so—that is, only subject to the Idea of a reason having full power over all subjective impulses to action). Here we have a practical proposition in which the willing of an action is not derived analytically from some other willing already presupposed (for we do not possess any such perfect will), but is on the contrary connected immediately with the concept of the will of a rational being as something which is not contained in this concept.

3. A *maxim* is a subjective principle of action and must be distinguished from an *objective principle*—namely, a practical law. The former contains a practical rule determined by reason in accordance with the conditions of the subject (often his ignorance or again his inclinations): It is thus a principle on which the subject *acts*. A law, on the other hand, is an objective principle valid for every rational being; and it is a principle on which he *ought to act*—that is, an imperative.

4. It should be noted that I reserve my division of duties entirely for a future *Metaphysic of Morals* and that my present division is therefore put forward as arbitrary (merely for the purpose of arranging my examples). Further, I understand here by a perfect duty one which allows no exception in the interests of inclination, and so I recognize among *perfect duties,* not only outer ones, but also inner. This is contrary to the accepted usage of the schools, but I do not intend to justify it here, since for my purpose it is all one whether this point is conceded or not.

The Principle of Generic Consistency

Alan Gewirth

3.2. Every agent must claim, at least implicitly, that he has rights of freedom and well-being for the sufficient reason that he is a prospective purposive agent. From the content of this claim it follows, by the principle of universalizability, that all prospective purposive agents have rights to freedom and well-being. If the agent denies this generalization, he contradicts himself. For he would then be in the position of both affirming and denying that being a prospective purposive agent is a sufficient condition of having rights to freedom and well-being.

As we also saw in the preceding chapter, the statement that some person or group of persons has a certain right entails a correlative 'ought'-judgment that all other persons ought at least to refrain from interfering with that to which the first person or group has the right. Since, then, the agent must accept the generalized rights-statement, 'All prospective purposive agents have rights to freedom and well-being,' he must, on pain of contradiction, also accept the judgment, 'I ought at least to refrain from interfering with the freedom and well-being of any prospective purposive agent.' The transition here from 'all' to 'any' is warranted by the fact that the 'all' in the generalization is distributive, not collective: it refers to each and hence to any prospective purposive agent.

Now the recipients of the agent's action are prospective purposive agents insofar as they can operate voluntarily and purposively, controlling their behavior by their unforced choice with a view to fulfillment of their purposes and having knowledge of relevant circumstances. When it is said that the recipients can operate in these ways, this 'can' is a dispositional one, referring to the long-range abilities (whatever their hereditary and environmental sources) that enter into such modes of operation. It would hence be irrelevant for an agent to argue that because he has previously assaulted someone or otherwise made him unable to operate freely and with basic well-being, his victim is not a prospective purposive agent and does not the rights referred to in the above generalization. The 'ought'-judgment entailed by the generalization logically must be accepted by the agent as binding on all his conduct toward other prospective agents, so that in coercing or harming any of them he violates a requirement he is rationally obliged to accept.

When some person is a recipient in a transaction, he does not actually choose or initiate and control his conduct with a view to fulfilling some purpose of his. Nevertheless, he is still a prospective agent who has purposes he

Alan Gewirth, *Reason and Morality* (Chicago: University of Chicago Press, 1978), pp. 133–139.

wants to fulfill, at least in the dispositional sense that he has wants or interests that are of concern to him. It would be incorrect to think that purposive participation is not attributable to the recipient because only agents have purposes. For someone to have a purpose it is not necessary that he actually try to achieve it; he may, like the recipient, be passive and quiescent. His purpose will correspondingly vary from the remotely dispositional and diffuse to the proximately occurrent and specific. In each of these kinds of situation, the recipient regards his purposes and objects as good. This goodness extends through the same range of basic, nonsubtractive, and additive goods as do the purposes of the agents: the recipient, too, regards as good and has as his at least dispositional purposes that he maintain the necessary preconditions of actions, that he not lose in transactions something that seems to him to be good, and that he gain in transactions something that seems to him to be good. For the recipient, too, his well-being consists especially in his having the general conditions and abilities required for his fulfilling such purposes.

3.3. Since the recipients of the agent's action are prospective agents who have purposes they want to fulfill, the agent must acknowledge that the generalization to which we saw that he is logically committed applies to his recipients: they too have rights to freedom and well-being. Their right to freedom means that just as the agent holds that he has a right to control whether or not he will participate in transactions, so his recipients have the right to control whether or not they will participate. Hence, the agent ought to refrain from interfering with their freedom by coercing them: their participation in transactions must be subject to their own consent, to their own unforced choice. The recipients' right to well-being means that just as the agent holds that he has a right to maintain the conditions and abilities required for purposive action, so his recipients also have the right to maintain these. Hence, the agent ought at least to refrain from harming his recipients by interfering with their basic, nonsubtractive, and additive goods, especially when these are viewed generically-dispositionally. In certain circumstances, moreover, when his recipients' well-being cannot otherwise be maintained through their own efforts, their right to well-being entails that the agent ought to act positively to assist them to have these conditions or abilities.

It follows from these considerations that every agent logically must acknowledge certain generic obligations. Negatively, he ought to refrain from coercing and from harming his recipients; positively, he ought to assist them to have freedom and well-being whenever they cannot otherwise have these necessary goods and he can help them at no comparable cost to himself. The general principle of these obligations and rights may be expressed as the following precept addressed to every agent: *Act in accord with the generic rights of your recipients as well as of yourself.* I shall call this the *Principle of Generic Consistency (PGC),* since it combines the formal consideration of consistency with the material consideration of rights to the generic features or goods of action. The two components of the *PGC,* requiring action in accord with the recipients' generic rights of freedom and of well-being, I shall call the *generic rules.*

The *PGC* is a necessary principle in two ways. It is formally or logically necessary in that for any agent to deny or violate it is to contradict himself, since he would then be in the position of holding that rights he claims for himself by virtue of having certain qualities are not possessed by other persons who have those qualities. The principle is also materially necessary, or categorical, in that, unlike other principles, the obligations of the *PGC* cannot be escaped by any agent by shifting his inclinations, interests, or ideals, or by appealing to institutional rules whose contents are determined by convention. Since the generic features of action are involved in the necessary structure of agency, and since the agent must hold that he has rights to these features simply insofar as he is a prospective purposive agent, he rationally must accept that his recipients also have these rights insofar as they too are prospective purposive agents. In this regard, the *PGC* is unlike those moral principles whose contents are contingent and normatively escapable in that they reflect the variable desires or opinions of agents.

I shall now try to explicate the *PGC*'s direct content somewhat more fully. To act in accord with someone's rights is to see to it, so far as one can, that one fulfills the correlative obligations. Since the rights have certain objects—they are rights to have or do something X—the content of the obligations, what the respondent B ought to do, is determined by what is required if the subject or the right-holder A is to have to do X. Sometimes, as in the case of the right to freedom of speech or movement, all that is required for B to act in accord with A's right is for B to refrain from interfering with A's speaking or moving. Here, then, the correlative obligation is only negative. At other times, however, the obligation is positive, as in the case of the right to have food where A is starving from lack of food and cannot obtain food by his own efforts. In such a case, for B to act in accord with A's right to food requires that B give food to A if he can. Positive obligations, requiring positive actions, clearly make more demands on the respondents than do negative obligations, so that the conditions of their fulfillment raise many more questions about comparative abilities, costs, causes, and other variables. The relevant assistance or positive action often requires a context of institutional arrangements, as against the negative obligations that may be independently fulfilled by respondents. I shall discuss these qualifications below.

What, then, does it mean for an agent to act in accord with his own generic rights? In such a case the agent is the subject or holder of the rights, but he is not necessarily also the respondent of the rights. Rather, in acting he sees to it that he at least occurrently maintains his own freedom and well-being so that these are not interfered with by other persons without his consent. Just as we have noted that the agent necessarily manifests or embodies the generic features of action in his conduct and necessarily claims at least implicitly to have freedom and well-being as his rights, so in his particular actions he necessarily acts in accord with his own generic rights. This is to say that at least on the particular occasions of his acting he maintains the essential conditions of his agency against any attempts by other persons to violate these conditions without his consent. Such violation may indeed occur, but then he is no longer an agent or acting in that situation.

That the agent acts in accord with his right to well-being does not mean that he is infallible in ascertaining what is required to fulfill his purposes and that he invariably acts conformably to this ascertainment. It means, rather, that he tries to fulfill his purposes and to see to it that without his consent other persons do not interfere with his maintaining the conditions that, so far as he is aware, are required for such purpose-fulfillment. Undoubtedly this process is marked by varying degrees of knowledge, rationality, and resoluteness among different agents. But this variation does not remove the generalization that, whatever their different purposes and abilities, agents act in accord with their own rights to freedom and well-being as required for their actions in pursuit of their purposes. Nor is this generalization removed by the fact that in some contexts persons may operate under conditions of compulsoriness and external threat; for in such cases there is forced choice rather than action in the strict sense. The generalization is not affected even by such an extreme case as that of suicide. For insofar as the would-be suicide maintains the conditions of action in the strict sense, including the absence of internal causes that remove his own control over his behavior, he still sees to it that other persons do not interfere with his freedom and well-being without his consent. It is also true, however, that in such a limiting case, where he intends to cease being an agent, he maintains these necessary goods only in the strictly temporary frame required for his final action aimed at losing them. This extreme, untypical case of agency does not, however, affect what holds true in the standard conditions and generic features of action.

From the preceding account of what it is to act in accord with someone's rights, it should also be clear what it is for the agent to act in accord with the generic rights of his recipients. In so acting, he refrains from interfering with their freedom and well-being without their consent, and he assists them to have these conditions where they would otherwise lack them and cannot maintain them by their own efforts. In contexts where this inability is widespread, the assistance in question should take the form of agents' supporting and contributing to institutions or social arrangements that more directly provide such assistance. It is necessarily true of the agent that he participates voluntarily and purposively in the transactions he initiates or controls with regard to his recipients, and that he claims for himself the rights to freedom and well-being in all such transactions. If the agent acts in accord with his recipients' generic rights, then, at least so far as his action is concerned, his recipients also participate voluntarily and purposively in their transactions with him so that their own freedom and well-being are also protected. Whether the recipient's participation in the transaction is voluntary or involuntary depends upon the agent, in that the latter can refrain from acting on his recipient until and unless the recipient has freely consented to participate. It also depends upon the agent whether the recipient's participation is purposive or contrapurposive, in that so far as concerns his action's intended and foreseeable effect on the recipient, the agent can see to it that he at least refrains from bringing about or contributing to a diminution of his recipient's well-being or capacity for purpose-fulfillment, and, in certain circumstances, he assists him to maintain well-being.

The obligations set by the *PGC* consist primarily in the modes of action just described, but they also involve correlated modes of respect. Every agent ought to respect his recipients' freedom and well-being as well as his own. Such respect includes not only action but also certain related dispositions: a recognition of the rights of others, a positive concern for their having the objects of these rights, and a positive regard for them as persons who have rights or entitlements equal to his own as well as the rational capacity to reflect on their purposes and to control their behavior in the light of such reflection.

Fulfillment of these obligations is also necessary for the agent's strict rational autonomy. Viewed etymologically, 'autonomy' means being a law (*nomos*) unto oneself (*auto*), or setting one's law for oneself. Now there may be many different kinds of law set by many different kinds of self. All cases of autonomy, nonetheless, are in a broad sense rational; but it is important to distinguish this broad sense from the strict sense. In the broad sense every person who sets laws for himself, or decides on his own principles of conduct, is rationally autonomous in that the law or principle he decides on is a general reason or criterion, and he subsumes particular cases under it. This criterion or principle, however, need not itself be rational, for it may be based on a faulty use of reason, including false but corrigible beliefs or invalid inferences. Thus a person who is rationally autonomous in the broad sense may use general criteria that reflect personal prejudices or benighted customs; he may be a racist, a perfervid nationalist, or otherwise wedded to irrational principles opposed to the *PGC*. Nevertheless, he will have chosen these reasons or principles for himself and may try to fashion a coherent plan of life on their basis.

If, on the other hand, one is rationally autonomous in the strict sense, then the general principle one chooses for oneself will have been arrived at by a correct use of reason, including true beliefs and valid inferences. In the strictest sense, these beliefs will reflect necessary features of the subject matter. This is the case with the agent who understands and accepts the *PGC* and with it the duty of respecting both the principle itself, as based on reason, and his recipients as having rights he rationally must respect. All normal human beings have the capacity to be rational in this strict sense, in that they have, at least in an elementary way, the empirical and logical abilities in question. Hence, they are all capable of being rationally autonomous in the strict sense, and it is to all of them that the *PGC* is addressed.

The Fundamental Principle of Morality
Alan Donagan

Both Jewish and Christian thinkers have always held that the numerous specific precepts of morality are all derivable from a few substantive general principles, even though the conception of those precepts as binding upon rational creatures as such is compatible with the new intuitionist doctrine that the fundamental principles from which they derive are many. No Jewish or Christian moralist would dispute that the part of morality having to do with duties to God, which lies outside the scope of this investigation, derives from the principle in the Mosaic Shema: that God is one, and is to be loved with one's whole mind and heart (Deut. 6:5). And most of them have held that the part having to do with rational creatures, in their relations with themselves and with one another, also derives from a single first principle. Here, however, tradition has diverged, and two different principles have each won some recognition as fundamental. Some traditional moralists have maintained that the two, despite their obvious differences, coincide at a deeper level. Of these, the most distinguished was Kant, whose first and second formulas of the fundamental principle of morality philosophically restate the two apparently different traditional principles, and who declared that those formulas "are at bottom merely . . . formulations of the very same law."

The more familiar of the two traditional candidates for recognition as the fundamental principle of morality, with respect to the relations of rational creatures to themselves and to one another, is also the more recent. In Judaism, its authority is talmudic. According to the Babylonian Talmud, a gentile once demanded of Hillel that he be taught the whole Law while he stood on one foot. "Do not do to your fellow what you hate to have done to you," Hillel told him. "This is the whole Law entire; the rest is explanation."[1] A similar saying of Jesus is preserved by Matthew: "All things whatsoever ye would that men should do to you, do ye even so to them" (Matt. 7:12). Although one of these formulations is negative and the other positive, they are in fact equivalent; for to forbid an action of a certain kind, and to command one of its contradictory kind, are equivalent. The precept formulated in these two ways has become known as "The Golden Rule."

Two objections are commonly made to receiving the Golden Rule as the fundamental principle of morality. First, it excludes the possibility that it may be right to do anything to another which you would hate to have done to you. Yet, as Kant pointed out, the Hebrew-Christian code calls upon parents, teachers, and judges to do many things to others, for their good or for the common good, which most plain men would hate to have done to them. How many judges would not hate to be sentenced, if they were guilty? Second, the Golden

The Theory of Morality (Chicago: University of Chicago Press, 1977), pp. 57–61.

Rule *prima facie* fails to condemn any action which affects the agent alone (as suicide may), or any action between consenting persons, to which there is no other party. Yet common morality as traditionally conceived certainly recognizes the existence of duties to oneself, and hence must forbid actions contributing to violations of those duties when done at the behest of somebody else.

Such objections can be forestalled by appropriate interpretations. For example, with respect to Hillel's formulation, a moralist might distinguish natural hating from unnatural; then, having laid it down that, in the Rule, hating is to be interpreted as natural hating, urge that it is unnatural either to hate getting one's just deserts or not to hate such wrongs to oneself as suicide. By such an interpretation, certain substantive principles of duty are in effect absorbed into the Rule. Other substantive principles can be introduced into it by other interpretations.

That the common objections to it can be forestalled by such interpretations, which are neither dishonest nor arbitrary, points to a characteristic of the Golden Rule which not only exposes its inadequacy as a first principle but also explains its ubiquity. For it is ubiquitous. The earliest known version of it, one very like Hillel's, is credited to Confucius; and others appear in all the major religions. It is a proverb in many languages. Nor does the evidence suggest that it was diffused from a single source.[2] The explanation is simple. What a man would or would not have another do to him is in part a function of the mores he has made his own. Hence in cultures whose mores differ radically, what the Golden Rule is taken to require or forbid will differ radically too. And so any system of conduct that can be put forward as rational can include it.

The variability of what, in different cultures, the Golden Rule is taken to require or forbid shows that it is accepted because of its form. It expresses the universality of the precepts of whatever system incorporates it. Its force is therefore, as Sidgwick pointed out, that of a principle of impartiality: in no system that incorporates it can it be permissible for A to treat B in a manner in which it would be impermissible for B to treat A, merely on the ground that they are two different individuals, and without there being any difference between the natures or the circumstances of the two which can be stated as a reasonable ground for difference of treatment."[3] In its original form, Kant's first formula, "Act only according to that maxim by which you can at the same time will that it should become a universal law," has the same force. It is a rubric for an act of self-examination by which anybody may verify whether his judgement of how he may treat another has a place in the system of conduct he accepts, or whether it is an exception made in his own interest. But, obviously, no principle of impartiality that is common to different systems of mores can serve as the substantive first principle that distinguishes any one of them from the others.

Although the Golden Rule has always enjoyed popular esteem and has recently been recognized as an adequate substantive principle by so eminent a moralist as R. M. Hare,[4] most traditional moral theologians and philosophers have attached more weight to the second of the two traditional candidates for recognition as the first principle of morality. It is presented in a well-known passage that precedes the parable of the Good Samaritan in Luke's gospel.

> And behold, a certain lawyer stood up, and tempted [Jesus], saying, Master, what shall I do to inherit eternal life? He said unto him, What is written in the Law? how readest thou? And he answering said, Thou shalt love the Lord thy God with all thy heart, and with all thy soul, and with all thy strength, and with all thy mind; and thy neighbor as thyself. And he said unto him, Thou hast answered right; this do, and thou shalt live (10:25–28).

With the approval of Jesus, the "lawyer" (that is, student of Torah) here offers, as the fundamental principle governing the relations of human beings to themselves and to one another, an injunction from Leviticus, 19:18, *Love your neighbor as yourself.*

Although Jesus went on to interpret "neighbor" as standing for any human being whatever, in the passage from Leviticus the term strictly refers only to one's countrymen, so that a Jew's neighbors in a Jewish state would be his fellow Jews. However, rabbinical teaching as codified in Maimonides' *Mishneh Torah* joined the passage in Leviticus to another in Deuteronomy, the two together being equivalent to the principle in Leviticus as Jesus interpreted it:

> 206. To love all human beings, who are of the covenant, as it is said, 'Thou shalt love thy neighbor as thyself' (*Lev.* 19:18).

> 207. To love the stranger, as it is said, 'Ye shall love the stranger' (*Deut.* 10:19).[5]

In his most revealing philosophical remarks about common morality, which are to be found in the treatise *de lege veteri* in his *Summa Theologiae,* Aquinas recognized the two precepts in the passage quoted from Luke as the first common principles of that morality (*prima et communia praecepta legis naturae*).[6] To these two precepts, all the precepts of the Mosaic decalogue, in which the whole of common morality is in some sense contained, are related as conclusions to common principles (*sicut conclusiones ad principia communia*).[7] The first common principles are self-evident (*per se nota*) to human reason, and the precepts of the decalogue can be known from them straight off with a little thought (*statim . . . modica consideratione*). As for the more specific precepts of morality, although they can be inferred from the precepts of the decalogue by diligent inquiry (*per diligentem inquisitionem*), only the wise are capable of carrying out such inquiries. Ordinary folk will therefore receive the more specific precepts by instruction (*mediante disciplina sapientium*).

In the system of morality thus sketched, confining attention to the part of it that is independent of any theological presupposition, there is a single fundamental principle, held by Aquinas to be *per se notum,* that human beings are to love one another as they love themselves. From this primary and common principle (which Aquinas also referred to as a *principium communissimum*)[8] all the precepts of the Mosaic decalogue that do not rest on a theistic premise, that is, all but the first four, can be derived with a little thought. And from the precepts of the decalogue, in turn, skilled moralists can derive the more specific precepts needed for resolving problems of casuistry.

A problem, however, remains. In his preliminary discussion of natural law in the treatise *de lege* (*Summa Theologiae*, I–II, 90–97, esp. 94, 2) Aquinas did not even mention what in *de lege veteri* he went on to recognize as its first and common precepts. Instead he described the natural law as deriving from a "first precept" which he also called "the first principle in practical reason (*primum principium in ratione practica*): namely, that "good is to be done and pursued, and evil shunned" (*bonum est faciendum et prosequendum, et malum vitandum*).[9] What was the relation, in Aquinas's mind, between this first principle and the nontheistic *principium communissimum* that one is to love one's fellow human beings as oneself?

Germain Grisez has offered the only answer known to me that is consistent with what Aquinas wrote about both principles. The principle that good is to be done and sought, and evil avoided, is not primarily moral. It defines the fundamental condition that any movement or abstention from movement must satisfy if it is to be accounted an action at all. For no bodily movement can intelligibly be called an action unless it is presented as seeking or attempting some good, or shunning some evil. Even actions contrary to practical reason require "at least a remote basis" in it.[10] Wrong actions, so far as they are actions at all, are done in pursuit of something that seems good to the agent. However, any human being who thinks clearly must recognize that there are certain goods fundamental to human flourishing—to a full human life as a rational being: they include life itself, communicable knowledge, and friendship. With regard to human beings, whether oneself or another, the principle that good is to be pursued and evil shunned first of all forbids any action whatever directed against those fundamental goods; secondarily, it commands every human being, as far as he reasonably can, to promote human good generally, both directly (by actions good in themselves, such as acquiring knowledge) and indirectly (by producing the means for human flourishing, such as growing food). But the disposition to act and abstain from action in accordance with these commands and prohibitions is what loving yourself and others consists in. Hence the primary and common principle of the natural law may also be formulated as: *Act so that the fundamental human goods, whether in your own person or in that of another, are promoted as may be possible, and under no circumstances violated*. It is a principle of what Kant thought of as respect (*Achtung*), but of respect for certain fundamental goods. And, so interpreted, it plainly follows immediately from the first principle of practical reason.

Aquinas implicitly distinguished the love (*dilectio, amor*) of our own and others' humanity demanded by natural reason from the theological virtue he called *caritas* ("charity"; in Greek, *agape*). For he declared that all natural virtues—all dispositions to act as the natural law requires—"are in us by nature as an undeveloped aptitude, and not as fully perfected" (*secundum aptitudinem et inchoationem, non . . . secundum perfectionem*), whereas the theological virtues, the greatest of which is charity, are infused by divine grace, "wholly from the outside."[11] Aquinas's doctrine of charity, which is fundamental to his moral theology, falls outside the scope of this inquiry. Roughly, he maintained that the virtues which are exhibited in actions done according to common morality, and are directed to natural human goods, must be "perfected" by directing them to man's ultimate supernatural end as divinely revealed, for which the infused theological virtue of charity is needed.[12] Charity comprehends every action demanded by the common morality required by natural reason, but directs them all to a further end, and an even more demanding one. Hence grace perfects nature. By affirming that the ends of theological virtues are not the same as those of the natural ones as such, but are more remote and comprehend more acts, Aquinas implied that his theory of the natural virtues—of common morality— does not logically presuppose his moral theology, and can be studied in its own right.

Although distinctions of this sort were once common property of orthodox Christianity in all its branches, there have recently been movements in Protestant moral theology to repudiate the doctrine that natural human reason can generate any moral laws at all: to proclaim *agape* (as theologians like to call it) as the sole valid guide for action; and, as the sole and sufficient rule of conduct, "Love, and do what you will!"

How this Augustinian injunction is supposed to guide conduct is far from clear, as W. K. Frankena has remarked; for the verb "to love" is desperately ambiguous.[13] In the mouths of orthodox theologians like St. Augustine or St. Thomas Aquinas, for whom traditional morality as embodied in the Mosaic decalogue is an expression of charity, one of the things enjoined is that the traditional moral law be obeyed. This position has been called "pure rule-agapism" by Paul Ramsey.[14] Others, taking what Frankena has judged "the clearest and most plausible view," have interpreted the law of love as a combination of a principle of benevolence, that we must produce good as such and prevent evil, with a principle of distributive justice.[15] Agapism of this sort would be a modified form of utilitarianism. Yet others have identified it with one or another of the pure forms of utilitarianism and have grappled with the familiar difficulties incurred. And finally, there are those who, confounding *agape* with diffuse affectionate sentiment, have reduced "Love, and do what you will!" to "Having ascertained the facts of your situation, allow nothing— and especially not the precepts of traditional morality—to deter you from what your affectionate sentiments may prompt!" It should surprise nobody that the results of this vulgar "situation ethics" are sloppy and incoherent.

Except for the first, all these positions are incompatible with the traditional doctrine that the system of common morality embodied in the Mosaic decalogue is strictly derivable from the primary and common principle that humanity is to be loved as such. And the first position, "pure rule-agapism," has to do, not with the rational character of common morality but with its relation to the theological virtue of charity. Our task is to inquire into the meaning of the primary and common principle, understood as knowable by ordinary human reason. And, as regards that inquiry, the only alternative to the interpretation of Aquinas proposed by Grisez, correctly, as I shall hereafter assume, is Kant's second formula of the fundamental principle of morality, *Act so that you treat humanity, whether in your own person or in that of another, always as an end, and never as a means only.* Although, like Aquinas's, according to the interpretation by Grisez which I accept, this formula is teleological, it takes the ends of actions to be human beings themselves, not the human goods that may be realized in them.

In recent generations, many British moralists have objected that humanity, or rational nature, is not the sort of thing that can be an end in itself. "[B]y an end," Sidgwick complained, "we commonly mean something to be realized, whereas 'humanity' is, as Kant says, a self-subsistent end."[16] Ross dilated upon this, arguing that "ends . . . in the ordinary sense of the word men are not. For an end is an object of desire, and an object of desire is something that does not yet exist." And on no better ground, he complacently pronounced "the notion of self-subsistent ends" to be "nothing but an embarrassment to Kant."[17]

Far from embarrassing Kant, it is more probable that such cavils would have astonished him. Nor do I think he would easily have been persuaded that, among Sidgwick's and Ross's countrymen, the belief that the ultimate end of an action is the existing being for whose sake it is done was any less common that it was among his own.

*   *   *

Kant's and Aquinas's versions of the primary common principle that humanity is to be loved for its own sake, although they converge, do not coincide. For while most acts of respecting human nature as an end in itself are also acts of respecting certain fundamental human goods as to be promoted and never violated, not all are. For example, respecting as an end in itself one human being who attacks the life of another, who is innocent, does not appear to exclude using deadly violence on him, if only so is the life or fundamental well-being of his innocent victim to be safeguarded. A man is not degraded to a mere manipulated means by being forcibly prevented from degrading somebody else to a mere manipulated means. But respecting every human life as an inviolable fundamental good does exclude using deadly violence on anybody, even to safeguard innocent lives. Hence Aquinas's version of the *principium communissimum* can only be reconciled with the received Christian doctrine that killing in self-defence or in defence of the innocent is licit, by such devices as confining its application to direct actions and drawing a distinction between direct and indirect killing.

There are three reasons for preferring Kant's interpretation of the primary and common principle to Aquinas's. First, it is simpler. If the principle that one is to love one's fellow human beings as oneself is to be understood as a principle of respect, as it must be to play the part it does in Jewish and Christian moral thinking, then it is most straightforwardly read as ordaining respect for human beings, not for fundamental human goods. Second, as the examples of self-defence and the safeguarding of innocent lives show, received Jewish and Christian moral conclusions are derivable more directly from the principle as Kant interpreted it. And finally, although the question itself will not be investigated until the final chapter, the principle appears to be more defensible in its Kantian form than in its Thomistic one.

In what follows, therefore, I take the fundamental principle of that part of traditional morality which is independent of any theological presupposition to have been expressed in the scriptural commandment, "Thou shalt love thy neighbor as thyself," understanding one's neighbor to be any fellow human being, and love to be a matter, not of feeling, but of acting in ways in which human beings as such can choose to act. The philosophical sense of this commandment was correctly expressed by Kant in his formula that one act so that one treats humanity always as an end and never as a means only. However, Kant was mistaken in thinking this formula to be equivalent to his formula of universal law, in which he captured the philosophical truth underlying the inaccurately stated Golden Rule.

Since treating a human being, in virtue of its rationality, as an end in itself, is the same as respecting it as a rational creature, Kant's formula of the fundamental principle may be restated in a form more like that of the scriptural commandment that is its original: *Act always so that you respect every human being, yourself or another, as being a rational creature.* And, since it will be convenient that the fundamental principle of the system to be developed be formulated in terms of the concept of permissibility analysed in the preceding section, the canonical form in which that principle will hereafter be cited is: *It is impermissible not to respect every human being, oneself or any other, as a rational creature.*

Notes

1. Babylonian Talmud, Shabbat, p. 31a.
2. Marcus G. Singer, "The Golden Rule" in *The Encyclopedia of Philosophy* ed. Paul Edwards, Vol. 3 (NY: Macmillan, 1967), pp. 365b–367a.
3. Sidgwick, *Methods of Ethics,* 7th ed. (London: Macmillan, 1907), p. 380.
4. R. M. Hare, *Freedom and Reason* (Oxford: Clarendon Press, 1963), pp. 86–111.
5. Mishneh Torah, List of Precepts 206, 207.
6. Aquinas, *Summa Theologiae* I-II, 1003 ad 1, and II ad 1.
7. Ibid.
8. Ibid.
9. Ibid.
10. Germain G. Grisez "The First Principles of Practical Reason: A Commentary on *Summa Theologiae,* 1–2, Question 94, Article 2" *Natural Law Forum* 10 (1965): 184–190.
11. Aquinas, *Summa Theologiae* I-II, 63, 1.
12. Ibid.
13. W. K. Frakena, *Ethics* (Englewood Cliffs, NJ: Prentice Hall, 1964), p. 44.
14. Paul Ramsey. *Deeds and Rules in Christian Ethics* (NY: Scribners, 1967), pp. 7–8, 111–113, 224–25.
15. Frakena, pp. 44–45.
16. Sidgwick, p. 390.
17. W. D. Ross. *Kant's Ethical Theory* (Oxford: Clarendon Press, 1954), p. 51.

▼ ## The Business Perspective

The Ethics of Responsibility

Peter Drucker

Countless sermons have been preached and printed on the ethics of business or the ethics of the businessman. Most have nothing to do with business and little to do with ethics.

One main topic is plain, everyday honesty. Businessmen, we are told solemnly, should not cheat, steal, lie, bribe, or take bribes. But nor should anyone else. Men and women do not acquire exemption from ordinary rules of personal behavior because of their work or job. Nor, however, do they cease to be human beings when appointed vice-president, city manager, or college dean. And there has always been a number of people who cheat, steal, lie, bribe, or take bribes. The problem is one of moral values and moral education, of the individual, of the family, of the school. But there neither is a separate ethics of business, nor is one needed.

All that is needed is to mete out stiff punishments to those—whether business executives or others—who yield to temptation. In England a magistrate still tends to hand down a harsher punishment in a drunken-driving case if the accused has gone to one of the well-known public schools or to Oxford or Cambridge. And the conviction still rates a headline in the evening paper: "Eton graduate convicted of drunken driving." No one expects an Eton education to produce temperance leaders. But it is still a badge of distinction, if not of privilege. And not to treat a wearer of such a badge more harshly than an ordinary workingman who has had one too many would offend the community's sense of justice. But no one considers this a problem of the "ethics of the Eton graduate."

The other common theme in the discussion of ethics in business has nothing to do with ethics.

Such things as the employment of call girls to entertain customers are not matters of ethics but matters of esthetics. "Do I want to see a pimp when I look at myself in the mirror while shaving?" is the real question.

It would indeed be nice to have fastidious leaders. Alas, fastidiousness has never been prevalent among leadership groups, whether kings and counts, priests or generals, or even "intellectuals" such as the painters and humanists of the Renaissance, or the "literati" of the Chinese tradition. All a fastidious man can do is withdraw personally from activities that violate his self-respect and his sense of taste.

Primum Non Nocere

The first responsibility of a professional was spelled out clearly, 2500 years ago, in the Hippocratic oath of the Greek physician: *primum non nocere*— "Above all, not knowingly to do harm."

No professional, be he doctor, lawyer, or manager, can promise that he will indeed do good for his client. All he can do is try. But he can promise that he will not knowingly do harm. And the client, in turn, must be able to trust the professional not knowingly to do him harm. Otherwise he cannot trust him at all. The professional has to have autonomy. He cannot be controlled, supervised, or directed by the client. He has to be private in that his knowledge and his judgment have to be entrusted with the decision. But it is the foundation of his autonomy, and indeed its rationale, that he see himself as "affected with the public interest." A professional, in other words, is private in the sense that he is autonomous and not subject to political or ideological control. But he is public in the sense that the welfare of his client sets limits to his deeds and words. And *primum non nocere,* "not knowingly to do harm," is the basic rule of professional ethics, the basic rule of an ethics of public responsibility.

There are important areas where managers, and especially business managers, still do not realize that in order to be permitted to remain autonomous and private they have to impose on themselves the responsibility of the professional ethic. They still have to learn that it is their job to scrutinize their deeds, words, and behavior to make sure that they do not knowingly do harm.

The manager who fails to think through and work for the appropriate solution to an impact of his business because it makes him "unpopular in the club" knowingly does harm. He knowingly abets a cancerous growth. That this is stupid has been said. That this always in the end hurts the business or the industry more than a little temporary "unpleasantness" would have hurt has been said too. But it is also a gross violation of professional ethics.

But there are other areas as well. American managers, in particular, tend to violate the rule not knowingly to do harm with respect to:

- executive compensation;
- the use of benefit plans to impose "golden fetters" on people in the company's employ; and
- in their profit rhetoric.

Their actions and their words in these areas tend to cause social disruption. They tend to conceal healthy reality and to create disease, or at least social hypochondria. They tend to misdirect and to prevent understanding. And this is grievous social harm.

Executive Compensation and Economic Inequality

Contrary to widespread belief, incomes have become far more equal in all developed countries than in any society of which we have a record. And they have tended to become steadily more equal as national and personal incomes increase. And, equally contrary to popular rhetoric, income equality is greatest in the United States.

The most reliable measure of income equality is the so-called Gini coefficient, in which an index of zero stands for complete equality of income and an index of 1 for total inequality in which one person in the population receives all the income. The lower the Gini coefficient, the closer a society is to income equality. In the U.S. the Gini in the early 1970s stood around 0.35—with about the same figure in Canada, Australia, and Great Britain, and probably also in Japan. West Germany and the Netherlands are about 0.40. France and Sweden are around 0.50.[1]

The main cause of the dangerous delusion of increasing inequality of income is the widely publicized enormous *pre-tax* incomes of a few men at the top of a few giant corporations, and the—equally widely publicized—"extras" of executive compensation, e.g., stock options.

The $500,000 a year which the chief executive of one of the giant corporations is being paid is largely "make-believe money." Its function is status rather than income. Most of it, whatever tax loopholes the lawyers might find, is immediately taxed away. And the "extras" are simply attempts to put a part of the executive's income into a somewhat lower tax bracket. Economically, in other words, neither serves much purpose. But socially and psychologically they "knowingly do harm." They cannot be defended.

One way to eliminate the offense is for companies to commit themselves to a maximum range of *after-tax* compensation. The 1 to 10 ratio that the great majority of Americans would consider perfectly acceptable, would, in fact, be wider than the actual range of most companies. (There should, I would argue, be room, however, for an occasional exception: the rare, "once-in-a-lifetime," very big, "special bonus" to someone, a research scientist, a manager, or a salesman who has made an extraordinary contribution.)

But equally important is acceptance of social responsibility on the part of managers to work for a rational system of taxation,[2] which eliminates the temptation of "tax gimmicks" and the need for them.

There is a strong case for adequate incentives for performing executives. And compensation in money is far preferable to hidden compensation such as perquisites. If he gets money, the recipient can choose what to spend it on rather than, as in the case of "perks," taking whatever the company provides, be it a chauffeur-driven car, a big house, or (as in the case of some Swedish companies) a governess for the children. Indeed it may well be that real incomes in American business are not sufficiently unequal and that the compression of income differentials in the years since 1950 has been socially and economically detrimental.

What is pernicious, however, is the delusion of inequality. The basic cause is the tax laws. But the managers' willingness to accept, and indeed to play along with, an antisocial tax structure is a major contributory cause. And unless managers realize that this violates the rule "not knowingly to do damage," they will, in the end, be the main sufferers.

The Danger of "Golden Fetters"

A second area in which the manager of today does not live up to the commitment of *primum non nocere* is closely connected with compensation.

Since World War II compensation and benefits have been increasingly misused to create "golden fetters."

Retirement benefits, extra compensation, bonuses, and stock options are all forms of compensation. From the point of view of the enterprise—but also from the point of view of the economy—these are "labor costs" no matter how they are labeled. They are treated as such by managements when they sit down to negotiate with the labor union. But increasingly, if only because of the bias of the tax laws, these benefits are being used to tie an employee to his employer. They are being made dependent on staying with the same employer, often for many years.

Golden fetters do not strengthen the company. They lead to "negative selection." People who know that they are not performing in their present employment—that is, people who are clearly in the wrong place—will often not move but stay where they know they do not properly belong. But if they stay because the penalty for leaving is too great, they resist and resent it. They know that they have been bribed and were too weak to say no. They are likely to be sullen, resentful, and bitter the rest of their working lives.

The fact that the employees themselves eagerly seek these benefits is no excuse. After all, medieval serfdom also began as an eagerly sought "employee benefit."

The Rhetoric of the Profit Motive

Managers, finally, through their rhetoric, make it impossible for the public to understand economic reality. This violates the requirement that managers, being leaders, not knowingly do harm. This is particularly true of the United States but also of Western Europe. For in the West, managers still talk constantly of the profit motive. And they still define the goal of their business as profit maximization. They do not stress the objective function of profit. They do not talk of risks—or very rarely. They do not stress the need for capital. They almost never even mention the cost of capital, let alone that a business has to produce enough profit to obtain the capital it needs at minimum cost.

Managers constantly complain about the hostility to profit. They rarely realize that their own rhetoric is one of the main reasons for this hostility. For indeed in the terms management uses when it talks to the public, there is no possible justification for profit, no explanation for its existence, no function it performs. There is only the profit motive, that is, the desire of some anonymous capitalists—and why that desire should be indulged in by society any more than bigamy, for instance, is never explained. But profitability is a crucial *need* of economy and society.

Managerial practice in most large American companies is perfectly rational. It is the rhetoric which obscures, and thereby threatens to damage both business and society. To be sure, few American companies work out profitability as a *minimum* requirement. As a result, most probably underestimate the profitability the company truly requires (let alone the inflationary erosion of capital). But they, consciously or not, base their profit planning on the twin objectives of ensuring access to capital needed and minimizing the cost of capital. In the American context, if only because of the structure of the U.S. capital market, a high "price/earnings ratio" is indeed a key to the minimization of the cost of capital; and "optimization of profits" is therefore a perfectly rational strategy which tends to lower, in the long run, the actual cost of capital.

But this makes it even less justifiable to keep on using the rhetoric of the profit motive. It serves no purpose except to confuse and to embitter.

If the society is to function, let alone if it is to remain a free society, the men we call managers will remain "private" in their institutions. No matter who owns them and how, they will maintain autonomy. But they will also have to be "public" in their ethics.

In this tension between the private functioning of the manager, the necessary autonomy of his institution and its accountability to its own mission and purpose, and the public character of the manager, lies the specific ethical problem of the society of organizations. *Primum non nocere* may seem tame compared to the rousing calls for "statesmanship" that abound in today's manifestos on social responsibility. But, as the physicians found out long ago, it is not an easy rule to live up to. Its very modesty and self-constraint make it the right rule for the ethics managers need, the ethics of responsibility.

Notes

1. On this see the article by Sanford Rose, "The Truth about Income and Equality in the U.S." in *Fortune,* December 1972.
2. We know the specifications of such a system—and they are simple: *no* preferential tax rates for *any* personal income, whether from salaries or from capital gains, and a limit on the maximum tax—say 50 percent of total income received.

 ## *CHECKLIST* for Deontology

The ethical checklists are short summaries meant to help students apply the theories they have been studying in the preceding section. They are not meant to stand alone nor are they meant to supplant deeper reading into primary sources of each ethical theory.

It also should be noted that **there is no single application of any theory that everyone will accept.** Therefore, the checklist below is just one version of the ethical theory presented. It is set down in this succinct format as a pedagogical aid for applying ethical theories that will be used in the Case Studies Reports.

Directions: Read the short epitome on deontology and then go through the steps outlined below. When you have finished the assignment, you will have constructed your own checklist for deontology.

▼
Deontology

Epitome:

Deontology is a moral theory based upon one's duty to adhere to a certain primitive moral principle(s). In the readings from this section you have three versions of a primitive moral principle (Kant, Gewirth, and Donagan). The moral principle is derived from and justified by the nature of reason and the structure of human action. Since its justification is general, so also is its scope general. The principle defines duty concerning moral situations in general. One way to understand this level of generality is to liken it to a scientific law. It is universal and absolute covering all societies in all historical epochs.

One difficulty people often face with such a general principle is that moral cases are presented to us as "particulars." In logic general or universal propositions are contrasted to particular or individual propositions. They are different logical types and cannot be directly compared. What you have to do is "translate" your moral problem into the same level of general language as the moral principle. This will allow you to arrive at a definitive outcome. However, this translation is not so easy. For example, take the case of Sally contemplating an abortion. All the particulars of Sally's individual situation must be translated into the general form of the categorical imperative.

Let us assume the first form of Kant's categorical imperative as our general principle. This principle—"act only on that maxim through which you can at the same time will that it should become a universal law"—prohibits murder.[1] This is because a universal law of murder in some society is logically contradictory. (If everyone murdered everyone else, then there would be no society.) Logically contradictory universal laws are immoral, therefore; murder is immoral.

Autonomy, however, is sanctioned by the categorical imperative and becomes the cornerstone of a formulation of the categorical imperative which addresses people as ends and not means only.

An example of this can be seen in the following: "How do we translate abortion?" Is abortion an instance of killing or of autonomy? If it is the former, it is prohibited. If it is the latter, it is permitted. The real debate rests in the translation. Once a moral situation is translated, the application to the moral law is easy. The moral law determines our duty in the situation, and we must do our duty or else we repudiate our human nature: rationality.

Application:

Step One: Choose a universal moral principle—either Kant's, Gewirth's, or Donagan's.

Step Two: Create a particular moral situation of your own which seems to involve a difficult choice of alternative actions. (Cases which pit two moral duties against each other are often good for this exercise.)

Step Three: Set out the possible alternative ways to translate the particular case into more general language, i.e., as an instance of truth telling, murder, autonomy, etc.

Step Four: Justify your translation while pointing out the flaws in alternative translations.

Step Five: Show how your translation fits a general corollary of the universal moral principle. Explain how you arrived at the corollary, and explain the outcome of translation to corollary. What sorts of attacks could people make against your translation, corollary derivation, or outcomes application? How would you defend yourself against these attacks?

Notes

1. The mode of this prohibition is that all moral maxims generated from the notion of a universal society of murderers are shown to be incoherent. This means that when you create a moral maxim such as, "It is permissable to murder" such a maxim is found to contain a logical contradiction. Like Plato, Kant believes that logical contradictions indicate immorality. This is because morality means, "the right and wrong in human action." 'Right' and 'wrong' are determined by reference to logic. Illogic, therefore, is wrong. This is the driving force behind the universality of the categorical imperative in its various forms.

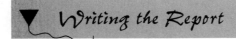

▼ *Writing the Report*

Choosing an Ethical Theory

Our goal is to write a report on the ethical impact of some critical factor in a business decision. Every business decision is composed of many elements. One of those elements is the ethical impact of the project/policy/action upon the company. At the end of the *Writing the Report* essays, you should be better prepared to do just that.

The business report approach allows you to employ techniques that you have been taught elsewhere along with those found in this text. Depending on your background in business, you can create a report that demonstrates your business acumen along with your sensitivity to the ethical dimensions found in the situation you are examining. Classes that have few business students will de-emphasize the nitty-gritty of business management.

The biggest difference between cases that you might prepare in regular business school classes and these cases is the additional component of ethics. This factor is too often discounted as: "Business is business." But this is wrong. The following essays will help you analyze the ethical and practical situation together. The approach will invoke a technique which rates a proposal as having three levels of complexity: surface, medium, and deep. The level of interaction allows you to see at a glance how the competing areas of "interest" and "ethical value" conflict.

There are five essays in this series that intend to sequentially lead you to a mastery of the business report: 1. Choosing an Ethical Theory; 2. Finding the Conflicts; 3. Assessing Embedded Levels; 4. Applying Ethical Theories; 5. Structuring the Essay.

At the end of each essay you will be presented with case studies with which you can apply your new found skills. By the end of the term you should be able to create an ethical impact statement of some sophistication.

In this first section you are presented with four of the most important ethical theories. The readings acquaint you with some of the philosophical complexities and general business applications. At the end of each theory you created a checklist that ensures you can apply the principles of that theory to some case which is presented to you.

In order to deal with any of the cases presented in the subsequent sections you will have to do two things: (a) Choose an ethical theory; and (b) Specify a viewpoint.

It is not my intent to force you into defending one ethical position for the rest of your life, but merely to recommend that you choose a single theory for your critical tool as you prepare for class. "How do I know which viewpoint to choose?" you might ask. This is a difficult question. It concerns the justification of the various ethical theories.

There are many criteria which can be used to justify an ethical theory. One of these is the issue of naturalism. Each theory presupposes a naturalistic or non-naturalistic epistemological standpoint. Naturalism is complicated. For our purposes let us describe naturalism as a view which holds that there are no entities or events which are, in principle, beyond the domain of scientific explanation. Cognitive claims are only valid if they are based upon accepted scientific modes.

Ethical naturalism states that moral judgments, too, are merely a subclass of facts about the natural world which can be studied scientifically. From this study we can determine moral correctness as a corollary of certain facts which can be scientifically investigated—e.g., how much pleasure various alternatives will produce for the group. Thus the utilitarians believe that moral judgments *are* judgments about which alternative will be most beneficial to some group's survival.

The Utilitarian would point to the scientific study of nature and might say that the instinct to pleasure is evidenced in all species. Further, there seems to be an evolutionary advantage to those species which act for the benefit of the group against those that do not.

Many socio–biologists make this sort of claim. The main imperative is that one's own genes be passed on to another filial generation. If passing on your own genes is impossible, then the next best thing is to pass on the genes of one's kin. Thus, seemingly altruistic behavior (such as a bird which stays behind in dangerous situations so that the group might survive) is really "selfish." It is selfish because helping the group *is* helping itself. Its genes (or those of its kin) are passed on.

Socio-biology, of course, is not universally accepted. Nor is it necessary for a utilitarian to be a socio-biologist. However, it does illustrate a type of justification that the utilitarian might make. He or she could move from the concept of group "happiness" in animals and extrapolate to humans. The supporting data are scientific, therefore; the theory is naturalistic.

Deontologists may or may not be naturalists. Since deontology involves a "duty based" ethics, the key question to be asked concerns how we know whether a binding duty exists to do such and such. Are all the moral "oughts" derivable from factual, scientifically ascertainable "is" statements? If they are, then the deontologist is a naturalist. If they are not, then the deontologist is not a naturalist.

Gewirth in his book *Reason and Morality* claims to derive "ought" from "is." There is no reference to knowledge claims that are not compatible with the scientific inquiry of natural objects. This would make Gewirth a naturalist.

Kant and Donagan are somewhat different. Each make reference to supernatural entities which are not scientifically supported. Kant spends considerable effort trying to define these boundaries in the "Transcendental Dialectic" section of his book *The Critique of Pure Reason*. This aside, neither Kant nor Donagan held there to be a problem about integrating the factual and the normative.

If you are inclined to view reality as an extention of evolutionary biology or that group advantage immediately entails a moral "ought," then you are leaning toward utilitarianism. However, if you think that people should act from pure duty alone without reference to anything except the rightness of the action, then deontology is probably your preference.

The "is-ought" problem was sharpened by intuitionist G. E. Moore.[1] Moore rejected ethical naturalism because he believed it contained a fallacy (which he dubbed "the naturalistic fallacy"). This fallacy claims it is false to define goodness in terms of any natural property. This is because "good" is not definable and because "good" is not subject to scientific examination. This is because the factual "is" realm is separate from the normative "ought" realm. The chasm between the two cannot be crossed.

"Good" for Moore is a unique, unanalyzable, non-natural property (as opposed, for example, to "yellow" which is a natural property). It is clear from this depiction that scientific methods will do no good. Science can tell us things about "yellow" but can tell us nothing about the meaning of "good."

Other intuitionists, too, hold that we understand important moral terms and/or moral maxims by cognitive means which are not scientific. Generally, these are immediate and cannot be justified in factual "is" language.

Intuitionism is therefore a non-naturalistic theory. Still, there are some remote connections to naturalism. For example, one can point to the *plausibility* of accepting certain common moral maxims—such as a prohibition against murder—by making reference to other societies. (In other words, since all societies prohibit murder, the prohibition against murder must be immediately apparent to all.) However, "plausibility" is not the same thing as exhaustive scientific demonstration. Justification in intuitionism lies in its alleged unarguable truth. This truth can be immediately seen by all.

If you are having trouble adopting any of the other theories and believe that acceptance or rejection of an ethical theory comes down to some sort of brute, immediate acceptance, then you will probably want to accept intuitionism as the justification for your ethical theory.

Finally, we turn to Virtue Ethics. This theory seems at first glance to be naturalistic. Aristotle, himself, lends credence to this when he talks about relying upon the common opinions of people about what is considered to be a virtue. The "common opinions" could be gathered and reviewed much as a sociologist or anthropologist might employ. This "scientific" method would yield definitive results. Aristotle believed that some common agreement existed about a core set of virtues.

Justification, therefore, was not an issue to Aristotle. If we accept a world view such as Aristotle presents, then we would all agree that "courage" (for example) is considered to be a virtue to everyone. The confirming data can be gathered and scientifically studied, ergo; it is naturalistic.

But what about today in our pluralistic society? Some might argue that there is no longer any consensus about the virtues. If there is no consensus as Aristotle envisioned, then what constitutes a Virtue may collapse into a form of intuitionism. For example, I think that X is a virtue. You think Y is a virtue. X and Y are mutually exclusive traits. You and I come from different societies, therefore, we cannot come to an agreement. All we can say is that, "I am right and you are wrong." Personal insight (intuitionism) is all we have.

If you believe that "courage," "wisdom," "self-control," "piety," and so forth are virtues to every society, then perhaps you will choose virtue ethics as your model.

To help you in making your choice of an ethical theory, try the following exercise. Examine one or more of the moral situations below and give: 1. An interpretation of what is right and wrong according to each of the four theories; 2. The manner of argument each might give; 3. Your own assessment of the strengths of each.

Situation One.   You are the constable of a small, remote, rural town in Northern Ireland. The town is divided into the Irish Catholics (20% minority) and the Irish Protestants (80% majority). All the Catholics live in one section of town which sits on a peninsula that juts out into the river just east of the main part of town.

One morning a young Protestant girl is found raped and murdered next to the town green. By general consensus it is concluded that a Catholic must have committed the crime. The Protestants form a citizens' committee that makes the following demand upon the constable: "We believe you to be a Catholic sympathizer. Therefore, we do not think you will press fast enough to bring this killer to justice. We know a Catholic did the crime. We have therefore sealed off the Catholic section of town. No one can go in or out. If you do not hand over the criminal by sundown, we will torch the entire Catholic section of town killing all 1000 people. Don't try to call for help. We've already disabled the telephone."

The constable worked hard all day in an effort to find out who did it. It was no use. He couldn't find out. It was now one hour before sundown. He didn't know what to do. His deputy said, "Why don't we just pick a random Catholic and tell them he did it? At least we'd be saving 999 lives."

"But then I'd be responsible for killing an innocent man!" returned the constable.

"Better one innocent die and 999 be saved. After all, there's no way the two of us can stop the mob. You have to give them a scapegoat."

Describe how all the ethical theories might handle this situation. Be sure your answer covers all the facets from your various ethical checklists.

Situation Two.   You are a railroad switchman. You sit in a tower and control a switch that will allow trains to travel over the regular track or will switch them over to a siding. One morning you are faced with a terrible dilemma. The N. Y. Zephyr is traveling at high speed on the main track. A school bus filled with children (at least fifty) has stalled on the main track as it crosses Elm Street. The bus driver is vainly trying to restart the engine, but the ignition has ceased to turn over. It is clear to you that it will not get off the track in time.

On the siding track is a homeless man who has fallen down and caught his foot on a rail tie. It is also clear that he is stuck.

In fifteen seconds the train will pass the switch which will allow you:
1. To send the train to the siding—thereby killing the homeless man—or
2. To do nothing and allow the train to take its normal course and thereby kill most if not all of the fifty school children on board.

Describe how all the ethical theories might handle this situation. Be sure your answer covers all the facets from your various ethical checklists.

Situation Three.   You are on the executive committee of the XYZ organization of insurance agents. Each year the committee gives an award to one of its members who displays high moral character in his or her work. This year you are among the four judges for the award. However, there is some disagreement among the judges about what constitutes a good person. The judges, besides yourself, are: Ms. Smith, Mrs. Taylor, and Mr. Jones. The candidates for the award are: Mr. Big and Mrs. Little.

Ms. Smith says that the award should go to Mr. Big because he saved the life of a man from drowning. However, Mr. Jones demurred saying that Mr. Big's motives are suspect considering the man he saved was in the midst of a very big business deal with Mr. Big. If the man had been allowed to drown, Mr. Big would have lost a lot of money. Ms. Smith said motives aren't important. It's the goodness of the act that counts and the man who was saved runs a big business in town. Many people besides Mr. Big would have been hurt if Mr. Big had not performed his feat.

Mr. Jones said the award should go to Mrs. Little because she performed a kind act of charity in chairing the town's United Way Campaign this last year. And surely such an act could not be said to benefit Mrs. Little in any way (unlike Mr. Big).

Mrs. Taylor says that she's somewhat unsure about either Mr. Big or Mrs. Little because both of them have been recommended on the basis of a single good act. Mrs. Taylor believes that it would be better to choose a candidate who has shown *over time* to have performed many good actions and to be of good character. "After all," she says, "a single swallow does not make a spring." Mr. Jones and Ms. Smith scratch their heads over this remark and turn to you. Who's right?

Describe how all the ethical theories might handle this situation. Be sure your answer covers all the facets from your various ethical checklists.

Notes:

1. I cannot stress too much that it is impossible to pigeonhole philosophers completely. In some important ways Moore was an intuitionist. This is because "good" had to be accepted as an unanalyzable, unnatural fact. But toward the end of *Principia Ethica* Moore sounds a lot like an "Agathistic Utilitarian." That is one who wishes to maximize the group's good. This mixture of labels among philosophers only shows that labels are limited in what they can do.

   Ross and Rawls have deontological and intuitionistic aspects to their theories. Therefore, one label alone cannot adequately capture the spirit of their philosophy. In an introductory text, such as this one, labels are used to simplify—but hopefully not obfuscate the dynamics present in these thinkers.

Part 2

Employer-Employee Relations

- ▶ **Privacy**
- ▶ **Affirmative Action**
- ▶ **Whistle Blowing**
- ▶ **Working Conditions**

CHAPTER *5*

Privacy

The Moral Contract between Employer and Employee

Norman E. Bowie

. . . My central thesis is that if a corporation or business is to treat its employees with dignity, it must recognize that these employees have certain rights that must be respected. In arguing for this thesis, I will contend that the "factors-of-production view of labor" is ethically unacceptable. Although I support David Ewing's strategy of extending constitutional rights to the workplace, I will argue on moral and conceptual rather than legal grounds. Specifically, I will claim that the very practice of business presupposes a recognition of employee rights on the part of the corporation. Hence I will conclude that the central issues are the identification and implementation of employee rights rather than the defense of them.

The Argument

The Contractual Context

One of the most useful devices in the practice of business is the notion of a business contract. The contract device is used in the hiring of employees, in the establishment of credit, in the ordering and supplying of goods, and in the issuing of a warranty. Now a contract is a kind of promise and, hence, is a

Adapted from Norman E. Bowie, "The Moral Contract between Employer and Employee," in *The Work Ethic in Business,* W. M. Hoffman and T. J. Wyly (Cambridge, Mass.: Oelgeschlager, Gunn, & Hair, 1981), pp. 195–202. Reprinted by permission.

moral device. In other words, since the use of contracts is central to business, the morality of promise keeping is central to business. Persons who are engaged in the making of contracts are essentially engaged in moral activity.

We can use the contract notion to establish the central thesis that business firms must admit that employees have certain rights which must be respected. The structure of the argument is as follows:

1. One person can enter a valid business contract only if the parties to the contract are responsible, autonomous adults.
2. If a person is a responsible, autonomous adult, then that person must view himself and be viewed by others as a moral agent.
3. A person can be a moral agent only if he has rights which he or she can press as claims against others.
4. Therefore, a person who enters a valid business contract is a person who has rights.
5. To recognize that a person has rights is to recognize that other persons entering the business contract have rights as well.
6. Therefore, a person entering a valid business contract must recognize the rights claims of the other contractees.

Let us examine this argument in some detail. Premise 1 asks who the promisers and promisees are. They are persons who must be considered to be responsible, autonomous agents. In other words, such persons are free adults who can be held accountable for their actions. Generally speaking, contracts with children, mental defectives, and criminals are not binding. The ideal contract maker is a responsible, autonomous adult.

Premise 2 exploits the conceptual relationship between being an autonomous responsible individual and being a moral individual. In considering yourself as a responsible autonomous being, you must consider yourself to be a moral being—an agent who can make moral claims against others. After all, what must a person be like to be capable of being a moral agent? He or she must be a rational person capable of making his or her own choices and willing to live by the consequences of the choices. In other words, a moral being is a rational, autonomous agent—just the kind of being who is capable of entering into contracts. When you enter into a contract with another person, you are treating that person as a responsible, autonomous contract maker. From the perspective of morality, parties to a contract are equals. Hence, arguing from a Kantian perspective, you must treat other contract makers in a similar way. You must recognize them as moral agents as well.

Premise 3 is the key to the argument. It asserts that one can be a moral agent only if he or she has rights which can be pressed as claims against others. The essential concepts in a defense of this premise are responsibility, dignity, and rights. A responsible being is one who can make choices according to his or her own insights. He or she is not under the control of others. He or she does not live simply for another. In other words, a responsible person is a person who has dignity and self-respect. But a person has dignity and self-respect when asserting himself or herself in the world. He can only have dignity and self-respect if he can say such things as "I may be wrong, but I am entitled to my opinion," "I will not change the research results because such behavior would violate the code of professional ethics which I have voluntarily adopted," or "What I do on my free time is none of the company's business." In uttering these remarks, he is asserting rights claims since rights are moral entitlements. What I have been arguing is that rights must be presupposed to account for our use of moral language and moral concepts. The following quotation captures my point exactly:

> Rights, we are suggesting, are fundamental moral commodities because they enable us to stand up on our own two feet, "to look others in the eye," and to feel in some fundamental way the equal of anyone. To think of oneself as the holder of rights is not to be unduly but properly proud, to have that minimal self-respect that is necessary to be worthy of the love and esteem of others. Conversely, to lack the concept of oneself as a rights bearer is to be bereft of a significant element of human dignity. Without such a concept, we could not view ourselves as beings entitled to be treated as not simply means but ends as well.[1]

Let me review the argument thus far. A person can enter a valid business contract only if he or she is a responsible, autonomous adult. But a responsible, autonomous adult is the paradigm case of a moral agent. He can be a moral agent, however, only if he has rights that can be pressed against others. Therefore, a person who enters a valid business contract is a person who has rights.

The remainder of the argument is rather simple. Premise 5 represents nothing more than the straightforward application of the moral principle of universalizability. What counts as a reason in one case must count as a reason in relevantly similar cases. The argument for our conclusion that persons entering a business contract must recognize the rights claims of others is now established as both valid and sound. Since the relation between an employer and an employee is essentially a contractual one, the thesis of this paper that an employer must recognize that his employees have certain rights has been established. Our analysis has shown that a focal point for any discussion of worker dignity in the corporation must be employee rights.

What Rights Do Employees Have?

To establish the conclusion that contractees must recognize the rights of other contractees is one thing. To argue what such recognition would amount to is something else. In this section I shall propose one analysis of what would constitute appropriate recognition. Our focus on contracts will continue to serve us well. Contract makers must look upon each other as rights bearers. What human right is closely associated with contract making? Surely it is the right to liberty. One cannot conclude a valid contract unless one is free to do so. That the market economy presupposes at least a negative right to liberty is accepted by almost the entire spectrum of political opinion from libertarians to welfare democrats.

To move from the claim that every human has a right to liberty to a list of specifications as to what the right to liberty entails is a difficult enterprise. On the most general formulation the right to liberty is a right to noninterference. But obviously that right to noninterference is not open-ended. We are not free to do whatever we want. The classic specification of a right to liberty is provided by John Stuart Mill:

> . . . the sole end for which mankind are warranted individually or collectively in interfering with the liberty of action of any of their number is self protection. That the only purpose for which power can be rightfully exercised over any member of a civilized community, against his will, is to prevent harm to others. His own good, either physical or mental is not a sufficient warrant.[2]

The concept of harm provides a wide escape clause, however. Corporations could and, indeed, have argued that apparent violations of individual liberty are necessary to prevent harm to the corporation. On the basis of that argument companies have regulated the dress, social life, family life, and political opinions of employees. Any employee action which adversely affects profit "harms" the corporation and could be restricted. The problems are not just theoretical. Let me amplify this analysis with some practical questions raised by the senior vice president of a major life insurance company as we discussed the issue of employee rights. . . . Consider freedom of religious conscience. Suppose a life insurance company acquires a health insurance company. This health insurance company pays medical bills for abortions. The claims processor from the parent company is a member of a church which holds abortion to be a deadly sin. On grounds of religious conscience, he or she refuses to process claims for medical expense to cover abortion. Does the company have a right to fire this person, and if the company did, would it violate the employee's freedom of religious conscience? Specifically, the company must balance the harm caused if it denies an employee an opportunity to exercise one of his liberties against the harm done if it doesn't deny the employee that opportunity. Such balancing must often be done if the employee's exercise of his or her liberty would not violate Mill's condition. Does this mean that companies have unlimited justification for limiting employee freedom of action whenever profits are adversely affected? Certainly not.

Business activity takes place within a social framework. Society permits business to seek profits only insofar as business plays by the rules society establishes. Hence, business activity should conform to the laws and basic moral norms of society. Once this background condition is understood, a business cannot restrict the freedom of an employee when that restriction requires the employee to perform some act which violates either the law or a basic moral norm of society. An employee cannot be ordered to falsify experimental data relating to product safety or to discriminate against a fellow employee on the basis of race. The fact that the falsification of the data or the discrimination would improve profits is irrelevant.

But what about restrictions on individual liberty that do not violate fundamental moral norms or statutes of law? Some further specification of the extent of a person's right to liberty is provided by the Constitution. It is here that the work of such writers as David Ewing is so important. Introducing constitutional rights shows how additional constraints can be placed on business. Since business activity takes place within American society, presumably business activity should be conducted consistently with the Bill of Rights which specifies our right to liberty. For example, free speech and freedom of religious conviction are specific examples of the right to liberty embodied in the Constitution. As such, these rights should be honored by business practice.

But what about those difficult cases where the rights of employees clash with the rights of management? After all, the employer is a party to the contract between employer and employee and the contract argument works just as well in establishing employer rights as it does in establishing employee rights. For example, it is already an established point at law that an employer has a legal right to loyalty. . . .

Both the interpretation of rights claims and the adjudication among competing rights claims rest with the courts or with other appropriate procedural mechanisms—e.g., the collective bargaining process. Moral philosophers cannot provide correct solutions to conflicting rights claims—neither can anyone else for that matter. As employees begin to press these rights claims, management has only two viable responses. It can allow the court to resolve such matters or it can provide the mechanism for resolving the conflicts within the corporate decision-making process itself. . . .

Notes

1. Norman E. Bowie and Robert L. Simon *The Individual and the Political Order* (Englewood Cliffs, NJ: Prentice-Hall, 1977), p. 78.
2. John Stuart Mill, *On Liberty,* Currin V. Shield (ed.), (Indianapolis: Bobbs-Merrill, Library of Liberal Arts Edition, 1956), p. 13.

Is Drug Testing Good or Bad?

Andrew Kupfer

Drug testing is the most hotly debated issue in employee rights today. At issue is whether or not workers should be forced to turn over a urine specimen—often produced under the watchful eyes of a witness to insure an untainted sample—which upon analysis will serve as proof that the worker is drug-free. This is a debate that weighs the privacy rights of individuals as opposed to the responsibility of employers to have their businesses operated by drug-free employees. This *Fortune* article asks the pivotal question of whether to randomly test all employees or just those whose jobs might be considered "safety-sensitive" such as airline pilots and railroad workers. It examines the reliability of drug tests and the problem of their false positives— results that tend to make those who are innocent appear guilty. It asks what use the tests will be put to by corporations. Will they fire those employees who fail? Will they make employee assistance programs available to help re-habilitate drug abusers who are exposed by the testing? How will American corporations assume and carry out the role of workplace policeman?

As the age of Aquarius turns to the age of abstinence, more and more com-panies are requiring job applicants and employees to take urine tests to prove they do not use drugs. Managers believe that drug-abusing workers cost mil-lions in lost productivity, absenteeism, and medical expenses. Companies re-sponsible for public safety live in fear of tragedies like the 1987 train wreck near Baltimore involving a Conrail engineer and brakeman who smoked mar-ijuana before a fatal collision with an Amtrak train. The Department of Trans-portation recently announced a plan to require random tests of four million railroad, trucking, and airline workers—and has already been challenged by the unions. The tests are becoming so common throughout industry that class-ified ads in the drug-culture magazine *High Times* offer products such as Uri-Clean that promise to beat the system.

For all this popularity, there is great confusion over what drug tests prove. Some companies report that absenteeism, medical costs, and produc-tivity have improved since they started testing job applicants and workers sus-pected of drug use. But these same companies say the tests were accompanied by a raft of managerial initiatives that may be equally responsible. The Navy, which performs more drug tests than any other American institution, has found only a low correlation between smoking marijuana, by far the most pop-ular drug, and performance. As yet there is no solid evidence that candidates who flunk preemployment tests are more likely to perform poorly than those who pass. Part of the problem is that the drug tests reject the casual weekend marijuana smoker as readily as the daily injector of heroin. Another part of the problem is less-than-perfect testing.

No wonder managers are confused. When do drug tests make sense and when don't they? One place they clearly make sense: corporations whose op-erations involve public safety. Airlines, railroads, bus companies, and electric utilities can't be too careful. They have good reason to test job applicants for the presence of drugs.

What about preemployment drug testing in less "safety-sensitive" in-dustries? Nearly half of all major U.S. companies, including IBM, Kodak, AT&T, Lockheed, 3M, and Westinghouse, require some or all job applicants to provide urine specimens. These companies say they have a responsibility to provide a safe, healthy, and productive environment for their workers and use preemployment drug tests in the hope of avoiding potential problems later on.

If they lose some excellent potential employees, they have many more eager, qualified applicants. Companies in low-paying service industries cannot be so selective. Drug tests could eliminate so many candidates that these employers cannot fill all their slots.

Once on the job, which employees should be tested for drugs? Again, the case is strongest for industries involving public safety. That may mean subjecting employees to drug tests, even by surprise and at random, to protect themselves, their coworkers, and the general welfare. The Nuclear Regulatory Commission is drawing up guidelines for the random testing of power plant operators. But random testing stirs employee resentment, is not likely to yield many offenders, and may be an invasion of privacy. Though the courts are leaning toward that interpretation, they have not ruled conclusively.

As for less safety-sensitive companies, managers should try to spot drug-related problems without testing the entire work force. However, if a worker's performance or absenteeism makes a manager suspect that he is using drugs, a test is an appropriate way to confirm those suspicions and lead him to treatment. After that, further tests can monitor an employee's progress as part of a broad program of counseling and rehabilitation—with firing the last resort for those who continue to fail.

American laboratories will process 15 million to 20 million drug tests [in 1988]. About half will be for companies, the rest for prisons, police, and public drug-treatment programs. Of the corporate tests, 85% will be for preemployment screening. Businesses will pay about $200 million in 1988 for drug testing, a figure some experts estimate will reach $500 million a year by 1991.

Besides trying to generally improve worker productivity, companies might begin preemployment testing for several reasons. Other employers in their area may have done so and they could fear being swamped by drug rejects. They may worry about being sued for negligent hiring if an employee using drugs causes an accident that harms the company, the public, or fellow employees. And they may simply be responding to a fundamental change in the zeitgeist. In the 1960s many people looked upon drugs as a way of enhancing the imagination without serious side effects; now people tend to see them as detracting from performance and downright dangerous.

While drug tests are reliable, they are far from foolproof. First, testers have to make sure that the urine sample belongs to the person who fills the bottle. The only way of knowing, as any baseball fan can attest, is to see the ball enter the glove. But because watching someone urinate is taboo, observers often avert their eyes and may not see a specimen being tampered with. The new guidelines for testing federal employees say that the donor may produce a urine sample "in the privacy of a stall." Besides the possibility of the old switcheroo, adding common table salt to a sample may sneak it past some initial screenings.

Urinalysis is better than blood tests at detecting the presence of drugs. Impurities are more highly concentrated in urine by a factor of 10. The telltale signs of drugs remain in urine much longer than they do in the bloodstream. (However, a blood test is more efficient in determining drug use within the past few hours.)

The urine test is a high-tech, two-part affair, increasingly performed by such companies as PharmChem Laboratories in Menlo Park, California, whose only business is drug testing. Samples arrive by overnight courier in sealed bottles with a label signed by both the donor and the person who collected the specimen. First the lab runs each sample through a screening test for an array of substances, including marijuana, cocaine, opiates, amphetamines, barbiturates, and hallucinogens. Screening exams are simple to run and relatively cheap, usually under $10 each. The most common screen is the enzyme multiplied immunoassay technique, or EMIT, which is made by Syva Co. EMIT uses ultraviolet light to tell if a target drug in the urine binds with a drug antibody in the test mixture.

Screening exams are extremely sensitive, but not very specific; that is, many legal substances—such as poppy seeds and cold medicines—can set off alarm bells. The International Olympic Committee in Seoul prematurely announced that British runner Linford Christie had failed a drug test only to recant and let him keep his silver medal when it found that the banned substance in his urine came from ginseng tea. Up to 10% of samples will register as false positives.

So all positive results should be presumed innocent until the lab runs a more accurate confirmatory exam. Still, according to Northwestern University's Lindquist-Endicott Report, one-third of companies do not retest if the initial test is positive.

Companies should ask applicants to list any medications that might cause a positive test result. But as Washington management consultant Theodore Rosen says, "If you don't remember that two weeks ago the doctor gave you Tylenol Plus 3—the 3 being codeine—you're on the hot seat." Employers do not usually tell applicants why they failed to get a job unless they ask, so they rarely have the chance to explain an innocent cross-reaction. For that reason such states as Connecticut, Minnesota, and Vermont require that test results be sent directly to the applicant.

The best confirmatory test is called gas chromotagraphy/mass spectrometry, or GC/MS, which uses $100,000 machines made by Hewlett-Packard or Perkin-Elmer. GC/MS makes a positive identification by breaking down drugs into their constituent molecules. The test is intricate and expensive, costing $40 to $70 each. But if the complex GC/MS test is not administered expertly, false negatives and false positives can still pop up. The National Institute on Drug Abuse is compiling a list of laboratories that conform to its standards; companies should use one that does.

Mistakes and misrepresentations aside, what can a urine sample tell potential employers? A test can show only past exposure to drugs. It cannot tell how much of the drug was consumed or when. It cannot prove drug addiction or the degree to which the drug impairs the faculties of the user, if at all. A true positive result does not mean that a person was under the influence of the drug at the time of the test, for the metabolic byproducts may remain in the urine for up to a month in the case of marijuana. At the same time, a person in the worst stages of cocaine withdrawal may show no trace of the drug because it leaves the system in about three days.

Some companies avoid preemployment drug testing because it could wipe out their worker pool. Drug use is highest among men 18 to 35 years old without college degrees, who include most applicants for low-paying jobs. Attorney Jerry Glassman, a partner in a New York City management-labor law firm, reports that a government agency in the Northeast, which he won't identify, recently gave drug tests to 1000 applicants for security guards: 980 failed. As it is, a general shortage of unskilled labor will hamstring business in the 1990s. Companies that need to fill a lot of these jobs face tough choices.

For all the problems with preemployment testing, some companies do it right. IBM requires a urine test of all job applicants. Unlike many corporations, IBM tells applicants if they failed the test and gives them a chance to come up with a solid medical reason. If they cannot, they can reapply after six months.

Companies that test job applicants often mistakenly assume that most employees with drug problems started using the substances before they were hired. But Thomas E. Backer, president of the Human Interaction Research Institute in Los Angeles, surveyed 1238 employee assistance programs—confidential services that help workers with personal problems—and found that on-the-job pressure led to a large number of drug-abuse referrals to the programs. Says Backer: "Self-medication for stress is the single most unrecognized and unexplored reason for abuse of drugs in the workplace, and one that companies can't screen out with preemployment tests."

Most controversial is random testing of all employees. While it is a strong deterrent to drug use, random testing is not necessarily good management practice. An official with a nuclear power company that tests employees only when suspicions warrant does not look forward to the random testing required by the proposed Nuclear Regulatory Commission regulations. He says: "Our supervisors have been brought along to be able to spot employees to test for cause. If random testing occurs, they might take a step backward and say, "Well, they'll get caught by the random test.'"

IBM does not perform random tests and tells managers to give employees every benefit of the doubt before recommending a drug test. If workers test positive, Big Blue offers treatment and gives them periodic drug tests during a one-year probationary period. If they fail during the year, or anytime thereafter, they may be fired.

Many companies say testing has helped lower costs and improve working conditions. The injury rate at Southern Pacific Transportation Co. is down over 60% since 1984, when it began preemployment and post-accident testing. Commonwealth Edison reports 25% to 30% lower absenteeism after six years with a drug program and a reduced rate of increase in medical costs. At Georgia Power sick days have fallen 23%, and serious accidents decreased from 39 in 1981, the year before drug testing was adopted, to 9 in 1987.

Georgia Power's program is unusual. The company encourages workers to go to its employee assistance program if they have a drug problem; if they do not come forward and managers suspect them of drug use, the company will order a drug test and dismiss them with no second chance if they fail. "You might say it's a nonrehabilitative approach, but we say the opposite," says labor relations coordinator Howard Winkler. "Since the price of detection is so high, it encourages employees to seek assistance before they're caught." The company has fired 75 to 100 employees who resisted the encouragement; 527 came forward for help. Over union objections, Georgia Power is about to start random testing of all employees. When it does, it will offer a second chance to those who fail.

Southern Pacific gives its drug tests total credit for the impressive improvement in its injury rate. At Commonwealth Edison and Georgia Power the drug program was part of wide-ranging attempts to curtail injuries and health costs and increase productivity.

To determine the relationship between drug testing and productivity, the U. S. Postal Service is conducting a novel study. Last year the post office told 5,400 job applicants in 20 cities that they had to take a urine test, which would be used for research only. The personnel managers doing the hiring had no access to the tests; they judged the applicants on other criteria. Only the Washington headquarters staff saw the results. The post office hired 4,156 of the people who took the test; 340 of them, or 8.2%, tested positive for drug use. The breakdown: 236 for marijuana, 71 for cocaine, and 33 for other illegal substances.

The post office will monitor the careers of the drug-positive hirees for two years to gauge their performance against that of other new workers. Lou Eberhardt, a post office spokesman, says that preliminary results will be available early in 1989, about halfway through the surveillance period.

When news of the study broke recently, union leaders complained about using workers as guinea pigs, and drug enforcement proponents criticized the government for hiring people known to take drugs. Both groups should cool down and wait for the results. On the one hand, the tests cost no potential union member a job. On the other, without the research there would have been no drug test, so the post office would have hired the drug-using applicants anyway.

*   *   *

An executive of a utility that routinely tests potential and current employees worries that companies are rushing to adopt drug testing without giving it much thought. "It's almost a case of managerial macho," he says. "If all you do is drug testing, if you don't train your supervisors to spot problems, or promote your employee assistance program, or communicate clearly and sympathetically with your employees, then you don't have a drug program."

Before joining the burgeoning ranks of willy-nilly drug testers, managers might want to consider the two companies that make the fancy mass spectrometers—Perkin-Elmer and Hewlett-Packard. Neither uses drug tests. They say that they know their employees, so they don't need to.

Privacy, Polygraphs and Work

George G. Brenkert*

The rights of prospective employees have been the subject of considerable dispute, both past and present. In recent years, this dispute has focused on the use of polygraphs to verify the claims which prospective employees make on employment application forms. With employee theft supposedly amounting to approximately ten billion dollars a year, with numerous businesses suffering sizeable losses and even being forced into bankruptcy by employee theft, significant and increasing numbers of employers have turned to the use of polygraphs.[1] Their right to protect their property is in danger, they insist, and the use of the polygraph to detect and weed out the untrustworthy prospective employee is a painless, quick, economical, and legitimate way to defend this right. Critics, however, have questioned both the reliability and validity of polygraphs, as well as objected to the use of polygraphs as demeaning, affronts to human dignity, violations of self-incrimination prohibitions, expressions of employers' mistrust, and violations of privacy.[2] Though there has been a great deal of discussion of the reliability and validity of polygraphs, there has been precious little discussion of the central moral issues at stake. Usually terms such as "dignity," "privacy," and "property rights" are simply bandied about with the hope that some favorable response will be evoked. The present paper seeks to redress this situation by discussing one important aspect of the above dispute—the supposed violation of personal privacy. Indeed, the violation of "a right to privacy" often appears to be the central moral objection to the use of polygraphs. However, the nature and basis of this claim have not yet been clearly established.[3] If they could be, there would be a serious reason to oppose the use of polygraphs on prospective employees.

There are three questions which must be faced in the determination of this issue. First, is the nature of the information which polygraphing seeks to verify, information which can be said to violate, or involve the violation of, a

Excerpted from "Privacy, Polygraphs and Work" by George G. Brenkert, *Business and Professional Ethics Journal*, Vol. 1, No. 1 (Fall 1981), pp. 19–35. Copyright © 1981 by George G. Brenkert. Reprinted by permission of the author.
*Department of Philosophy, the University of Tennessee.

person's privacy? Second, does the use of the polygraph itself as the means to corroborate the responses of the job applicant violate the applicant's privacy? Third, even if—for either of the two preceding reasons—the polygraph does violate a person's privacy, might this violation still be justified by the appeal to more weighty reasons, e.g., the defense of property rights?

I

In order to determine what information might be legitimately private to an individual who seeks employment we must consider the nature of the employer/(prospective) employee relationship. The nature of this relationship depends upon the customs, conventions and rules of the society. These, of course, are in flux at any time—and particularly so in the present case. They may also need revision. Further, the nature of this relationship will depend upon its particular instances—e.g., that of the employer of five workers or of five thousand workers, the kind of work involved, etc. In essence, however, we have a complex relationship in which an employer theoretically contracts with a person(s) to perform certain services from which the employer expects to derive a certain gain for himself. In the course of the employee's performance of these services, the employer entrusts him with certain goods, money, etc.; in return for such services he delivers to the employee a certain remuneration and (perhaps) benefits. The goals of the employer and the employee are not at all, on this account, necessarily the same. The employee expects his remuneration (and benefits) even if the services, though adequately performed, do not result in the end the employer expected. Analogously, the employer expects to derive a certain gain for the services the employee has performed even if the employee is not (fully) satisfied with his work or remuneration. On the other hand, if the employer is significantly unable to achieve the ends sought through the contract with the employee, the latter may not receive his full remuneration (should the employer go bankrupt) and may even lose his job. There is, in short, a complicated mixture of trust and antagonism, connectedness and disparity of ends in the relation between employer and employee.

Given this (brief) characterization of the relationship between employer and employee, the information to which the employer qua employer is entitled about the (prospective) employee is that information which regards his possible acceptable performance of the services for which he might be hired. Without such information the employer could not fulfill the role which present society sanctions. There are two aspects of the information to which the employer is entitled given the employer/employee relationship. On the one hand, this information will relate to and vary in accordance with the services for which the person is to be hired. But in any case, it will be limited by those services and what they require. In short, one aspect of the information to which the employer is entitled is "job relevant" information. Admittedly the criterion of job relevancy is rather vague. Certainly there are few aspects of a person which might not affect his job performance—aspects including his sex life, etc. How then does the "job relevancy" criterion limit the questions asked or the information sought? It does so by limiting the information sought to that which is directly connected with the job description. If a typist is sought, it is job relevant to know whether or not a person can type—typing tests are legitimate. If a store manager is sought, it is relevant to know about his abilities to manage employees, stock, etc. That is, the description of the job is what determines the relevancy of the information to be sought. It is what gives the employer a right to know certain things about the person seeking employment. Accordingly, if a piece of information is not "job relevant" then the employer is not entitled qua employer to know it. Consequently, since sexual practices, political beliefs, associational activities, etc. are not part of the description of most jobs, that is, since they do not directly affect one's job performance, they are not legitimate information for an employer to know in the determination of the hiring of a job applicant.[4]

However, there is a second aspect to this matter. A person must be able not simply to perform a certain activity, or provide a service, but he must also be able to do it in an acceptable manner—i.e., in a manner which is approximately as efficient as others, in an honest manner, and in a manner compatible with others who seek to provide the services for which they were hired. Thus, not simply one's abilities to do a certain job are relevant, but also aspects of one's social and moral character are pertinent. A number of qualifications are needed for the purport of this claim to be clear. First, that a person must be able to work in an acceptable manner is not intended to legitimize the consideration of the prejudices of other employees. It is not legitimate to give weight in moral deliberations to the immoral and/or morally irrelevant beliefs which people hold concerning the characteristics of others. That one's present employees can work at a certain (perhaps exceptional) rate is a legitimate consideration in hiring other workers. That one's present employees have prejudices against certain religions, sexes, races, political views, etc. is not a morally legitimate consideration. Second, it is not, or should not be, the motives, beliefs, or attitudes underlying the job relevant character traits, e.g., honest, efficient, which are pertinent, but rather the fact that a person does or does not perform according to these desirable character traits. This is not to say, it should be noted, that a person's beliefs and attitudes about the job itself, e.g., how it is best to be done, what one knows or believes about the job, etc., are irrelevant. Rather it is those beliefs, attitudes and motives underlying one's desired character traits which are not relevant. The contract of the employer with the employee is for the latter to perform acceptably certain services—it is not for the employee to have certain underlying beliefs, motives, or attitudes. If I want to buy something from someone, this commercial relation does not entitle me to probe the attitudes, motives, and beliefs of the person beyond his own statements, record of past actions, and the observations of others. Even the used car salesman would correctly object that his right to privacy was being violated if he was required to submit to Rorschach tests, an attitude survey test, truth serums, and/or the polygraph in order to determine his real beliefs about selling cars. Accordingly, why the person acts the way in which he acts ought not to be the concern of the employer. Whether a person is a good working colleague simply because he is congenial, because his ego needs the approval of others, or because he has an oppressive superego is, in this instance, morally irrelevant. What is relevant is whether this person has, by his past actions, given some indication that he may work in a manner compatible with others.

Consequently, a great deal of the information which has been sought in preemployment screening through the use of polygraph tests has violated the privacy of individuals. Instances in which the sex lives, for example, of applicants have been probed are not difficult to find. However, privacy violations have occurred not simply in such generally atypical instances but also in standard situations. To illustrate the range of questions asked prospective employees and the violations of privacy which have occurred we need merely consider a list of some questions which one of the more prominent polygraph firms includes in its current tests:

> Have you ever taken any of the following without the advice of a doctor? If Yes, please check: Barbiturates, Speed, LSD, Tranquilizers, Amphetamines, Marijuana, Others.

> In the past five years about how many times, if any, have you bet on horse races at the race track?

> Do you think that policemen are honest? Did you ever think about committing a robbery?

> Have you been refused credit or a loan in the past five years?

> Have you ever consulted a doctor about a mental condition?

> Do you think that it is okay to get around the law if you don't actually break it?

> Do you enjoy stories of successful crimes and swindles?[5]

Such questions, it follows from the above argument, are for any standard employment violations of one's right to privacy. An employer might ask if a person regularly takes certain narcotic drugs, if he is considering him for a job which requires handling narcotics. An employer might ask if a person has been convicted of a larceny, etc. But whether the person enjoys stories about successful larcenists, whether a person has ever taken any prescription drugs without the advice of a doctor, or whether a person bets on the horses should be considered violations of one's rightful privacy.

The upshot of the argument in the first two sections is, then, that some information can be considered rightfully private to an individual. Such information is rightfully private or not depending on the relationship in which a person stands to another person or institution. In the case of the employer/employee relationship, I have argued that that information is rightfully private which does not relate to the acceptable performance of the activities as characterized in the job description. This excludes a good many questions which are presently asked in polygraph tests, but does not, by any means, exclude all such questions. There still remain many questions which an employer might conceivably wish to have verified by the use of the polygraph. Accordingly, I turn in the next section to the question whether the verification of the answers to legitimate questions by the use of the polygraph may be considered a violation of a person's right to privacy. If it is, then the violation obviously does not stem from the questions themselves but from the procedure, the polygraph test, whereby the answers to those questions are verified.

II

A first reason to believe that use of the polygraph occasions a violation of one's right to privacy is that, even though the questions to be answered are job relevant, some of them will occasion positive, lying reactions which are not necessarily related to any past misdeeds. Rather, the lying reaction indicated by the polygraph may be triggered because of unconscious conflicts, fears and hostilities a person has. It may be occasioned by conscious anxieties over other past activities and observations. Thus, the lying reaction indicated by the polygraph need not positively identify actual lying or the commission of illegal activities. The point, however, is not to question the validity of the polygraph. Rather, the point is that the validity of the polygraph can only be maintained by seeking to clarify whether or not such reactions really indicate lying and the commission of past misdeeds. But this can be done only by the polygraphist further probing into the person's background and inner thoughts. However, inasmuch as the questions can no longer be restrained in this situation by job relevancy considerations, but must explore other areas to which an employer is not necessarily entitled knowledge, to do this will violate a person's right to privacy.

A second reason why the polygraph must be said to violate a job applicant's right to privacy relates to the monitoring of a person's physiological responses to the questions posed to him. By measuring these responses, the polygraph can supposedly reveal one's mental processes. Now even though the questions posed are legitimate questions, surely a violation of one's right to privacy occurs. Just because I have something which you are entitled to see or know, it does not follow that you can use any means to fulfill that entitlement and not violate my privacy. Consider the instance of two good friends, one of whom has had some dental work done which puts him in a situation such that he can tune in the thoughts and feelings of his friend. Certain facts about, and emotional responses of, his friend—aspects which his friend (we will assume) would usually want to share with him—simply now stream into his head. Even though the friendship relation generally entitles its members to know personal information about the other person, the friend with the dental work is not entitled to such information in this direct and immediate way. This manner of gaining this information simply eliminates any private reserves of the person; it wholly opens his consciousness to the consciousness of another. Surely this would be a violation of his friend's right to privacy, and his friend would rightfully ask that such dental work be modified. Even friends do not have a right to learn in this manner of each other's inner thoughts and feelings.

Such fancy dental work may, correctly, be said to be rather different from polygraphs. Still the point is that though one is entitled to some information about another, one is not entitled to use any means to get it. But why should the monitoring by an employer or his agent of one's physiological responses to legitimate questions be an invasion of privacy—especially if one has agreed to take the test? There are several reasons.

First, the claim that one freely agrees or consents to take the test is surely, in many cases, disingenuous.[6] Certainly a job applicant who takes the polygraph test is not physically forced or coerced into taking the exam. However, it is quite apparent that if he did not take the test and cooperate during the test, his application for employment would either not be considered at all or would be considered to have a significant negative aspect to it. This is surely but a more subtle form of coercion. And if this be the case, then one cannot say that the person has willingly allowed his reactions to the questions to be monitored. He has consented to do so, but he has consented under coercion. Had he a truly free choice, he would not have done so.

Now the whole point of the polygraph test is, of course, not simply to monitor physiological reactions but to use these responses as clues, indications, or revelations of one's mental processes and acts. The polygraph seeks to make manifest to others one's thoughts and ideas. However, unless we freely consent, we are entitled to the privacy of our thoughts, that is, we have a prima facie right not to have our thoughts exposed by others, even when the information sought is legitimate. Consider such analogous cases as a husband reading his wife's diary, a person going through a friend's desk drawers, a stranger reading personal papers on one's desk, an F.B.I. agent going through one's files. In each of these cases, a person attempts to determine the nature of someone else's thoughts by the use of clues and indications which those thoughts left behind. And, in each of these cases, though we may suppose that the person seeks to confirm answers to legitimate questions, we may also say that, if the affected person's uncoerced consent is not forthcoming, his or her right to privacy is violated. Morally, however, there is no difference between ascertaining the nature of one's thoughts by the use of a polygraph, or reading notes left in a drawer, going through one's diary, etc. Hence, unless there are overriding considerations to consent to such revelations of one's thoughts, the use of the polygraph is a violation of one's right to privacy.[7]

Second, if we value privacy not simply as a barrier to the intrusion of others but also as the way by which we define ourselves as separate, autonomous persons, individuals with an integrity which lies at least in part in the ability to make decisions, to give or withhold information and access, then the polygraph strikes at this fundamental value.[8] The polygraph operates by turning part of us over which we have little or no control against the rest of us. If a person were an accomplished yogi, the polygraph would supposedly be useless—since that person's physiological reactions would be fully under his control. The polygraph works because most of us do not have that control. Thus, the polygraph is used to probe people's reactions which they would otherwise protect, not expose to others. It uses part of us to reveal the rest of us. It takes the "shadows" consciousness throws off within us and reproduces them for other people. As such, the use of the polygraph undercuts the decision-making aspect of a person. It circumvents the person. The person says such and such, but his uncontrolled reactions may say something different. He does not know—even when honest— what his reactions might say. Thus it undercuts and demeans that way by which we define ourselves as autonomous persons—in short, it violates our privacy. Suppose one said something to another—but his Siamese and undetached twin, who was given to absolute truth and who correctly knew every thought, past action, and feeling of the person said: "No, he does not really believe that." I think the person would rightfully complain that his twin had better remain silent. Just so, I have a right to complain when my own feelings are turned on me. This subtle form of self-incrimination is a form of invading one's privacy. An employer is entitled to know certain facts about one's background, but this relationship does not entitle him—or his agents—to probe one's emotional responses, feelings, and thoughts.

Thus, it follows that even if the only questions asked in a polygraph test are legitimate ones, the use of the polygraph for the screening of job applicants still violates one's privacy. In this case, the violation of privacy stems from the procedure itself, and not the questions. Accordingly, one can see the lameness of the defense of polygraphing which maintains that if a person has nothing to hide, he should not object to the polygraph tests. Such a defense is mistaken at least on two counts. First, just because someone believes something to be private does not mean that he believes that what is private is wrong, something to be ashamed about or to be hidden. Second, the polygraph test has been shown to violate a person's privacy, whether one person has really something to hide or not—whether he is dishonest or not. Consequently, if the question is simply whether polygraphing of prospective employees violates their privacy the answer must be affirmative.

III

There remains one possible defense of the use of polygraphs for screening prospective employees. This is to admit that such tests violate the applicant's privacy but to maintain that other considerations outweigh this fact. Specifically, in light of the great amount of merchandise and money stolen, the right of the employers to defend their property outweighs the privacy of the applicant. This defense is specious, I believe, and the following arguments seek to show why.

First, surely it would be better if people who steal or are dishonest were not placed in positions of trust. And if the polygraphs were used in only these cases, one might well maintain that the use of the polygraph, though it violates one's privacy, is legitimate and justified. However, the polygraph cannot be so used, obviously, only in these cases—it must be used more broadly on both honest and dishonest applicants. Further, if a polygraph has a 90% validity then out of 1,000 interviewees, a full 100 will be misidentified.[9] Now if 10% of the interviewees are thieves, then 10 out of the 100 will steal, but 90 would not; in addition 90 out of the 900 would be thieves, and supposedly correctly identified. This means that 90 thieves would be correctly identified, 10 thieves would be missed, and 90 honest people would be said not to have cleared the test. Thus, for every thief "caught," one honest person would also be "caught"—the former would be correctly identified as one who would steal, while the latter could not be cleared of the suspicion that he too would steal. The point, then, is that this means of defending property rights is one that excludes not simply thieves but honest people as well—and potentially in equal numbers. Such a procedure certainly appears to constitute not simply a violation of privacy rights, but also, and more gravely, an injustice to those honest people stigmatized as not beyond suspicion and hobbled in their competition with others to get employment. If then using polygraph tests to defend property rights is not simply like preventing a thief from breaking into the safe, but more like keeping a thief from the safe plus binding the leg of an innocent bystander in his competition with others to gain employment, then one may legitimately doubt that this procedure to protect property rights is indeed defensible.[10]

Second, it has been claimed that just as the use of blood tests on suspected drunken drivers and the use of baggage searches at the airport are legitimate, so too is the polygraphing of prospective employees. Both of the former kinds of searches may also be said to violate a person's privacy; still they are taken to be justified whether the appeal is to the general good they produce or to the protection of the rights of other drivers or passengers and airline employees. However, neither the blood test nor the baggage search is really analogous to the use of the polygraph on job applicants. Blood tests are only administered to those drivers who have given police officers reason to believe that they (the drivers) are driving while under the influence of alcohol. The polygraph, however, is not applied only to those suspected of past thefts; it is applied to others as well. Further, the connection between driving while drunk and car accidents is quite direct; it immediately endangers both the safety and lives of others. The connection between polygraph tests of a diverse group of applicants (some honest and some dishonest) and future theft is not nearly so direct nor do the thefts endanger the lives of others. Baggage searches are a different matter. They are similar to polygraphing in that they are required of everyone. They are dissimilar in that they are made because of fears concerning the safety of other people. Further, surely there is a dissimilarity between officials searching one's baggage for lethal objects which one is presently trying to sneak on board, and employers searching one's mind for the true nature of one's past behavior which may or may not lead to future criminal intentions. Finally, there are signs at airports warning people, before they are searched, against carrying weapons on airplanes; such weapons could at that time be declared and sent, without prejudice, with the regular baggage. There is no similar aspect to polygraph tests. Thus, the analogies suggested do not hold. Indeed, they suggest that we allow for a violation of privacy only in very different circumstances than those surrounding the polygraphing of job applicants.

Third, the corporate defense of polygraphs seems one-sided in the sense that employers would not really desire the universalization of their demands. Suppose that the businesses in a certain industry are trying to get a new government contract. The government, however, has had difficulties with other corporations breaking the rules of other contracts. As a result it has lost large sums of money. In order to prevent this in the present case it says that it is going to set up devices to monitor the reactions of board members and top managers when a questionnaire is sent to them which they must answer. Any business, of course, need not agree to this procedure but if it does then it will be noted in their file regarding this and future government contracts. The questionnaire will include questions about the corporations' past fulfillment of contracts, competency to fulfill the present contract, loopholes used in past contracts, collusion with other companies, etc. The reactions of the managers and board members, as they respond to these questions, will be monitored and a decision on the worthiness of that corporation to receive the contract will be made in part on this basis.

There can be little doubt, I think, that the management and directors of the affected corporations would object to the proposal even though the right of the government to defend itself from the violation of its contracts and serious financial losses is at stake. It would be said to be an unjustified violation of the privacy of the decision-making process in a business; an illegitimate encroachment of the government on free enterprise. But surely if this is the legitimate response for the corporate job applicant, the same kind of response would be legitimate in the case of the individual job applicant.

Finally, it is simply false that there are not other measures which could be taken which could not help resolve the problem of theft. The fact that eighty percent of industry does not use the polygraph is itself suggestive that business does not find itself absolutely forced into the use of polygraphs. It might be objected that that does not indicate that certain industries might need polygraphs more than others—e.g., banks and drug companies more than auto plants and shipyards. But even granting this point there are other measures which businesses can use to avoid the problem of theft. Stricter inventory controls, different kinds of cash registers, educational programs, hot lines, incentives, etc. could all be used. The question is whether the employer, management, can be imaginative and innovative enough to move in these directions.

Notes

1. Cf. Harlow Unger, "Lie Detectors: Business Needs Them to Avoid Costly Employee Rip-Offs," *Canadian Business,* Vol. 51 (April, 1978), p. 30. Other estimates may be found in "Outlaw Lie-Detector Tests?", *U.S. News & World Report,* Vol. 84, No. 4, (January 1978), p. 45, and Victor Lipman, "New Hiring Tool: Truth Tests," *Parade* (October 7, 1979), p. 19.

2. Both the AFL-CIO and the ACLU have raised these objections to the use of the polygraph for screening job applicants; cf. *AFL-CIO Executive Council Statements and Reports: 1956–1975* (Westport, Conn.: Greenwood Press, 1977), p. 1422. See also ACLU Policy #248.

3. See, for example, Alan F. Westin, *Privacy and Freedom* (New York: Antheneum, 1967), p. 238.

4. This would have to be qualified for security jobs and the like.

5. John E. Reid and Associates, *Reid Report* (Chicago: By the author, 1978), passim.

6. The reasons why people do not submit to the polygraph are many and various. Some might have something to hide; others may be scared of the questions, supposing that some of them will not be legitimate; some may feel that they are being treated like criminals; others may fear the jaundiced response of the employer to the applicant's honest answers to legitimate questions; finally some may even object to the polygraph on moral grounds, e.g., it violates one's right to privacy.

7. See Section III below.

8. Cf. Jeffrey H. Reiman, "Privacy, Intimacy, and Personhood," *Philosophy and Public Affairs,* Vol. VI (Fall, 1976).

9. Estimates of the validity of the polygraph range widely. Professor David Lykken has been reported as maintaining that the most prevalent polygraph test is correct only two-thirds of the time (cf. Bennett H. Beach, "Blood, Sweat and Fears," *Time,* September 8, 1980, p. 44). A similar figure of seventy percent is reported by Richard A. Sternbach et. al., "Don't Trust the Lie Detector," *Harvard Business Review,* Vol. XL (Nov.–Dec., 1962), p. 130. Operators of polygraphs, however, report figures as high as 95% accuracy; cf. Sternbach, p. 129.

10. This argument is suggested by a similar argument in David T. Lykken, "Guilty-Knowledge Test: The Right Way to Use a Lie Detector," *Psychology Today,* (March, 1975), p. 60.

A Bill of Rights for Employees and Employers

Patricia H. Werhane

In her provocative work *Persons, Rights and Corporations,* (1985) business ethicist Patricia Werhane argues that one can modify the relationship between corporations and their employees in such a way that justice can be done to both; so that employees can exercise their rights as human beings and corporations can still reap the benefits of the free-enterprise system. Her program for reform entails a recognition of the importance of moral rights in the workplace, which serves as the basis for this mutual relationship. Reprinted here is

Patricia H. Werhane, *Persons, Rights and Corporations,* © 1985, pp. 168–170. Reprinted with permission of Prentice-Hall, Inc., Englewood Cliffs, NJ.

the appendix to her book, where she lists the kinds of moral rights she believes are necessary for both employees and employers, if workplace injustice is to be eradicated.

Employee Rights

1. Every person has an equal right to a job and a right to equal consideration at the job. Employees may not be discriminated against on the basis of religion, sex, ethnic origin, race, color, or economic background.
2. Every person has the right to equal pay for work, where "equal work" is defined by the job description and title.
3. Every employee has rights to his or her job. After a probation period of three to ten years every employee has the right to his or her job. An employee can be dismissed only under the following conditions:

    a. He or she is not performing satisfactorily the job for which he or she was hired.
    b. He or she is involved in criminal activity either within or outside the corporation.
    c. He or she is drunk or takes drugs on the job.
    d. He or she actively disrupts corporate business activity without a valid reason.
    e. He or she becomes physically or mentally incapacitated or reaches mandatory retirement age.
    f. The employer has publicly verifiable economic reasons for dismissing the employee, e.g., transfer of the company, loss of sales, bankruptcy, etc.
    g. Under no circumstances can an employee be dismissed or laid off without the institution of fair due process procedures.

4. Every employee has the right to due process in the workplace. He or she has the right to a peer review, to a hearing, and if necessary, to outside arbitration before being demoted or fired.
5. Every employee has the right to free expression in the workplace. This includes the right to object to corporate acts that he or she finds illegal or immoral without retaliation or penalty. The objection may take the form of free speech, whistle-blowing, or conscientious objection. However, any criticism must be documented or proven.
6. The Privacy Act, which protects the privacy and confidentiality of public employees, should be extended to all employees.
7. The polygraph should be outlawed.
8. Employees have the right to engage in outside activities of their choice.
9. Every employee has the right to a safe workplace, including the right to safety information and participation in improving work hazards. Every employee has the right to legal protection that guards against preventable job risks.

10. Every employee has the right to as much information as possible about the corporation, about his or her job, work hazards, possibilities for future employment, and any other information necessary for job enrichment and development.

11. Every employee has the right to participate in the decision-making processes entailed in his or her job, department, or in the corporation as a whole, where appropriate.

12. Every public and private employee has the right to strike when the foregoing demands are not met in the workplace.

Employer Rights

1A. Any employee found discriminating against another employee or operating in a discriminatory manner against her employer is subject to employer reprimand, demotion, or firing.

2A. Any employee not deserving equal pay because of inefficiency should be shifted to another job.

3A. No employee who functions inefficiently, who drinks or takes drugs on the job, commits felonies or acts in ways that prevent carrying out work duties has a right to a job.

4A. Any employee found guilty under a due process procedure should be reprimanded (e.g., demoted or dismissed), and, if appropriate, brought before the law.

5A. No employer must retain employees who slander the corporation or other corporate constituents.

6A. The privacy of employers is as important as the privacy of employees. By written agreement employees may be required not to disclose confidential corporate information or trade secrets unless not doing so is clearly against the public interest.

7A. Employers may engage in surveillance of employees at work (but only at work) with their foreknowledge and consent.

8A. No employee may engage in activities that literally harm the employer, nor may an employee have a second job whose business competes with the business of the first employer.

9A. Employees shall be expected to carry out job assignments for which they are hired unless these conflict with common moral standards or unless the employee was not fully informed about these assignments or their dangers before accepting employment. Employers themselves should become fully informed about work dangers.

10A. Employers have rights to personal information about employees or prospective employees adequate to make sound hiring and promotion judgments so long as the employer preserves the confidentiality of such information.

11A. Employers as well as employees have rights. Therefore the right to participation is a correlative obligation on the part of *both* parties to respect mutual rights. Employers, then, have the right to demand efficiency and productivity from their employees in return for the employee right to participation in the workplace.

12A. Employees who strike for no reason are subject to dismissal.

Any employee or employer who feels he or she has been unduly penalized under a bill of rights may appeal to an outside arbitrator.

Drug Testing and Corporate Responsibility: The "Ought Implies Can" Argument

Jennifer Moore

In the past few years, testing for drug use in the workplace has become an important and controversial trend. Approximately 30% of Fortune 500 companies now engage in some sort of drug testing or screening, as do many smaller firms. The Reagan administration has called for mandatory testing of all federal employees. Several states have already passed drug testing laws; others will probably consider them in the future. While the Supreme Court has announced its intention to rule on the testing of federal employees within the next few months, its decision will not settle the permissibility of testing private employees. Discussion of the issue is likely to remain lively and heated for some time.

Most of the debate about drug testing in the workplace has focused on the issue of privacy rights. Three key questions have been: Do employees have privacy rights? If so, how far do these extend? What kinds of considerations outweigh these rights? I believe there are good reasons for supposing that employees do have moral privacy rights,[1] and that drug testing usually (though not always) violates these, but privacy is not my main concern in this paper. I wish to examine a different kind of argument, the claim that because corporations are responsible for harms committed by employees while under the influence of drugs, they are entitled to test for drug use.

This argument is rarely stated formally in the literature, but it can be found informally quite often.[2] One of its chief advantages is that it seems, at least at first glance, to bypass the issue of privacy rights altogether. There seems to be no need to determine the extent or weight of employees' privacy rights to make the argument work. It turns on a different set of principles altogether, that is, on the meaning and conditions of responsibility. This is an important asset, since arguments about rights are notoriously difficult to settle. Rights claims frequently function in ethical discourse as conversation-stoppers or non-negotiable demands.[3] Although it is widely recognized that

Jennifer Moore, "Drug Testing and Corporate Responsibility: The 'Ought Implies Can' Argument, *Journal of Business Ethics* **8**: 1989, 279–287.

rights are not absolute, there is little consensus on how far they extend, what kinds of considerations should be allowed to override them, or even how to go about settling these questions. But it is precisely these thorny problems that proponents of drug testing must tackle if they wish to address the issue on privacy grounds. Faced with the claim that drug testing violates the moral right to privacy of employees, proponents of testing must either (1) argue that drug testing does not really violate the privacy rights of employees,[4] (2) acknowledge that drug testing violates privacy rights, but argue that there are considerations that override those rights, such as public safety; or (3) argue that employees have no moral right to privacy at all.[5] It is not surprising that an argument that seems to move the debate out of the arena of privacy rights entirely appears attractive.

In spite of its initial appeal, however, I will maintain that the argument does not succeed in circumventing the claims of privacy rights. Even responsibility for the actions of others, I will argue, does not entitle us to do absolutely anything to control their behavior. We must look to rights, among other things, to determine what sorts of controls are morally permissible. Once this is acknowledged, the argument loses much of its force. In addition, it requires unjustified assumptions about the connection between drug testing and the prevention of drug-related harm.

An "Ought Implies Can" Argument

Before we can assess the argument, it must be set out more fully. It seems to turn on the deep-rooted philosophical connection between responsibility and control. Generally, we believe that agents are not responsible[6] for acts or events that they could not have prevented. People are responsible for their actions only if, it is often said, they "could have done otherwise". Responsibility implies some measure of control, freedom, or autonomy. It is for this reason that we do not hold the insane responsible for their actions. Showing that a person lacked the capacity to do otherwise blocks the normal moves of praise or blame and absolves the agent of responsibility for a given act.

For similar reasons, we believe that persons cannot be obligated to do things that they are incapable of doing, and that if they fail to do such things, no blame attaches to them. Obligation is empty, even senseless, without capability. If a person is obligated to perform an action, it must be within his or her power. This principle is sometimes summed up by the phrase "ought implies can". Kant used it as part of a metaphysical argument for free will, claiming that if persons are to have obligations at all, they must be autonomous, or capable of acting freely.[7] The argument we examine here is narrower in scope, but similar in principle. If corporations are responsible for harms caused by employees under the influence of drugs, they must have the ability to prevent these harms. They must, therefore, have the freedom to test for drug use.

But the argument is still quite vague. What exactly does it mean to say that corporations are "responsible" for harms caused by employees? There are several possible meanings of "responsible". Not all of these are attributable to corporations, and not all of them exemplify the principle that "ought implies can". The question of how or whether corporations are "responsible" is highly complex, and we cannot begin to answer it in this paper.[8] There are, however, four distinct senses of "responsible" that appear with some regularity in the argument. They can be characterized, roughly, as follows: (a) legally liable; (b) culpable or guilty; (c) answerable or accountable; (d) bound by an obligation. The first is purely legal; the last three have a moral dimension.

Legal Liability

We do hold corporations legally liable for the negligent acts of employees under the doctrine of *respondeat supèrior* ("let the master respond"). If an employee harms a third party in the course of performing his or her duties for the firm, it is the corporation which must compensate the third party. *Respondeat superior* is an example of what is frequently called "vicarious liability". Since the employee was acting on behalf of the firm, and the firm was acting through the employee when the harmful act was committed, liability is said to "transfer" from the employee to the firm. But it is not clear that such liability on the part of the employer implies a capacity to have prevented the harm. Corporations are held liable for accidents caused by an employee's negligent driving, for example, even if they could not have foreseen or prevented the injury. While some employee accidents can be traced to corporate negligence,[9] there need be no fault on the part of the corporation for the doctrine of *respondeat superior* to apply. The doctrine of *respondeat superior* is grounded not in fault, but in concerns of public policy and utility. It is one of several applications of the notion of liability without fault in legal use today.

  Because it does not imply fault, and its attendant ability to have done otherwise, legal liability or responsibility **a** cannot be used successfully as part of an "ought implies can" argument. Holding corporations legally liable for harms committed by intoxicated employees while at the same time forbidding drug-testing is not inconsistent. It could simply be viewed as yet another instance of liability without fault. Of course, one could argue that the notion of liability without fault is itself morally unacceptable, and that liability ought not to be detached from moral notions of punishment and blame. This is surely an extremely important claim, but it is beyond the scope of this paper. The main point to be made here is that we must be able to attribute more than legal liability to corporations if we are to invoke the principle of "ought implies can". Corporations must be responsible in sense **b, c,** or **d**—that is, *morally* responsible—if the argument is to work.

Moral Responsibility

Are corporations morally responsible for harms committed by intoxicated employees? Perhaps the most frequently used notion of moral responsibility is sense **b,** what I have called "guilt" or "culpability".[10] I have in mind here the strongest notion of moral responsibility, the sense that is prevalent in criminal law. An agent is responsible for an act in this sense if the act can be imputed to him or her. An essential condition of imputability is the presence in the agent of an intention to commit the act, or *mens rea*.[11] But does an employer whose workers use drugs satisfy the *mens rea* requirement? The requirement probably would be satisfied if it could be shown that the firm intended the resulting harms, ordered its employees to work under the influence of drugs, or even, perhaps (though this is less clear) turned a blind eye to blatant drug abuse in the workplace.[12] But these are all quite farfetched possibilities. It is reasonable to assume that most corporations do not intend the harms caused by their employees, and that they do not order employees to use drugs on the job. Drug use is quite likely to be prohibited by company policy. If corporations are morally responsible for drug-related harms committed by employees, then, it is not in sense **b**.

Corporations might, however, be morally responsible for harms committed by employees in another sense. An organization acts through its employees. It empowers its employees to act in ways in which they otherwise would not act by providing them with money, power, equipment, and authority. Through a series of agreements, the corporation delegates its employees to act on its behalf. For these reasons, one could argue that corporations are responsible, in the sense of "answerable" or "accountable" (responsibility **c**), for the harmful acts of their employees. Indeed, it could be argued that if corporations are not morally responsible for these acts, they are not morally responsible for any acts at all, since corporations can only act through their employees.[13] To say that corporations are responsible for the harms of their employees in sense **c** is to say more than just that a corporation must "pay up" if an employee causes harm. It is to assign fault to the corporation by virtue of the ways in which organizational policies and structures facilitate and direct employees' actions.[14]

Moreover, corporations presumably have the same obligations as other agents to avoid harm in the conduct of their business. Since they conduct their business through their employees, it could plausibly be argued that corporations have an obligation to anticipate and prevent harms that employees might cause in the course of their employment. If this reasoning is correct, corporations are morally responsible for the drug-related harms of employees in sense **d**—that is, they are under an obligation to prevent those harms. The "ought implies can" argument, then, may be formulated as follows:

1. If corporations have obligations, they must be capable of carrying them out, on the principle of "ought implies can".
2. Corporations have an obligation to prevent harm from occurring in the course of conducting their business.
3. Drug use by employees is likely to lead to harm.
4. Corporations must be able to take steps to eliminate (or at least reduce) drug use by employees.
5. Drug testing is an effective way to eliminate/reduce employee drug use.
6. Therefore corporations must be permitted to test for drugs.[15]

The Limits of Corporate Autonomy

This is surely an important argument, one that deserves to be taken seriously. The premise that corporations have an obligation to prevent harm from occurring in the conduct of their business seems unexceptionable and consistent with the actual moral beliefs of society. There is not much question that drug use by employees, especially regular drug use or drug use on the job, leads to harms of various kinds. Some of these are less serious than others, but some are very serious indeed: physical injury to consumers, the public, and fellow employees—and sometimes even death.[16]

Moreover, our convictions about the connections between responsibility or obligation and capability seem unassailable. Like other agents, if corporations are to have obligations, they must have the ability to carry them out. The argument seems to tell us that corporations are only able to carry out their obligation to prevent harm if they can free themselves of drugs. To prevent corporations from drug testing, it implies, is to prevent them from discharging their obligations. It is to cripple corporate autonomy just as we would cripple the autonomy of an individual worker if we refused to allow him to "kick the habit" that prevented him from giving satisfactory job performance.

But this analogy between corporate and individual autonomy reveals the initial defect in the argument. Unlike human beings, corporations are never fully autonomous selves. On the contrary, their actions are always dependent upon individual selves who are autonomous. Human autonomy means self-determination, self-governance, self-control. Corporate autonomy, at least as it is understood here, means control over others. Corporate autonomy is essentially derivative. But this means that corporate acts are not the simple sorts of acts generated by individual persons. They are complex. Most importantly, the members of a corporation are frequently not the agents, but the objects, of "corporate" action. A good deal of corporate action, that is, necessitates doing something not only *through* corporate employees, but *to* those employees.[17] The act of eliminating drugs from the workplace is an act of this sort. A corporation's ridding itself of drugs is not like an individual person's "kicking the habit". Rather, it is one group of persons making another group of persons give up drug use.

This fact has important implications for the "ought implies can" argument. The argument is persuasive in situations in which carrying out one's obligations requires only *self*-control, and does not involve controlling the behavior of others. Presumably there are no restrictions on what one may do to oneself in order to carry out an obligation.[18] But a corporation is not a genuine "self", and there *are* moral limits on what one person may do to another. Because this is so, we cannot automatically assume that the obligation to prevent harm justifies employee drug testing. Of course this does not necessarily mean that drug testing is *unjustified*. But it does mean that before we can determine whether it is justified, we must ask what is permissible for one person or group of persons to do to another to prevent a harm for which they are responsible.

Are there any analogies available that might help to resolve this question? It is becoming increasingly common to hold a hostess responsible (both legally and morally) for harm caused by a drunken guest on the way home from her party. In part, this is because she contributes to the harm by serving her guest alcohol. It is also because she knows that drunk driving is risky, and has a general obligation to prevent harm. What must she be allowed to do to prevent harms of this kind? Persuade the guest to spend the night on the couch? Surely. Take her car keys away from her? Perhaps. Knock her out and lock her in the bathroom until morning? Surely not.

Universities are occasionally held legally and morally responsible for harms committed by members of fraternities—destruction of property, gang rapes, and injuries or death caused by hazing. What may they do to prevent such harms? They may certainly withdraw institutional recognition and support from the fraternity, refusing to let it operate on the campus. But may they expel students who live together off-campus in fraternity-like arrangements? Have university security guards police these houses, covertly or by force? These questions are more difficult to answer.

We sometimes hold landlords morally (though not legally) responsible for tenants who are slovenly, play loud music, or otherwise make nuisances of themselves. Landlords are surely permitted to cancel the leases of such tenants, and they are justified in asking for references from previous landlords to prevent future problems of this kind. But it is not clear that a landlord may delve into a tenant's private life, search his room, or tap his telephone in order to anticipate trouble before it begins.

Each of these situations is one in which one person or group of persons is responsible, to a greater or a lesser degree, for the prevention of harm by others, and needs some measure of control in order to carry out this responsibility.[19] In each case, there is a fairly wide range of actions which we would be willing to allow the first party, but there are some actions which we would rule out. Having an obligation to prevent the harms of others seems to permit us some forms of control, but not all. At least one important consideration in deciding what kinds of actions are permissible is the *rights* of the controlled parties.[20] If these claims are correct, we must examine the rights of employees in order to determine whether drug testing is justified. The relevant right in the case of drug testing is the right to privacy. The "ought implies can" argument, then, does not circumvent the claims of privacy rights as it originally seemed to do.

The Agency Argument

A proponent of drug testing might argue, however, that the relation between employers and employees is significantly different from the relation between hosts and guests, universities and members of fraternities, or landlords and tenants. Employees have a special relation with the firm that employs them. They are *agents,* hired and empowered to act on behalf of the employer. While they act on the business of the firm, it might be argued, they "are" the corporation. The restrictions that apply to what one independent agent may do to another thus do not apply here.

But surely this argument is incorrect, for a number of reasons. First, if it were correct, it would justify anything a corporation might do to control the behavior of an employee—not merely drug testing, but polygraph testing, tapping of telephones, deception, psychological manipulation, whips and chains, etc.[21] There are undoubtedly some people who would argue that some of these procedures are permissible, but few would argue that all of them are. The fact that even some of them appear not to be suggests that we believe there are limits to what corporations may do to control employees, and that one consideration in determining these limits is the employees' rights.

Secondly, the argument implies that employees give up their own autonomy completely when they sign on as agents, and become an organ or piece of the corporation. But this cannot be true. Agency is a moral and contractual relationship of the kind that can only obtain between two independent, autonomous parties. This relationship could not be sustained if the employee ceased to be autonomous upon signing the contract. Employees are not slaves, but autonomous agents capable of upholding a contract. Moreover, we expect a certain amount of discretion in employees in the course of their agency. Employees are not expected to follow illegal or immoral commands of their employers, and we find them morally and legally blameworthy when they do so. That we expect such independent judgment of them suggests that they do not lose their autonomy entirely.[22]

Finally, if the employment contract were one in which employees gave up all right to be treated as autonomous human beings, then it would not be a legitimate or morally valid contract. Some rights are considered "inalienable"—people are forbidden from negotiating them away even if it seems advantageous to them to do so. The law grants recognition to this fact through anti-discrimination statutes, minimum wage legislation, workplace health and safety standards, etc. Even if I would like to, I may not trade away, for example, my right not to be sexually harassed or my right to know about workplace hazards.

Again, these arguments do not show that drug testing is unjustified. They do show, however, that if drug testing is justified, it is not because the "ought implies can" argument bypasses the issue of employee rights, but because drug testing does not impermissibly violate those rights.[23] To think that obligation, or responsibility for the acts of others, can circumvent rights claims is to misunderstand the import of the "ought implies can" principle. The principle tells us that there is a close connection between obligation or responsibility and capability. But it does not license us to disregard the rights of others any more than it guarantees us the physical conditions that make carrying out our obligations possible. It may well prove that employees' right to privacy, assuming they have such a right, is secondary to some more weighty consideration. I take up this question briefly below. What has been shown here is that the issue of the permissibility of drug testing will not and cannot be settled *without* a close scrutiny of privacy rights. If we are to decide the issue, we must eventually determine whether employees have privacy rights, how far they extend, and what considerations outweigh them—precisely the difficult questions the "ought implies can" argument sought to avoid.

Is Drug Testing Necessary?

The "ought implies can" argument also has another serious flaw. The argument turns on the claim that forbidding drug testing prevents corporations from carrying out their obligation to prevent harm. But this is only true if drug testing is *necessary* for preventing drug-related harm. If it is merely one option among many, then forbidding drug testing still leaves a corporation free to prevent harm in other ways. For the argument to be sound, in other words, premise 5 would have to be altered to read, "drug testing is a necessary element in any plan to rid the workplace of drugs."

But it is not at all clear that drug testing *is* necessary to reduce drug use in the workplace. Its necessity has been challenged repeatedly. In a recent article in the *Harvard Business Review,* for example, James Wrich draws on his experience in dealing with alcoholism in the workplace and suggests the use of broadbrush educational and rehabilitative programs as alternatives to testing. Corporations using such programs to combat alcohol problems, Wrich reports, have achieved tremendous reductions in absenteeism, sick leave, and on-the-job accidents.[24] Others have argued that impaired performance likely to result in harm could be easily detected by various sorts of performance-oriented tests—mental and physical dexterity tests, alertness tests, flight simulation tests, and so on. These sorts of procedures have the advantage of not being controversial from a rights perspective.[25]

Indeed, many thinkers have argued that drug testing is not only unnecessary, but is not even an effective way to attack drug use in the workplace. The commonly used and affordable urinalysis tests are notoriously unreliable. They have a very high rate both of false negatives and of false positives. At best the tests reveal, not impaired performance or even the presence of a particular drug, but the presence of metabolites of various drugs that can remain in the system long after any effects of the drug have worn off.[26] Because they do not measure impairment, such tests do not seem well-tailored to the purpose of preventing harm—which, after all, is the ultimate goal. As Lewis Maltby, vice president of a small instrumentation company and an opponent of drug testing, puts it,

> . . . [T]he fundamental flaw with drug testing is that it tests for the wrong thing. A realistic program to detect workers whose condition put the company or other people at risk would test for the condition that actually creates the danger.[27]

If these claims are true, there is no real connection between the obligation to prevent harm and the practice of drug testing, and the "ought implies can" argument provides no justification for drug testing at all.[28]

Conclusion

I have made no attempt here to determine whether drug testing does indeed violate employees' privacy rights. The analysis on p. 146 above suggests that we have reason to believe that employees have some rights. Once we accept the notion of employee rights in general, it seems likely that a right to privacy would be among them, since it is an important civil right and central for the protection of individual autonomy. There are also reasons, I believe, to think that most drug testing violates the right to privacy. These claims need much more defense than they can be given here, and even if they are true, this does not necessarily mean that drug testing is unjustified. It does, however, create a *prima facie* case against drug testing. If drug testing violates the privacy rights of employees, it will be justified only under very strict conditions, if it is justified at all. It is worth taking a moment to see why this is so.

It is generally accepted in both the ethical and legal spheres that rights are not absolute. But we allow basic rights to be overridden only in special cases in which some urgent and fundamental good is at stake. In legal discourse, such goods are called "compelling interests".[29] While there is room for some debate about what counts as a "compelling interest," it is almost always understood to be more than a merely private interest, however weighty. Public safety might well fall into this category, but private monetary loss probably would not. While more needs to be done to determine what kinds of interests justify drug testing, it seems clear that if testing does violate the basic rights of employees, it is only justified in extreme cases—far less often that it is presently used. Moreover, we believe that overriding a right is to be avoided wherever possible, and is only justified when doing so is *necessary* to serve the "compelling interest" in question. If it violates rights, then drug testing is only permissible if it is necessary for the protection of an interest such as public safety and if there is no other, morally preferable, way of accomplishing the same goal. As we have seen above, however, it is by no means clear that drug testing meets these conditions. There may be better, less controversial ways to prevent the harm caused by drug use; if so, these must be used in preference to drug testing, and testing is unjustified. And if the attacks on the effectiveness of drug testing are correct, testing is not only unnecessary for the protection of public safety, but does not serve any "compelling interest" at all.

What do these conclusions tell us about the responsibility of employers for preventing harms caused by employees? If it is decided that drug testing is morally impermissible, then there can be no duty to use it to anticipate and prevent harms. Corporations who fail to use it cannot be blamed for doing so. They cannot have a moral obligation to do something morally impermissible. Moreover, if it turns out that there is no other effective way to prevent the harms caused by drug use, then it seems to me we may not hold employers morally responsible for those harms. This seems to me unlikely to be the case—there probably are other effective measures to control drug abuse in the workplace. But corporations can be held responsible only to the extent that they are permitted to act. It would not be inconsistent, however, to hold corporations legally liable for the harms caused by intoxicated employees under the doctrine of *respondeat superior,* even if drug testing is forbidden, for this kind of liability does not imply an ability to have done otherwise.

Notes

1. Employees do not, of course, have legal privacy rights, although the courts seem to be moving slowly in this direction. Opponents of testing usually claim that employees have *moral* rights to privacy, even if these have not been given legal recognition. See, for example, Joseph Des Jardins and Ronald Duska, "Drug Testing in Employment," in *Business Ethics: Readings and Cases in Corporate Morality,* 2nd Ed, *ed.* W. M. Hoffman and J. M. Moore (McGraw-Hill, forthcoming).

2. See, for example, "Work-Place Privacy Issues and Employer Screening Policies," Richard Lehr and David Middlebrooks, *Employee Relations Law Journal* 11, 407. Lehr and Middlebrooks cite the argument as one of the chief justifications for drug testing used by employers. I have also encountered the argument frequently in discussion with students, colleagues, and managers.

3. Ronald Dworkin has referred to rights as moral "trumps." This kind of language tends to suggest that rights overwhelm all other considerations, so that when they are flourished, all that opponents can do is subside in silence. Rights are frequently asserted this way in everyday discourse, and in this sense rights claims tend to close, rather than open, the door to fruitful ethical dialogue.

4. In his article "Privacy, Polygraphs, and Work," *Business and Professional Ethics Journal* 1, Fall, 1981, 19, George Brenkert has developed the idea that my privacy is violated when someone acquires information about me that they are not entitled, by virtue of their relationship to me, to have. My mortgage company, for example, is entitled to know my credit history; a prospective sexual partner is entitled to know if I have any sexually transmitted diseases. Thus their knowledge of this information does not violate my privacy. One could argue that employers are similarly entitled to the information obtained by drug tests, and that drug testing does not violate privacy for this reason. A somewhat different move would be to argue that testing does not violate privacy because employees give their "consent" to it drug testing as part of the employment contract. For a sustained attack on these and other Type 1 arguments, see Joseph Des Jardins and Ronald Duska, "Drug Testing in Employment."

5. One might defend this position on the ground that the employer "owns" the job and is therefore entitled to place any conditions he wishes on obtaining or keeping it. The problem with this argument is that it seems to rule out *all* employee rights, including such basic ones as the right to organize and bargain collectively, or the right not to be discriminated against, which have solid legal as well as ethical grounding. It also implies that ownership overrides all other considerations, and it is not at all clear that this is true. One might take the position that by accepting a job, an employee has agreed to give up all his rights save those actually specified in the employment contract. But this makes the employment contract look like an agreement in which employees sell themselves and accept the status of things without rights. And it overlooks the fact that we believe there are some things ("inalienable" rights) that persons ought not to be permitted to bargain away. Alex Michalos has discussed some of the limitations of the employment contract in "The Loyal Agent's Argument," in *Ethical Theory and Business,* 2nd edition, ed. Tom L. Beauchamp and Norman E. Bowie (Englewood Cliffs, NJ: Prentice-Hall, 1983), p. 247.

6. The term "responsibility" is deliberately left ambiguous here. Several different meanings of it are examined below.

7. See Immanuel Kant, *Critique of Practical Reason,* trans. Lewis White Beck (Indianapolis: Bobbs-Merrill, 1956), p. 30.

8. In this paper I have tried to avoid getting embroiled in the question of whether or not corporations are themselves "moral agents," which has been the question to dominate the

corporate responsibility debate. The argument I offer here does, I believe, have important implications for the problem of corporate agency, but does not require me to take a stand on it here. I am content to have those who reject the notion of corporations as moral agents read my references to corporate responsibility as shorthand for some complex form of individual or group responsibility.

9. One example would be negligent hiring, which is an increasingly frequent cause of action against an employer. Employers can also be held negligent if they give orders that lead to harms that they ought to have foreseen. Domino's Pizza is now under suit because it encouraged its drivers to deliver pizzas as fast as possible, a policy that accident victims claim should have been expected to cause accidents.

10. This understanding of moral responsibility often seems to overshadow other notions. In an article on corporate responsibility, for example, Manuel Velasquez concludes that because corporations are not responsible in this sense, they are "not responsible for anything they do." "Why Corporations Are Not Responsible For Anything They Do," *Business and Professional Ethics Journal* **2**, Spring, 1983, 1.

11. There is also an *actus reus* requirement for this type of responsibility—that is, the act must be traceable to the voluntary bodily movements of the agent. Obviously, corporations do not have bodies, but the people who work for them do. The question, then, has become when may we call an act by one member of the corporation a "corporate act." If it is possible to do so at all, the decisive feature is probably the presence of some sort of corporate "intention." This is why I focus on intention here, and why intention has been central to the discussion of corporate responsibility.

12. There are some, like Velasquez, who hold that a corporation can never satisfy the *mens rea* requirement because this would require a collective mind. If this were true, the argument would collapse at the outset. Others believe that a *mens rea* can be attributed to corporations metaphorically, if it can be shown that company policy includes an "intention" to harm, and it is this model I follow here.

13. There are, of course, those who take precisely this position. See Velasquez, "Why Corporations Are Not Responsible For Anything They Do."

14. See, for example, Peter French, *Collective and Corporate Responsibility* (New York: Columbia University Press, 1984).

15. It is tempting to conclude from this argument that drug testing is not only permissible, but obligatory, but this is not the case. The reason why it is not provides a clue to one of the major weaknesses of the argument. Drug testing would be obligatory only if it were *necessary* for the prevention of harm due to drug use, but it is not clear that this is so. But also means that it is not clear that corporations are deflected from their duty to prevent harm by a prohibition against drug testing. See below for a fuller discussion of this problem.

16. For example, it has been claimed that employees who use drugs cause four times as many work-related accidents as do other employees. The highly publicized Conrail crash in 1987 was determined to be drug-related. Of course there are harms to the company itself as well, in the form of higher absenteeism, lowered productivity, higher insurance costs, etc. But since these types of harm raise the question of what a company may do to preserve its self-interest, rather than what it may do to prevent harms to others for which they are responsible, I focus here on harm to employees, consumers, and the public.

17. In our eagerness to assign "corporate responsibility," this fact has frequently been overlooked. This in turn has led, I believe, to an oversimplified view of corporate action. I discuss this problem more fully in a paper in progress entitled "The Paradox of Corporate Autonomy."

18. It is an interesting question whether there are limitations on what individuals can do to themselves to control their own behavior. What about individuals who undergo hypnosis, or who have their jaws wired shut in order to *lose* weight? Are they violating their own rights? Undermining their own autonomy? It could be argued plausibly that these kinds of things are not permissible, on the Kantian ground that we have a duty not to treat ourselves as merely as means to an end. Of course, if there are such restrictions, it makes the "ought implies can" argument as applied to corporations even weaker.

19. None of these analogies is perfect. In the case of the hostess and guest, for example, the guest is clearly intoxicated. This is rarely true of employees who are tested for drugs; if the employee were visibly intoxicated, there would be no need to test. Moreover, in the hostess/guest case the hostess contributes directly to the intoxication. There are important parallels, however. In each case one party is held morally (and in two of the cases, legally) responsible for harms caused by others. Moreover, the first parties are responsible in close to the same way that employers are responsible for the acts of their employees: they in some sense "facilitate" the harmful acts, they have some capacity to prevent those acts, and they are thus viewed as having an obligation to prevent them. One main difference, of course, is that employees are "agents" of their employers. See p. 146.

20. There are other, utility-related considerations, as well—for example, harm to employees who are unjustly dismissed, a demoralized workforce, the costs of testing, etc. I concentrate here on rights because they have been the primary focal point in the drug testing debate.

21. The assumption here is that persons are entitled to do whatever they wish to themselves. See Note 18.

22. See Michalos, "The Loyal Agent's Argument."

23. Some violations of right, of course, are permissible. See p. 148.

24. James T. Wrich, "Beyond Testing: Coping with Drugs at Work," *Harvard Business Review* Jan–Feb 1988, 120.

25. See Des Jardins and Duska, "Drug Testing in Employment," and Lewis Maltby, "Why Drug Testing is a Bad Idea," *Inc.,* June 1987. While other sorts of tests also have the potential to be abused, they are at least a direct measurement of something that an employer is entitled to know—performance capability. Des Jardins and Duska offer an extended defense of this sort of test.

26. See Edward J. Imwinkelreid, "False Positive," *The Sciences,* Sept.–Oct. 1987, **22.** Also David Bearman, "The Medical Case Against Drug Testing," *Harvard Business Review* Jan–Feb. 1988, 123.

27. Maltby, "Why Drug Testing Is a Bad Idea," pp. 152–153.

28. It could still be argued that drug testing *deters* drug use, and thus has a connection with preventing harm, even though it doesn't directly provide any information that enables companies to prevent harm. This is an important point, but it is still subject to the restrictions discussed in the previous section. Not everything that has a deterrent value is permissible. It is possible that a penalty of capital punishment would provide a deterrent for rapists, or having one's hand removed deter shoplifting, but there are very few advocates for these penalties. Effectiveness is not the only issue here; rights and justice are also relevant.

29. The principle that fundamental rights may not be overridden by the state unless doing so is necessary to serve a "compelling state interest" is a principle of constitutional law, but it also reflects our moral intuitions about when it is appropriate to override rights. The legal principle would not apply to all cases of drug testing in the workplace because many of these involve private, rather than state, employees. But the principle does provide us with useful guidelines in the ethical sphere. Interestingly, Federal District Judge George Revercomb recently issued an injunction blocking the random drug testing of Justice Department employees on the ground that it did not serve a compelling state interest. Since there was no evidence of a drug problem among the Department's employees, the Judge concluded, there is no threat that would give rise to a compelling interest. See "Judge Blocks Drug Testing of Justice Department Employees," *New York Times* July 30, 1988, 7.

Department of Philosophy,
University of Delaware,
Newark,
Delaware 19716,
U.S.A.

CHAPTER 6

Affirmative Action

Preferential Hiring

Judith Jarvis Thomson

Many people are inclined to think preferential hiring an obvious injustice.[1]
I should have said "feel" rather than "think": it seems to me the matter has
not been carefully thought out, and that what is in question, really, is a gut
reaction.

I am going to deal with only a very limited range of preferential hirings:
that is, I am concerned with cases in which several candidates present themselves for a job, in which the hiring officer finds, on examination, that all are
equally qualified to hold that job, and he then straightway declares for the
black, or for the woman, because he or she *is* a black or a woman. And I shall
talk only of hiring decisions in the universities, partly because I am most familiar with them, partly because it is in the universities that the most vocal and
articulate opposition to preferential hiring is now heard—not surprisingly,
perhaps, since no one is more vocal and articulate than a university professor
who feels deprived of his rights.

I suspect that some people may say, Oh well, in *that* kind of case it's all
right, what we object to is preferring the less qualified to the better qualified.
Or again, What we object to is refusing even to consider the qualifications of
white males. I shall say nothing at all about these things. I think that the argument I shall give for saying that preferential hiring is not unjust in the cases
I do concentrate on can also be appealed to to justify it outside that range of

Judith Jarvis Thomson, "Preferential Hiring," *Philosophy & Public Affairs 2,* no. 4 (Summer
1973). Copyright © 1973 by Princeton University Press. Excerpts reprinted by permission.

cases. But I won't draw any conclusions about cases outside it. Many people do have that gut reaction I mentioned against preferential hiring in *any* degree or form; and it seems to me worthwhile bringing out that there is good reason to think they are wrong to have it. Nothing I say will be in the slightest degree novel or original. It will, I hope, be enough to set the relevant issues out clearly.

I

But first, something should be said about qualifications.

I said I would consider only cases in which the several candidates who present themselves for the job are equally qualified to hold it; and there plainly are difficulties in the way of saying precisely how this is to be established, and even what is to be established. Strictly academic qualifications seem at a first glance to be relatively straightforward: the hiring officer must see if the candidates have done equally well in courses (both courses they took, and any they taught), and if they are recommended equally strongly by their teachers, and if the work they submit for consideration is equally good. There is no denying that even these things are less easy to establish than first appears: for example, you may have a suspicion that Professor Smith is given to exaggeration, and that this "great student" is in fact less strong than Professor Jones's "good student"—but do you *know* that this is so? But there is a more serious difficulty still: as blacks and women have been saying, strictly academic indicators may themselves be skewed by prejudice. My impression is that women, white and black, may possibly suffer more from this than black males. A black male who is discouraged or down-graded for being black is discouraged or down-graded out of dislike, repulsion, a desire to avoid contact; and I suspect that there are very few teachers nowadays who allow themselves to feel such things, or, if they do feel them, to act on them. A woman who is discouraged or down-graded for being a woman is not discouraged or down-graded out of dislike, but out of a conviction she is not serious. . . .

II

. . . Suppose two candidates for a civil service job have equally good test scores, but that there is only one job available. We could decide between them by coin-tossing. But in fact we do allow for declaring for A straightway, where A is a veteran, and B is not.[2] It may be that B is a nonveteran through no fault of his own: perhaps he was refused induction for flat feet, or a heart murmur. That is, those things in virtue of which B is a nonveteran may be things which it was no more in his power to control or change than it is in anyone's power to control or change the color of his skin. Yet the fact is that B is not a veteran and A is. On the assumption that the veteran has served his country, the country owes him something. And it seems plain that giving him preference is a not unjust way in which part of that debt of gratitude can be paid.

And now, . . . we should turn to those debts which are incurred by one who wrongs another. It is here we find what seems to me the most powerful argument for the conclusion that the preferential hiring of blacks and women is not unjust.

I obviously cannot claim any novelty for this argument: it's a very familiar one. Indeed, not merely is it familiar, but so are a battery of objections to it. It may be granted that if we have wronged A, we owe him something: we should make amends, we should compensate him for the wrong done him. It may even be granted that if we have wronged A, we must make amends, that justice requires it, and that a failure to make amends is not merely callousness, but injustice. But (a) are the young blacks and women who are amongst the current applicants for university jobs amongst the blacks and women who were wronged? To turn to particular cases, it might happen that the black applicant is middle class, the son of professionals, and has had the very best in private schooling; or that the woman applicant is plainly the product of feminist upbringing and encouragement. Is it proper, much less required, that the black or woman be given preference over a white male who grew up in poverty, and has to make his own way and earn his encouragements? Again, (b), did we, the current members of the community, wrong any blacks or women? Lots of people once did; but then isn't it for them to do the compensating? That is, if they're still alive. For presumably nobody now alive owned any slaves, and perhaps nobody now alive voted against women's suffrage. And (c) what if the white male applicant for the job has never in any degree wronged any blacks or women? If so, *he* doesn't owe any debts to them, so why should *he* make amends to them?

These objections seem to me quite wrong-headed.

Obviously the situation for blacks and women is better than it was a hundred and fifty, fifty, twenty-five years ago. But it is absurd to suppose that the young blacks and women now of an age to apply for jobs have not been wronged. Large-scale, blatant, overt wrongs have presumably disappeared; but it is only within the last twenty-five years (perhaps the last ten years in the case of women) that it has become at all widely agreed in this country that blacks and women must be recognized as having, not merely this or that particular right normally recognized as belonging to white males, but all of the rights and respect which go with full membership in the community. Even young blacks and women have lived through down-grading for being black or female: they have not merely not been given that very equal chance at the benefits generated by what the community owns which is so firmly insisted on for white males, they have not until lately even been felt to have a right to it.

And even those who were not themselves down-graded for being black or female have suffered the consequences of the down-grading of other blacks and women: lack of self-confidence, and lack of self-respect. For where a community accepts that a person's being black, or being a woman, are right and proper grounds for denying that person full membership in the community, it can hardly be supposed that any but the most extraordinarily independent black or woman will escape self-doubt. All but the most extraordinarily independent of them have had to work harder—if only against self-doubt—then all but the most deprived white males, in the competition for a place amongst the best qualified.

If any black or woman has been unjustly deprived of what he or she has a right to, then of course justice does call for making amends. But what of the blacks and women who haven't actually been deprived of what they have a right to, but only made to suffer the consequences of injustice to other blacks and women? *Perhaps* justice doesn't require making amends to them as well; but common decency certainly does. To fail, at the very least, to make what counts as public apology to all, and to take positive steps to show that it is sincerely meant, is, if not injustice, then anyway a fault at least as serious as ingratitude.

Opting for a policy of preferential hiring may of course mean that some black or woman is preferred to some white male who as a matter of fact has had a harder life than the black or woman. But so may opting for a policy of veterans' preference mean that a healthy, unscarred, middle class veteran is preferred to a poor, struggling, scarred, nonveteran. Indeed, opting for a policy of settling who gets the job by having all equally qualified candidates draw straws may also mean that in a given case the candidate with the hardest life loses out. Opting for any policy other than hard-life preference may have this result.

I have no objection to anyone's arguing that it is precisely hard-life preference that we ought to opt for. If all, or anyway all of the equally qualified, have a right to an equal chance, then the argument would have to draw attention to something sufficiently powerful to override that right. But perhaps this could be done along the lines I followed in the case of blacks and women: perhaps it could be successfully argued that we have wronged those who have had hard lives, and therefore owe it to them to make amends. And then we should have in more extreme form a difficulty already present: how are these preferences to be ranked? shall we place the hard-lifers ahead of blacks? both ahead of women? and what about veterans? I leave these questions aside. My concern has been only to show that the white male applicant's right to an equal chance does not make it unjust to opt for a policy under which blacks and women are given preference. That a white male with a specially hard history may lose out under this policy cannot possibly be any objection to it, in the absence of a showing that hard-life preference is not unjust, and, more important, takes priority over preference for blacks and women.

Lastly, it should be stressed that to opt for such a policy is not to make the young white male applicants themselves make amends for any wrongs done to blacks and women. Under such a policy, no one is asked to give up a job which is already his; the job for which the white male competes isn't his, but is the community's, and it is the hiring officer who gives it to the black or woman in the community's name. Of course the white male is asked to give up his equal chance at the job. But that is not something he pays to the black or woman by way of making amends; it is something the community takes away from him in order that *it* may make amends.

Still, the community does impose a burden on him: it is able to make amends for its wrongs only by taking something away from him, something which, after all, we are supposing he has a right to. And why should *he* pay the cost of the community's amends-making?

If there were some appropriate way in which the community could make amends to its blacks and women, some way which did not require depriving anyone of anything he has a right to, then that would be the best course of action for it to take. Or if there were anyway some way in which the costs could be shared by everyone, and not imposed entirely on the young white male job applicants, then that would be, if not best, then anyway better than opting for a policy of preferential hiring. But in fact the nature of the wrongs done is such as to make jobs the best and most suitable form of compensation. What blacks and women were denied was full membership in the community; and nothing can more appropriately make amends for that wrong than precisely what will make them feel they now finally have it. And that means jobs. Financial compensation (the cost of which could be shared equally) slips through the fingers; having a job, and discovering you do it well, yield—perhaps better than anything else—that very self-respect which blacks and women have had to do without.

But of course choosing this way of making amends means that the costs are imposed on the young white male applicants who are turned away. And so it should be noticed that it is not entirely inappropriate that those applicants should pay the costs. No doubt few, if any, have themselves, individually, done any wrongs to blacks and women. But they have profited from the wrongs the community did. Many may actually have been direct beneficiaries of policies which excluded or down-graded blacks and women—perhaps in school admissions, perhaps in access to financial aid, perhaps elsewhere; and even those who did not directly benefit in this way had, at any rate, the advantage in the competition which comes of confidence in one's full membership, and of one's rights being recognized as a matter of course.

Of course it isn't only the young white male applicant for a university job who has benefited from the exclusion of blacks and women: the older white male, now comfortably tenured, also benefited, and many defenders of preferential hiring feel that he should be asked to share the costs. Well, presumably we can't demand that he give up his job, or share it. But it seems to me in place to expect the occupants of comfortable professorial chairs to contribute in some way, to make some form of return to the young white male who bears the cost, and is turned away. It will have been plain that I find the outcry now heard against preferential hiring in the universities objectionable; it would also be objectionable that those of us who are now securely situated should placidly defend it, with no more than a sigh of regret for the young white male who pays for it.

III

One final word: "discrimination." I am inclined to think we so use it that if anyone is convicted of discriminating against blacks, women, white males, or what have you, then he is thereby convicted of acting unjustly. If so, and if I am right in thinking that preferential hiring in the restricted range of cases we have been looking at is *not* unjust, then we have two options: (a) we can simply reply that to opt for a policy of preferential hiring in those cases is not to opt for a policy of discriminating against white males, or (b) we can hope to get usage changed—e.g., by trying to get people to allow that there is discriminating against and discriminating against, and that some is unjust, but some is not.

Best of all, however, would be for that phrase to be avoided altogether. It's at best a blunt tool: there are all sorts of nice moral discriminations [*sic*] which one is unable to make while occupied with it. And that bluntness itself fits it to do harm: blacks and women are hardly likely to see through to what precisely is owed them while they are being accused of welcoming what is unjust.

Notes

1. This essay is an expanded version of a talk given at the Conference on the Liberation of Female Persons, held at North Carolina State University at Raleigh, on March 26–28, 1973, under a grant from the S & H Foundation. I am indebted to James Thomson and the members of the Society for Ethical and Legal Philosophy for criticism of an earlier draft.
2. To the best of my knowledge, the analogy between veterans' preference and the preferential hiring of blacks has been mentioned in print only by Edward T. Chase, in a Letter to the Editor, *Commentary,* February 1973.

Preferential Hiring: A Reply to Judith Jarvis Thomson

Robert Simon

Judith Jarvis Thomson has recently defended preferential hiring of women and black persons in universities.[1] She restricts her defense of the assignment of preference to only those cases where candidates from preferred groups and their white male competitors are equally qualified, although she suggests that her argument can be extended to cover cases where the qualifications are unequal as well. The argument in question is compensatory; it is because of pervasive patterns of unjust discrimination against black persons and women that justice, or at least common decency, requires that amends be made.

While Thomson's analysis surely clarifies many of the issues at stake, I find it seriously incomplete. I will argue that even if her claim that compen-

Robert Simon, "Preferential Hiring: A Reply to Judith Jarvis Thomson," *Philosophy & Public Affairs 3*, no. 3 (Spring 1974). Copyright © 1974 by Princeton University Press. Excerpts reprinted by permission.

sation is due victims of social injustice is correct (as I think it is), it is questionable nevertheless whether preferential hiring is an acceptable method of distributing such compensation. This is so, even if, as Thomson argues, compensatory claims override the right of the white male applicant to equal consideration from the appointing officer. For implementation of preferential hiring policies may involve claims, perhaps even claims of right, other than the above right of the white male applicant. In the case of the claims I have in mind, the best that can be said is that where preferential hiring is concerned, they are arbitrarily ignored. If so, and if such claims are themselves warranted, then preferential hiring, while *perhaps* not unjust, is open to far more serious question than Thomson acknowledges.

A familiar objection to special treatment for blacks and women is that, if such a practice is justified, other victims of injustice or misfortune ought to receive special treatment too. While arguing that virtually all women and black persons have been harmed, either directly or indirectly, by discrimination, Thomson acknowledges that in any particular case, a white male may have been victimized to a greater extent than have the blacks or women with which he is competing. However, she denies that other victims of injustice or misfortune ought automatically to have priority over blacks and women where distribution of compensation is concerned. Just as veterans receive preference with respect to employment in the civil service, as payment for the service they have performed for society, so can blacks and women legitimately be given preference in university hiring, in payment of the debt owed them. And just as the former policy can justify hiring a veteran who in fact had an easy time of it over a nonveteran who made great sacrifices for the public good, so too can the latter policy justify hiring a relatively undeprived member of a preferred group over a more disadvantaged member of a nonpreferred group.

But surely if the reason for giving a particular veteran preference is that he performed a service for his country, that same preference must be given to anyone who performed a similar service. Likewise, if the reason for giving preference to a black person or to a woman is that the recipient has been injured due to an unjust practice, then preference must be given to anyone who has been similarly injured. So, it appears, there can be no relevant *group* to which compensation ought to be made, other than that made up of and only of those who have been injured or victimized.[2] Although, as Thomson claims, all blacks and women may be members of that latter group, they deserve compensation *qua* victim and not *qua* black person or woman.

There are at least two possible replies that can be made to this sort of objection. First, it might be agreed that anyone injured in the same way as blacks or women ought to receive compensation. But then, "same way" is characterized so narrowly that it applies to no one except blacks and women. While there is nothing logically objectionable about such a reply, it may nevertheless be morally objectionable. For it implies that a nonblack male who has been terribly injured by a social injustice has less of a claim to compensation than a black or woman who has only been minimally injured. And this implication may be morally unacceptable.

A more plausible line of response may involve shifting our attention from compensation of individuals to collective compensation of groups.[3] Once this shift is made, it can be acknowledged that as individuals, some white males may have stronger compensatory claims than blacks or women. But as compensation is owed the group, it is group claims that must be weighed, not individual ones. And surely, at the group level, the claims of black persons and women to compensation are among the strongest there are.

Suppose we grant that certain groups, including those specified by Thomson, are owed collective compensation. What should be noted is that the conclusion of concern here—that preferential hiring policies are acceptable instruments for compensating groups—does not directly follow. To derive such a conclusion validly, one would have to provide additional premises specifying the relation between collective compensation to groups and distribution of that compensation to individual members. For it does not follow from the fact that some group members are compensated that the group is compensated. Thus, if through a computer error, every member of the American Philosophical Association was asked to pay additional taxes, then if the government provided compensation for this error, it would not follow that it had compensated the Association. Rather it would have compensated each member *qua* individual. So what is required, where preferential hiring is concerned, are plausible premises showing how the preferential award of jobs to group members counts as collective compensation for the group.

Thomson provides no such additional premises. Moreover, there is good reason to think that if any such premises were provided, they would count against preferential hiring as an instrument of collective compensation. This is because although compensation is owed to the group, preferential hiring policies award compensation to an arbitrarily selected segment of the group; namely, those who have the ability and qualifications to be seriously considered for the jobs available. Surely, it is far more plausible to think that collective compensation ought to be equally available to all group members, or at least to all kinds of group members.[4] The claim that although compensation is owed collectively to a group, only a special sort of group member is eligible to receive it, while perhaps not incoherent, certainly ought to be rejected as arbitrary, at least in the absence of an argument to the contrary.

Accordingly, the proponent of preferential hiring faces the following dilemma. Either compensation is to be made on an individual basis, in which case the fact that one is black or a woman is irrelevant to whether one ought to receive special treatment, or it is made on a group basis, in which case it is far from clear that preferential hiring policies are acceptable compensatory instruments. Until this dilemma is resolved, assuming it can be resolved at all, the compensatory argument for preferential hiring is seriously incomplete at a crucial point.

Notes

1. Judith Jarvis Thomson, "Preferential Hiring," *Philosophy & Public Affairs,* 2, no. 4 (Summer 1973), 364–384.
2. This point also has been argued for recently by J. L. Cowen, "Inverse Discrimination," *Analysis,* 33, no. I (1972), 10–12.
3. Such a position has been defended by Paul Taylor, in his "Reverse Discrimination and Compensatory Justice," *Analysis,* 33, no. 4 (1973), 177–182.
4. Taylor would apparently agree, *ibid,* 180.

In Defense of Hiring Apparently Less Qualified Women

Laura M. Purdy*

> *A Man's mind—what there is of it—has always the advantage of being mascu-line—as the smallest birchtree is of higher kind than the most soaring palm—and even his ignorance is of a sounder quality.*
>
> George Elliot, *Middlemarch,* ch. 2

There are relatively few women in academe, and it is reasonable to believe that discrimination—conscious and unconscious, subtle and overt, individual and institutional—is responsible for this state of affairs.[1] Affirmative action programs have been promoted to try to neutralize this discrimination. One form requires academic departments to search actively for female candidates; if a woman with qualifications at least as good as those of the leading male contender is found, she is to be hired.

Does this policy create new and serious injustice, as some contend?[2] If a woman and a man were equally qualified, and one could be sure that prejudice against women played no part in the decision to hire, such a policy would certainly be an imposition on the department's freedom to hire the most compatible-seeming colleague. (This is not to say that such an imposition could never be justified: we might, for example, believe that the importance of creating role models for female students justifies some loss of freedom on the part of departments.) However, it is widely conceded that there is prejudice against women among academics, with the result that women are not getting the appointments they deserve. My intent here is to consider how this happens. I will argue that women are often not perceived to be as highly qualified as they really are. Thus when the qualifications of candidates are compared, a woman may not be thought equally (or more highly) qualified, even when she is. Affirmative action programs which require hiring of equally qualified women will therefore be ineffective: the hiring of women perceived to be less qualified is needed if discrimination against women is to cease.

Excerpted from "In Defense of Hiring Apparently Less Qualified Women" by Laura M. Purdy. *Journal of Social Philosophy,* Vol. 15 (Summer 1984), pp. 26–33. Reprinted with permission of the author and publisher.
*Department of Philosophy, Wells College.

Some people think that the latter course is both unnecessary and unfair. Alan Goldman, for instance, maintains that it is unnecessary because the procedural requirements of good affirmative action programs are sufficient to guarantee equal opportunity. He also believes it to be unfair because it deprives the most successful new Ph.D.'s of their just reward—a good job.[3] I will argue that neither of these claims is true and that there is a good case for hiring women perceived to be less well qualified than their male competitors.

The general difficulty of forming accurate assessments of candidates' merit is well-known, and it is probable that the better candidate has sometimes been taken for the worse. It is reasonable to believe, however, that the subjective elements in evaluations lead to systematic lowering of women's perceived qualifications. I have two arguments for this claim. The first is that past prejudice biases the evidence and the second is that present prejudice biases perception of the evidence. Let us examine each in turn.

Why then may women be better qualified than their records suggest? One principal reason is that many men simply do not take women seriously:

> You might think that the evaluation of the specific performance would be an objective process, judged on characteristics of performance itself rather than on assumptions about the personality or ability of the performer. Yet performance is rarely a totally objective process. Two people may view the same event and interpret it differently. In the same way, it is possible for someone to view two people acting in exactly the same way and yet come to different conclusions about that behavior.[4]

Studies by Rosenthal and Jacobson provide experimental support for this claim. They found that students reported one group of rats to run mazes faster than another identical group, when they had previously been told that the first group was brighter. Ann Sutherland Harris quite plausibly concludes that such studies have important implications for women:

> If male scholars believe that women are intellectually inferior to men—less likely to have original contributions to make, less likely to be logical, and so on—will they not also find the evidence to support their beliefs in the women students in their classes, evidence of a far more sophisticated nature than the speed at which one rat finds its way through a maze? Their motives will be subconscious. Indeed, they will firmly believe that their judgment is rational and objective.[5]

What grounds are there for maintaining that this does not occur whenever women are evaluated? Other studies suggest additional hurdles for women that bias the evidence upon which they are judged. For instance, male students (though not female ones) rate identical course syllabi higher when the professor is said to be a man.[6]

Sociologist Jessie Bernard suggests that bias occurs whether women present accepted ideas or novel ones. In one study, a man and a woman taught classes using the same material. The man engaged the students' interest: he was thought both more biased and more authoritative than the equally competent woman. According to Bernard, she was taken less seriously because she did not "look the part."[7] To support her position that novel ideas are less well received from women than men, Bernard mentions the case of Agnes Pockels, whose discoveries in physics were ignored for years. She cites this as an example of the general inability to see women in "the idea-man or instrumental role. We are simply not used to looking for innovation and originality from women."[8] The consequences of failing to take new ideas seriously may be even more detrimental to women than the failure to be taken seriously as a teacher. Bernard argues: "The importance of priority . . . highlights the importance of followers, or, in the case of science, of the public qualified to judge innovations. If an innovation is not recognized—even if recognition takes the form of rejection and a fight—it is dead."[9]

Additional persuasive evidence that women's ideas are not taken seriously by men comes from a study by Daryl and Sandra Bem, replicating a previous study by Philip Goldberg with women. A number of scholarly articles were submitted to a group of undergraduate men, who were to judge how good they were. Each paper was read by each man, but the paper read by half the students was attributed to a man, that read by the other half, to a woman. The results were striking: the "man's" article was rated higher than the "woman's" in most cases.[10] Does this prejudice continue to operate at more advanced levels?

One significant study showed more papers by women were chosen for presentation at the annual meeting of a national professional organization when they were submitted anonymously.[11] This suggests that whether a woman's work is published or not will also depend more on the reviewers' conception of women than upon the merits of the piece—at least until blind reviewing becomes the rule. Furthermore, there is evidence that even when a woman is recognized as having done a good job at some task, her performance is more likely than a man's to be attributed to factors other than ability. Hence others are less likely to expect future repeated success on her part.[12] And, unsuccessful performance by a male is more likely than that of a female to be attributed to bad luck.[13] Studies have also shown that male applicants for scholarship funds were judged more intelligent and likeable than their female counterparts,[14] and that males were favored over females for study abroad programs.[15] In addition, until very recently, recommendations written for women were more likely to mention personal appearance in an undermining way (as well as marital status) than those written for men.[16] These facts have obvious repercussions for candidates' overall records. Hence if the hypotheses considered so far here are true, then women are systematically undervalued with respect to some of the most widely-used indicators of quality.

[Women also] run the risk of having their already undervalued qualifications devalued again when they are candidates for a position. This conclusion is supported by a study which showed that the same dossier was often ranked higher by academic departments when it was attributed to a man than when it was attributed to a woman.[17] Research on interviews also suggests that both men and women are systematically biased against women.[18]

I have been arguing that women are likely to be more highly qualified than they seem. This fact alone would support a policy of hiring women perceived to be less qualified. However, I think there is another sound argument for such a policy. Women may sometimes be less qualified than their male competitors because as students they faced stumbling-blocks the men did not. Hence some women probably deserve their weak recommendations and dearth of publications because their work is less fully developed and their claims less well supported than a man's might be. This can occur because women's social role often precludes opportunities for informal constructive criticism; it may also be the result of the lack of a mentor to push her to her limits. Finally, a woman is likely to have had to work in a debilitating environment of lowered expectations.[19]

Goldman argues that it would be wrong to hire such a woman if there were a more qualified candidate: ". . . the white male who has successfully met the requirements necessary to attaining maximal competence attains some right to that position. It seems unjust for society to set standards of achievement and then to thwart the expectations of those who have met those standards."[20]

But surely hiring is ultimately intended to produce the best scholar and teacher, not to reward the most successful graduate student. Consequently, if there are grounds for believing that women turn into the former, despite not having been the latter according to the traditional criteria, it is reasonable to hold that they should sometimes be hired anyway. And there are such grounds.

The obstacles encountered by women in academe are well-documented and there is no need to elaborate at length upon them here. What matters is the nature of the person they create. Until very recently, at every stage of schooling, fewer girls than boys continued.[21] There is considerable evidence that women graduate students have higher academic qualifications than their male counterparts.[22] This appears to be because only the very highly qualified get into graduate school.[23] Harris argues that it ". . . is worth remembering that women candidates for graduate school are the survivors of a long sifting process—only the very best of the good students go on to graduate school."[24] A report issued by women at the University of Chicago supports this claim— the grade averages of women students entering graduate school were significantly higher than those of men.[25]

Once there, women have somewhat higher attrition rates than men. But Harris thinks that this is "largely explained by the lack of encouragement and the actual discouragement experienced by women graduate students for their career plans. . . . It is not surprising that some women decide that they are not cut out to be scholars and teachers."[26] She argues that if women were not highly committed, the attrition rate would be much higher: ". . . only the hardiest survive."[27]

In light of all these facts, a temporary policy of hiring women perceived to be less well qualified would be reasonable, to see if the hypothesis that they will bloom is borne out. Such a policy is less risky than it might seem since junior faculty members are on probation and can be fired if they do not start to fulfill their promise.

In conclusion, there are good grounds for at least a trial of the policy I am proposing with regard to hiring in academe, since existing affirmative action programs have not been and cannot be effective.[28] I have tried to show why women may often seem less qualified than they really are, and why they may be more promising than they seem. Unless faculty members take these factors into account, no improvements in the position of women can be expected, for women are likely to seem less worthy of being hired than their male competitors when they are judged in the usual manner. Requiring departments to hire women perceived to be less well qualified may well turn out to be the most efficacious way to force departments to recognize and remedy the situation. It might also have a more generally beneficial side-effect of promoting faculty members' awareness of their own biases as they struggle to distinguish between truly mediocre women and those merely perceived to be so!

Notes

1. The general trend continues to be that the more prestigious the post or institution, the fewer women there are to be found. See, for instance, "Status of Female Faculty Members, 1979–80," *The Chronicle of Higher Education,* 29 September 1980.
2. See Alan Goldman, "Affirmative Action," *Philosophy and Public Affairs,* Vol. 5, n. 2 (Winter 1976), 178.
3. Ibid.
4. Kay Deaux, *The Behavior of Women and Men,* (Monterey, CA: Brooks/Cole Publishing Co., 1976), p. 24.
5. Ann Sutherland Harris reports this study in "The Second Sex in Academe" in *And Jill Came Tumbling After: Sexism in American Education,* ed. Judith Stacey et al., (New York: 1974), p. 299.
6. Jessie Bernard, *Academic Women,* (New York: Meridian Press, 1965), pp. 255–57. "The 'teachers' were selected by the department as being of about equal competence in communications skills. They were given two written lectures to deliver to sections of Sociology I. . . . both young people were given the lectures in advance, and they agreed on how to interpret all major points in their presentations, which were to be identical. One spoke to each section and a week later each spoke to the other section" (p. 256).
7. Ibid.
8. Ibid.
9. Ibid.
10. Reported by Deaux, p. 25.
11. This study appeared in "On Campus with Women," March 1977, Association of American Colleges, and was reported in *Ms.,* Vol. 7, n. 5 (November 1978), 87. *Ms.* writes: "In 1973, at the last annual conference held before the policy was initiated, 6.3 percent of the papers selected were from women scholars. In 1975, 17 percent of the papers selected were from women scholars." The organization in question is the Archaeological Institute of America.
12. Veronica F. Nieva and Barbara Gutek, "Sex Effects on Evaluation," *Academy of Management Review,* Vol. 5, n. 2 (1980), p. 267.
13. Ibid., p. 270.
14. Ibid., p. 268.
15. Ibid.
16. Jennie Farley, "Academic Recommendations: Males and Females as Judges and Judged," *AAUP Bulletin,* Vol. 64, n. 2 (May 1978). p. 84.
17. L. S. Fidell, "Empirical Verification of Sex Discrimination in Hiring Practices in Psychology," *American Psychologist,* Vol. 60 (1970), 1049–98.

18. Robert L. Dipboye, Richard D. Arvey, and David E. Terpstra, "Sex and Physical Attractiveness of Raters and Applicants as Determinants of Resume Evaluations," *Journal of Applied Psychology*, Vol. 62, n. 3 (June 1977), p. 288. This study was limited to undergraduate students, however, so it should not be assumed that it can be generalized to the educated population we are concerned with here.
19. Nieva and Gutek, p. 271.
20. Goldman, p. 191.
21. See Harris and Barnard in Stacey et al., pp. 302–5.
22. Harris, pp. 304–5.
23. Ibid.
24. Ibid.
25. Ibid.
26. Ibid.
27. Ibid. My own experience at the prestigious Ivy League institution where I took my Ph.D. was far from encouraging. When I arrived, there were no women faculty members. The class before mine, numbering about 10, contained no women, and I was the only woman in my class of about 10. Twice in my first year I was present in groups addressed by professors as "Gentlemen." One of these occasions was especially fraught with emotion. I and four men gathered at a professor's office to return one of the crucial 4-hour field exams required of first-year students. The professor beamed at us and said, "Well, we'll see how you did, gentlemen!"
28. See *Sex Discrimination in Higher Education,* ed. Jennie Farley, (Ithaca: ILR Publications, 1981).

Is Turn About Fair Play?

Barry R. Gross

. . . The balance of argument weighs against reverse discrimination for four interrelated sets of reasons. First, the procedures designed to isolate the discriminated are flawed. Second, the practice has undesirable and dangerous consequences. Third, it fails to fit any of the models of compensation or reparations. Fourth, it falls unjustly upon both those it favors and those it disfavors. I conclude that if to eliminate discrimination against the members of one group we find ourselves discriminating against another, we have gone too far.

Sociologically, groups are simply not represented in various jobs and at various levels in percentages closely approximating their percentage of the population. When universities in general and medical schools in particular discriminated heavily against them, Jews were represented in the medical profession in far greater percentages than their percentage of the population. At the same time, they were represented in far lower percentages in banking, finance, construction, and engineering than their percentage in the population, especially the population of New York City. A similar analysis by crudely drawn group traits—Jew, Roman Catholic, WASP, Irish, and so forth—of almost any trade, business or profession would yield similar results.

From *Reverse Discrimination,* ed. Barry R. Gross (Buffalo, NY: Prometheus Books, 1977); reprinted from the *Journal of Critical Analysis,* Vol. 5 (Jan.-Apr. 1975).

But the argument from population percentages may be meant not as an analysis of what is the case, but as an analysis of what ought to be the case. A proponent might put it this way: It is true that groups are not usually represented in the work force by their percentage in the population at large, but minority C has been systematically excluded from the good places. Therefore, in order to make sure that they get some of them, we should systematically include them in the good places, and a clear way of doing it is by their percentage in the population. Or we might conclude instead: therefore, in order to make up for past exclusion, they should be included in the good places as reparation, and an easy way to do it is by their percentage in the population.

If the definition of a minority discriminated against is ipso facto their representation in certain jobs in percentages less than their percentage in the general population, then one has to remark that the reasoning is circular. For we are trying to prove: (1) that minority C is discriminated against.

We use a premise (3) that minority C is underrepresented in good jobs. Since (1) does not follow from (3) (mere underrepresentation not being even prima facie evidence of discrimination), it is necessary to insert (2) that their underrepresentation is due to discrimination. But this completes the circle.

A critic might reply that we know perfectly well what is meant. The groups discriminated against are blacks, Puerto Ricans, Mexican-Americans, American Indians, and women. He is correct, though his answer does not tell us *how to find out* who is discriminated against. The critic, for example, left out Jews and Orientals. If he should reply that Jews and Orientals do well enough, we point out that the question was not "Who fails to do well?" but rather, "Who is discriminated against?" This argument shows that the mechanisms for identifying the victims of discrimination and for remedying it are seriously deficient.

Even if we allow that the percentage of the group in the work force versus its percentage in the population is the criterion of discrimination, who is discriminated against will vary depending upon how we divide the groups. We may discover that Republicans are discriminated against by our literary or intellectual journals—*New York Review, Dissent, Commentary.* We may also discover that wealthy Boston residents are discriminated against by the Los Angeles Dodgers, that women are discriminated against by the Army, and that idiots (we hope) are discriminated against by universities.

What employment or profession a person chooses depends upon a number of variables—background, wealth, parents' employment, schooling, intelligence, drive, ambition, skill, and not least, luck. Moreover, the analysis will differ depending upon what group identification or stratification you choose. None seems to have priority over the others. Every person can be typed according to many of these classifications. It seems, therefore, that the relevant analysis cannot even be made, much less justified.

In addition, some proponents of the population-percentage argument seem to hold: (4) From the contingent fact that members of the group C were discriminated against, it follows necessarily that they are underrepresented in the good positions. They then go on to assert (5) if members of group C were not discriminated against they would not be underrepresented, or (6) if they are underrepresented, then they are discriminated against.

But clearly (4) is itself a contingent, not a necessary truth. Clearly also neither (5) nor (6) follows from it, (5) being the fallacy of denying the antecedent and (6) the fallacy of affirming the consequent. Lastly, neither (5) nor (6) is necessarily true. The members of a group might simply lack interest in certain jobs (for example, Italians in the public-school system are in short supply). Could one argue that, even though neither (4), (5), nor (6) is *necessarily* true, the mere fact of underrepresentation in certain occupations does provide evidence of discrimination? The answer is no—no more than the fact of "overrepresentation" in certain occupations is evidence of favoritism.

At most, underrepresentation can be used to support the contention of discrimination when there is *other* evidence as well.

Fair Play: Ought We to Discriminate in Reverse?

There are at least three difficulties with reverse discrimination: first, it is inconsistent; second, it licenses discrimination; third, it is unfair.

If we believe the principle that equal opportunity is a right of everyone, then if members of group C are excluded from enjoying certain opportunities merely because they are members of group C, their right is being abrogated. They are entitled to this right, but so is everybody else, even those persons who presently deny it to them. If both are made to enjoy equal opportunity, then both are enjoying their right. To give either oppressors or oppressed more than equal opportunity is equally to deny the rights of one or the other in violation of the principle of equal opportunity.

Proponents of reverse discrimination seem to be caught on the horns of a dilemma: either discrimination is illegitimate or it is not. If it is illegitimate, then it ought not to be practiced against anyone. If it is not, then there exists no reason for *now* favoring blacks, Puerto Ricans, Chicanos, Indians, women, and so forth over whites.

Two strategies present themselves. Either we can analyze one disjunct with a view to showing that distinctions can be made which require compensation or reparations in the form of reverse discrimination to be made to wronged individuals or groups; or we can try to soften one of the disjuncts so as to make a case for exceptions in favor of the wronged. The first appeals both to our reason and our sense of justice. The second appeals to our emotions. I shall argue that neither strategy works.[1]

Now reverse discrimination can take several forms, but I think that what many of its proponents have in mind is a strong form of compensation—a form which requires us to discriminate against non-C members and favor C members even if less qualified. One may well wonder whether there is not a little retribution hidden in this form of compensation.

The "Softened" General Principle

The argument for construing reverse discrimination as compensation or reparation has a great appeal which can be brought out by contrasting it with another approach. One might agree that as a general rule reverse discrimination is illegitimate but that it need not be seen as universally illegitimate. In particular, in the case where people have been so heavily discriminated against as to make it impossible for them now to gain a good life, there is no possibility of their having a fair chance, no possibility of their starting out on anything like equal terms, then and only then is it legitimate to discriminate in their favor and hence against anyone else.

Against this "softened" general principle I shall urge two sorts of objections which I call respectively "practical" and "pragmatic." Against the reparations type of argument, I shall urge first that there is some reason to think the conditions for exacting and accepting them are lacking, and second that, owing to the peculiar nature of the reparations to be exacted (reverse discrimination), the very exaction of them is unreasonable and unfair to both parties—exactors and exactees.

I mention briefly two sorts of practical objections to the "softened" general principle. First, it is simply the case that when discrimination is made in favor of someone regardless of his qualifications, there is the greatest possible danger that the person getting the position will not be competent to fill it. Second, when a person is placed in a position because of discrimination in his favor, he may come to feel himself inferior.[2] This may easily lead to the permanent conferral of inferior status on the group, an inferiority which is all the stronger because it is self-induced. Its psychological effects should not be underestimated.

The pragmatic objection to the "softened" general principle is much stronger. Discrimination in any form is invidious. Once licensed, its licenses rebound upon its perpetrators as well as others. Principles tend to be generalized without consideration of restrictions or the circumstances to which they were intended to apply. Students of the Nazi movement will have noticed that in licensing the discrimination, isolation, persecution, and "final solution" of the Jews, the Nazis (foreign and German) licensed their own. (Hitler's plans for extermination included political groups, for example, the Rohm faction of the SA, as well as other racial groups, for example, Slavs and Balts who fought on the German side.) It is necessary to be quite careful what principles one adopts. In view of the long and bloody history of discrimination, one ought to be very chary of sanctioning it.

Compensations, Reparations, and Restitution

Because it escapes most of these objections, the reparations argument becomes very attractive. What is more obvious than the principle that people ought to be compensated for monetary loss, pain and suffering inflicted by others acting either as agents of government or as individuals? From the negligence suit to reparations for war damage, the principle is comfortable, familiar, and best of all, legal. For victims of broken sidewalks, open wells, ignored stop signs, the conditions under which damages are awarded are quite clear. (1) There is specific injury, specific victim, specific time and place. (2) A specific individual or set of individuals must be found responsible either (a) by actually having done the injury, or (b) by failing to act in such a way (for example, repairing the sidewalk, sealing the well) so as to remove a particular potential source of injury on their property. (3) A reasonable assessment of the monetary value of the claim can be made. In such cases no moral blame is attached to the person forced to pay compensation.

But reparations are somewhat less clear. How much does Germany owe France for causing (losing?) World War I? Can we say that *Germany* caused the war? Germany did pay, at least in part, based upon rough calculations of the cost of the Allied armies, including pensions, the loss of allied GNP, indemnities for death and for the destruction of property. . . .

Inapplicability of These Paradigms

Can reverse discrimination be construed to fit any of these paradigms? Can favoring blacks, Chicanos, Indians, women, and so forth over whites or males be seen as compensation, reparations, or restitution? The answer is no for two general reasons and for several which are specific to the various paradigms. The general reasons are, first, that responsibility for discrimination past and present and for its deleterious consequences is neither clearly assigned nor accepted. Some seem to think that the mere fact of its existence makes all whites (or males in the case of antifeminism) responsible.[3] But I do not know an analysis of responsibility which bears out this claim. Second, there is a great difficulty, if not an impossibility, in assigning a monetary value to the damage done and compensation allegedly owed—that is to say, reverse discrimination.

If we turn to the negligence paradigm, all the conditions seem to fail. *Specific* injury is lacking, *specific* individual responsibility is lacking, and there is no way to assess the monetary value of the "loss." Indeed, in the case of reverse discrimination it is not monetary value which is claimed but preferential treatment. Under the large-scale reparations paradigm two conditions beyond responsibility are lacking. There are no governments or government-like agencies between which the transfer could take place, and there is no *modus agendi* for the transfer to take place.

Where the transfer is to be of preferential treatment, it is unclear how it is even to be begun. So we come to the third paradigm: individual restitution. This is much closer, for it deals with compensating individual victims of persecution. Again, however, it fails to provide a model, first, because reverse discrimination cannot be looked at in monetary terms, and second, even if it could, the restitution is designed to bring a person back to where he was before deprivation. In the case of the minorities in question, there can be no question of restoring them to former positions or property. Precisely, the point of the reparation is to pay them for what they, because of immoral social practices, never had in the first place. . . .

Justice

Finally, if we ignore all that has been said and simply go ahead and discriminate in reverse, calling it reparation, it remains to ask whether it would be either reasonable or just? I think the answer is no. It is possible to hold that in some set of cases, other things being equal, compensation is required and yet to argue either that since other things are not equal compensation is not required, or that even if some compensation is required it ought not to take the form of reverse discrimination. Certainly, from the fact that some form of compensation or reparation must be made it does not follow that any *specific* form of compensation is in order. If X is discriminated against in awarding professorships because he is a member of C group, it scarcely follows that if compensation is in order it *must* take the form of his being discriminated in favor of for another professorship, at least not without adopting the principle of 'an eye for an eye" (and only an *eye* for an eye?). Consider X being turned down for an apartment because he is a C member. Must compensation consist just in his being offered another ahead of anybody else? Even if he has one already? To go from the relatively innocuous principle that where *possible* we ought to compensate for damages, to sanction reverse discrimination as the proper or preferred form of redress, requires us to go beyond mere compensation to some principle very much like "let the punishment mirror the crime." But here the person "punished," the person from which the compensation is exacted, is often not the "criminal." Nor will it help to say that the person deprived of a job or advancement by reverse discrimination is not really being punished or deprived, since the job did not belong to him in the first place. Of course it didn't; nor did it belong to the successful candidate. What belonged to both is equal consideration, and that is what one of them is being deprived of.[4]

There is an element of injustice or unfairness in all reparations. The money derived from taxes paid by all citizens is used for reparations regardless of whether they were responsible for, did nothing about, opposed, or actually fought the policies or government in question. Yet we say that this is the only way it can be done, that the element of unfairness is not great, and that on the whole it is better that this relatively painless way of appropriating money from Jones, who is innocent, be used than that the victims of persecution or crime go uncompensated. But the consequences of reverse discrimination are quite different, especially when it is based upon group membership rather than individual desert. It is possible and is sometimes the case that though most C members are discriminated against, Y is a C member who has met with no discrimination at all. Under the principle that all C members should be discriminated in favor of, we would offer "compensation" to Y. But what are we compensating him *for*? By hypothesis he was no victim of discrimination. Do we compensate him for what happened to others? Do we pay Jones for what we buy from Smith? We seem to be compensating him for being a C member, but why? Do we secretly hold C members inferior? Some claim that society as a whole must bear the burden of reparation. But then reverse discrimination will hardly do the trick. It does not exact redress from the government, or even from all white (responsible?) citizens equally, but falls solely against those who apply for admissions, or jobs *for which blacks or other minorities are applying at the same time.* By the same token, it does not compensate or "reparate" all minority persons equally but merely those applying for admission, jobs, promotions, and so forth. Those whose positions are secure would not be paid. A white person who fought for civil rights for blacks may be passed over for promotion or displaced, a victim of reverse discrimination, while a Ku Klux Klan man at the top of the job ladder pays nothing. This would be a laughably flawed system if it were not seriously advocated by responsible people, and partly implemented by the government. Surely, it violates the principles of both compensatory and distributive justice.

Notes

1. For examples of these strategies, see the article by J. W. Nickel . . . herein.
2. *Contra* this objection see Irving Thalberg, "Justifications of Institutional Racism," *The Philosophical Forum,* Winter 1972.
3. See Thalberg. For an interesting catalogue of "irresponsible use of 'responsibility'" see Robert Stover, "Responsibility for the Cold War—A Case Study in Historical Responsibility," *History and Theory,* 1972. For a clear-cut analysis that more than mere presence on the scene is required to show responsibility, see S. Levinson, "Responsibility for Crimes of War," *Philosophy and Public Affairs,* Spring 1973.
4. See Gertrude Ezorsky, "It's Mine," *Philosophy and Public Affairs,* Spring 1974.

Affirmative Action: An Ethical Evaluation

Bill Shaw

I. Introduction

Affirmative action has been defined as "a public or private program designed to equalize hiring and admissions opportunities for historically disadvantaged groups by taking into consideration those very characteristics which have been used to deny them equal treatment."[1] As comprehensive as this definition may

Bill Shaw, "Affirmative Action: An Ethical Evaluation," *Journal of Business Ethics* (7) (1988) 763–770.

be, it is obvious that, in the employment area, affirmative action plans often encompass more than equalized hiring opportunities. Such programs often seek to increase the number of minorities and women in higher level/higher paying jobs by equalizing their promotion opportunities and protecting them from being laid off under the "last hired, first fired" rule of seniority. In all three of these situations—hiring, promotion and layoff—the effect is to deprive some individual, normally white males, of a "potential benefit, or opportunity, in order to enhance the opportunities of others," i.e., minorities and females.[2]

While one would think that this "redistribution of potentials"[3] would be less controversial than a redistribution of actual wealth, this is simply not the case. Unlike social welfare programs, affirmative action has given rise to rigorous debate.[4] In truth, even the coalition responsible for Civil Rights legislation is in disagreement over how the U.S. should remedy the effects of past discrimination.

Opponents of affirmative action adhere to a policy of strict colorblindness. They believe that all governmental distinctions based on race should be presumed illegal unless the distinctions pass the stringent requirements of "strict scrutiny."[5] Proponents of affirmative action contend that only malign distinctions based on race should be abolished; benign distinctions that favor minorities and women should be allowed. This is because, "in order to get beyond racism, we must first take race into account," and "in order to treat some people equally, we must treat them differently."[6]

Initially, the affirmative action debate was not aided by the Supreme Court's seemingly contradictory rulings.[7] And the controversy intensified when Reagan Administration officials, most notably Attorney General Edwin Meese and Assistant Attorney General for Civil Rights William Bradford Reynolds, voiced their opposition to affirmative action programs. Mr. Reynolds attempted to persuade fifty-one localities to abandon their affirmative action hiring and promotion programs, and announced his intention to ask the Supreme Court to overturn *United States Steelworkers v. Weber*,[8] which authorized companies and unions to adopt voluntary affirmative action programs. Pitted against the Administration's position are various civil rights and women's groups who view affirmative action as an appropriate remedy for redressing past discrimination, and as a way to open the doors for blacks and women to professions which have historically excluded them.

The Supreme Court re-addressed the issue of affirmative action and, in recent major decisions,[9] reaffirmed race- and gender-conscious hiring and promotion preferences in the work-place. These pronouncements signal a rejection of the Reagan Administration's stance on affirmative action. However, despite the Supreme Court's rulings, it is apparent that the controversy over affirmative action continues, and there are strong arguments to be met on both sides. Rather than examining the affirmative action debate from a purely legal viewpoint, this paper will look at it from an ethical perspective. The question this paper will address is, how can affirmative action be ethically justified?

II. The Problem of Discrimination

Affirmative action seeks to remedy the problem of the strong, persistent, and irrational discriminations made by large portions of society.[10] Irrational discrimination is taken to mean the use of such irrelevant characteristics as color or gender to judge an individual's human worth or capability.

In the past, women and minorities have been blatantly excluded from the process of attaining jobs sought by white males, and the effects of this discrimination continue today. For example, because blacks have historically been relegated to lower paying jobs, today's seniority systems, which effectively lock blacks into these jobs, perpetuate past discrimination against the entire group.[11] Affirmative action seeks to remedy the effects of this irrational discrimination by "alter[ing] our environment so as to weaken or extinguish such discriminations, or at least to break up the stratifications."[12]

III. Affirmative Action Mechanisms

There are two mechanisms by which affirmative action programs have been implemented.[13] One applies a fairly rigid formula or quota to determine how many minority group members should be granted a benefit.[14] For example, under the quota system, a given number of minority workers will be hired until the proportion of minority employees reaches the minimum percentage within the overall labor pool. Because a quota system precludes nonminority employees from consideration, this mechanism is viewed as inequitable and has been highly criticized; legally it is permissible only as a last resort effort to remedy egregious discrimination.[15]

Hiring goals, the second mechanism for affirmative action, does not designate positions for minorities only; in contrast to a quota system, a system utilizing hiring goals only requires that employers make every effort to hire minorities, but nonminorities are not barred from competition.[16] Quite understandably, hiring goals are less controversial, and more equitable, than quotas. The mechanism for affirmative action that this paper will be referring to is a hiring goal system.

IV. Ethical Arguments For and Against Affirmative Action[17]

A. Colorblind v. Race-Conscious Plans

As stated earlier, affirmative action seeks to remedy the problem of irrational discriminations. However, as opponents of affirmative action argue, if race/gender is morally irrelevant, it should never be a consideration in hiring, promotions and other job related situations because to prefer one employee over another on this basis cannot be morally justified. The law, they argue, should be "colorblind" and totally neutral.

There are several responses to this argument. First, it is obvious that our culture has never considered race or gender irrelevant to employment decisions. A cursory reading of American history bears out this contention.[18] Thus opponents of affirmative action, by stripping the historical context from our employment practices with the demand for race- and gender-blind laws, favor a policy that will tolerate the effects of past discrimination for years to come. To suggest otherwise is simply to ignore a social reality.[19]

Second, if the social order which subjected groups on the basis of race or sex was unjust, why is it unjust to redefine that social order to fashion group remedies for group injuries? "To ignore the fact that a person is [black] would be to ignore the fact that there had been a social practice in which unjust actions were directed toward [black] persons as such."[20] It is obvious that our earlier social practices worked to the benefit of white males who attained and maintain an unfair advantage of the expense of blacks and women. To disregard collective injury, then, would be "morally speaking . . . the most hideous aspect of the injustices of human history: those carried out systematically and directed toward whole groups of men and women as groups."[21]

Third, in examining the historical income distribution in the United States, it becomes apparent that the disparity between races cannot be correlated to such morally relevant characteristics as "rights, deserts, merits, contributions and needs of recipients."[22] Under a distributive justice theory of affirmative action, group members are entitled to preferential treatment, not because society is admitting and paying for past errors, but because those persons deserve a greater "shot" at the limited resources available simply in virtue of being members of the human community.[23] Distributive theories require no admission of social or collective guilt; they merely require the acknowledgement that, from this time forward, society's resources be distributed on the basis of morally relevant factors.

Given this concept of justice, considering an applicant's race as part of the bundle of traits that constitute "merit" is entirely consistent with the understanding of merit as a unique combination of factors that best meets society's needs.[24] This understanding is buttressed by the observation that getting ahead in American society has often turned on quite obviously nonmeritocratic factors.[25]

Where does it end, and when? It ends when the proportion of women and minorities in unskilled positions approximates that of the population generally, and when their proportion in the ranks of skilled and professional positions approximates their appearance in the pool of qualified applicants. Affirmative action is not committed to maintain those targets. Once they are reached, it becomes a matter of personal choice for group members to decide whether they will seek these positions. If they do not, that is an issue that can be addressed (or not addressed) when it arises, and on a basis that will have no necessary connection with the reasons here advanced in support of affirmative action.

B. Individual v. Group Protection

If affirmative action is supposed to remedy the effects of past discrimination, opponents of such programs often ask, what of the fact that many of the victims of discrimination are dead? Further, are not many nonvictims receiving underserved compensation for injuries they never experienced?

First, it is apparent that historical injuries cannot be separated from the present effects of history.[26] The classic example involves seniority systems: in the past, black employees were relegated to the lowest paying positions in a company with no chance of elevating themselves. The higher paying jobs were restricted to "whites only." After civil rights legislation prohibited such segregation in the work place, blacks were allowed to compete for and attain higher level positions. However, when it came to receiving employment benefits and avoiding layoffs, black employees suffered by virtue of past segregation. Due to their lack of seniority, black employees were denied employment benefits and fell victim to the "last hired, first fired rule of seniority."[27] Then, as the "badges of slavery" continue, it becomes irrelevant whether affirmative action redresses past discrimination or the present effects of past discrimination.[28]

Second, it is also apparent that racial discrimination is "all encompassing." An examination of early American attitudes toward blacks documents the fact that race discrimination is directed not at individuals, but blacks as a group.[29] By way of illustration, note the language from *Scott v. Sandford*[30] referring to negroes as a "race fit for slavery." Further, Jim Crow laws stamped all blacks as the inferior race. The all encompassing nature of discrimination was further documented by the Supreme Court in *Brown v. Board of Education.*[31] Thus, it is almost inconceivable that individual group members did not suffer humiliation and injury.[32]

Next, the argument that affirmative action frequently aids those who need it least ignores the extent affirmative action has opened up opportunities for blue collar workers.[33] It also assumes that affirmative action should be provided only to the most deprived strata of the black community, or those who can best document their victimization. To the contrary, however, affirmative action operates at its most effective level in assisting the efforts of those with threshold ability to integrate the trades and professions. After all, if it cannot be utilized to assist those on the verge of breaking through, i.e., those who will serve as role models for the remainder of the community, this may mean that additional social intervention to address unmet needs may be required for those left untouched by affirmative action.[34]

Finally, even if some individual group members managed to escape injury, affirmative action can be justified on the ground of administrative convenience.[35] The correlation between race or sex and relative inequality of opportunity is sufficiently high that it justifies use of such traits for the efficient administration of this policy.[36]

C. Unfair Burden on Present Generation of White Workers

Opponents of affirmative action also argue that, even if blacks and women deserve compensation, it is unfair to extract that compensation through the imposition of harm on innocent white males. Or, to phrase the issue in terms of utility rather than fairness, affirmative action causes unqualified persons to be placed in jobs that would otherwise be held by those of greater skills and abilities, and this is socially harmful because our resources are not producing "the greatest good for the greatest number."

In addressing both the unfairness and inefficiency claims of affirmative action opponents, note first that whatever injury white males incur does not give rise to a constitutional claim because the damage "does not derive from a scheme animated by racial prejudice."[37] The lessened opportunity that white males face is simply an incidental consequence of addressing a compelling societal need. If white males are deprived of anything, it is the expectation of unearned position. Only because they stand to gain so much from past discrimination do they stand to lose from affirmative action. But white males are not excluded on the basis of racial prejudice, they are excluded "because of a rational calculation about the socially most beneficial use of limited resources. . . ."[38]

This paper does not undertake an analysis of the constitutionality of affirmative action plans, but recent observations of the Supreme Court in this context are supportive of a fairness evaluation. Justice Brennan, writing for the Court in *U.S. v. Paradise*,[39] related that governmental bodies, including courts, "may constitutionally employ racial classifications essential to remedy unlawful treatment of racial . . . groups subject to discrimination."[40] The following criteria will be employed to assess the constitutionality of racial classifications:

(1) The necessity for relief and the efficacy of alternative remedies,
(2) The flexibility and duration of relief including the availability of waiver provisions to be utilized in the event there are no qualified minority candidates,
(3) The relationship of the numerical goals to the relevant labor market,
(4) The impact of the relief on non-minority applicants.[41]

With regard to the issue of burdening white males who did not discriminate, it should be noted that, while these individuals may not have discriminated, they have received the benefits of a society that has discriminated and has supplied them better education and better economic conditions. Under these circumstances, a white male, aware of the discrimination against women and blacks, who insisted on being hired, would essentially endorse and condone prior discrimination. Even if a white male was ignorant of past discrimination against women and minorities, given our historical record, the assumption should be that these groups were discriminated against.

One way of analyzing the situation is by way of a hypothetical. Imagine two runners at the starting line. If one runner is somehow weighted-down but the other runner is not, it is obvious that, once the race begins, the first runner is at a severe disadvantage. Even if that runner is released halfway through the race, he or she is still far behind. In order to equalize the first runner's position with that of the second, the second needs to be handicapped in some way. The opportunity to catch up and to become competitive is only fair under the circumstances.

However, even upon applying this reasoning in support of affirmative action, opponents may argue that it results in the advancement of incompetent workers. This argument can be addressed by setting up certain minimum standards of competence that every applicant must meet, i.e., applicants must demonstrate some basic degree of proficiency in order to qualify for the labor pool.[42] Affirmative action does not require employers to hire unqualified individuals, nor does it require the discharge of white employees, i.e., white employees do not lose their entitlements.[43]

It should be noted that by opening up opportunities for women and minorities, affirmative action broadens the talent base of business and leads to a recognition of the potential of these groups. A utilitarian argument would demonstrate that a refusal to employ these talents to their best use is "wasteful," and further that affirmative action would benefit the general welfare by (1) promoting minority role models, and (2) improve services for minority communities. For example, blacks who become doctors and lawyers are more likely to meet minority needs than white doctors and lawyers.[44]

> Suppose for example that there is a need for a great increase in the number of black doctors, because the health needs of the black community are unlikely to be met otherwise. And suppose that at the present average level of premedical qualifications among black applicants, it would require a huge expansion of total medical school enrollment to supply the desirable absolute number of black doctors without adopting differential admissions standards. Such an expansion may be unacceptable either because of its cost or because it would produce a total supply of doctors, black and white, much greater than the society requires. This is a strong argument for accepting reverse discrimination, not on grounds of justice but on grounds of social utility. (In addition, there is the salutary effect on the aspirations and expectation of other blacks, from the visibility of exemplars in formerly inaccessible positions.)[45]

Further, the virtual absence of black policemen helped spark the ghetto rebellions of the 1960s. However, after the police force became integrated through strong affirmative action, relations between the minority communities and the police improved.[46]

D. Preference Cheapens Real Achievement of Women and Minorities

Finally, there is always the argument that affirmative action stigmatizes the preferred group and causes others to denigrate their achievements. Although affirmative action probably causes some white to denigrate black achievements, it is unrealistic to argue that these programs cause most white disparagement of black abilities. Such disparagement was around long before affirmative action.[47] Given this inevitable resistance, one must be wary of the fear of backlash to limit necessary reforms. Further, it is apparent that affirmative action can help combat disparagement of these achievements by breaking down stereotypes and changing people's attitudes. Thus, the uncertain extent to which affirmative action diminishes the accomplishments of women and minorities in the eyes of some people must be balanced against the stigmatization that occurs when they are virtually absent from important societal institutions.

Opponents of affirmative action argue that such programs sap the internal morale of blacks, i.e., their not truly earned positions cause them to lower their expectations of themselves. Again, although this might be true in some cases, it is incorrect to say that affirmative action undermines the morale of the black community. Most black beneficiaries view affirmative action programs as "rather modest compensation" for the many years of racial subordination; for them, affirmative action is a form of social justice.[48]

It is also apparent that many blacks view claims of meritocracy, as it applies to attaining employment, dubiously. The over-exclusion of blacks from public and private educational and employment institutions is an indictment of the concept of meritocracy. It is clear that many non-objective, non-meritocratic factors influence the distribution of opportunity. Most people realize the thoroughly political nature of merit, i.e., that it is a malleable concept determined by the perceived needs of society.[49]

Lastly, most blacks and women are aware that, in the absence of affirmative action, they would not receive equal consideration with white males. Racism and sexism continue, and the "rules" are not impartial. For example, many women are socialized to seek marriage and motherhood from birth. Additionally, as human beings identify most easily with members of the own race and sex, a white male employer may be unable to judge a black or female applicant objectively. Affirmative action forces employers to consider the qualifications and potentialities of these individuals.

V. Conclusion

This paper has examined four major arguments advanced by opponents of affirmative action and attempted to rebut them on the basis of moral considerations. It is clear that the problem of past racial/gender discrimination has not disappeared; its effects linger, resulting in a wide disparity in opportunities and attainments between blacks/women and white males. Affirmative action, although not the "perfect solution," is by far the most viable method of redressing the effects of past discrimination. Thus it cannot be dismissed lightly by way of arguing for mere colorblindness.

Notes

1. Duncan, "The Future of Affirmative Action: A Jurisprudential/legal Critique," 17 HARV.CR.—C.L. L. REV. 503 (1982).
2. Barton, "Affirmative Action: Making Decisions," 83 W. VA. L. REV. 47 (1980).
3. *Id.*
4. *Id.* at 60–61. As Barton notes, social welfare programs guarantee that, henceforth, no person shall suffer the consequences of any discrimination based on race, color, sex, age, ethnicity, or creed. Social welfare programs do not seek to correct existing inequities or to prevent the making of discrimination. Affirmative action, on the other hand, seeks to compensate for past harm by redistributing certain opportunities. Affirmative action seeks to prevent the effects and the making of unjust discrimination by, inter alia, changing the way people think.
5. Kennedy, "Persuasion and Distrust: A Comment on the Affirmative Action Debate," 99 HARV. L. REV. 1327, 1334 (1986).
6. Regents of the University of California v. Bakke, 438 U.S. 265, 407 (1978) (Blackmun, J., plurality opinion).
7. Cf. United Steelworkers v. Weber, 443 U.S. 193 (1979) (5–2) holding that Title VII does not prohibit all private, voluntary race conscious affirmative action plans, and Fullilove v. Klutznick, 448 U.S. 448 (1980) (6–3), approving a 10% set aside for minority contractors under federal law, with Regents of University of California v. Bakke, 438 U.S. 265, 407 (1978) (5–4), holding that the admissions program of the University of California (Davis) which set aside 16 class positions for minority students to be unlawful, and Memphis Firefighters Local #1784 v. Stotts, 467 U.S. 561 (1984) (6–3), holding that the Civil Rights Act bars a federal judge from ordering that recently hired blacks can keep their jobs while whites with more seniority were being laid off except on evidence that the blacks were actual victims of illegal discrimination.
8. Robinson, "A Record of Hostility" 71 ABAJ 39, 40 (Oct. 1985); "Justice Official Terms Court's Ruling a Disappointment and Unfortunate," *NEW YORK TIMES,* Thurs. July 3, 1986, page 13, col. 3.
9. Local 93, International Association of Firefighters v. City of Cleveland, 106 S. Ct. 3063 (1986) (6–3), held that lower federal courts have broad discretion to approve consent decrees in which employers, over the objections of white employees, settle discrimination suits by agreeing to preferential hiring or promotion of minority group members. The Court upheld a decree where Cleveland agreed to settle a job discrimination suit by temporarily promoting black and Hispanic workers ahead of whites who had more seniority and higher test scores. In Local 28, Sheet Metal Workers v. EEOC, 106 S. Ct. 3019 (1986) (5–4), the Court approved a lower court order requiring NYC sheet metal workers union to meet a 20% minority membership goal by 1987. The Court also held, 6–3, that judges may order racial preferences in union membership and other contexts if necessary to rectify especially "egregious" discrimination. During its next session, the court held, in U.S. v. Paradise, 107 S. Ct. 1053 (1987) (5–4), that because of the Alabama State Police's long history of egregious discrimination coupled with a strong federal interest in supporting prior judicial decrees, the enforcement of numerical quotas (one black promotion for every white), for as long as the upper ranks of the department had a smaller percentage of blacks than the lower ranks, was appropriate. In a companion case involving gender-based discrimination, Johnson v. Santa Clara County Transportation Agency, 55 U.S.L. W. 4379 (daily ed., Mar. 25, 1987), the court upheld a voluntary affirmative action plan that promoted a female instead of a male, though both were qualified for the job. The plan was based on a comparison of the county's work force with the

level of women and minorities qualified for higher level positions rather than general population statistics.

10. Barton, *supra* n. 2 at 50.

11. E.g., Local 189 United Papermakers and Paperworkers v. United States, 416 F.2d 980 (5th Cir. 1969); Teamsters v. United States, 431 U.S. 324 (1977) (relying on §703(h) of Title VII, 42 U.S.C. §2000e–2(h), the Court held that absent their having been entered into and maintained with a discriminatory purpose, such systems, regardless of their impact, do not violate Title VII. Individual claimants may, however, obtain relief in the form of back pay or retroactive seniority.)

12. Barton, *supra* no. 2 at 51. In Barton's view, there are 4 ways society can respond to discrimination: (1) institutionalize it via legislation, (2) ignore it, (3) articulate principles prohibiting people from acting on their discrimination, yet take no affirmative steps to extinguish discrimination, (4) adopt affirmative measures to end existing stratification and extinguish the discrimination which strengthened the stratification. *Id.* at 49, n. 6.

13. Specific methods often suggested to remedy the effects of historical discrimination in the workplace include: (1) retroactive seniority, (2) front pay (3) inverse seniority, (4) work sharing, (5) plantwide seniority, (6) governmental intervention. This paper will not examine specific mechanisms in implementing affirmative action, but will concentrate on the broader concepts of quotas and goals.

14. Duncan, *supra* n. 1 at 507–508.

15. *Id.* at 508; Local 28, Sheet Metal Workers v. EEOC, 106 S. Ct. 3019 (1986); U.S. v. Paradise, 107 S. Ct. 1053 (1987).

16. Duncan, *supra* n. 1 at 508.

17. Throughout this paper the following ethical concepts will be advanced to evaluate the worth of targets or goals as they are required by affirmative action programs: compensatory and distributive justice, and utility or utilitarianism. See Nickel, Preferential Policies in Hiring and Admissions: Jurisprudential Approach, 75 COLUM. L. REV. 534 (1975). Although these three theories will be referred to throughout this paper, the format is designed to set out the ethical arguments levelled at affirmative action, and to rebut them.

18. M. Wasserstrom, *Philosophy and Social Issues* (1980), p. 14.

19. *Id.* at 12.

20. Taylor, "Reverse Discrimination and Compensatory Justice" *Analysis* **33** (1973), p. 179.

21. *Id.* at 181–182.

22. R. K. Greenawalt, Discrimination and Reverse Discrimination—Essay and Materials in Philosophy and Law (1979), pp. 65–67. Statistics do not conclusively establish distributive injustice however, because careers are a function of individual priorities. Greenawalt, Judicial Scrutiny of "Benign" Racial Preferences in Law School Admissions, 75 COLUM L. REV. 559, 589 n. 129 (1975).

23. This is the distributive justice theory of affirmative action. It looks to the future, not to the past as compensatory justice does. Benefits and burdens are distributed in accordance with such relevant considerations as the rights, merits, contributions, needs and deserts of recipients. Nickel, *supra* n. 17 at 539. Duncan, *supra* n. 1 at 521.

24. For the most part, with regard to hiring or admission policy, the institution will develop a benchmark/minimally qualified score consisting of aptitude test, admission score, grade point average, interview (subjective evaluation) and the like. If sex or race will enable a person to do a job better in the judgment of the hiring authority/admission committee, i.e., bring better medical care to the black community or break down the stereotypic image of women in the construction industry, then race or sex may well qualify as a meritocratic quality. The fact that race or sex may be a socially useful trait in particular circumstances should not be confused "with the very different and despicable idea that one race [or sex] may be inherently more worthy than another." Dworkin, The Rights of Alan Bakke, *The New York Review of Books* (1977), in J. DesJardins and J. McCall, *Contemporary Issues in Business Ethics* (1985), pp. 407, 411.

25. After all, "Would anyone claim that Henry Ford II was head of the Ford Motor Company because he was the most qualified person for the job?" Wasserstrom, Rascism, Sexism,

and Preferential Treatment: An Approach to the Topics, 24 U.C.L.A. L. REV. 581, 619 (1977).

26. Duncan, *supra* n. 1 at 510. Present day discrimination in hiring is a "but for" result of historical practices. It contributes to housing patterns which in turn result in *de facto* school segregation. U.S. Commission on Civil Rights, Affirmative Action in the 1980's: Dismantling the Process of Discrimination 11 (1981).

27. Teamsters v. United States, 431 U.S. 324 (1977); Firefighters Local Union No. 1784 v. Stotts, 467 U.S. 561 (1984); Wygant v. Jackson Board of Education, 106 S. Ct. 1842 (1986).

28. See City of Memphis v. Greene, 101 S. Ct. 1584, 1610–13 (1981) (Marshall, J., dissenting); Sullivan v. Little Hunting Park, 396 U.S. 229 (1969); Jones v. Alfred H. Mayer Co., 391 U.S. 409 (1968).

29. Duncan, *supra* n. 1 at 516.

30. 60 U.S. 393, 407 (1856).

31. 347 U.S. 483 (1954).

32. Even on the argument that some blacks have overcome losses and humiliation through their own efforts and are not deserving of compensation, affirmative action can still be justified on a group basis for reasons of administrative convenience. Nickel, Discrimination and Morally Relevant Characteristics, *Analysis* **32** (1972), pp. 113, 114; Dworkin, *supra* n. 24 at 411.

33. See, e.g., Firefighters Local Union No. 1784 v. Stotts, 467 U.S. 561 (1984) (affirmative action for firefighters); United Steelworkers v. Weber, 443 U.S. 193 (1979) (affirmative action for craft workers).

34. Kennedy, *supra* n. 5 at 1333.

35. Nickel, *supra* n. 17 at 538.

36. Although 11.2% of the U.S. population is black, blacks (and other minorities) comprise only 4.2% of the legal professional and account for only 5.9% of engineers. Only 5.2% of the nation's managers and administrators and 5.1% of its sales workers are nonwhite. 27.5% of cleaning workers, 25.3% of taxi drivers and chauffeurs, and 43.1% of garbage collectors are black. Similarly, 99.1% of secretaries and 80.1% of clerical workers in general are women. Domestic cleaners and servants are 96.9% women, 53.4% black. Statistical Abstract of the U.S. (1981) at 402–404.

37. Kennedy, *supra* n. 5 at 1336.

38. R. Dworkin, *A Matter of Principle* (1985), p. 301.

39. 107 S. Ct. 1053 (1987).

40. *Id*. at 1065.

41. *Id*. This framework is similar, though not identical, to that applicable to private sector, voluntary affirmative action plans such as the one approved in United Steelworkers v. Weber, 443 U.S. 193 (1979).

42. *Supra* n. 9.

43. Wygant v. Jackson Board of Education, 106 S. Ct. 1842 (1986).

44. Nickel, *supra* n. 17 at 545.

45. Nagel, "Equal Treatment and Compensatory Discrimination," *Philosophy and Public Affairs* **2** (1973), p. 348.

46. Kennedy, *supra* n. 5 at 1329.

47. *Id*. at 1331–1332.

48. *Id*.

49. *Supra* n. 24.

College of Business,
University of Texas,
Austin, TX 78712-1175,
U.S.A.

Justice in Preferential Hiring

M. S. Singer and A. E. Singer

The issue of preferential hiring or reverse discrimination in selection has received considerable attention in both the ethics and psychology literatures. In the literature of ethics, theoretical analyses of the rights and wrongs of preferential hiring have been well documented. Three major justifications have been put forward. First, preferential hiring obeys the compensatory justice principles and is a form of compensation to the minorities for past discriminations they have suffered (e.g., Broxhill, 1972; Minas, 1977; Taylor, 1973; Thomson, 1973). Second, preferential hiring is a means to promote social welfare and to achieve distributive justice in future employment opportunities (e.g., Fiss, 1976; Nagel, 1973; Sher, 1975). Third, preferential hiring avoids wastage of minority abilities and helps to broaden the talent pool of organisations (Shaw, 1988). It also benefits the general welfare by improving social services for minority communities (e.g., Kennedy, 1986; Nagel, 1973; Nickel, 1975). Opponents have, however, argued against the program on four grounds. First, selection should be based on job-relevant merits or qualifications, rather than on irrelevant factors such as sex or ethnic origin (e.g., Garrett and Klonoski, 1986). Merit-based selections result in greater efficiency in terms of the utility of human resources in organisations (e.g., Black, 1974; Schmitt & Noe, 1986). Second, compensation for past ills should not be required of all members of majority groups, nor should reparation go to all members of minority groups. The principles of compensatory justice requires that reparation be paid only to those injured by the very ones who inflict the injuries (e.g., Goldman, 1975; Karst & Horowitz, 1974; Nickel, 1974). Third, preferential hiring itself violates the principle of equality by discriminating against white males (e.g., Cohen, 1975; Newton, 1973). Fourth, preferential hiring may have unintentional adverse effects on minority members in that it implies minorities are inferior, hence are in need of help (e.g., Goldman, 1976), and that it causes people to denigrate real achievements of minorities (e.g., Shaw, 1988).

The psychological literature of preferential hiring provides empirical data on two key issues; the utility of preferential hiring in terms of organizational productivity, and the social psychological consequences of the program. Several studies (e.g., Cronback *et al.*, 1980; Schmitt *et al.*, 1984; Schmitt & Noe, 1986) have applied utility analyses to estimate, in dollar terms, net gains or losses associated with preferential hiring. The general conclusion was that utilities associated with the goal of optimizing organizational productivity and

M. S. Singer and A. E. Singer, "Justice in Preferential Hiring," *Journal of Business Ethics* **10** 1991, 797–803.

the goal of preferential hiring were almost certain to be in conflict with each other (e.g., Gross and Su, 1975; Schmitt, 1989).

Several studies have demonstrated that preferential hiring may have adverse social and psychological consequences. Jacobson and Koch (1977) examined the effect of selection method of leaders on leader performance evaluation. It was found that sex-based preferential hiring had negative impact on subordinates' judgment of leader performance. In a correlational analysis, Chacko (1982) reported that women managers' organizational commitment, job satisfaction and role stress were adversely associated with their beliefs that their own selections were sex-based rather than merit-based. Heilman and Herlihy (1984) found that women's jobs were devalued when others thought that their selections were based on preferential treatment. In a laboratory study concerning leadership, Heilman *et al.* (1987) found that sex-based selection had negative effects on woman leaders' self-perceptions and self-evaluations of leadership performance. These studies are convergent in demonstrating that preferential hiring may harm the very people it was intended to benefit (Sowell, 1978).

One empirical question which is perhaps of central significance in the debate over the justice of preferential hiring (and has received no attention to our knowledge) concerns the perceived fairness of the program. Rawls (1971) has considered justice in terms of fairness. Recent organizational justice theories (see Greenberg, 1987, for a review) have also operationalised "justice" as "perceived fairness." In the following sections, we report two studies designed to examine the perceived fairness of preferential hiring.

Study 1

Design of Study 1

A 22-item survey questionnaire was designed for the study. Each item represented a hypothetical case of selecting between two finalist candidates for a training course. Respondents were told that selection decisions were made by a training director and that the decisions were primarily based on candidates' scores on a general trainability test which was a required test for all candidates. Respondents were further told that the training director was extremely concerned with the fact that so far few candidates from minority groups (as defined by sex and ethnic origins) have been selected for the training course. Because minority members would benefit greatly from this course, the training director took into account candidates' minority membership status in the selection decisions. For each item, the trainability scores of the two finalist candidates (*A* and *B*), together with the training director's decision (of selecting *A* or *B*) were given. Respondents were also told that candidate *A* belongs to a majority group and candidate *B* belongs to a minority group (see the samples of respondents for further specifications). Respondents were then required to rate the fairness of each decision on a 7-point scale with "1" labelled as "extremely fair." "4" as "not fair nor unfair" and "7" as "extremely unfair." The independent variable was the score discrepancy between candidate A and B. Five discrepancy scores (4, 8, 12, 16, 20) were used to represent the differences in candidate A and B's trainability scores.

In this design, "preferential selection" was represented by the five items depicting the selection of candidate B (a minority member) who had a *lower* trainability score than candidate A (a majority member).

Selection decisions representing conventional discrimination were depicted by the five items stating that candidate B (minority) had a *higher* score but that candidate A (majority) was selected. Two other items in the questionnaire represented the two cases (select A and select B) with both candidates having the same trainability score. The remaining 10 items represented cases of merit-based selections whereby the higher scoring candidate was selected.

Subjects of Study 1

Two independent samples of respondents were given this questionnaire with different instructions concerning the minority membership status of the candidates. Sample 1 was used to gather data on respondents' fairness perceptions of "ethnicity-based" selection. The respondents were 108 (39 males and 69 females) Europeans. All respondents were undergraduate psychology students with a mean age of 20 years and 6 months. All respondents were told that candidate A was a European and that candidate B was member of an ethnic-minority group. Sample 2 was used to collect data on male vs. female respondents' fairness perceptions of "sex-based" selection. The respondents were a different group of 44 male and 70 female undergraduate psychology students with a mean age of 20 years and 11 months. They were instructed that candidate A was a male and candidate B was a female.

Results of Study 1

The mean fairness ratings for both samples are presented in Table I. All the mean ratings, except for those that have "0" discrepancy scores, were significantly lower than a null mean of "4" which represented the neutral point (neither fair nor unfair) on the 7-point scale. This indicates that, similar to conventional discrimination, preferential hiring based on either sex or ethnicity was perceived as unfair.

To test for the effects of respondents' sex, discrepancy scores and the type of discrimination, a 2 (respondent sex) × 6 (score discrepancy: 0, 4, 8, 12, 16 and 20) × 2 (preferential selection vs. conventional discrimination) Analysis of Variance with repeated measures on the last two factors was carried out on fairness ratings. For ethnicity-based selections, the only significant result concerned the main effect for score discrepancy: $F(5, 530)$ 8.69, $p < 0.01$. None of the other effects was found significant. The ANOVA results for sex-based selection were similar to this. The only significant effect

Table I.   Mean Ratings for Ethnicity-Based and Sex-Based Preferential Selection

Score Discrepancy	Preferential Selection (Select B When Score A > Score B)	Conventional Discrimination (Select A When Score B > Score A)
Ethnicity-Based Preferential Selection (N = 108)		
0	3.81 (0.92)	3.81 (0.87)
4	3.21 (1.22)	2.55 (1.16)
8	2.54 (1.09)	2.49 (1.00)
12	2.48 (1.41)	2.17 (1.32)
16	2.03 (1.20)	2.12 (1.22)
20	1.66 (1.26)	1.73 (1.33)

Score Discrepancy	Males (N = 44)	Females (N = 70)	Males (N = 44)	Females (N = 70)
Sex-Based Preferential Selection (N = 114)				
0	3.90 (1.11)	4.05 (1.30)	3.70 (1.03)	3.73 (1.16)
4	3.00 (1.16)	3.13 (1.20)	2.58 (0.92)	2.61 (1.10)
8	2.54 (0.97)	2.64 (1.02)	2.41 (0.88)	2.49 (0.94)
12	2.24 (1.25)	2.22 (1.21)	1.93 (1.00)	1.96 (0.99)
16	1.80 (0.86)	1.85 (1.20)	1.97 (1.01)	1.99 (1.11)
20	1.46 (0.69)	1.48 (1.25)	1.48 (1.15)	1.51 (0.92)

SDs in parentheses

was the main effect for score discrepancy: $F(5, 560)$ 9.80. $p < 0.01$. None of the other effects was significant.

These results indicate first, preferential selection was perceived as unfair, irrespective of whether it was based on candidate's sex or ethnic origin; and second, the degree of perceived unfairness was associated with the score discrepancy between the two hypothetical candidates, the less qualified the minority candidate, the more the selection was seen as unfair.

One limitation of study 1 concerned the use of a within-subjects design. The two sets of findings might be in part due to subjects making direct comparisons among the outcomes of the 22 hypothetical cases. In study 2, a between-subjects design was used in which subjects were required to evaluate the fairness of only one case of preferential selection. The purpose was to cross validate the findings of study 1 in an experimental context which calls for absolute rather than relative judgements.

In addition, study 2 also aimed to ascertain whether the provision of *explanatory justifications* for preferential selection would have an effect on fairness perceptions. Bies (1987a) has recently argued that perceptions of justice are the product of "a process of argumentation or persuasion" (p. 304). Perceptions of justice or injustice of an outcome are influenced more by the provision of a social account for the outcome, rather than solely by the favorability of the final outcome. Bies further argued that perceptions of injustice associated with unfavorable outcomes are primarily due to the inadequacy or absence of justifications; when adequate justifications are provided, feelings of injustice would be significantly reduced. Empirical findings are in general supportive of this claim (Bies, 1987a; 1987b; Bies and Shapiro, 1988).

Two types of justifications for preferential selection are used in study 2: "ethical" or "legislative" justification. As reviewed previously, proponents of preferential selection have provided three major reasons (i.e., to correct past ills, to promote fair employment distributions, and to utilize minority talents). These are based on moral reasoning and hence can be used as an "ethical" justification for preferential selection. As an alternative, recruiting organizations could provide a "legislative" justification claiming legislation policies as the reason for their implementing the preferential program. According to Bies (1987a), it was expected that either justification would reduce the perceived injustice observed in study 1 when no justification was provided.

Study 2

Design of Study 2

A 3 (type of justification: none, ethical, legislation) × 4 (score discrepancy: 2, 4, 7, 10) factorial design was used. Both factors were between-subjects factors. A hypothetical case of selection was designed for this study:

> This case concerns the recruiting practice of a large computer consultancy firm. The firm advertised a position for a computer programmer. All applicants were required to sit for the Computer Programmer Aptitude Test (CPAT) which was specially designed by personnel selection experts for the firm. Previous research has shown that the test is a valid predictor of later job performance. The top 10 scorers on the CPAT were then interviewed by the personnel department. Here are the names of the 10 final candidates, together with their CPAT scores (out of 100):
>
> > John H. (95), Fu–Tuk S. (90), Bruce N. (86), Jerry T. (81), Alan B. (75), Chie-Min R. (72), Don T. (67), Rob A. (61), Paul P. (56), and Sandy D. (50).
>
> All candidates were between 21 and 23 years of age. All had a B.Sc. degree and a similar academic record. All candidates had some previous working experience, but none of them had worked as a computer programmer or in a related job.
>
> The position was offered to Fu-Tuk S.

The independent variable of "score discrepancy" was manipulated by placing the successful candidate, Fu-Tak S., at 2nd (CPAT score=90), 4th (81),

7th (67) or the 10th (50) place in the list. For the condition of "4th-place," the list of the 10 final candidates remained the same except for Jerry T. filling in the 2nd place. For the conditions of "7th- and "10th-places," the name Chie-Min R. was excluded from the list and the name Simon R. filled in the 10th and 9th places for the two conditions respectively. The aim was to keep Fu-Tak S. as the highest scoring minority candidate.

Subjects receiving ethical justifications were also given this information:

> In justifying the decision, the personnel department wrote in the letter to all rejected candidates, that the firm has been concerned with the very small number of ethnic-minority members currently working as computer programmers. Because historically ethnic-minority members have been disadvantaged, the firm is interested in correcting such past ills. The firm is also committed to promote a fair distribution of employment opportunities as well as to broaden the overall talent pool by actively seeking qualified minority employees. The decision to appoint Fu-Tuk S. was primarily due to the fact that he was the highest scoring ethnic minority candidate.

Subjects receiving legislation justifications were given this information:

> In justifying the decision, the personnel department wrote in the letter to all rejected candidates, that in recent years there has been an increasing number of graduates of ethnic minority origins, who majored in computer programming or related fields. Equal employment legislation stipulates that ethnic minority candidates be given equal employment opportunities without discrimination. The firm therefore feels obliged to actively seek qualified minority programmers to join its staff. The decision to offer the position to Fu-Tuk S. was primarily due to the fact that he was the highest scoring ethnic minority candidate.

Respondents were then required to go through 11 items evaluating the case. Among these, three items assessed "outcome fairness" of the decision: "In your view, how fair was the selection outcome?," "In your view, how would most of the unsuccessful job candidates judge the fairness of the decision?," and "In your view, how would most people judge the fairness of the decision?"

Subjects made their responses on an 10-point rating scale with "1" labelled as "extremely unfair" and "10" as "extremely fair."

Subjects and Procedure of Study 2

The subject sample consisted of 216 (155 male and 61 female) undergraduate students at the universities of Western Australia, Curtin and Murdoch in Western Australia. All subjects were of European origin. The age range was between 17 and 34 years old. Of the 216 respondents, 135 completed the questionnaire in a first year commerce lecture at the University of Western Australia. The remaining respondents were undergraduate students recruited from the libraries and campus cafes in the three universities.

Results of Study 2

For each subject, a score of outcome fairness was calculated by averaging the ratings on the three items assessing the variable. The cell means for each of the 12 treatment conditions are presented in Table II. A 3×4 (justification $\times$ score discrepancy) ANOVA was performed. Justification had a significant main effect on fairness ratings: $F(2, 199)=5.66$, $p < 0.01$. The cell means were 4.42 (no justification), 3.96 (ethical justification) and 3.43 (legislative justification). This indicates that when no justification was given, the decision was considered as the most fair; when legislation was given as justification the same decision was considered as the least fair.

Score discrepancy also had a significant main effect on fairness ratings: $F(3, 199)=11.19$, $p < 0.01$. The cell means were 4.43, 4.79, 3.42 and 3.07 for the score discrepancy conditions of 2, 4, 7 and 10, respectively. To test whether European respondents would perceive ethnic-based selection as unfair, these means were compared to the null mean of 5 (the neutral point on the 11-point rating scale). All four means were significantly lower than 5 at $p < 0.05$; $t(53)= -2.79, -2.03, -3.64$ and -4.11 respectively. This suggests that all four selection decisions were considered as unfair by the European respondent sampled.

The justification $\times$ score discrepancy interaction effect was not significant: $F(6, 199)=1.64$.

Discussion

The two studies using different methodology have provided convergent evidence that preferential selection was perceived as unfair, regardless of whether it was based on the candidate's sex or ethnic origin. The level of perceived injustice was directly related to the discrepancy in merits between the two candidates. The less "qualified" the minority candidate as compared with the majority candidate, the more the selection was perceived as unfair.

The results further showed that the provision of either an ethical or a legislative justification, rather than reducing the perceived injustice as expected,

Table II.   Mean Fairness Ratings: Study 2

Score Discrepancy	None (N = 72)	Justification Ethical (N = 72)	Legislative (N = 72)
2	5.26 (1.99)	4.48 (1.62)	3.56 (1.68)
4	4.89 (1.92)	5.30 (2.52)	4.19 (1.72)
7	3.55 (1.07)	3.06 (1.91)	3.65 (1.85)
10	3.98 (1.36)	2.98 (1.56)	2.32 (1.35)

SDs in parentheses

exacerbated feelings of injustice due to preferential selection. This finding appeared inconsistent with several earlier studies showing a significant reduction in perceptions of injustice when a justification was provided for the unfavorable outcome (e.g., Bies, 1987b; Bies & Shapiro, 1988). Two interpretations are plausible: First, in previous studies observing a justification effect in reducing felt injustice, the outcome of the allocations involved no "winner." That is, no candidate was offered the job in Bies and Shapiro's (1988) study; and similarly, in the Folger *et al.* (1983) study in a competitive game context, subjects were told that the rules of the game changed and no one had won the competition. In the present study, the selection outcome involved making the job offer to a particular candidate (i.e., the winner). The presence of such a winner referent is significant for judgements of justice. Central to most theories of distributive justice (e.g., equity theories and the theory of relative deprivation) are the referent comparison process and the relative nature of fairness judgements. In the absence of a winner referent, the allocation appears to have left everyone "in the same boat," hence by comparison, the unfavorable outcome may not seem too bad. However, in the presence of a winner referent, the result of the inevitable referent comparison process would be more likely to exacerbate feelings of injustice, when the winner referent was not seen as being the most qualified or merited.

The second possible interpretation concerned the issue of minority employment. History is replete with incidents of racial tension due to "foreigners" stealing away employment opportunities from "locals." Any attempt in justifying such outcomes might be inevitably met with "psychological reactance" (Brehm, 1966). This line of reasoning would further predict that the use of a hard line approach in implementing preferential selection (e.g., through legislation) would induce greater resistance than an approach based on grounds of humanity. This is consistent with the present finding in study 2 that preferential selection outcomes were seen as even more unfair under the condition of legislative justification than the ethical justification condition.

Two additional findings are worth noting: First, although fairness perceptions in both studies were primarily concerned with those of the disadvantaged target groups (i.e., males' perceptions of sex-based selection and Europeans' perceptions of ethnic-based selection), there was evidence in study 1 showing that females perceived sex-based selection as equally unfair as their male counterparts. This indicates that minority members (females) who are the beneficiaries of such preferential treatment, also perceived such selection programs as unfair.

Second, results of study 1 showed that either sex-based or ethnicity-based preferential hiring was perceived as equally unfair as conventional discrimination against minorities. However, the distinction between these two types of discrimination could be made in terms of "expected pessimistic" injustice and "unexpected optimistic" injustice (Martin, 1981). Because of the differences in the underlying "expectations," the two forms of discrimination may have differential effects on behavior. Future research could examine possible behavioral consequences of perceived injustice due to preferential selection.

The practical implication of the findings appears clear: At least so far as these respondent groups are concerned, it would be difficult to theoretically justify preferential selection in terms of fairness perceptions. One weakness of the study concerns the use of student subjects. Although this could pose problems for the generalizability of the findings, fairness perceptions of students are nonetheless significant in view of the fact that their future employment prospects may be adversely affected by such preferential selection programs.

Acknowledgements

The authors wish to thank Evelyn Shackley, Elif Oral, Clare Lange, Chris Burt and Peter Gurney for their assistance in study 1; Tanya Detrick, Chris Chelliah and Andy Hoggard for their assistance in study 2. The project was supported by a research grant from the University of Canterbury to the first author.

References

Bies, R. J.: 1987a, "The Predicament of Injustice: The Management of Moral Outrage," in L. L. Cummings and B. M. Staw, (Eds.), *Research in Organizational Behavior* (Vol. 9) (JAI Press, Greenwich, CT), pp. 289–319.

Bies, R. J.: 1987b, "Beyond Voice: The Influence of Decision-Maker Justification and Sincerity on Procedural Fairness Judgments," *Representative Research in Social Psychology* **17**, pp. 3–14.

Bies, R. J. and Shapiro, D. L.: 1988, "Voice and Justification: Their Influence on Procedural Fairness Judgments," *Academy of Management Journal* **31**, pp. 676–685.

Black, V.: 1974, "The Erosion of Legal Principles in the Creation of Legal Policies," *Ethics* **84**, pp. 72–74.

Brehm, J. W.: 1966, *A Theory of Psychological Reactance* (Academic Press, New York).

Broxhill, B.: 1972, "The Morality of Reparations," *Social Theory and Practice* **2**, pp. 113–122.

Chacko, T. I.: 1982, "Women and Equal Employment Opportunity: Some Unintended Effects," *Journal of Applied Psychology* **67**, pp. 119–123.

Cohen, C.: 1975, "Race and the Constitution," *The Nation* **8** Feb., 1975.

Cronbach, L. J., Yalow, E., and Schaeffer, G. A.: 1980, "A Mathematical Structure for Analyzing Fairness in Selection," *Personnel Psychology* **33**, pp. 693–704.

Fiss, O. M.: 1976, "Groups and the Equal Protection Clause," *Philosophy and Public Affairs* **5**, pp. 150–151.

Folger, R., Rosenfield, D., and Robinson, T.: 1983, "Relative Deprivation and Procedural Justifications," *Journal of Personality and Social Psychology* **45**, pp. 268–273.

Garrett, T. M. and Klonoski, R. J.: 1986, *Business Ethics* (2nd Ed.) (Prentice-Hall, Englewood Cliffs, NJ).

Goldman, A. H.: 1975, "Limits to the Justification of Reverse Discrimination," *Social Theory and Practice* **3**, pp. 110–113.

Goldman, A. H.: 1976, "Affirmative Action," *Philosophy and Public Affairs* **5**, p. 187.

Greenberg, J.: 1987, "A Taxonomy of Organisational Justice Theories," *Academy of Management Review* **12**, pp. 9–22.

Gross, A. L. and Su W.: 1975, "Defining a 'Fair' or 'Unbiased' Selection Model: A Question of Utilities," *Journal of Applied Psychology* **60**, pp. 345–351.

Heilman, M. E. and Herlihy, J. N.: 1984, "Affirmative Action, Negative Reaction? Some Moderating Conditions," *Organizational Behavior and Human Performance* **33**, pp. 204–213.

Heilman, M. E., Simon, M. C., and Repper, D. P.: 1987, "Intentionally Favored, Unintentionally Harmed? Impact of Sex-based Preferential Selection on Self-perceptions and Self-evaluations," *Journal of Applied Psychology* **72**, pp. 62–68.

Jacobson, M. B. and Koch W.: 1977, "Women as Leaders: Performance Evaluation as a Function of Method of Leader Selection," *Organizational Behavior and Human Performance* **20**, pp. 149–157.

Karst, K. L. and Horowitz, H. W.: 1974, "Affirmative Action and Equal Protection," *Virginia Law Review* **60**, pp. 955–974.

Kennedy, R.: 1986, "Persuasion and Distrust: A Comment in the Affirmative Action Debate," *Harvard Law Review* **99**, pp. 1327–1334.

Martin, J.: 1981, "Relative Deprivation: A Theory of Distributive Justice for an Era of Shrinking Resources," in L. L. Cummings and B. M. Staw, (Eds.), *Research in Organizational Behavior* (Vol. 3) (JAI Press, Greenwich, CT), pp. 53–107.

Minas, A. C.: 1977, "How Reverse Discrimination Compensates Women," *Ethics* **88**, pp. 74–79.

Nagel, T.: 1973, "Equal Treatment and Compensatory Discrimination," *Philosophy and Public Affairs* **2**, pp. 348–363.

Newton, L. H.: 1973, "Reverse Discrimination as Unjustified," *Ethics* **83**, pp. 308–312.

Nickel, J. W.: 1974, "Classification by Race in Compensatory Programs," *Ethics* **84**, pp. 146–150.

Nickel, J. W.: 1975, "Preferential Policies in Hiring and Admissions: A Jurisprudential Approach," *Columbia Law Review* **75**, pp. 534–558.

Rawls, J.: 1971, *A Theory of Justice* (Clarendon Press, Oxford).

Schmitt, N., Gooding, R. Z., Noe, R. A., and Kirsch, M.: 1984, "Meta-analyses of Validity Studies Published Between 1964 and 1982 and the Investigation of Study Characteristics," *Personnel Psychology* **37**, pp. 407–422.

Schmitt, N. and Noe, R. A.: 1986, "Personnel Selection and Equal Employment Opportunity," in C. L. Cooper and I. T. Robertson, (Eds.), *International Review of Industrial and Organizational Psychology* (Wiley, New York).

Schmitt, N.: 1989, "Fairness in employment selection," in M. Smith and I. Robertson (Eds.), *Advances in Personnel Selection and Assessment* (Wiley, Chichester).

Shaw, B.: 1988, "Affirmative Action: An Ethical Evaluation," *Journal of Business Ethics* **7**, pp. 763–770.

Sher, G.: 1975, "Justifying Reverse Discrimination in Employment," *Philosophy and Public Affairs* **4**, pp. 159–170.

Sowell, T.: 1978, "Are Quotas Good for Blacks?," *Commentary* **65**, pp. 39–43.

Taylor, P. W.: 1973, "Reverse Discrimination and Compensatory Justice," *Analysis* **33**, pp. 177–182.

Thomson, J. J.: 1973, "Preferential Hiring," *Philosophy and Public Affairs* **2**, p. 381.

University of Canterbury,
Dept. of Psychology,
Christchurch 1,
New Zealand.

University of Canterbury,
Dept. of Management,
Christchurch 1,
New Zealand

CHAPTER 7

Whistle Blowing

The Anatomy of Whistle-Blowing

Ralph Nader

Probably no other issue can cause so much consternation to a manager who wants to do the right thing in his or her career as that of deciding whether or not to blow the whistle on his or her organization or coworkers. In this selection, consumer advocate Ralph Nader takes up the essential issue of whistle-blowing and managerial responsibility. Nader's approach is to argue that managers and all corporate employees have an overriding duty to public safety that must supersede loyalties to their organizations. He then goes on to list eight important questions the potential whistle-blower must contemplate; and he calls for workplace protections for those who do find it necessary to report violations of law and ethics in their midst. There is thus a need for what Nader labels a "new whistle-blower ethic," because the whistle-blower is the "last line of defense" the public has in its confrontation with massive institutions that wield such great power over the lives of ordinary citizens.

Americans believe that they have set for themselves and for the rest of the world a high example of individual freedom. That example inevitably refers to the struggle by a minority of aggrieved citizens against the royal tyranny of King George III. Out of the struggle that established this nation some chains were struck off and royal fiats abolished. Americans became a nation with the

Ralph Nader, Peter J. Petkas, and Kate Blackwell, editors, *Whistle Blowing* (NY: Grossman Publishers, 1972). Reprinted with permission of the author.

conviction that arbitrary government action should not restrict the freedom of individuals to follow their own consciences.

Today arbitrary treatment of citizens by powerful institutions has assumed a new form, no less insidious than that which prevailed in an earlier time. The "organization" has emerged and spread its invisible chains. Within the structure of the organization there has taken place an erosion of both human values and the broader value of human beings as the possibility of dissent within the hierarchy has become so restricted that common candor requires uncommon courage. The large organization is lord and manor, and most of its employees have been desensitized much as were medieval peasants who never knew they were serfs. It is true that often the immediate physical deprivations are far fewer, but the price of this fragile shield has been the dulling of the senses and perceptions of new perils and pressures of a far more embracing consequence.

Some of these perils may be glimpsed when it is realized that our society now has the numbing capacity to destroy itself inadvertently by continuing the domestic chemical and biological warfare against its citizens and their environments. Our political economy has also developed an inverted genius that can combine an increase in the gross national product with an increase in the gross national misery. Increasingly, large organizations—public and private—possess a Medea-like intensity to paralyze conscience, initiative, and proper concern for people outside the organization.

Until recently, all hopes for change in corporate and government behavior have been focused on external pressures on the organization, such as regulation, competition, litigation, and exposure to public opinion. There was little attention given to the simple truth that the adequacy of these external stimuli is very significantly dependent on the internal freedom of those within the organization.

Corporate employees are among the first to know about industrial dumping of mercury or fluoride sludge into waterways, defectively designed automobiles, or undisclosed adverse effects of prescription drugs and pesticides. They are the first to grasp the technical capabilities to prevent existing product or pollution hazards. But they are very often the last to speak out, much less to refuse to be recruited for acts of corporate or governmental negligence or predation. Staying silent in the face of a professional duty has direct impact on the level of consumer and environmental hazards. But this awareness has done little to upset the slavish adherence to "following company orders."

Silence in the face of abuses may also be evaluated in terms of the toll it takes on the individuals who in doing so subvert their own consciences. For example, the twenty-year collusion by the domestic automobile companies against development and marketing of exhaust control systems is a tragedy, among other things, for engineers who, minionlike, programmed the technical artifices of the industry's defiance. Settling the antitrust case brought by the Justice Department against such collusion did nothing to confront the question of subverted engineering integrity.

The key question is, at what point should an employee resolve that allegiance to society (e.g., the public safety) must supersede allegiance to the organization's policies (e.g., the corporate profit), and then act on that resolve by informing outsiders or legal authorities? It is a question that involves basic issues of individual freedom, concentration of power, and information flow to the public. These issues in turn involve daily choices such as the following.

To report or not to report:

1. defective vehicles in the process of being marketed to unsuspecting consumers;
2. vast waste of government funds by private contractors;
3. the industrial dumping of mercury in waterways;
4. the connection between companies and campaign contributions;
5. a pattern of discrimination by age, race, or sex in a labor union or company;
6. mishandling the operation of a workers' pension fund;
7. willful deception in advertising a worthless or harmful product;
8. the sale of putrid or adulterated meats, chemically camouflaged in supermarkets;
9. the use of government power for private, corporate, or industry gain;
10. the knowing nonenforcement of laws being seriously violated, such as pesticide laws;
11. rank corruption in an agency or company;
12. the suppression of serious occupational disease data.

It is clear that hundreds and often thousands of people are privy to such information but choose to remain silent within their organizations. Some are conscience-stricken in so doing and want guidance. Actually, the general responsibility is made clear for the professional by codes of ethics. These codes invariably etch the primary allegiance to the public interest, while the Code of Ethics for United States Government Service does the same: "Put loyalty to the highest moral principles and to country above loyalty to persons, party, or Government department." The difficulty rests in the judgment to be exercised by the individual and its implementation. Any potential whistle-blower has to ask and try to answer a number of questions:

1. Is my knowledge of the matter complete and accurate?
2. What are the objectionable practices and what public interest do they harm?
3. How far should I and can I go inside the organization with my concern or objection?
4. Will I be violating any rules by contacting outside parties and, if so, is whistle-blowing nevertheless justified?
5. Will I be violating any laws or ethical duties by *not* contacting external parties?

6. Once I have decided to act, what is the best way to blow the whistle—anonymously, overtly, by resignation prior to speaking out, or in some other way?
7. What will be likely responses from various sources—inside and outside the organization— to the whistle-blowing action?
8. What is expected to be achieved by whistle-blowing in the particular situation?

. . . The decision to act and the answers to all of these questions are unique for every situation and for every individual. Presently, certitudes are the exception.

There is a great need to develop an ethic of whistle-blowing which can be practically applied in many contexts, especially within corporate and governmental bureaucracies. For this to occur, people must be permitted to cultivate their own form of allegiance to their fellow citizens and exercise it without having their professional careers or employment opportunities destroyed. This new ethic will develop if employees have the right to due process within their organizations and if they have at least some of the rights—such as the right to speak freely—that now protect them from state power. In the past . . . whistle-blowing has illuminated dark corners of our society, saved lives, prevented injuries and disease, and stopped corruption, economic waste, and material exploitation. Conversely, the absence of such professional and individual responsibility has perpetuated these conditions. In this context whistle-blowing, if carefully defined and protected by law, can become another of those adaptive, self-implementing mechanisms which mark the relative difference between a free society that relies on free institutions and a closed society that depends on authoritarian institutions.

Indeed, the basic status of a citizen in a democracy underscores the themes implicit in a form of professional and individual responsibility that places responsibility to society over that to an illegal or negligent or unjust organizational policy or activity. These themes touch the right of free speech, the right to information, the citizen's right to participate in important public decisions, and the individual's obligation to avoid complicity in harmful, fraudulent, or corrupt activities. Obviously, as in the exercise of constitutional rights, abuses may occur. But this has long been considered an acceptable risk of free speech within very broad limits. . . .

. . . The willingness and ability of insiders to blow the whistle is the last line of defense ordinary citizens have against the denial of their rights and the destruction of their interests by secretive and powerful institutions. As organizations penetrate deeper and deeper into the lives of people—from pollution to poverty to income erosion to privacy invasion—more of their rights and interests are adversely affected. This fact of contemporary life has generated an ever greater moral imperative for employees to be reasonably protected in upholding such rights regardless of their employers' policies. The corporation, the labor unions and professional societies to which its employees belong, the government in its capacity as employer, and the law must all change or be changed to make protection of the responsible whistle-blower possible.

Each corporation should have a bill of rights for its employees and a system of internal appeals to guarantee these rights. As a condition of employment, workers at every level in the corporate hierarchy should have the right to express their reservations about the company's activities and policies, and their views should be accorded a fair hearing. They should have the right to "go public," and the corporation should expect them to do so when internal channels of communication are exhausted and the problem remains uncorrected.

Unions and professional societies should strengthen their ethical codes—and adopt such codes if they do not already have them. They should put teeth into mechanisms for implementing their codes and require that they be observed not only by members but also by organizations that employ their members. Unions should move beyond the traditional "bread and butter" issues, the societies should escape their preoccupation with abstract professionalism, and both should apply their significant potential power to protecting members who refuse to be automatons. Whistle-blowers who belong to labor unions have fared only slightly better than their unorganized counterparts, except when public opinion and the whistle-blower's fellow workers are sufficiently aroused. This is partly a result of the bureaucratized cooptation of many labor leaders by management and the suppression of rank and file dissent within the union or local. . . .

All areas of the law touching upon the employee-employer relationship should be reexamined with an eye to modifying substantially the old rule that an employer can discharge an employee for acts of conscience without regard to the damage done to the employee. Existing laws that regulate industry should be amended to include provisions protecting employees who cooperate with authorities. The concept of trade secrecy is now used by business and government alike to suppress information that the public has a substantial need to know. A sharp distinction must be drawn between individual privacy and corporate secrecy, and the law of trade secrecy is a good place to begin. The Freedom of Information Act, which purports to establish public access to all but the most sensitive information in the hands of the federal government, can become a toothless perversion because civil servants who release information in the spirit of the act are punished while those who suppress it are rewarded.

Whistle-blowing is encouraged actively by some laws and government administrators to assist in law enforcement. Under the recently rediscovered Refuse Act of 1899, for example, anyone who reports a polluter is entitled to one-half of any fine collected—even if the person making the report is an employee of the polluting company. And corporations constantly probe government agencies to locate whistle-blowers on their behalf. Consumers need routine mechanisms to encourage the increased flow of information that deals with health, safety, environmental hazards, corruption, and waste inside corporate and governmental institutions. Whistle-blowing can show the need for such systemic affirmations of the public's right to know. . . .

The rise in public consciousness among the young and among minority groups has generated a sharper concept of duty among many citizens, recalling Alfred North Whitehead's dictum, "Duty arises from our potential control over the course of events." But loyalties do not end at the boundaries of an organization. "Just following orders," was an attitude that the United States military tribunals rejected in judging others after World War II at Nuremberg. And for those who set their behavior by the ethics of the great religions, with their universal golden rule, the right to appeal to a higher authority is the holiest of rights.

The whistle-blowing ethic is not new; it simply has to begin flowering responsibly in new fields where its harvests will benefit people as citizens and consumers. . . . The realistic tendency of such an internal check within General Motors or the Department of the Interior will be to assist traditional external checks to work more effectively in their statutory or market-defined missions in the public interest. . . .

However, the exercise of ethical whistle-blowing requires a broader, enabling environment for it to be effective. There must be those who listen and those whose potential or realized power can utilize the information for advancing justice. Thus, as with any democratic institutions, other links are necessary to secure the objective changes beyond the mere exposure of the abuses. The courts, professional and citizen groups, the media, the Congress, and honorable segments throughout our society are part of this enabling environment. They must comprehend that the tyranny of organizations, with their excessive security against accountability, must be prevented from trammeling a fortified conscience within their midst. Organizational power must be insecure to some degree if it is to be more responsible. A greater freedom of individual conviction within the organization can provide the needed deterrent—the creative insecurity which generates a more suitable climate of responsiveness to the public interest and public rights.

Corporate Responsibility and the Employee's Duty of Loyalty and Obedience

Phillip I. Blumberg

This article constitutes a preliminary inquiry into aspects of a problem that the author believes will become an area of dynamic change in the corporate organization and in time will produce significant change in established legal concepts. It is concerned with the impact of the new view of the corporation

From "Corporate Responsibility and the Employee's Duty of Loyalty and Obedience: A Preliminary Inquiry," Phillip Blumberg, in *Oklahoma Law Review* vol 24. no. 3. August 1971. Reprinted by permission of *Oklahoma Law Review*.

upon traditional concepts of the duties of loyalty and obedience of the employee to his employer, firmly recognized in the law of agency. This impact has been illustrated by a number of recent developments, which have a common core: the right of the employee of the large public corporation to take action adverse to the interests of his employer in response to the employee's view as to the proper social responsibility of his corporate employer. . . .

The Restatement of Agency

A review of the relevant provisions of the *Restatement of Agency* provides an obvious starting point for consideration of the new view of the role and duties of the employee.[1]

A. The Duty of Obedience

Section 383 and Section 385 state the agent's duty to obey the principal. Section 385(1) imposes upon the agent "a duty to obey all reasonable directions" of the principal.[2] Comment *a* points out:

> In determining whether or not the orders of the principal to the agent are reasonable . . . *business or professional ethics* . . . are considered. [Emphasis added.]

Comment *a* continues:

> In no event would it be implied that an agent has a duty to perform acts which . . . are *illegal or unethical* . . . [Emphasis added.]

Thus, Comment *a* expressly excludes matters contrary to "business or professional ethics" or "illegal or unethical" acts from those which an agent would be required to perform. This frees the agent from participation in such behavior and authorizes him to withdraw from the agency relation if the principal persists. It in no way authorizes him to disclose such directions of the principal, or not to comply with an instruction of the principal not to disclose any information about the principal's affairs, even in those cases where he is privileged not to perform in accordance with the principal's instructions. The duty exists not only so long as the agent remains an agent but continues after the agency has been terminated as well.

Section 385(2) provides:

> (2) Unless he is privileged to protect his own or another's interests, an agent is subject to a duty not to act in matters entrusted to him on account of the principal contrary to the directions of the principal. . . .

The Comments make it clear that "an interest" which the agent is privileged to protect refers only to an economic interest, such as a lien or his business reputation. There is no suggestion that an interest which "he is privileged to protect" includes the public interest.

B. The Duty of Loyalty

Section 387 expresses the general principle that:

> an agent is subject to a duty to his principal to act solely for the benefit of the principal in all matters connected with his agency.

Comment *b* emphasizes the high degree of the duties of loyalty of the agent by stating that they "are the same as those of a trustee to his beneficiaries." It provides, however, that:

> The agent is also under a duty not to act or speak disloyally . . . except in the protection of his own interests or those of others. He is not, however, necessarily prevented from acting in good faith outside his employment in a manner which injuriously affects his principal's business.

and provides the following illustration:

> 3. A, employed by P, a life insurance company, in good faith advocates legislation which would require a change in the policies issued by the company. A has violated no duty to P.

Thus, the agent is free to act "in good faith outside his employment," even in a manner which injures his principal's business, but is subject to a duty identical with that of a trustee with respect to "all matters connected with his agency." Under the comment and illustration, the General Motors employee may campaign in good faith for legislation imposing costly antipollution or product safety controls on automobile manufacturers, but he occupies a position equivalent to a trustee with respect to information about General Motors operations which he has acquired in the course, or on account, of his employment.

Section 394 prohibits the agent from acting:

> for persons whose interests conflict with those of the principal in matters in which the agent is employed.

The numerous examples in the comments relate to competitors or adverse parties in commercial transactions or parties with adverse claims and make it plain that the reference to conflicting "interests" means economic interests.

C. The Duty of Confidentiality

Section 395 imposes a duty upon the agent:

> not to use or to communicate information confidentially given him by the principal or acquired by him during the course of or on account of his agency . . . to the injury of the principal, on his own account or on behalf of another . . . unless the information is a matter of general knowledge.

Comment *a* emphasizes that the agency relation "permits and requires great freedom of communication between the principal and the agent." It expands the agent's duty by stating that the agent:

> also has a duty not to use information acquired by him as agent . . . for any
> purpose likely to cause his principal harm or to interfere with his business,
> although it is information not connected with the subject matter of his
> agency.

Comment *b* extends the duty beyond "confidential" communications to "information which the agent should know his principal would not care to have revealed to others." Both Comments *a* and *b* refer to protection of the principal against competition, but it is clear that this is merely one of the interests of the principal protected by the section.

Comment *f* creates a privilege, significantly enough for a public, not an economic, interest:

> An agent is privileged to reveal information confidentially acquired . . . in
> the protection of a superior interest of himself or of a third person. Thus, if
> the confidential information is to the effect that the principal is committing
> or is about to commit a crime, the agent is under no duty not to reveal it.

This is the only illustration in the *Restatement* that the term "interest" may embrace something of a noneconomic nature. The public interest in law enforcement is deemed a "superior interest" giving rise to a privilege to reveal otherwise confidential information.

If construed to include disclosure to any person, and not solely to law enforcement agencies, Comment *f* would support the "public interest disclosure" proposal to the extent it relates to "illegal" matters, without regard to the nature or seriousness of the offense. *Section 395,* Comment *f,* however, refers only to commission of a "crime." This contrasts with *Section 385(1)* relating to the duty of obedience which refers not only to "illegal" but also to "unethical" acts and to "business or professional ethics." The inclusion of these latter elements in *Section 385(1)* and their omission in *Section 395* would indicate that the release of confidential information privileged under *Section 395* does not extend beyond criminal acts.

Although *Section 395* refers only to the agent's use or communication of information "on his own account or on behalf of another" and does not literally prohibit use or communication of such information for the benefit of the public, Comment *a* prohibits such use "for any purpose likely to cause his principal harm or to interfere with his business." Comment *a* thus would appear to expand the duty of the agent beyond acts "on his own account or on behalf of another" to include disclosures made to advance the "public interest," which were not related to commission of a "crime" privileged under Comment *f.* . . .

In summary, except in the single area of "crime," the *Restatement* provides no support for the view that the employee may disclose nonpublic information about his employer acquired as a result of the employment relationship in order to promote the superior interest of society. . . . The reference in *Section 395,* Comment *f* permitting the agent to disclose confidential information concerning a criminal act committed or planned by the principal is the sole exception to a system of analysis that is otherwise exclusively concerned with matters relating to the economic position of the parties. Thus, the question may fairly be asked to what extent the *Restatement* and the common-law decisions are useful in the analysis of a proposal that rests on the concept of an agent's primary obligation as a citizen to the society, transcending his economic duty to the principal.

Are doctrines resting on a policy of protecting the economic position of the principal against impairment by reasons of an agent's effort to achieve economic gain properly applicable to the employee who releases nonpublic information about his employer without intent to obtain economic advantage for himself—and motivated by a desire to promote the public good rather than to injure the principal (although such injury may in fact result)?

The duties of loyalty and obedience on the part of the agent are unquestionably central to the agency relationship, irrespective of economic considerations. But these duties, as the *Restatement* itself recognizes, have limitations. To paraphrase Mr. Justice Frankfurter's well-known admonition:[3] To say that an agent has duties of loyalty and obedience only begins analysis; it gives direction to further inquiry. It is thus not enough to say that the agent has duties of loyalty and obedience which will be impaired. One must inquire more deeply and ascertain the outer perimeter of the agent's obligations by balancing the conflicting considerations. On this critical question of how far the duties of loyalty and obedience extend, the *Restatement* enunciating the traditional rules in their economic setting provides limited guidance. . . .

The Changing Role of the Corporate Employee

. . . In the balance of the conflicting rights of the government employee as citizen and the objective of government for efficient administration, the courts have placed a lesser value on the traditional duties of loyalty and obedience and have subordinated these duties to the employees' right of free speech in order to enable the employee to play a role as a citizen in matters of public controversy. Similarly, one may inquire whether, in time, erosion of the traditional employer-employee relation and the traditional concepts of loyalty and obedience will not also occur within the major American corporation. . . .

In an illuminating article,[4] Dean Blades has reexamined the traditional concept of employment at will and the employer's traditional power to discharge the employee at any time for any reason (or indeed for no reason) and has suggested that in time the doctrine—already hedged in by statute and collective bargaining agreements—will be modified, possibly by the legislatures, perhaps by the courts, to protect the employee against discharge for exercise of those personal rights which have no legitimate connection with the employment relationship. . . .

As one moves from the theoretical level to the practical level, one may inquire whether the employer's right of discharge has not already been impaired at least in those cases where public sympathy is squarely behind the employee, as in the case of the Eastern Airlines pilot who placed his concern with air pollution above obedience to company regulations. The rules of law may condemn such activity as a clear breach of the duty of loyalty and obedience. The corporation may be tempted to exercise its right of discharge, but its freedom of action (without regard to obligations under any union contract) will be severely restricted by the climate of public opinion which may well have been significantly influenced by the publicity attending the affair.

In the arena of public opinion, the issue will involve the merits of the conduct of the employee, not whether the conduct was contrary to instructions. In the Eastern Airlines case, the intentional violation of regulations and the impracticability of allowing each of the 3700 Eastern Airlines pilots to "make his own rules" were not the issues before the public. The subject of the public debate was the impact of the Eastern Airlines practice on air pollution. Unless the corporation can prevail in the battle for public opinion on the merits of the conduct in issue, it must yield to public clamor or face the consequences of unfavorable public reaction. Moreover, if the employer is unionized, it is unlikely that the union efforts on behalf of the employee will be limited to the legal question of whether the conduct constitutes "just cause" for discharge under the collective agreement.

At this stage, whatever the traditional legal doctrines, the corporation's right of discharge may be illusory. The major corporation must recognize that it has become a public institution and must respond to the public climate of opinion. Thus, whether or not the major corporation in the law of the future comes to be regarded as a quasi-governmental body for some purpose, it operates today as a political as well as economic institution, subject to political behavior by those affected by it and to public debate over those of its actions which attain public visibility.

The pervasive public concern with corporate social responsibility will unquestionably lead to employee response to an appeal for disclosures of confidential information tending to show corporate participation in the creation of social or environmental problems. It is only realistic, therefore, to anticipate the appearance of the government-type "leak" in the major corporation. Whether or not it violates traditional agency concepts, a "public interest clearing house" may be expected to transact considerable business. Aggrieved employers are hardly going to feel free to resort to theoretically available legal or equitable remedies for redress so long as the unauthorized disclosures relate to "antisocial" conduct and do not reflect economic motivation. The corporation that is guilty of environmental abuse reported to the "clearing house" will not be well-advised to compound its conduct by instituting action against the "clearing house" or the employee (if it can identify him) and thereby assure even greater adverse publicity with respect to its objectionable environmental activities. . . .

Another aspect of the proposal for a "public interest clearing house" has considerable merit. This is the objective to provide protection through exposure to public opinion for corporate employees discharged for refusal to participate in illegal, immoral, or unprofessional acts. Involving no breach of confidentiality, this is a laudable effort to translate into reality the theoretical legal rights of the employee recognized at common law and in the *Restatement of Agency* in the face of the grave economic inequality between the individual employee and the giant corporate employer. Such an effort should receive the support of all interested in raising the standards of industrial morality. . . .

Statutory relief is another possible method to achieve appropriate protection for the rights of employees covering unionized and nonunionized employees alike. Antidiscrimination employment statutes already prohibit discrimination on the basis of "race, color, religion, sex, or national origin," age, or union membership. They might well be extended to make unlawful discrimination for political, social or economic views even when publicly expressed in opposition to an employer's policy. Similarly, statutory prohibition of discharge for refusal to participate in acts that are illegal or contrary to established canons of professional ethics, or for cooperation with governmental law-enforcement, legislative or executive agencies, deserves serious consideration.

Conclusion

The duties of loyalty and obedience are essential in the conduct of any enterprise—public or private. Yet, they do not serve as a basis to deprive government employees of their rights as citizens to participate in public debate and criticism of their governmental employer and should not be utilized to deprive corporate employees of similar rights.

As employee attitudes and actions reflect the increased public concern with social and environmental problems and the proper role of the corporation in participating in their solution, traditional doctrines of the employee's duties of loyalty and obedience and the employer's right of discharge will undergo increasing change. The pressure of "public interest" stockholder groups for increased corporate social responsibility will also be reflected by employees. At some point in the process, disagreement with management policies is inevitable. When the employees persist in their disagreement and the disagreement becomes public, an erosion of the traditional view of the duties of loyalty and obedience will have occurred. Yet, this hardly seems a fundamental problem for the corporation or undesirable from the point of view of the larger society. The real question is to establish civilized perimeters of permissible conduct that will not silence employees from expressing themselves on the public implications of their employers' activities in the social and environmental arena and at the same time will not introduce elements of breach of confidentiality and impairment of loyalty that will materially impair the functioning of the corporation itself. A balancing of interests, not a blind reiteration of traditional doctrines, is required. It is hoped that this preliminary review will suggest some possible solutions to the problem.

Notes

1. For the purposes of this paper, "agent" should be regarded as interchangeable with "employee."
2. *Restatement (Second) of Agency* (1958), §385(1) (hereinafter cited as *Restatement*).
3. See Mr. Justice Frankfurter in SEC v. Chenery Corp., 318 U.S. 80, 85-86, 63 S.Ct. 454, 458, 87 L.Ed. 626, 632 (1943).
4. See Blades, "Employment At Will v. Individual Freedom: or Limiting the Allusive Exercise of Employer Power," 67, *Columbia Law Review,* 1404 (1967).

Whistle Blowing

Richard T. De George*

We shall restrict our discussion to a specific sort of whistle blowing, namely, *nongovernmental, impersonal, external whistle blowing.* We shall be concerned with (1) employees of profit-making firms, who, for moral reasons, in the hope and expectation that a product will be made safe, or a practice changed, (2) make public information about a product or practice of the firm that due to faulty design, the use of inferior materials, or the failure to follow safety or other regular procedures or state of the art standards (3) threatens to produce serious harm to the public in general or to individual users of a product. We shall restrict our analysis to this type of whistle blowing because, in the first place, the conditions that justify whistle blowing vary according to the type of case at issue. Second, financial harm can be considerably different from bodily harm. An immoral practice that increases the cost of a product by a slight margin may do serious harm to no individual, even if the total amount when summed adds up to a large amount, or profit. (Such cases can be handled differently from cases that threaten bodily harm.) Third, both internal and personal whistle blowing cause problems for a firm, which are for the most part restricted to those within the firm. External, impersonal whistle blowing is of concern to the general public, because it is the general public rather than the firm that is threatened with harm.

As a paradigm, we shall take a set of fairly clear-cut cases, namely, those in which serious bodily harm—including possible death—threatens either the users of a product or innocent bystanders because of a firm's practice, the design of its product, or the action of some person or persons within the firm. (Many of the famous whistle-blowing cases are instances of such situations.) We shall assume clear cases where serious, preventable harm will result unless a company makes changes in its product or practice.

Cases that are less clear are probably more numerous, and pose problems that are difficult to solve, for example, how serious is *serious*, and how does one tell whether a given situation is serious? We choose not to resolve such issues, but rather to construct a model embodying a number of distinctions that will enable us to clarify the moral status of whistle blowing, which may, in turn, provide a basis for working out guidelines for more complex cases.

Finally, the only motivation for whistle blowing we shall consider here is moral motivation. Those who blow the whistle for revenge, and so on, are not our concern in this discussion.

Corporations are complex entities. Sometimes those at the top do not want to know in detail the difficulties encountered by those below them. They wish lower-management to handle these difficulties as best they can. On the other hand, those in lower-management frequently present only good news to those above them, even if those at the top do want to be told about difficulties. Sometimes, lower-management hopes that things will be straightened out without letting their superiors know that anything has gone wrong. For instance, sometimes a production schedule is drawn up, which many employees along the line know cannot be achieved. Each level has cut off a few days of the production time actually needed, to make his projection look good to those above. Because this happens at each level, the final projection is weeks, if not months, off the mark. When difficulties develop in actual production, each level is further squeezed and is tempted to cut corners in order not to fall too far behind the overall schedule. The cuts may be that of not correcting defects in a design, or of allowing a defective part to go through, even though a department head and the workers in that department know that this will cause trouble for the consumer. Sometimes a defective part will be annoying; sometimes it will be dangerous. If dangerous, external whistle blowing may be morally mandatory.

The whistle blower usually fares very poorly at the hands of his company. Most are fired. In some instances, they have been blackballed in the whole industry. If they are not fired, they are frequently shunted aside at promotion time, and treated as pariahs. Those who consider making a firm's wrongdoings public must therefore be aware that they may be fired, ostracized, and condemned by others. They may ruin their chances of future promotion and security; and they also may make themselves a target for revenge. Only rarely have companies praised and promoted such people. This is not surprising, because the whistle blower forces the company to do what it did not want to do, even if, morally, it was the right action. This is scandalous. And it is ironic that those guilty of endangering the lives of others—even of indirectly killing them—frequently get promoted by their companies for increasing profits.

Because the consequences for the whistle blower are often so disastrous, such action is not to be undertaken lightly. Moreover, whistle blowing may, in some cases, be morally justifiable without being morally mandatory. The position we shall develop is a moderate one, and falls between two extreme positions: that defended by those who claim that whistle blowing is always morally justifiable, and that defended by those who say it is never morally justifiable.

Whistle Blowing as Morally Permitted

The kind of whistle blowing we are considering involves an employee somehow going public, revealing information or concerns about his or her firm in the hope that the firm will change its product, action, or policy, or whatever it is that the whistle blower feels will harm, or has harmed others, and needs to be rectified. We can assume that when one blows the whistle, it is not with the consent of the firm, but against its wishes. It is thus a form of disloyalty and of disobedience to the corporation. Whistle blowing of this type, we can further assume, does injury to a firm. It results in either adverse publicity or in an investigation of some sort, or both. if we adopt the principle that one ought not to do harm without sufficient reason, then, if the act of whistle blowing is to be morally permissible, some good must be achieved that outweighs the harm that will be done.

There are five conditions, which, if satisfied, change the moral status of whistle blowing. If the first three are satisfied, the act of whistle blowing will be morally justifiable and permissible. If the additional two are satisfied, the act of whistle blowing will be morally obligatory.

Whistle blowing is morally permissible if—

> 1. The firm, through its product or policy, will do serious and considerable harm to the public, whether in the person of the user of its product, an innocent bystander, or the general public.

Because whistle blowing causes harm to the firm, this harm must be offset by at least an equal amount of good, if the act is to be permissible. We have specified that the potential or actual harm to others must be serious and considerable. That requirement may be considered by some to be both too strong and too vague. Why specify "serious and considerable" instead of saying, "involve more harm than the harm that the whistle blowing will produce for the firm?" Moreover, how serious is "serious?" And how considerable is "considerable?"

There are several reasons for stating that the potential harm must be serious and considerable. First, if the harm is not serious and considerable, if it will do only slight harm to the public, or to the user of a product, the justification for whistle blowing will be at least problematic. We will not have a clear case. To assess the harm done to the firm is difficult; but though the harm may be rather vague, it is also rather sure. If the harm threatened by a product is slight or not certain, it might not be greater than the harm done to the firm. After all, a great many products involve some risk. Even with a well-constructed hammer, one can smash one's finger. There is some risk in operating any automobile, because no automobile is completely safe. There is always a trade-off between safety and cost. It is not immoral not to make the safest automobile possible, for instance, and a great many factors enter into deciding just how safe a car should be. An employee might see that a car can be made slightly safer by modifying a part, and might suggest that modification; but not making the modification is not usually grounds for blowing the whistle. If serious harm is not threatened, then the slight harm that is done say by the use of a product, can be corrected after the product is marketed (e.g., as a result of customer complaint). Our society has a great many ways of handling minor defects, and these are at least arguably better than resorting to whistle blowing.

To this consideration should be added a second. Whistle blowing is frequently, and appropriately, considered an unusual occurrence, a heroic act. If the practice of blowing the whistle for relatively minor harm were to become a common occurrence, its effectiveness would be diminished. When serious harm is threatened, whistle blowers are listened to by the news media, for instance, because it is news. But relatively minor harm to the public is not news. If many minor charges or concerns were voiced to the media, the public would soon not react as it is now expected to react to such disclosures. This would also be the case if complaints about all sorts of perceived or anticipated minor harm were reported to government agencies, although most people would expect that government agencies would act first on the serious cases, and only later on claims of relatively minor harm.

There is a third consideration. Every time an employee has a concern about possible harm to the public from a product or practice we cannot assume that he or she makes a correct assessment. Nor can we assume that every claim of harm is morally motivated. To sift out the claims and concerns of the disaffected worker from the genuine claims and concerns of the morally motivated employee is a practical problem. It may be claimed that this problem has nothing to do with the moral permissibility of the act of whistle blowing; but whistle blowing is a practical matter. If viewed as a technique for changing policy or actions, it will be justified only if effective. It can be trivialized. If it is, then one might plausibly claim that little harm is done to the firm, and hence the act is permitted. But if trivialized, it loses its point. If whistle blowing is to be considered a serious act with serious consequences, it should be reserved for disclosing potentially serious harm, and will be morally justifiable in those cases.

Serious is admittedly a vague term. Is an increase in probable automobile deaths, from 2 in 100,000 to 15 in 100,000 over a one-year period, serious? Although there may be legitimate debate on this issue, it is clear that matters that threaten death are prima facie serious. If the threatened harm is that a product may cost a few pennies more than otherwise, or if the threatened harm is that a part or product may cause minor inconvenience, the harm— even if multiplied by thousands or millions of instances—does not match the seriousness of death to the user or the innocent bystander.

The harm threatened by unsafe tires, which are sold as premium quality but that blow out at 60 or 70 mph, is serious, for such tires can easily lead to death. The dumping of metal drums of toxic waste into a river, where the drums will rust, leak, and cause cancer or other serious ills to those who drink the river water or otherwise use it, threatens serious harm. The use of sub-standard concrete in a building, such that it is likely to collapse and kill people, poses a serious threat to people. Failure to x-ray pipe fittings, as required in building a nuclear plant, is a failure that might lead to nuclear leaks; this involves potential serious harm, for it endangers the health and lives of many.

The notion of *serious* harm might be expanded to include serious financial harm, and kinds of harm other than death and serious threats to health and body. But as we noted earlier, we shall restrict ourselves here to products and practices that produce or threaten serious harm or danger to life and health. The difference between producing harm and threatening serious danger is not significant for the kinds of cases we are considering.

> 2. Once an employee identifies a serious threat to the user of a product or to the general public, he or she should report it to his or her immediate superior and make his or her moral concern known. Unless he or she does so, the act of whistle blowing is not clearly justifiable.

Why not? Why is not the weighing of harm sufficient? The answer has already been given in part. Whistle blowing is a practice that, to be effective, cannot be routinely used. There are other reasons as well. First, reporting one's concerns is the most direct, and usually the quickest, way of producing the change the whistle blower desires. The normal assumption is that most firms do not want to cause death or injury, and do not willingly and knowingly set out to harm the users of their products in this way. If there are life-threatening defects, the normal assumption is, and should be, that the firm will be interested in correcting them—if not for moral reasons, at least for prudential reasons, viz., to avoid suits, bad publicity, and adverse consumer reaction. The argument from loyalty also supports the requirement that the firm be given the chance to rectify its action or procedure or policy before it is charged in public. Additionally, because whistle blowing does harm to the firm, harm in general is minimized if the firm is informed of the problem and allowed to correct it. Less harm is done to the firm in this way, and if the harm to the public or the users is also averted, this procedure produces the least harm, on the whole.

The condition that one report one's concern to one's immediate superior presupposes a hierarchical structure. Although firms are usually so structured, they need not be. In a company of equals, one would report one's concerns internally, as appropriate.

Several objections may be raised to this condition. Suppose one knows that one's immediate superior already knows the defect and the danger. In this case reporting it to him or her would be redundant, and condition two would be satisfied. But one should not presume without good reason that one's superior does know. What may be clear to one individual may not be clear to another. Moreover, the assessment of risk is often a complicated matter. To a person on one level what appears as unacceptable risk may be defensible as legitimate to a person on a higher level, who may see a larger picture, and knows of offsetting compensations, and the like.

However, would not reporting one's concern effectively preclude the possibility of anonymous whistle blowing, and so put one in jeopardy? This might of course be the case; and this is one of the considerations one should weigh before blowing the whistle. We will discuss this matter later on. If the reporting is done tactfully, moreover, the voicing of one's concerns might, if the problem is apparent to others, indicate a desire to operate within the firm, and so make one less likely to be the one assumed to have blown the whistle anonymously.

By reporting one's concern to one's immediate superior or other appropriate person, one preserves and observes the regular practices of firms, which on the whole promote their order and efficiency; this fulfills one's obligation of minimizing harm, and it precludes precipitous whistle blowing.

> 3. If one's immediate superior does nothing effective about the concern or complaint, the employee should exhaust the internal procedures and possibilities within the firm. This usually will involve taking the matter up the managerial ladder, and, if necessary—and possible—to the board of directors.

To exhaust the internal procedures and possibilities is the key requirement here. In a hierarchically structured firm, this means going up the chain of command. But one may do so either with or without the permission of those at each level of the hierarchy. What constitutes exhausting the internal procedures? This is often a matter of judgment. But because going public with one's concern is more serious for both oneself and for the firm, going up the chain of command is the preferable route to take in most circumstances. This third condition is satisfied of course if, for some reason, it is truly impossible to go beyond any particular level.

Several objections may once again be raised. There may not be time enough to follow the bureaucratic procedures of a given firm; the threatened harm may have been done before the procedures are exhausted. If, moreover, one goes up the chain to the top and nothing is done by anyone, then a great deal of time will have been wasted. Once again, prudence and judgment should be used. The internal possibilities may sometimes be exhausted quickly, by a few phone calls or visits. But one should not simply assume that no one at any level within the firm will do anything. If there are truly no possibilities of internal remedy, then the third condition is satisfied.

As we mentioned, the point of the three conditions is essentially that whistle blowing is morally permissible if the harm threatened is serious, and if internal remedies have been attempted in good faith but without a satisfactory result. In these circumstances, one is morally justified in attempting to avert what one sees as serious harm, by means that may be effective, including blowing the whistle.

We can pass over as not immediately germane the questions of whether in nonserious matters one has an obligation to report one's moral concerns to one's superiors, and whether one fulfills one's obligation once one has reported them to the appropriate party.

Whistle Blowing as Morally Required

To say that whistle blowing is morally permitted does not impose any obligation on an employee. Unless two other conditions are met, the employee does not have a moral obligation to blow the whistle. To blow the whistle when one is not morally required to do so, and if done from moral motives (i.e., concern for one's fellow man) and at risk to oneself, is to commit a supererogatory act. It is an act that deserves moral praise. But failure to so act deserves no moral blame. In such a case, the whistle blower might be considered a moral hero. Sometimes he or she is so considered, sometimes not. If one's claim or concern turns out to be ill-founded, one's subjective moral state may be as praiseworthy as if the claim were well-founded, but one will rarely receive much praise for one's action.

For there to be an obligation to blow the whistle, two conditions must be met, in addition to the foregoing three.

> 4. The whistle blower must have, or have accessible, documented evidence that would convince a reasonable, impartial observer that one's view of the situation is correct, and that the company's product or practice poses a serious and likely danger to the public or to the use of the product.

One does not have an obligation to put oneself at serious risk without some compensating advantage to be gained. Unless one has documented evidence that would convince a reasonable, impartial observer, one's charges or claims, if made public, would be based essentially on one's word. Such grounds may be sufficient for a subjective feeling of certitude about one's charges, but they are not usually sufficient for others to act on one's claims. For instance, a newspaper is unlikely to print a story based simply on someone's undocumented assertion.

Several difficulties emerge. Should it not be the responsibility of the media or the appropriate regulatory agency or government bureau to carry out an investigation based on someone's complaint? It is reasonable for them to do so, providing they have some evidence in support of the complaint or claim. The damage has not yet been done, and the harm will not, in all likelihood, be done to the complaining party. If the action is criminal, then an investigation by a law-enforcing agency is appropriate. But the charges made by whistle blowers are often not criminal charges. And we do not expect newspapers or government agencies to carry out investigations whenever anyone claims that possible harm will be done by a product or practice. Unless harm is imminent, and very serious (e.g., a bomb threat), it is appropriate to act on evidence that substantiates a claim. The usual procedure, once an investigation is started or a complaint followed up, is to contact the party charged.

One does not have a moral obligation to blow the whistle simply because of one's hunch, guess, or personal assessment of possible danger, if supporting evidence and documentation are not available. One may, of course, have the obligation to attempt to get evidence if the harm is serious. But if it is unavailable—or unavailable without using illegal or immoral means—then one does not have the obligation to blow the whistle.

> 5. The employee must have good reason to believe that by going public the necessary changes will be brought about. The chance of being successful must be worth the risk one takes and the danger to which one is exposed.

Even with some documentation and evidence, a potential whistle blower may not be taken seriously, or may not be able to get the media or government agency to take any action. How far should one go, and how much must one try? The more serious the situation, the greater the effort required. But unless one has a reasonable expectation of success, one is not obliged to put oneself at great risk. Before going public, the potential whistle blower should know who (e.g., government agency, newspaper, columnist, TV reporter) will make use of his or her evidence, and how it will be handled. He or she should have good reason to expect that the action taken will result in the kind of change or result that he or she believes is morally appropriate.

The foregoing fourth and fifth conditions may seem too permissive to some and too stringent to others. They are too permissive for those who wish everyone to be ready and willing to blow the whistle whenever there is a chance that the public will be harmed. After all, harm to the public is more serious than harm to the whistle blower, and, in the long run, if everyone saw whistle blowing as obligatory, without satisfying the last two conditions, we would all be better off. If the fourth and fifth conditions must be satisfied, then people will only rarely have the moral obligation to blow the whistle.

If, however, whistle blowing were mandatory whenever the first three conditions were satisfied, and if one had the moral obligation to blow the whistle whenever one had a moral doubt or fear about safety, or whenever one disagreed with one's superiors or colleagues, one would be obliged to go public whenever one did not get one's way on such issues within a firm. But these conditions are much too weak, for the reasons already given. Other, stronger conditions, but weaker than those proposed, might be suggested. But any condition that makes whistle blowing mandatory in large numbers of cases, may possibly reduce the effectiveness of whistle blowing. If this were the result, and the practice were to become widespread, then it is doubtful that we would all be better off.

Finally, the claim that many people very often have the obligation to blow the whistle goes against the common view of the whistle blower as a moral hero, and against the commonly held feeling that whistle blowing is only rarely morally mandatory. This feeling may be misplaced. But a very strong argument is necessary to show that although the general public is morally mistaken in its view, the moral theoretician is correct in his or her assertion.

A consequence of accepting the fourth and fifth conditions stated is that the stringency of the moral obligation of whistle blowing corresponds with the common feeling of most people on this issue. Those in higher positions and those in professional positions in a firm are more likely to have the obligation to change a firm's policy or product—even by whistle blowing, if necessary—than are lower-placed employees. Engineers, for instance, are more likely to have access to data and designs than are assembly-line workers. Managers generally have a broader picture, and more access to evidence, than do nonmanagerial employees. Management has the moral responsibility both to see that the expressed moral concerns of those below them have been adequately considered and that the firm does not knowingly inflict harm on others.

The fourth and fifth conditions will appear too stringent to those who believe that whistle blowing is always a supererogatory act, that is always moral heroism, and that it is never morally obligatory. They might argue that, although we are not permitted to do what is immoral, we have no general moral obligation to prevent all others from acting immorally. This is what the whistle blower attempts to do. The counter to that, however, is to point out that whistle blowing is an act in which one attempts to prevent harm to a third party. It is not implausible to claim both that we are morally obliged to prevent harm to others at relatively little expense to ourselves, and that we are morally obliged to prevent great harm to a great many others, even at considerable expense to ourselves.

The five conditions outlined can be used by an individual to help decide whether he or she is morally permitted or required to blow the whistle. Third parties can also use these conditions when attempting to evaluate acts of whistle blowing by others, even though third parties may have difficulty determining whether the whistle blowing is morally motivated. It might be possible successfully to blow the whistle anonymously. But anonymous tips or stories seldom get much attention. One can confide in a government agent, or in a reporter, on condition that one's name not be disclosed. But this approach, too, is frequently ineffective in achieving the results required. To be effective, one must usually be willing to be identified, to testify publicly, to produce verifiable evidence, and to put oneself at risk. As with civil disobedience, what captures the conscience of others is the willingness of the whistle blower to suffer harm for the benefit of others, and for what he or she thinks is right.

Precluding the Need for Whistle Blowing

The need for moral heroes shows a defective society and defective corporations. It is more important to change the legal and corporate structures that make whistle blowing necessary than to convince people to be moral heroes.

Because it is easier to change the law than to change the practices of all corporations, it should be illegal for any employer to fire an employee, or to take any punitive measures, at the time or later, against an employee who satisfies the first three aforementioned conditions and blows the whistle on the company. Because satisfying those conditions makes the action morally justifiable, the law should protect the employee in acting in accordance with what his or her conscience demands. If the whistle is falsely blown, the company will have suffered no great harm. If it is appropriately blown, the company should suffer the consequences of its actions being made public. But to protect a whistle blower by passing such a law is no easy matter. Employers can make life difficult for whistle blowers without firing them. There are many ways of passing over an employee. One can be relegated to the back room of the firm, or be given unpleasant jobs. Employers can find reasons not to promote one or to give one raises. Not all of this can be prevented by law, but some of the more blatant practices can be prohibited.

Second, the law can mandate that the individuals responsible for the decision to proceed with a faulty product or to engage in a harmful practice be penalized. The law has been reluctant to interfere with the operations of companies. As a result, those in the firm who have been guilty of immoral and illegal practices have gone untouched even though the corporation was fined for its activity.

A third possibility is that every company of a certain size be required, by law, to have an inspector general or an internal operational auditor, whose job it is to uncover immoral and illegal practices. This person's job would be to listen to the moral concerns of employees, at every level, about the firm's practices. He or she should be independent of management, and report to the audit committee of the board, which, ideally, should be a committee made up entirely of outside board members. The inspector or auditor should be charged with making public those complaints that should be made public if not changed from within. Failure on the inspector's part to take proper action with respect to a worker's complaint, such that the worker is forced to go public, should be prima facie evidence of an attempt to cover up a dangerous practice or product, and the inspector should be subject to criminal charges.

In addition, a company that wishes to be moral, that does not wish to engage in harmful practices or to produce harmful products, can take other steps to preclude the necessity of whistle blowing. The company can establish channels whereby those employees who have moral concerns can get a fair hearing without danger to their position or standing in the company. Expressing such concerns, moreover, should be considered a demonstration of company loyalty and should be rewarded appropriately. The company might establish the position of ombudsman, to hear such complaints or moral concerns. Or an independent committee of the board might be established to hear such complaints and concerns. Someone might even be paid by the company to present the position of the would-be whistle blower, who would argue for what the company should do, from a moral point of view, rather than what those interested in meeting a schedule or making a profit would like to do. Such a person's success within the company could depend on his success in precluding whistle blowing, as well as the conditions that lead to it.

Whistleblowing and Professional Responsibility

Sissela Bok

"Whistleblowing" is a new label generated by our increased awareness of the ethical conflicts encountered at work. Whistleblowers sound an alarm from within the very organization in which they work, aiming to spotlight neglect or abuses that threaten the public interest.

The stakes in whistleblowing are high. Take the nurse who alleges that physicians enrich themselves in her hospital through unnecessary surgery; the engineer who discloses safety defects in the braking systems of a fleet of new rapid-transit vehicles; the Defense Department official who alerts Congress to military graft and overspending: all know that they pose a threat to those whom they denounce and that their own careers may be at risk.

Moral Conflicts

Moral conflicts on several levels confront anyone who is wondering whether to speak out about abuses or risks or serious neglect. In the first place, he must try to decide whether, other things being equal, speaking out is in fact in the public interest. This choice is often made more complicated by factual uncertainties: Who is responsible for the abuse or neglect? How great is the threat? And how likely is it that speaking out will precipitate changes for the better?

In the second place, a would-be whistleblower must weigh his responsibility to serve the public interest against the responsibility he owes to his colleagues and the institution in which he works. While the professional ethic requires collegial loyalty, the codes of ethics often stress responsibility to the public over and above duties to colleagues and clients. Thus the United States Code of Ethics for Government Servants asks them to "expose corruption wherever uncovered" and to "put loyalty to the highest moral principles and to country above loyalty to persons, party, or government."[1] Similarly, the largest professional engineering association requires members to speak out against abuses threatening the safety, health, and welfare of the public.[2]

A third conflict for would-be whistleblowers is personal in nature and cuts across the first two: even in cases where they have concluded that the facts warrant speaking out, and that their duty to do so overrides loyalties to colleagues and institutions, they often have reason to fear the results of carrying out such a duty. However strong this duty may seem in theory, they know that, in practice, retaliation is likely. As a result, their careers and their ability to support themselves and their families may be unjustly impaired.[3] A government handbook issued during the Nixon era recommends reassigning "undesirables" to places so remote that they would prefer to resign.

Adapted from Sissela Bok, "Whistleblowing and Professional Responsibility," *New York University Education Quarterly* Vol. II, 4 (1980), 2–7. Reprinted with permission.

Whistleblowers may also be downgraded or given work without responsibility or work for which they are not qualified; or else they may be given many more tasks than they can possibly perform. Another risk is that an outspoken civil servant may be ordered to undergo a psychiatric fitness-for-duty examination,[4] declared unfit for service, and "separated" as well as discredited from the point of view of any allegations he may be making. Outright firing, finally, is the most direct institutional response to whistleblowers.

Add to the conflicts confronting individual whistleblowers the claim to self-policing that many professions make, and professional responsibility is at issue in still another way. For an appeal to the public goes against everything that "self-policing" stands for. The question for the different professions, then, is how to resolve, insofar as it is possible, the conflict between professional loyalty and professional responsibility toward the outside world. The same conflicts arise to some extent in all groups, but professional groups often have special cohesion and claim special dignity and privileges.

The plight of whistleblowers has come to be documented by the press and described in a number of books. Evidence of the hardships imposed on those who chose to act in the public interest has combined with a heightened awareness of professional malfeasance and corruption to produce a shift toward greater public support of whistleblowers. Public service law firms and consumer groups have taken up their cause; institutional reforms and legislation have been proposed to combat illegitimate reprisals.[5]

Given the indispensable services performed by so many whistleblowers, strong support is often merited. But the new climate of acceptance makes it easy to overlook the dangers of whistleblowing: of uses in error or in malice; of work and reputations unjustly lost for those falsely accused; of privacy invaded and trust undermined. There comes a level of internal prying and mutual suspicion at which no institution can function. And it is a fact that the disappointed, the incompetent, the malicious, and the paranoid all too often leap to accusations in public. Worst of all, ideological persecution throughout the world traditionally relies on insiders willing to inform on their colleagues or even on their family members, often through staged public denunciations or press campaigns.

No society can count itself immune from such dangers. But neither can it risk silencing those with a legitimate reason to blow the whistle. How then can we distinguish between different instances of whistleblowing? A society that fails to protect the right to speak out even on the part of those whose warnings turn out to be spurious obviously opens the door to political repression. But from the moral point of view there are important differences between the aims, messages, and methods of dissenters from within.

Nature of Whistleblowing

Three elements, each jarring, and triply jarring when conjoined, lend acts of whistleblowing special urgency and bitterness: dissent, breach of loyalty, and accusation.

Like all dissent, whistleblowing makes public a disagreement with an authority or a majority view. But whereas dissent can concern all forms of disagreement with, for instance, religious dogma or government policy or court decisions, whistleblowing has the narrower aim of shedding light on negligence or abuse, or alerting to a risk, and of assigning responsibility for this risk.

Would-be whistleblowers confront the conflict inherent in all dissent: between conforming and sticking their necks out. The more repressive the authority they challenge, the greater the personal risk they take in speaking out. At exceptional times, as in times of war, even ordinarily tolerant authorities may come to regard dissent as unacceptable and even disloyal.[6]

Furthermore, the whistleblower hopes to stop the game; but since he is neither referee nor coach, and since he blows the whistle on his own team, his act is seen as a violation of loyalty. In holding his position, he has assumed certain obligations to his colleagues and clients. He may even have subscribed to a loyalty oath or a promise of confidentiality. Loyalty to colleagues and to clients comes to be pitted against loyalty to the public interest, to those who may be injured unless the revelation is made.

Not only is loyalty violated in whistleblowing, hierarchy as well is often opposed, since the whistleblower is not only a colleague but a subordinate. Though aware of the risks inherent in such disobedience, he often hopes to keep his job.[7] At times, however, he plans his alarm to coincide with leaving the institution. If he is highly placed, or joined by others, resigning in protest may effectively direct public attention to the wrongdoing at issue.[8] Still another alternative, often chosen by those who wish to be safe from retaliation, is to leave the institution quietly, to secure another post, and then to blow the whistle. In this way, it is possible to speak with the authority and knowledge of an insider without having the vulnerability of that position.

It is the element of accusation, of calling a "foul," that arouses the strongest reactions on the part of the hierarchy. The accusation may be of neglect, of willfully concealed dangers, or of outright abuse on the part of the colleagues or superiors. It singles out specific persons or groups as responsible for threats to the public interest. If no one could be held responsible—as in the case of an impending avalanche—the warning would not constitute whistleblowing.

The accusation of the whistleblower, moreover, concerns a present or an imminent threat. Past errors or misdeeds occasion such an alarm only if they still affect current practices. And risks far in the future lack the immediacy needed to make the alarm a compelling one, as well as the close connection to particular individuals that would justify actual accusations. Thus an alarm can be sounded about safety defects in a rapid-transit system that threaten or will shortly threaten passengers, but the revelation of safety defects in a system no longer in use, while of historical interest, would not constitute whistleblowing. Nor would the revelation of potential problems in a system not yet fully designed and far from implemented.[9]

Not only immediacy, but also specificity, is needed for there to be an alarm capable of pinpointing responsibility. A concrete risk must be at issue rather than a vague foreboding or a somber prediction. The act of whistle-blowing differs in this respect from the lamentation or the dire prophecy. An immediate and specific threat would normally be acted upon by those at risk. The whistleblower assumes that his message will alert listeners to something they do not know, or whose significance they have not grasped because it has been kept secret.

The desire for openness inheres in the temptation to reveal any secret, sometimes joined to an urge for self-aggrandizement and publicity and the hope for revenge for past slights or injustices. There can be pleasure, too—righteous or malicious—in laying bare the secrets of co-workers and in setting the record straight at last. Colleagues of the whistleblower often suspect his motives: they may regard him as a crank, as publicity-hungry, wrong about the facts, eager for scandal and discord, and driven to indiscretion by his personal biases and shortcomings.

For whistleblowing to be effective, it must arouse its audience. Inarticulate whistleblowers are likely to fail from the outset. When they are greeted by apathy, their message dissipates. When they are greeted by disbelief, they elicit no response at all. And when the audience is not free to receive or to act on the information—when censorship or fear of retribution stifles response—then the message rebounds to injure the whistleblower. Whistleblowing also requires the possibility of concerted public response: the idea of whistle-blowing in an anarchy is therefore merely quixotic.

Such characteristics of whistleblowing and strategic considerations for achieving an impact are common to the noblest warnings, the most vicious personal attacks, and the delusions of the paranoid. How can one distinguish the many acts of sounding an alarm that are genuinely in the public interest from all the petty, biased, or lurid revelations that pervade our querulous and gossip-ridden society? Can we draw distinctions between different whistle-blowers, different messages, different methods?

We clearly can, in a number of cases. Whistleblowing may be starkly inappropriate when in malice or error, or when it lays bare legitimately private matters having to do, for instance, with political belief or sexual life. It can, just as clearly, be the only way to shed light on an ongoing unjust practice such as drugging political prisoners or subjecting them to electroshock treatment. It can be the last resort for alerting the public to an impending disaster. Taking such clearcut cases as benchmarks, and reflecting on what it is about them that weighs so heavily for or against speaking out, we can work our way toward the admittedly more complex cases in which whistleblowing is not so clearly the right or wrong choice, or where different points of view exist regarding its legitimacy—cases where there are moral reasons both for concealment and for disclosure and where judgments conflict. Consider the following cases:[10]

A. As a construction inspector for a federal agency, John Samuels (not his real name) had personal knowledge of shoddy and deficient construction practices by private contractors. He knew his superiors received free vacations and entertainment, had their homes remodeled and found jobs for their relatives—all courtesy of a private contractor. These superiors later approved a multimillion no-bid contract with the same "generous" firm.

Samuels also had evidence that other firms were hiring nonunion laborers at a low wage while receiving substantially higher payments from the government for labor costs. A former superior, unaware of an office dictaphone, had incautiously instructed Samuels on how to accept bribes for overlooking sub-par performance.

As he prepared to volunteer this information to various members of Congress, he became tense and uneasy. His family was scared and the fears were valid. It might cost Samuels thousands of dollars to protect his job. Those who had freely provided Samuels with information would probably recant or withdraw their friendship. A number of people might object to his using a dictaphone to gather information. His agency would start covering up and vent its collective wrath upon him. As for reporters and writers, they would gather for a few days, then move on to the next story. He would be left without a job, with fewer friends, with massive battles looming, and without the financial means of fighting them. Samuels decided to remain silent.

B. Engineers of Company "A" prepared plans and specifications for machinery to be used in a manufacturing process and Company "A" turned them over to Company "B" for production. The engineers of Company "B," in reviewing the plans and specifications, came to the conclusion that they included certain miscalculations and technical deficiencies of a nature that the final product might be unsuitable for the purposes of the ultimate users, and that the equipment, if built according to the original plans and specifications, might endanger the lives of persons in proximity to it. The engineers of Company "B" called the matter to the attention of appropriate officials of their employer who, in turn, advised Company "A." Company "A" replied that its engineers felt that the design and specifications for the equipment were adequate and safe and that Company "B" should proceed to build the equipment as designed and specified. The officials of Company "B" instructed its engineers to proceed with the work.

C. A recently hired assistant director of admissions in a state university begins to wonder whether transcripts of some applicants accurately reflect their accomplishments. He knows that it matters to many in the university community, including alumni, that the football team continue its winning tradition. He has heard rumors that surrogates may be available to take tests for a fee, signing the names of designated applicants for admission, and that some of the transcripts may have been altered. But he has no hard facts. When he brings the question up with the director of admissions, he is told that the rumors are unfounded and asked not to inquire further into the matter.

Individual Moral Choice

What questions might those who consider sounding an alarm in public ask themselves? How might they articulate the problem they see and weigh its injustice before deciding whether or not to reveal it? How can they best try to make sure their choice is the right one? In thinking about these questions it helps to keep in mind the three elements mentioned earlier: dissent, breach of loyalty, and accusation. They impose certain requirements—of accuracy and judgment in dissent; of exploring alternative ways to cope with improprieties that minimize the breach of loyalty; and of fairness in accusation. For each, careful articulation and testing of arguments are needed to limit error and bias.

Dissent by whistleblowers, first of all, is expressly claimed to be intended to benefit the public. It carries with it, as a result, an obligation to consider the nature of this benefit and to consider also the possible harm that may come from speaking out: harm to persons or institutions and, ultimately, to the public interest itself. Whistleblowers must, therefore, begin by making every effort to consider the effects of speaking out versus those of remaining silent. They must assure themselves of the accuracy of their reports, checking and rechecking the facts before speaking out; specify the degree to which there is genuine impropriety; consider how imminent is the threat they see, how serious, and how closely linked to those accused of neglect and abuse.

If the facts warrant whistleblowing, how can the second element—breach of loyalty—be minimized? The most important question here is whether the existing avenues for change within the organization have been explored. It is a waste of time for the public as well as harmful to the institution to sound the loudest alarm first. Whistleblowing has to remain a last alternative because of its destructive side effects: it must be chosen only when other alternatives have been considered and rejected. They may be rejected if they simply do not apply to the problem at hand, or when there is not time to go through routine channels, or when the institution is so corrupt or coercive that steps will be taken to silence the whistleblower should he try the regular channels first.

What weight should an oath or a promise of silence have in the conflict of loyalties? One sworn to silence is doubtless under a stronger obligation because of the oath he has taken. He has bound himself, assumed specific obligations beyond those assumed in merely taking a new position. But even such promises can be overridden when the public interest at issue is strong enough. They can be overridden if they were obtained under duress or through deceit. They can be overridden, too, if they promise something that is in itself wrong or unlawful. The fact that one has promised silence is no excuse for complicity in covering up a crime or a violation of the public's trust.

The third element in whistleblowing—accusation—raises equally serious ethical concerns. They are concerns of fairness to the persons accused of impropriety. Is the message one to which the public is entitled in the first place? Or does it infringe on personal and private matters that one has no right to invade? Here, the very notion of what is in the public's best "interest" is at issue: "accusations" regarding an official's unusual sexual or religious experiences may well appeal to the public's interest without being information relevant to the "public interest."

Great conflicts arise here. We have witnessed excessive claims to executive privilege and to secrecy by government officials during the Watergate scandal in order to cover up for abuses the public had every right to discover. Conversely, those hoping to profit from prying into private matters have become adept at invoking "the public's right to know." Some even regard such private matters as threats to the public: they voice their own religious and political prejudices in the language of accusation. Such a danger is never stronger than when the accusation is delivered surreptitiously. The anonymous accusations made during the McCarthy period regarding political beliefs and associations often injured persons who did not even know their accusers or the exact nature of the accusations.

From the public's point of view, accusations that are openly made by identifiable individuals are more likely to be taken seriously. And in fairness to those criticized, openly accepted responsibility for blowing the whistle should be preferred to the denunciation or the leaked rumor. What is openly stated can more easily be checked, its source's motives challenged, and the underlying information examined. Those under attack may otherwise be hard put to defend themselves against nameless adversaries. Often they do not even know that they are threatened until it is too late to respond. The anonymous denunciation, moreover, common to so many regimes, places the burden of investigation on government agencies that may thereby gain the power of a secret police.

From the point of view of the whistleblower, on the other hand, the anonymous message is safer in situations where retaliation is likely. But it is also often less likely to be taken seriously. Unless the message is accompanied by indications of how the evidence can be checked, its anonymity, however safe for the source, speaks against it.

During this process of weighing the legitimacy of speaking out, the method used, and the degree of fairness needed, whistleblowers must try to compensate for the strong possibility of bias on their part. They should be scrupulously aware of any motive that might skew their message: a desire for self-defense in a difficult bureaucratic situation, perhaps, or the urge to seek revenge, or inflated expectations regarding the effect their message will have on the situation. (Needless to say, bias affects the silent as well as the outspoken. The motive for holding back important information about abuses and injustice ought to give similar cause for soul-searching.)

Likewise, the possibility of personal gain from sounding the alarm ought to give pause. Once again there is then greater risk of a biased message. Even if the whistleblower regards himself as incorruptible, his profiting from revelations of neglect or abuse will lead others to question his motives and to put less credence in his charges. If, for example, a government employee stands to make large profits from a book exposing the iniquities in his agency, there is danger that he will, perhaps even unconsciously, slant his report in order to cause more of a sensation.

A special problem arises when there is a high risk that the civil servant who speaks out will have to go through costly litigation. Might he not justifiably try to make enough money on his public revelations—say, through books or public speaking—to offset his losses? In so doing he will not strictly speaking have *profited* from his revelations: he merely avoids being financially crushed by their sequels. He will nevertheless still be suspected at the time of revelation, and his message will therefore seem more questionable.

Reducing bias and error in moral choice often requires consultation, even open debate:[11] methods that force articulation of the moral arguments at stake and challenge privately held assumptions. But acts of whistleblowing present special problems when it comes to open consultation. On the one hand, once the whistleblower sounds his alarm publicly, his arguments will be subjected to open scrutiny: he will have to articulate his reasons for speaking out and substantiate his charges. On the other hand, it will then be too late to retract the alarm or to combat its harmful effects, should his choice to speak out have been ill-advised.

For this reason, the whistleblower owes it to all involved to make sure of two things: that he has sought as much and as objective advice regarding his choice as he can *before* going public; and that he is aware of the arguments for and against the practice of whistleblowing in general, so that he can see his own choice against as richly detailed and coherently structured a background as possible. Satisfying these two requirements once again has special problems because of the very nature of whistleblowing: the more corrupt the circumstances, the more dangerous it may be to seek consultation before speaking out. And yet, since the whistleblower himself may have a biased view of the state of affairs, he may choose not to consult others when in fact it would be not only safe but advantageous to do so; he may see corruption and conspiracy where none exists.

Notes

1. Code of Ethics for Government Service passed by the U.S. House of Representatives in the 85th Congress (1958) and applying to all government employees and office holders.
2. Code of Ethics of the Institute of Electrical and Electronics Engineers, Article IV.
3. For case histories and descriptions of what befalls whistleblowers, see: Rosemary Chalk and Frank von Hippel, "Due Process for Dissenting Whistle-Blowers," *Technology Review* 81 (June-July 1979): 48-55; Alan S. Westin and Stephen Salisbury, eds., *Individual Rights in the Corporation* (New York: Pantheon, 1980); Helen Dudar, "The Price of Blowing the Whistle," *New York Times Magazine,* 30 October 1979, pp. 41-54; John Edsall, *Scientific Freedom and Responsibility* (Washington, D.C.: American Association for the Advancement of Science, 1975), p. 5; David Ewing, *Freedom Inside the Organization* (New York: Dutton, 1977); Ralph Nader, Peter Petkas, and Kate Blackwell, *Whistle Blowing* (New York: Grossman, 1972); Charles Peter and Taylor Branch, *Blowing the Whistle* (New York: Praeger, 1972).
4. Congressional hearings uncovered a growing resort to mandatory psychiatric examinations. See U.S. Congress, House Committee on Post Office and Civil Service, Subcommittee on Compensation and Employee Benefits *Forced Retirement/Psychiatric Fitness for Duty Exams,* 95th Cong., 2nd sess., 3 November 1978, pp. 2-4. See also the Subcommittee hearings of 28 February 1978. Psychiatric referral for whistleblowers has become

institutionalized in government service, but it is not uncommon in private employment. Even persons who make accusations without being "employed" in the organization they accuse have been classified as unstable and thus as unreliable witnesses. See, e.g., Jonas Robitscher, "Stigmatization and Stone-Walling: The Ordeal of Martha Mitchell," *Journal of Psychohistory,* 6, 1979, pp. 393-407.

5. For an account of strategies and proposals to support government whistleblowers, see Government Accountability Project, *A Whistleblower's Guide to the Federal Bureaucracy* (Washington, D.C.: Institute for Policy Studies, 1977).

6. See, e.g., Samuel Eliot Morison, Frederick Merk, and Frank Friedel, *Dissent in Three American Wars* (Cambridge: Harvard University Press, 1970).

7. In the scheme worked out by Albert Hirschman in *Exit, Voice and Loyalty* (Cambridge: Harvard University Press, 1970), whistleblowing represents "voice" accompanied by a preference not to "exit," though forced "exit" is clearly a possibility and "voice" after or during "exit" may be chosen for strategic reasons.

8. Edward Weisband and Thomas N. Franck, *Resignation in Protest* (New York: Grossman, 1975).

9. Future developments can, however, be the cause for whistleblowing if they are seen as resulting from steps being taken or about to be taken that render them inevitable.

10. Case A is adapted from Louis Clark, "The Sound of Professional Suicide," *Barrister,* Summer 1978, p. 10; Case B is Case 5 in Robert J. Baum and Albert Flores, eds., *Ethical Problems of Engineering* (Troy, N.Y.: Rensselaer Polytechnic Institute, 1978), p. 186.

11. I discuss these questions of consultation and publicity with respect to moral choice in chapter 7 of Sissela Bok, *Lying* (New York: Pantheon, 1978); and in *Secrets* (New York: Pantheon Books, 1982) Ch. IX and XV.

CHAPTER 8

Working Conditions

Of Acceptable Risk

William W. Lowrance

Few headlines are so alarming, perplexing, and personal in their implications as those concerning safety. Frightening stories jolt our early morning complacency so frequently that we wonder whether things can really be *that* bad. We are disturbed by what sometimes appear to be haphazard and irresponsible regulatory actions, and we can't help being suspicious of all the assaults on our freedoms and our pocketbooks made in the name of safety. We hardly know which cries of "Wolf!" to respond to; but we dare not forget that even in the fairy tale, the wolf really did come.

The issues: X-rays, cosmetics, DDT, lead, pharmaceuticals, toys, saccharin, intrauterine contraceptive devices, power lawn mowers, air pollutants, noise. . . .

The questions: How do we determine how hazardous these things are? Why is it that cyclamates one day dominate the market as the principal calorie-cutting sweetener in millions of cans of diet drinks, only to be banned the next day because there is a "very slight chance" they may cause cancer? Why is it that one group of eminent experts says that medical X-rays (or food preservatives, or contraceptive pills) are safe and ought to be used more widely, while another group of authorities, equally reputable, urges that exposure to the same things should be restricted because they are unsafe? At what point do debates such as that over DDT stop being scientific and objective and start being political and subjective? How can anyone gauge the public's willingness to accept risks? . . .

Judging Safety

. . . Safety is not measured. *Risks* are measured. Only when those risks are weighed on the balance of social values can safety be judged: *a thing is safe if its attendant risks are judged to be acceptable.*

Determining safety, then, involves two extremely different kinds of activities. . . .

Measuring risks—measuring the probability and severity of harm—is an empirical, scientific activity;

Judging safety—judging the acceptability of risks—is a normative, political activity.

Although the difference between the two would seem obvious, it is all too often forgotten, ignored, or obscured. This failing is often the cause of the disputes that hit the front pages.

We advocate use of this particular definition for many reasons. It encompasses the other, more specialized, definitions. By employing the word "acceptable," it emphasizes that safety decisions are relativistic and judgmental. It immediately elicits the crucial questions, "Acceptable in whose view?" and "Acceptable in what terms?" and "Acceptable for whom?" Further, it avoids all implication that safety is an intrinsic, absolute, measurable property of things.

In the following two examples, risk-measuring activity is described in Roman type, and safety-judging in italics. . . .

A scientific advisory committee is charged by the government with recommending radiation exposure standards. The committee reviews all the animal experiments, the occupational medical record, the epidemiological surveys of physicians and patients exposed to X-rays, and the studies of the survivors of the Nagasaki and Hiroshima explosions. It inventories the modes of exposure; it reviews present radiation standards, including those of other nations and international organizations; and it examines the practical possibility of reducing exposures. *It weighs all the risks, costs, and benefits, and then decides that the allowed exposure has been unacceptably high; it recommends that because the intensity of some major sources, such as medical X-rays, can be reduced at reasonable cost and with little loss of effectiveness, the standards should be made more restrictive.*

Over a three-year period, William Ruckelshaus, administrator of the Environmental Protection Agency, considered many different petitions from the various interested parties before acting on his agency's inquiry into the use of DDT. Finally, in 1972, he ruled that the scientific evidence led him to conclude that DDT is "an uncontrollable, durable chemical that persists in the aquatic and terrestrial environments" and "collects in the food chain," and that although the evidence regarding human tumorogenicity and other long-term effects was inconclusive, there was little doubt that DDT has serious ecological effects. Ruckelshaus reviewed the benefits of DDT in the protection of cotton and other crops and affirmed that other equally effective pesticides were available. *Summing the arguments, then, he ruled that "the long-range risks of continued use of DDT for use on cotton and most other crops is unacceptable and outweighs any benefits. . . ."[1]*

. . . In heading down the slopes a skier attests that he accepts the risks; at a later stage of his life he may reject those very same risks because of changes in his awareness, his physical fragility, or his responsibilities to family or firm. While one woman may accept the side effects of oral contraceptives because she doesn't want to risk pregnancy, another woman may so fear the pill that she judges a diaphragm to be a more acceptable compromise among the several risks. Even though he is fully aware of the mangled fingers, chronic coughs, or damaged eyes or ears of those around him, a worker may accept those risks rather than endure the daily nuisance and tedium of blade guards, respirators, goggles, or ear protectors; but his employer, for reasons of cost, paternalism, or government requirement, may find this risky behavior unacceptable. . . .

Acceptance may be just a passive, or even stoical, continuance of historical momentum, as when people accept their lot at a dangerous traditional trade or continue to live near a volcano. Acceptance may persist because no alternatives are seen, as in the case of automobiles and many other technological hazards. Acceptance may result from ignorance or misperception of risk: variations on "I didn't know the gun was loaded" and "It won't happen to me" show up in every area. Acceptance may be simply acquiescence in a majority decision, such as a referendum-based decision on fluoridation, or in a decision by some governing elite, as with the average person's tacit approval of most public standards. Acceptance may even be an expression of preference for modern but known risks over perhaps smaller but less well understood risks, as with preference for coal- and oil-fired power plants over nuclear plants. . . . It is important to appreciate that such decisions may or may not be—and are certainly not necessarily—fair, just, consistent, efficient, or rational.

There is a great deal of overlap between the two decisionmaking domains implied by our definition of safety. Scientists, engineers, and medical people are called upon by political officials to judge the desirability of certain courses for society. Panels of scientists recommend exposure limits. Physicians prescribe medicines and diets. Engineers design dams, television sets, toasters, and airplanes. All of these decisions are heavily, even if only implicitly, value-laden.

On the other hand, by adopting particular risk data in their deliberations, political and judiciary agents at least implicitly rule on the correctness of measurements. The business of determining risk must often be settled operationally in hearings or other political deliberations, because the day-to-day management of society can't always wait for scientists to complete their cautious, precise determinations, which may take years. Congressional committees and regulatory agencies conduct hearings and issue rulings on the risks of food additives and air pollutants. Courts rule on the dangers of DDT. Risk and its acceptability are weighed by both manufacturers and consumers in the push-and-pull of the marketplace.

Between the two activities—measuring risk and judging safety—lies a discomforting no-man's-land . . . or every-man's-land. Scientists on the fringe of the political arena, attempting to avoid charges of elitism, are looking for more objective ways to appraise society's willingness to accept various risks. At the same time, political officials confronted by scientifically controversial "facts" that never seem to gain the clarity promised by textbooks are exploring the possibilities of advisory assistance, fact-finding hearings, and formal technology assessments.

Guides to Acceptability

"Reasonableness." This is by far the most commonly cited and most unimpeachable principle in safety judgments. For instance, the legislative charter of the Consumer Product Safety Commission directs it to "reduce unreasonable risk of injury" associated with consumer goods.[2] Panels of experts frequently invoke a "rule of reason" in rendering advice. The concept of reasonableness pervades economic analyses of hazard reduction and the structures of legal liability.

Unfortunately, reference to reasonableness is in a sense a phantom citation. It provides little specific guidance for public decisionmakers, for whom reasonableness is presumably a requirement for staying in office. Not surprisingly, the Consumer Product Safety Act does not venture to define reasonableness. As guidance, the Safety Commission quotes the description given by the final report of its progenitor, the National Commission on Product Safety:

> Risks of bodily harm to users are not unreasonable when consumers understand that risks exist, can appraise their probability and severity, know how to cope with them, and voluntarily accept them to get benefits that could not be obtained in less risky ways. When there is a risk of this character, consumers have reasonable opportunity to protect themselves; and public authorities should hesitate to substitute their value judgments about the desirability of the risk for those of the consumers who choose to incur it.
>
> But preventable risk is not reasonable
>
> (a) when consumers do not know that it exists; or
>
> (b) when, though aware of it, consumers are unable to estimate its frequency and severity; or
>
> (c) when consumers do not know how to cope with it, and hence are likely to incur harm unnecessarily; or
>
> (d) when risk is unnecessary in . . . that it could be reduced or eliminated at a cost in money or in the performance of the product that consumers would willingly incur if they knew the facts and were given the choice.[3]

The point of safety judgments is indeed to decide what is reasonable; it's just that any rational decision will have to be made on more substantive bases, such as the following, which are in a sense criteria for reasonableness.

Custom of usage. The Food and Drug Administration has designated hundreds of food additives as "generally recognized as safe" (GRAS). The GRAS list, established in 1958, includes such substances as table salt, vitamin A, glycerin, and baking powder, whose long use has earned them wide and generally unquestioned acceptance.[4] Being classified as GRAS exempts those substances from having to pass certain premarket clearances. From time to time this sanction is challenged, but most critics of the GRAS list have argued not so much that it should be abandoned as that individual items should be subjected to periodic review. In 1969, following its decision to ban the popular artificial sweetener cyclamate (until then GRAS), the Food and Drug Administration initiated a full review of the GRAS list. That review is still in progress, and "so far nothing has been found to lead to any further bans similar to the one on cyclamate."[5]

Prevailing professional practice. Long established as the criterion for physicians' clinical practice, this principle is increasingly being invoked in evaluating the protection that engineers, designers, and manufacturers provide their clients. Buildings are said to conform to the "prevailing local standards." Toys are "of a common design." X-ray machines are operated "at normal intensities." In many instances the wisdom of such deference to convention can be questioned. The underlying assumption is that if a thing has been in common use it must be okay, since any adverse effects would have become evident, and that a thing sanctioned by custom is safer than one not tested at all.

Best available practice, highest practicable protection, and lowest practicable exposure. Air and water quality regulations have stipulated that polluters control their emissions by the "best available means." So have noise abatement laws. Obviously, although such a requirement does provide the public regulator with a vague rationale, he must still exercise judgment over what constitutes "best" practice for every individual case and what economic factors should be considered in defining "practicable." Hardware for pollution control or noise abatement may exist, but only at a cost that many allege to be prohibitive; is it to be considered "available"? . . .

"No detectable adverse effect." Although such a principle is applied frequently in our everyday lives, and although it has a certain operational value, it is a weak criterion which may amount to little more than an admission of uncertainty or ignorance. Many hazards now recognized, such as moderate levels of X-rays or asbestos or vinyl chloride, could at an earlier time have been said to have "no detectable adverse effect." . . .

The threshold principle. If it can be proven that there is indeed a level of exposure below which no adverse effect occurs, subthreshold exposures might be considered safe. But determining whether there really is a threshold, for the especially vulnerable as well as for the average populace, is usually a nearly impossible task. As we mentioned earlier, for loud noises there are clearly thresholds of annoyance, pain, and ear damage. But whether there are thresholds for effects of radiation, chemical carcinogens, and mutagens has never been firmly established. . . .

On Being, and Being Held, Responsible

In essence the issue is posed by the following questions: Should technically trained people be expected to bear any social responsibilities different from those borne by others? Why? What are the unique obligations? And further, can all the obligations be met simply by individuals working alone, or are there in addition some responsibilities requiring technical people to act collectively? . . .

Scientists, engineers, designers, architects, physicians, public health experts, and other technically trained people *do* have special responsibilities to the rest of society with respect to personal safety. Some principal kinds of risks which ought to be taken upon the conscience of the technical community are:

1. Technically complex risks whose intricacies are comprehensible only to highly trained people;
2. Risks that can be significantly reduced by applying new technology or by improving the application of existing technology;
3. Risks constituting public problems whose technical components need to be distinguished explicitly from their social and political components so that responsibilities are assigned properly;
4. Technological intrusions on personal freedom made in the pursuit of safety; and
5. Risks whose possible consequences appear so grave or irreversible that prudence dictates the urging of extreme caution, even before the risks are known precisely.

Notice that we have said that these problems *should be taken as matters of conscience* by the technical community. Whether the verb describing the action should be *protecting,* or *watching over,* or *looking out for,* or *issuing a warning,* depends on the situation. The specific response might be doing an experiment, raising an issue before a professional society, blowing the whistle on an employer, exerting political leverage, or aiding a legislator or administrator in untangling the parts of a public issue.

. . . These responsibilities have several deep origins. Basically they arise, in congruence with all major moral philosophies, from the conviction that every person has a general responsibility for the well-being of his fellow men. Reflecting this, the common law has held through the centuries that anyone who becomes aware of the possibility of danger has a responsibility to warn those at risk. But we are obliged to push further and ask whether, in this age of cultural specialization, there isn't more to the issue—for if we don't press, we may be left simply making vague exhortations to virtue.

When we examine what society expects, we find that it does look to the technical community for warning, guidance, and protection, in the kinds of situations we have described and in others as well. Highly trained people are definitely seen as having special status. Given this, a key to developing a compelling ethical argument, and to understanding why the lay public feels as it does, seems to reside in the notion of professionalism.

Over the years a tacit but nonetheless real compact has developed. Society *invests in* training and professional development of scientists and other technical people. It invests heavily; substantial public subsidy of one form or another goes to virtually every college, university, medical school, field station, and research facility in the United States. By and large the professions are left free to govern themselves, control admission to membership, choose their direction of research, enforce the quality of work, and direct the allocation of public funds within their subject area.

Concomitantly, society *invests with* the professions and their institutions certain trusts, among them a trust that the professions will watch over the well-being of society, including its safety. As Berkeley sociologist William Kornhauser has expressed it, "Professional responsibility is based on the belief that the power conferred by expertise entails a fiduciary relationship to society."[6] This "fiduciary relationship," or what we have called a tacit compact, is what gives rise to the ethical "oughts."

. . . As this century has careened along it has brought an increasing need for a collective shouldering of responsibility. The one-to-one personal relationships that once governed ethical conduct have been supplanted by more diffuse ones involving many intermediaries. Industrial scientists plan their research by committee. Engineers who design tunnels and dams interact with their ultimate public clients only indirectly, through managers, attorneys, and the officials who supervise public contracts. Physicians may still carry the wand of Aesculapius, but they do so in the context of one of the nation's largest businesses. Two sorts of diffuseness enlarge the collective dimension. First, the cliency is expanding, often in the interest of social justice: a national health care system that intends to reach every citizen has quite different ethical dimensions from a free-market private physician system. And second, as we confront hazards that are more diffuse, we often realize that *nobody* has considered that the problem was specifically his concern: there is no International Agency for the Supervision of the Ozone Layer.

We try to manage these problems by government action, building in mechanisms of accountability where possible; and we test the justice of specific actions in the courts, as when people feel that they are being unfairly denied medical care. Beyond that, and usually leading it, we have to depend on action by communities of scholars and coteries of professionals—hence the obligations we listed earlier.

Two current cases exemplify some of the difficulties. Three engineers in California, backed to a limited extent by several engineering societies, have pressed suit against the Bay Area Rapid Transit (BART) system for firing them after they publicly protested that the automatic train control systems their companies were developing for BART were inadequate and not up to the best professional standards with regards to passenger safety. The dispute raises complex questions about how great the risks really were, whether they should have been considered acceptable, how engineers should play their roles, how corporations should handle dissension, and what the professional societies should do.[7] In another case, an international group of biologists has voluntarily convened itself to discuss whether and how to control certain genetics experiments that would have bizarre, disastrous consequences if they ran amok.[8]

There is little precedent for either case, so it is not surprising that neither has been handled with assurance. In the BART case, the engineering societies were not well prepared to act and could muster only limited support. Perhaps for lack of experience and guidance, the three engineers party to the suit were not able to pursue the case through the courts to completion; the case has reportedly had to be settled out of court, thus setting only weak legal precedent. In the genetic experiments case, the scientists involved continue to suffer the anguish of not even being able to reach a firm consensus on the issue, and they are hard pressed to take any action other than to issue stern pronouncements, plead for prudence, and cross their collective fingers that researchers will be careful.

We have developed the above arguments because we believe they are important. They are by no means the sole guide to action. There can be no substitute for honesty, courage, sacrifice, and the other manifestations of high morality. Nor should legal and other sanctions fail to be applied: enforceable building codes can be adopted to supplement voluntary action; duties can be made a matter of contractual responsibility; and falsification of records is cause for lawsuit. There are many obligations in addition to ethical ones. The ethical ones are of a special sort, though, and urgently deserve to be developed.

The great questions of responsibility will remain with us. Is simply providing information or issuing warnings a sufficient response, or ought those with the knowledge do more? How is responsibility passed up through administrative and managerial hierarchies? In what sense is tacit acquiescence in a misleading scheme irresponsible (as when corporate scientists who know better say nothing when their company makes false claims for its products or evades pollution control laws)? To what extent should those who generate scientific and technological innovations be responsible for their subsequent application?

Notes

1. U.S. Environmental Protection Agency, "Consolidated DDT hearings," *37 Federal Register,* 13369–13376 (July 7, 1972).
2. Consumer Product Safety Act, *Public Law 82-573* (1972).
3. National Commission on Product Safety, *Final Report,* 11 (1970).
4. 21 *U.S. Code of Federal Regulations,* 121.101 (subpart B).
5. Alan T. Spiher, Jr., "Food ingredient review: Where it stands now," *FDA Consumer,* 23–26 (June 1974).

6. William Kornhauser, *Scientists in Industry,* 1 (University of California Press, Berkeley, 1962).

7. Gordon D. Friedlander, *IEEE Spectrum,* 11, 69–76 (October 1974); Gordon D. Friedlander, "Fixing BART," *IEEE Spectrum,* 12, 43–45 (February 1975).

8. Nicholas Wade, "Genetics: Conference sets strict controls to replace moratorium," *Science* 187, 931–935 (1975); Stuart Auerbach, "And man created risks," *Washington Post* (March 9, 1975.)

Working Conditions

Vincent Barry

The conditions under which people work are as morally significant as wages. Considerable legislation and enlightened business leadership have significantly reduced the dinginess that often characterized the work place in former years. Nevertheless, problems remain. Safety laws and company policies cannot keep pace with the dangers that employees face as a result of modern technology and equipment. In brief, working conditions easily can violate the ideal of noninjury.

For example, at a Shell location not too long ago, a refinery employee nearly lost an arm while using a high-pressure lubricating gun. The incident began harmlessly enough when the worker inadvertently got his forearm in the way of the spray jetting from the gun's nozzle. He wiped the grease off, unmindful of the serious injury he had sustained. Later the arm swelled and became painful, and surgery was required. For a while surgeons thought the arm would have to be amputated.

What had happened? Grease, usually a soft substance, when propelled to high velocity can become like needles that penetrate the skin. In this instance the grease penetrated the skin, depositing foreign material up to the worker's elbow. The material, insoluble in blood, could be removed only by surgery.

Was this a bizarre, remote occurrence? Not exactly. With the widespread use of a similar tool, the high-pressure airless paint gun, such incidents have become common enough for concern. Indeed, a recent survey by the Consumer Product Safety Commission's Bureau of Epidemiology indicated that an estimated 847 surgeons and hand specialists have treated at least one injury caused by injection from high-pressure grease guns or airless spray paint guns. Ninety-six percent of the patients were professional painters.[1]

Modern technology has also introduced another threat to worker health and safety heretofore unacknowledged: noise. So serious a threat has noise become in many occupational settings that the 1970 Occupational Safety and Health Act proposed that 85 decibels be the maximum noise level to which a

From Vincent Barry, *Moral Issues in Business,* 2nd ed. (Belmont, CA: Wadsworth, 1983), pp. 129–132.

worker may be exposed during an eight-hour day. Many companies don't think this goal is enforceable or realistic. Nevertheless, worker health and safety is an ethical concern to which employers must address themselves, even in the absence of legislation.

Despite legislation the scope of occupational hazards remains awesome and generally unrecognized. Thus, although the thrust of the 1970 Occupational Safety and Health Act is ". . . to ensure so far as possible every working man and woman in the nation safe and healthful working conditions," implementation of the act has been spotty. Consider the fact that there are fewer than 100 qualified Occupational Safety and Health Administration (OSHA) industrial hygienists and approximately 500 OSHA inspectors for about 4 million work places. Add to this fact that OSHA has established only one permanent standard—for asbestos, recognizing the epidemic of asbestosis and asbestos-induced lung and other cancers, especially among insulation workers. What's more, of 80 million workers, there are over 7 million annual work-related diseases and injuries, of which 2 million are disabling and 14,000 fatal. Estimates of losses run as high as 250 million person-working days, costing $1.5 billion in wages and an annual loss to the gross national product (GNP) of $8 billion.[2] Before presuming that things are getting better, reflect on the fact that the incidence of disabling injuries in manufacturing industries was 20 percent greater in the late 1970s than it was in 1958.

Although of paramount importance, worker health and safety represent just one facet of working conditions that both affects the work environment and raises moral questions. There are numerous others: forcing employees to participate in questionable legal or moral activity, showing favoritism in dealing with employees, and transferring workers great distances without sharing costs. In some cases, working conditions can raise multiple moral concerns. Take, for example, forced overtime, which is the practice of compelling workers to work beyond their regular hours or shifts. Occurring on an occasional basis, forced overtime is rarely injurious but rather can be beneficial in helping workers meet basic maintenance needs. But what about when forced overtime becomes a regular practice? In some instances workers must put in so much overtime that they lack time to fill vital personal needs, such as tending to their families or restoring themselves through recreation. The implications are serious not only for workers but for the firm and consumers as well because efficiency, productivity, and quality can suffer. The moral implications of forced overtime grow even more serious when the practice is used to avoid hiring additional workers. Here questions of justice and social responsibility invariably crop up.

Management Styles

How managers conduct themselves on the job can often do more to enhance or diminish the work environment than any other facet of employer-employee relations. Partially influencing this conduct are the general assumptions managers make about human beings and the subsequent leadership styles they adopt.

The late Douglas McGregor proposed two basic sets of assumptions about human beings that he observed managers take.[3] He called these Theories X and Y. We describe them here because so many moral problems that arise relative to managerial treatment of employees have their roots in these assumptions. In order to evaluate intelligently the morality of specific behavior, it's frequently necessary to evaluate the underlying assumptions about people that give rise to it. For example, if a male chauvinist manager treats female subordinates unequally and unfairly, the immorality of his behavior is ultimately rooted in his assumptions about women generally. If he weren't sexually prejudiced, he probably wouldn't behave the way he does. Given his assumptions about women, however, his behavior is altogether consistent and, in his mind, moral. After all, he believes women are inherently unequal and inferior to men. If you would consider his behavior immoral, it's likely because you believe his assumptions are unsound.

According to McGregor, managers who espouse Theory X believe that workers essentially dislike work and will do everything they can to avoid it. As a result, such workers must be coerced and bullied in order to make their efforts conform to organizational objectives. Such managers insist that the average person wishes to avoid responsibility, lacks ambition, and primarily values security above everything else.

Managers who espouse Theory Y believe that workers essentially like work and view it as something natural and potentially enjoyable. As a result, these managers don't believe that strict control and direction is the only way to achieve organizational goals. Similarly, they view workers as being motivated by self-fulfillment goals as well as by promise of more money. Workers don't eschew responsibility but accept it and seek it out.

These assumptions inspire different and often divergent managerial conduct toward employees, which is perhaps best observed in the leadership styles that managers adopt. For example, Theory X managers likely provide autocratic leadership. They closely shepherd employees by giving orders and directions to subordinates, and they rarely solicit ideas about how tasks should be performed. They tell employees what to do and how to do it. They expect little more of employees than that they follow orders. Theory Y managers, on the other hand, are likely to be more democratic. While informing employees of the tasks to be performed, they also solicit new ideas from them regarding the execution of the tasks. They use this input to refine their own ideas about how to perform tasks. Theory Y managers might also tend to be laissez-faire in their approach to work, providing minimum direction for employees and leaving to them decisions on work methods. Laissez-faire managers generally view themselves as resource persons, trouble shooters, and supporters rather than directors of the work force.

As suggested, many moral problems in management-employee relations can be traced to basic managerial assumptions about workers. Moral issues crop up when managers routinize themselves to a leadership role regardless of the idiosyncrasies of the employees they deal with. This is analogous to the question of justice that arises in subjecting everyone to the same intelligence test despite the fact that the test has been devised with a select group in mind. In both cases not only are legitimate individual differences overlooked, but these differences become the basis of punitive treatment. Thus, it's very tempting for managers, even of the non-Theory X variety, to assume an autocratic style for unskilled workers, laissez-faire for highly skilled ones, and democratic for employees who fall somewhere in between. But unfortunately human nature defies such glib pigeonholing and stereotyping. Some employees at whatever level respond to and need little managerial orchestration; others need and want close supervision. When managers overlook this, they overlook people's needs and run risks of creating a work atmosphere that's not only hostile to workers but also unconducive to optimum productivity. They invite injustice into the work place as well, for injustice can arise as much from treating people identically as treating them unequally. If these problems are to be avoided, it seems that managers must choose a style of leadership suitable to the needs, abilities, and predilections of those in their charge.

Whereas the preceding topics—hiring, promotions, discipline, discharge, wages, and working conditions—are areas of perennial management concerns, today's managers must also deal with new challenges that have grown out of recent and profound social and cultural changes. One of these challenges concerns the treatment of special employees such as women, who increasingly are entering the American work force.

Notes

1. *Reported in Robert E. Swindle,* Fundamentals of Modern Business (*Belmont, CA: Wadsworth Publishing Co., 1977*), p. 72.
2. *See Rollin H. Simonds,* "OSHA Compliance: Safety Is Good Business," Personnel, July-August, 1973.
3. *Douglas McGregor,* The Human Side of Enterprise (*NY: McGraw-Hill, 1960*).

Managerial Secrecy: An Ethical Examination
Victor Pompa

In these tough economic times many employers are faced with tremendous cost pressures, and they often reduce costs by restructuring organizations, reorganizing work, eliminating jobs and letting people go. This requires management planning and hence foreknowledge of events which will effect certain employees. Managers, in general, become responsible in two senses for certain

Victor Pompa, "Managerial Secrecy: An Ethical Examination," Journal of Business Ethics **11** (1992) 147–156.

employees becoming unemployed. In the first sense, managers have the positional authority to trim the workforce. In the second sense, they are the people who actually decide who will lose a job. In my business experience, managers tend to withhold foreknowledge of impending organizational changes, especially when the changes will limit or eliminate jobs.

This paper will be an attempt to describe such an organizational situation, and derive ethical conditions for releasing or withholding foreknowledge about the elimination of jobs. First, I will provide general ethical arguments against management secrecy in layoff situations, then a scenario of just such an incident to include specific management justifications for secrecy. This second section may be regarded as the rebuttal to the general case. Third, I will provide philosophical justifications for secrecy and finally an ethical analysis of the reasons to withhold information presented in Section Two.

The Prima Facie Case against Management Secrecy

I believe that the presumption should be against withholding information about layoffs on both consequentialist and deontological grounds. However, there may be specific situations in which secrecy is justified and the analysis will attempt to define those conditions. This paper will not be a discussion about the ethics of laying people off, although that is in itself a significant ethical issue.

In consequentialist terms, two kinds of significant harm are caused by withholding information about an upcoming layoff: financial and psychological. People (employees, managers) and the company are harmed.

Employees who are laid off without warning are harmed because they are poorly prepared to respond to their sudden loss of income. In this day and age, few working people (even white collar employees) can face loss of income with equanimity. Basic necessities, such as shelter, food, transportation and healthcare require an enormous amount of money, even for the frugal. The stress of meeting financial commitments is a major burden of life for most. Losing a job is ranked at the top of stress producing situations, along with the death of a spouse or divorce. The less notice you have, the more harm can occur. You don't have time to save, to cut back or to avoid further financial commitments. You have less time to find another job, while you still have an income.

Sometimes, it is true, people who are laid off experience change that leads them to a better life—financially, emotionally or in their orientation to work. For example, a corporate manager may have an orientation to work which includes the image of a successful career, including steady promotion, increasing staff size, regular merit pay increases. She may choose to put work issues before family and social life. She may also include subordinating personal, and intellectual interests to the needs of the organization. After a layoff, this person might rearrange her priorities and find herself happier and more productive. She might like her new career much better, do a kind of work which is more personally satisfying, or spend more time with her family.

From a consequentialist point of view, these events must be considered uncommon, fortuitous and certainly not foreseeable. Otherwise more people would make these radical changes voluntarily, rather than under the press of necessity. In any case, whether the benefits of the change outweigh the pain of the transition is not a calculation that can be made for some time after the event. It certainly cannot be included in these calculations when managers decide to withhold information about the impending layoff. In other words, a manager can't, in good conscience say "I know my employee, (an accountant for example), will be happier as an artist or a shoe salesman, so being laid off will actually be a net benefit to him."

From this perspective, to the degree that withholding the information impairs an employee from managing the hardship and stress which follows the loss of a job, it is unjustified.

The negative consequences for the company are also significant. As a human enterprise, with purpose and social dimension, successful business organizations depend on a measure of trust between managers and employees. Withholding critical information about job security will breach trust in the eyes of employees. Those who remain after a layoff are generally shaken. They have the feeling that they could be next. They will become suspicious and wonder when (not *if*) the manager will withhold information again. This will hinder business operations since employees will discount future management communications and spend time and energy trying to uncover what managers are *really* planning. Some will also spend time nursing grievances, spreading rumors and looking for ways to take advantage of the company before it takes advantage of them.

Consequently, managers will have to follow one of two paths in the attempt to restore employee performance. They may practice a much more open form of management, disclosing considerable amounts of background information before every decision to demonstrate that nothing significant is hidden. Or, they may take a more autocratic and coercive stance to try to ensure that work gets done. The latter has a tendency to produce *malicious obedience,* that behavior which is characterized by following orders to the letter, especially when initiative would be beneficial. Think of it as "working to rule," doing only what is expressly stipulated. Just the normal number of everyday, unexpected events will create enormous amounts of extra work for the manager, since he or she will need to give explicit instructions for each new event. In either case, normal communications and work interactions will become more time consuming and complex. Little that is said or done will be taken at face value. Work life will be suffused with tension as people try to protect themselves. This degrades the work environment over the long term.

To sum up, withholding information is not justifiable because it will be viewed as breaking trust and the consequences to the company will reduce employee performance and hence success in the marketplace. I have presented only the harm done by withholding information thus far. In section 2, "The Situation," I will present what I believe is a fair representation of the benefits of withholding the information.

Deontologically, if withholding information constitutes deception which limits employees' informed choice about their work status, then it violates the Kantian imperative to treat others as ends in themselves, not merely as means. Sisela Bok argues that deception is more subtly controlling than force, but coercive nonetheless, because it "works on belief as well as action."[1] That is, it creates false understanding and impairs the capacity for judgment, as well as the capacity to act. It is thus doubly demeaning.

Withholding the layoff information is deceptive because it is an attempt to make it seem to employees that the work situation has not changed; that their jobs are as secure as they were previously. Employees are led to believe they can maintain existing behaviors and count on continuing income and all the tangible and intangible benefits attached to steady work, when managers know this is not true, at least for some employees. This isn't to say that managers can be expected to promise endless security and stability to their employees. That isn't possible, or even desirable. But it is to say that allowing people to believe what is not true by maintaining silence is a form of deception. It is disrespectful of employees and violates their status as ends in themselves.

Having given the general ethical case against withholding the information, I will now look at a hypothetical situation and describe what specific reasons managers would use to justify holding back information.

The Situation

Sheila is the manager of a group of ten professionals in a large corporation. They are non-union. The corporation has a reputation as a good company to work for, for treating its employees with respect. Employees relations policies are above average, and they are applied consistently. Pay and benefits are in the top third of the industry. Sheila has a deserved reputation as a good manager, one who gets the work done and takes care of her people. The work group has above average productivity.

Unfortunately, Sheila has been told by her superior that because of long-term, structural changes in the industry, she will have to downsize her unit by two or three people. There will be a modest severance package. Sheila has two to three weeks to determine who will be released. The criteria for selection do not make the choice automatic. Sheila has both flexibility and responsibility for choosing among employees who have roughly equal work histories, skills and potential. She is unhappy about the task, but accepts the responsibility as part of her managerial role.

Sheila has also been told that she may tell her employees about the situation when she is ready. Sharing accurate information, equally, with all employees would not be damaging in potential law suits, so there is no valid legal reason to withhold the information. The discretion allowed Sheila to disclose or withhold information should be interpreted in this situation as a sign that her superior will trust her good judgment on this issue, and also hold her accountable for the consequences. Those who are familiar with large, corporate organizations might be tempted to interpret the fact that Sheila has options as either an attempt by her manager to avoid responsibility for events or as an indication that her decision is inconsequential: that her boss really believes the information can be released without harm. But, Sheila's choice in this situation is not trivial.

After talking with managerial colleagues and agonizing through a night of reflection, Sheila decides that she will not say anything to her staff, until the day the people are dismissed. She feels until action has to be taken about who will go, there is nothing really to say. She believes she can keep the activity secret. She fears the following consequences if she releases the information:

(1) Productivity will drop because people will be so upset they won't concentrate on work.
(2) There could be sabotage to company assets.
(3) The wrong people will begin looking for work, rather than waiting to see who is let go.
(4) That her own productivity will be hampered by people continuously asking her for updated information.
(5) That her people will tell others and create wider morale problems.
(6) The company's downsizing plans will leak to the press and damage the corporation's competitive situation.
(7) Giving out the information early will only upset the staff needlessly.
(8) Finally, she fears anger and even violence directed toward herself.

The consequences Sheila fears may be grouped in several ways, but for this exercise, it is convenient to think of one through six as being harmful to the company, tangibly and intangibly. Reason seven is harmful to the employees themselves and reason eight is harmful to Sheila, separate from the harm to her performance noted earlier in reason four. This grouping roughly corresponds to the areas of discussion noted in Section One, the general arguments against withholding the information.

Each reason is plausible, so none can be dismissed out of hand, though some are extremely unlikely. Probability of their occurrence will be a factor in the analysis. But before moving on to discuss each reason, we should take some time to understand the legitimate uses of secrecy. When is secrecy ethically justified? How do those justifications apply in the business setting?

Justifications for Secrecy

In *Secrets,* Sissela Bok provides four prima facie justifications for individual or personal secrecy. Each of them is subject to qualification. First, she notes that secrecy is not the same as privacy, it is "an additional layer of protection"[2] for private lives. Secrecy is first meant to allow individuals a measure of control over the boundaries between themselves and the world. It protects individuality and the bonds of intimacy. Intimate relationships, which are essential to human existence, cannot survive without the promise of protection from disclosure, according to Bok. By retaining secrets, people keep to themselves what they do not want others to know. Without that ability, all is open to scrutiny and few are strong enough or pure enough to be that open.

Second and third, secrecy protects plans and their execution, especially when they take time to mature or when they are of a creative or fragile nature which cannot flourish in public.[3] Chess strategy is a good example of a plan which requires secrecy to execute. Exposed in advance, the strategy is worthless, since one's opponent need not consider defenses against alternative plans.

Finally, secrecy is justified to protect individual property, when property is viewed as an extension of the self.[4] Without property, at least in our times, one is incapable of initiating and executing projects, which limits one's ability to influence the world and maintain an individual identity. Secrecy is thus ethically justified when used to keep one's property safe (in most cases.)

Bok recognizes a mild presumption *for* personal secrecy in the ordinary course of events. That is, one needs substantial reason to penetrate the secrecy protecting private information. Without compelling considerations, it is ethically impermissible to reveal or attempt to penetrate a person's secrets. Bok recognizes that secrecy is not justified in protecting immoral plans and actions. "Secrecy is essential in the planning of every form of injury to human beings,"[5] and so it is dangerous.

Bok sees a radical difference between the justifiable secrecy attached to protecting individuality and institutional secrecy, or secrecy used in the pursuit of institutional goals. She argued that "it is fallacious to argue from individual privacy to corporate privacy"[6] and the presumption shifts away from secrecy in the institutional setting. Institutional secrecy just creates too many abuses and has too many dangers to be easily condoned. For example, institutional secrecy is often used to cover abuses of power and permits riskier decision making based on lessening of personal responsibility.[7] Institutional secrecy also "debilitates judgment,"[8] since it screens plans from public scrutiny, which limits the range of perspective applied to a decision.

Bok recognizes that there are legitimate uses of secrecy in large institutions—say in the protection of negotiating strategies, or in trade secrets—but she also alerts us to the danger that secrecy tends to expand beyond its original sphere, frequently creating an insider/outsider mentality which degrades the outsiders and justifies otherwise immoral actions toward them.

Bok's assessment is useful as we return to consider Sheila's choice to withhold information about the impending layoff in her department. Before discussing each of her reasons, it will be helpful to determine the type of secrecy she plans to maintain—personal or corporate—so we can better assess her justifications.

In trying to categorize which type of secrecy is being applied, I recognize that it is frequently difficult to separate personal from organizational interests. For example, if Sheila mishandles the layoffs, her personal success may be in jeopardy. But she is not keeping personal secrets. She is keeping the company's secrets. Sheila may have to weigh the personal consequences to herself in the decision. Yet, it does not mean the information being kept secret should receive the same presumption for secrecy that Sheila could claim if her people asked her what her salary was, or had she ever had an extra marital affair.

Because there are potential personal consequences to the handling of company secrets, managers, like Sheila, tend to treat the information personally. Attaching personal consequences to the handling of secrets is one of the ways organizations bind their agents to their purposes. But that does not mean the information is personal and protected.

Sheila is acting as agent for the corporation and is obligated to perform her assigned duties to the best of her ability, within the constraints of law and moral judgment. So we should recognize that (with one exception, reason eight) Sheila is using secrecy to protect the institution, not herself. Hence, we should presume against the use of secrecy unless there are overriding reasons for it.

We should also note that Sheila does have the latitude to tell her staff about the upcoming layoff. She is thus not relieved of ethical responsibility for her actions. (In my business experience, it is not uncommon for subordinate managers to find themselves in both types of situations—those in which they are absolutely forbidden to reveal information and therefore relieved of some measure of moral responsibility and others in which they have discretion to choose their course of action.)

Let's now look at Sheila's reasons for silence and determine the ethical weight of each.

I. Loss of Employee Productivity

Sheila's reasoning rests on two arguments. First, that the company is obligated to deliver goods and services for which customers have paid. Second, that as long as the company pays an employee's salary, regardless of whether employment will continue, the employee is obligated to perform assigned duties to an acceptable level.

Sheila would argue that telling her people about the layoff will inevitably diminish their allegiance to the company's goals and lessen their commitment to the company, so it is justified not to tell them until the last possible minute.

The first argument appears to be a strong justification for withholding information. But the presumption against secrecy requires Sheila to explore other ways of meeting obligations rather than deceiving her people. After the layoff, the group will have diminished resources anyway and the obligations will still remain. She will have to devise methods to get work done with fewer people in the near future. She is equally obligated to devise methods to get work done with full staff, even if not all of them are entirely motivated and emotionally involved in the work of the company because of the anxiety of job loss.

The other argument is less defensible since it ignores one of the conditions of a voluntary employment relationship: each party needs to have relevant information which may affect their choice about continuing the agreement. Without that information, the agreement does not rest on informed consent. Someone might object that employees have no decision to make until those to be laid off are named, but that is not correct. Sheila will be practicing deception by allowing her staff to believe that work conditions are as they were before—relatively secure, stable and continuous when in fact they are not. A substantive change has occurred.

I would argue then that the first reason does not justify withholding the information. Sheila has a primary responsibility not to deceive her employees. Sheila has an additional obligation to find ways to meet the company's commitments in the face of diminished unit capacity. When she cannot, it is the company's obligation to find additional means.

II. Sabotage and Damage to Company Property

Is Sheila justified in withholding information because someone in the group might damage company assets? It is necessary and ethical to protect the company's assets, and there is a case to be made for precautions. But again, it is incumbent upon Sheila to ascertain the real dimensions of the problem, rather than making a blanket assumption that sabotage is likely. Her general fear of sabotage is like a general fear of driving because auto accidents occur. This may be a reasonable fear even though the probability of an accident is small on any one occasion, but we don't cease driving because accidents sometimes happen.

Also, it is not likely that someone will commit sabotage until they know they are being dismissed. They would have no incentive for damaging the company unless they were leaving. Presumably, when they are notified, they will also be asked to leave the premises. Sheila will be telling people in advance only that plans are underway to reduce headcount, but that does not create an incentive for any employee to start damaging the company.

Sheila needs to determine if any of her staff is likely to take revenge on the company physically. Her assessment needs to be based on the best knowledge she has and any other valid information available through other sources in the company. Is there a particular individual prone to react the way she fears? Why does she think so? Next there should be a realistic assessment of the damage which could be done. This needs to be balanced against the harm to be done to the employees by not giving them information. Even after the utilitarian calculation, Sheila is still obligated to ask if she is violating the Kantian imperative to treat people as ends in themselves. This would override all the utilitarian calculations.

If Sheila determines that someone is likely to sabotage work, then she needs to devise strategies for protecting assets from the person. For example, she might involve security, reduce access to files, prohibit after hours work, increase the frequency of file backups. If she determines that the number of people likely to sabotage assets is large, and the strategies for prevention were exorbitantly expensive or impossible to execute, she might then be justified in withholding the information. It is my experience, however, that the fear of sabotage is far greater than the reality.

III. The Wrong People Will Go

Sheila's justification assumes that the company has the right to maintain the best people and anything which causes those people to leave is detrimental to the company. This clearly conflicts with the Kantian imperative to treat each person as an end in herself, not just as a means to one's own ends. Sheila can use justifiable means to retain good employees, but deception is not one of the means since all employees are independent agents temporarily and freely associated with the company for mutual benefit.

We should also note that this is a special case of a general pattern of behavior. If we examine the larger pattern, it may be easier to see the fallacy in Sheila's reasoning. Employees decide to leave companies every day, for a variety of reasons. Pay or working conditions may be inadequate; they may not agree with product direction or policies toward consumers. It is conventional wisdom among managers that it is often the better people, people who have greater ambition or energy, that leave companies which are beginning to be in trouble. The employees who leave make their decisions based on all the information available to them. We would not say it is ethical to restrict their general knowledge of the company because it might cause them to leave. So there is something unsavory about trying to withhold critical information.

This is analogous to the argument for restricting information about potential side effects of a drug because it could discourage people from using it. Drug users may still choose to use the drug after they know of the potential side effects, but it will be an informed choice. We no longer generally accept the right of drug companies to withhold negative information from consumers. There is no substantial difference between information about drug side effects and the potential negative effects of working for a particular company. Both consumers and employees have the expectation not to be deceived, so they can make informed decisions.

Where reasons one and two appear to have some merit, if they are qualified carefully, I have argued that Sheila's reasoning in this instance has little or no merit.

IV. Sheila Loses Productivity

Once Sheila tells the group that downsizing is underway, it is certainly true that she will have to spend considerable time explaining what is happening, comforting her staff, giving updates and listening to their concerns. It should be clear, however, that these tasks are her normal responsibilities as a manager.

As business conditions shift, managers will shift their attention from one task to another. At the end of the fiscal year they may be totally absorbed in closing the books, while during the introduction of a new product they may be heavily involved in customer contacts. In times of organizational change, a manager's main focus is the morale and productivity of the staff. Managerial success is measured by maintaining a productive and motivated workforce. Sheila, like any other manager, needs to be prepared to take time for staff.

It might be argued that by telling her staff ahead of time she is creating an unnecessary problem. But that isn't true. She is merely revealing a problem that already exists: the company believes her group's work can be done with fewer people. True, if she reveals the information she might have to respond to the concerns of ten people for an extra two weeks, whereas she will only have to deal with the concerns of seven or eight after the event if she keeps silent. But, that is not a qualification that makes an ethical difference. She can't predict who will need help and who won't. She can't predict who of the ten might become support for the others either, thus actually increasing her productivity. And Sheila needs to consider that the reactions of the survivors will be more difficult to deal with if the layoffs come as a complete surprise. In addition, she needs to consider the amount of inconvenience she may suffer in comparison with the harm done to those to be laid off. Finally, she needs to consider the damage to her productivity after the layoff, if her people learn not to trust her based on her actions surrounding the layoff.

In short, though Sheila would possibly be inconvenienced by releasing the information, balanced against the harm done to individuals and her future management effectiveness, the extra work is not justification for withholding the information.

V. Create Wider Morale Problems

This is a seductive argument; one that many managers would support. Anyone who has worked in a large organization could make this case by describing the disruptive power of false rumors and true but unpleasant facts. In bad times morale is low, employees are anxious, and bad news is magnified. People spend more time discussing their concerns and complaining. The more bad news there is on the grapevine, the more productivity slumps and the less trust there is for management judgment and communications. There could be a point where the sheer number of fearful and angry employees creates so much harm to the organization and to the employees that silence is justified.

Seductive as it is, this argument is flawed because it allows secrecy to prevail in instances where even a remotely plausible case might be made that large numbers of people would become involved in disruptive behavior if the secret were let out. In other words, it justifies all or none type decision making that obliterates more subtle ethical distinctions about real harms and real benefits.

The following situation should be useful in understanding the problem with this argument. Suppose a small work group has been exposed to a possible workplace health hazard of some sort—say naturally occurring radon gas in an isolated facility. The group manager wants to withhold the information until further tests are done, in part for fear these employees will tell employees working in other facilities and they will become concerned about their work environment. Let's further assume that none of the other workers were exposed so they have not been harmed.

It seems reasonable to say that withholding the information is unethical, even if the word did spread to other non-involved employees. Even if those employees did become concerned and did cause the company some harm through disruption in the work, we still would say the ethical course was to reveal the information out of respect to the potentially harmed workers.

The one difference between this situation and the layoff is the inclusion of a physical health risk, compared to loss of income. Some might argue that this crosses over a threshold of harm that makes it more damaging and thus makes secrecy less justifiable. If there is such a threshold, I think it is a very low one, which really does little to divide the two cases. The layoff, like radon gas, could cause physical harm (emotional reaction, even heart attack). We also know that loss of one's job is a critical blow to self esteem. Being laid off causes real harm to most workers. If it wouldn't be ethical to withhold one type of information, it would not be ethical to withhold the other.

We need to remember that in the layoff situation we are not concerned about people in other groups rioting or causing other mayhem. We are anticipating a modest increase in the level of workplace tension and inattention to work. These are not insignificant and they will cost the company something. But the presumption still needs to be that most employees will manage themselves and their concerns with a reasonable amount of dignity and appropriate behavior. The exaggeration of negative consequences to a wider audience does not justify silence.

VI. Harm the Company's Competitive Standing

The argument here is that it is ethically justifiable to withhold information about the state of the company from employees in order to prevent them from giving the information to outsiders. This could harm the company's competitive standing, perhaps by damaging its reputation or persuading outsiders to doubt the competence of management.

It must be acknowledged that damage to the company's reputation would be real damage. But, as argued above, the company has an obligation to establish to the best of its ability the dimensions of the damage that could be done, and the likelihood of any of the affected employees actually leaking the information. The smaller the amount of damage envisioned, and the lower the probability of anyone actually leaking the information, the less justification this reason provides. Proportion should also be kept in mind when considering the size of the layoff. If a few employees in isolated departments are being let go, the damage to the company's standing would be insignificant. Normal attrition accounts for hundreds of separations per week from any Fortune 100 company. If the layoff is massive, then financial analysts and the business media would have been predicting the action long in advance, and layoffs sometimes enhance the prospects of companies in Wall Street's eyes.

Meanwhile, there is a corporate obligation to release accurate financial information on a timely basis, at least to stockholders. While there is no direct connection between the company's financial statements and the plan to lay off a few people in Sheila's department, there is a thread of reasoning that Sheila is using which implies that the longer one delays releasing negative information about the company, the better it is for the company. On the other hand, from the point of view of one who would receive the information later, rather than sooner, there is a diminution of trust in those who have held the information. This could cause greater harm to the company than any caused by the early public awareness that financial difficulties are causing change.

This does not seem to be a solid argument against releasing the information. It appears that this is another instance of exaggerating negative consequences.

VII. Upset the Staff

Sheila's underlying premise is that her employees should not suffer emotional turmoil by facing employment uncertainty; it is wrong to upset the staff. The implication is that her responsibility is to protect the staff from worry, even if events should be worrisome.

While the solicitude could be appreciated, it does not appear justifiable ethically. From the deontological point of view, Sheila is not treating the staff with dignity. She is treating them not as adults with the capacity to face their difficulties, but as children who need to be sheltered from the realities surrounding them. Second, while some of the staff will worry needlessly, since they will not be laid off, some of the staff do have something tangible to worry about. They will be laid off and they are being denied information which could be crucial to making informed choices about work and about providing for themselves and their families. Sheila is restricting their ability to take care of themselves.

Finally, Sheila may actually be doing positive harm to some members of her staff. Suppose she decided to release the information early in the management selection process. In her mind, Sheila has determined that five of the staff are equally eligible to be laid off, but she hasn't decided which ones will actually go yet. News of the layoff is the final push for one of the five, who resigns to go back to college. That person might not have been one of those Sheila would eventually choose. But the volunteer has protected the job of another and eliminated the harm to that person. Thus by giving out information, Sheila would be treating people as ends in themselves and possibly diminishing the amount of harm done.

The point is not that this event is likely to happen, or that Sheila could guarantee that it would happen. But it is at least as likely as some other scenario which Sheila is using as justification for not releasing the information. So the speculative projections about the emotional states of employees used to justify silence might also support release of the information. This argument also fails to justify silence.

VIII. Fear of Personal Violence

Sheila's concern for her personal safety does justify some caution in the release of information which may anger employees. Managers have no obligation to expose themselves to physical harm doing their jobs. This concern is even more serious than concern for damage to the company's assets because the danger is to a person, not just to property.

Sheila needs to perform the same sort of probability analysis as she would regarding damage to assets. Which employee, if any, is Sheila afraid of? Is her fear based on good information? What makes this seem a probable conclusion? It is also preferable that even if a violent reaction might be probable from one employee, the information could still be released, if things can be arranged to protect the person (Sheila or a substitute) releasing the information. That is, if Sheila feels she needs protection while doing her job, the company needs to provide it.

I would argue for a lower threshold of probability that something could happen, which gives the benefit of credence of Sheila's concern for her physical safety. That is, be a little more wary of employees if personal safety is involved. Interestingly, secrecy in this case seems to shift away from Bok's concept of collective secrecy and over toward personal secrecy, to protect Sheila's person. We would like to presume for secrecy in that situation. But in this hybrid type of secrecy we need to separate the kind of secret being protected from the person who needs to be protected. Sheila's secret is not a personal secret so the information still needs to be released. However, Sheila may not have to be the one to release it, at least not alone. Other agents of the company may have to be involved in order to ensure safety and ethical behavior.

Collective Justification

Of all the arguments made, only three have even limited merit in justifying silence about the impending layoff. Those three are, if the action would cause harm to Sheila, harm to assets of the company and perhaps some broader disruption in the company, resulting from the news spreading. Would silence be justified if one could show that all of these would occur? Or some combination of these and the other reasons?

Tackling the second point first, if individual beliefs do not justify a course of action, then a collection of those beliefs do not justify action either. It is analogous to the police arresting a small time career criminal for a series of crimes even though they have no evidence to connect him to any single one. They are sure these are the kind of crime he would commit so they arrest him because, even though they can't prove guilt in any one instance, maybe the number of crimes will show he's guilty. There is not evidence of wrongdoing, just enough suspicion to look like evidence. That is how I think of the collection of inadequate justifications. There is a weight of discomfort about releasing the information which seems to make it acceptable not to make the information public.

Could a combination of all three of the slightly justifiable reasons justify secrecy in our situation? I would have to say that if the probability of violence to persons, disruption and sabotage or damage to company assets was truly significant then it might be justifiable to withhold the information.

As an aside, I would also add that such a scenario would be a clear indication that the company itself was substantially out of control, that the workplace was so tense or hostile that a normal working environment no longer existed. It would be like a city devastated by a natural disaster. Normal standards of behavior had broken down and the normal methods of control were replaced by curfew and the National Guard.

It would probably be prudent to avoid inflaming a very tense situation. The injunction to respect persons as ends in themselves would still be strong though, so this would be a marginally ethical decision.

Summary

In this paper I described what is currently a typical management situation in the United States with the intention of analyzing the ethics of withholding information about an impending layoff. I provided a common scenario and typical management thinking regarding the decision to release the information. I also presented the philosophical justifications for secrecy—both personal and collective, then analyzed each reason to test its ethical validity.

I concluded that there is little ethical justification for withholding information about an impending layoff, unless it is not reasonably possible to protect persons and property from violent reactions to the news. I also conclude that the possibility of multiple, violent and disruptive responses to the news could justify secrecy. But short of a total civil breakdown in the workplace, it appears unethical to withhold information about impending layoffs for two reasons. It violates the Kantian imperative to treat individuals as ends in themselves, and, in general, the harms to be done by releasing information are usually exaggerated and more than balanced by the good to be done for the people facing sudden loss of work.

Notes

1. Bok, S.: 1978, *Lying* (Vintage Books, New York) p. 19.
2. Bok, S.: 1982, *Secrecy* (Pantheon Books, New York) p. 13.
3. Bok, *Secrecy,* p. 22.

4. Bok, *Secrecy,* p. 24.
5. Bok, *Secrecy,* p. 26.
6. Bok, *Secrecy,* p. 10.
7. Bok, *Secrecy,* p. 109.
8. Bok, *Secrecy,* p. 109.

Fielding Institute,
Santa Barbara,
CA,
U.S.A.

Should Unions Participate in Quality of Working Life Activities?

Edward Cohen-Rosenthal*

Who would be against participating in a quality of working life effort? After all, being for a program aimed at improving the workplace is like supporting motherhood and apple pie. Yet when one searches for actual activity, the review does not reveal that quality of working life programs are the norm among companies and governments in the United States and Canada. The same is true among unions. There are a number of reasons for the scarcity of actual "quality of working life" or QWL programs. This is especially true when we define the topic to mean intentionally designed efforts to bring about increased labor-management cooperation to jointly solve the problem of improving organizational performance and employee satisfaction.

This article examines the issues of why organizations do or do not participate in quality of working life improvement programs. In exploring this topic, the perspective of the trade union is highlighted. At the outset, two caveats should be laid bare. First, though supportive, I do not believe that QWL programs are for everyone. There may be perfectly legitimate practical or philosophical reasons for non-participation. Secondly, I recognize that most workplaces do make some attempts to improve the quality of working life in one way or another. To focus on the more comprehensive and intentional efforts does not deny either the existence of alternative strategies or more isolated or informal efforts. Nor does it contest that other approaches may also have a positive impact.

Excerpted from "Should Unions Participate in Quality of Working Life Activities?", *Quality of Working Life: The Canadian Scene,* vol. 3, no. 4 (January 1980). Copyright © by Edward Cohen-Rosenthal. Reprinted by permission of the author.
*President, ECR Associates, and assistant to the president for educational programs, Bricklayers International Union.

Ways to Think about Possible Participation

The Theory of Competing Interests

Under our economic system, management has a responsibility to represent the interests of capital. The stockholders demand it. The management of a company is accountable for obtaining the best possible return on investment and managing the company in a manner which would guarantee it. If they did not, investors would put their money elsewhere and the company would go bankrupt. Unions are there to represent the interests of labor. They are the safeguard of the rights of workers in a workplace or company. Unions provide a collective voice for the demands and concerns of workers both for a fair share of the revenues of the company and for fair treatment at work. The workers demand it. Recognizing that management wants to get the most for its stockholders and labor for the employees, we have a classic presentation of the interests of labor pitted against the interests of capital. Many labor and management people alike are reluctant to blur the distinctions between the two roles.

Yet, the facts of the matter are that the two interests are not distinct but are interdependent. If the company goes bottom up then the workers have nothing. If the workers do not produce the products then the shareholders cannot obtain a return on their investment. Those involved with quality of working life look for the interdependencies as the grounds for activity while maintaining that there may be fundamental differences in orientation between the two parties.

Sometimes we make too much out of the adversarial nature of collective bargaining. Too often, the image is of two gunfighters squaring off against each other in a dusty Western town. In truth, collective bargaining is a method of conflict resolution. The aim is to reach a reasonable compromise. There are a set of rules and possible sanctions which each side can use. But it is their interdependence and need for compromise which compels them to come together and helps them come to an agreement.

Zero Sum Power Game

The power theory of why people balk at quality of working life programs is relatively simple. People who hold this view believe that there is only so much "power" in a situation. Therefore, the more one side has, the less the other side must have. Curiously, this belief tends to work in two directions. On the one hand, management is reluctant to involve the union for fear of enhancing its influence—and consequently diminishing management's authority. Yet at the same time, many unions are concerned because they do not want to allow more influence over the workers by management—and therefore weaken the union role. There is no way to buy out of this dilemma as long as power and authority are viewed as a struggle over a fixed power configuration. Yet the Maginot line view of industrial relations often is an imaginary view of the nature and possibilities of power and authority in the workplace.

The goal in the workplace in terms of power is the same as it is with any other power source. It is to provide the energy to make something happen. The power in the workplace can be employed to work together or it can be expended in fighting one another. Authority can be the kind associated with fear or it can be associated with positive attachment to the mutual goals of the union and the company. The aim in a QWL project is to create more power and greater authority by directing energies in a mutually beneficial manner. Often it is the workplaces with the greatest fights over turf power where QWL can have the greatest success by rechanneling the antagonistic energy into constructive activity.

Industrial Democracy

Since Sidney and Beatrice Webb at the turn of the century, industrial democracy has been a guiding phrase for trade unionists. There are many shapes to the call for greater industrial democracy. Collective bargaining has been correctly seen as a major step forward in the development of industrial democracy. Others have also employed the term in promoting equal employment opportunity. Co-determination is viewed as another avenue. All of the forms seek to broaden the franchise and improve the representation of workers. When Irving Bluestone of the United Automobile Workers discusses QWL, it is as much in terms of democratic rights as in any other manner. European trade unionists have used industrial democracy as a rallying cry for greater trade union and worker power in making decisions within corporations. Both union leaders and some managers have been attracted to new workplace change activities through a commitment to the idea of participation. They seek a new order of economic justice. An industrial democrat doesn't need justifications of productivity improvements or employee satisfaction. It's the moral justification which counts. Yet for the very same reasons, there are those who refuse to become involved with the slightest activity for fear that it will lead to ever increasing demands for industrial democracy and threaten the current power structure.

Risks and Benefits of Union Participation in QWL Programs

The following discussion of benefits and risks have been developed over the past few years as I have talked with and observed trade unionists and managers both considering and undertaking programs. To be fair, let's look at the possible pitfalls before assessing possible benefits.

Risks

There are a whole series of potentially negative problems which surround the issue of the union's role. My basic premise is that the union must maintain its clear identity as the representative of the workers. If this isn't clear, then problems are compounded. If the union becomes an apologist for management decisions or simply a prod for productivity (unfortunately, this has happened in some cases even without QWL), then it loses its authority as the workers' representative. This diminishes their effectiveness as a union and paradoxically makes them less useful to management. Involvement in quality of working life activities ought to be no preamble to softness in negotiations over traditional collective bargaining matters such as wages and benefits. Though an impact of QWL may be to increase the size of the pie available for negotiation, it rarely is the forum for the hard fights over who is to get what from whom. If the union allows communication to go directly to the membership without the union's involvement and acknowledgement of their role, then there is a danger of weakening union allegiance within the workforce. In almost all cases, employees like the new programs and if the union is perceived as an ogre or not heard from, then membership estrangement can occur. All of these matters have to do with maintaining an adequate perception of the union as the workers' voice.

A union needs to determine, before going into a program, whether the company is doing it for the legitimate purpose of improving the operation and morale at the worksite or for union busting. In a few cases, companies have instituted programs in their unionized plants and then transported their ideas to their non-union facilities as a way to contain union growth. However, more often than not, in developing QWL programs companies which have many unionized sections have ignored the unionized parts in favor of non-union facilities or new plants. This is probably the most insidious form of union busting since it provides the benefits of QWL to non-union and not to union employees. The lesson for a union is that you can get hurt by not doing it as much as by doing it.

Some unionists are concerned about the diverse nature of the treatment of employees in QWL programs thereby contradicting work rules developed in the union contract. There may be a long history of developing uniform rules to combat capriciousness in treatment and/or to encourage solidarity among workers in an industry. The issue of flexibility vs. protection is a difficult one. Some joint projects have sidestepped this issue by finding other areas of more common ground to attack.

A look at the record of the failures of union-management projects points out that the greatest problem is not the lack of sufficient results. It has to do with internal union politics. In some unions with powerful minority caucuses and fractured support, even the best program could provide ammunition for internal political opposition. Several projects I have run across in mining and woodworking were voted out in hastily called meetings packed with opponents.

There are other pitfalls to watch out for including possible violations of the contract, job loss due to increased productivity, speedup, arbitrary changes in job classifications and responsibilities without proper pay adjustments and loss of comparability in an industry. Another difficult question surrounds the potential liability of the union for the decisions it jointly entered into with management.

Benefits

Clearly there are many things that can go wrong with a quality of working life effort. If simple machines can go on the blink, then how many more possibilities are there for problems in complicated relationships, testing out new ground? Each of the items mentioned above have remedies. Yet an honest appraisal would say that in certain situations a QWL initiative may not be possible. With proper and sustained attention, things can turn out quite well with many benefits to the company and the union. Here we concentrate on the positive impact on the union.

Given that the union is able to fend off all of the possible difficulties, especially the internal politics, then there are many benefits for the union. Some of these derive from the process directly through increased access to information and pre-notification of changes in work arrangements or machinery. Hopefully, the additional input can help avoid management errors or decisions which would have a negative impact on the membership.

Some of the other benefits come from increased representation of membership concerns. In almost all programs, grievances have gone down—sometimes dramatically. Those grievances which were filed were generally handled faster and at a lower step. This represents a substantial savings in time and money for both the union and the management especially in avoiding arbitration and labor board cases. The membership finds that their concerns are being resolved much more quickly. The grievances which disappear first are the petty grievances caused by poor communication and lack of respect. Another measure of member interest is attendance at union meetings. At present, most union meetings are chronically under-attended. In a number of cases, attendance at union meetings has gone up when a QWL project has been instituted.

Of course, there are a variety of other ways that a successful program better assists the membership. Their work satisfaction may increase. The union may be helping to address a broader range of personal concerns which extend beyond the economic. Workers tend to learn more under participative programs and health and safety is often improved. Stress caused by poor supervision and unnecessary ropes to jump may be alleviated. Better communication with fellow workers may result. The impact on stress and working conditions applies to union leaders as well as rank-and-file.

The increased visibility of the union in a joint project helps its image both internally and externally. The membership sees the union taking a lead on a variety of non-economic issues which affects them. The union is advocating another dimension of human dignity in addition to compensation justice. Often employees organize into a union because of the lack of respect and fair treatment they may receive. Too often, the questions of human dignity get sidetracked after an election is won. This kind of program fulfills the promises made in organizing. A cooperative spirit aimed at increased customer service and quality can also win applause in the industry and the public.

In a political organization like a union, elections are the true test of success. In the General Motors plants with joint QWL programs, every local UAW administration which stood for reelection won. This may be in part due to increased representation and it may also reflect some of the new skills of listening, problem solving and cooperation learned in the project. To my knowledge, nobody has lost an election solely because of QWL.

A final set of benefits has to do with the broad impacts of QWL programs. By helping improve the performance of the company, several benefits may be derived. There may be more money which could go for higher wages and benefits, or for modernization, expansion or health and safety improvement among other possibilities. Increasing the pool of money does not have to be done through the loss of jobs but rather the expansion of the market and cutting non-personnel costs. The improved condition of the company may result in saving jobs which may have been lost from falling into an uncompetitive position. In some cases, a QWL project has resulted in more jobs than before.

In the final analysis, real situations involve varying degrees of the benefits and the headaches. What will be the exact configuration in a local setting has to do with the conditions going in and the energy and imagination in the implementation.

Conclusion

The answer to the question of whether or not unions should participate in QWL programs is a definite maybe. Each union needs to weigh for itself its own situation. It needs to determine whether cooperation is consistent with the needs and goals of the membership and the values of the union. The situation surrounding the initiative needs to be examined and considered carefully to determine the sincerity of management and the possibilities of success. Internal union political situations need to be judged and accommodated. The potential benefits for the union, the membership, the company and the public need to be measured against the probable pitfalls. Sometimes the issue is not whether to respond to the initiatives of management but whether the union should take the issue up first. In this case, the motivation may be an ideological commitment to the spread of industrial democracy or a concern that the continued mismanagement of the company will seriously jeopardize the membership. A blind and naive adoption of quality of working life programs is ill advised. The answer to the initial question of whether one should be in favor of quality working life improvements is of course yes. But the next questions are how, by whom and at what cost. Many roads and strategies can be employed in seeking a common goal of an effective, healthy and dignifying workplace.

▶ *Employer-Employee Relations*

Each of the applied ethics sections of this text (Parts 2–5) includes an interview with a key figure who is prominent in his/her field. The purpose of these interviews is to bridge the gap between theory and practice and offer the student an exposure to how people in the "real world" confront practical, ethical issues.

RODERICK A. DeARMENT is currently a partner in the Washington, D.C. law firm of Covington & Burling. Rod served as Deputy Secretary of Labor from 1989 through 1991 and previously served as Chief of Staff to the Senate Majority Leader and as Chief Counsel and Staff Director of the Senate Finance Committee. Rod is a graduate of Trinity College (Hartford) and of the University of Virginia Law School.

Q: *What do you think are the most pressing issues in Employer-Employee relations today?*

A: From the employee's viewpoint, one of the most pressing issues is job security. Job security is the central issue in the current national coal strike and certainly is on all employees' minds as one major corporation after another announces massive employment downsizing plans. The cost and availability of health care coverage is another pressing issue. The cost of health care has certainly been a frequent and difficult bargaining issue in labor-management negotiations in recent years. Wages have receded somewhat as a front burner issue primarily because the low inflation rate has taken some pressure off of living expenses and the job security issue has displaced wages as a concern in an otherwise anemic labor market.

From an employer's standpoint, worker productivity and product quality might be two of the most pressing issues. Many employers are seeking greater worker participation in an effort to improve productivity and quality so that U.S. businesses remain internationally competitive. Greater worker participation through quality circles, employee self-management and the like has lead to reductions in mid-level supervisory management.

Q: *What ethical standard, if any, do you think should be applied to employer-employee relations?*

A: I think the guiding ethical principle should be one of mutual respect and fundamental fairness in employer-employee interaction. What I mean by fairness is honest and open dealings by both sides. Each side has its own interest and point of view, but there should be a significant overlap of mutual self-interest. For example, it is strongly in each side's mutual interest to have an efficient, profitable company. Nevertheless, mistrust frequently develops and labor and management get into direct confrontations. Usually neither side is well served by such confrontations. One need only look to the example of

Eastern Airlines to see that is graphically illustrated. Eastern Airlines was destroyed as a company because management and the machinist union locked themselves in a death struggle which both sides lost.

Q: *What kinds of employment situations can give rise to problems that have an "ethical" dimension?*

A: One example is the issue of employee privacy. Mandatory drug testing has raised hotly debated employee privacy concerns. Some unions have opposed drug testing even to protect public safety. They argue that employees' dignity and right to privacy should be absolutely protected and forced drug testing assumes guilt. However, there have been several tragic accidents in which operators of public transportation were shown to have been under the influence of drugs or alcohol. These accidents have intensified the debate and many argue that privacy rights have to give way to concerns for the safety of the public and co-workers.

Employee privacy concerns have also been raised by the use of surveillance cameras in parking garages and other semi-public areas. These were installed to allow detection of theft and personal assault. Nevertheless, some employees argue they constitute an invasion of privacy.

A third example involves the electronic monitoring of employee's work such as monitoring telephone calls by sales persons or information operators. Employers feel that such monitoring is important to make certain they are giving polite, accurate telephone service. Many employees argue that such monitoring puts extra stress on them and invades their privacy. This is an area where legislation has been proposed to deal with employees' concerns.

Where both sides have legitimate concerns, it is often difficult for employers and employees to work together to resolve these issues. These conflicts obviously put a strain on the "fairness" principle.

Q: *Do all parties perceive fairness in the same way?*

A: Not when you are dealing in outcomes only. If I were the CEO of a company and I could not deliver for my stockholders (for whom I have a fiduciary responsibility), then I might categorize all the intervening factors as "unfair." They are unfair in the sense that they prevent me from attaining my goal.

Likewise, the union member whose real earning power is diminished because of foreign competition which is out of his or her company's control may also feel that this is "unfair" since it decreases his ability to be as materially comfortable as in the past.

These are examples of fairness as applied to outcomes. However, the kind of fairness I have in mind is fairness of *process*. If there is a fair process, then all dissatisfaction will be directed to those exterior forces beyond the control of employer or employee. In this scenario the employer and employee would do all in their power to deal honestly and openly with each other. They would obey the spirit as well as the letter of the applicable laws and they will go beyond the law to deal with each other in an honest effort to resolve mutual problems.

Q: *Can you give me an example on the micro and macro levels which demonstrates what you mean?*

A: Yes. On the macro level a good example is how work force "downsizing" is handled. Downsizing is an all too common occurrence in our competitive global economy. The easier cases are those where the adjustment can be made slowly. When you can plan a few years in advance, then downsizing can be handled by attrition and early retirement. In these circumstances the only ones who are really "hurt" are people who will not get a chance to work for the company.

The more difficult cases involve situations in which real pain is being distributed among an identifiable group of workers. Then the question is, "Who will get how much of the pain?" Let's examine three strategies:

(a) Layoff by seniority
(b) Layoff by productivity
(c) Layoff collectively

In (a) you are saying that the employees who have worked at your plant the longest have the most "invested" in the company and therefore deserve the most consideration. This has been a traditional strategy and is embedded into many union contracts. The down side is that the younger workers tend to be the ones let go and they may be the most productive. Also seniority-based layoffs often disproportionately hurt female and minority workers. If you are left with a less productive work force, then the manager has not fulfilled his obligation to the company and the company's stockholders.

In (b) you keep your productive workers, but you may also be viewed as being heartless to those who have given their working lives to the company. Your most productive workers of today look and see what might be happening to them in a few years. It will bother them to see senior people let go merely because times are tough. Therefore, morale may fall and with it, productivity.

Perhaps the best answer is (c), if enough savings can be achieved this way. Let everyone take a little time off together and share the pain collectively. It is important that if you adopt (c) as a strategy, that salaried management is not exempted. Too often managers have unwisely taken large bonuses at the time that they were asking rank and file employees to absorb layoffs and pay reductions. This can have a devastating effect on morale and productivity.

Q: *In this case fairness dictates that all share the pain equally. Isn't this difficult to do when a dollar to an upper management type is not the same as a dollar to a line worker?*

A: It is impossible to make a shared sacrifice mathematically identical. The important point is that everybody is asked to participate.

Q: *What about a micro case example?*

A: Well, as I mentioned earlier, a good example would be a manager investigation of a dispute of sexual harassment complaint, which is certainly a hot topic today. As the investigating manager, you have a duty to each party to make sure that the facts are uncovered and then company policy and the applicable law is fairly and even-handedly applied.

One particular difficulty in sexual harassment cases is that the complaint may reflect other agendas operating between the parties. This can make objective fact-gathering difficult. For example the boss who is the subject of the complaint might have a hidden agenda of breaking down the subordinate for some reason and the sexual harassment may be the means of this. Or in the opposite situation the subordinate may be trying to displace or otherwise harm the superior.

If only the two of the individuals were involved, and there is no other corroborating evidence, or witnesses, it becomes very difficult to gather objective data. Without sufficient data one cannot be confident of a fair result. And yet if no action is taken, a grievous wrong will go unpunished. Nevertheless, it is the manager's responsibility to do everything in his or her power to create a fair process that sensitively deals with both sides of a dispute.

Q: *Wouldn't it be easier for a company only to look at the bottom line and forget ethical considerations? After all, they may constrain the ability of the company to make a profit. If this were the case, then why be ethical?*

A: Perhaps in some cases, a company can make short term gains through unethical practices. For example, by unfairly exploiting workers some advantages might be gained on competitors—in the short term. But these results are likely to be only temporary. I believe fair and ethical policies will pay off in the long run. It pays not only in "psychic" happiness, but also in dollars and cents. The company that strives toward fair and ethical treatment of its workers will be likely to have a workforce that does not turn over as quickly. It will be more highly skilled and more loyal to the company. Loyalty is an important commodity that often shows itself in times of adversity. I would go so far as to say that ethical business practices (including but not confined to employer-employee relations) are a necessary condition for having a successful company. That is, without ethical practices, it is only a matter of time before short-term benefits begin to unravel.

This is not, however, the only element of business success. One can have an outstanding workforce and model employee-employer relations, but if consumers do not like the product, you are still out of business. There are obviously a host of other important business factors in creating a good company. These factors *along with* ethical considerations go into fashioning a company that will last.

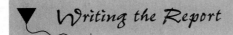

Writing the Report

Finding the Conflicts

After one has established an ethical point of view, he or she is ready to approach cases. The first stage in handling cases effectively is to analyze the situation into two categories: Cost Issues and Ethical Issues. Obviously there are times when the cost issues and the ethical issues will not contradict each other. At other times they will. It is your job to determine when this occurs.

Let's take an example.

Case 1: You run an old fashioned hardware store in which most items appear unpackaged on the shelves or in bulk. Your store employees select goods for the customer based upon their particular needs and put them into brown paper bags which they mark with a price before directing the customers toward the cashiers.

Lately, you have been suffering from "shrinkage" (a euphemism for theft). Inventory, especially larger ticket items, has been disappearing. You don't believe that customers are taking these goods because you have three cashiers who must be passed before exiting the store. The items missing are large and bulky and would be noticed by the cashiers.

The other option is that your employees are stealing from you. Your son-in-law, Bubba Bean, knows someone who will run regular polygraph tests on employees to determine who is telling the truth about theft (cost $100 per session—90% effective when used over a year time frame). Your own daughter, Sarah, suggests that you create a system whereby you encourage fellow employees to turn each other in if they notice suspicious activities ($2,500 for employee rewards). Your wife, Judy, thinks you ought to hire a private detective to spy on the store and see who's doing it (cost $2,500 per week—estimated time to solve the case four weeks with an almost 100% chance for success—based upon this man's past performance).

The thefts are becoming costly, $350 per week. What should you do? The problem is employee theft. The cost to you is $350 per week. This amounts to $18,200 per year. The three solutions are:

(a) lie detector tests—weekly evaluations would amount to $5,200 per year (less if the problem could be "solved" earlier). Effectiveness almost 90%.
(b) employee rewards for turning in fellow employees—$2,500. Effectiveness unknown.
(c) private investigator—$2,500 per week times estimated four weeks = $10,000. Effectiveness almost 100%.

Considering only cost, (b) comes out on top followed by (a) and (c), by far the costliest. If one were to consider both cost and benefit, (b) would still win unless (a) could solve the problem in less than six months.

But are cost issues the only consideration? You have found from the readings in Part 2 on privacy that the use of a lie detector is controversial. Also, the use of informants may cause some difficulties. But what kind of difficulties? How does one determine just what the ethical implications are?

This is a difficult question. Often managers operate from a position of intuitionism here. If they feel "funny" about a particular solution, then they shy away from it. However, if your boss does not feel uncomfortable about the same class of actions, then you have a problem.

Ethical issues are perceived as one applies his or her moral theory to a given situation. Since there are several theories of morality, it follows that what one theory depicts as ethically sanctioned may be prohibited by another. In the real world you will face people with different moral theories and different levels of understanding within those theories. What is a person to do?

It is my contention that you must remain true to your own moral theory. If the moral theory you have chosen for yourself sanctions a particular action you must obey that sanction. This may put you in uncomfortable situations if your theory is more restrictive in some situations than someone else's (for example your boss's). Facility with other moral theories and how they work can help you to bridge the gap (as much as possible). You begin by assessing the situation according to your own moral theory. Next, you assess the situation through the other person's moral theory (it is probably the case that the other person has not ever set out his or her positions in any systematic way). Finally, you explain to the other individual why you must act as you do, and where the theoretical differences occur. This will not guarantee that the other person will accept your solution, but it will lift the argument away from the situation at hand and place it on a higher level of abstraction. Most people are more tolerant of variances at the theoretical level than they are at the level of some particular action.

Let us return to the case at hand. You are in the situation of determining whether there are any moral issues at stake in the choices that are presented. If there are none, then you could act purely according to your cost analysis.

How do you know if there are any moral issues at stake? As we have said above, the ultimate test is the application of your moral theory. However, as an aid in application try completing the following checklist of questions. If the answer to either of the questions is "yes," then it is probable that some ethical issues are present that need to be addressed.

CHECKLIST for Detecting Ethical Issues

Directions: 1. Read over your case carefully. 2. Determine what point of view you will adopt in the case. This involves both the person whose point of view you have chosen to illustrate and the ethical theory you will adopt to examine the case. 3. Ask the following questions of the person whose point of view you have chosen. If the answer to either question is "yes," then proceed to use your ethical theory to determine an ethical judgment.

1. *Is Any Party Being Exploited Solely for the Advantage of Another?* (Exploitation can include instances of lying, injuring, deliberate falsification, creating an unequal competitive environment and so forth.)

2. *Is Every Effort Being Made to Assist and Affirm the Human Dignity of All Parties Involved?* (Affirming human dignity can include instances of encouraging the fulfillment of legal and human rights as well as taking personal responsibility for results that are consonant with these principles. Thus #2 does not allow you to hide behind non-functioning rules.)

Question #1 concerns "prohibitions," i.e., actions which you must refrain from doing. Question #2 concerns "obligations," i.e., actions which you are required to do. Whatever is not an ethical obligation or a prohibition, is a "permission," i.e., actions which you may do if you choose. Thus, if the case you present to the checklist does not invoke a prohibition or an obligation, then you may act solely according to the dictates of your cost analysis.

Let us return to the example at hand and submit it to the checklist. Alternative (a) involves using a lie detector. Does using a lie detector exploit the employee? [Answer this question for discussion in class.]

What about the second point? Is this a situation in which you might assist or affirm the human dignity of your employees by using or not using the lie detector? [Answer this question for discussion in class.]

Repeat this test for the other two alternatives as well. Once you have completed this preliminary ethical assessment you are in a position to go further in your evaluation by returning to the ethical theory you have adopted and to determine further *how* and the reasons *why* the prohibitions and obligations are applicable.

Once you have done this, you have completed the "finding-the-conflicts" step. You have created two lists: a cost issues list and an ethical issues list. Each prescribes independently at this stage. In the next chapter we will work at integrating these two lists.

As you go through the macro and micro cases in this section follow the procedures listed above as you create a cost issues list and an ethical issues list for each.

Macro and Micro Cases

The cases section of this book are divided into two categories: macro and micro. Each type of case employs a different point of view.

Macro Case. The macro case takes large institutional entities as its focus. For example, one might examine Beechnut and the ersatz apple juice or BCCI and international money laundering. The purpose of the macro case is to get you thinking about how corporations should act in their environment. You will take the perspective of a high level official and make judgments which will affect many thousands.

Micro Case. The micro case examines individuals working within business as its focus. For example, one might look at a mid-level manager's approach to end of the year sales reports, or an engineer's decision to be a "whistle blower." The attraction of these cases is that you can project yourself realistically into these cases. It is probable that you will be in positions similar to the Micro Case descriptions (whereas only a fraction of people will ever really be a Macro Case decisionmaker).

Case Development. The word 'case' is used in different ways by different people. This book will suggest one form of case response. The method for preparing and developing these cases is suggested in the essays entitled: "Writing the Report" which can be found at the end of each section in the book. Your professor may also have specific guidelines of his/her own.

For those who wish to use it, this approach offers a bridge between traditional approaches to case studies taught in business schools and a philosophical method that emphasizes essay development. The intention throughout is that you expand your mind with the general essays and develop a practical skill in applying an ethical theory to thorny moral/cost conflicts through writing a business report that defends a particular course of action.

Please note that though most of the cases presented here have fictional venues, they are based upon composites of real Corporate America.

acro Cases

Case 2.1—Plant Closing at Alpha Corporation

Alpha Corporation is composed of two divisions: one manufactures custom-made machine parts, the other modifies existing robotic systems to increase efficiency and improve quality. The parts factory was built in 1947 and modernized in 1975. Because of declining sales in the custom parts division it was decided to close down the plant.

The parts plant is located on the south side of Chicago in a declining urban industrial area. The robotics systems operation is centered in Durham, North Carolina in an emerging high tech research triangle. The wage scale in North Carolina is substantially lower than in Chicago. Further, the workers in the parts plant have assembly line manufacturing skills. The North Carolina operation requires computer programming and application skills. A comparison of the typical worker at each plant is as follows:

Category Operation	Chicago Parts Plant	North Carolina Robotics
Average Age	46 years old	28 years old
Average time with company	17 years	3 years
Average Education	11.8 years	15.2 years
Contract type	union	non-union
Racial Mix: Black/White	75%/25%	5%/95%

It is not an open issue *whether* the plant will be closed or not. It will be closed according to all relevant laws on plant closures. However, there is some dissention among the senior management on the way to handle the layoffs. The positions expressed have been these:

Position One. Close the plant in Chicago following only the relevant laws on plant closures (notification, mandatory liaison with state social services agencies, etc. Estimated cost of the "bare bones" closure is $2,500,000).

Position Two. Close the plant in Chicago. Offer a sliding scale lump sum payment for all workers who have been with the company at least one year. The amount of the payment would vary from one to six months salary. [The highest going to those who have been with the company for over twenty years. Cost of the lump sum payment is $15,000,000 in addition to the "bare bones" costs.]

Position Three. The North Carolina operation is expanding by 250 jobs per year. There are 1000 jobs in the Chicago operation. Make a commitment to retrain and reassign one-fourth of your Chicago operation. For the rest of the employees offer a sliding scale of lump sum payments. Since the average payments for redundancy are only slightly lower than the cost or retraining, position three appears to cost the same as position two. However, it is estimated that position three (the retraining option) will be most popular to younger workers who would have lower redundancy payments. Thus the estimated cost of position three is $20,000,000 in addition to the "bare bones" costs.

Among other factors to consider are these: 1. There may be additional relocation costs involved in creating a friendly environment to the Chicago workers who move to North Carolina [possible cost $250,000.] 2. The North Carolina operation had a real net last year of $28,000,000. 3. There will have to be an allocation formula in case more workers want to relocate than there are positions for them. Three formulas have been suggested: (a) By Seniority; (b) By Productivity; (c) Randomly. 4. It might be possible to hire more than 250 employees if the wages were generally lowered in the North Carolina operation. However, this might hurt morale and lower the output of that facility.

You are commissioned to write a report to senior management about what course Alpha Corporation should take. Weigh both cost and ethical issues in making your decision.

Case 2.2—Implementing an Affirmative Action Program at Smith Pharmaceuticals

Smith Pharmaceuticals is a small company which specializes in manufacturing a limited line of generic drugs for mail order drug companies. Smith has its headquarters in Atlanta, Georgia. The composition of Smith's work force is as follows:

Work Force Analysis of Smith Pharmaceuticals

	Gross	Male/Female		Ave. Wage
Total Workers	100	70	30	$27,959.90
Factory Workers	40	35	5	$24,000.00
Scientists	6	6	0	$47,000.00
Warehouse/Drivers	7	7	0	$18,000.00
Maintenance	5	2	3	$15,000.00
Sales	25	15	10	$30,000.00
Clerical—total	17	5	12	$35,470.00
Clerical support	12	0	12	$19,000.00
Clerical management	5	5	0	$75,000.00

	Gross	Black/White		Ave. Wage
Total Workers	100	59	41	$27,959.90
Factory Workers	40	37	3	$24,000.00
Scientists	6	0	6	$47,000.00
Warehouse/Drivers	7	6	1	$18,000.00
Maintenance	5	5	0	$15,000.00
Sales	25	3	22	$30,000.00
Clerical—total	17	8	9	$35,470.00
Clerical support	12	8	4	$19,000.00
Clerical management	5	0	5	$75,000.00

The company is publicly owned and at a recent shareholders meeting there arose a fight over the company's hiring practices. The irate stockholder said he would sue the company to get it into compliance with affirmative action legislation. The shareholder noted a recent court decision in Savannah that forced a company to change its hiring practices. "In that case (like this one)," said the stockholder, "the company did a considerable amount of work for the government. Since our largest account is the Postal Handlers Insurance Plan, and since this is a federal health program, we have an obligation to meet more than the letter of the law."

The company president, Phillip Denton, replied that the company has an admirable affirmative action record. Over half of the employees are African American. Thirty percent are women. There is a policy not to discriminate in hiring. Federal Equal Opportunity Commission language is used in any job advertisement. No qualified minority who has applied for a position has *ever* been turned away. "The plain fact is that certain jobs attract certain people," the president said.

The irate stockholder said this was not enough. The president agreed to hire an outside consulting firm to report on its affirmative action policies.

You are the outside consultant who will write the report. You find your job somewhat hampered by lack of clear records of who has applied for positions, but through your interviews you find that in job categories which are disproportionately represented by one group, the president's assertion that women and minorities simply haven't applied, is true. Given the two tables on page 263 and your interview information, construct your report.

Case 2.3—Fetal Protection Policies

Your lawn chemical plant faces a similar problem to the well documented case of the American Cyanamid Company: what to do about the dilemma of having a production process that is well within the federal (OSHA, Occupational Safety and Health Act) guidelines for adult workers, but will not be within medical guidelines for pregnant women. Your company is considering adopting an exclusionary policy of its own for pregnant women and is asking you to analyze one of the more important cases on female exclusionary policies in recent years: The American Cyanamid Company.

Senior management will review your report and policy recommendations in making their policy decision.

Survey of American Cyanamid Company[1]

The Company: The American Cyanamid Company produces pigments, dyestuffs, animal feed supplements, melamine, platinum catalysts, plastic antioxidants, and specialty chemicals. It is located in an otherwise depressed socio-economic region of West Virginia.

The Problem: The lead pigments production contained exposure to five chemicals thought to be especially hazardous to fetuses: hydrazine hydrate, hydrazine sulfate, lead, Thiotepa and Methotrexate. Though the exposure to these chemicals was well within OSHA guidelines for adults, it was too elevated for fetuses. Particularly offensive was the exposure to lead. Changing Federal guidelines regarding lead and children/fetuses was constantly altering to lower and lower levels.

The company envisioned a lawsuit from a child who had been injured when his mother was exposed to these chemicals while in the lead chromate pigment manufacturing area.

Even if workers were appraised of the dangers involved, it was possible for inadvertent exposure [since women don't know they are pregnant for at least one month at the earliest]. It is also true that exposure during the first trimester of pregnancy can cause the most severe birth defects and is when most miscarriages occur. Clearly the company felt at risk having women of childbearing age working in the lead chromate pigment manufacturing area.

The Solution: In January 1978 the company announced to its employees that it was implementing a "fetus protection" policy. This policy stated that women between the ages of 16 and 50 could not work in production jobs involving lead pigments unless they could prove they had been surgically sterilized.

Results of the Policy: Between February and July 1978 the five women employed in the lead pigments manufacturing area submitted to surgical sterilization at a hospital not associated with American Cyanamid. The women said the company told them that there were not enough jobs to go around. The implication being that if they did not submit to the sterilization, they might lose employment.

The company denies this, saying that offers of comparable jobs at comparable pay were made.

The Law: Two laws were thought to be relevant to this case. First, Federal Law contained in the OSHA Act of 1970 and the Toxic Substances Control Act of 1977 differentiated between "teratogens" and "mutagens." Teratogens affected the fetus when a pregnant women was exposed to them. Mutagens affected the fetus by affecting adults in such a way that future offspring will be damaged.

Lead is a mutagen. It is unclear whether it affects women at lower levels than it does men. There is a level at which both would be harmed. But this documented level was not approached in this instance. Thus, it is an open scientific question whether both men and women or simply women or neither would be adversely affected by the exposure to lead. But recent scientific studies suggest that any exposure to lead may be detrimental to both men and women.

Second, Title VII of the 1964 Civil Rights Act prohibits wrongful discrimination on the basis of sex. If Cyanamid's program picked out women and caused them to suffer intimidation and pressure to terminate their reproductive capacity [while not affecting men in the same way], then the program might be liable to civil damages and restoration of job and promotional opportunities.

The Company's Liability Exposure: If the company were found to have injured or to have exposed to disease an employee (male or female) while in the process of doing one's job, and if the company operated its manufacturing plant within established guidelines, and if there is no other indication of flagrant disregard for employee safety, then the maximum exposure for each incident is $100,000 to an annual aggregate of $500,000 as stipulated by the model ISO Workers Compensation Law.

The amount of these damages would be paid by an insurance company and there would be no excess exposure.

Thus, any damage to an employee would probably indicate a minimal exposure to the company.

Bodily injury to unborn fetuses, however, is the grounds for a personal injury lawsuit. If the grounds of this personal injury are found to be a pollution exposure, it is probably excluded by the company's insurance policy under the model ISO General Liability Definitions. In any event, the size of the suit and its impact upon the company is substantially greater from this sort of lawsuit.

Thus, the company has more to lose from injuring a fetus than it does from injuring one of its own workers on the job.

Discrimination suits can also entail high costs.

The Result: An initial fine of $10,000 was assessed by OSHA. This was reversed by the Occupational Safety and Health Review Commission. The basis of the reversal was that it was determined that the fetal protection policy did not lie within OSHA's jurisdiction. [Another exclusionary policy at Bunker Hill was similarly dismissed.]

The EEOC action was "settled." Thus, no definitive opinion was rendered.

Case 2.4—Changing the Corporate Culture at MBI

You have just been hired as vice-president for Human Resource Development at MBI, a giant computer firm. Your being hired is a part of a wholesale change at the computer giant which once ruled the computer marketplace, but which now is steadily losing market share as the "mainframe" computer is being replaced by mini and micro computers.

As a result of the entirely new senior management team, many policies of the past are being re-examined. The Board of Directors has commissioned you to assess the present corporate culture and report back on your recommendations before the next Board meeting in February. What you have found is the following set of facts.

Origins of the Company: MBI was originally a typewriter and office machine company. It had an autocratic leader who wanted to create a model employee "image." The company prospered and moved into the lucrative computer market. The company's success was not due to superior computers, but to superior marketing and service. It is this commitment, along with the company "image," that the founder believed engendered the success of the company.

The Company Image: The unwritten doctrine goes like this: Men employees will wear short, conservative hair cuts. No beards nor mustaches. White shirts will be worn with conservative ties. No flashy or trendy apparel. Black or navy suits preferred, but charcoal will be accepted.

   Women are encouraged to wear thick, white cotton blouses which are to be buttoned to the neck. All skirts and dresses should fall below the knee. Only use that amount of make-up that is unobtrusive. No sexually provocative hair styles—tight and back is the best example.

   Employees are encouraged to maintain tranquil domestic relations. Above all, *no scandalous behavior.* No alcohol or drug use. Cigarettes only during off hours and at personal lunches. Employees are encouraged to accept all transfers and promotions or face repercussions. Employees found wanting in any of these areas will be subjected to living hell until they quit. After all, no one is ever laid off at MBI.

Advocates of the Image: The image creates a disciplined sales and service force (and this was what made the company great). Those people who balk at the regimented "clean cut" image of the company will be the sort who lower morale for the rest of the company and are basically "losers." After all, if they don't like the rules, they don't have to work here. No one put a gun to their heads. A company is entitled to create whatever corporate culture it wants to. With military precision, strict enforcement of "the image" can lead MBI to future success. MBI will thus succeed through the sheer force of "the image's" imposed moral excellence.

Detractors of the Image: There is not one type of "good person" that fits all people. Alternate life styles are a right under the Constitution of the United States. Any and all attempts to stifle diversity are not ethically correct. Other companies have made good money with the gays and lesbians that MBI has let go because they didn't fit the corporate mold. It is time to break the mold and become profitable again.

Company Survey: Two company surveys done one and three years ago, respectively, suggest that the employees at MBI are happy with the corporate culture the way it is. The conclusion of those reports was, "Why change something people are happy with?"

Does the image encourage moral behavior in an albeit paternalistic way through extrinsic inducements? Does it help its employees be all they can be despite frailties of human nature? Or does it encourage hiding and cheating? Is paternalism justified in a corporate culture, even if it was founded with good intentions? What weight do you place on the fact that the employees seem to like the "image" and the culture it fosters?

Case 2.5—Sexual Harassment at XYZ Department Store

You are the personnel manager at XYZ Department Store. The store is located in a medium-sized city and sells clothes and furniture. The people involved in the complaint are Fred Feinstein, the floor manager in men's apparel and Bill Neal, a salesclerk in men's apparel.

Bill Neal has come to you claiming that Mr. Feinstein has made numerous unwanted sexual advances on him. Mr. Neal further claims that since Mr. Feinstein is his superior, it has been difficult for him to do his job effectively. Mr. Neal is afraid of retributive action that might be taken against him by Mr. Feinstein.

According to company policy you have Mr. Neal file a formal complaint using the standard company format (a two page document which is designed to state the pertinent facts while informing the employee of his/her rights under the law). Once this is done you assure Mr. Neal that according to company policy, no one can be fired for one year after a complaint has been filed. (The only grounds for dismissal during this period would be: (a) being found guilty of a crime or (b) non performance of one's duties, i.e., not showing up for work.) Mr. Neal appeared satisfied as he returned to his job.

Next, you invite Mr. Feinstein into your office. You confront him with the fact that one of his subordinates had said that he has sexually harassed him.

"It's that son-of-a-bitch Neal. I knew he'd try to fix me."

You ask Mr. Feinstein to explain.

"Neal has been doing a poor job lately. He makes personal phone calls and often disappears for long periods in the stockroom. Recently, I have searched for him when he was absent on the floor. I found him sitting down with his feet up. Says all the walking makes him tired.

'Well, that's what you're paid to do,' I say. 'You get your ass in gear, buddy, or you are history around here.'"

"Can anyone confirm these conversations?"

"Hell no. I told you: he goes off by himself into the back room. What am I supposed to do? Take another producing employee with me so that the department is completely empty?"

"The employee says you make unwanted sexual advances upon him."

"Advances! That's homosexuality. Look, I'm a husband and a father. I'm no homosexual. Besides that, I'm an Orthodox Jew and I believe that homosexuality is outlawed in the Bible. If you go any farther with this, people are going to think, 'Where there's smoke, there's fire.' I'll be smeared. My reputation will be down the toilet. And for what? A good-for-nothing lazy employee. I tell you this: if you go any farther with this, I'll sue you and this store for all you're worth."

"Think about that before you start putting ideas into people's head and thereby smear me by innuendo. Think about whether some lazy greaseball who has only been with us for six months is worth all that. I'll be waiting."

You decide that this is a very difficult problem and take it to your boss, Shiela Mann, the president of XYZ. Ms. Mann tells you that she pays you a good salary to make decisions like this. But before you do, she advises you to see her again with the company attorney.

Now you must prepare a report for your meeting. What should you do?

Case 2.6—FBI Informant: To Be or Not to Be?

You work for LTD Construction of New Jersey, Inc. LTD is a large general contractor out of Patterson who bids exclusively on public works projects. When you came to work for LTD almost a year ago you were very impressed at some of the people who called on the principles of the agency, Vito and Robert Gambini (brothers). Vito was the president of the firm and he received calls from congressmen, federal judges and other important sounding people. No wonder LTD was always getting contracts.

Your job at LTD is as office manager. You keep everything hopping and ensure that everyone works productively.

The office has two fax machines. One machine is in the general office and the other is in Robert Gambini's private office. This latter machine carries confidential correspondence and is never read by anyone save the Gambini brothers.

One day Robert and Vic leave to go to an important contract meeting in Manhattan. Before he leaves Robert locks the double door that leads to both of the brothers' offices. You think nothing about it until the building maintenance man comes by to check on some leaking pipes. Leaking pipes are serious matters and must be attended to immediately.

The maintenance man goes up into the ceiling and works at it for some time. You forget about him and go about your office manager business. Finally, you notice the maintenance man coming out of the Gambinis's office. He has a big smile upon his face. The leak was found and fixed. It had been in the ceiling of Robert Gambini's office.

"I didn't leak water anywhere, but I almost got some papers on the fax machine wet. Here. I picked them up so they wouldn't get soaked." The maintenance man handed you the faxes and left. Immediately, you took the faxes back into Mr. Gambini's office. He would be furious if he knew that his faxes had been disturbed. It then occurred to you that you had better make sure the pages were in order or else it would tip off the Gambinis that someone had been into their papers.

As you turned the pages you discover something that is very disturbing. It is a communication that indicates that your bosses are engaging in bribery and extortion. Immediately you become frightened. On instinct you copy the faxes on the bosses's private copier and set the copies in the file folder you are carrying.

Then you replace the faxes on the machine just as they would have come in. The doors are locked and you wait until you get home to review the documents again. There was no mistake. You decide to talk to your brother who is a lawyer.

He looks at the documents, too. "I think these Gambinis are into Organized Crime. You've got to go to the FBI."

"I don't want any trouble. Can't I just quit my job?"

"Then the Gambinis would get suspicious."

"Can't I go on as if nothing had happened?"

"Then you become an accessory to their crimes."

"But won't they kill me if I give evidence?"

"The witness protection program has a very good record for keeping witnesses alive."

"But then my whole life would change. We'd have to change our name. The kids. My spouse. Everything would be so different."

"But these Gambinis are 'bad guys.' They have to be put away. They're hurting countless people by their activities."

"I could get myself fired."

My brother thought for a moment. "I guess that's an option. But can you live with the knowledge that you could have put criminals away and didn't?"

What should you do? Create a report which would justify one of the options to yourself and to your spouse.

Case 2.7—An African American at Sunshine News

You are an African American named Michael. Six months ago you were hired as a senior news writer at Sunshine News, a local television station with affiliation to one of the national networks. You come to the job with the following qualifications: 1. Student intern at *The Wall Street Journal* for three summers while an undergraduate; 2. A masters degree from Columbia University's school of journalism; 3. Two years doing 'weekend weather' for a New Jersey television station, 4. One year as a junior news writer with the *Associated Press* in Washington, D. C.

When the job at Sunshine News came you were excited. There are only two senior news writers on the news team. You are one step below the producer and two steps below the news director (both jobs to which you aspire). You also have three junior writers who work under you.

The Problem began early. The other senior news writer, named Swen, told you that all assignments came from the news director via the producer, that each of you had his team of writers, but that there were times when some "borrowing" would have to go on when one writer was overloaded.

Then a big national story broke. At the same time a prominent local story also came to the fore. You were assigned the national story, but could only use one of your junior writers. Nevertheless, you worked very hard. You stayed up much of the night doing background and creating a piece which would complement the network coverage. The next day you waited with expectation.

Nothing happened. The national story ran as a network footage only. All the station's attention went to the local story.

Therein began The Problem. Time after time you were given lousy stories, or good stories which never ran—or if they ran they did so only in part and often at low audience times. Frequently two-thirds of your staff was commandeered. The only writer you could depend upon was a fresh graduate from college with no experience.

You made an appointment to see the news director, Molly Hammer. "I think I am not getting a fair deal in the news assignments," you began.

"Nonsense," was her reply.

"Look, I have documented what Swen's gotten and what I've gotten over the past six months. Whenever I've been given any decent story, it's either killed or whacked to pieces and placed in the daytime 'news update' mini slots." You hand her your list. She looks at it for at least six seconds and sets it atop a pile of other papers.

"Look, Michael you're new to the station. I have to break you in."

"It's been six months, Ms. Hammer. I think with my background, I'm broken in well enough."

"That's my call, Michael."

"Look at my resumé. No other writer on the staff has anywhere near my qualifications."

"I know all about your resumé, Michael. That's why we hired you. We've been thinking about having you read the station editorials on the evening time slot."

"Now that's more like it," you say. "I have good experience in writing pointed rhetorical pieces. Why at Columbia—"

"Maybe in time *you can* both write the pieces and read them. For now, I thought you'd read Swen's copy. It'd give us a fresh face before the camera."

You wanted to say, "A black face, you mean. A real two-fer: hire one African American and count him twice. Once as a so-called senior writer and once as an on-camera personality." *Instead you say,* "Well, I'll think that over, Ms. Hammer. But my point about writing assignments still stands."

When you get home you are overwhelmed by a mixture of nausea and anger. This is the 1990s. Why are they doing this to you? You are the only African American at the station who is not a janitor or a typist. You feel used and abused. But what should you do? 1. File a grievance with the Civil Rights Commission? 2. Try other ways to make your point to management? [You've already tried the direct approach and failed. It could get worse if they decided to get mean.] 3. Openly fight Swen and keep your writing team together? [Make it an 'us-them' confrontation.] 4. Job hunt? 5. Some other option?

This problem keeps you up most of the night. The next day you vow to make a report to yourself to clarify your options. You are a rational person and don't want to be swayed by a hasty, emotional decision. *Write Michael's report.*

Case 2.8—An Accountant's Dilemma[2]

You are an accountant at one of the Big Eight Firms. You have been in the job for just over a year. One of the things that you took very seriously in your training as an accountant was the rigorous code of ethics of the American Institute of Certified Public Accountants (AICPA). This code suggests that accountants maintain independence from clients and they bear equal responsibility for reporting unlawful or misleading information when normal accounting practice would show to the accountant that such information was questionable or false. These guidelines were also a part of your auditing exam.

The situation is this: you have been brought in to perform an audit of a very good client. The client is a holding company with a real estate subsidiary. Your supervisor, Bill Howe, wants to go over your work (which is not unusual since you are still in your two-year review period).

You begin the project and encounter a number of difficulties which you work hard to reconcile. You are successful in solving all the problems save one: there is a property whose value is declared to be 2.5 million by the real estate subsidiary. You believe this to be far overvalued. At best you believe the property to be worth $200,000. The property is a strip shopping center in a run-down part of an inner city which had recently been ravaged by riots. There are only two current tenants and one is twelve months' delinquent in his rents. Comparable properties have been selling for $150,000 to $200,000.

The intent of the holding company is to write down the inflated value of the property on their taxes. This write down would have a 7% impact on the taxes of the subsidiary and a 1% impact on the holding company.

AICPA regulations require differences of opinion between client and public accountant which affect the income statement by more than 3% to be considered material and to be disclosed in the CPA's opinion.

Because of this you attach a "subject-to-opinion" designation on the valuation of the property as well as attaching your own documentation that suggests that $200,000 is a more accurate price.

Your supervisor reacts by asking you to remove the "subject-to-opinion" and replace it with "clean opinion." Also, you are instructed to remove the pages which support your own estimation of the property. It was, after all, really the holding company which counted and not the real estate subsidiary; therefore, these changes should not be of any consequence to you.

You refuse to alter your findings citing your interpretation of AICPA regulations. However, you find that Bill Howe (on his own) made the changes anyway.

You are unsure what you should do in these circumstances. You believe that what Bill Howe did was wrong. You also know that Bill Howe is your supervisor and that you are in a two-year probationary period after which you will be dismissed unless you have a good recommendation from your supervisor (Bill Howe).

If something were discovered and the case investigated, you do have your own computer files documenting your version of the case. It is possible that computer files can be tampered with and you are unsure whether such tampering can be detected should a full scale investigation occur.

If such a questionable practice happened once, it could happen again. You would have to change *yourself* in order to work in such a situation. The job market for accountants at this moment is rather tight. Getting another job would be difficult (especially if you had the reputation as a "troublemaker").

It is possible to take such issues to an independent review board. If you acted promptly you could protect yourself and get the matter aired in a professional setting. There are "whistle blower" protections in such proceedings. However, you aren't really sure they can protect you. When you are on "probation" they can always find a way to get rid of you.

You decide to write a report recommending a personal course of action.

Notes

1. Much of this case is based upon Oil, Chemical, and Atomic Workers International Union and Local 3-499, Oil, Chemical and Atomic Workers, Petitioners vs. American Cyanamid Company, respondent No. 81-1687/ United States Court of Appeals, District of Columbia Circuit/ Argued 10/4/83/ Decided 8/24/84. See also Harvard Business School Case 9-181-131, 1981.

2. See also a similar case in Harvard Business School case 9-380-185, 1980.

Consumer Issues

▶ Health Care
▶ Advertising
▶ The Consumer
▶ The Environment

CHAPTER 9

Health Care

Address to Congress on Health Care Reform

President Bill Clinton

My fellow Americans, tonight we come together to write a new chapter in the American story.

Our forebears enshrined the American dream—life, liberty, the pursuit of happiness. Every generation of Americans has worked to strengthen that legacy, to make our country a place of freedom and opportunity, a place who—where people who work hard can rise to their full potential and a place where their children can have a better future. . . .

Our purpose in this dynamic age must be to change, to make change our friend and not our enemy. If Americans are to have the courage to change in a difficult time, we must first be secure in our most basic needs. Tonight I want to talk to you about the most critical thing we can do to build that security.

This health-care system of ours is badly broken and it is time to fix it. Despite the dedication of literally millions of talented health care professionals, our health care is too uncertain and too expensive, too bureaucratic and too wasteful. It has too much fraud and too much greed.

At long last, after decades of false starts, we must make this our most urgent priority: giving every American health security, health care that can never be taken away, health care that is always there.

So tonight I want to talk to you about the principles that I believe must embody our efforts to reform America's health care system: Security, simplicity, savings, choice, quality and responsibility.

Security for All

Millions of Americans are just a pink slip away from losing their health insurance, and one serious illness away from losing all their savings. Millions more are locked into the jobs they have now just because they or someone in their family had once been sick and they have what is called a preexisting condition. And on any given day, over 37 million Americans—most of them working people and their little children—have no health insurance at all. And in spite of all this, our medical bills are growing at over twice the rate of inflation, and the United States spends over a third more of its income on health care than any other nation on Earth. . . .

My fellow Americans, we must fix this system, and it has to begin with congressional action.

The proposal that I describe tonight borrows many of the principles and ideas that have been embraced in plans introduced by both Republicans and Democrats in this Congress. For the first time in this century leaders of both political parties have joined together around the principle of providing universal, comprehensive health care. It is a magic moment, and we must seize it.

And so tonight let me ask all of you: every member of the House, every member of the Senate, each Republican and each Democrat. Let us keep this spirit and let us keep this commitment until this job is done. We owe it to the American people.

Now if I might, I would like to review the six principles I mentioned earlier and describe how we think we can best fulfill those principles.

First and most important, security. Security means that those who do not now have health care coverage will have it. And for those who have it, it will never be taken away. We must achieve that security as soon as possible.

Under our plan every American would receive a health-care security card that will guarantee a comprehensive package of benefits over the course of an entire lifetime roughly comparable to the benefit package offered by most Fortune 500 companies.

This health-care security card will offer this package of benefits in a way that can never be taken away. So let us agree on this: Whatever else we disagree on, before this Congress finishes its work next year, you will pass and I will sign legislation to guarantee this security to every citizen of this country.

Simplifying the System

The second principle is simplicity. Our health care system must be simpler for the patients and simpler for those who actually deliver health care: our doctors, our nurses, our other medical professionals. Today we have more than 1,500 insurers with hundreds and hundreds of different forms. . . . The medical-care industry is literally drowning in paperwork. In recent years the number of administrators in our hospitals has grown by four times the rate that the number of doctors has grown.

A hospital ought to be a house of healing, not a monument to paperwork and bureaucracy.

Under our proposal there would be one standard insurance form, not hundreds of them. We will simplify also—and we must—the government's rules and regulations, because they are a big part of this problem.

The third principle is savings. Reform must produce savings in this health care system—it has to. We are spending over 14% of our income on health care; Canada's at 10; nobody else is over nine. We're competing with all these people for the future and the other major countries, they cover everybody. And they cover them with services as generous as the best company policies here in this country. . . .

Our competitiveness, our whole economy, the integrity of the way the government works, and ultimately our living standards, depend upon our ability to achieve savings without harming the quality of health care. So how will we achieve these savings? First, to give groups of consumers and small businesses the same market bargaining power that large corporations and large groups of public employees now have.

We want to let market forces enable plans to compete. We want to force these plans to compete on the basis of price and quality, not simply to allow them to continue making money by turning people away who are sick or old, or performing mountains of unnecessary procedures. . . .

We want to create what has been missing in this system for too long . . . ; To have a combination of private market forces and a sound public policy that will support that competition but limit the rate at which prices can exceed the rate of inflation and population growth, if the competition doesn't work, especially in the early going.

The second thing I want to say is, that unless everybody is covered . . . we will never be able to fully put the brakes on health-care inflation. Why is that? Because when people don't have health insurance they will get health care, but they get it when it's too late, when it's too expensive, often from the most expensive place of all, the emergency room.

Third thing we can do to save money is simply by simplifying the system. . . . freeing the health care providers from these costly and unnecessary paperwork and administrative decisions will save tens of billions of dollars.

We also have to crack down on fraud and abuse in the system. That drains millions of dollars a year. It is a very large figure, according to every health-care expert I've ever spoken to. . . .

The fourth principle is choice. . . . We propose to give every American a choice among high-quality plans. You can stay with your current doctor, join a network of doctors and hospitals or join a health maintenance organization. If you don't like your plan, every year you'll have the chance to choose a new one. The choice will be left to the American citizen, the worker, not the boss and certainly not some government bureaucrat.

We also believe that doctors should have a choice as to what plans they practice in. Otherwise, citizens may have their own choices limited. We want to end the discrimination that is now growing against doctors and to permit them to practice in several different plans. Choice is important for doctors and it is absolutely critical for our consumers.

The fifth principle is quality. . . . Our proposal will create report cards on health plans so that consumers can choose the highest-quality health-care providers and reward them with their business. At the same time, our plan will track quality indicators so that doctors can make better and smarter choices of the kind of care they provide.

The sixth and final principle is responsibility.

We need to restore a sense that we're all in this together and that we all have a responsibility to be a part of the solution. Responsibility has to start with those who profit from the current system.

It . . . should apply to anybody who abuses this system and drives up the cost for honest, hard-working citizens and undermines confidence in the honest, gifted health-care providers we have.

Taking Responsibility

But let me say this—and I hope every American will listen—because this is not an easy thing to hear. Responsibility in our health-care system isn't just about them. It's about you. It's about me. It's about each of us.

Too many of us have not taken responsibility for our own health care and for our own relations to the health-care system. Many of us who've had fully paid health-care plans have used the system whether we needed it or not without thinking what the costs were. Many people who use this system don't pay a penny for their care even though they can afford to. I think those who don't have any health insurance should be responsible for paying a portion of their new coverage. There can't be any something for nothing, and we have to demonstrate that to people. This is not a free system. . . .

Forty years from now, our grandchildren will . . . find it unthinkable that there was a time in this country when hard-working families lost their homes, their savings, their businesses—lost everything simply because their children got sick or because they had to change jobs. Our grandchildren will find such things unthinkable tomorrow if we have the courage to change today.

This is our chance. This is our journey. And when our work is done, we will know that we have answered the call of history and met the challenge of our time.

Some Practical and Moral Issues in Health-Care Reform
Michael Boylan

Most of us need health care at one time or the other in our lives. In one sense it is an "invisible" commodity because it is not really apparent to us until we need it. With the advances in medical science in the last seventy-five years there is increasingly more that can be done for us by modern medicine. All of this has a price tag. And the price tag is staggering. But not all Americans have actual access to health care. ("Actual Access" means the ability to utilize appropriate health care providers for the remedy of health conditions.) This lack of actual access is generally due to lack of insurance. Health insurance is not cheap. Therein lies the genesis of the problem. If comprehensive health care is a right, then presently it is not accessible to all. For these reasons and others President Clinton has made an initial stab at overhauling the country's health care system.

Because health care is over 15% of our economy (thus constituting a cluster of businesses in themselves) and because virtually every business is confronted with the health insurance issue, some careful thinking on these issues is very important. The purpose of this essay is: 1. To outline the strengths and weaknesses of the current health care system; 2. To sketch the ethical arguments on human rights and health care; and 3. To set out some of the practical issues involved in comprehensive universal coverage.

The Present System.   When my grandfather was in medical school, around the turn of the twentieth century, there were still classes that used Galen as their basis. I am a great admirer of Galen, but the medical world that Galen knew depicted the physician as one who set broken bones, helped delivering babies, prescribed diet/exercise, and suggested herbs to balance the four humors of the body.[1]

With the twentieth century, Galenic medicine became a thing of the past. Medicine advanced rapidly on two fronts: (a) pharmacology, and (b) surgery. The former was stirred by advances in specialized medical research and the latter by advances in technique (including ways to keep the patient alive both during and after an operation) and biomedical technology (including prosthetics, improved surgical equipment and monitoring apparati). The "new medicine" enabled miracles to be performed that were thought to be impossible in my grandfather's medical school days.

With the new medicine came a greater price tag. Most of this price tag was associated with hospitalization. To enable people to be able to afford expensive hospitalization, medical insurance was promoted. Originally health insurance was designed for catastrophes. (Insurance often works best when it protects its policy holders against an unlikely catastrophe—as in home owners' insurance.)

In the post World War II period health insurance gradually began adding other features to its coverages: pregnancy and childbirth, office visits, and prescription drugs. At the same time medical advances were increasing rapidly. Hospitals bought new and expensive machines which had to be paid for by each and every patient who entered the door—whether he/she needed those services or not. Medical accountability also rose as the litigious climate heated up. Each and every time that things "went badly," it has to be "somebody's fault." (Somebody's fault means a malpractice suit.) This created a climate in which both physicians and hospitals had to establish careful guidelines about what the "prudent practitioner" would do in such and such situation. If anyone varied from this, then he/she was liable for malpractice.

Hospitals had to add layers of administrative staff to comply with the demands of high accountability. This meant an increasingly larger price tag.

Insurance companies, who had routinely paid every bill presented to them in the fifties and sixties, were now auditing bills more carefully for mistakes and fraud. This also increased the costs.

The good news is that health care has enabled people to live longer lives. The bad news is that this aging population has greatly increased health-care needs. Medicare was established to help meet these needs, but Medicare pays only a fraction of what procedures actually cost on the open market. This meant that younger patients (and their insurance companies) were forced to subsidize the difference. It is an invisible tax.

The late 1980s saw an explosion of health insurance costs which were caused by a similar rise in health-care costs. More people were getting knee and back operations instead of hobbling around as their parents had. Americans were using their health insurance as they never had before because it really improved the quality of their lives.

By the 1990s health insurance was too expensive for many Americans. Family coverage was often as costly as the rent or mortgage. Americans were not used to paying such a high percentage of their income on health insurance. For many there was no choice. They could not afford the high premiums and went without coverage. This gamble works so long as you don't need to go to the hospital. But if you do, then you can find yourself forced to go to public hospitals which are over crowded and often without the latest medical equipment.

For the very poor Medicaid is available. Eligibility varies according to each state, but like Medicare, it does not reimburse at the market rate. The difference is made up by "paying customers" (meaning people with insurance).

Types of Health Insurance

1. **Traditional indemnity insurance.** Under this type of coverage the policy holder pays an annual deductible and then is reimbursed under a co-insurance arrangement with the insurance company (usually 80%–20%). When the policy holder's expenses reach a "stop-loss" limit, the company pays 100% up to the limits of the policy (usually one million to five million). Coverage is available only for accident or sickness (pregnancy is generally treated as any other illness). In most cases there is no preventative care coverage.

   One feature that is very controversial about indemnity plans in small groups (under 100 employees) is the "pre-existing condition clause." This clause generally excludes pre-existing medical conditions for up to twelve months. (Sometimes they are permanently excluded from coverage.) It is possible in very small health groups that a person can be turned down entirely for a pre-existing medical condition. This means that even if he or she has the money, he or she may not be able to purchase health insurance. [Some states have passed laws forbidding insurance companies from discriminating against those with pre-existing conditions.]

2. **HMO.** Health maintenance organizations are either set-up as full service centers (like Kaiser Permanente) or networks of physicians (like individual practice associations). In either case the patient generally has no deductible except a small office payment (usually $5 to $20). Routine coverages are broader in an HMO. Every routine coverage that an indemnity plan covers are covered in an HMO with the addition of preventative care coverage. Further, in federally qualified HMOs there are no pre-existing condition limitations.

   In return for expanded routine coverages, the patient gives up some control of his or her health-care choices. The primary care physician decides whether you need to see a specialist. If that primary care physician says "no," then you don't go.

   It is this "managed care" feature that makes HMOs more economical than indemnity plans. The economical advantages and broader coverages are balanced against less control over one's own health care decisions.

   There are also some restrictions on who one sees for treatment. One *must* see a participating member of that particular HMO. If the doctor you want is taking no more new patients, or if you do not like any of the physicians in the HMO, then you are out of luck. This is another distinction from the traditional indemnity plans which allow you to choose any doctor who has a license to practice medicine.

   Finally, managed care is generally more restrictive on the types of "big ticket items" it will pay for. Many exclude transplants all together. Most have annual caps on the amount of prescription drugs they will pay for. In a survey I did among twenty HMO's in the Washington, D.C. area the average prescription drug cap was $3000 per year. There are a substantial number of physical afflictions which require more than $250 per month ($3000 per year). The patient must make up the difference.

   To offer a real incentive for cost containment, many HMO primary care physicians are given a "budget" that varies according to how many patients they oversee. If they are under their "budget," then they receive all or some of the difference. Thus, the physician has a financial interest in holding down the number of tests and expensive procedures he/she allows you to have.

3. **PPO.** The PPO is a variant of the traditional indemnity plan. In the PPO there is a list of participating physicians (much like the IPA–HMO outlined above). These physicians agree to charge pre-determined prices to PPO patients. In return, they are listed in the directory and presumably get more business. The insurance company knows in advance what its costs will be. Whenever an insurance company can fill in an unknown figure with a known figure, its costs decrease. Thus a PPO is more economical than the traditional indemnity plan, but it is not as economical as the HMO.

Like the indemnity plan, the PPO does not cover preventative care. Like the indemnity plan there are more permissible "high ticket treatments" that are covered. And like indemnity plans there is the pre-existing condition clause.

Unlike the indemnity plan there is less choice. One must choose a physician in the network. However, there is no primary care physician. Virtually all choice for medical treatment lies in the patient's hands. Like the HMO there is generally no deductible—save for a modest co-payment for an office visit.

There seems to be a scale which equates choice of doctors and treatment with greater cost. Patient empowerment/autonomy is expensive. Thus, the indemnity plan is the most expensive, followed by the PPO and the HMO is the most cost efficient.

4. **Opt out plans.** Because patient empowerment/autonomy is so popular to consumers, many HMO and PPO plans now have an "opt out" feature. This means that if you don't want to use the HMO or the PPO, you can opt out of the plan and your health insurance becomes a traditional indemnity plan.

To encourage policy holders to use the HMO or PPO, insurance companies often add some restrictions to the opt out option. This is important to the insurance companies so that they can avoid "adverse selection." (Adverse selection occurs when two or more plans exist and there are incentives for the sicker members of the population to utilize one plan to the exclusion of the others.)

Health Insurance in Other Countries

The following two plans are the most popular alternatives to health care as practiced in the United States.

5. **Government run health plans.** Many countries in the world have government run health plans. In these plans physicians are really employees of the government. They have a quota of patients for a practice and see people on their list whenever those people are in need of health care.

There are a number of attractive features in government run health plans:
(a) there is universal, comprehensive coverage;
(b) since physicians are employees of the government, the litigious malpractice climate is largely eliminated;
(c) because physicians work on salary, they do not have to have their minds distracted with running a business and can concentrate on practicing medicine.

There are some disadvantages to government run health plans:
(a) because physicians are employees of the government, their salaries are far less than those of private practice physicians. Some say that this is

a disincentive for the "best and brightest" to enter medicine. (That is, if we assume that *high compensation* is a critical incentive for people entering medicine as a career.) If the compensation incentive is correct, then a country with a government run health plan will have less able physicians than countries which rely upon private practice physicians. (That is, if we assume that the best and brightest make the best physicians.)

(b) To lower costs, many physicians have large practices and this can lead to long waiting times to see doctors. This "clinic" atmosphere may discourage some from going to the doctor—even when they need to. They might not have an hour or two to sit waiting.

(c) Most countries that have government run health plans also have private practice physicians who are hired only by the rich. This creates a "two tier" health system. The average person may rightly perceive that he or she is getting a different level of care than the rich. In the United States, those with health insurance, may be on a more "even playing field." (However, this disregards those who have no health insurance and are not covered by Medicare or Medicaid.)

6. **Single payer plans.** In a single payer model private practice physicians are maintained. They are paid by insurance. The difference is that there is only one insurance company: the Government. With one payer there is only one set of regulations and guidelines. Sub-units of the country (provinces or states) are given health care "budgets" (much like the budgets mentioned above in the HMO's). Once one's budget has been exhausted there is severe pressure to limit further services (though further services are never completely "cut off.") If one's budget has money at the end of the year, the health care community may share in this surplus.

Like a planned economy in economics, the single payer system has the advantages of central control. Health policy can be uniform. Most theories of distributive justice promote treating "like cases" in the same way.

Like a planned economy in economics, the single payer system has the disadvantages of central control. Centrally controlled economies are less efficient. The converse suggests that "small," diverse, and competitive models are more efficient because they can adapt to market conditions more readily.

Many view the single payer system as having the advantages of government run health care (such as comprehensive universal coverage) without the drawbacks.

Human Rights and Health Care. Obviously one important part of the health care debate is whether or not a citizen of a country has a right to health care. If he or she does, then it is the government's correlative duty to provide this good to the individual.[2] Thus, if all citizens have a right to health care, then the government has the correlative duty to provide it.

Therefore, it is an important question whether or not individuals have a right to health care. This brief exposition does not attempt to fully explore this issue, but merely raises some important issues and point to the way that the question might be answered. To this end let us first address two theories for the basis of human rights: (a) natural rights theory; (b) community rights theory.

Natural Rights Theory.   There are a number of versions of natural rights theory. There is even disagreement about when it was first enunciated in the Western tradition.[3] What concerns us here is a form of the theory which states that there is some characteristic that all people possess that justifies their claim to that good as a right. This good is thus claimed solely on the basis of the claimant's status as a human being (or in some cases an "adult" human being).

There are several persuasive writers in the natural rights tradition that, at least, began with John Locke (if not earlier.)[4] For our purposes let us borrow from Alan Gewirth who uses contemporary action theory to create a dialectically necessary argument to support the claim that all people have the rights to freedom and well being (see the Gewirth article in the theory section of this book).[5]

In short, this argument contends that for myself I must claim freedom and well being in order to act. I must logically recognize that I do not differ in this respect from other humans. Thus, in my claiming this right for myself, I am also claiming it for all other humans as well.

The question then becomes whether or not health care is an essential good of well being. Using a sort of Kantian reasoning this question could be rephrased as, "Can I will myself not to have adequate health care coverage without violating a universal law of nature?"[6] The answer would seem to be, "No." For if I were to deny myself such a good, I would be willing my misfortune and/or destruction. And to do that would be to violate a universal law of nature.

On this compressed analysis I *must* claim the right to adequate (i.e., comprehensive) health care coverage. Because *I* must claim the good (as an essential element of my well being), then I must acknowledge that *all* can claim it. Thus, everyone has a right to adequate (comprehensive) health care coverage.

Community Rights Theory.   Community rights theories may have their origin in Hegel.[7] One contemporary version of the argument has been presented by Beth Singer.[8] Briefly, we can characterize rights as operative or not operative. This means that a human community recognizes the rights or does not recognize them. On this view, the "rights relation" is a social institution governed by the attitudes of a normative community. It is, in one sense, an empty question to ask what rights one has that are not exhibited. This is because "having" and "taking" are different modes. Rights that are not already possessed (by being recognized in the human community) must be "taken" in order to be operative. This is a political, sociological, and historical truism.

The discussion of rights—not operative—must turn on *how* and *by what means* they will, in the future, be "taken."

Once taken, these claims are in the repertoire of rights recognized by the community.

It is clear that citizens in the United States do not now have universal, comprehensive health care. Thus, they have no right to universal, comprehensive health care until such time as the reciprocal attitudes of the individual and the community change on this subject.

The Right to Health Care.   Depending upon the theory you have chosen to depict human rights, you have two different answers to whether there is a "right" to health care. If one accepts my adaptation of Kant and Gewirth, then there is a right to comprehensive universal health care (based on a natural rights theory).

If one takes the community rights viewpoint, then there is not a *right* to health care (yet), but there still may be good reasons for citizens to band together to convince the society that such a right should be recognized.

I would side with the advocates of the natural right to health care. But this still leaves one question open that must be addressed: the Kantian doctrine that "ought implies can." Under this doctrine no one can be said to have a binding moral duty to perform something that is practically impossible for him to do. This maxim is important to Kant for without it, his theory is doomed to inconsistency.[9]

Thus, the question may be whether the United States can institute comprehensive universal health care. If they can, then they should.

But what lies behind this "can"? Does the "can" mean (1) "logically possible" or (2) "practically possible" or (3) "comfortable to implement" or (4) "may be implemented without raising taxes or cutting other programs" or (5) "politically easy to bring about." Obviously the answers to these interpretations of "can" are different. Therein lies a large part of the practical implementation of any health care reform.

Practical Issues Involved in Comprehensive Universal Coverage.   The number of practical impediments to establishing a comprehensive universal health care system in the United States is very large. It is not difficult to sketch some of them. First, there are the vested interests which will be disturbed. These include: 1. hospitals, 2. doctors, 3. pharmaceutical companies, 4. insurance companies, 5. the myriad of medical support facilities. It is a political fact that entrenched interests are difficult to overcome in a democracy. This is one aspect of the "can" described in the last section.

A second element of the "can" equates to "economically afford." This, in turn, requires a specification of "afford." Clearly this word implies a value system that ranks alternatives. If one puts comprehensive universal health care at the top of the list, then the United States can certainly afford it. But few people seem inclined to do so. Much of the current dissatisfaction with health care revolves around the *cost* of health care. Americans seem reluctant to put it very high on the list of priorities. Many people want the "best available care," but at the same time do not want to pay for it. Unless there is a will to rank health care high, comprehensive universal coverage will never occur. This is because it is very costly. How costly is difficult to determine, but in a peacetime economy it is likely to be the largest single item in the federal budget (after payment on the national debt).

Few really believe that comprehensive coverage can be obtained without either raising taxes significantly or cutting existing programs. This latter alternative always sounds great because each of us has a different idea of which programs are ripe for cutting. (Those programs which don't benefit us, personally, are usually those that we think are ripe for cutting.)

The establishment of "political will" is a job for politicians. Unless the American people accept that comprehensive universal health coverage is important, it will never pass—no matter how "right" it is.

The third sense of "can" involves what sort of health care we want. Do we desire everyone to have access to the "best available care" or will we settle for a rationing formula? If so, then what sort of formula? If the rationing formula is too restrictive, then it may not be an improvement over what we presently have. Again, the "can" is involved with people making a conscious decision about whether they believe "best available care" is an integral part of their well being (or at least a more integral part of their well being than a second car, boat, or summer home).

The last sense of "can" involves *who* will pay for it. At the writing of this essay (1994), the most popular candidate is business. When health care was inexpensive, it became a standard fringe benefit of most employers. As health insurance became more and more costly, employees have taken on an increasingly greater share of the premium payments.

There is often a false sense among individuals that if payment for some good does not come directly out of their pockets, then they are not paying for it. Thus government and big business are thought to be able to provide fringe benefits "free of cost" to the average person. This, of course, is untrue. The government depends upon taxes for its revenue and business passes on its expenses to consumers. We all pay.

Some have suggested that we take the mechanism of health insurance out of the workplace and make it like car insurance, which is privately purchased though, at the same time, mandatory in most states.

Small businesses are most vocal for this option citing the thin margins on which they work and the limited reserve capital they have at any given time. Indeed, it has been small businesses who have been the greatest critics of comprehensive universal coverage because they feel it will put them out of business.

It is hard to assess this claim. But if it is true, then some sort of accommodation must be made for small business.

What about sole proprietors? These individuals have no employees but themselves. These people make up the largest percentage of the present uninsured population. How can these people be monitored so that they are compelled to purchase health insurance. These hardworking individuals—be they painters, carpenters or whatever—have often made the choice in the present situation not to purchase health insurance. What makes us think that they will purchase health insurance under a different scenario? They will say they have no money left after rent, food, and clothing to purchase insurance. Tax "write-offs" are not significant to people with little money coming in and no appreciable savings. This sort of argument is a further dimension of the "ought implies can" dilemma.

There are a considerable number of difficulties associated with establishing comprehensive universal health care coverage in the United States. The task will not be an easy one. But then large changes are never easy. It seems to me that the moral "ought" supports the change. There are many candidates for this "ought" being overridden by practical problems (the "can"). I do not believe these practical difficulties are definitive. I believe we ought to go forward with comprehensive universal coverage in some form.

Notes

1. "Galen's Conception Theory" *Journal of the History of Biology* 19.1 (1986). "The Hippocratic and Galenic Challenges to Aristotle's Conception Theory" *Journal of the History of Biology* 15.1 (1982).

2. This idea of correlative rights is derived from Wesley N. Hohfeld, *Fundamental Legal Conceptions* (New Haven Conn., Yale University Press, 1919). In that work Hohfeld describes a "claims right." A claim is a right with a specific correlative duty of the form "x has a right to y against z in virtue of p." In this case x and z are individuals. Z has a duty to give x some good, y, because of p (some institution which validates the transaction). Thus, if x lends $10 to z, then because of the institution of paying debts, x has a right to that $10 at some specified time from z. In this way, rights and duties are correlative. A right of one agent is identified as the duty of some other agent. A right is a duty seen from another standpoint.

3. Some articles to note on this controversy are: H.L.A Hart, "Are There Any Natural Rights?" *Philosophical Review* 64 (1955): 176–177; W.W. Buckland, *A Text–Book of Roman Law from Augustus to Justinian* (rpt. Cambridge: Cambridge University Press, 1963), p. 58; *Elementary Principles of the Roman Private Law* (Cambridge: Cambridge University Press, 1912), pp. 9, 61–62; *A Manual of Roman Private Law* (Cambridge: Cambridge University Press, 1925), p. 155; Michel Villey, *Lecons d'historie de la philosophie du droit* (Paris: Vrin, 1957), chs. 11 and 14; S.I. Benn and R.S. Peters, *Social Principles and the Democratic State* (London: George Allen and Unwin, 1959); Michael Boylan, "Seneca and Moral Rights" *The New Scholasticism* 53.3 (1979): 362–374.

4. The literature is rich here. See especially A.I. Melden, *Rights and Persons* (Berkeley, CA: University of California Press, 1977); Jacques Maritain, *Les droits de l'homme et la loi naturelle* (rpt. N.Y.: Editions de la Maison Francais, 1942); Roscoe Pound, *Jurisprudence* (St. Paul, MN: West Publishing Co., 1959).

5. It is not my desire to discuss this argument at length but only to use it as an example of a natural rights theory. For a thorough discussion of Gewirth's argument see: Deryck Beyleveld, *The Dialectical Nature of Necessity* (Chicago: University of Chicago Press, 1991).

6. This is intended to be an application of the so-called imperfect duties—Kant, *Groundwork of the Metaphysics of Morals,* tr H.J. Paton (rpt. N.Y.: Harper Torchbooks, 1964) Royal Prussian Academy p. 421 "Act as if the maxim of your action were to become through

your will a universal law of nature." See also examples #3 and #4 which Kant uses on p. 423. For a discussion of this puzzling distinction of perfect and imperfect duties see: H.J. Paton (1964), p. 31; R. Chisholm, "Supererogation and Offence" *Ratio* 5 (1963): p. 4; and Alan Donagan, *The Theory of Morality* (Chicago, University of Chicago Press, 1977), pp. 154–155.

7. See Hegel's *The Philosophy of Right,* tr T.M. Knox (Oxford: Clarendon Press, 1942); see also Michael Oakeshott, *Rationalism in Politics* (London: Methuen and Co., 1962). The sociological angle is developed by George Herbert Mead in *Mind, Self, and Society* (Chicago: University of Chicago Press, 1934).

8. Beth Singer, *Operative Rights* (Albany, N.Y.: SUNY Press, 1993).

9. The inconsistency is this: on the one hand one may have a duty to do x, yet on the other hand it is impossible to do x. Thus the individual is put in the position of a moral dilemma. No matter what one does, he is immoral. If he tries to do his duty and fails (which must happen if doing his duty is impossible), then he is immoral. If he ignores his duty, then he is immoral.

   For a discussion of the consequences of moral inconsistency for Kant (or similar systems) see Donagan (1977), ch. 5.

Alternatives to Federal Regulatory Realignment of Health Care

Christopher J. Kalkhof, CHE, NHA

Healthcare Reform

The current crisis in the U.S. healthcare system may be more one of perception than fact. While it is true that in certain areas of the country and for some segments of the population there are real healthcare access and coverage problems, coverage *is* available in most places and for most individuals. The magnitude of the crisis may not be significant enough to justify the major changes in the healthcare delivery system that will result from present reform proposals.

Many changes are needed in the healthcare system. The system needs to become more effective, physicians and hospitals need to become more cost efficient and price competitive, duplication of services needs to be eliminated, and hospitals need to focus on assuring the appropriateness of care rather than filling beds.

These changes can be accomplished, however, without government-directed healthcare reform. Moreover, healthcare reform proposals themselves raise a serious question: Will any of the proposals adequately address healthcare access for the varied population segments of America?

The most widely discussed reform proposal is the Clinton administration's managed competition approach. Other proposals for reform advocate a

Christopher J. Kalkhof, "Alternatives to Federal Regulatory Realignment of Health Care," *Health Care Financial Management.*

Canadian-type, single-payer system—an approach supported by a number of members of Congress and some lobbying groups—and several alternative versions of managed competition.

The common thread among these reform initiatives is the focus on healthcare benefits coverage. The rationale behind these initiatives is that benefits coverage will ensure access to health care. However, benefits coverage in and of itself will not necessarily guarantee that medical care will be accessible, acceptable, available, and affordable for the individual who has the coverage. Nor does it assure continuity of treatment and quality of services.

It is likely that the Clinton plan or a modified version of the managed competition approach to healthcare reform eventually will be passed by Congress. Adoption of a managed competition approach will create a heavily regulated healthcare system. The Clinton plan, for example, calls for creating massive healthcare alliances, one in each state or geographic region or for each major corporation. These alliances will act as insurance pools for large numbers of healthcare consumers and spread risks among providers. As a result, alliances will be able to collect premiums from all employers or welfare funds, contract with designated healthcare plans for the provision of services, enroll eligibles, and enforce cost-cutting directives. In addition, the Clinton proposal will impose a global budget on healthcare spending, restricting increases in insurance premiums to the general rate of inflation by 1999.

If it can be assumed, however, that healthcare delivery and financing processes already are undergoing fundamental systemic change as a result of competitive market forces. The question then becomes: Will the introduction of government-mandated managed competition into the current market-driven evolutionary process increase or decrease the probability of improving provider accessibility, availability, acceptability, affordability, continuity, and quality of care for the individuals the system is intended to serve—the patients?

Healthcare Utilization Factors

The following variables have been found to promote or prohibit the utilization of healthcare services by families:

- Need, which may be defined as the perceived seriousness of illnesses, chronic activity limitations, and disability;
- Predisposition, which includes behavior, sex, age, education, marital status, race, lifestyle, and so forth;
- Enabling factors, which include economic considerations (e.g., income, out-of-pocket cost, health insurance); organizational opportunities (e.g., existing regional/community delivery systems); and accessibility (e.g., urban vs. rural residence, distance to services, regularly available care when needed, and an adequate supply of healthcare services in the community).[1]

The Clinton proposal and other current reform proposals primarily address economic enabling factors; they do not consider to any great extent organizational or accessibility factors or need and predisposition. The practical impact from a market perspective of a program of healthcare reform that focuses on economic enabling factors or healthcare benefits coverage is a significant increase in demand for services. Increased demand, however, leads to increased production of healthcare services, and thus higher costs. Higher costs run counter to one of the core objective of national healthcare reform, namely, to reduce expenditures as a percentage of the gross national product and reduce the rate of growth of expenditures.

The managed care aspects of healthcare reform initiatives should reduce average inpatient admission rates and lengths of stays as well as the frequency of unnecessary ambulatory services. Nevertheless, expenditures will rise rapidly because the benefits coverage aspects of reform will increase consumer demand for healthcare services.

If anticipated cost containment or global budgetary goals are not achieved by an alliance in a given geographic area, pressure to reduce expenses will mount. Additional price reductions will be sought from physicians and hospitals, or hospitals and physicians will be required to accept more of the financial risk associated with the delivery of healthcare services within the parameters of a defined budget. The practical implication of such financing relationships with providers is financial insolvency if providers cannot reduce the per-unit cost of health service production and delivery.

Negative Impact of Regulatory Realignment

Before endorsing any of the proposed reform strategies, affected parties should consider the impact that a government-developed and government-regulated national healthcare system will have on the nation's healthcare delivery and insurance systems, the population in general, and employers.

Proponents of government-sponsored national healthcare reform programs support their positions or views by noting that other industrialized countries, such as Canada and Germany, have national health programs. What proponents of national healthcare reform overlook is that most of these countries adopted their programs thirty or more years ago, when little realignment of the healthcare industry was required.

In present day America, however, millions of individuals work directly in or are peripherally connected with the healthcare industry; indeed, health care is one of the single largest economic industries in the United States. Proponents of government intervention in the structure and operation of the U.S. healthcare delivery and financing mechanisms argue that a nationalized program in this country will *not* reduce the portion of the GNP consumed by health care as these programs do in other industrialized countries. Moreover, their argument ignores the negative effects national healthcare reform will have on a principal sector of the economy. Hundreds of thousands of healthcare workers may lose their jobs when healthcare facilities and insurance companies close and business suppliers of healthcare goods and services downsize.

The Healthcare System in Transformation

Many medical professionals as well as healthcare and health insurance executives contend that the U.S. healthcare system already is in the process of evolving into a more cost-effective and cost-efficient structure. This evolution appears to be driven by two principal segments of the healthcare industry: Insurers who must become more cost effective and efficient to remain competitive in the market, and provider organizations choosing to define their futures proactively rather than waiting to react to market trends after-the-fact. The emphasis placed on healthcare reform by President Clinton and intense media attention given to healthcare issues over the past two years have fostered this evolution by making providers realize they cannot maintain the status quo.

The mature managed care market environments found on the West Coast appear to have progressed the most toward creating and implementing more efficient and effective delivery and financing systems. More integrated systems also have been developed in some of the large urban areas in Illinois, Arizona, Massachusetts, and Michigan. Because of the demonstrated success of these models, other communities and provider organizations are beginning to tailor such systems for their communities and markets.

The development of integrated provider delivery systems has accelerated because of the likelihood of healthcare reform. Many purchasers of healthcare services have actively urged or otherwise influenced providers to develop more structured service delivery networks and to share the financial risk of providing services. Providers, in turn, have looked past the short-term horizon and attempted to define and organize delivery systems that meet the needs of their communities and markets. Additionally, many state governments have undertaken important initiatives, such as mandating community rating for small businesses and placing Medicaid programs under managed care, to encourage the creation of more accessible and affordable provider delivery systems.

It may be argued, therefore, that the U.S. healthcare system is reforming itself at the local level with varying degrees of success, depending on the coordination of providers, insurers, and employers in specific geographic regions. It might also be argued that the role of the government, therefore, should be to concentrate on maintaining the momentum for change by encouraging competitive market forces rather than attempting to dismantle or reconfigure the existing healthcare system through legislative reform action and subsequent government administration.

A Competitive Alternative

If government regulatory realignment is not the best approach for increasing healthcare accessibility and affordability, what approach is preferable for meeting the healthcare needs of the population of the United States? No single approach can address the multifaceted aspects of the U.S. healthcare system, the constituent groups it serves, and the financing mechanisms that support it. However, some broad insights have been gained over the last twenty years from the market experience of the managed care, insurance, and provider industries. These insights indicate that healthcare industry realignment may be driven by competitive market forces to meet the needs of employed individuals as well as those individuals who receive health benefits coverage under Medicare or Medicaid. A market-driven healthcare services and financing realignment scenario that responds to these three macro-market segments of the population may be considered an alternative to managed competition or other government-directed reform schemes.

This type of market-driven realignment would ensure that:

- Healthcare providers and private/public health insurers operate in a competitive, free-market environment under necessary market or regulatory restraints that ensure appropriate business practices (e.g., financial solvency requirements, licensing, etc.);
- The competitiveness of healthcare delivery systems would be driven by the ability of organizations to assure the satisfaction of customers, the value of services, and the accessibility, acceptability, affordability, availability, continuity, and quality of health care; and
- The competitiveness of health insurance plans would be based on the satisfaction of customers and the value and price of benefits products.

The role of the government, under such a scenario, would be to modify existing policies and provide incentives to facilitate the development of integrated provider delivery and financing systems and create a more level competitive playing field between not-for-profit and for-profit insurers in the market (e.g., remove anti-trust barriers to integration, minimize "cherry picking" and underpricing marketing strategies).

Design of the Healthcare Benefit Package

In a market driven scenario, competitive market forces would lead to the development of a healthcare benefits package that would be acceptable to the majority of constituent groups in a given market area, regardless of financing source (e.g., employer or state government for Medicaid). This type of benefits design package would incorporate the best features of the four existing types of healthcare plans—health maintenance organizations (HMOs), preferred provider organizations (PPOs), point-of-service (POS) plans, or traditional indemnity fee-for-service plans. It also would include standard quality assurance procedures and credentialing criteria for selecting participating providers used by managed care organizations.

A competitively driven healthcare system realignment would allow the market strategies of healthcare insurers and purchasers and the designs of their benefits plans to shift to paid-in-full coverage (subject to applicable co-payments and/or deductibles), if insured parties use participating providers.

In cases where nonparticipating providers would be used, services covered by the benefits plan would be reimbursed according to a fixed schedule of allowances. The individually insured member who chose to obtain the services of a nonparticipating provider would be responsible for paying the difference between the provider's actual charges and the indemnified reimbursement.

Elements of managed care would be employed to control costs. However, the managed care process would not use the primary care physician as the access control point for healthcare delivery. Nor would the process require enrolled members to select a primary care physician as their assigned physician. Rather, enrolled members would be able to see any participating provider at the member's discretion for covered services without first obtaining an approved referral by an assigned primary care physician.

Traditional managed care features, such as hospital precertification, would be employed. However, the enrolled member, not a primary care physician, would be required to obtain the precertification. A financial penalty (in the form of a per-admission deductible) would be assessed against members who did not secure precertification before hospitalization for a nonemergency.

By applying managed care in this manner, the healthcare benefits plan would maintain the integrity of the patient-physician relationship. It would not insist that an outside third-party intercede between physician and patient in the healthcare delivery process; it would not question the physician's or the patient's decision regarding medical treatment; yet it would still inject an element of cost control.

Additionally, a healthcare benefit plan of this nature would not require participating physicians to seek approval from the insuring entity for an initial referral to a specialist or for subsequent treatment by a specialist. Rather, the participating physician, in conjunction with the patient, would be able to make a referral to any participating or nonparticipating physician.

Provider Delivery Systems

If insurers and providers are given incentives to compete on the basis of quality and cost effectiveness, regional provider delivery systems that are structured along a continuum of care spectrum could be developed. To be most attractive to payers in a competitive market environment, healthcare providers would need to bring together—in one local delivery system or contracting block—all types of necessary healthcare services, eliminating costly duplication of services and technology. Alliances could form between hospitals and physicians and, depending on the community, with other groups, such as nursing homes, home healthcare agencies, rehabilitation facilities, and so forth.

Healthcare insurers and purchasers also could seek contractual arrangements that have participating providers share financial risk. These arrangements could take several forms: capitation, fixed allowances for outpatient services and bundled pricing for inpatient services, or allocation of a percentage of the premium dollar.

These payment mechanisms might appear to be similar to price setting or global budgeting. However, when based on free-market forces, contractual arrangements such as these would be negotiated on a case-by-case basis among individual provider groups and insurers for a specific market environment; they would not be determined by government intercession as managed competition cost controls would.

These payment schemes, at least initially, might not receive support of physicians because they would signal the end of charge-based, fee-for-service medicine. Truly integrated provider delivery and financing systems would turn hospitals from revenue centers into cost centers. Because of the repositioning of roles and status, this change would meet resistance from the hospital industry. The healthcare market of the 1990s and beyond, however, will demand payment mechanisms such as these to assure product/service value, product differentiation, price competitiveness, and customer satisfaction.

Small Employers

As many surveys have indicated, the majority of the millions of uninsured and underinsured individuals in this country work for small businesses that cannot afford to offer healthcare benefit programs to their employees. One way of achieving a more level competitive field from the standpoint of premium affordability would be to encourage community rating for small to medium-sized employer market segments (i.e., employers with 200 or fewer employees), but to disallow medical underwriting and exclusions from coverage eligibility based on preexisting medical conditions.

Community rating of employers in this size range would include 95 percent or more of all employers in a region or market. It would pool the claims experience of all small group businesses for an insurer and improve the predictability of their health insurance claims and utilization. It also would make health insurance more affordable because a single large claim by one employee would not be held against the individual employer's experience alone; it would be directed against the experience of the pool as a whole.

Unlike managed competition, this approach would not eliminate the opportunity for employers, welfare funds, and insurers to choose alternative financing arrangements if they desired. It would not require the development of quasigovernmental healthcare purchasing groups; rather, it would take advantage of trade association and chambers of commerce groups that are used currently by many small businesses to purchase healthcare coverage.

Just as with healthcare reform, increased coverage through community rating might increase the demand for services among consumers and the volume of services to be delivered by many providers. However, these increases would be offset by the managed care features contained in employer healthcare benefit plans. Nevertheless, the need to make insurance products price competitive would require insurers to seek provider reimbursement arrangements based on fixed prices and bundled services. Insurers also would seek additional risk sharing among providers.

Medicare and Medicaid

Medicare and Medicaid recipients perhaps could benefit the most from a competitively driven realignment of the healthcare system. Today, Medicare and Medicaid programs consume a large portion of the national healthcare dollar. Yet the programs are fraught with excessive utilization, and Medicaid in particular does not assure accessibility to healthcare services.

Most healthcare reform proposals essentially fold Medicaid into a restructured framework for healthcare delivery based on managed competition principles and allow states to request that Medicare recipients retain coverage under the existing Federal program or participating in the new healthcare plans.

A competitive, market-driven realignment of the healthcare system also could be applied to the Medicare and Medicaid populations. In this case, Federal and State governments could send out requests for proposals (RFP) to all insurers in a given state or region asking for bids on providing coverage to individuals eligible for Medicare and Medicaid in the area. The goal would be to offer several healthcare plans and integrated provider delivery system alternatives, depending on the size of the area, the total number of Medicare and Medicaid recipients in the market area, and the nature of the market (i.e., urban or rural). By contracting with insurers and providers through a competitive market process, Federal and State governments would become the single largest purchaser of healthcare services in the country and the single largest customer of insurers and providers. The enormous market power of the government would ensure the accessibility and affordability of healthcare services for the Medicare and Medicaid segments of the population. Insurers and providers would not only make changes in their operations and delivery systems to accommodate the public sector of their business. They also would change the way they do business for all buyers or purchasers of their services.

Use of healthcare benefit products that offer for paid-in-full coverage of services given by participating providers would improve the revenue portfolios of providers because it would bring to an end the practice of shifting costs to private sector insurers and purchasers when reimbursements from the public sector are inadequate.

Conclusion

A cost-effective, cost-efficient integrated provider delivery and financing system for the provision of healthcare services to all segments of the population can be created without direct government intervention. Many such systems already exist at the local level. The government's role in healthcare reform should be to facilitate the proliferation of these systems nationwide and foster further evolution of the present market-driven healthcare system. Rather than become the manager of change, the government should offer incentives that would accelerate the pace of the change that is occurring and encourage insurers and providers to engage in cooperative efforts to make the health-care system more accessible, available, affordable, and acceptable in terms of continuity and quality of care to all individuals.

Notes

1. Anderson R: *A Behavioral Model of Families' Use of Health Services,* Chicago, Ill.: University of Chicago Center of Health Administration Studies, 1968, pp. 14–19.

The Oregon Priority-Setting Exercise: Quality of Life and Public Policy

David C. Hadorn

In 1989 the Oregon State legislature passed the Oregon Basic Health Services Act, which created a Health Services Commission charged with "developing a priority list of health services, ranging from the most important to the least important for the entire population to be served."[1] The goal of this legislation was to permit the expansion of Medicaid to 100 percent of all Oregonians living in poverty by covering only services deemed to be of sufficient importance or priority.

The Oregon Health Services Commission (OHSC) initially interpreted "for the entire population to be served" as suggesting the use of cost-effectiveness principles for developing the priority list. These principles are based on the utilitarian quest for "the greatest good for the greatest number" and tend to devalue adverse effects of a policy on specific individuals.[2] By the lights of cost-effectiveness, the "importance" of a health service depends not only on the expected outcomes of treatment (such as prolongation of life, reduction of pain), but also on the cost of that service and on the number of patients who can benefit from it. Thus, even very beneficial treatments might not be considered important if the costs of providing those treatments are high or if only a few people benefit from them.

In keeping with their interpretation of the statute, the OHSC initially conducted a cost-effectiveness analysis of over 1600 health services ranging from appendectomies to treatment of colds and flu. Predictably, the resulting draft list rated outpatient office visits for minor problems as the "most important" services; the cost of these visits was estimated at $98.51. Indeed, the first ninety-four items on Oregon's initial list were for office visits, for often self-limiting conditions such as thumb-sucking and low back pain. By contrast, certain life-saving surgeries, such as appendectomies, were rated relatively low because of their higher associated costs.

David C. Hadorn, "The Oregon Priority-Setting Exercise," *Hastings Center Report* 21, no. 3, supplement (1991): 11–16.

This counterintuitive priority order (and negative public reaction to it[3]) led the OHSC to abandon cost-effectiveness analysis for purposes of developing its final priority list.[4] Instead, the OHSC developed a set of seventeen health service "categories," which described either a specific type of service (for example, maternity care, preventive services) or, more generically, the expected outcomes of care (for example, "treatment of life-threatening illness where treatment restores life-expectancy and return to previous health"). Commissioners formally ranked these seventeen categories in order of importance according to three subjective criteria: value to the individual, value to society, and whether the category seemed "necessary."

Each treatment was then assigned to the single most appropriate category, based on Commissioners' judgment. Services were ranked within categories according to the degree of benefit expected from treatment. Finally, the OHSC rearranged apparently misplaced services "by hand," for example, moving obviously important services rated low by the method higher on the final list.

This alternate methodology produced a much more intuitively sensible final priority list than the earlier draft list, although more work may be needed before the "final" list can serve as the basis for public policy, particularly with respect to better specifying treatments and indications for treatment.[5]

At the time of this writing, independent actuaries are estimating the costs of providing services on the final list. The Oregon legislature will then decide whether to accept the list as the basis for expanding the State's Medicaid program, as per the Oregon Basic Health Services Act. If so, the legislature will draw a line somewhere on the list to separate the services that will be covered under Medicaid from those that will not. Finally, if this step is taken, Oregon will appeal to the federal government for a Medicaid waiver, which must be granted if the plan is to proceed.

Role of Quality of Life

The Oregon priority-setting process is significant in many ways, particularly with respect to its implications for social policy. Some of the most important of these implications, discussed in the accompanying article by Charles Dougherty, relate to questions of distributive justice, including Rawlsian attempts to identify the least advantaged members of society and to assess how the Oregon process affects them. (For my money, the uninsured poor are the worst off and the Oregon process improves their lot.) In addition, the fact that cost-effectiveness analysis failed to produce a reasonable priority list has significant implications for future efforts to set health care priorities.[6]

Another important story concerning the Oregon priority-setting exercise remains to be told, however. This story concerns the critical role played by quality of life judgments in constructing Oregon's final priority list. Estimates of how treatments affect quality of life were by far the single most important factor in determining the priority order on that list. Most of the service categories that constituted the principal method of prioritization were explicitly defined in terms of quality of life or, in what was generally treated as an equivalent term, "health status." Furthermore, the secondary (within-category) rank-ordering was performed by reference to the "net benefit" from treatment, which, as we shall see, was an explicit *numerical* estimate of the impacts of treatment on quality of life.

Lack of understanding about the role of quality of life in formulating the final priority list has already led to erroneous interpretations of the list. For example, a spokesperson for Children's Defense Fund in Washington, D.C., criticized the fact that treatment for extremely premature infants (less than 500 grams and less than twenty-three weeks gestation) was rated next to last on the list (just prior to treatment for infants born without a brain), saying, "If you're looking at it from a purely economic view, it makes sense not to cover those infants. Of course, we think it's completely unethical to do that."[7]

In fact, however, economic considerations had little or nothing to do with placement of this (or any other) treatment on the *final* list; rather, like most items near the bottom of the list, treatment of extremely premature infants was rated low because it had been assigned to the lowest-ranked service category: treatments offering "minimal or no improvement in QWB," or Quality of Well-Being, the OHSC's term for quality of life. It was a consideration of the *outcomes* (in this case, severe retardation and cerebral palsy) of treating extremely premature infants that led the OHSC to make this category assignment—and in turn determined placement on the final list.

Similarly, active medical or surgical treatments for terminally ill patients were rated near the bottom of the list by virtue of having been assigned to the same poor-outcome category just described. Terminally ill patients were defined (problematically, perhaps) as those with less than a 10 percent chance of surviving five years, even with treatment, and included patients suffering from "cancer with distant metastases" or "terminal HIV disease." Comfort care for these patients, including hospice programs and pain medication, was ranked relatively high, however—at 164 out of 709 total items—as was the longevity- and quality-of-life-enhancing drug AZT for patients with HIV disease, at 158.

Background

Before describing the method used by the OHSC to obtain explicit estimates of quality-of-life outcomes (the basis for within-category ranking of services) a little background is required, both historical and philosophical. The focus on quality of life as a principal factor in health care resource allocation has a long history in Oregon, most of which concerns the activity of a community grass-roots bioethics project known as Oregon Health Decisions (OHD).[8] For several years preceding creation of the OHSC, OHD had held hundreds of citizen meetings around the state to discuss health care and resource allocation issues. In September 1988 a Citizens Health Care Parliament was held in Portland in which fifty delegates met for a day and a half to develop "a set of public policy principles which are intended to be guideposts for the state legislature and other policy-makers concerned with health care resource allocation."[9] The principles developed by the parliament focused on quality of life to a remarkable extent. Indeed, the first six (of fifteen) principles contained explicit references to the importance of quality of life in making health care allocation decisions. Of particular interest are these:

1. The responsibility of government in providing health care resources is to improve the overall quality of life of people by acting within the limits of available financial and other resources.
4. Health care activities should be undertaken to increase the length of life and/or the health-related quality of life during one's life span.
5. Quality of life should be used as one of the ethical standards when allocating health care expenditures with insurance or government funds.
6. Health-related quality of life includes physical, mental, social, cognitive, and self-care functions, as well as a perception of pain and sense of well-being.

As part of the process of developing its priority list, the OHSC commissioned OHD to hold a series of public meetings to discuss people's values concerning the outcomes of care. OHD used a set of service categories similar to those ultimately adopted by the OHSC to elicit relative preferences for different treatments. Quality of life again emerged as a major priority.

Ethical Considerations

One final, critical clarification is required before describing the OHSC's approach to measuring quality of life. The use of quality of life information to develop public policy is potentially problematic from a couple of perspectives. First, the use of purely objective measures of quality of life, such as the degree of assistance required to walk or level of independence in self-care activities, does not correlate well with *perceived* quality of life. For example, Najman and Levine reviewed an extensive literature in which quality of life reports were obtained from patients who were "objectively" living restricted lives. Almost invariably, perceived quality of life was higher than might have been predicted.[10]

Second, judging others' quality of life may place us on a slippery slope. In the *Encyclopedia of Bioethics,* Reich notes that judgments of "unacceptable quality of life" are often determined by the "social acceptability" of various diseases or conditions.[11] Similarly, Harris worries about the use of quality of life for resource allocation policy:

> If for example some people were given life-saving treatment in preference to others because they had a better quality of life than those others, or more dependents and friends, or because they were considered more useful, this would amount to regarding such people as more valuable than others on that account. Indeed it would be tantamount, literally, to sacrificing the lives of others so that they might continue to live. . . . To discriminate between

people on the grounds of quality of life . . . is as unwarranted as it would be to discriminate on the grounds of race or gender.[12]

There is, however, a key distinction between underestimating quality of life or using the concept to bring about invidious discrimination, on the one hand, and Oregon's use of it on the other. Specifically, the concerns expressed in the previous paragraphs involve judgments made about a person's quality of life at a given point in time—independent of any medical or surgical treatments. Such judgments are *inappropriate* bases upon which to ground resource allocation policy.

By contrast, the *appropriate,* nondiscriminatory way to deal with quality-of-life information (and the approach adopted by the OHSC) is to focus on the *change* in quality of life expected with the use of a specific treatment or procedure. How much *better or worse* (if at all) is a patient's quality of life likely to be with application of a particular health service? This focus permits appropriate consideration to be given to the important impacts of treatments on quality of life which, as described earlier, are of considerable importance to the public in determining fair and rational systems of resource allocation. At the same time, the potential for discrimination is eliminated because treatments for handicapped or "poor quality of life" patients are evaluated on the same basis as are treatments for everyone else. It is the *change* in quality of life, or net benefit, realized from a *treatment* that matters, not the *point-in-time* quality of life of a *patient*.

Quality-Adjusted Life Years

After consulting with advisors at Oregon Health Decisions, the OHSC decided to incorporate quality of life considerations into the priority-setting process using the "quality-adjusted life year" (QALY) approach.[13] This method permits integration of the quality-of-life effects of treatment with its associated impacts on life expectancy. Some treatments, such as appendectomies, are valued not for any improvements in quality of life, but rather for their substantial positive effects in life expectancy: in the case of appendicitis, going from perhaps two weeks to normal. Other treatments have significant impact on quality of life, but little or no effect on life expectancy—such as medication or surgery for arthritis, or prostatectomy for benign obstruction. Still other treatments involve trade-offs between quality and quantity of life, where a longer life expectancy may come at the expense of various side effects from treatment, resulting in a possible decrease in quality of life.

Use of the QALY approach requires the explicit estimation of "percentage of normal quality of life." One year of "normal" quality of life is considered equivalent in value to two years of "one-half normal" quality of life: moreover, two treatments offering these respective outcomes would be valued equally (other things being equal). The QALY concept is useful primarily because it reminds us of a few key principles:

Necessity. We have no choice but to consider both quality and quantity of life in some integrative fashion to properly evaluate health care services.

Common Sense. Other things being equal, treatments offering fewer net benefits in terms of either quality of life, longevity, or both, should be valued less highly than treatments offering more such benefits. Thus, if two treatments each offer about a year of additional life, the one that offers greater benefits in terms of quality of life should be favored.

Proportionate Value. Building on the last concept, treatments should be valued *roughly in proportion to the degree of benefit they offer to patients.* Thus, we should be able to distinguish between treatments that offer highly valued outcomes, such as comfort and the relief of pain that is characteristic of hospice programs, from treatments that provide less-valued outcomes, such as the marginal prolongation of life with severe side effects characteristic of many aggressive treatments for terminally ill patients. The QALY approach in theory permits this sort of distinction to be made.

Several problems with the QALY concept have so far caused it to remain merely a heuristic device, by limiting real-world application:

Questionable Assumption. The QALY method assumes that people see no difference between, say, one year of normal-quality life and ten years of life at one-tenth quality (whatever *that* is). The QALY approach assumes that a short, good life is of equal value to a long, ailing one. This assumption seems unlikely to be valid.

Equity Problems. The QALY approach suffers from a limitation common to any purely utilitarian construct: our intuitive rejection of conclusions to the effect that one person should be treated rather than many. In particular, QALY logic supposes that if a choice comes down to treating one person who stands to gain ten QALYs, or nine people who each stand to gain one QALY, then the single person should be treated.

Measurement Problems. What does it mean to speak of someone having a "one-tenth normal" quality of life? How could we come up with such an overall numerical estimate? Anyway, how can we quantify a *quality,* especially one so amorphous and ill-defined as quality of life?

The first two of these problems speak to the fact that QALYs cannot be used as the sole basis for resource allocation decisionmaking. This conclusion is hardly new; even the staunchest advocates of the QALY concept realize that the conflict between individual and societal preferences and issues of justice and equity must also be entered into the resource allocation equation.

It is the measurement problem that is responsible for the fact that QALYs have had so little impact on the health care system since their introduction almost twenty years ago. And it is here that the OHSC made its greatest methodological contribution to the goal of setting health care priorities. As such, the Oregon process represents the first large-scale effort in the United States to operationalize the QALY concept for purposes of resource allocation policy.

The OHSC Method for Quality of Life Measurement

The methodology adopted by the OHSC for estimating QALYs was based on a set of descriptions of poor health or impaired quality of life borrowed (after slight modification) from a set of generic quality-of-life states developed by Kaplan and Bush.[14] These states consist of descriptions of physical or emotional symptoms and of different degrees of limitations or impairment in mobility, physical activity, and social activity.

To derive a numerical estimate of the quality-of-life benefit from treatments, local physicians predicted which problems, if any, patients would experience *five years* after diagnosis, both *with* and *without* treatment. (The five-year window was selected as a reasonable yardstick against which to standardize the expected benefit of different treatments and procedures.) The numerical difference between the aggregate values of the treated compared to untreated health states was considered to be the *net benefit* from treatment.

The impact of treatment on *life-expectancy*—the other component of the QALY measure—was integrated in two ways. First, life expectancy was factored into the equation by virtue of the "zero quality of life" status assigned to the percentage of patients estimated to die in each group. Second, the net-benefit component was multiplied by the expected duration of that benefit for computation of cost-effectiveness ratios, although the "net-benefit" component alone—without multiplication by expected duration of benefit—was used to prioritize services within categories for creating the final priority list.

Analysis of the Oregon Process

Several features of the described method for setting priorities are of interest. Most fundamentally, perhaps, the QALY approach to priority setting was a systematic alternative to more traditional methods of involving the public in health care resource allocation. More typically, citizens are asked which *programs* they prefer: neonatal intensive care units, transplant surgery programs, screening for high blood pressure, hospice care, and so on. This approach is limited by the fact that most people know very little about the expected health outcomes associated with these programs, or about associated costs and other important factors that should shape public policy. By contrast, the method adopted by the OHSC asked people about their preferences for the *outcomes* of care, including various states of ill health and disability. Everyone has been ill at one time or another and has experienced at least temporary periods of disability. Most people are in a position to recall what care can do, and therefore can offer opinions about various states of health that are better informed than their opinions about programs.

Several questions arise, however, regarding (1) the process of asking people to imagine a state of poor health and to apply a rating to that state and (2) the subsequent process of aggregating individual ratings. I take up these problems more fully elsewhere,[15] but a couple of issues deserve brief mention here. First, I believe that Oregon was correct in surveying generally healthy citizens, rather than actively ill patients, because the inevitable biases of the latter group would hopelessly confound the rating process. True, people may have difficulty imagining states of poor health or of impaired quality of life, but by surveying enough people (and 1000 randomly selected individuals is more than enough) an adequate indication of public preferences can probably be obtained. Moreover, in related work we have found that the task of imagining and rating health states can be substantially facilitated by using visual representations of the various states, and by using paired comparisons in addition to simple ratings of individual health states.[16]

But what about the prototypical problem of the "happy quadriplegic"? How can we account for the fact that many patients with chronic illnesses or disabilities adjust emotionally to those states? This is a common enough finding. Might it be a mistake, therefore, to label a severely impaired or painful health state as less desirable than one without impairment or pain? Surely no, for although people in wheelchairs may adjust to their situation, it does not follow that they would not value a procedure that enabled them to walk again. This consideration relates again to the importance of focusing on *changes* in quality of life brought about by health services.

Another important observation is that OHSC's use of *generic health states* (those that can be applied to any illness or condition, rather than illness- or treatment-specific outcomes) enabled all types of health services to be denominated in terms of a "common currency" of benefits and harms. This is a critical consideration from the perspective of health care resource allocation,[17] since it is necessary to compare directly the outcomes of, say, coronary bypass surgery with those of chemotherapy to assess the relative value of these two procedures.

Thus, Oregon's process—explicitly estimating generic treatment outcomes, weighted according to empirically derived public values for those outcomes—was a sophisticated exercise in priority setting, congruent with contemporary thinking. Just this sort of approach is required if public values are to be meaningfully incorporated into the priority-setting process.

Inevitably, however, the Oregon effort to implement a preference-for-outcomes approach was limited by imperfections in available methods. A couple of examples will suffice. The described health states are very broad, often encompassing a wide variety of problems and conditions. For example, the "trouble talking" state incorporates everything from a slight lisp to total mutism. Moreover, the decrement values assigned to the states often do not make sense; "unable to use transportation outside the home" was rated the same as "bed-bound," while "burn over large areas of the body" was rated the same as an "upset stomach."

The rating problem may be due in part to the simplified telephone rating task used to obtain decrement values. Raters were asked to assign a numerical rating between 0 and 100 (0=death, 100=good health) to each of 10 health states. A typical scenario was: "You can go anywhere and have no limitations on physical or other activity but have stomach aches, vomiting, or diarrhea." (Ratings were then rescaled to a decrement value between 0 and 1, with higher numbers associated with more serious, lower-rated problems.) Thus, only one problem at a time was stipulated to be present in each scenario; everything else was assumed to be normal. Obviously, this assumption is problematic, since illness and disability tend to occur together. It is difficult to imagine a patient with a large burn, for example, who is not limited in mobility and social activity. In related work, we have observed that the use of a similar one-dimensional, direct rating approach failed to produce valid preference ratings.

A related potential problem with OHSC's quality-of-life measurement method is that the decrement values of the various problems and conditions are assumed to be cumulative in their effect on overall quality of life. There is evidence, however, that the interactions among quality of life problems is more complicated than simple addition would suggest.[18]

These methodological limitations notwithstanding, the Oregon priority-setting exercise was a remarkably farsighted and sophisticated effort to incorporate quality of life measurement into resource allocation policy. The OSHC correctly focused on the *change* in quality of life afforded by *treatments,* rather than on *point-in-time* quality of life assessments of *patients* or on people's feelings about health care *programs.* The method selected by the OHSC properly included the explicit estimation of (generic) outcomes of treatment and empirically derived preferences for those outcomes.

Only the details of this process—among them, better specification of health states—need change in subsequent iterations of the Oregon process. In the meantime, can Oregon's final list serve as a legitimate basis for public policy? The answer to this question is unclear, and may depend on whether and how Oregon better specifies treatments and indications for treatment.[19] Much more will be known in a few months, after the Oregon legislature has considered the list and federal action is taken on a Medicaid waiver. The events in Oregon are critically important for American health and social policy; they will bear close watching over the coming months and years.

Acknowledgment

Preparation of this article was supported by a grant from the Pew Charitable Trusts.

Notes

1. Oregon Senate Bill 27.
2. Milton Weinstein and William Stason, "Foundations of Cost-effectiveness Analysis for Health and Medical Practices," *NEJM* 296 (1976): 716–21.
3. T. Egan, "Problems Could Delay Proposal by Oregon to Ration Health Care," *New York Times,* 30 July 1990.
4. David Hadorn, "Setting Health Care Priorities in Oregon: Cost-effectiveness Meets the Rule of Rescue," *JAMA* 265 (1991): 2218–25.
5. Hadorn, "Setting Health Care Priorities."
6. Hadorn, "Setting Health Care Priorities."

7. Dean Mayer and Merit Kimball, "Oregon Commission OKs Medicaid Pecking Order," *Healthweek,* 25 February 1991, pp. 1, 36.

8. Brian Hines, "Health Policy on the Town Meeting Agenda," *Hastings Center Report* 16, no. 2 (1986): 5–7; Bruce Jennings, "Community Health Decisions: A Grassroots Movement in Bioethics," *Hastings Center Report* 18, no. 5, Special Supplement (1988).

9. "Quality of Life in Allocating Health Care Resources," adopted by the Citizens Health Care Parliament, 23–24 September 1988, Portland, Oregon.

10. Jackob Najman and Sol Levine, "Evaluating the Impact of Medical Care and Technologies on the Quality of Life: A Review and Critique," *Social Science and Medicine* 15 (1981): 107–15.

11. Warren Reich, "Life: Quality of Life," *Encyclopedia of Bioethics* (New York: The Free Press, 1978), pp. 829–40, at 837.

12. John Harris, "QALYifying the Value of Life," *Journal of Medical Ethics* 13 (1987): 117–23, at 121.

13. Graham Loomes and Lynda McKenzie, "The Use of QALYs in Health Care Decision Making," *Social Science and Medicine* 28 (1989): 299–308.

14. Robert Kaplan and James Bush, "Health-Related Quality of Life Measurement for Evaluation Research and Policy Analysis," *Health Psychology* 1 (1982): 61–80.

15. David Hadorn, "The Role of Public Values in Setting Health Care Priorities," *Social Science and Medicine* 52 (1991): 773–81.

16. David Hadorn, T. Hauber, and Ron Hays, "Improving Task Comprehension in the Measurement of Health State Preferences: A Trial of Informational Cartoon Figures and a Paired-Comparison Task." Unpublished.

17. Hadorn, "The Role of Public Values."

18. David Hadorn and Ron Hays, "Multitrait-multimethod Analysis of Health-related Quality of Life Measures," *Medical Care* 1991, forthcoming.

19. G. Torrance, M. Boyle, and S. Horwood, "Application of Multi-Attribute Utility Theory to Measure Social Preferences for Health States," *Operations Research* 30 (1982): 1043–69.

Oregon's Denial: Disabilities and Quality of Life

Paul T. Menzel

In using quality of life as a guide to rationing health services, Oregon laid itself open to charges of bias against the disabled—charges that cannot be dismissed out of hand.

Many observers were surprised, even stunned, by the Department of Health and Human Services' 3 August denial of Oregon's request for approval of its demonstration health plan for Medicaid. Admittedly the plan was gutsy and, for the United States, groundbreaking. To expand Medicaid coverage to more persons, 122 of 709 services (treatment-condition pairs) were excluded from coverage after a complex, many-layered process of surveys and public discussion about health care priorities.[1] But despite the plan's laudable extension of

Paul T. Menzel, "Oregon's Denial: Disabilities and Quality of Life," *Hastings Center Report* 22, no. 6 (1992): 21–25.

coverage to a wider segment of the state's low-income population, its most vigorous critics generally came from the political left; the plan, after all, made the poor the first targets of explicit rationing, and it did little to control provider fees or physician incomes. Predisposed toward state variety and experimentation rather than federal homogeneity and centralized national health programs, the Bush administration seemed poised to give it its blessing.

The unexpected rejection letter from Louis Sullivan, Secretary of Health and Human Services, focused only on conflicts with the Americans with Disabilities Act (ADA).[2] It noted particular components of the prioritization process likely to contain bias against the disabled, especially the Quality of Well-Being scale[3] derived from a telephone survey ranking six functional impairments and twenty-three symptomatic conditions, and it cited specific statements in the primary report of the Oregon Health Services Commission.

How cogent are these complaints? Is bias against the disabled inherent in the use of quality of life measurements to ration health services? Is the concern for people with disabilities only a smokescreen for the Bush administration's election-year reticence to admit that the problems with our health care system are so serious that explicit rationing may be the next order of the day? While I believe that the Oregon plan can be defended against the accusation that it is unfair to the poor,[4] and while the administration's complaints harbor some serious potential confusions, I will argue that the federal rejection notes a legitimate point of fundamental difficulty in any rationing scheme that gives quality of life measurement a significant role. Though the difficulty is not necessarily fatal, it should command thoughtful recognition.

The Main Complaint

Secretary Sullivan's main complaint is that the prioritized list of 709 condition-treatment pairs was "based in substantial part on the premise that the value of the life of a person with a disability is less than the value of the life of a person without a disability." He cited two segments of the prioritization process—the telephone survey and last-stage "hand adjustments" by commissioners.

The Department of Health and Human Services claims that the quality of life data derived from the survey "quantifies stereotypic assumptions about persons with disabilities" by giving heavy weight to the responses of persons who had not experienced such conditions. The analysis accompanying Sullivan's letter quotes Oregon's own acknowledgment that "those who had experienced the problem did not feel it was as severe as those who had not experienced the problem."[5] It notes that Oregon's submissions did not deny the potential for bias in constructing the Quality of Well-Being scale out of the telephone survey; the state only claimed that the telephone survey's impact on the final list was "limited." In turn Sullivan cites Oregon's own statistical analysis that the survey had allowed 120 condition-treatment pairs to move at least thirty places on the final list, and more than fifty pairs to move at least fifty places.

One of the administration's specific claims about the telephone survey is clearly misleading. For only five of the twenty-nine symptomatic conditions and impairments of function on which the survey focused did Oregon acknowledge that respondents who had experienced the condition rated it a less severe diminution of the quality of life than those who had not experienced it.[6] Moreover, only two of these conditions—cognitive difficulties and trouble with breathing—noticeably overlap with disabilities covered by the ADA. Oregon was aware of the problem of variations in ranking quality of life with different experiences, took the trouble to find out whether the responses to its survey differed significantly on the basis of respondents' experience of the condition categories, and thought it had found little that was disturbing.

Nonetheless, the problem here is difficult and fundamental. If the people whose Quality of Well-Being is ranked low do not themselves share in that judgment of their condition, then certainly something is wrong with the claim that what is being ranked is the "real quality" of people's lives; the conceptual starting point for serious, nonbiased claims about quality of life must surely be people's own perceptions thereof. Thus, for example, my perception of the quality of life in being paraplegic is only as good for the whole ranking enterprise as its accuracy in representing how I would actually feel about paraplegic life, compared to other states, were I paraplegic. Quality of Well-Being rankings are dangerous indeed if they represent some people rating *other* people's lives—especially lives of which they know little and whose conditions they never anticipate sharing. The Quality of Well-Being scale should reflect how people rank their own lives and the quality of the various states in which they might someday find themselves.[7] This is a problem at the core of using measurements of relative quality of life in rationing scarce services among different individuals, some of whom will suffer irreversible disadvantages from a given allocation. The solution is to insure that those who initially contribute the preferences are both reasonably knowledgeable about the conditions they are asked to rank and that they realize the utter personal seriousness of their responses—that their rankings may contribute to either others' or their own disadvantage in later allocations.

Stating the required solution this way actually deepens the difficulty even further, however. Suppose the condition being ranked is largely a congenital one—congenital, at least, in the loose sense of early onset. Oregon decisionmakers—commissioners or survey respondents who did not have this condition—would then be dealing with a condition they knew they would not one day have. That is, they would not be making their rationing choices in a fair, risk-taking state of ignorance about how the resulting allocations will turn out individually for them in particular. Many such long-standing, relatively early onset conditions, indeed, are precisely the quintessential cases of disability that the ADA is intended to protect. To be sure, it is not clear that on the actual Oregon prioritization list, any such disabilities (paired with treatments) fell below the number 587 funding cut-off line *because* the Quality of Well-Being in that condition measured by the survey generated too low a net benefit of therapy, but the danger of this happening in a way that disadvantages disabled people is obvious.

The extent of this difficulty is not fully appreciated by David C. Hadorn in an otherwise very useful recent discussion. Hadorn claims that to insist that the "preferences of disabled persons should govern the evaluation of health states and of outcomes used to set priorities . . . is at odds with . . . the 'insurance principle'" requiring before-the-fact assessments of the value of curative or compensatory measures.[8] To be sure, we render prior consent to risk useless in setting priorities if we insist that it be forthcoming from the point in time at which the risk has already come about; one only needs to know and understand what one might be getting oneself into. But it is not sufficient to require only "full implementation of the insurance principle," including "adequate representation of all interested parties" in some collective enterprise. The problem is that persons with early onset disabilities have not been able to share in the before-the-fact, risk-taking perspective from which people can make fair quality of life assessments and implicit rationing decisions. For them, we have no fair alternative to placing the act of assessment closer to their current condition. That can be done by asking disabled persons themselves, or if that too completely eliminates the risk element required by the insurance principle, by at least asking persons who are directly familiar with disability conditions.

This difficulty in the use of quality of life rankings for congenital and nearly lifelong disabilities must be kept in perspective. We cannot dismiss entirely the use of these rankings even for persons with long-standing disability conditions that rank low. The most accurate Quality of Well-Being measurements in the world are likely to disadvantage disabled persons *when the question is one of services that might save or extend their lives,* but they can still gain something else from the whole business of such ranking. With quality of life adjustments, *non-lifesaving services that improve their condition are more likely to come out ahead* in any rationing competition precisely because the initial quality of life from which the disabled patient moved is rated low, which increases the net *gain* attributed to a service that pushes them to a given level higher up.[9] It is not clear what disabled people themselves would say about this tradeoff. Will they endorse a bargain in which they gain some prospective advantage in competing for quality-enhancing measures for their lives but lose credits in the competition for scarce lifesaving resources? That is an open question, whose answer is neither obviously affirmative—endorsing Oregon's use of an at least accurately constructed Quality of Well-Being scale—nor obviously negative, pitting the ADA against virtually any plan infused by considerations of quality of life.

Hand Adjustments

The commissioners' last-stage "hand adjustments" of the priorities it generated with the help of Quality of Well-Being ratings greatly exacerbated the problem the federal government perceived. According to the Oregon report, commissioners used a "reasonableness" test involving "public health impact, cost of medical treatment, incidence of condition, effectiveness of treatment, social costs, and cost of non-treatment." Commissioners also "observed that it was not reasonable—logically or economically—to rank preventable or readily treatable conditions in relatively unfavorable positions. In other words, where severe or exacerbated conditions were ranked in a relatively favorable position compared to prevention of disease, disability or exacerbation, these occurrences were reversed."[10] The Department of Health and Human Services analysis jumps on this, taking particular offense at the apparent downgrading of "severe or exacerbated conditions," a wording that it noted was almost "the very definition of a disability."

It could be, of course, that the "severe and exacerbated conditions" that got downgraded on the list were linked with the treatments that could benefit persons with those conditions only very marginally, if at all. Then it would be the relative futility of therapy for a severe and exacerbated condition, not the severity and exacerbation itself, that would explain a low position on the list. But Oregon left itself open to other suspicions. Take "low incidence," for example: suppose it led to a particular last-stage reordering. Why, separate from cost-per-benefit differences, should we care a whit about whether a condition is rare or common when we prioritize services? If a condition is rare but costs no more *per case* to treat and generates equal per-case benefits, it is surely forgetful of individual recipients to downgrade services for relatively low-incidence conditions.

The point can be illustrated with a simple hypothetical example. Why should we prefer treatment one for condition A, costing $10 for each of 100 people, over treatments two through eleven for conditions B through K, each of which also costs $10, but where each of the conditions affects only 10 people? In either case we are gaining the same benefit for 100 people for $1000. To prefer the common disease is surely an irrational bias against people and problems that come in small groups. We don't have an "ism" with which to label such a preference, but it surely is unjustifiable in the absence of other factors (like greater danger of contagion for the more common disease).

This is one example of what may be a general bias in the Oregon model against individuals and their plights and toward community perceptions of their situations. Oregon ought to be lauded for bringing rationing out of the closet in the consciousness of its citizens. We all ought to be thinking about the priorities by which we would really like to be governed, as long as we share the risks and do not lord our preferences over people who know much more about their situation than we do. But we can easily get so caught up in the "community" nature of the discussion and the framework in which it is conducted that we unfairly ignore certain individuals. There may indeed need to be an opportunity for some kind of last-stage adjustments of the outcome of any initial, more highly structured prioritization process, but that should not be a vehicle for the biases and powers of popular majorities.

Other Federal Criticisms

Only two particular condition-treatment pairs on the final Oregon list were specifically mentioned in the federal analysis. Understandably, given their sole mention, they have been featured prominently in news coverage of the denial. Liver transplants for alcoholic cirrhosis patients were excluded as item 690, while similar transplants for "cirrhosis of liver or biliary tract without mention of alcohol" were funded as item 367. Life support for low-birthweight babies under 500 grams and under 23 weeks' gestation was the second-lowest item (708), while medical therapy (presumably including life support) for low-birthweight infants of at least 500 grams was highly ranked (item 22).

The Department of Health and Human Services observes that the differential listing of the two types of potential liver transplant patients seems to be "made entirely on the basis of a disabling condition (alcoholism)" since "similarly situated" individuals without that condition would receive treatment. The analysis acknowledges that entirely consistently with the ADA, Oregon could exclude transplant coverage in cases where the patient is not only alcoholic but shows little evidence of alcohol use rehabilitation. Presumably any transplant's chances of success are markedly lower if the alcoholic patient is not effectively rehabilitated. This is not a difficult problem for the Oregon plan; it can meet ADA standards by simply referring to *unrehabilitated* alcoholism in its excluded condition-transplant pair. It would of course have to cover transplants for alcoholic patients likely to stay rehabilitated unless as a category they too have sufficiently lower chances of success.[11]

It is crucial that this interpretation of the liver transplant case govern the interpretation of an earlier, more general passage in the department's analysis. After its pointed criticism of the "reasonableness" test for last-stage adjustments, the department acknowledges the many factors such as the cost of medical procedures and the length of hospital stays that Oregon may consider in allocating medical resources consistent with the ADA. Then it states the general standard: "Oregon may consider . . . any content neutral factor that does not take disability into account *or that does not have a particular exclusionary effect on persons with disabilities*."[12]

This sounds right, but what counts as having "a particular exclusionary effect on persons with disabilities"? Take condition-treatment pair 686, medical therapy for progressive dementia and organic brain syndrome (Alzheimer's is one form). Suppose even the most knowledgeable and sympathetic people looking forward to the possibility of such dementia deem the quality of life in that condition so low that what would otherwise be sufficiently high-benefit care can here be classified as not worth funding. Infusing quality of life concerns into the process does indeed have a "particular exclusionary effect on persons with that disability." Just previously the department's analysis makes another statement of what the ADA prohibits: "any methodology that would intentionally ration health care resources by associating quality of life considerations with disabilities." The use of the Quality of Well-Being scale would seem to end up rationing out life-supporting medical therapy for patients with severe organic brain syndrome, and a focus on the behavioral conditions necessary for a good chance of medical success will probably end up rationing out liver transplants for unrehabilitated alcoholics. Quality of life considerations as well as likelihood of medical success sometimes do get associated with disabilities (though not *only* with disabilities). Such considerations must not be seen as biased against persons with disabilities just because they catch disabilities in their net. They ought to be regarded as inconsistent with the ADA only if we would reject them as legitimate considerations at all were they not sometimes to deny care to persons with disabilities. This is a tough distinction for many to accept, for it means that even with the ADA, particular disabled individuals will end up disadvantaged. It is, however, a distinction utterly essential to maintain if we are going to have any significant rationing at all.[13]

The objection to excluding life-support for under-500-gram babies may also not turn out to be a fundamental sticking point as the Oregon plan is revised. It has long been acknowledged that physicians and families can let very low-chance infants die without running afoul of the Child Abuse Amendments of 1984 if they stay in the plausible enough range of nontreatment to avoid their own *state* child abuse agency's investigation. To be sure, the administration's Oregon waiver rejection is suspicious in that it is linked to a hardline "save any baby at all costs" point of view during an election year in which every right-to-life watchdog is waiting to pounce on the least sign of administration backsliding. Oregon, however, can undoubtedly just give in to Secretary Sullivan on this one and use the language of the 1984 Child Abuse Amendments to state its inclusions and exclusions; doing so will not end up in any practical requirement that physicians and families go all out to save babies weighing less than 500 grams.

A Necessary Risk

Rationing that considers quality of life must be allowed to go forward even if at times it happens to disadvantage some persons with disabilities. Indeed, it is questionable whether we could ever devise a system of priority-setting that was not informed in some measure by assessments of quality of life. Disadvantage, however, is not the same thing as the invidious discrimination the ADA seeks to preclude. We can live with some outcomes disadvantageous to some persons with disabilities—so long as quality of life measures adequately take into account the judgments of those who experience disabling conditions at first hand, and so long as any such disadvantages are significantly driven by medical outcomes data and not disability per se. Nevertheless, the flags that the Department of Health and Human Services saw in the Oregon plan for reforming Medicaid and eventually more of its health care system were real danger flags. Properly qualified and interpreted, the questions about consistency with the ADA that the department has asked raise important fundamental issues about the fairness of different methods of measuring quality of life for use

in allocating health services. It is disturbing to see across-the-board opponents of any and all rationing apparently get some of the administration's ear,
and it must have been terribly maddening for Oregon officials not to have been
consulted earlier about the department's potential objections, but the administration has reinserted an appropriate consideration of the disadvantaged
individual back into what might have become Oregon's too narrow reflection
of dominantly "communal" values.

Notes

1. For two relatively comprehensive descriptions and discussions of the Oregon plan, see
   Michael Garland, "Justice, Politics, and Community: Expanding Access and Rationing
   Health Services in Oregon," *Law, Medicine, and Health Care* 20, nos. 1–2 (1992): 67–81;
   and Charles J. Dougherty, "Setting Health Care Priorities: Oregon's Next Steps," special
   supplement, *Hastings Center Report* 21, no. 3 (1991): 1–10. The plan itself is reported by
   the Oregon Health Services Commission, *Prioritization of Health Services: A Report to the
   Governor and the Legislature* (Salem, Oregon, 1991), hereafter OHSC Report.

2. Letter of 3 August 1992 from Louis W. Sullivan, Secretary of Health and Human Services,
   to Oregon Governor Barbara Roberts, with accompanying three-page "Analysis Under the
   Americans with Disabilities Act ('ADA') of the Oregon Reform Demonstration."

3. Detailed in the OHSC Report, ch. 2 and appendices C and G. See also David Hadorn,
   "The Oregon Priority-Setting Exercise: Quality of Life and Public Policy," special supplement, *Hastings Center Report* 21, no. 3 (1991): S11–S16. For the basic framework
   within which the Oregon plan was working, see Robert M. Kaplan and J. P. Anderson, "A
   General Health Policy Model: Update and Applications," *Health Services Research* 23
   (1988): 203–35; and Kaplan and Anderson, "The General Health Policy Model: An Integrated Approach," in *Quality of Life Assessments in Clinical Trials,* ed. B. Spilker (New
   York: Raven Press, 1990), pp. 131–49.

4. Paul Menzel, "Some Ethical Costs of Rationing," *Law, Medicine, and Health Care* 20,
   nos. 1–2 (1992): 57–66, at 62–64. For another defense of the plan against this criticism,
   see Leonard M. Fleck, "The Oregon Medicaid Experiment: Is It Just Enough?" *Business
   and Professional Ethics Journal* 9, nos. 3–4 (1990): 201–17. A more nuanced and cautious discussion is Norman Daniels, "Is the Oregon Rationing Plan Fair?" *JAMA* 265,
   no. 17 (1 May 1991): 2232–35.

5. OHSC Report, C-11.

6. Numbers 4, "trouble learning, remembering or thinking clearly"; 10, "coughed, wheezed
   or had trouble breathing"; 18, "prescribed medication or diet for health reasons"; 19,
   "wear glasses or contact lens"; and 21, "trouble with sexual performance." OHSC Report,
   C-11.

7. This point is developed at greater length in Menzel, "Some Ethical Costs," pp. 59–62,
   and in Menzel, *Strong Medicine: The Ethical Rationing of Health Care* (New York: Oxford
   University Press, 1990), pp. 84–91. For a vigorous argument that measurements of quality of life cannot meet this test of representing accurately the real value of life to the
   people whose lives get ranked relatively low, see John Harris, "QALYfying the Value of
   Life," *Journal of Medical Ethics* 13, no. 3 (1987): 117–23.

8. David C. Hadorn, "The Problem of Discrimination in Health Care Priority Setting,"
   JAMA 268, no. 11 (16 September 1992): 1454–59, at 1455–56.

9. A point noted at greater length and with illustration in Menzel, *Strong Medicine,*
   pp. 80–81; also see Hadorn's "Point 5" in "The Problem of Discrimination," p. 1456.

10. OHSC Report, p. 28. The entire passage quoted here is also quoted in the DHHS
    analysis.

11. What is not allowed by the ADA, apparently, is any differential of the sort argued for by
    Moss and Siegler: both for reasons of fairness and the need for public support for organ

donation and transplantation, nonalcoholic patients who cannot even remotely be alleged to have brought their end-stage liver disease on themselves ought to stand ahead of alcoholic patients for the very scarce number of available livers. See Alvin H. Moss and Mark Siegler, "Should Alcoholics Compete Equally for Liver Transplantation?" *JAMA* 265, no. 10 (13 March 1991): 1295–98.

12. Emphasis added. At this point *Alexander v. Choate*, 469 U.S. 287 (1985) at 302, is cited; there the court allowed a reduction in the number of hospital days covered by a state program from 24 to 20.

13. Perhaps some of the organized disability groups whose representatives met with Secretary Sullivan not long before his announcement of the Oregon denial wanted to disable any deliberate rationing of health care. *U.S. News and World Report,* in fact, claimed precisely that ("To Ration or Not to Ration?" 10 August 1992, p. 26).

Do the Right Thing: Minnesota's HealthRight Program

Arthur L. Caplan and Paul A. Ogren

By the spring of 1992 a clear consensus had emerged among politicians, policy makers, and pundits in Washington, D.C. The nation's health care system was dying. Escalating costs, combined with diminishing access for the poor and underinsured, were strangling the system.

Individual states have been forced to bear the dire consequences of federal inaction. A few states—Massachusetts, Oregon, Vermont, New York, and Minnesota—have decided they can no longer wait for the federal government to act and have started down the road of health reform on their own. Massachusetts, Oregon, and Minnesota have taken the biggest steps toward systematic reform. Their efforts merit attention since they are likely to serve as both a stimulus and a template for other states and the federal government.

In April 1988 Massachusetts enacted a plan to provide universal access to all state residents through a "play or pay" scheme. Small businesses were mandated by law to provide health insurance to their employees, but the plan collapsed in the face of economic recession. The business community asked for and received a delay in all mandated reforms until 1995.

Oregon took a bold step toward reform two years later with its plan to increase access for the poor and uninsured through a combination of mandates on small businesses to provide insurance and a scheme to increase Medicaid eligibility by rationing services explicitly for those in Oregon's Medicaid program. The decision to increase access for the poor through limits in benefits coverage elicited a storm of criticism over the morality of rationing health care for the poor. The controversy delayed the requisite federal waivers for implementing Oregon's health reform plan.

Arthur L. Caplan and Paul A. Ogren, "Do the Right Thing: Minnesota's HealthRight Program," *Hastings Center Report* 22, no. 5 (1992): 4–5.

The most recent effort to effect health care reform is occurring in Minnesota. On 21 April 1992 the governor signed into law a health care reform plan called HealthRight. This complex legislation (185 pages, single-spaced!), adopted with broad public and bipartisan support, represents a novel approach to the twin problems of skyrocketing costs and inadequate access.

Unlike Massachusetts, the Minnesota plan does not mandate coverage or require small business to foot the bill for health insurance. Unlike Oregon, HealthRight does not explicitly ration care for the poor to expand access. Instead the Minnesota plan seeks to increase access by implementing a number of structural and institutional reforms to contain costs.

What Does HealthRight Do?

HealthRight does not entitle any Minnesotan to health care. The legislation seeks to expand access to health care by making health insurance more affordable. Those who are uninsured—roughly 370,000, or 8.6 percent of the population, will be able to buy health insurance at subsidized prices. Money for subsidies is obtained from new taxes on health care providers, including doctors, dentists, drug wholesalers, hospitals (2% added to their bills, with Medicaid and Medicare revenues exempted), HMOs, and not-for-profit health services corporations such as Blue Cross (1% on premiums). In addition, there is a five-cent increase in the cigarette tax.

The amount of subsidy available is linked to personal income. A family of three earning $10,000 a year will pay roughly $12 a month and receive a state subsidy of $300 a month toward the purchase of insurance. A family of three earning roughly $30,000 a year can buy into the play by paying approximately $300 a month without any subsidy.

The benefits covered under the subsidized insurance plan are very limited. Those who purchase state-subsidized insurance are covered for all outpatient physician and hospital services, hearing aids, immunizations, well child checkups, and ambulance services. Preventive dental care, eyeglasses, and prescriptions are available with small copayments. There is very limited coverage for mental health, chemical dependency, and in-patient hospital care ($10,000 cap per year). In weighing the needs of those now uninsured against the importance of cost containment, benefits are strongly and intentionally skewed toward preventive and maintenance services. Those who have only HealthRight insurance but incur catastrophic costs must still "spend down" to the poverty level to qualify for Medicaid.

HealthRight also expands access to the uninsured and underinsured by requiring private insurers to offer cheaper health insurance plans to small businesses and individual purchasers. This is done by eliminating or restricting insurance rating practices based on gender, age, geography, and preexisting disease conditions in favor of community rating practices. Pooling larger groups should enable companies to get lower premium rates. The HealthRight plan prohibits failure to renew policies for the sick or disabled and requires group policies to be open to all employees. The state also creates a buying pool for employers and access to a reinsurance association for large claims to give small business more clout in negotiating premium rates and benefits coverage.

Greater access for the underinsured and uninsured is also encouraged by a number of other reforms aimed at containing costs. A newly created state commission has the authority to collect information on prices and large capital investments in a standardized manner. A health care analysis unit has been created to collect blinded data on every patient in the state in order to promulgate outcome-based practice guidelines that can be used both to modify inefficient provider behavior and to serve as practice standards for use in defending against charges of malpractice. The state health commissioner has the power to limit overall spending on health care to 10 percent annually based upon the targets, findings, and strategies recommended by these bodies. The state will offer its own managed care plan for those on Medicaid and other state programs.

HealthRight further expands access by making Medicare assignment mandatory and eliminating balanced billing. All hospitals, doctors, dentists, and HMOs must accept Medicaid and HealthRight patients if they wish to participate in workman's compensation or the state's high-risk reinsurance pool, or to sell their services to state employees.

Minnesota is the first state to try to expand insurance coverage using a variety of substantive economic and structural reforms. HealthRight does not ration existing benefits. The plan does not impose mandates on business. Nor does it provide every state resident with a right to health care. HealthRight tries to redress or eliminate financial barriers to access in the existing system by driving down costs for both the uninsured and the underinsured.

Is HealthRight Right?

The most innovative element of HealthRight is the use of what amounts to health excise taxes in combination with a variety of other cost-containment measures to generate revenue that will lower the cost of insurance. Many providers are extremely unhappy with the imposition of health excise taxes, arguing that they represent an unfair burden on providers and the sick. But ultimately, at least part of the cost of provider taxes will be passed along to third-party payers, representing a transfer of resources from the insured to the uninsured. Taxing providers and insurers rather than using mandates on small business, as proposed in Massachusetts and Oregon, serves as a powerful incentive to providers to become more efficient and to restrain increases in prices and costs.

The insurance, structural, and regulatory reforms imposed in the legislation are aimed at lowering the cost of private insurance for those who obtain it through their employment. The collection of information on the prices and outcomes associated with care, with a fixed limit on overall annual price increases, should allow for the more prudent purchase of services in the years to come while restraining escalating overall costs.

If HealthRight is economically sound, is it ethically sound? This is more difficult to assess, since there are many values against which the legislation can be evaluated. Minnesota claims to want to help the uninsured and under-insured obtain greater access to health care, so it seems fair to assess the morality of HealthRight on the basis of whether it can meet this critical goal and whether the benefits and burdens of increasing access are distributed fairly.

HealthRight does provide access to many more people but—as currently designed and funded—does not provide universal access to needed health care to all Minnesotans. It makes the purchase of insurance more attractive to individuals and families by lowering cost. But some families and small businesses may still choose not to buy insurance even if the price is significantly reduced. Those who are self-employed or who lack insurance may still choose to take their chances and go without insurance. Small businesses may not find the price of insurance low enough to be attractive or affordable.

There is a further problem in lowering the cost of insurance to broaden access to care. Access depends upon the availability of competent providers and the quality of care they can provide. While HealthRight takes some tentative steps toward assuring the availability of providers and improving the quality of care, it does not guarantee either.

Finally, HealthRight tolerates significant differences in the insurance coverage that is available to Minnesotans, depending upon how they receive it. Those who buy the newly created, subsidized insurance will have benefits that are far less comprehensive than are available to those on Medicaid or Medicare, or to those who are enrolled in state-regulated private insurance plans or private managed-care plans. The uninsured poor will find it easier to insure against the costs of preventive and maintenance health care services, but they will have limited access to acute and chronic institutional services.

The most persuasive moral argument in favor of the approach Minnesota has taken is that the reforms do not ask sacrifices of the poorest of the poor to increase access for others. HealthRight requires those who have coverage to fund greater access for those who lack it. The plan also relies on the exercise of individual responsibility rather than mandating the purchase of insurance. Most importantly, Minnesota is premising its reforms on the belief that all participants in the health care system ought to bear some of the burden of using existing resources to generate funds to significantly lower the cost of insurance for the uninsured and underinsured. Voltaire said, "The best is the enemy of the good." Minnesota is trying hard to do good. Time will tell whether the state has gotten it right.

CHAPTER 10

Advertising

The Dependence Effect

John Kenneth Galbraith*

The theory of consumer demand, as it is now widely accepted, is based on two broad propositions, neither of them quite explicit but both extremely important for the present value system of economists. The first is that the urgency of wants does not diminish appreciably as more of them are satisfied or, to put the matter more precisely, to the extent that this happens it is not demonstrable and not a matter of any interest to economists or for economic policy. When man has satisfied his physical needs, then psychologically grounded desires take over. These can never be satisfied or, in any case, no progress can be proved. The concept of satiation has very little standing in economics. It is neither useful nor scientific to speculate on the comparative cravings of the stomach and the mind.

The second proposition is that wants originate in the personality of the consumer or, in any case, that they are given data for the economist. The latter's task is merely to seek their satisfaction. He has no need to inquire how these wants are formed. His function is sufficiently fulfilled by maximizing the goods that supply the wants.

The notion that wants do not become less urgent the more amply the individual is supplied is broadly repugnant to common sense. It is something to be believed only by those who wish to believe. Yet the conventional wisdom must be tackled on its own terrain. Intertemporal comparisons of an individual's state of mind do rest on doubtful grounds. Who can say for sure that the deprivation which afflicts him with hunger is more painful than the deprivation which afflicts him with envy of his neighbour's new car? In the time that has passed since he was poor his soul may have become subject to a new and deeper searing. And where a society is concerned, comparisons between marginal satisfactions when it is poor and those when it is affluent will involve not only the same individual at different times but different individuals at different times. The scholar who wishes to believe that with increasing affluence there is no reduction in the urgency of desires and goods is not without points for debate. However plausible the case against him, it cannot be proved. In the defence of the conventional wisdom this amounts almost to invulnerability.

However, there is a flaw in the case. If the individual's wants are to be urgent they must be original with himself. They cannot be urgent if they must be contrived for him. And above all they must not be contrived by the process of production by which they are satisfied. For this means that the whole case for the urgency of production, based on the urgency of wants, falls to the ground. One cannot defend production as satisfying wants if that production creates the wants.

Were it so that man on arising each morning was assailed by demons which instilled in him a passion sometimes for silk shirts, sometimes for kitchenware, sometimes for chamber-pots, and sometimes for orange squash, there would be every reason to applaud the effort to find the goods, however odd, that quenched this flame. But should it be that his passion was the result of his first having cultivated the demons, and should it also be that his effort to allay it stirred the demons to ever greater and greater effort, there would be question as to how rational was his solution. Unless restrained by conventional attitudes, he might wonder if the solution lay with more goods or fewer demons.

So it is that if production creates the wants it seeks to satisfy, or if the wants emerge *pari passu* with the production, then the urgency of the wants can no longer be used to defend the urgency of the production. Production only fills a void that it has itself created.

The even more direct link between production and wants is provided by the institutions of modern advertising and salesmanship. These cannot be reconciled with the notion of independently determined desires, for their central function is to create desires—to bring into being wants that previously did not exist.[1] This is accomplished by the producer of the goods or at his behest. A broad empirical relationship exists between what is spent on production of consumers' goods and what is spent in synthesizing the desires for that production. A new consumer product must be introduced with a suitable advertising campaign to arouse an interest in it. The path for an expansion of output must be paved by a suitable expansion in the advertising budget. Outlays for the manufacturing of a product are not more important in the strategy of modern business enterprise than outlays for the manufacturing of demand for the product. None of this is novel. All would be regarded as elementary by the most retarded student in the nation's most primitive school of business administration. The cost of this want formation is formidable. In 1956 total advertising expenditure—though, as noted, not all of it may be assigned to the synthesis of wants—amounted to about ten thousand million dollars. For some years it had been increasing at a rate in excess of a thousand million dollars a year. Obviously, such outlays must be integrated with the theory of consumer demand. They are too big to be ignored.

But such integration means recognizing that wants are dependent on production. It accords to the producer the function both of making the goods and of making the desires for them. It recognizes that production, not only passively through emulation, but actively through advertising and related activities, creates the wants it seeks to satisfy.

The businessman and the lay reader will be puzzled over the emphasis which I give to a seemingly obvious point. The point is indeed obvious. But it is one which, to a singular degree, economists have resisted. They have sensed, as the layman does not, the damage to established ideas which lurks in these relationships. As a result, incredibly, they have closed their eyes (and ears) to the most obtrusive of all economic phenomena, namely modern want creation.

This is not to say that the evidence affirming the dependence of wants on advertising has been entirely ignored. It is one reason why advertising has so long been regarded with such uneasiness by economists. Here is something which cannot be accommodated easily to existing theory. More previous scholars have speculated on the urgency of desires which are so obviously the fruit of such expensively contrived campaigns for popular attention. Is a new breakfast cereal or detergent so much wanted if so much must be spent to compel in the consumer the sense of want? But there has been little tendency to go on to examine the implications of this for the theory of consumer demand and even less for the importance of production and productive efficiency. These have remained sacrosanct. More often the uneasiness has been manifested in a general disapproval of advertising and advertising men, leading to the occasional suggestion that they shouldn't exist. Such suggestions have usually been ill received.

And so the notion of independently determined wants still survives. In the face of all the forces of modern salesmanship it still rules, almost undefiled, in the textbooks. And it still remains the economist's mission—and on few matters is the pedagogy so firm—to seek unquestioningly the means for filling these wants. This being so, production remains of prime urgency. We have here, perhaps, the ultimate triumph of the conventional wisdom in its resistance to the evidence of the eyes. To equal it one must imagine a humanitarian who was long ago persuaded of the grievous shortage of hospital facilities in the town. He continues to importune the passers-by for money for more beds and refuses to notice that the town doctor is deftly knocking over pedestrians with his car to keep up the occupancy.

And in unravelling the complex we should always be careful not to overlook the obvious. The fact that wants can be synthesized by advertising, catalysed by salesmanship, and shaped by the discreet manipulations of the persuaders shows that they are not very urgent. A man who is hungry need never be told of his need for food. If he is inspired by his appetite, he is immune to the influence of Messrs. Batten, Barton, Durstine and Osborn. The latter are effective only with those who are so far removed from physical want that they do not already know what they want. In this state alone men are open to persuasion.

The general conclusion of these pages is of such importance for this essay that it had perhaps best be put with some formality. As a society becomes increasingly affluent, wants are increasingly created by the process by which they are satisfied. This may operate passively. Increases in consumption, the counterpart of increases in production, act by suggestion or emulation to create wants. Or producers may proceed actively to create wants through advertising and salesmanship. Wants thus come to depend on output. In technical terms it can no longer be assumed that welfare is greater at an all-round higher level of production than at a lower one. It may be the same. The higher level of production has, merely, a higher level of want creation necessitating a higher level of want satisfaction. There will be frequent occasion to refer to the way wants depend on the process by which they are satisfied. It will be convenient to call it the Dependence Effect.

The final problem of the productive society is what it produces. This manifests itself in an implacable tendency to provide an opulent supply of some things and a niggardly yield of others. This disparity carries to the point where it is a cause of social discomfort and social unhealth. The line which divides our area of wealth from our area of poverty is roughly that which divides privately produced and marketed goods and services from publicly rendered services. Our wealth in the first is not only in startling contrast with the meagreness of the latter, but our wealth in privately produced goods is, to a marked degree, the cause of crisis in the supply of public services. For we have failed to see the importance, indeed the urgent need, of maintaining a balance between the two.

This disparity between our flow of private and public goods and services is no matter of subjective judgment. On the contrary, it is the source of the most extensive comment which only stops short of the direct contrast being made here. In the years following World War II, the papers of any major city—those of New York were an excellent example—told daily of the shortages and shortcomings in the elementary municipal and metropolitan services. The schools were old and overcrowded. The police force was under strength and underpaid. The parks and playgrounds were insufficient. Streets and empty lots were filthy, and the sanitation staff was under-equipped and in need of men. Access to the city by those who work there was uncertain and painful and becoming more so. Internal transportation was overcrowded, unhealthful, and dirty. So was the air. Parking on the streets had to be prohibited, and there was no space elsewhere. These deficiencies were not in new and novel services but in old and established ones. Cities have long swept their streets, helped their people move around, educated them, kept order, and provided horse rails for vehicles which sought to pause. That their residents should have a non-toxic supply of air suggests no revolutionary dalliance with socialism.

The contrast was and remains evident not alone to those who read. The family which takes its mauve and cerise, air-conditioned, power-steered, and power-braked car out for a tour passes through cities that are badly paved, made hideous by litter, blighted buildings, billboards, and posts for wires that should long since have been put underground. They pass on into a countryside that has been rendered largely invisible by commercial art. (The goods which the latter advertise have an absolute priority in our value system. Such aesthetic considerations as a view of the countryside accordingly come second. On such matters we are consistent.) They picnic on exquisitely packaged food from a portable icebox by a polluted stream and go on to spend the night at a park which is a menace to public health and morals. Just before dozing off on an air-mattress, beneath a nylon tent, amid the stench of decaying refuse, they may reflect vaguely on the curious unevenness of their blessings. Is this, indeed, the American genius?

The case for social balance has, so far, been put negatively. Failure to keep public services in minimal relation to private production and use of goods is a cause of social disorder or impairs economic performance. The matter may now be put affirmatively. By failing to exploit the opportunity to expand public production we are missing opportunities for enjoyment which otherwise we might have had. Presumably a community can be as well rewarded by buying better schools or better parks as by buying bigger cars. By concentrating on the latter rather than the former it is failing to maximize its satisfactions. As with schools in the community, so with public services over the country at large. It is scarcely sensible that we should satisfy our wants in private goods with reckless abundance, while in the case of public goods, on the evidence of the eye, we practice extreme self-denial. So, far from systematically exploiting the opportunities to derive use and pleasure from these services, we do not supply what would keep us out of trouble.

The conventional wisdom holds that the community, large or small, makes a decision as to how much it will devote to its public services. This decision is arrived at by democratic process. Subject to the imperfections and uncertainties of democracy, people decide how much of their private income and goods they will surrender in order to have public services of which they are in greater need. Thus there is a balance, however rough, in the enjoyments to be had from private goods and services and those rendered by public authority.

It will be obvious, however, that this view depends on the notion of independently determined consumer wants. In such a world one could with some reason defend the doctrine that the consumer, as a voter, makes an independent choice between public and private goods. But given the dependence effect—given that consumer wants are created by the process by which they are satisfied—the consumer makes no such choice. He is subject to the forces of advertising and emulation by which production creates its own demand. Advertising operates exclusively, and emulation mainly, on behalf of privately produced goods and services.[2] Since management and emulative effects operate on behalf of private production, public services will have an inherent tendency to lag behind. Car demand which is expensively synthesized will inevitably have a much larger claim on income than parks or public health or even roads where no such influence operates. The engines of mass communication, in their highest state of development, assail the eyes and ears of the community on behalf of more beer but not of more schools. Even in the conventional wisdom it will scarcely be contended that this leads to an equal choice between the two.

The competition is especially unequal for new products and services. Every corner of the public psyche is canvassed by some of the nation's most talented citizens to see if the desire for some merchantable product can be cultivated. No similar process operates on behalf of the nonmerchantable services of the state. Indeed, while we take the cultivation of new private wants for granted we would be measurably shocked to see it applied to public services. The scientist or engineer or advertising man who devotes himself to developing a new carburetor, cleanser, or depilatory for which the public recognizes no need and will feel none until an advertising campaign arouses it, is one of the valued members of our society. A politician or a public servant who dreams up a new public service is a wastrel. Few public offences are more reprehensible.

So much for the influences which operate on the decision between public and private production. The calm decision between public and private consumption pictured by the conventional wisdom is, in fact, a remarkable example of the error which arises from viewing social behavior out of context. The inherent tendency will always be for public services to fall behind private production. We have here the first of the causes of social imbalance.

Notes

1. Advertising is not a simple phenomenon. It is also important in competitive strategy and want creation is, ordinarily, a complementary result of efforts to shift the demand curve of the individual firm at the expense of others or (less importantly, I think) to change its shape by increasing the degree of product differentiation. Some of the failure of economists to identify advertising with want creation may be attributed to the undue attention that its use in purely competitive strategy has attracted. It should be noted, however, that the competitive manipulation of consumer desire is only possible, at least on any appreciable scale, when such need is not strongly felt.

2. Emulation does operate between communities. A new school or a new highway in one community does exert pressure on others to remain abreast. However, as compared with

the pervasive effects of emulation in extending the demand for privately produced consumers' goods there will be agreement, I think, that this intercommunity effect is probably small.

The *Non Sequitur* of the "Dependence Effect"

Friedrich A. von Hayek*

For well over a hundred years the critics of the free enterprise system have resorted to the argument that if production were only organized rationally, there would be no economic problem. Rather than face the problem which scarcity creates, socialist reformers have tended to deny that scarcity existed. Ever since the Saint-Simonians their contention has been that the problem of production has been solved and only the problem of distribution remains. However absurd this contention must appear to us with respect to the time when it was first advanced, it still has some persuasive power when repeated with reference to the present.

The latest form of this old contention is expounded in *The Affluent Society* by Professor J. K. Galbraith. He attempts to demonstrate that in our affluent society the important private needs are already satisfied and the urgent need is therefore no longer a further expansion of the output of commodities but an increase of those services which are supplied (and presumably can be supplied only) by government. Though this book has been extensively discussed since its publication in 1958, its central thesis still requires some further examination.

I believe the author would agree that his argument turns upon the "Dependence Effect." The argument of this chapter starts from the assertion that a great part of the wants which are still unsatisfied in modern society are not wants which would be experienced spontaneously by the individual if left to himself, but are wants which are created by the process by which they are satisfied. It is then represented as self-evident that for this reason such wants cannot be urgent or important. This crucial conclusion appears to be a complete *non sequitur* and it would seem that with it the whole argument of the book collapses.

The first part of the argument is of course perfectly true: we would not desire any of the amenities of civilization—or even of the most primitive culture—if we did not live in a society in which others provide them. The innate wants are probably confined to food, shelter, and sex. All the rest we learn to desire because we see others enjoying various things. To say that a desire is not

Excerpted from "The *Non Sequitur* of the 'Dependence Effect'" by F. A. von Hayek, *Southern Economic Journal* (April 1961). Copyright © 1961. Reprinted by permission of the publisher.
*Professor Emeritus of Economics, University of Chicago and University of Freiburg.

important because it is not innate is to say that the whole cultural achievement of man is not important.

This cultural origin of practically all the needs of civilized life must of course not be confused with the fact that there are some desires which aim, not as a satisfaction derived directly from the use of an object, but only from the status which its consumption is expected to confer. In a passage which Professor Galbraith quotes, Lord Keynes seems to treat the latter sort of Veblenesque conspicuous consumption as the only alternative "to those needs which are absolute in the sense that we feel them whatever the situation of our fellow human beings may be." If the latter phrase is interpreted to exclude all the needs for goods which are felt only because these goods are known to be produced, these two Keynesian classes describe of course only extreme types of wants, but disregard the overwhelming majority of goods on which civilized life rests. Very few needs indeed are "absolute" in the sense that they are independent of social environment or of the example of others, and that their satisfaction is an indispensable condition for the preservation of the individual or of the species. Most needs which make us act are needs for things which only civilization teaches us to exist at all, and these things are wanted by us because they produce feelings or emotions which we would not know if it were not for our cultural inheritance. Are not in this sense probably all our esthetic feelings "acquired tastes"?

How complete a *non sequitur* Professor Galbraith's conclusion represents is seen most clearly if we apply the argument to any product of the arts, be it music, painting, or literature. If the fact that people would not feel the need for something if it were not produced did prove that such products are of small value, all those highest products of human endeavor would be of small value. Professor Galbraith's argument could be easily employed without any change of the essential terms, to demonstrate the worthlessness of literature or any other form of art. Surely an individual's want for literature is not original with himself in the sense that he would experience it if literature were not produced. Does this then mean that the production of literature cannot be defended as satisfying a want because it is only the production which provokes the demand? In this, as in the case of all cultural needs, it is unquestionably, in Professor Galbraith's words, "the process of satisfying the wants that creates the wants." There have never been "independently determined desires for" literature before literature has been produced and books certainly do not serve the "simple mode of enjoyment which requires no previous conditioning of the consumer." Clearly my taste for the novels of Jane Austen or Anthony Trollope or C. P. Snow is not "original with myself." But is it not rather absurd to conclude from this that it is less important than, say, the need for education? Public education indeed seems to regard it as one of its tasks to instill a taste for literature in the young and even employs producers of literature for that purpose. Is this want creation by the producer reprehensible? Or does the fact that some of the pupils may possess a taste for poetry only because of the efforts of their teachers prove that since "it does not arise in spontaneous consumer need and the demand would not exist were it not contrived, its utility or urgency, ex contrivance, is zero?"

The appearance that the conclusions follow from the admitted facts is made possible by an obscurity of the wording of the argument with respect to which it is difficult to know whether the author is himself the victim of a confusion or whether he skillfully uses ambiguous terms to make the conclusion appear plausible. The obscurity concerns the implied assertion that the wants of the consumers are determined by the producers. Professor Galbraith avoids in this connection any terms as crude and definite as "determine." The expressions he employs, such as that wants are "dependent on" or the "fruits of" production, or that "production creates the wants" do, of course, suggest determination but avoid saying so in plain terms. After what has already been said it is of course obvious that the knowledge of what is being produced is one of the many factors on which it depends what people will want. It would scarcely be an exaggeration to say that contemporary man, in all fields where he has not yet formed firm habits, tends to find out what he wants by looking at what his neighbours do and at various displays of goods (physical or in catalogues or advertisements) and then choosing what he likes best.

In this sense the tastes of man, as is also true of his opinions and beliefs and indeed much of his personality, are shaped in a great measure by his cultural environment. But though in some contexts it would perhaps be legitimate to express this by a phrase like "production creates the wants," the circumstances mentioned would clearly not justify the contention that particular producers can deliberately determine the wants of particular consumers. The efforts of all producers will certainly be directed towards that end; but how far any individual producer will succeed will depend not only on what he does but also on what the others do and on a great many other influences operating upon the consumer. The joint but uncoordinated efforts of the producers merely create one element of the environment by which the wants of the consumers are shaped. It is because each individual producer thinks that the consumers can be persuaded to like his products that he endeavours to influence them. But though this effort is part of the influences which shape consumers' tastes, no producer can in any real sense "determine" them. This, however, is clearly implied in such statements as that wants are "both passively and deliberately the fruits of the process by which they are satisfied." If the producer could in fact deliberately determine what the consumers will want, Professor Galbraith's conclusions would have some validity. But though this is skillfully suggested, it is nowhere made credible, and could hardly be made credible because it is not true. Though the range of choice open to the consumers is the joint result of, among other things, the efforts of all producers who vie with each other in making their respective products appear more attractive than those of their competitors, every particular consumer still has the choice between all those different offers.

A fuller examination of this process would, of course, have to consider how, after the efforts of some producers have actually swayed some consumers, it becomes the example of the various consumers thus persuaded which will influence the remaining consumers. This can be mentioned here only to emphasize that even if each consumer were exposed to pressure of only one producer, the harmful effects which are apprehended from this would soon be offset by the much more powerful example of his fellows. It is of course fashionable to treat this influence of the example of others (or, what comes to the same thing, the learning from the experience made by others) as if it amounted all to an attempt of keeping up with the Joneses and for that reason was to be regarded as detrimental. It seems to me that not only the importance of this factor is usually greatly exaggerated but also that it is not really relevant to Professor Galbraith's main thesis. But it might be worthwhile briefly to ask what, assuming that some expenditure were actually determined solely by a desire of keeping up with the Joneses, that would really prove? At least in Europe we used to be familiar with a type of persons who often denied themselves even enough food in order to maintain an appearance of respectability or gentility in dress and style of life. We may regard this as a misguided effort, but surely it would not prove that the income of such persons was larger than they knew how to use wisely. That the appearance of success, or wealth, may to some people seem more important than many other needs, does in no way prove that the needs they sacrifice to the former are unimportant. In the same way, even though people are often persuaded to spend unwisely, this surely is no evidence that they do not still have important unsatisfied needs.

Professor Galbraith's attempt to give an apparent scientific proof for the contention that the need for the production of more commodities has greatly decreased seems to me to have broken down completely. With it goes the claim to have produced a valid argument which justifies the use of coercion to make people employ their income for those purposes of which he approves. It is not to be denied that there is some originality in this latest version of the old socialist argument. For over a hundred years we have been exhorted to embrace socialism because it would give us more goods. Since it has so lamentably failed to achieve this where it has been tried, we are now urged to adopt it because more goods after all are not important. The aim is still progressively to increase the share of the resources whose use is determined by political authority and the coercion of any dissenting minority. It is not surprising, therefore, that Professor Galbraith's thesis has been most enthusiastically received by the intellectuals of the British Labour Party where his influence bids fair to displace that of the late Lord Keynes. It is more curious that in this country it is not recognized as an outright socialist argument and often seems to appeal to people on the opposite end of the political spectrum. But this is probably only another instance of the familiar fact that on these matters the extremes frequently meet.

Advertising and Ethics
Phillip Nelson

The Market System and Advertising

There are two possible routes one can take to ethics. One can exhort others to take account of social well-being in their behavior—"to love one another" and act accordingly. Or one can try to design institutions such that people will, indeed, benefit society, given the motivations that presently impel their behavior. Most economists, whatever their political position, adopt the latter view; ethical behavior is behavior that, in fact, benefits society, not necessarily behavior that is motivated to benefit society.

Those of us who advocate the market as an appropriate institution are following the lead of Adam Smith: that the market, more or less, acts as if there were an invisible hand, converting individual actions motivated by the pursuit of private gain into social benefit. The selfish employer, for example, callously firing employees when he no longer needs them, helps in the reallocation of labor to activities where it is more useful.

This is not the stuff of poetry. In novels—and quite possibly in the interpersonal relations upon which novels generally focus—selfish people act in ways disastrous to those around them. But novels are hardly the basis for determining social policy, though novelists and their compatriots, literary critics, are often in the forefront in the espousal of "social causes." They have been the consciences of society. Because of their focus on motivation, they have generated a guilt complex when guilt is totally unjustified.

It must be admitted that the market is not a perfect instrument, that the invisible hand wavers a bit. Some individual actions will not lead to social well-being. However, popular perceptions tend to exaggerate market imperfections. For example, the available evidence indicates that the monopoly problem is not terribly serious in the United States. More importantly, the popular view fails to evaluate the problems of alternative institutions. The record of government regulation to make the market behave has been distinguished by case after case where the cure has been worse than the disease, where often there has been no disease at all.

I want to look at the ethics of advertising, given this perspective. Advertising is ethical not because of the motivations of its practitioners but because of the consequences of its operation. The invisible hand strikes again! The market power of consumers will force advertisers to act in ways that benefit society. Advertising will by no means be an "ideal" institution. But it will do an effective job of getting information to consumers.

Advertising bothers its critics not only because its practitioners are selfishly motivated. The advertising itself is often distasteful. Celebrities endorse that brand that pays them the highest price. Advertisers lie if it pays. Advertisers often make empty statements. Nobel prizes for literature have not yet been awarded to the classics of the advertising art. But the crucial question is not whether advertising is aesthetically satisfying, or whether its practitioners are noble, or even whether they occasionally lie. The question is whether advertising generates social well-being. Some of the former questions are not irrelevant in determining the answer to the latter question. In particular, as I discuss later, the role that truth plays in generating socially useful advertising is an important question.

Advertising and Information

Before resolving the fundamental ethical issue about advertising, it is important to understand how advertising behaves. I support a simple proposition about the behavior of advertising: that all advertising is information. This is not a statement with which the critics of advertising would agree. What bothers them is that advertising is paid for by the manufacturers of the brands whose products are being extolled. How can information be generated by such a process? Clearly, some kind of mechanism is required to make the self-interested statements of manufacturers generate information. But such a mechanism exists—consumer power in the product markets.

The nature of consumer control over advertising varies with the character of consumer information. Consumers can get some information about certain qualities of products prior to purchase. For example, they can try on a dress, find out about the price of a product, or see how new furniture looks. I call these "search qualities." In the case of search qualities, a manufacturer is almost required by the nature of his business to tell the truth. The consumer can determine before he buys the product whether indeed this is the dress or the piece of furniture that has been advertised; and in consequence, it will pay the advertiser to be truthful. This is a situation where the famous ditty of Gilbert and Sullivan would be appropriate:

This haughty youth, he tells the truth
Whenever he finds it pays;
And in this case, it all took place
Exactly like he says.

Now, there are other qualities that the consumer cannot determine prior to purchase. It is very difficult for the consumer to determine the taste of a brand of tuna fish before he buys the tuna fish, or to determine how durable a car will be until he's experienced it; but even in these cases, the consumer can get information about a product. The character of his experiences when using the brand will generate information to the consumer. This information will not be useful for initial purchases, but it will govern whether the consumer repeatedly purchases the brand or not. The repeat purchase of consumers provides the basis of consumer control of the market in the case of "experience qualities."

In this case, there will be certain characteristics of the advertising which are truthful. It will pay the advertiser to relate correctly the function of the brand. It pays the manufacturer of Pepto-Bismol to advertise his brand as a stomach remedy rather than as a cure for athlete's foot because, obviously, he is going to be able to get repeat purchases if Pepto-Bismol does something for stomachs and people are taking it for stomachs. If they're taking the stomach remedy for athlete's foot, they're in trouble. So the effort to get repeat purchasers will generate a lot of truthfulness in advertising. Another example: it pays the manufacturer of unsweetened grapefruit juice to advertise the product as unsweetened. This is the effective way to get repeat purchases; hence people can believe it.

There are other qualities about the brand for which the incentive of truthfulness does not exist. It pays the manufacturer of Pepto-Bismol to advertise his brand as the most soothing stomach remedy even if it were the least soothing stomach remedy around. It pays somebody to say that a piece of candy tastes best even if the candy has an unpleasant taste. Even here, however, there is information for the consumer to obtain through advertising. The advertising message is not credible, but the fact that the brand is advertised is a valuable piece of information to the consumer. The consumer rightly believes that there is a positive association between advertising and the better buy. The more advertising he sees of the product, the more confidence he has prior to purchasing the product. Simply put, it pays to advertise winners. It does not pay to advertise losers. In consequence, the brands that are advertised the most heavily are more likely to be the winners.

The mechanism that is operating is the repeat purchasing power of the consumer. Brands that are good after purchase will be brands that consumers buy more. In consequence, there is a negatively sloped demand curve. People buy more as the price per unit of utility of a good goes down, even when it takes experience on the part of consumers to determine this utility. As quantity goes up, the amount of advertising will also go up. This is a well-established relationship.[1] The positive association between quantity and advertising and the negative association between quantity and price per unit of utility generates a negative association between advertising and price per unit of utility. In other words, the "better buys" advertise more; and, in consequence, the *amount* of advertising provides information to consumers.

Considering that we have no direct measure of "better buys," there is a good deal of evidence to support this proposition. First, it pays a firm to expand its sales if it can produce what consumers want more cheaply than other firms. It can increase its sales either by increasing advertising or lowering prices. I maintain that it does both at the same time, just as plants usually increase both their capital and their labor when they expand output on a permanent basis. But the critics say that the larger selling brand advertises more; therefore, it charges more to cover the costs of advertising.

The only way the critics could be right is if diminishing returns in advertising did not exist. By diminishing returns in advertising, I mean that the more a manufacturer spends on advertising, the less he gets in additional sales per dollar of advertising. When there are diminishing returns, the advertising of the larger selling brand is less efficient; it gets fewer sales per dollar. When advertising is less efficient in that sense, the larger advertiser will have a greater incentive to get additional sales by lowering the price. With diminishing returns in advertising, then, the larger selling brand both advertises more and gives greater value per dollar. There is considerable evidence that there are, indeed, diminishing returns in advertising.[2]

There is a second strand of evidence in support of my position. One can successfully predict which products get advertised more intensively by assuming that advertising provides information in the way I have described. It can be shown that it requires more advertising to provide the indirect advertising for experience goods than the direct advertising of search goods. Indeed, the advertising/sales ratios are greater for experience goods than search goods.

There is another important piece of evidence that winners are advertised more. If it is true that the larger-selling brand provides better value per dollar on the average than smaller-selling brands, wouldn't it pay a brand to advertise its rank in its product class more, the higher the rank? Consumers would prefer to buy top sellers rather than bottom sellers. The evidence is overwhelming that more brands say that they are Number One than declare any other rank.

One could argue, I suppose, that consumers are brainwashed into believing that larger-selling brands are better, when the contrary is true. But how could this be? A lot more advertisers have an interest in brainwashing the consumers into believing the contrary. Yet, the "big is beautiful" message wins. The only reasonable explanation is that this is the message which is confirmed by the consumers' own experiences. The brainwashing explanation is particularly hard to accept, given the industries in which brands most frequently advertise their Number One status. It pays consumers to make much more thoughtful decisions about durables than non-durables because the cost to them of making a mistake is so much greater in that case. Yet, the "I am Number One" advertising occurs more frequently for durables than for non-durables.[3] Even more convincing is the evidence that the advertising of Number One rank is not confined to possibly gullible consumers. That same message is used in advertising directed to businessmen. They too must have been brainwashed if the critics are right. But such soft-headed businessmen could hardly survive in the market.

The evidence seems inescapable: larger-selling brands do, on the whole, provide the better value per dollar. The evidence also shows—and all would admit—that larger-selling brands advertise more. In consequence, the more advertised brands are likely to be the better buys.

It is frequently alleged that advertised brands are really no better than non-advertised brands. A case that is often cited in this connection is Bayer Aspirin. But aspirins do, indeed, vary in their physical characteristics. Soft aspirins dissolve in the stomach both more rapidly and more certainly than hard aspirins. In consequence, the soft aspirin are better. They are also more expensive to produce. It is no accident that the most heavily advertised brand of aspirin is a soft aspirin. Of course, there are also non-advertised soft aspirins that sell for less than Bayer Aspirin. But the issue is not whether the best unadvertised aspirin is as good as the most heavily advertised aspirin. The issue is whether purchasing one of the more heavily advertised aspirins at random gives one a better product, on the average, than getting an unadvertised aspirin at random. The existence of unadvertised soft aspirin, when the consumer does not know which aspirin fits into that category, is of little help to the consumer.

Advertising can provide this information without consumers being aware of its doing so. Advertising as information does not require intelligent consumer response to advertising, though it provides a basis for such intelligent response. Consumers who actually believe paid endorsements are the victims of the most benign form of deception. They are deceived into doing what they should do anyhow.

It does not pay consumers to make very thoughtful decisions about advertising. They can respond to advertising for the most ridiculous, explicit reasons and still do what they would have done if they made the most careful judgments about their behavior. "Irrationality" is rational if it is cost-free.

Whatever their explicit reasons, consumers' ultimate reason for responding to advertising is their self-interest in so doing. That is, it is no mere coincidence that thoughtful and unthoughtful judgments lead to the same behavior. If it were not in consumers' self-interest to respond to advertising, they would no longer pay attention to advertising. . . .

Notes

1. This is borne out by data from the Internal Revenue Service *Source Book of Income,* 1957. For every industry, firms with larger sales advertise more.
2. See Phillip Nelson, "Advertising as Information Once More," *Journal of Political Economy* 4 (1982), 729–774.
3. In the May, 1955, issue of *Life* magazine, there were twelve durable and three non-durable, "I am Number One" advertisements.

The Morality (?) of Advertising

Theodore Levitt*

This year Americans will consume about $20 billion of advertising, and very little of it because we want it. Wherever we turn, advertising will be forcibly thrust on us in an intrusive orgy of abrasive sound and sight, all to induce us to do something we might not ordinarily do, or to induce us to do it differently. This massive and persistent effort crams increasingly more commercial noise into the same, few, strained twenty-four hours of the day. It has provoked a reaction as predictable as it was inevitable: a lot of people want the noise stopped, or at least alleviated.

And they want it cleaned up and corrected. As more and more products have entered the battle for the consumer's fleeting dollar, advertising has increased in boldness and volume. Last year, industry offered the nation's supermarkets about 100 new products a week, equal, on an annualized basis, to the total number already on their shelves. Where so much must be sold so hard, it is not surprising that advertisers have pressed the limits of our credulity and generated complaints about their exaggerations and deceptions.

Only classified ads, the work of rank amateurs, do we presume to contain solid, unembellished fact. We suspect all the rest of systematic and egregious distortion, if not often of outright mendacity.

The attack on advertising comes from all sectors. Indeed, recent studies show that the people most agitated by advertising are precisely those in the higher income brackets whose affluence is generated by the industries that create the ads.[1] While these studies show that only a modest group of people are preoccupied with advertising's constant presence in our lives, they also show that distortion and deception are what bother people most.

This discontent has encouraged Senator Philip Hart and Senator William Proxmire to sponsor consumer-protection and truth-in-advertising legislation. People, they say, want less fluff and more fact about the things they buy. They want description, not distortion, and they want some relief from the constant, grating, vulgar noise.

Legislation seems appropriate because the natural action of competition does not seem to work, or at least not very well. Competition may ultimately flush out and destroy falsehood and shoddiness, but "ultimately" is too long for the deceived—not just the deceived who are poor, ignorant, and dispossessed,

*Carter Professor of Business Administration, Harvard Business School, and editor, *Harvard Business Review*.

but also all the rest of us who work hard for our money and can seldom judge expertly the truth of conflicting claims about products and services.

The consumer is an amateur, after all; the producer is an expert. In the commercial arena, the consumer is an impotent midget. He is certainly not king. The producer is a powerful giant. It is an uneven match. In this setting, the purifying power of competition helps the consumer very little—especially in the short run, when his money is spent and gone, from the weak hands into the strong hands. Nor does competition among the sellers solve the "noise" problem. The more they compete, the worse the din of advertising.

A Broad Viewpoint Required

Most people spend their money carefully. Understandably, they look out for larcenous attempts to separate them from it. Few men in business will deny the right, perhaps even the wisdom, of people today asking for some restraint on advertising, or at least for more accurate information on the things they buy and for more consumer protection.

Yet, if we speak in the same breath about consumer protection and about advertising's distortions, exaggerations, and deceptions, it is easy to confuse two quite separate things—the legitimate purpose of advertising and the abuses to which it may be put. Rather than deny that distortion and exaggeration exist in advertising, in this article I shall argue that embellishment and distortion are among advertising's legitimate and socially desirable purposes; and that illegitimacy in advertising consists only of falsification with larcenous intent. And while it is difficult, as a practical matter, to draw the line between legitimate distortion and essential falsehood, I want to take a long look at the distinction that exists between the two. This I shall say in advance—the distinction is not as simple, obvious, or great as one might think.

The issue of truth versus falsehood, in advertising or in anything else, is complex and fugitive. It must be pursued in a philosophic mood that might seem foreign to the businessman. Yet the issue at base *is* more philosophic than it is pragmatic. Anyone seriously concerned with the moral problems of a commercial society cannot avoid this fact. I hope the reader will bear with me—I believe he will find it helpful, and perhaps even refreshing.

What Is Reality?

What, indeed? Consider poetry. Like advertising, poetry's purpose is to influence an audience; to affect its perceptions and sensibilities; perhaps even to change its mind. Like rhetoric, poetry's intent is to convince and seduce. In the service of that intent, it employs without guilt or fear of criticism all the arcane tools of distortion that the literary mind can devise. Keats does not offer a truthful engineering description of his Grecian urn. He offers, instead, with exquisite attention to the effects of meter, rhyme, allusion, illusion, metaphor, and sound, a lyrical, exaggerated, distorted, and palpably false description. And he is thoroughly applauded for it, as are all other artists, in whatever medium, who do precisely this same thing successfully.

Commerce, it can be said without apology, takes essentially the same liberties with reality and literality as the artist, except that commerce calls its creations advertising, or industrial design, or packaging. As with art, the purpose is to influence the audience by creating illusions, symbols, and implications that promise more than pure functionality. Once, when asked what his company did, Charles Revson of Revlon, Inc. suggested a profound distinction: "In the factory we make cosmetics; in the store we sell hope." He obviously has no illusions. It is not cosmetic chemicals women want, but the seductive charm promised by the alluring symbols with which these chemicals have been surrounded—hence the rich and exotic packages in which they are sold, and the suggestive advertising with which they are promoted.

Commerce usually embellishes its products thrice: first, it designs the product to be pleasing to the eye, to suggest reliability, and so forth; second, it packages the product as attractively as it feasibly can; and then it advertises this attractive package with inviting pictures, slogans, descriptions, songs, and so on. The package and design are as important as the advertising.

The Grecian vessel, for example, was used to carry liquids, but that function does not explain why the potter decorated it with graceful lines and elegant drawings in black and red. A woman's compact carries refined talc, but this does not explain why manufacturers try to make these boxes into works of decorative art.

Neither the poet nor the ad man celebrates the literal functionality of what he produces. Instead, each celebrates a deep and complex emotion which he symbolizes by creative embellishment—a content which cannot be captured by literal description alone. Communication, through advertising or through poetry or any other medium, is a creative conceptualization that implies a vicarious experience through a language of symbolic substitutes. Communication can never be the real thing it talks about. Therefore, all communication is in some inevitable fashion a departure from reality.

Everything Is Changed . . .

Poets, novelists, playwrights, composers, and fashion designers have one thing more in common. They all deal in symbolic communication. None is satisfied with nature in the raw, as it was on the day of creation. None is satisfied to tell it exactly "like it is" to the naked eye, as do the classified ads. It is the purpose of all art to alter nature's surface reality, to reshape, to embellish, and to augment what nature has so crudely fashioned, and then to present it to the same applauding humanity that so eagerly buys Revson's exotically advertised cosmetics.

Few, if any, of us accept the natural state in which God created us. We scrupulously select our clothes to suit a multiplicity of simultaneous purposes, not only for warmth, but manifestly for such other purposes as propriety, status, and seduction. Women modify, embellish, and amplify themselves with colored paste for the lips and powders and lotions for the face; men as well as women use devices to take hair off the face and others to put it on the head. Like the inhabitants of isolated African regions, where not a single whiff of advertising has ever intruded, we all encrust ourselves with rings, pendants, bracelets, neckties, clips, chains, and snaps.

Man lives neither in sackcloth nor in sod huts—although these are not notably inferior to tight clothes and overheated dwellings in congested and polluted cities. Everywhere man rejects nature's uneven blessings. He molds and repackages to his own civilizing specifications an otherwise crude, drab, and generally oppressive reality. He does it so that life may be made for the moment more tolerable than God evidently designed it to be. As T. S. Eliot once remarked, "Human kind cannot bear very much reality."

. . . Into Something Rich and Strange

No line of life is exempt. All the popes of history have countenanced the costly architecture of St. Peter's Basilica and its extravagant interior decoration. All around the globe, nothing typifies man's materialism so much as the temples in which he preaches asceticism. Men of the cloth have not been persuaded that the poetic self-denial of Christ or Buddha—both men of sackcloth and sandals—is enough to inspire, elevate, and hold their flocks together. To amplify the temple in men's eyes, they have, very realistically, systematically sanctioned the embellishment of the houses of the gods with the same kind of luxurious design and expensive decoration that Detroit puts into a Cadillac.

One does not need a doctorate in social anthropology to see that the purposeful transmutation of nature's primeval state occupies all people in all cultures and all societies at all stages of development. Everybody everywhere wants to modify, transform, embellish, enrich, and reconstruct the world around him—to introduce into an otherwise harsh or bland existence some sort of purposeful and distorting alleviation. Civilization is man's attempt to transcend his ancient animality; and this includes both art and advertising.

Let us assume for the moment that there is no objective, operational difference between the embellishments and distortions of the artist and those of the ad man—that both men are more concerned with creating images and feelings than with rendering objective, representational, and informational descriptions. The greater virtue of the artist's work must then derive from some subjective element. What is it?

It will be said that art has a higher value for many because it has a higher purpose. True, the artist is interested in philosophic truth or wisdom, and the ad man is selling his goods and services. Michelangelo, when he designed the Sistine chapel ceiling, had some concern with the inspirational elevation of man's spirit, whereas Edward Levy, who designs cosmetics packages, is interested primarily in creating images to help separate the unwary consumer from his loose change.

But this explanation of the difference between the value of art and the value of advertising is not helpful at all. For is the presence of a "higher" purpose all that redeeming?

Perhaps not; perhaps the reverse is closer to the truth. While the ad man and designer seek only to convert the audience to their commercial custom, Michelangelo sought to convert its soul. Which is the greater blasphemy? Who commits the greater affront to life—he who dabbles with man's erotic appetites, or he who meddles with man's soul? Which act is the easier to judge and justify?

The Audience's Demands

This compulsion to rationalize even art is a highly instructive fact. It tells one a great deal about art's purposes and the purposes of all other communication. As I have said, the poet and the artist each seek in some special way to produce an emotion or assert a truth not otherwise apparent. But it is only in communion with their audiences that the effectiveness of their efforts can be tested and truth revealed. It may be academic whether a tree falling in the forest makes a noise. It is *not* academic whether a sonnet or a painting has merit. Only an audience can decide that.

Where have we arrived? Only at some common characteristics of art and advertising. Both are rhetorical, and both literally false; both expound an emotional reality deeper than the "real"; both pretend to "higher" purposes, although different ones; and the excellence of each is judged by its effect on its audience—its persuasiveness, in short. I do not mean to imply that the two are fundamentally the same, but rather that they both represent a pervasive, and I believe *universal,* characteristic of human nature—the human audience *demands* symbolic interpretation in everything it sees and knows. If it doesn't get it, it will return a verdict of "no interest."

To get a clearer idea of the relation between the symbols of advertising and the products they glorify, something more must be said about the fiat the consumer gives to industry to "distort" its messages.

Symbol and Substance

As we have seen, man seeks to transcend nature in the raw everywhere. Everywhere, and at all times, he has been attracted by the poetic imagery of some sort of art, literature, music, and mysticism. He obviously wants and needs the promises, the imagery, and the symbols of the poet and the priest. He refuses to live a life of primitive barbarism or sterile functionalism.

Consider a sardine can filled with scented powder. Even if the U.S. Bureau of Standards were to certify that the contents of this package are identical with the product sold in a beautiful paisley-printed container, it would not sell. The Boston matron, for example, who has built herself a deserved reputation for pinching every penny until it hurts, would unhesitatingly turn it down. While she may deny it, in self-assured and neatly cadenced accents, she obviously desires and needs the promises, imagery, and symbols produced by hyperbolic advertisements, elaborate packages, and fetching fashions.

The need for embellishment is not confined to personal appearance. A few years ago, an electronics laboratory offered a $700 testing device for sale. The company ordered two different front panels to be designed, one by the engineers who developed the equipment and one by professional industrial designers. When the two models were shown to a sample of laboratory directors with Ph.D.'s, the professional design attracted twice the purchase intentions that the engineer's design did. Obviously, the laboratory director who has been baptized into science at M.I.T. is quite as responsive to the blandishments of packaging as the Boston matron.

And, obviously, both these customers define the products they buy in much more sophisticated terms than the engineer in the factory. For a woman, dusting powder in a sardine can is not the same product as the identical dusting powder in an exotic paisley package. For the laboratory director, the test equipment behind an engineer-designed panel just isn't as "good" as the identical equipment in a box designed with finesse.

But all promises and images, almost by their very nature, exceed their capacity to live up to themselves. As every eager lover has ever known, the consummation seldom equals the promises which produced the chase. To forestall and suppress the visceral expectation of disappointment that life has taught us must inevitably come, we use art, architecture, literature, and the rest, and advertising as well, to shield ourselves, in advance of experience, from the stark and plain reality in which we are fated to live. I agree that we wish for unobtainable unrealities, "dream castles." But why promise ourselves reality, which we already possess? What we want is what we do *not* possess!

Everyone in the world is trying in his special personal fashion to solve a primal problem of life—the problem of rising above his own negligibility, of escaping from nature's confining, hostile, and unpredictable reality, of finding significance, security, and comfort in the things he must do to survive. Many of the so-called distortions of advertising, product design, and packaging may be viewed as a paradigm of the many responses that man makes to the conditions of survival in the environment. Without distortion, embellishment, and elaboration, life would be drab, dull, anguished, and at its existential worst.

But still, the critics may say, commercial communications tend to be aggressively deceptive. Perhaps, and perhaps not. The issue at stake here is more complex than the outraged critic believes. Man wants and needs the elevation of the spirit produced by attractive surroundings, by handsome packages, and by imaginative promises. He needs the assurances projected by well-known brand names, and the reliability suggested by salesmen who have been taught to dress by Oleg Cassini and to speak by Dale Carnegie. Of course, there are blatant, tasteless, and willfully deceiving salesmen and advertisers, just as there are blatant, tasteless, and willfully deceiving artists, preachers, and even pro-fessors. But, before talking blithely about deception, it is helpful to make a dis-tinction between things and descriptions of things.

The Question of Deceit

Poetic descriptions of things make no pretense of being the things themselves. Nor do advertisements, even by the most elastic standards. Advertisements are the symbols of man's aspirations. They are not the real things, nor are they intended to be, nor are they accepted as such by the public. A study some years ago by the Center for Research in Marketing, Inc. concluded that deep down inside the consumer understands this perfectly well and has the attitude that an advertisement is an ad, not a factual news story.

Even Professor Galbraith grants the point when he says that ". . . be-cause modern man is exposed to a large volume of information of varying de-grees of unreliability . . . he establishes a system of discounts which he applies to various sources almost without thought. . . . The discount becomes nearly total for all forms of advertising. The merest child watching television dismisses the health and status-giving claims of a breakfast cereal as 'a commercial.'"[2]

This is not to say, of course, that Galbraith also discounts advertising's effectiveness. Quite the opposite: "Failure to win belief does not impair the effectiveness of the management of demand for consumer products. Manage-ment involves the creation of a compelling image of the product in the mind of the consumer. To this he responds more or less automatically under cir-cumstances where the purchase does not merit a great deal of thought. For building this image, palpable fantasy may be more valuable than circumstan-tial evidence."[3]

Linguists and other communications specialists will agree with the con-clusion of the Center for Research in Marketing that "advertising is a symbol system existing in a world of symbols. Its reality depends upon the fact that it is a symbol . . . the content of an ad can never be real, it can only say some-thing about reality, or create a relationship between itself and an individual which has an effect on the reality life of an individual."

Consumer, Know Thyself!

Consumption is man's most constant activity. It is well that he understands himself as a consumer.

The object of consumption is to solve a problem. Even consumption that is viewed as the creation of an opportunity—like going to medical school or taking a singles-only Caribbean tour—has as its purpose the solving of a prob-lem. At a minimum, the medical student seeks to solve the problem of how to lead a relevant and comfortable life, and the lady on the tour seeks to solve the problem of spinsterhood.

The "purpose" of the product is not what the engineer explicitly says it is, but what the consumer implicitly demands that it shall be. Thus the consumer consumes not things, but expected benefits—not cosmetics, but the satisfactions of the allurements they promise; not quarter-inch drills, but quarter-inch holes; not stock in companies, but capital gains; not numerically controlled milling machines, but trouble-free and accurately smooth metal parts; not low-cal whipped cream, but self-rewarding indulgence combined with sophisticated convenience.

The significance of these distinctions is anything but trivial. Nobody knows this better, for example, than the creators of automobile ads. It is not the generic virtues that they tout, but more likely the car's capacity to enhance its user's status and his access to female prey.

Whether we are aware of it or not, we in effect expect and demand that advertising create these symbols for us to show us what life *might* be, to bring the possibilities that we cannot see before our eyes and screen out the stark reality in which we must live. We insist, as Gilbert put it, that there be added a "touch of artistic veri-similitude to an otherwise bald and unconvincing narrative."

Understanding the Difference

In a world where so many things are either commonplace or standardized, it makes no sense to refer to the rest as false, fraudulent, frivolous, or immaterial. The world works according to the aspirations and needs of its actors, not according to the arcane or moralizing logic of detached critics who pine for another age—an age which, in any case, seems different from today's largely because its observers are no longer children shielded by protective parents from life's implacable harshness.

To understand this is not to condone much of the vulgarity, purposeful duplicity, and scheming half-truths we see in advertising, promotion, packaging, and product design. But before we condemn, it is well to understand the difference between embellishment and duplicity and how extraordinarily uncommon the latter is in our times. The noisy visibility of promotion in our intensely communicating times need not be thoughtlessly equated with malevolence.

Thus the issue is not the prevention of distortion. It is, in the end, to know what kinds of distortions we actually want so that each of our lives is, without apology, duplicity, or rancor, made bearable. This does not mean we must accept out of hand all the commercial propaganda to which we are each day so constantly exposed, or that we must accept out of hand the equation that effluence is the price of affluence, or the simple notion that business cannot and government should not try to alter and improve the position of the consumer vis-á-vis the producer. It takes a special kind of perversity to continue any longer our shameful failure to mount vigorous, meaningful programs to protect the consumer, to standardize product grades, labels, and packages, to improve the consumer's information-getting process, and to mitigate the vulgarity and oppressiveness that is in so much of our advertising.

But the consumer suffers from an old dilemma. He wants "truth," but he also wants and needs the alleviating imagery and tantalizing promises of the advertiser and designer.

Business is caught in the middle. There is hardly a company that would not go down in ruin if it refused to provide fluff, because nobody will buy pure functionality. Yet, if it uses too much fluff and little else, business invites possibly ruinous legislation. The problem, therefore, is to find a middle way. And in this search, business can do a great deal more than it has been either accustomed or willing to do:

> It can exert pressure to make sure that no single industry "finds reasons" why it should be exempt from legislative restrictions that are reasonable and popular.

> It can work constructively with government to develop reasonable standards that will assure a more amenable commercial environment.

> It can support legislation to provide the consumer with the information he needs to make easy comparison with products, packages, and prices.

> It can support and help draft improved legislation on quality stabilization.

> It can support legislation that gives consumers easy access to strong legal remedies where justified.

> It can support programs to make local legal aid easily available, especially to the poor and undereducated who know so little about their rights and how to assert them.

> Finally, it can support efforts to moderate and clean up the advertising noise that dulls our senses and assaults our sensibilities.

It will not be the end of the world or of capitalism for business to sacrifice a few commercial freedoms so that we may more easily enjoy our own humanity. Business can and should, for its own good, work energetically to achieve this end. But it is also well to remember the limits of what is possible. Paradise was not a free-goods society. The forbidden fruit was gotten at a price.

Notes

1. See Raymond A. Bauer and Stephen A. Greyser, *The Consumer View* (Boston, Division of Research, Harvard Business School, 1968); see also Gary A. Steiner, *The People Look at Television* (New York, Alfred A. Knopf, Inc., 1963).
2. John Kenneth Galbraith, *The New Industrial State* (Boston, Houghton-Mifflin Company, 1967), pp. 325–326.
3. *Ibid.*, p. 326.

CHAPTER 11

The Consumer

The Consumer's Need for Safety and Product Quality

Vincent Barry

Areas of Business Responsibility to Consumers

Most consumer advocates and commentators on business view business responsibilities to consumers as falling into four main categories: needs, information, safety, and quality. We will consider each of these.

Needs

Business's responsibility for understanding and providing for consumer needs derives from the fact that citizen-consumers are completely dependent on business to satisfy their needs. This dependence is particularly true in our highly technological society, characterized as it is by a complex economy, intense specialization, and urban concentration. Contrast these conditions with those prevailing in the United States when the country was primarily agrarian, composed of people who could satisfy most of their own needs. In those times one had little difficulty practicing the virtues of self-reliance, independence, and rugged individualism in providing for oneself and one's family.

Today, however, we find ourselves parts of an economic and social network of interdependency. More and more we rely on others to provide the wherewithal for our survival and prosperity. We no longer make our own clothing, produce our own food, provide our own transportation, manufacture

From Vincent Barry, *Moral Issues in Business* (Belmont, CA: Wadsworth, 1983), pp. 274–287.

our own tools, or construct our own homes. At one time, for example, Americans could provide their own entertainment, but today's urban sprawl has in many instances covered recreational commons. Whereas opportunities for exercise and recreation were once as near as the front door, now they're often only as near (or as far) as gyms, health spas, tracks, bike paths, or other designated zones of exercise.

Obviously business alone does not shoulder the responsibility for our total well-being, but it does carry the lion's share for determining what commodities to produce and in what numbers, how these will be produced and for whom. But responsibilities for production decisions in the operation of a market economy cannot be divorced from the problems of procuring raw materials to sustain the consumer's society. Already the United States lacks the domestic reserves to meet more than only a small and shrinking fraction of American needs. Where will we get the raw materials U.S. industry needs to provide for domestic needs? The answer seems to lie in the Third World nations of Asia, Africa, and Latin America. If this is so, serious moral concerns will inevitably arise.

Information

The responsibility to provide consumers with product information derives from much of what we've just said. The complex and highly specialized nature of today's economy makes it impossible for consumers to become self-made experts on all the products and services they need. Without enormous business input consumers can't even become knowledgeable. Because business is often the sole source of consumer information, it has an obligation to provide *clear, accurate,* and *adequate* product and service information.

When business communicates clearly, it does so in a direct, straightforward way, relying neither on deception nor psychological manipulation. When it communicates accurately, it provides truths, not half-truths; it avoids gross exaggeration and innuendo. When it communicates adequately, it provides consumers enough information to make the best choice with respect to quality and price. The nature of these descriptions should indicate that determining what's clear, accurate, and adequate communication isn't easy. Perhaps the best way of illuminating these obligations is to consider marketing areas where moral issues relative to information are present. Two of the main areas are advertising and labeling.

Advertising.   Most moral issues related to advertising exist because of a conflict between its informative and persuasive functions. On the one hand, advertising functions to provide consumers information about the goods and services available to them. On the other hand, it serves to persuade them to purchase one product rather than another. These two functions are not always compatible. In an attempt to persuade, advertisers often obfuscate, misrepresent, or even lie. Moral issues arise when, in an attempt to persuade, advertisers are ambiguous, conceal facts, exaggerate, or employ psychological appeals. Let's look at each of these aspects of advertising.

Ambiguity. When ads are ambiguous, they can be deceiving. Suppose, for example, a government study found that Grit filter cigarettes were lower in tar and nicotine than their filter-tip competitors. As part of its advertising, Grit claims, "Government Supported Grit Filters." "Supported" here is ambiguous. It cannot only mean that government research supports Grit's claim that it's lower in tar and nicotine than its competitors but also that the government endorses the use of Grit. The Continental Baking Company was charged with such ambiguity by the Federal Trade Commission (FTC). In advertising its Profile Bread, Continental implied that eating the bread would lead to weight loss. The fact was that Profile had about the same number of calories per ounce as other breads but each slice contained seven fewer calories only because it was sliced thinner than most breads. Continental issued a corrective advertisement.

In all aspects of advertising, much potential moral danger lies in the interpretation. The Profile ad is a good example. A large number of people interpreted that ad to mean that eating Profile Bread would lead to a weight loss.[1] Likewise, for years consumers have inferred from its advertisements that Listerine mouthwash effectively fought bacteria and sore throats. Not so; in 1978 the FTC ordered Listerine to run a multimillion-dollar disclaimer. In such cases, advertisers and manufacturers invariably deny intending the inference that consumers draw. But sometimes the ad is so ambiguous that a reasonable person couldn't infer anything else. Thus, when a cold tablet advertises, "At the first sign of a cold or flu—Coricidin," what is the consumer likely to think? The fact is that neither Coricidin nor any other cold remedy can cure the common cold. At best it can only provide temporary symptomatic relief. But a consumer is left to draw his or her own conclusion, and it's likely to be the wrong one.

A striking example of this "open-to-interpretation" aspect of ambiguity can be seen in the battle over a seemingly harmless topic—buying a tire. Uniroyal advises consumers to buy the numbers: use the numbers and letter molded into the sidewalls under a federally mandated tire-grading system to select the best tire value. Goodyear counters that the numbers are misleading and that the only reliable way to buy a tire is by brand name and dealer recommendations. (It is hardly any coincidence, of course, that Uniroyal has the highest tread-wear number on its first-line radials, those supplied to auto dealers; and Goodyear has the best-known brand, the biggest advertising budget, and the most stores and dealers.)

The dispute is long-standing. In the mid-60s the government responded to concern about quality and safety by proposing a quality grading system. Producers fought tire grading for over ten years, but a 1979 court decision forced them to start using grade labels. Under the law, each manufacturer can grade its own tires, and the government randomly checks to see that the tires measure up to the ratings. Although grading began with the bias-ply tires, in 1980 tire makers also had to begin putting separate A, B, or C grade ratings on radials for traction and ability to withstand heat buildup from high-speed driving. In response, tire makers simply put on a number to indicate expected wear and left it at that.

But early in 1981 Uniroyal, which had rated its "Steeler" at 220 (indicating 66,000 miles of useful life[2]), started advertising that its Steelers were better than Goodyear's Custom Polysteel, which had been rated at 170 (51,000 miles), and other competing brands. As a result, Goodyear, Firestone Tire and Rubber, B.F. Goodrich, and General Tire were put in the ludicrous position of having to convince tire dealers and motorists that their grade ratings were really meaningless, and that no one should take them seriously.

Each of these companies insisted that the test results on which the ratings were based are so variable that they are not reliable. Goodyear, for example, said tests on its Polysteel tires ranged from 160 to 420, with a 13-inch size ranking the lowest. Goodyear therefore assigned a grade of 160 for 13-inch tires and 170 for 14- and 15-inch sizes to assure that all tires met the grade. Fair or not, Goodyear began running ads declaring that, in comparative tests, its Custom Polysteel Tires averaged 229 and 329 ratings in 14- and 15-inch sizes, higher than the 250 and 277 averaged for Uniroyal's Steelers. For its part, Uniroyal insisted that the records of the tests they had run showed that the Goodyear tires didn't test as well as the Steelers.

What, then, does a tire grade mean? What kind of information does it provide the consumer? You be the judge.

Aiding and abetting ambiguity in ads is the use of "weasel" words, words used to evade or retreat from a direct or forthright statement or position. Consider the weasel *help*. *Help* means "aid" or "assist" and nothing else. Yet, as one author has observed, "'help' is the one single word which, in all the annals of advertising, has done the most to say something that couldn't be said."[3] Because the word *help* is used to qualify, once it's used almost anything can be said after it. Thus, we're exposed to ads for products that "help us keep young," "help prevent cavities," "help keep our houses germ-free." Consider for a moment how many times a day you hear or read phrases like these: "helps stop," "helps prevent," "helps fight," "helps overcome," "helps you feel," "helps you look." And, of course, "help" is hardly the only weasel. "Like," "virtual" or "virtually," "can be," "up to" (as in "provides relief *up to* eight hours"), "as much as" (as in "saves *as much as* one gallon of gas"), and numerous other weasels function to say what can't be said.

That ads are open to interpretation doesn't exonerate advertisers from the obligation to provide clear information. Indeed, this fact intensifies the responsibility, because the danger of misleading through ambiguity increases as the ad is subject to interpretation. At stake is not only people's money but also their health, loyalties, and expectations. The potential harm a misleading ad can cause is great, not to mention its cavalier treatment of the truth. For these reasons ambiguity in ads is of serious moral concern.

A final word about this topic. As far back as 1944 the United States Supreme Court, speaking about the issue of truthful advertisement, proposed a standard whose spirit might still be used in evaluating ads. In insisting on the literal truthfulness of an ad, the Court recommended "a form of advertising clear enough so that, in the words of the prophet Isaiah, 'wayfaring men, though fools, shall not err therein.'"[4]

Concealed facts. When advertisers conceal facts, they suppress information which is unflattering to their products. Put another way, a fact is concealed when its availability would probably make the desire, purchase, or use of the product less likely than in its absence. The case of Pertussin is a case in point. Surely if consumers had known of the potentially fatal ingredients the vaporizer contained, they'd have been less likely to purchase the product than they apparently were. Concealed facts concern us in ethics not only because they can exploit by misleading as much as ambiguity can but also because they wantonly undermine truth telling.

Truth rarely seems foremost in the minds of advertisers. As Samm Sinclair Baker writes in *The Permissible Lie:* "Inside the agency the basic approach is hardly conducive to truth telling. The usual thinking in forming a campaign is first what can we say, true or not, that will sell the product best? The second consideration is, how can we say it effectively and get away with it so that (1) people who buy won't feel let down by too big a promise that doesn't come true, and (2) the ads will avoid quick and certain censure by the FTC."[5] In this observation we see the business person's tendency to equate what's legal with what's moral, an attitude we previously alluded to. It's precisely this outlook that leads to advertising behavior of dubious morality.

One needn't look far to find examples of concealed facts in ads. You may recall the old Colgate-Palmolive ad for its Rapid Shave Cream. It showed Rapid Shave being used to shave "sandpaper": "Apply, soak, and off in a stroke." This was an impressive ad for any man who's ever scraped his way awake. Unfortunately, what Colgate concealed was that the sandpaper in the ad was actually Plexiglas and that actual sandpaper had to be soaked in Rapid Shave for about eighty minutes before it came off in a stroke.[6]

More recently Campbell vegetable soup ads showed pictures of a thick, rich brew calculated to whet even a gourmet's appetite. Supporting the soup were clear glass marbles deposited into the bowl to give the appearance of solidity.

Then there's the whole area of feminine deodorant sprays (FDS), one rife with concealed facts. Currently an industry in excess of $55 million, FDS ads not only fail to mention that such products in most cases are unnecessary but that they frequently produce unwanted side effects: itching, burning, blistering, and urinary infections. A Food and Drug Administration (FDA) "caution" now appears on these products.

If business has obligations to provide clear, accurate, and adequate information, we must wonder if it meets this charge when it hides facts relevant to the consumer's need and desire for or purchase of a product. Hiding facts raises serious moral concerns relative to truth telling and consumer exploitation. This exploitation takes the form of real injuries that can result to users of products and also of abridgements to consumers' personal freedom. When consumers are deprived of comprehensive knowledge about a product, their choices are constricted.

Exaggeration. Advertisers can mislead through exaggeration; that is, by making claims unsupported by evidence. For example, claims that a pain reliever provides "extra pain relief" or is "50% stronger than aspirin," that it "upsets the stomach less frequently," or that it's "superior to any other non-prescription pain killer on the market" contradict evidence which indicates that all analgesics are effective to the same degree.[7]

In recent years the FTC has been making numerous companies substantiate their claims, as in the Profile and Listerine cases. In the tire industry, the FTC has questioned Goodyear's claim that its Double-Eagle Polysteel Tires can be driven over ax blades without suffering damage. It has also asked Sears, Roebuck and Company to prove its claim that its steel-belted radial tires can give 60,000 to 101,000 miles of service. In the auto industry, the FTC has questioned Volkswagen's claim that its squareback sedan gets about twenty-five miles per gallon and that it gives drivers 200 gallons of gas more a year compared with the average domestic compact. In addition, the FTC has asked General Motors to verify its claim that its Vega's ground beams provide more side-impact collision protection than those of any other comparable compact. And it has questioned Chrysler's claim that its electronic system never needs tuning.[8]

Clearly the line between deliberate deception and what advertising mogul David Ogilvy has termed "puffery" is not always clear. By *puffery* Ogilvy means the use of "harmless" superlatives. Thus advertisers frequently boast of the merits of their products by using words such as *best, finest,* or *most.* In many instances the use of such puffery is indeed harmless, as in the claim that a soap is the "best loved in America." Other times, however, it's downright misleading, as in the Dial soap ad which claimed that Dial was "the most effective deodorant soap you can buy." When asked to substantiate that claim, Armour-Dial Company insisted that it was not claiming product superiority; all it meant was that Dial soap was *as effective as* any other soap.

Of moral importance in determining the line between puffery and deliberate deception would seem to be the advertiser's intention and the likely interpretation of the ad. Are the claims intended as no more than verbal posturing, or are they intended to sell through deceptive exaggeration? Are advertisers primarily interested in saying as much as they can without drawing legal sanction or in providing consumers with accurate information? But even when the intention is harmless, advertisers must consider how the ad is likely to be interpreted. What conclusion is the general consuming public likely to draw about the product? Is that conclusion contrary to likely performance? Without raising questions like these about their ads, advertisers and manufacturers run risks of warping truth and injuring consumers, two significant moral concerns.

Psychological appeals. A psychological appeal is one that aims to persuade exclusively by appealing to human emotions and emotional needs and not to reason.

This is potentially the area of greatest moral concern in advertising. An automobile ad that presents the product in an elitist atmosphere peopled by members of the "in" set appeals to our need and desire for status. A life insurance ad that portrays a destitute family woefully struggling in the aftermath of a provider's death aims to persuade through pity and fear. Reliance on such devices, although not unethical per se, raises moral concerns because rarely do such ads fully deliver what they promise.

Ads that rely extensively on pitches to power, prestige, sex, masculinity, femininity, acceptance, approval, and the like aim to sell more than a product. They are peddling psychological satisfaction.

Psychological messages raise serious moral questions about inner privacy. Perhaps the best example is the increasingly explicit and pervasive use of sexual pitches in ads.

> SCENE: An artist's skylit studio. A young man lies nude, the bedsheets in disarray. He awakens to find a tender note on his pillow. The phone rings and he gets up to answer it.
> WOMAN'S VOICE: 'You snore.'
> ARTIST (SMILING): 'And you always steal the covers.'

More cozy patter between the two. Then a husky-voiced announcer intones: 'Paco Rabanne. A cologne for men. What is remembered is up to you.'[9]

Although sex has always been used to sell products, it has never before been used as explicitly in advertising as it is today. And the sexual pitches are by no means confined to products like cologne. The California Avocado Commission supplements its "Love Food From California" recipe ads with a campaign featuring leggy actress Angie Dickinson, who is sprawled across two pages of some eighteen national magazines to promote the avocado's nutritional value. The copy line reads: "Would this body lie to you?" Similarly, Dannon Yogurt recently ran an ad featuring a bikini-clad beauty and the message: "More nonsense is written on dieting than any other subject—except possibly sex."

Some students of marketing claim that ads like these appeal to the subconscious mind of both marketer and consumer. Purdue University psychologist and marketing consultant Jacob Jacoby contends that marketers, like everyone else, carry around sexual symbols in their subconscious that, intentionally or not, they use in ads. A case in point: the widely circulated Newport cigarette "Alive with Pleasure" campaign. One campaign ad featured a woman riding the handlebars of a bicycle driven by a man. The main strut of the bike wheel stands vertically beneath her body. In Jacoby's view, such symbolism needs no interpretation.

Author Wilson Bryan Key, who has extensively researched the topic of subconscious marketing appeals, claims that many ads take a subliminal form. *Subliminal advertising is advertising that communicates at a level beneath our conscious awareness,* where some psychologists claim that the vast reservoir of human motivation primarily resides. Most marketing people would likely deny that such advertising occurs. Key disagrees. Indeed, he goes so far as to claim:

"It is virtually impossible to pick up a newspaper or magazine, turn on a radio or television set, read a promotional pamphlet or the telephone book, or shop through a supermarket without having your subconscious purposely massaged by some monstrously clever artist, photographer, writer, or technician."[10]

Concern with the serious nature of psychological appeals is what the California Wine Institute seemed to have in mind when it adopted an advertising code of standards. The following restrictions are included:

> No wine ad shall present persons engaged in activities with appeal particularly to minors. Among those excluded: amateur or professional sports figures, celebrities, or cowboys; rock stars, race car drivers.

> No wine ad shall exploit the human form or "feature provocative or enticing poses or be demeaning to any individual."

> No wine ad shall portray wine in a setting where food is not presented.

> No wine ad shall present wine in "quantities inappropriate to the situation."

> No wine ad shall portray wine as similar to another type of beverage or product such as milk, soda, or candy.

> No wine ad shall associate wine with personal performance, social attainment, achievement, wealth, or the attainment of adulthood.

> No wine ad shall show automobiles in a way that one could construe their conjunction.

As suggested, the code seems particularly sensitive to the subtle implications that wine ads often carry. In a more general sense it alerts us to the psychological nuances of ads. In adopting such a rigorous code of advertising ethics, the California Wine Institute recognizes the inextricable connection between *what* is communicated and *how* it is communicated. In other words, as media expert Marshall McLuhan always insisted, content cannot be distinguished from form, nor form from content. Sensitivity to this proposition would go far toward raising the moral recognition level in advertising and toward alerting businesspeople to the moral overtones of psychological appeals.

Labeling and Packaging.   Business's general responsibility to provide clear, accurate, and adequate information undoubtedly applies to product labeling and packaging. The reason is that, despite the billions of dollars spent annually on advertising, a product's label and package remain the consumer's primary source of product information. Specifically, a product's label and package either succeed in providing or fail to provide information that consumers need to make the best choice of price and quality.

To illustrate the nature and dimensions of the moral overtones in this area, consider a representative study made up of five randomly selected housewife-shoppers.[11] Each shopper shared the characteristics of a college education and extensive family marketing experience. The five women were taken to a supermarket, where they were handed ten dollars each and asked to purchase fourteen items, the average number of purchases that shoppers make. When they finished, their selections were compared with the merchandise available in the supermarket. Of the seventy items chosen, thirty-six were the "best buys"; that is, the most economical selections available of products of comparable quality. Even granting that the sample here is too small to draw firm conclusions, the results suggest that some shoppers are fooled by such things as labeling and packaging.

Together with advertising, then, product labeling and packaging represents an area of uppermost concern relative to consumer information. Although this responsibility is an important one, there are others that deserve equal consideration. One is consumer safety.

Safety

We have seen that the increasing complexity of today's economy and the growing dependence of consumers on business for their survival and enrichment have heightened business responsibilities in the area of consumer information. The same factors apply to product safety. From toys to tools, consumers use products believing that they won't be harmed or injured by them. Since consumers are not in a position of technical expertise to judge the sophisticated products which are necessary for contemporary life, they must rely primarily on the conscionable efforts of business to ensure consumer safety. This extreme dependency underscores business's obligations in the area of consumer safety.

Today consumers who suffer product-related injuries and sue have a good chance of winning. In recent years courts have become especially liberal in awarding damages. A remarkable example is the recent case of a California youth who was tragically burned over 80 percent of his body as a result of an auto accident in which the gas tank of his car exploded. A court held Ford Motor Company accountable for the potentially dangerous location of the tank and awarded the young man in excess of $20 million. Ford is appealing the decision.

In addition, under the doctrine of privity of contract, an injured consumer may sue any or all persons in the product distribution chain of command. The doctrine once stressed direct contractual relationships, holding that producers could avoid responsibility for product failure if a product was purchased from someone other than the producer. But the doctrine of privity of contract has been expanded. Today it includes persons who endorse products, such as celebrities. Also, under strict liability laws, manufacturers have limited liability for unfit or unsafe products that injure consumers or workers. What's more, negligence does not have to be proved. Suit can be brought as long as it can be established that the manufacturers made a defective or unsafe product. In effect, strict liability laws ensure that the cost of product-related injuries will be borne by the manufacturers of a product rather than by the injured party. The point is, business owes it to itself and its stockholders to be safety conscious, apart from any concerns for protecting consumers.

When discussions of product safety arise, such glamour items as the automobile attract the most attention. While it's true that in the area of product safety consumerism has given considerable attention to automobile safety beginning with Ralph Nader's book *Unsafe at Any Speed* (1965), statistics show that numerous other products are associated with more injury-producing accidents than the automobile. In 1973 the Consumer Product Safety Commission listed the most hazardous products as the bicycle and bicycle equipment: 372,000 accidents; stairs, ramps, and landings: 356,000 accidents; nails, carpet tacks, screws, and thumbtacks: 275,000 accidents; sports-related equipment and apparel: 75,000 injuries. Obviously not all or even the majority of these injuries and accidents resulted from defective products. But the point is that the potential for accidents and injuries is everywhere. Thus business bears a general responsibility to ensure the safety of all products.

Whether business people discharge their responsibility in the area of consumer safety depends almost entirely on what, if anything, they do to ensure a safe product. Abiding by the following steps would do much to help business behave morally with respect to consumer safety.

1. *Business can give safety the priority warranted by the product*. This is an important factor because businesses often base safety considerations strictly on cost factors. Thus, if the margin of safety can be increased without significantly insulting budgetary considerations, fine. If not, then safety questions are shelved. Moreover, businesses frequently allow the law to determine to what extent they'll ensure safety. Although both cost and the law are factors in safety control, two other considerations seem of more moral importance. One factor is the seriousness of the injury the product can cause. The automobile, for example, can cause severe injury or death; thus it should be an item of the highest priority. Other products which can cause serious injury, such as power tools, pesticides, and chemicals, also deserve high priority. The second factor to consider is the frequency of occurrence. How often is a particular product involved in an accident? When a product scores high on both the seriousness and frequency tests, it would warrant the highest priority as a potential safety hazard.

2. *Business should abandon the misconception that accidents occur exclusively as a result of product misuse and abuse*. At one time such a belief may have been valid, but in using today's highly sophisticated products, numerous people have followed product instructions explicitly and still were injured. For example, in the Greenman v. Yuba Power Products, Inc., case, plaintiff Greenman's lawyer was able to show that the power tool which caused Greenman serious head injury was unsafe when used in the manner recommended by the company. The point is that the company shares the responsibility of product safety together with the consumer. Rather than insisting that consumers' abuse of products leads to most accidents and injuries, firms would probably accomplish more by carefully pointing out how their products can be used safely. If the product poses a potentially serious threat, a company may need to take extraordinary measures to

ensure continued safe usage of it. Determining the extent to which the company must go, however, isn't an easy task. Sometimes a firm's moral responsibility for ensuring safety doesn't reach much beyond the sale of the product. Other times it may extend well beyond that. Consider, for example, the case of a power tool company. Users of its products can easily fall into bad and dangerous habits while using the firm's machinery. Some would argue, therefore, that the company has an obligation to follow up the sale of such a product, perhaps by visiting consumers to see if they've developed hazardous shortcuts.

3. *Business must monitor the manufacturing process itself.* Frequently firms fail to control key variables during the manufacturing process, resulting in product defects. Of moral relevancy in this case is whether companies periodically review working conditions and the competence of key personnel. It's just as pertinent that at the design stage of the process personnel be able to predict ways that the product will fail and the consequences of this failure. Again, with respect to the materials used in production, companies ordinarily can select those that have been pretested or certified as flawless. If a company fails to do this, then we must question the priority that company gives safety. Similar questions arise when companies do not make use of research available about product safety. When none is available, a company really interested in safety can generate its own. In doing this, however, or in making use of safety research and studies, companies should rely on the findings of independent research groups. Studies by these groups ensure impartial and disinterested analysis and are usually more reliable than studies by in-house programs.

4. *When a product is ready to be marketed, companies should have their product safety staff review advertising for safety-related content.* This step not only ensures accuracy and completeness but also provides consumers with vital purchase information. A corollary to this rule would be informing salespeople about the product's hazardous aspects.

5. *When a product reaches the marketplace, firms should make available to consumers in writing everything relative to the product's performance.* This information should include operating instructions, the product's safety features and under what conditions it will fail, a complete list of the ways the product can be used, and a cautionary list of the ways it should not be used.

6. *Companies should investigate consumer complaints.* This process encourages firms to deal fairly with consumers and to utilize the most effective source of product improvement: the opinions of those who use it.

Even if firms seriously tended to each of these safety considerations, they couldn't guarantee an absolutely safe product. Some hazards invariably will attach to numerous products, heroic efforts notwithstanding. But business must acknowledge and discharge moral responsibilities in this area. Morally speaking, no one's asking for an accident- and injury-proof product—only that a manufacturer do everything reasonable to approach that ideal.

Product Quality

Most would agree that business bears a general responsibility to ensure that the quality of a product measures up to the claims made about it and to reasonable consumer expectations. They would undoubtedly see this responsibility as deriving primarily from the consumer's basic right to get what he or she pays for. But it seems that business's obligation for product quality also stems from its general responsibility to protect owners' interests, for just as the burden of product safety has shifted to the producer, so has product performance. This realization means a toughening of product liability law and a softening of judicial resistance to consumer complaints. In increasing numbers consumers are going to court when products don't perform. What's more, the courts often uphold their complaints. As a result, the area of product performance incurs serious financial risks to stockholders who must increase business's responsibility in this area.

One way that business tries to meet its responsibilities is through *warranties, obligations that sellers assure to purchasers.* We generally speak of two kinds of warranties, expressed and implied. Expressed warranties are the claims that sellers explicitly state. They include assertions about the product's characteristics, assurances of product durability, and statements that generally appear on a warranty card or statements placed on labels, wrappers, packages, or in the advertising of the product. Of moral concern here is that the manufacturer ensure that a product live up to its billing. Just as important, however, is the question of reparation. When a product fails to perform as promoted, whether and how the manufacturer "makes good" the consumer loss raises moral concerns. In some cases, the manufacturer may issue a refund or a new product; in others, much more reparation may be required.

Implied warranties include the implicit claim that a particular product is fit for the ordinary use for which it is likely to be employed. Again, serious moral questions of reparation arise when injury or harm results from the failure of a product to perform as it should. Suppose, for example, that Eleanor Solano buys a new automobile. After she drives the car around for a few days under normal conditions, its steering mechanism fails and she is severely injured. In such a case, a company may bear far-reaching moral as well as legal responsibilities, even if on purchase Solano signed a disclaimer limiting the company's liability to replacement of defective parts.

In sum, business has a general responsibility to ensure the quality of its product. Where there are discrepancies between explicit or implicit claims and performance, moral questions about reparation arise. At the same time it is important to note that business's responsibility for product quality and its obligation to provide clear, accurate, and adequate information to ensure product safety are tied to questions that reach beyond consumer dissatisfaction with unsafe or inferior merchandise. Obligations in this area invite serious consideration by business about its attitude toward people, about its priorities, and about whether it's cultivating a marketplace atmosphere conducive to fair treatment for all consumers, no matter what their socioeconomic standings.

Notes

1. See "Mea Culpa, Sort Of," *Newsweek,* September 27, 1971, p. 98.
2. A rating of 100 supposedly equals 30,000 miles of useful life.
3. Paul Stevens, "Weasel Words: God's Little Helpers," in *Language Awareness,* ed. Paul A. Eschhol, Alfred A. Rosa, Virginia P. Clark (New York: St. Martin's Press, 1974), p. 156.
4. "Charles of the Ritz District Corporation v. FTC, 143, F.2d 276 (2d Cir. 1944)," in David A. Aaken and George S. Day, *Consumerism: Search for the Consumer Interest* (New York: The Free Press, 1974), p. 140.
5. Samm Sinclair Baker, *The Permissible Lie* (New York: World Publishing Co., 1968), p. 16.
6. *Ibid.*
7. The editors of *Consumer Reports, The Medicine Show* (Mt. Vernon, N.Y.: Consumers Union, 1972), p. 14.
8. Fred Luthans and Richard M. Hodgetts, *Social Issues in Business* (New York: Macmillan, 1976), p. 353.
9. Gail Bronson, "Sexual Pitches in Ads Become More Explicit and Pervasive," *The Wall Street Journal,* November 18, 1980, p. 1.
10. Wilson Bryan Key, *Subliminal Seduction* (New York: New American Library, 1972), p. 11.
11. E. B. Weiss, "Marketers Fiddle While Consumers Burn," *Harvard Business Review,* July–August, 1968, p. 48.

Crimes, Lies and Prudential-Bache

Kurt Eichenwald

The champagne flowed freely aboard the Queen Elizabeth 2 as a group of Prudential-Bache brokers and their spouses steamed out of New York harbor for a weeklong cruise celebrating another year of big sales and fat commissions.

Their host, Clifton S. Harrison, a Dallas developer who made millions selling real estate partnerships through Prudential's retail network, told them money was no object on the all-expenses-paid trip to London. They agreed, ordering sumptuous meals not even on the ship's lavish menus.

But as they indulged during that week in May 1986, the brokers spoke bitterly of their host. For while Mr. Harrison threw fabulous parties, the deals they sold for him performed terribly, straining relationships with top clients. The brokers decided to stop getting burned. "Almost to a broker, we vowed on that trip never to do another one of his deals," said one broker, speaking on condition of anonymity.

There would be no more deals. Even as the QE2 headed to sea, Mr. Harrison's real estate empire was sinking, a victim partly of excessive spending and bad management. Indeed, Mr. Harrison would not even be able to afford the bill for the cruise; instead, he negotiated an installment plan.

New York Times. Sunday, October 10, 1993.

A Troubling Record

The documents and interviews show:

- After not disclosing Mr. Harrison's conviction in filings, lawyers for Prudential supported his efforts to mislead others about it in sworn statements.
- Before backing Mr. Harrison in 1980, the firm failed to interview his former business partners, who believed he had cheated them and had not been rehabilitated after his conviction.
- Some partnership disclosure documents were riddled with critical omissions. On one document, the signature of one of Mr. Harrison's former partners was apparently forged.
- Prudential repeatedly bailed out Mr. Harrison from problems caused by his excessive spending, at times through deals that masked payments to him.
- Many businessmen who played key roles in Mr. Harrison's deals with Prudential have since been imprisoned for financial crimes unrelated to the deals.
- A Texas savings and loan institution recruited to lend to a Harrison deal may have been cheated by the deal's general partners. And, according to sworn testimony and a personal diary, a Prudential executive later tried to influence other lending decisions by the institution and attempted to arrange loan swaps to help an Arkansas thrift largely owned by another developer sponsored by the firm.

Responding to inquiries about the Harrison deals, Prudential, a subsidiary of the Prudential Insurance Company of America, said in a statement that "the reporting concerning Prudential-Bache's sale of partnerships in the 80's does not represent an accurate reflection of how Prudential Securities does business in the 90's."

Mr. Harrison, now living in Moscow, declined to comment on matters in litigation. But, in a phone interview, he expressed some regret. "We made mistakes," he said. "There was a rush to do business, Prudential-Bache was making a lot of money, and a lot of deals were done that shouldn't have been. If we had it all to do over, we would have disclosure in two-inch letters."

Prudential's reputation has been stained of late by more than just the Harrison deals. Accusations of securities-law violations among brokers at branch offices, including those in Dallas, Atlanta and Newport Beach, Calif., are under Government investigation.

The Crimes

Fraud, Then a Pardon by the White House

For a man who would one day control more than half a billion dollars in real estate, Clifton Harrison had modest beginnings. A native of Amarillo, Tex., he attended three colleges without graduating.

Entering business in 1963 through a training program at First National Bank in Dallas, he soon was handling national accounts. But Mr. Harrison, a boisterous, glad-handing man often seen in expensive clothes and fast cars, earned a reputation for rich tastes that worried bank executives. In 1966, "senior officers requested an investigation after they determined that Harrison was spending more money than he was making," said a 1980 security report prepared for Prudential.

In 1967, bank officers, shocked by wrongdoing found in their investigation, alerted prosecutors. Mr. Harrison was arrested, and later confessed to brazen crimes: In 1964 he had begun defrauding two financial institutions. In the scheme, he reported stock certificates he owned as missing, later selling the replacements. Then he pledged the worthless originals as collateral on loans he never repaid.

His crimes grew in 1966 after he received lending authority. Mr. Harrison made $25,000 in loans to imaginary customers, depositing the money in an account he controlled.

Mr. Harrison pleaded guilty to fraud and embezzlement, and his sentence was fixed at three years. While in prison, he obtained a degree from Southern Methodist University. After eighteen months, he was paroled.

He continued his studies, focusing on real estate, and earned his M.B.A. at S.M.U. in 1970. An admiring professor, Sydney Reagan, helped Mr. Harrison find work selling limited partnerships with Irving Klein, a scrappy local real estate investor.

Through that job Mr. Harrison met the Dallas elite, with successful deals through Mr. Klein winning fans like Herman Ulevitch, a prominent doctor, and Raymond Freedman, a corporate executive. When Mr. Klein died in the early 1970s, Mr. Harrison had a fat Rolodex and a good reputation.

Bolstered by success, Mr. Harrison applied for a Presidential pardon for his crimes. With Mr. Reagan, Mr. Freedman, Dr. Ulevitch and others offering character references, he was pardoned by President Gerald Ford on Oct. 9, 1974, a month after Richard Nixon's pardon.

With that new beginning, Mr. Harrison persuaded Mr. Freedman and Dr. Ulevitch to invest in a firm to be called Harrison Freedman Associates, a real estate syndicator and developer. Business grew, and Mr. Harrison attracted Dutch institutional investors.

The Extravagance
Living the Good Life as Deals Went Bad

But his partners grew uncomfortable with his extravagance. "There was a feeling of being lavish—extra lavish," Mr. Freedman said. "He became carried away with the fact that he had the money to spend. And obviously he spent more than he was making."

Worse, some of Harrison Freedman's Texas deals collapsed. An office park in Dallas was foreclosed upon, and shopping centers in Lewisville and Bowie, Tex., defaulted.

The Bowie default shattered the partners' relationship. Mr. Harrison failed to pay $434,000 owed on the note he arranged and signed; Dr. Ulevitch and Mr. Freedman, his minority-share partners, paid the debt.

The partnership came apart about 1979, amid concerns that Mr. Harrison had not been rehabilitated and that his dealings were "not quite Kosher," Mr. Freedman said in a deposition. Mr. Harrison agreed to buy Mr. Freedman's shares, signing an i.o.u. for $100,000. The debt remains unpaid.

But Mr. Harrison was moving up. His Dutch and other European contacts attracted the attention of executives at Bache & Company, Prudential-Bache's predecessor, who approached him about doing business.

Had the firm asked at the time, Mr. Freedman said recently, he would have given his assessment of Mr. Harrison: "Hell, no. Do not invest with this man."

But no one from the firm ever called.

The Prudential Link

A Profitable Alliance, but Not for Investors

Paul J. Proscia faced big pressure. Brokers at Bache were already demoralized by the firm's scandalous extensions of credit to the Hunt Brothers for the Texas billionaires' attempt to corner the silver market in 1980. Now, in April 1981, Mr. Proscia, a Bache executive, was planning how to rally brokers around another Texan, Clifton Harrison.

Bache executives, envious of Mr. Harrison's ties to Europe and his experience in limited partnerships, were already sold, having used him in one overseas deal. Even descriptions of Mr. Harrison's crimes and business troubles in a security report they commissioned did not dissuade them.

But without broker support, Mr. Harrison's partnerships would not sell. Mr. Proscia wrote James J. Darr, who headed the limited-partnership division, describing Mr. Harrison's "positives" for brokers: the "Bache Harrison subsidiary," a venture created for a European deal that earned fees; his European ties, and special investments for big-ticket brokers. Each translated into how he could make them all money.

By 1982, brokers were meeting Mr. Harrison to listen to why their clients should invest with him. The timing could not have been better: Demand for limited-partnership tax shelters had boomed because of generous real estate deductions in the 1981 tax act.

That helped Prudential's partnership division, called direct investments, to sell numerous Harrison partnerships that renovated or built commercial properties, including the Federal Archives building and Barbizon Hotel in

Manhattan and the Brazilian Court Hotel in Palm Beach, Fla. By 1986, Prudential had raised almost $300 million from top clients, including Frank Cary, a former chairman of I.B.M., and John Emery, a former chairman of Emery Air Freight.

The pitch was simple: By purchasing an interest at a cost that could exceed $100,000, investors became limited partners, sharing in depreciation deductions. They could also see a profit on the sale of the property.

If a deal faces financial problems, like low occupancy rates, the partnership investment deteriorates. That makes the general partner, who packages and runs the partnership for a fee, as important as the property.

While clients learned about the Harrison properties, Prudential never told them or their brokers about the criminal background of the man they were trusting with their money. The S.E.C. requires disclosure of an investment's material facts, but Prudential lawyers decided that the pardon made disclosure unnecessary, a position that won approval from New York's Attorney General.

But Mr. Harrison's background was destined to surface as his deals came apart. While partnership tax shelters suffered after the changes to tax laws in 1986, and from the eventual real estate collapse, Mr. Harrison's deals were troubled long before. The troubles included incomplete financing, failure to meet loan terms and construction delays.

Some problems were not disclosed. For example, partnership documents often did not mention Mr. Harrison's business failures. And flaws were sometimes hidden. In the 1982 Archives deal, for example, documents disclosed that the partnership had $40 million in bank credit. They did not mention that only $30 million was available at any point, creating a cash shortfall, or that the loan had requirements that were never met.

The Archives partnership suffered from other problems. For example, Archives documents had signatures by Mr. Freedman. In testimony, Mr. Freedman said he never signed them, raising the specter of forgery.

As investors lost millions, Prudential raked it in. Brokers earned $1.2 million in commissions, from the doomed Archives project, while the firm received fat fees.

Records show that partnership money was spent on limousines, expensive restaurants and hotels for Mr. Harrison and Prudential executives.

The spending raised suspicions. A Prudential report in 1988 said William B. Petty Jr., a former employee, accused Mr. Darr of receiving $200,000 in benefits from Mr. Harrison. No details were offered. Mr. Darr dismissed the charge as the unsubstantiated accusation of a disgruntled former employee.

Mr. Harrison's expenditures were undeniable. According to his charge-card slips and court records, in six months in 1986 he billed $50,000 for food, limousines, hotels and apartments. Expenses included a $712 meal and $177 tip at Lutèce in Manhattan, $2,000 for limousines and $9,000 in first-class air travel.

Mr. Harrison also spent in excess of his more than $1 million in annual partnership management fees on loan interest, flower bills and alimony resulting from four divorces, people who reviewed his records said.

Prudential bailed out Mr. Harrison. For example, when Prudential sold stakes in the Fountain Square Limited Partnership, a Cincinnati project, in 1983, it did not disclose that Mr. Harrison had borrowed $1.2 million from the partnership and repaid it by charging $1.2 million when the property was sold.

When Mr. Harrison had trouble in 1984, five Prudential executives, including Mr. Darr, Mr. Proscia and Robert Sherman, head of retail sales, became the sole investors in a partnership that assumed control of a Harrison brownstone and a $1.25 million debt Mr. Harrison owed. The brownstone sold for $360,000, with the proceeds and large tax deductions going to the executives.

The Deceptions

As Deals Fall Apart, Truth Is Concealed

Jim Darr's memo meant business. "I expect $6,000,000 in sales on the Madison Plaza transaction by the end of the production month," said the 1984 note to a regional manager in San Diego. "Get it done."

Mr. Darr had good reason to apply pressure. Madison Plaza, a partnership investing in buildings at Madison Avenue and 42nd Street in Manhattan, had the potential to be one of Prudential's most profitable deals.

But Madison Plaza, the most complex Harrison deal Prudential ever sold, was destined to destroy any shred of credibility the developer had with the firm's brokers.

The deal began with another general partner: Carnegie Realty Capital, with principals Bernhard F. Manko and Jon Edelman. Despite Madison Plaza's prime location, Mr. Manko and Mr. Edelman could not get brokers interested. The deal could not close until every unit was sold.

Prudential recruited Mr. Harrison as another general partner to help sell brokers on it. But even with his sales charm, Madison Plaza stumped him; its closing date was repeatedly changed. Months later, that was memorialized on a T-shirt brokers received at a volleyball party for them on the Caribbean island of Antigua celebrating the closing. The shirt read: "I Survived Madison Plaza," followed by nine closing dates, eight of them scratched out.

In 1984, Mr. Harrison, looking for someone to purchase $15 million in unsold units, met John H. Roberts Jr., president of the now-defunct Summit Savings Association of Plainview, Tex. After describing his fruitful relationship with Prudential, Mr. Harrison introduced Mr. Roberts to Mr. Darr, and the men discussed whether Mr. Roberts would buy the units through Summit's investment arm. Mr. Roberts was assured that Summit would receive a fee and that Prudential would quickly resell the units.

A day later, without a loan application, or appraisal, Summit lent $15 million, and Mr. Roberts joined as a general partner.

The loan's terms required that Summit be paid before the general partners received fees. But those terms were ignored, court records show, with Mr. Harrison and Carnegie each receiving $300,000 days after the closing without Mr. Roberts's knowledge. Summit's loan was never repaid in full.

After Madison Plaza closed, Mr. Darr and Mr. Roberts frequently discussed potential deals. In a telephone call in 1984, Mr. Roberts's diaries show, they discussed whether Summit could swap loans with First South Savings and Loan Association, in Arkansas.

First South's largest shareholders were principals of Watson & Taylor, a general partner in other Prudential deals. First South had ties with Mr. Darr, having lent him $1.8 million for a house in Connecticut.

At the time, court records show, auditors were criticizing tens of millions of dollars in First South loans to Watson & Taylor, and First South had begun an illegal scheme to hide the problems. The diaries are not clear whether the First South loan swaps discussed involved Watson & Taylor loans, but George Watson, a principal, was mentioned in the talk between Mr. Darr and Mr. Roberts.

By February 1985, no loan swaps had occurred. Mr. Darr called Summit again, reaching James M. Holbrook, a Summit lawyer. In a recent deposition, Mr. Holbrook quoted Mr. Darr saying Mr. Roberts "made commitments to have Summit buy loans from First South," and then lend Watson & Taylor $10 million.

"He wanted to know why those weren't being funded," Mr. Holbrook testified. "He did it in a demanding way, as if I was a loan officer refusing to make a loan and the president of the bank was coming in saying, 'You will make this loan.'"

Mr. Darr, who left Prudential in 1988, denied making the demands. "I could not and would not direct Mr. Holbrook to do anything," he said. "And Pru-Bache would never have undertaken any transaction unless it passed due diligence standards."

But Mr. Roberts was gone, having been ousted by Federal regulators. In 1989 he pleaded guilty to bank fraud for having taken $1.5 million from Summit to buy an airplane. That same year Mr. Manko and Mr. Edelman were indicted and later convicted of a tax fraud involving another business. The next year, Howard J. Weichern Jr., the chief executive of First South, was convicted of bank fraud involving Watson & Taylor loans.

By then, Mr. Harrison's secret past had emerged. In 1989, John C. McNulty, an Archives investor, sued, and in a deposition, with a Prudential lawyer watching, Mr. Harrison was asked about his background. He decided to deceive.

Why did he leave the bank in 1967, he was asked. "We had major disagreements." What did he do then? "I was a carpenter," a job he did hold— in prison.

Later, Mr. McNulty's lawyer discovered bank documents revealing Mr. Harrison's criminal record. Prudential lawyers attempted to block their admission, but failed. Mr. McNulty was awarded his entire claim. Prudential had other ideas. The firm offered Mr. McNulty better terms to settle if he would allow the verdict to be "vacated," as if it never existed. He agreed, and investors have never officially been told of the verdict.

But even as the settlement was reached, copies of the decision were in circulation. In a seminal article in 1991 on Prudential partnerships, Business Week reported the McNulty decision and Harrison conviction.

By then, a new general partner was at Madison Plaza. In 1988, Prudential and Mr. Harrison recruited Edward Strasser, manager of Harvard's real estate, to take over some Harrison deals. Mr. Strasser said he agreed only after receiving assurances from Prudential that it would help financially if the deals had more trouble. After all, Mr. Strasser says he was told, Prudential would want to protect its investors. Prudential has denied ever making a financial commitment.

In 1991, with the real estate depression crippling Madison Plaza, Mr. Strasser returned to Prudential seeking a loan. After months of negotiation, the firm refused.

The partnerships' troubles, Prudential executives said, were not their responsibility.

Strict Products Liability and Compensatory Justice

George G. Brenkert*

I

Strict products liability is the doctrine that the seller of a product has legal responsibilities to compensate the user of that product for injuries suffered because of a defective aspect of the product, even when the seller has not been negligent in permitting that defect to occur.[1] Thus, even though a manufacturer, for example, has reasonably applied the existing techniques of manufacture and has anticipated and cared for nonintended uses of the product, he may still be held liable for injuries a product user suffers if it can be shown that the product was defective when it left the manufacturer's hands.[2]

To say that there is a crisis today concerning this doctrine would be to utter a commonplace which few in the business community would deny. The development of the doctrine of strict products liability, according to most business people, threatens many businesses financially.[3] Furthermore, strict

Written for the first edition of this book. Copyright © 1984 by George G. Brenkert. Reprinted by permission of the author.
*Department of Philosophy, the University of Tennessee.

products liability is said to be a morally questionable doctrine, since the manufacturer or seller has not been negligent in permitting the injury-causing defect to occur. On the other hand, victims of defective products complain that they deserve full compensation for injuries sustained in using a defective product whether or not the seller is at fault. Medical expenses and time lost from one's job are costs no individual should have to bear by himself. It is only fair that the seller share such burdens.

In general, discussions of this crisis focus on the limits to which a business ought to be held responsible. Much less frequently, discussions of strict products liability consider the underlying question of whether the doctrine of strict products liability is rationally justifiable. But unless this question is answered it would seem premature to seek to determine the limits to which business ought to be held liable in such cases. In the following paper I discuss this underlying philosophical question and argue that there is a rational justification for strict products liability which links it to the very nature of the free enterprise system.

II

It should be noted at the outset that strict products liability is not absolute liability. To hold a manufacturer legally (and morally) responsible for any and all injuries which product users might sustain would be morally perverse. First, it would deny the product user's own responsibility to take care in his actions and to suffer the consequences when he does not. It would therefore constitute an extreme form of moral and legal paternalism.

Second, if the product is not defective, there is no significant moral connection between anything the manufacturer has done or not done and the user's injuries other than the production and sale of the product. This provides no basis for holding the manufacturer responsible for the user's injuries. If, because of my own carelessness, I cut myself with my new pocket knife, the fact that I just bought my knife from Blade Manufacturing Company provides no moral reason to hold Blade Manufacturing responsible for my injury.

Finally, though the manufacturer's product might be said to have harmed the person,[4] it is wholly implausible, when the product is not defective and the manufacturer not negligent, to say that the manufacturer has harmed the user. Thus, there would seem to be no moral basis upon which to maintain that the manufacturer has any liability to the product user. Strict products liability, on the other hand, holds that the manufacturer can be held liable when the product can be shown to be defective, even though the manufacturer himself has not been negligent.[5]

Two justifications of strict products liability are predominant in the literature. Both, I believe, are untenable. They are:

1. To hold producers strictly liable for defective products will cut down on the number of accidents and injuries which occur by forcing manufacturers to make their products safer.[6]

2. The manufacturer is best able to distribute to others the costs of injuries which users of his defective products suffer.[7]

There are several reasons why the first justification is unacceptable. First, it has been argued plausibly that almost everything that can be attained through the use of strict liability to force manufacturers to make their products safer can also be attained in other ways through the law.[8] Hence, to hold manufacturers strictly liable will not necessarily help reduce the number of accidents. The incentive to produce safer products already exists, without invoking the doctrine of strict products liability.

Second, at least some of the accidents which have been brought under strict liability have been caused by features of the products which the manufacturers could not have foreseen or controlled. At the time the product was designed and manufactured, the technological knowledge required to discover the hazard and take steps to minimize its effects was not available. It is doubtful that in such cases the imposition of strict liability upon the manufacturer could reduce accidents.[9] Thus, again, this justification for strict products liability fails.[10]

Third, the fact that the imposition of legal restraints and/or penalties would have a certain positive effect—for example, reduce accidents—does not show that the imposition of those penalties would be just. It has been pointed out before that the rate of crime might be cut significantly if the law would imprison the wives and children of men who break the law. Regardless of how correct that claim may be, to use these means in order to achieve a significant reduction in the crime rate would be unjust. Thus, the fact—if fact it be—that strict liability would cut down on the amount of dangerous and/or defective products placed on the market, and thus reduce the number of accidents and injuries, does not justify the imposition of strict liability on manufacturers.

Finally, the above justification is essentially a utilitarian appeal which emphasizes the welfare of the product users. It is not obvious, however, that those who use this justification have ever undertaken the utilitarian analysis which would show that greater protection of the product user's safety would further the welfare of product users. If emphasis on product user safety would cut down on the number and variety of products produced, the imposition of strict liability might not enhance product user welfare; rather, it might lower it. Furthermore, if the safety of product users is the predominant concern, massive public and private education safety campaigns might do as much or more to lower the level of accidents and injuries as strict products liability.

The second justification given for strict products liability is also utilitarian in nature. Among the factors cited in favor of this justification are the following:

1. "An individual harmed by his or her use of a defective product is often unable to bear the loss individually."
2. "Distribution of losses among all users of a product would minimize both individual and aggregate loss."

3. "The situation of producers and marketers in the marketplace enables them conveniently to distribute losses among all users of a product by raising prices sufficiently to compensate those harmed (which is what in fact occurs where strict liability is in force)."[11]

This justification is also defective.

First, the word "best" in the phrase "best able to distribute to others the cost" is usually understood in a nonmoral sense; it is used to signify that the manufacturer can most efficiently pass on the costs of injuries to others. Once this use of "best" is recognized, surely we may ask why these costs ought to be passed on to other consumers and/or users of the same product or line of products. Even if the imposition of strict liability did maximize utility, it might still be unjust to use the producer as the distributor of losses.[12] Indeed, some have objected that to pass along the costs of such accidents to other consumers of a manufacturer's products is unjust to them.[13] The above justification is silent with regard to these legitimate objections.

Second, manufacturers may not always be in the best (that is, most efficient and economical) position to pass costs on to customers. Even in monopoly areas, there are limitations. Furthermore, some products are subject to an elastic demand, preventing the manufacturer from passing along the costs.[14] Finally, the present justification could justify far more than is plausible. If the reason for holding the manufacturer liable is that the manufacturer is the "best" administrator of costs, one might plausibly argue that the manufacturer should pay for injuries suffered not only when he is not negligent but also when the product is not defective. Theoretically, at least, this argument could be extended from cases of strict liability to that of absolute liability.

Whether this argument holds up depends upon contingent facts concerning the nature and frequency of injuries people suffer using products, the financial strength of businesses, and the kinds and levels of products liability insurance available to them. It does not depend on any morally significant elements in the relationship between the producer and the product user. Such an implication, I believe, undercuts the purported moral nature of this justification and reveals it for what it is: an economic, not a moral, justification.

Accordingly, neither of the major current justifications for the imposition of strict liability appears to be acceptable. If this is the case, is strict products liability a groundless doctrine, willfully and unjustly imposed on manufacturers?

III

This question can be asked in two different ways. On the one hand, it can be asked within the assumptions of the free enterprise system. On the other hand, it could be raised with the premise that the fundamental assumptions of that socioeconomic system are also open to revision and change. In the following, I will discuss the question *within* the general assumptions of the free enterprise system. Since these assumptions are broadly made in legal and business circles it is interesting to determine what answer might be given within these constraints. Indeed, I suggest that only within these general assumptions can strict products liability be justified.

To begin with, it is crucial to remember that what we have to consider is the relationship between an entity doing business and an individual.[15] The strict liability attributed to business would not be attributed to an individual who happened to sell some product he had made to his neighbor or a stranger. If Peter sold an article he had made to Paul and Paul hurt himself because the article had a defect which occurred through no negligence of Peter's, we would not normally hold Peter morally responsible to pay Paul's injuries.

Peter did not claim, we may assume, that the product was absolutely risk-free. Had he kept it, he himself might have been injured by it. Paul, on the other hand, bought it. He was not pressured, forced, or coerced to do so. Peter mounted no advertising campaign. Though Paul might not have been injured if the product had been made differently, he supposedly bought it with open eyes. Peter did not seek to deceive Paul about its qualities. The product, both its good and bad qualities, became his when he bought it.

In short, we assume that both Peter and Paul are morally autonomous individuals capable of knowing their own interests, that such individuals can legitimately exchange their ownership of various products, that the world is not free of risks, and that not all injuries one suffers in such a world can be blamed on others. To demand that Peter protect Paul from such dangers and/or compensate him for injuries resulting from such dangers is to demand that Peter significantly reduce the risks of the product he offers to Paul and to protect Paul from encountering those risks. However, this demand smacks of paternalism and undercuts our basic moral assumptions about such relations. Hence, in such a case, Peter is not morally responsible for Paul's injuries or, because of this transaction, obligated to aid him. Perhaps Peter owes Paul aid because Paul is an injured neighbor or person. Perhaps for charitable reasons Peter ought to help Paul. But Peter has no moral obligation stemming from the sale itself to provide aid.

It is different for businesses. They have been held to be legally and morally obliged to pay the victim for his injuries. Why? What is the difference? The difference is that when Paul is hurt by a defective product from corporation X, he is hurt by something produced in a socioeconomic system purportedly embodying free enterprise. In other words, among other things:

1. Each business and/or corporation produces articles or services it sells for profit.
2. Each member of this system competes with other members of the system in trying to do as well as it can for itself not simply in each exchange, but through each exchange for its other values and desires.
3. Competition is to be "open and free, without deception or fraud."

4. Exchanges are voluntary and undertaken when each party believes it can benefit thereby. One party provides the means for another party's ends if the other party will provide the first party the means to its ends.[16]
5. The acquisition and disposition of ownership rights—that is, of private property—is permitted in such exchanges.
6. No market or series of markets constitutes the whole of a society.
7. Law, morality, and government play a role in setting acceptable limits to the nature and kinds of exchange in which people may engage.[17]

What is it about such a system which would justify claims of strict products liability against businesses? Calabresi has suggested that the free enterprise system is essentially a system of strict liability.[18] Thus the very nature of the free enterprise system justifies such liability claims. His argument has two parts. First, he claims that "bearing risks is both the function of, and justification for, private enterprise in a free enterprise society."[19] "Free enterprise is prized, in classical economics, precisely because it fosters the creation of entrepreneurs who will take such uninsurable risks, who will, in other words, gamble on uncertainty and demonstrate their utility by surviving—by winning more than others."[20]

Accordingly, the nature of private enterprise requires individual businesses to assume the burden of risk in the production and distribution of its products. However, even if we grant that this characterization of who must bear the risks "in deciding what goods are worthy of producing and what new entrants into an industry are worth having" is correct, it would not follow that individual businesses ought to bear the burden of risk in cases of accidents.

Calabresi himself recognizes this. Thus in the second part of his argument he maintains that there is a close analogy which lets us move from the regular risk-bearing businesses must accept in the marketplace to the bearing of risks in accidents: "although . . . [the above characterization] has concerned *regular* entrepreneurial-product risks, not accident risks, the analogy is extremely close."[21] He proceeds to draw the analogy, however, in the following brief sentence: "As with product-accident risks, our society starts out by allocating ordinary product-production risks in ways which try to maximize the chances that incentives will be placed on those most suited to 'manage' these risks."[22] In short, he asserts that the imposition of strict products liability on business will be the most effective means of reducing such risks.

But such a view does not really require, as we have seen in the previous section, any assumptions about the nature of the free enterprise system. It could be held independently of such assumptions. Further, this view is simply a form of the first justificatory argument we discussed and rejected in the previous section. We can hardly accept it here just by attaching it to the nature of free enterprise.

Nevertheless, Calabresi's initial intuitions about a connection between the assumptions of the free enterprise system and the justification of strict products liability are correct. However, they must be developed in the following, rather different, manner. In the free enterprise system, each person and/or business is obligated to follow the rules and understandings which define this socioeconomic system. Following the rules is expected to channel competition among individuals and businesses to socially positive results. In providing the means to fulfill the ends of others, one's own ends also get fulfilled.

Though this does not happen in every case, it is supposed to happen most of the time. Those who fail in their competition with others may be the object of charity, but not of other duties. Those who succeed, qua members of this socioeconomic system, do not have moral duties to aid those who fail. Analogously, the team which loses the game may receive our sympathy but the winning team is not obligated to help it to win the next game or even to play it better. Those who violate the rules, however, may be punished or penalized, whether or not the violation was intentional and whether or not it redounded to the benefit of the violator. Thus, a team may be assessed a penalty for something that a team member did unintentionally to a member of the other team but which injured the other team's chances of competition in the game by violating the rules.

This point may be emphasized by another instance involving a game that brings us closer to strict products liability. Imagine that you are playing table tennis with another person in his newly constructed table tennis room. You are both avid table tennis players and the game means a lot to both of you. Suppose that after play has begun, you are suddenly and quite obviously blinded by the light over the table—the light shade has a hole in it which, when it turned in your direction, sent a shaft of light unexpectedly into your eyes. You lose a crucial point as a result. Surely it would be unfair of your opponent to seek to maintain his point because he was faultless—after all, he had not intended to blind you when he installed that light shade. You would correctly object that he had gained the point unfairly, that you should not have to give up the point lost, and that the light shade should be modified so that the game can continue on a fair basis. It is only fair that the point be played over.

Businesses and their customers in a free enterprise system are also engaged in competition with each other.[23] The competition here, however, is multifaceted as each tries to gain the best agreement he can from the other with regard to the buying and selling of raw materials, products, services, and labor. Such agreements must be voluntary. The competition which leads to them cannot involve coercion. In addition, such competition must be fair and ultimately result in the benefit of the entire society through the operation of the proverbial invisible hand.

Crucial to the notion of fairness of competition are not simply the demands that the competition be open, free, and honest, but also that each person in a society be given an equal opportunity to participate in the system in order to fulfill his or her own particular ends. Friedman formulates this notion in the following manner:

> . . . the priority given to equality of opportunity in the hierarchy of values
> . . . is manifested particularly in economic policy. The catchwords were free
> enterprise, competition, laissez-faire. Everyone was to be free to go into any

business, follow any occupation, buy any property, subject only to the agreement of the other parties to the transaction. Each was to have the opportunity to reap the benefits if he succeeded, to suffer the costs if he failed. There were to be no arbitrary obstacles. Performance, not birth, religion, or nationality, was the touchstone.[24]

What is obvious in Friedman's comments is that he is thinking primarily of a person as a producer. Equality of opportunity requires that one not be prevented by arbitrary obstacles from participating (by engaging in a productive role of some kind or other) in the system of free enterprise, competition, and so on in order to fulfill one's own ends ("reap the benefits"). Accordingly, monopolies are restricted, discriminatory hiring policies have been condemned, and price collusion is forbidden.

However, each person participates in the system of free enterprise *both* as a worker/producer *and* as a consumer. The two roles interact; if the person could not consume he would not be able to work, and if there were no consumers there would be no work to be done. Even if a particular individual is only (what is ordinarily considered) a consumer, he or she plays a theoretically significant role in the competitive free enterprise system. The fairness of the system depends upon what access he or she has to information about goods and services on the market, the lack of coercion imposed on that person to buy goods, and the lack of arbitrary restrictions imposed by the market and/or government on his or her behavior.

In short, equality of opportunity is a doctrine with two sides which applies both to producers and to consumers. If, then, a person as a consumer or a producer is injured by a defective product—which is one way his activities might arbitrarily be restricted by the action of (one of the members of) the market system—surely his free and voluntary participation in the system of free enterprise will be seriously affected. Specifically, his equal opportunity to participate in the system in order to fulfill his own ends will be diminished.

Here is where strict products liability enters the picture. In cases of strict liability the manufacturer does not intend for a certain aspect of his product to injure someone. Nevertheless, the person is injured. As a result, he is at a disadvantage both as a consumer and as a producer. He cannot continue to play either role as he might wish. Therefore, he is denied that equality of opportunity which is basic to the economic system in question just as surely as he would be if he were excluded from employment by various unintended consequences of the economic system which nevertheless had racially or sexually prejudicial implications. Accordingly, it is fair for the manufacturer to compensate the person for his losses before proceeding with business as usual. That is, the user of a manufacturer's product may justifiably demand compensation from the manufacturer when its product can be shown to be defective and has injured him and harmed his chances of participation in the system of free enterprise.

Hence, strict liability finds a basis in the notion of equality of opportunity which plays a central role in the notion of a free enterprise system.

That is why a business which does *not* have to pay for the injuries an individual suffers in the use of a defective article made by that business is felt to be unfair to its customers. Its situation is analogous to that of a player's unintentional violation of a game rule which is intended to foster equality of competitive opportunity.

A soccer player, for example, may unintentionally trip an opposing player. He did not mean to do it; perhaps he himself had stumbled. Still, he has to be penalized. If the referee looked the other way, the tripped player would rightfully object that he had been treated unfairly. Similarly, the manufacturer of a product may be held strictly liable for a product of his which injures a person who uses that product. Even if he is faultless, a consequence of his activities is to render the user of his product less capable of equal participation in the socioeconomic system. The manufacturer should be penalized by way of compensating the victim. Thus, the basis upon which manufacturers are held strictly liable is compensatory justice.

In a society which refuses to resort to paternalism or to central direction of the economy and which turns, instead, to competition in order to allocate scarce positions and resources, compensatory justice requires that the competition be fair and losers be protected.[25] Specifically, no one who loses should be left so destitute that he cannot reenter the competition. Furthermore, those who suffer injuries traceable to defective merchandise or services which restrict their participation in the competitive system should also be compensated.

Compensatory justice does not presuppose negligence or evil intentions on the part of those to whom the injuries might ultimately be traced. It is not perplexed or incapacitated by the relative innocence of all parties involved. Rather, it is concerned with correcting the disadvantaged situation an individual experiences due to accidents or failures which occur in the normal working of that competitive system. It is on this basis that other compensatory programs which alleviate the disabilities of various minority groups are founded. Strict products liability is also founded on compensatory justice.

An implication of the preceding argument is that business is not morally obliged to pay, as such, for the physical injury a person suffers. Rather, it must pay for the loss of equal competitive opportunity—even though it usually is the case that it is because of a (physical) injury that there is a loss of equal opportunity. Actual legal cases in which the injury which prevents a person from going about his or her daily activities is emotional or mental, as well as physical, support this thesis. If a person were neither mentally nor physically harmed, but still rendered less capable of participating competitively because of a defective aspect of a product, there would still be grounds for holding the company liable.

For example, suppose I purchased and used a cosmetic product guaranteed to last a month. When used by most people it is odorless. On me, however, it has a terrible smell. I can stand the smell, but my co-workers and most other people find it intolerable. My employer sends me home from work until it wears off. The product has not harmed me physically or mentally. Still, on the above argument, I would have reason to hold the manufacturer liable. Any cosmetic product with this result is defective. As a consequence my opportunity to participate in the socioeconomic system is curbed. I should be compensated.

IV

There is another way of arriving at the same conclusion about the basis of strict products liability. To speak of business or the free enterprise system, it was noted above, is to speak of the voluntary exchanges between producer and customer which take place when each party believes he has an opportunity to benefit. Surely customers and producers may miscalculate their benefits; something they voluntarily agreed to buy or sell may turn out not to be to their benefit. The successful person does not have any moral responsibilities to the unsuccessful person—at least as a member of this economic system. If, however, fraud is the reason one person does not benefit, the system is, in principle, undermined. If such fraud were universalized, the system would collapse. Accordingly, the person committing the fraud does have a responsibility to make reparations to the one mistreated.

Consider once again the instance of a person who is harmed by a product he bought or used, a product that can reasonably be said to be defective. Has the nature of the free enterprise system also been undermined or corrupted in this instance? Producer and consumer have exchanged the product but it has not been to their mutual benefit; the manufacturer may have benefited, but the customer has suffered because of the defect. Furthermore, if such exchanges were universalized, the system would also be undone.

Suppose that whenever people bought products from manufacturers the products turned out to be defective and the customers were always injured, even though the manufacturers could not be held negligent. Though one party to such exchanges might benefit, the other party always suffered. If the rationale for this economic system—the reason it was adopted and is defended—were that in the end both parties share the equal opportunity to gain, surely it would collapse with the above consequences. Consequently, as with fraud, an economic system of free enterprise requires that injuries which result from defective products be compensated. The question is: Who is to pay for the compensation?

There are three possibilities. The injured party could pay for his own injuries. However, this is implausible since what is called for is compensation and not merely payment for injuries. If the injured party had simply injured himself, if he had been negligent or careless, then it is plausible that he should pay for his own injuries. No compensation is at stake here. But in the present case the injury stems from the actions of a particular manufacturer who, albeit unwittingly, placed the defective product on the market and stands to gain through its sale.

The rationale of the free enterprise system would be undermined, we have seen, if such actions were universalized, for then the product user's equal opportunity to benefit from the system would be denied. Accordingly, since the rationale and motivation for an individual to be part of this socioeconomic system is his opportunity to gain from participation in it, justice requires that the injured product user receive compensation for his injuries. Since the individual can hardly compensate himself, he must receive compensation from some other source.

Second, some third party—such as government—could compensate the injured person. This is not wholly implausible if one is prepared to modify the structure of the free enterprise system. And, indeed, in the long run this may be the most plausible course of action. However, if one accepts the structure of the free enterprise system, this alternative must be rejected because it permits the interference of government into individual affairs.[26]

Third, we are left with the manufacturer. Suppose a manufacturer's product, even though the manufacturer wasn't negligent, always turned out to be defective and injured those using his products. We might sympathize with his plight, but he would either have to stop manufacturing altogether (no one would buy such products) or else compensate the victims for their losses. (Some people might buy and use his products under these conditions.) If he forced people to buy and use his products he would corrupt the free enterprise system. If he did not compensate the injured users, they would not buy and he would not be able to sell his products. Hence, he could partake of the free enterprise system—that is, sell his products—only if he compensated his user/victims. Accordingly, the sale of this hypothetical line of defective products would be voluntarily accepted as just or fair only if compensation were paid the user/victims of such products by the manufacturer.

The same conclusion follows even if we consider a single defective product. The manufacturer put the defective product on the market. Because of his actions others who seek the opportunity to participate on an equal basis in this system in order to benefit therefrom are unable to do so. Thus, a result of his actions, even though unintended, is to undermine the system's character and integrity. Accordingly, when a person is injured in his attempt to participate in this system, he is owed compensation by the manufacturer. The seller of the defective article must not jeopardize the equal opportunity of the product user to benefit from the system. The seller need not guarantee that the buyer/user will benefit from the purchase of the product; after all, the buyer may miscalculate or be careless in the use of a nondefective product. But if he is not careless or has not miscalculated, his opportunity to benefit from the system is illegitimately harmed if he is injured in its use because of the product's defectiveness. He deserves compensation.

It follows from the arguments in this and the preceding section that strict products liability is not only compatible with the system of free enterprise but that if it were not attributed to the manufacturer the system itself would be morally defective. And the justification for requiring manufacturers to pay compensation when people are injured by defective products is that the demands of compensatory justice are met.[27]

Notes

1. This characterization of strict products liability is adapted from Alvin S. Weinstein et al., *Products Liability and the Reasonably Safe Product* (New York: John Wiley & Sons, 1978), ch. 1. I understand the seller to include the manufacturer, the retailer, distributors, and wholesalers. For the sake of convenience, I will generally refer simply to the manufacturer.

2. Cf. John W. Wade, "On Product 'Design Defects' and Their Actionability," 33 *Vanderbilt Law Review* 553 (1980); Weinstein et al., *Products Liability and the Reasonably Safe Product,* pp. 8, 28–32; Reed Dickerson, "Products Liability: How Good Does a Product Have to Be?" 42 *Indiana Law Journal* 308–316 (1967). Section 402A of the Restatement (Second) of Torts characterizes the seller's situation in this fashion: "the seller has exercised all possible care in the preparation and sale of his product."

3. Cf. John C. Perham, "The Dilemma in Product Liability," *Dun's Review,* 109 (1977), pp. 48–50, 76; W. Page Keeton, "Products Liability—Design Hazards and the Meaning of Defect," 10 *Cumberland Law Review* 293–316 (1979); Weinstein et al., *Products Liability and the Reasonably Safe Product,* ch. 1.

4. More properly, of course, the person's use of the manufacturer's product harmed the product user.

5. Clearly one of the central questions confronting the notion of strict liability is what is to count as "defective." With few exceptions, it is held that a product is defective if and only if it is unreasonably dangerous. There have been several different standards proposed as measures of the defectiveness or unreasonably dangerous nature of a product. However, in terms of logical priorities, it really does not matter what the particular standard for defectiveness is unless we know whether we may justifiably hold manufacturers strictly liable for defective products. That is why I concentrate in this paper on the justifiability of strict products liability.

6. Michel A. Coccia, John W. Dondanville, and Thomas R. Nelson, *Product Liability: Trends and Implications* (New York: American Management Association, 1970), p. 13; W. Page Keeton, "The Meaning of Defect in Products Liability Law—A Review of Basic Principles," 45 *Missouri Law Review* 580 (1980); William L. Prosser, "The Assault Upon the Citadel (Strict Liability to the Consumer)," 69 *The Yale Law Journal* 119 (1960).

7. Coccia, Dondanville, and Nelson, *Product Liability: Trends and Implications,* p. 13; Keeton, "The Meaning of Defect in Products Liability Law—A Review of Basic Principles," pp. 580–581; David G. Owen, "Rethinking the Policies of Strict Products Liability," 33 *Vanderbilt Law Review* 686 (1980); Prosser, "The Assault Upon the Citadel (Strict Liability to the Consumer)," p. 1120.

8. Marcus L. Plant, "Strict Liability of Manufacturers for Injuries Caused by Defects in Products—An Opposing View," 24 *Tennessee Law Review* 945 (1957); Prosser, "The Assault Upon the Citadel (Strict Liability to the Consumer)," pp. 1114, 1115, 1119.

9. Keeton, "The Meaning of Defect in Products Liability Law—A Review of Basic Principles," pp. 594–595; Weinstein et al., *Products Liability and the Reasonably Safe Product,* p. 55.

10. An objection might be raised that such accidents ought not to fall under strict products liability and hence do not constitute a counterexample to the above justification. This objection is answered in Sections III and IV.

11. These three considerations are formulated by Michael D. Smith, "The Morality of Strict Liability in Tort," *Business and Professional Ethics Newsletter,* 3 (1979), p. 4. Smith himself, however, was drawing upon Guido Calabresi, "Some Thoughts on Risk Distribution and the Law of Torts," 70 *Yale Law Journal* 499–553 (1961).

12. Smith, "The Morality of Strict Liability in Tort," p. 4. Cf. George P. Fletcher, "Fairness and Utility in Tort Theory," 85 *Harvard Law Review* 537–573 (1972).

13. Rev. Francis E. Lucey, S. J., "Liability Without Fault and the Natural Law," 24 *Tennessee Law Review* 952–962 (1957); Perham, "The Dilemma in Product Liability," pp. 48–49.

14. Plant, "Strict Liability of Manufacturers for Injuries Caused by Defects in Products—An Opposing View," pp. 946–947. By "elastic demand" is meant "a slight increase in price will cause a sharp reduction in demand or will turn consumers to a substitute product" (pp. 946–947).

15. Cf. Prosser, "The Assault Upon the Citadel (Strict Liability to the Consumer)," pp. 1140–1141; Wade, "On Product 'Design Defects' and Their Actionability," p. 569; Coccia, Dondanville, and Nelson, *Product Liability: Trends and Implications,* p. 19.

16. F. A. Hayek emphasizes this point in "The Moral Element in Free Enterprise," in *Studies in Philosophy, Politics, and Economics* (New York: Simon and Schuster, 1967), p. 229.

17. Several of these characteristics have been drawn from Milton Friedman and Rose Friedman, *Free to Choose* (New York: Avon Books, 1980).

18. Calabresi, "Product Liability: Curse or Bulwark of Free Enterprise," 27 *Cleveland State Law Review* 325 (1978).

19. *Ibid.,* p. 321.

20. *Ibid.*

21. *Ibid.,* p. 324.

22. *Ibid.*

23. Cf. H. B. Acton, *The Morals of Markets* (London: Longman Group Limited, 1971), pp. 1–7, 33–37; Milton Friedman and Rose Friedman, *Free to Choose.*

24. Milton Friedman and Rose Friedman, *Free to Choose,* pp. 123–124.

25. I have drawn heavily, in this paragraph, on the fine article by Bernard Boxhill, "The Morality of Reparation," reprinted in *Reverse Discrimination,* ed. Barry R. Gross (Buffalo, New York: Prometheus Books, 1977), pp. 270–278.

26. Cf. Calabresi, "Product Liability: Curse or Bulwark of Free Enterprise," pp. 315–319.

27. I would like to thank the following for providing helpful comments on earlier versions of this paper: Betsy Postow, Jerry Phillips, Bruce Fisher, John Hardwig, and Sheldon Cohen.

Manufacturing the Audi Scare

Peter W. Huber

If you're the kind of driver who sometimes has trouble finding the brakes in your car, you should be driving an Audi. Last month, in 35-mph crash tests of an airbag-equipped Audi 100, the mannequin in the driver's seat suffered the lowest crash force ever recorded by the National Highway and Traffic Safety Administration, NHTSA, in this kind of test.

And yet, according to the Center for Auto Safety—a self-styled public interest organization that sells its research to plaintiffs' lawyers—the Audi 100's predecessor, the Audi 5000, was as deadly as the Audi 100 is safe. It exhibited "sudden acceleration," a fatal propensity to take off at full speed even as the terrified driver rammed the brake pedal to the floor.

CBS's "60 Minutes" ran a devastating expose of the Audi 5000. Audi customers fled. Lawyers cashed in. The American public was saved, yet again,

The Wall Street Journal. Monday, December 18, 1989.

from the perils of technology gone awry. Only one little noticed footnote remains at the end: There was nothing wrong with the car.

The Audi story is, by now, dismally familiar. "Sudden acceleration" accidents occurred when the transmission was shifted out of "park." The driver always insisted he was standing on the brake, but after the crash the brakes always worked perfectly. A disproportionate number of accidents involved drivers new to the vehicle. When an idiot-proof shift was installed so that a driver could not shift out of park if his foot was on the accelerator, reports of sudden acceleration plummeted.

But a story to the effect that cars accelerate when drivers step on the accelerator doesn't boost television ratings or jury verdicts. And driver error is understandably hard to accept for a mother whose errant foot killed her six-year-old son. So with the help of such mothers, CAS and CBS knitted together a tissue of conjecture, insinuation and calumny. The car's cruise control was at fault. Or maybe the electronic idle. Or perhaps the transmission.

"60 Minutes," in one of journalism's most shameful hours, gave air time in November 1986 to a self-styled expert who drilled a hole in an Audi transmission and pumped in air at high pressure. Viewers didn't see the drill or the pump—just the doctored car blasting off like a rocket.

Junk science of this kind moves fast. Real science takes time to catch up with this kind of intellectual cockroach and squash it. Government agencies in Japan and Canada, as well as in the U.S., conducted painstaking studies. The Canadians who are franker about such things, called it "driver error." In America, where we can't attach blame to anyone whose name doesn't end with Inc., it was called "pedal misapplication." And unsurprisingly, it's not just Audi drivers who commit it.

So, in the long run, the truth does come out. In the short run, the lawyers swoop in. Most soon recognized that they couldn't prove any defect in the Audi's engine or transmission. But our liability system today is a master of the bait and switch—the switch was to "pedal misdesign."

No doubt about it, the original Audi, like other European cars, placed brake and accelerator pedals slightly closer together than is usual in many American designs. This allows the good driver to move faster between the pedals in high-speed emergency. Perhaps it also makes it easier for the bad driver to mix up the pedals. Nobody, including NHTSA, is quite sure whether, overall, the old Audi pedal placement was marginally better or marginally worse. End of case? Hardly. With Audi shell-shocked and vulnerable from the earlier junk-engineering claims, the pedal placement lawyers moved in.

The "60 Minutes" story starred a mother who had run over her six-year-old son. On the air, she insisted that she had had her foot on the brake the whole time. When her $48 million claim came to court in Akron, Ohio, in June 1988 the investigating police officer and witnesses at the scene testified that after the accident the distraught mother had admitted that her foot had slipped off the brake. The jury found no defect in the car.

Trial judges in New Jersey and New York have overturned bad-pedal-design verdicts against Audi. Last July a federal court in Pennsylvania issued a summary judgment for Audi. And that should have been the end of Audi's legal troubles.

Except that it wasn't. An appellate court reinstated the New Jersey verdict; an appeal is pending. The New York case was settled before retrial. A California jury returned a $3.5 million verdict against Audi on a pedal-placement theory, after the plaintiff's lawyers abandoned a sudden-acceleration claim. Another appeal is pending. Today, Audi is reportedly defending itself in more than 140 different suits, and damage claims are in excess of $5 billion. Not that the aggregate claims have the slightest connection with reality, of course. At one point, a single demented plaintiff in New York filed identical $5 billion claims in both federal and state courts; both have since been thrown out.

How about the U.S. government safety report? In July, 1989, shortly after the report was released, Audi ran a hopeful advertisement titled "Case Closed." "The case is not closed," responded Robert Lisco, a Chicago plaintiffs' attorney. "Those guys must be smoking something." "60 Minutes" never even acknowledged the final U.S. findings; it did grudgingly note identical conclusions of an earlier, blue-ribbon study, and then proceeded to rebroadcast inflammatory videos from the earlier segment. CAS denounced the government study and cheerfully cranked up yet another sudden acceleration smear, this one against Cadillacs. Lawyers for the "Audi Victims Network" brazenly declared that the report strengthened their clients' cases.

They may be right. The largest suit now pending against Audi is an Illinois class action, ostensibly representing 300,000 or so Audi 5000 owners. The charge? That because of the sudden acceleration controversy, Audis have lost resale value.

Yes, sudden acceleration is real. A powerful engine kicks into gear without warning or reason. It crashes through a respected business, ruins the livelihood of hundreds of innocent dealers, and devalues the property of hundreds of thousands of bewildered car owners. The windfall goes to those who destroy and then successfully blame others for the wreckage. For heaven's sake, where are the brakes?

CHAPTER 12

The Environment

Should Trees Have Standing?—Toward Legal Rights for Natural Objects

Christopher D. Stone

Throughout legal history, each successive extension of rights to some new entity has been, theretofore, a bit unthinkable. We are inclined to suppose the rightlessness of rightless "things" to be a decree of Nature, not a legal convention acting in support of some status quo. It is thus that we defer considering the choices involved in all their moral, social, and economic dimensions. And so the United States Supreme Court could straight-facedly tell us in *Dred Scott* that Blacks had been denied the rights of citizenship "as a subordinate and inferior class of beings, who had been subjugated by the dominant race. . . ."[1] In the nineteenth century, the highest court in California explained that Chinese had not the right to testify against white men in criminal matters because they were "a race of people whom nature has marked as inferior, and who are incapable of progress or intellectual development beyond a certain point . . . between whom and ourselves nature has placed an impassable difference."[2] The popular conception of the Jew in the 13th century contributed to a law which treated them as "men *ferae naturae*, protected by a quasi-forest law. Like the roe and the deer, they form an order apart."[3] Recall, too, that it was not so long ago that the foetus was "like the roe and the deer." In an early suit attempting to establish a wrongful death action on behalf of a negligently killed foetus (now widely accepted practice), Holmes, then on the

From *Southern California Law Review*, vol. 45 (1972), pp. 453–460, 463–464, 480–481, 486–487. Reprinted by permission.

Massachusetts Supreme Court, seems to have thought it simply inconceivable "that man might owe a civil duty and incur a conditional prospective liability in tort to one not yet in being."[4] The first woman in Wisconsin who thought she might have a right to practice law was told that she did not, in the following terms:

> The law of nature destines and qualifies the female sex for the bearing and nurture of the children of our race and for the custody of the homes of the world. . . . [A]ll life-long callings of women, inconsistent with these radical and sacred duties of their sex, as is the profession of the law, are departures from the order of nature; and when voluntary, treason against it. . . . The peculiar qualities of womanhood, its gentle graces, its quick sensibility, its tender susceptibility, its purity, its delicacy, its emotional impulses, its subordination of hard reason to sympathetic feeling, are surely not qualifications for forensic strife. Nature has tempered woman as little for the juridical conflicts of the court room, as for the physical conflicts of the battle field. . . .[5]

The fact is, that each time there is a movement to confer rights onto some new "entity," the proposal is bound to sound odd or frightening or laughable. This is partly because until the rightless thing receives its rights, we cannot see it as anything but a *thing* for the use of "us"—those who are holding rights at the time. In this vein, what is striking about the Wisconsin case above is that the court, for all its talk about women, so clearly was never able to see women as they are (and might become). All it could see was the popular "idealized" version of *an object it needed*. Such is the way the slave South looked upon the Black. There is something of a seamless web involved: there will be resistance to giving the thing "rights" until it can be seen and valued for itself; yet, it is hard to see it and value it for itself until we can bring ourselves to give it "rights"—which is almost inevitably going to sound inconceivable to a large group of people.

The reason for this little discourse on the unthinkable, the reader must know by now, if only from the title of the paper. I am quite seriously proposing that we give legal rights to forests, oceans, rivers and other so-called "natural objects" in the environment—indeed, to the natural environment as a whole.

As strange as such a notion may sound, it is neither fanciful nor devoid of operational content. In fact, I do not think it would be a misdescription of recent developments in the law to say that we are already on the verge of assigning some such rights, although we have not faced up to what we are doing in those particular terms. We should do so now, and begin to explore the implications such a notion would hold.

Toward Rights for the Environment

Now, to say that the natural environment should have rights is not to say anything as silly as that no one should be allowed to cut down a tree. We say human beings have rights, but—at least as of the time of this writing—they can be executed. Corporations have rights, but they cannot plead the fifth amendment; *In re Gault* gave 15-year-olds certain rights in juvenile proceedings, but it did not give them the right to vote. Thus, to say that the environment should have rights is not to say that it should have every right we can imagine, or even the same body of rights as human beings have. Nor is it to say that everything in the environment should have the same rights as every other thing in the environment.

But for a thing to be *a holder of legal rights,* something more is needed than that some authoritative body will review the actions and processes of those who threaten it. As I shall use the term, "holder of legal rights," each of three additional criteria must be satisfied. All three, one will observe, go towards making a thing *count* jurally—to have a legally recognized worth and dignity in its own right, and not merely to serve as a means to benefit "us" (whoever the contemporary group of rights-holders may be). They are, first, that the thing can institute legal actions *at its behest;* second, that in determining the granting of legal relief, the court must take *injury to it* into account; and, third, that relief must run to the *benefit of it.*

The Rightlessness of Natural Objects at Common Law

Consider, for example, the common law's posture toward the pollution of a stream. True, courts have always been able, in some circumstances, to issue orders that will stop the pollution. . . . But the stream itself is fundamentally rightless, with implications that deserve careful reconsideration.

The first sense in which the stream is not a rights-holder has to do with standing. The stream itself has none. So far as the common law is concerned, there is in general no way to challenge the polluter's actions save at the behest of a lower riparian—another human being—able to show an invasion of *his* rights. This conception of the riparian as the holder of the right to bring suit has more than theoretical interest. The lower riparians may simply not care about the pollution. They themselves may be polluting, and not wish to stir up legal waters. They may be economically dependent on their polluting neighbor. And, of course, when they discount the value of winning by the costs of bringing suit and the chances of success, the action may not seem worth undertaking. . . .

The second sense in which the common law denies "rights" to natural objects has to do with the way in which the merits are decided in those cases in which someone is competent and willing to establish standing. At its more primitive levels, the system protected the "rights" of the property owning human with minimal weighing of any values: "*Cujus est solum, ejus èst usque ad coelum et ad infernos.*" Today we have come more and more to make balances—but only such as will adjust the economic best interests of identifiable humans.

. . . None of the natural objects, whether held in common or situated on private land, has any of the three criteria of a rights-holder. They have no standing in their own right; their unique damages do not count in determining outcome; and they are not the beneficiaries of awards. In such fashion, these objects have traditionally been regarded by the common law, and even by all but the most recent legislation, as objects for man to conquer and master and use—in such a way as the law once looked upon "man's" relationships to African Negroes. Even where special measures have been taken to conserve them, as by seasons on game and limits on timber cutting, the dominant motive has been to conserve them *for us*—for the greatest good of the greatest number of human beings. Conservationists, so far as I am aware, are generally reluctant to maintain otherwise. As the name implies, they want to conserve and guarantee *our* consumption and *our* enjoyment of these other living things. In their own right, natural objects have counted for little, in law as in popular movements. . . .

As I mentioned at the outset, however, the rightlessness of the natural environment can and should change; it already shows some signs of doing so.

Toward Having Standing in Its Own Right

It is not inevitable, nor is it wise, that natural objects should have no rights to seek redress in their own behalf. It is no answer to say that streams and forests cannot have standing because streams and forests cannot speak. Corporations cannot speak either; nor can states, estates, infants, incompetents, municipalities or universities. Lawyers speak for them, as they customarily do for the ordinary citizen with legal problems. One ought, I think, to handle the legal problems of natural objects as one does the problems of legal incompetents—human beings who have become vegetable. If a human being shows signs of becoming senile and has affairs that he is de jure incompetent to manage, those concerned with his well-being make such a showing to the court, and someone is designated by the court with the authority to manage the incompetent's affairs. The guardian (or "conservator" or "committee"—the terminology varies) then represents the incompetent in his legal affairs. Courts make similar appointments when a corporation has become "incompetent"—they appoint a trustee in bankruptcy or reorganization to oversee its affairs and speak for it in court when that becomes necessary.

On a parity of reasoning, we should have a system in which, when a friend of a natural object perceives it to be endangered, he can apply to a court for the creation of a guardianship. . . .

. . . One reason for making the environment itself the beneficiary of a judgment is to prevent it from being "sold out" in a negotiation among private litigants who agree not to enforce rights that have been established among themselves. Protection from this will be advanced by making the natural object a party to an injunctive settlement. Even more importantly, we should make it a beneficiary of money awards. . . .

The idea of assessing damages as best we can and placing them in a trust fund is far more realistic than a hope that a total "freeze" can be put on the environmental status quo. Nature is a continuous theatre in which things and species (eventually man) are destined to enter and exit. In the meantime, co-existence of man and his environment means that *each* is going to have to compromise for the better of both. Some pollution of streams, for example, will probably be inevitable for some time. Instead of setting an unrealizable goal of enjoining absolutely the discharge of all such pollutants, the trust fund concept would (a) help assure that pollution would occur only in those instances where the social need for the pollutant's product (via his present method of production) was so high as to enable the polluter to cover *all* homocentric costs, plus some estimated costs to the environment *per se,* and (b) would be a corpus for preserving monies, if necessary, while the technology developed to a point where repairing the damaged portion of the environment was feasible. Such a fund might even finance the requisite research and development.

I do not doubt that other senses in which the environment might have rights will come to mind, and, as I explain more fully below, would be more apt to come to mind if only we should speak in terms of their having rights, albeit vaguely at first. "Rights" might well lie in unanticipated areas. It would seem, for example, that Chief Justice Warren was only stating the obvious when he observed in *Reynolds v. Sims* that "legislators represent people, not trees or acres." Yet, could not a case be made for a system of apportionment which *did* take into account the wildlife of an area? It strikes me as a poor idea that Alaska should have no more congressmen than Rhode Island primarily *because there are in Alaska all those trees and acres, those waterfalls and forests.* I am not saying anything as silly as that we ought to overrule *Baker v. Carr* and retreat from one man-one vote to a system of one man-or-tree one vote. Nor am I even taking the position that we ought to count each acre, as we once counted each slave, as three-fifths of a man. But I am suggesting that there is nothing unthinkable about, and there might on balance even be a prevailing case to be made for, an electoral apportionment that made some systematic effort to allow for the representative "rights" of non-human life. And if a case can be made for that, which I offer here mainly for purpose of illustration, I suspect that a society that grew concerned enough about the environment to make it a holder of rights would be able to find quite a number of "rights" to have waiting for it when it got to court.

Notes

1. Dred Scott v. Sandford, 60 U.S. (19 How.) 396, 404–5 (1856).
2. People v. Hall, 4 Cal. 399, 405 (1854).
3. Schechter, "The Rightlessness of Medieval English Jewry," 45 *Jewish Q. Rev.,* 121, 135 (1954) quoting from M. Bateson, *Medieval England,* 139 (1904).
4. Dietrich v. Inhabitants of Northampton, 138 Mass. 14, 16 (1884).
5. *In re* Goddell, 39 Wisc. 232, 245 (1875).

The Case for Economic Growth

Wilfred Beckerman

For some years now it has been very unfashionable to be in favor of continued long-run economic growth. Unless one joins in the chorus of scorn for the pursuit of continued economic growth, one is in danger of being treated either as a coarse Philistine, who is prepared to sacrifice all the things that make life really worth living for vulgar materialist goods, or as a shortsighted, complacent, Micawber who is unable to appreciate that the world is living on the edge of a precipice. For it is widely believed that if growth is not now brought to a halt in a deliberate orderly manner, either there will be a catastrophic collapse of output when we suddenly ran out of key raw materials, or we shall all be asphyxiated by increased pollution. In other words, growth is either undesirable or impossible, or both. Of course, I suppose this is better than being undesirable and inevitable, but the antigrowth cohorts do not seem to derive much comfort from the fact. . . .

Hence it is not entirely surprising that the antigrowth movement has gathered so much support over the past few years even though it is 99 percent nonsense. Not 100 percent nonsense. There does happen to be a one percent grain of truth in it.

This is that, in the absence of special government policies (policies that governments are unlikely to adopt if not pushed hard by communal action from citizens), pollution will be excessive. This is because—as economists have known for many decades—pollution constitutes what is known in the jargon as an "externality." That is to say, the costs of pollution are not always borne fully—if at all—by the polluter. The owner of a steel mill that belches smoke over the neighborhood, for example, does not usually have to bear the costs of the extra laundry, or of the ill-health that may result. Hence, although he is, in a sense, "using up" some of the environment (the clean air) to produce his steel he is getting this particular factor of production free of charge. Naturally, he has no incentive to economize in its use in the same way as he has for other factors of production that carry a cost, such as labor or capital. In all such cases of "externalities," or "spillover effects" as they are sometimes called, the normal price mechanism does not operate to achieve the socially desirable pattern of output or of exploitation of the environment. This defect of the price mechanism needs to be corrected by governmental action in order to eliminate excessive pollution.

But, it should be noted that the "externality" argument, summarized above, only implies that society should cut out "excessive" pollution; not *all* pollution. Pollution should only be cut to the point where the benefits from

Wilfred Beckerman, "The Case for Economic Growth," *Public Utilities Fortnightly,* Sept. 26, 1974, abridged and reprinted by permission of the publisher.

reducing it further no longer offset the costs to society (labor or capital costs) of doing so.

Mankind has always polluted his environment, in the same way that he has always used up some of the raw materials that he has found in it. When primitive man cooked his meals over open fires, or hunted animals, or fashioned weapons out of rocks and stones, he was exploiting the environment. But to listen to some of the extreme environmentalists, one would imagine that there was something immoral about this (even though God's first injunction to Adam was to subdue the earth and every living thing that exists on it). If all pollution has to be eliminated we would have to spend the whole of our national product in converting every river in the country into beautiful clear-blue swimming pools for fish. Since I live in a town with a 100,000 population but without even a decent swimming pool for the humans, I am not prepared to subscribe to this doctrine.

Anyway, most of the pollution that the environmentalists make such a fuss about, is not the pollution that affects the vast mass of the population. Most people in industrialized countries spend their lives in working conditions where the noise and stench cause them far more loss of welfare than the glamorous fashionable pollutants, such as PCB's or mercury, that the anti-growth lobby makes such a fuss about. Furthermore, such progress as has been made over the decades to improve the working conditions of the mass of the population in industrialized countries has been won largely by the action of working-class trade unions, without any help from the middle classes that now parade so ostentatiously their exquisite sensibilities and concern with the "quality of life."

The extreme environmentalists have also got their facts about pollution wrong. In the Western world, the most important forms of pollution are being reduced, or are being increasingly subjected to legislative action that will shortly reduce them. In my recently published book (*"In Defense of Economic Growth"*)[1] I give the facts about the dramatic decline of air pollution in British cities over the past decade or more, as well as the improvement in the quality of the rivers. I also survey the widespread introduction of antipollution policies in most of the advanced countries of the world during the past few years, which will enable substantial cuts to be made in pollution. By comparison with the reductions already achieved in some cases, or envisaged in the near future, the maximum pollution reductions built into the computerized calculations of the Club of Rome[2] can be seen to be absurdly pessimistic.

The same applies to the Club of Rome's assumption that adequate pollution abatement would be so expensive that economic growth would have to come to a halt. For example, the dramatic cleaning up of the air in London cost a negligible amount per head of the population of that city. And, taking a much broader look at the estimates, I show in my book that reductions in pollution many times greater than those which the Club of Rome purports to be the upper limits over the next century can, and no doubt will, be achieved over the next decade in the advanced countries of the world at a cost of only about one percent to 2 percent of annual national product.

When confronted with the facts about the main pollutants, the antigrowth lobby tends to fall back on the "risk and uncertainty" argument. This takes the form, "Ah yes, but what about all these new pollutants, or what about undiscovered pollutants? Who knows, maybe we shall only learn in a 100 years' time, when it will be too late, that they are deadly." But life is full of risk and uncertainty. Every day I run the risk of being run over by an automobile or hit on the head by a golf ball. But rational conduct requires that I balance the probabilities of this happening against the costs of insuring against it. It would only be logical to avoid even the minutest chance of some catastrophe in the future if it were costless to do so. But the cost of stopping economic growth would be astronomic. This cost does not merely comprise the loss of any hope of improved standards of living for the vast mass of the world's population, it includes also the political and social costs that would need to be incurred. For only a totalitarian regime could persist on the basis of an antigrowth policy that denied people their normal and legitimate aspirations for a better standard of living.

But leaving aside this political issue, another technical issue which has been much in the public eye lately has been the argument that growth will be brought to a sudden, and hence catastrophic, halt soon on account of the impending exhaustion of raw material supplies. This is the "finite resources" argument; i.e., that since the resources of the world are finite, we could not go on using them up indefinitely.

Now resources are either finite or they are not. If they are, then even zero growth will not save us in the longer run. Perhaps keeping Gross National Product at the present level instead of allowing it to rise by, say, 4 percent per annum, would enable the world's resources to be spread out for 500 years instead of only 200 years. But the day will still come when we would run out of resources. (The Club of Rome's own computer almost gave the game away and it was obliged to cut off the printout at the point where it becomes clear that, even with zero growth, the world eventually begins to run out of resources!) So why aim only at zero growth? Why not cut output? If resources are, indeed, finite, then there must be some optimum rate at which they should be spread out over time which will be related to the relative importance society attaches to the consumption levels of different generations. The "eco-doomsters" fail to explain the criteria that determine the optimum rate and why they happen to churn out the answer that the optimum growth rate is zero.

And if resources are not, after all, finite, then the whole of the "finite resources" argument collapses anyway. And, in reality, resources are not finite in any meaningful sense. In the first place, what is now regarded as a resource may not have been so in the past decades or centuries before the appropriate techniques for its exploitation or utilization had been developed. This applies, for example, to numerous materials now in use but never heard of a century ago, or to the minerals on the sea bed (e.g., "manganese nodules"), or even the sea water itself from which unlimited quantities of certain basic minerals can eventually be extracted.

In the second place, existing known reserves of many raw materials will never appear enough to last more than, say, twenty or fifty years at current rates of consumption, for the simple reason that it is rarely economically worthwhile to prospect for more supplies than seem to be salable, at prospective prices, given the costs of exploitation and so on. This has always been the case in the past, yet despite dramatic increases in consumption, supplies have more or less kept pace with demand. The "finite resource" argument fails to allow for the numerous ways that the economy and society react to changes in relative prices of a product, resulting from changes in the balance between supply and demand.

For example, a major United States study in 1929 concluded that known tin resources were only adequate to last the world ten years. Forty years later, the Club of Rome is worried because there is only enough to last us another fifteen years. At this rate, we shall have to wait another century before we have enough to last us another thirty years. Meanwhile, I suppose we shall just have to go on using up that ten years' supply that we had back in 1929.

And it is no good replying the demand is growing faster now than ever before, or that the whole scale of consumption of raw materials is incomparably greater than before. First, this proposition has also been true at almost any time over the past few thousand years, and yet economic growth continued. Hence, the truth of such propositions tells us nothing about whether the balance between supply and demand is likely to change one way or the other. And it is this that matters. In other words, it may well be that demand is growing much faster than ever before, or that the whole scale of consumption is incomparably higher, but the same applies to supply. For example, copper consumption rose about fortyfold during the nineteenth century and demand for copper was accelerating, around the turn of the century, for an annual average growth rate of about 3.3 percent per annum (over the whole century) to about 6.4 percent per annum during the period 1890 to 1910. Annual copper consumption had been only about 16,000 tons at the beginning of the century, and was about 700,000 tons at the end of it; i.e., incomparably greater. But known reserves at the end of the century were greater than at the beginning.

And the same applies to the postwar period. In 1946 world copper reserves amounted to only about 100 million tons. Since then the annual rate of copper consumption has trebled and we have used up 93 million tons. So there should be hardly any left. In fact, we now have about 300 million tons!

Of course, it may well be that we shall run out of some individual materials; and petroleum looks like one of the most likely candidates for exhaustion of supplies around the end of this century—if the price did not rise (or stay up at its recent level). But there are two points to be noted about this. First, insofar as the price does stay up at its recent level (i.e., in the $10 per barrel region) substantial economies in oil use will be made over the next few years, and there will also be a considerable development of substitutes for conventional sources, such as shale oil, oil from tar sands, and new ways of using coal reserves which are, of course, very many times greater than oil reserves (in terms of common energy units).

Secondly, even if the world did gradually run out of some resources it would not be a catastrophe. The point of my apparently well-known story about "Beckermonium" (the product named after my grandfather who failed to discover it in the nineteenth century) is that we manage perfectly well without it. In fact, if one thinks about it, we manage without infinitely more products than we manage with! In other words, it is absurd to imagine that if, say, nickel or petroleum had never been discovered, modern civilization would never have existed, and that the eventual disappearance of these or other products must, therefore, plunge us back into the Dark Ages.

The so-called "oil crisis," incidentally, also demonstrates the moral hypocrisy of the antigrowth lobby. For leaving aside their mistaken interpretation of the technical reasons for the recent sharp rise in the oil price (i.e., it was not because the world suddenly ran out of oil), it is striking that the antigrowth lobby has seized upon the rise in the price of oil as a fresh argument for abandoning economic growth and for rethinking our basic values and so on. After all, over the past two or three years the economies of many of the poorer countries of the world, such as India, have been hit badly by the sharp rise in the price of wheat. Of course, this only means a greater threat of starvation for a few more million people in backward countries a long way away. That does not, apparently, provoke the men of spiritual and moral sensibility to righteous indignation about the values of the growth-oriented society as much as does a rise in the price of gasoline for our automobiles!

The same muddled thinking is behind the view that mankind has some moral duty to preserve the world's environment or supplies of materials. For this view contrasts strangely with the antigrowth lobby's attack on materialism. After all, copper, oil, and so on are just material objects, and it is difficult to see what moral duty we have to preserve indefinitely the copper species from extinction.

Nor do I believe that we have any overriding moral duty to preserve any particular animal species from extinction. After all, thousands of animal species have become extinct over the ages, without any intervention by mankind. Nobody really loses any sleep over the fact that one cannot now see a live dinosaur. How many of the people who make a fuss about the danger that the tiger species may disappear even bother to go to a zoo to look at one? And what about the web-footed Beckermanipus, which has been extinct for about a million years. . . .

In fact, I am not even sure that the extinction of the human race would matter. The bulk of humanity leads lives full of suffering, sorrow, cruelty, poverty, frustration, and loneliness. One should not assume that because nearly everybody has a natural animal instinct to cling to life they can be said, in any meaningful sense, to be better off alive than if they had never been born. Religious motivations apart, it is arguable that since, by and large (and present company excepted, of course), the human race stinks, the sooner it is extinct the better. . . .

Whilst economic growth alone may never provide a simple means of solving any of these problems, and it may well be that, by its very nature, human society will always create insoluble problems of one kind or another, the absence of economic growth will only make our present problems a lot worse.

Notes

1. Jonathan Cape, London. The U.S.A. edition, under the title "*Two Cheers for the Affluent Society,*" was published by the St. Martins Press in the fall of 1974.
2. The Club of Rome is an informal international organization of educators, scientists, economists, and others which investigates what it conceives to be the overriding problems of mankind. Its study, "The Limits to Growth," has become the bible of no-growth advocates (Potomac Associates, 1707 L Street, N.W., Washington, D.C., $2.75). The study assembled data on known reserves of resources and asked a computer what would happen if demand continued to grow exponentially. Of course, the computer replied everything would break down. The theory of "Beckermonium" lampoons this. Since the author's grandfather failed to discover "Beckermonium" by the mid-1800's, the world has had no supplies of it at all. Consequently, if the Club's equations are followed, the world should have come to a halt many years ago. "Beckermonium's" foundation is that the things man has not yet discovered are far more numerous and of greater importance than what has been discovered. (Editor's of *Public Utilities Fortnightly* Note.)

Ethics and Ecology

William T. Blackstone*

Much has been said about the right to a decent or livable environment. In his 22 January 1970 state of the union address, President Nixon stated: "The great question of the seventies is, shall we surrender to our surroundings, or shall we make our peace with Nature and begin to make the reparations for the damage we have done to our air, our land, and our water? . . . Clean air, clean water, open spaces—these would once again be the birthright of every American; if we act now, they can be." It seems, though, that use of the term *right* by President Nixon, under the rubric of a "birthright" to a decent environment, is not a strict sense of the term. That is, he does not use this term to indicate that one has or should have either a legal right or a moral right to a decent environment. Rather he is pointing to the fact that in the past our environmental resources have been so abundant that all Americans did in fact inherit a livable environment, and it would be *desirable* that this state of affairs again be the case. Pollution and the exploitation of our environment is precluding this kind of inheritance.

Few would challenge the desirability of such a state of affairs or of such a "birthright." What we want to ask is whether the right to a decent environment can or ought to be considered a right in a stricter sense, either in a legal or moral sense. In contrast to a merely desirable state of affairs, a right entails a correlative duty or obligation on the part of someone or some group to accord one a certain mode of treatment or to act in a certain way.[1] Desirable states of affairs do not entail such correlative duties or obligations.

The Right to a Livable Environment as a Human Right

Let us first ask whether the right to a livable environment can properly be considered to be a human right. For the purposes of this paper, however, I want to avoid raising the more general question of whether there are any human rights at all. Some philosophers do deny that any human rights exist.[2] In two recent papers I have argued that human rights do exist (even though such rights may properly be overridden on occasion by other morally relevant reasons) and that they are universal and inalienable (although the actual exercise of such rights on a given occasion is alienable).[3] My argument for the existence of universal human rights rests, in the final analysis, on a theory of what it means to be human, which specifies the capacities for rationality and freedom as essential, and on the fact that there are no relevant grounds for excluding any human from the opportunity to develop and fulfill his capacities (rationality and freedom) as a human.

If the right to a livable environment were seen as a basic and inalienable human right, this could be a valuable tool (both inside and outside of legalistic frameworks) for solving some of our environmental problems, both on a national and on an international basis. Are there any philosophical and conceptual difficulties in treating this right as an inalienable human right? Traditionally we have not looked upon the right to a decent environment as a human right or as an inalienable right. Rather, inalienable human or natural rights have been conceived in somewhat different terms; equality, liberty, happiness, life, and property. However, might it not be possible to view the right to a livable environment as being entailed by, or as constitutive of, these basic human or natural rights recognized in our political tradition? If human rights, in other words, are those rights which each human possesses in virtue of the fact that he is human and in virtue of the fact that those rights are essential in permitting him to live a human life (that is, in permitting him to fulfill his capacities as a rational and free being), then might not the right to a decent environment be properly categorized as such a human right? Might it not be conceived as a right which has emerged as a result of changing environmental conditions and the impact of those conditions on the very possibility of human life and on the possibility of the realization of other rights such as liberty and equality? Let us explore how this might be the case.

Given man's great and increasing ability to manipulate the environment, and the devastating effect this is having, it is plain that new social institutions and new regulative agencies and procedures must be initiated on both national and international levels to make sure that the manipulation is in the public interest. It will be necessary, in other words, to restrict or stop some practices and the freedom to engage in those practices. Some look upon such additional state planning, whether national or international, as unnecessary further intrusion on man's freedom. Freedom is, of course, one of our basic values, and few would deny that excessive state control of human action is to be avoided. But such restrictions on individual freedom now appear to be necessary in the interest of overall human welfare and the rights and freedoms of *all* men. Even John Locke with his stress on freedom as an inalienable right recognized that this right must be construed so that it is consistent with the equal right to freedom of others. The whole point of the state is to restrict unlicensed freedom and to provide the conditions for equality of rights for all. Thus it seems to be perfectly consistent with Locke's view and, in general, with the views of the founding fathers of this country to restrict certain rights or freedoms when it can be shown that such restriction is necessary to insure the equal rights of others. If this is so, it has very important implications for the rights to freedom and to property. These rights, perhaps properly seen as inalienable (though this is a controversial philosophical question), are not properly seen as unlimited or unrestricted. When values which we hold dear conflict (for example, individual or group freedom and the freedom of all, individual or group rights and the rights of all, and individual or group welfare and the welfare of the general public) something has to give; some priority must be established. In the case of the abuse and waste of environmental resources, less individual freedom and fewer individual rights for the sake of greater public welfare and equality and rights seem justified. What in the past had been properly regarded as freedoms and rights (given what seemed to be unlimited natural resources and no serious pollution problems) can no longer be so construed, at least not without additional restrictions. We must recognize both the need for such restrictions and the fact that none of our rights can be realized without a livable environment. Both public welfare and equality of rights now require that natural resources not be used simply according to the whim and caprice of individuals or simply for personal profit. This is not to say that all property rights must be denied and that the state must own all productive property, as the Marxist argues. It is to insist that those rights be qualified or restricted in the light of new ecological data and in the interest of the freedom, rights, and welfare of all.

The answer then to the question, Is the right to a livable environment a human right? is yes. Each person has this right *qua* being human and because a livable environment is essential for one to fulfill his human capacities. And given the danger to our environment today and hence the danger to the very possibility of human existence, access to a livable environment must be conceived as a right which imposes upon everyone a correlative moral obligation to respect.

The Right to a Livable Environment as a Legal Right

If the right to a decent environment is to be treated as a legal right, then obviously what is required is some sort of legal framework which gives this right a legal status. Such legal frameworks have been proposed. Sen. Gaylord Nelson, originator of Earth Day, proposed a Constitutional Amendment guaranteeing every American an inalienable right to a decent environment.[4] Others want to formulate an entire "environmental bill of rights" to assist in solving our pollution problems. Such a bill of rights or a constitutional revision would provide a legal framework for the enforcement of certain policies bearing on environmental issues. It would also involve the concept of "legal responsibility" for acts which violate those rights. Such legal responsibility is beginning to be enforced in the United States.

Others propose that the right to a decent environment also be a cardinal tenet of international law. Pollution is not merely a national problem but an international one. The population of the entire world is affected by it, and a body of international law, which includes the right to a decent environment and the accompanying policies to save and preserve our environmental resources, would be an even more effective tool than such a framework at the national level. Of course, one does not have to be reminded of the problems involved in establishing international law and in eliciting obedience to it. Conflicts between nations are still settled more by force than by law or persuasion. The record of the United Nations attests to this fact. In the case of international conflict over environmental interests and the use of the environment, the possibility of international legal resolution, at least at this stage of history, is somewhat remote; for the body of enforceable international law on this topic is meager indeed. This is not to deny that this is the direction in which we should (and must) move.

A good case can be made for the view that not all moral or human rights should be legal rights and that not all moral rules should be legal rules. It may be argued that any society which covers the whole spectrum of man's activities with legally enforceable rules minimizes his freedom and approaches totalitarianism. There is this danger. But just as we argued that certain traditional rights and freedoms are properly restricted in order to insure the equal rights and welfare of all, so also it can plausibly be argued that the human right to a livable environment should become a legal one in order to assure that it is properly respected. Given the magnitude of the present dangers to the environment and to the welfare of all humans, and the ingrained habits and rules, or lack of rules, which permit continued waste, pollution, and destruction of our environmental resources, the legalized status of the right to a livable environment seems both desirable and necessary.

It is essential that government step in to prevent the potentially dire consequences of industrial pollution and the waste of environmental resources. Such government regulations need not mean the death of the free enterprise system. The right to private property can be made compatible with the right to a livable environment, for if uniform antipollution laws were applied to all industries, then both competition and private ownership could surely continue. But they would continue within a quite different set of rules and attitudes toward the environment. This extension of government would not be equivalent to totalitarianism. In fact it is necessary to insure equality of rights and freedom, which is essential to a democracy.

Ecology and Economic Rights

We suggested above that it is necessary to qualify or restrict economic or property rights in the light of new ecological data and in the interest of the freedom, rights, and welfare of all. In part, this suggested restriction is predicated on the assumption that we cannot expect private business to provide solutions to the multiple pollution problems for which they themselves are responsible. Some companies have taken measures to limit the polluting effect of their operations, and this is an important move. But we are deluding ourselves if we think that private business can function as its own pollution police. This is so for several reasons: the primary objective of private business is economic profit. Stockholders do not ask of a company, "Have you polluted the environment and lowered the quality of the environment for the general public and for future generations?" Rather they ask, "How high is the annual dividend and how much higher is it than the year before?" One can hardly expect organizations whose basic norm is economic profit to be concerned in any great depth with the long-range effects of their operations upon society and future generations or concerned with the hidden cost of their operations in terms of environmental quality to society as a whole. Second, within a free enterprise system companies compete to produce what the public wants at the lowest possible cost. Such competition would preclude the spending of adequate funds to prevent environmental pollution, since this would add tremendously to the cost of the product—unless all other companies would also conform to such antipollution policies. But in a free enterprise economy such policies are not likely to be self-imposed by businessmen. Third, the basic response of the free enterprise system to our economic problems is that we must have greater economic growth or an increase in gross national product. But such growth many ecologists look upon with great alarm, for it can have devastating long-range effects upon our environment. Many of the products of uncontrolled growth are based on artificial needs and actually detract from, rather than contribute to, the quality of our lives. A stationary economy, some economists and ecologists suggest, may well be best for the quality of man's environment and of his life in the long run. Higher GNP does not automatically result in an increase in social well-being, and it should not be used as a measuring rod for assessing economic welfare. This becomes clear when one realizes that the GNP

> aggregates the dollar value of all goods and services produced—the ciga-
> rettes as well as the medical treatment of lung cancer, the petroleum from
> offshore wells as well as the detergents required to clean up after oil spills,
> the electrical energy produced and the medical and cleaning bills resulting
> from the air-pollution fuel used for generating the electricity. The GNP
> allows no deduction for negative production, such as lives lost from unsafe
> cars or environmental destruction perpetrated by telephone, electric and gas
> utilities, lumber companies, and speculative builders.[5]

To many persons, of course, this kind of talk is not only blasphemy but subversive. This is especially true when it is extended in the direction of additional controls over corporate capitalism. (Some ecologists and economists go further and challenge whether corporate capitalism can accommodate a stationary state and still retain its major features.[6]) The fact of the matter is that the ecological attitude forces one to reconsider a host of values which have been held dear in the past, and it forces one to reconsider the appropriateness of the social and economic systems which embodied and implemented those values. Given the crisis of our environment, there must be certain fundamental changes in attitudes toward nature, man's use of nature, and man himself. Such changes in attitudes undoubtedly will have far-reaching implications for the institutions of private property and private enterprise and the values embodied in these institutions. Given the crisis we can no longer look upon water and air as free commodities to be exploited at will. Nor can the private ownership of land be seen as a lease to use that land in any way which conforms merely to the personal desires of the owner. In other words, the environmental crisis is forcing us to challenge what had in the past been taken to be certain basic rights of man or at least to restrict those rights. And it is forcing us to challenge institutions which embodied those rights.

Ethics and Technology

I have been discussing the relationship of ecology to ethics and to a theory of rights. Up to this point I have not specifically discussed the relation of technology to ethics, although it is plain that technology and its development is responsible for most of our pollution problems. This topic deserves separate treatment, but I do want to briefly relate it to the thesis of this work.

It is well known that new technology sometimes complicates our ethical lives and our ethical decisions. Whether the invention is the wheel or a contraceptive pill, new technology always opens up new possibilities for human relationships and for society, for good and ill. The pill, for example, is revolutionizing sexual morality, for its use can preclude many of the bad consequences normally attendant upon premarital intercourse. *Some* of the strongest arguments against premarital sex have been shot down by this bit of technology (though certainly not all of them). The fact that the use of the pill can prevent unwanted pregnancy does not make premarital sexual intercourse morally right, nor does it make it wrong. The pill is morally neutral, but its existence does change in part the moral base of the decision to engage in premarital sex. In the same way, technology at least in principle can be neutral—neither necessarily good nor bad in its impact on other aspects of the environment. Unfortunately, much of it is bad—very bad. But technology can be meshed with an ecological attitude to the benefit of man and his environment.

I am not suggesting that the answer to technology which has bad environmental effects is necessarily more technology. We tend too readily to assume that new technological developments will always solve man's problems. But this is simply not the case. One technological innovation often seems to breed a half-dozen additional ones which themselves create more environmental problems. We certainly do not solve pollution problems, for example, by changing from power plants fueled by coal to power plants fueled by nuclear energy, if radioactive waste from the latter is worse than pollution from the former. Perhaps part of the answer to pollution problems is less technology. There is surely no real hope of returning to nature (whatever that means) or of stopping *all* technological and scientific development, as some advocate. Even if it could be done, this would be too extreme a move. The answer is not to stop technology, but to guide it toward proper ends, and to set up standards of antipollution to which all technological devices must conform. Technology has been and can be used to destroy and pollute an environment, but it can also be used to save and beautify it.

Notes

1. This is a dogmatic assertion in this context. I am aware that some philosophers deny that rights and duties are correlative. Strictly interpreted this correlativity thesis is false, I believe. There are duties for which there are no correlative rights. But space does not permit discussion of this question here.
2. See Kai Nielsen's, "Skepticism and Human Rights," *Monist*, 52, no. 4 (1968): 571–594.
3. See my "Equality and Human Rights," *Monist*, 52, no. 4 (1968): 616–639; and my "Human Rights and Human Dignity," in Laszlo and Gotesky, eds., *Human Dignity*.
4. *Newsweek*, 4 May 1970, p. 26.
5. See Melville J. Ulmer, "More Than Marxist," *New Republic*, 26 December 1970, p. 14.
6. See Murdock and Connell, "All about Ecology," *Center Magazine*, 3, no. 1 (January–February 1970): 63.

The Place of Nonhumans in Environmental Issues

Peter Singer

Not for Humans Only

When we humans change the environment in which we live, we often harm ourselves. If we discharge cadmium into a bay and eat shellfish from that bay, we become ill and may die. When our industries and automobiles pour noxious fumes into the atmosphere, we find a displeasing smell in the air, the long-term results of which may be every bit as deadly as cadmium poisoning. The harm that humans do the environment, however, does not rebound solely, or even chiefly, on humans. It is nonhumans who bear the most direct burden of human interference with nature.

By "nonhumans" I mean to refer to all living things other than human beings, though for reasons to be given later, it is with nonhuman animals, rather than plants, that I am chiefly concerned. It is also important, in the context of environmental issues, to note that living things may be regarded either collectively or as individuals. In debates about the environment the most important way of regarding living things collectively has been to regard them as species. Thus, when environmentalists worry about the future of the blue whale, they usually are thinking of the blue whale as a species, rather than of individual blue whales. But this is not, of course, the only way in which one can think of blue whales, or other animals, and one of the topics I shall discuss is whether we should be concerned about what we are doing to the environment primarily insofar as it threatens entire species of nonhumans, or primarily insofar as it affects individual nonhuman animals.

The general question, then, is how the effects of our actions on the environment of nonhuman beings should figure in our deliberations about what we ought to do. There is an unlimited variety of contexts in which this issue could arise. To take just one: Suppose that it is considered necessary to build a new power station, and there are two sites, A and B, under consideration. In most respects the sites are equally suitable, but building the power station on site A would be more expensive because the greater depth of shifting soil at that site will require deeper foundations; on the other hand to build on site B will destroy a favored breeding ground for thousands of wildfowl. Should the presence of the wildfowl enter into the decision as to where to build? And if so, in what manner should it enter, and how heavily should it weigh?

In a case like this the effects of our actions on nonhuman animals could be taken into account in two quite different ways: directly, giving the lives and welfare of nonhuman animals an intrinsic significance which must count in any

From P. Singer, "The Place of Nonhumans in Environmental Issues," in *Ethics and Problems of the 21st Century,* eds. K. E. Goodpaster and K. M. Sayre (Notre Dame, Ind.: University of Notre Dame Press, 1979), pp. 191–198. Reprinted by permission.

moral calculation; or indirectly, so that the effects of our actions on nonhumans are morally significant only if they have consequences for humans. . . .

The view that the effects of our actions on other animals has no direct moral significance is not as likely to be openly advocated today as it was in the past; yet it is likely to be accepted implicitly and acted upon. When planners perform cost-benefit studies on new projects, the costs and benefits are costs and benefits for human beings only. This does not mean that the impact of the power station or highway on wildlife is ignored altogether, but it is included only indirectly. That a new reservoir would drown a valley teeming with wildlife is taken into account only under some such heading as the value of the facilities for recreation that the valley affords. In calculating this value, the cost-benefit study will be neutral between forms of recreation like hunting and shooting and those like bird watching and bush walking—in fact hunting and shooting are likely to contribute more to the benefit side of the calculations because larger sums of money are spent on them, and they therefore benefit manufacturers and retailers of firearms as well as the hunters and shooters themselves. The suffering experienced by the animals whose habitat is flooded is not reckoned into the costs of the operation; nor is the recreational value obtained by the hunters and shooters offset by the cost to the animals that their recreation involves.

Despite its venerable origins, the view that the effects of our actions on nonhuman animals have no intrinsic moral significance can be shown to be arbitrary and morally indefensible. If a being suffers, the fact that it is not a member of our own species cannot be a moral reason for failing to take its suffering into account. This becomes obvious if we consider the analogous attempt by white slaveowners to deny consideration to the interests of blacks. These white racists limited their moral concern to their own race, so the suffering of a black did not have the same moral significance as the suffering of a white. We now recognize that in doing so they were making an arbitrary distinction, and that the existence of suffering, rather than the race of the sufferer, is what is really morally significant. The point remains true if "species" is substituted for "race." The logic of racism and the logic of the position we have been discussing, which I have elsewhere referred to as "speciesism," are indistinguishable; and if we reject the former then consistency demands that we reject the latter too.[1]

It should be clearly understood that the rejection of speciesism does not imply that the different species are in fact equal in respect of such characteristics as intelligence, physical strength, ability to communicate, capacity to suffer, ability to damage the environment, or anything else. After all, the moral principle of human equality cannot be taken as implying that all humans are equal in these respects either—if it did, we would have to give up the idea of human equality. That one being is more intelligent than another does not entitle him to enslave, exploit, or disregard the interests of the less intelligent being. The moral basis of equality among humans is not equality in fact, but the principle of equal consideration of interests, and it is this principle that, in consistency, must be extended to any nonhumans who have interests.

There may be some doubt about whether any nonhuman beings have interests. This doubt may arise because of uncertainty about what it is to have an interest, or because of uncertainty about the nature of some nonhuman beings. So far as the concept of "interest" is the cause of doubt, I take the view that only a being with subjective experiences, such as the experience of pleasure or the experience of pain, can have interests in the full sense of the term; and that any being with such experiences does have at least one interest, namely, the interest in experiencing pleasure and avoiding pain. Thus consciousness, or the capacity for subjective experience, is both a necessary and a sufficient condition for having an interest. While there may be a loose sense of the term in which we can say that it is in the interests of a tree to be watered, this attenuated sense of the term is not the sense covered by the principle of equal consideration of interests. All we mean when we say that it is in the interests of a tree to be watered is that the tree needs water if it is to continue to live and grow normally; if we regard this as evidence that the tree has interests, we might almost as well say that it is in the interests of a car to be lubricated regularly because the car needs lubrication if it is to run properly. In neither case can we really mean (unless we impute consciousness to trees or cars) that the tree or car has any preference about the matter.

The remaining doubt about whether nonhuman beings have interests is, then, a doubt about whether nonhuman beings have subjective experiences like the experience of pain. I have argued elsewhere that the commonsense view that birds and mammals feel pain is well founded,[2] but more serious doubts arise as we move down the evolutionary scale. Vertebrate animals have nervous systems broadly similar to our own and behave in ways that resemble our own pain behavior when subjected to stimuli that we would find painful; so the inference that vertebrates are capable of feeling pain is a reasonable one, though not as strong as it is if limited to mammals and birds. When we go beyond vertebrates to insects, crustaceans, mollusks and so on, the existence of subjective states becomes more dubious, and with very simple organisms it is difficult to believe that they could be conscious. As for plants, though there have been sensational claims that plants are not only conscious, but even psychic, there is no hard evidence that supports even the more modest claim.[3]

The boundary of beings who may be taken as having interests is therefore not an abrupt boundary, but a broad range in which the assumption that the being has interests shifts from being so strong as to be virtually certain to being so weak as to be highly improbable. The principle of equal consideration of interests must be applied with this in mind, so that where there is a clash between a virtually certain interest and a highly doubtful one, it is the virtually certain interest that ought to prevail.

In this manner our moral concern ought to extend to all beings who have interests. Unlike race or species, this boundary does not arbitrarily exclude any being; indeed it can truly be said that it excludes nothing at all, not even "the most contemptible clod of earth" from equal consideration of interests—for full consideration of no interests still results in no weight being given to whatever was considered, just as multiplying zero by a million still results in zero.[4]

Giving equal consideration to the interests of two different beings does not mean treating them alike or holding their lives to be of equal value. We may recognize that the interests of one being are greater than those of another, and equal consideration will then lead us to sacrifice the being with lesser interests, if one or the other must be sacrificed. For instance, if for some reason a choice has to be made between saving the life of a normal human being and that of a dog, we might well decide to save the human because he, with his greater awareness of what is going to happen, will suffer more before he dies; we may also take into account the likelihood that it is the family and friends of the human who will suffer more; and finally, it would be the human who had the greater potential for future happiness. This decision would be in accordance with the principle of equal consideration of interests, for the interests of the dog get the same consideration as those of the human, and the loss to the dog is not discounted because the dog is not a member of our species. The outcome is as it is because the balance of interests favors the human. In a different situation—say, if the human were grossly mentally defective and without family or anyone else who would grieve for it—the balance of interests might favor the nonhuman.[5]

The more positive side of the principle of equal consideration is this: where interests are equal, they must be given equal weight. So where human and nonhuman animals share an interest—as in the case of the interest in avoiding physical pain—we must give as much weight to violations of the interest of the nonhumans as we do to similar violations of the human's interest. This does not mean, of course, that it is as bad to hit a horse with a stick as it is to hit a human being, for the same blow would cause less pain to the animal with the tougher skin. The principle holds between similar amounts of felt pain, and what this is will vary from case to case.

It may be objected that we cannot tell exactly how much pain another animal is suffering, and that therefore the principle is impossible to apply. While I do not deny the difficulty and even, so far as precise measurement is concerned, the impossibility of comparing the subjective experiences of members of different species, I do not think that the problem is different in kind from the problem of comparing the subjective experiences of two members of our own species. Yet this is something we do all the time, for instance when we judge that a wealthy person will suffer less by being taxed at a higher rate than a poor person will gain from the welfare benefits paid for by the tax; or when we decide to take our two children to the beach instead of to a fair, because although the older one would prefer the fair, the younger one has a stronger preference the other way. These comparisons may be very rough, but since there is nothing better, we must use them; it would be irrational to refuse to do so simply because they are rough. Moreover, rough as they are, there are many situations in which we can be reasonably sure which way the balance of interests lies. While a difference of species may make comparisons rougher still, the basic problem is the same, and the comparisons are still often good enough to use, in the absence of anything more precise. . . .

The difficulty of making the required comparison will mean that the application of this conclusion is controversial in many cases, but there will be some situations in which it is clear enough. Take, for instance, the wholesale poisoning of animals that is euphemistically known as "pest control." The authorities who conduct these campaigns give no consideration to the suffering they inflict on the "pests," and invariably use the method of slaughter they believe to be cheapest and most effective. The result is that hundreds of millions of rabbits have died agonizing deaths from the artificially introduced disease, myxomatosis, or from poisons like "ten-eighty"; coyotes and other wild dogs have died painfully from cyanide poisoning; and all manner of wild animals have endured days of thirst, hunger, and fear with a mangled limb caught in a leg-hold trap.[6] Granting, for the sake of argument, the necessity for pest control—though this has rightly been questioned—the fact remains that no serious attempts have been made to introduce alternative means of control and thereby reduce the incalculable amount of suffering caused by present methods. It would not, presumably, be beyond modern science to produce a substance which, when eaten by rabbits or coyotes, produced sterility instead of a drawn-out death. Such methods might be more expensive, but can anyone doubt that if a similar amount of human suffering were at stake, the expense would be borne?

Another clear instance in which the principle of equal consideration of interests would indicate methods different from those presently used is in the timber industry. There are two basic methods of obtaining timber from forests. One is to cut only selected mature or dead trees, leaving the forest substantially intact. The other, known as clear-cutting, involves chopping down everything that grows in a given area, and then reseeding. Obviously when a large area is clear-cut, wild animals find their whole living area destroyed in a few days, whereas selected felling makes a relatively minor disturbance. But clear-cutting is cheaper, and timber companies therefore use this method and will continue to do so unless forced to do otherwise. . . .[7]

It is not merely the act of killing that indicates what we are ready to do to other species in order to gratify our tastes. The suffering we inflict on the animals while they are alive is perhaps an even clearer indication of our speciesism than the fact that we are prepared to kill them.[8] In order to have meat on the table at a price that people can afford, our society tolerates methods of meat production that confine sentient animals in cramped, unsuitable conditions for the entire durations of their lives. Animals are treated like machines that convert fodder into flesh, and any innovation that results in a higher "conversion ratio" is liable to be adopted. As one authority on the subject has said, "cruelty is acknowledged only when profitability ceases."[9] So hens are crowded four or five to a cage with a floor area of twenty inches by eighteen inches, or around the size of a single page of the *New York Times*. The cages have wire floors, since this reduces cleaning costs, though wire is unsuitable for the hens' feet; the floors slope, since this makes the eggs roll down for easy collection, although this makes it difficult for the hens to rest comfortably. In these conditions all the birds' natural instincts are thwarted: They cannot stretch their wings fully, walk freely, dust-bathe, scratch the ground, or build a nest. Although they have never known other conditions, observers have noticed that the birds vainly try to perform these actions. Frustrated at their inability to do so, they often develop what farmers call "vices," and peck each other to death. To prevent this, the beaks of young birds are often cut off.

This kind of treatment is not limited to poultry. Pigs are now also being reared in cages inside sheds. These animals are comparable to dogs in intelligence, and need a varied, stimulating environment if they are not to suffer from stress and boredom. Anyone who kept a dog in the way in which pigs are frequently kept would be liable to prosecution, in England at least, but because our interest in exploiting pigs is greater than our interest in exploiting dogs, we object to cruelty to dogs while consuming the produce of cruelty to pigs. Of the other animals, the condition of veal calves is perhaps worst of all, since these animals are so closely confined that they cannot even turn around or get up and lie down freely. In this way they do not develop unpalatable muscle. They are also made anaemic and kept short of roughage, to keep their flesh pale, since white veal fetches a higher price; as a result they develop a craving for iron and roughage, and have been observed to gnaw wood off the sides of their stalls, and lick greedily at any rusty hinge that is within reach.

Since, as I have said, none of these practices cater to anything more than our pleasures of taste, our practice of rearing and killing other animals in order to eat them is a clear instance of the sacrifice of the most important interests of other beings in order to satisfy trivial interests of our own. To avoid speciesism we must stop this practice, and each of us has a moral obligation to cease supporting the practice. Our custom is all the support that the meat industry needs. The decision to cease giving it that support may be difficult, but it is no more difficult than it would have been for a white Southerner to go against the traditions of his society and free his slaves; if we do not change our dietary habits, how can we censure those slaveholders who would not change their own way of living?

Notes

1. For a fuller statement of this argument, see my *Animal Liberation* (New York: A New York Review Book, 1975), especially ch. 1.
2. *Ibid.*
3. See, for instance, the comments by Arthur Galston in *Natural History,* 83, no. 3 (March 1974): 18, on the "evidence" cited in such books as *The Secret Life of Plants.*
4. The idea that we would logically have to consider "the most contemptible clod of earth" as having rights was suggested by Thomas Taylor, the Cambridge Neo-Platonist, in a pamphlet he published anonymously, entitled *A Vindication of the Rights of Brutes* (London,

1792) which appears to be a satirical refutation of the attribution of rights to women by Mary Wollstonecroft in her *Vindication of the Rights of Women* (London, 1792). Logically, Taylor was no doubt correct, but he neglected to specify just what interests such contemptible clods of earth have.

5. Singer, *Animal Liberation*, pp. 20–23.

6. See J. Olsen, *Slaughter the Animals, Poison the Earth* (New York: Simon and Schuster, 1971), especially pp. 153–164.

7. See R. and V. Routley, *The Fight for the Forests* (Canberra: Australian National University Press, 1974), for a thoroughly documented indictment of clear-cutting in Australia; and for a recent report of the controversy about clear-cutting in America, see *Time*, May 17, 1976.

8. Although one might think that killing a being is obviously the ultimate wrong one can do to it, I think that the infliction of suffering is a clearer indication of speciesism because it might be argued that at least part of what is wrong with killing a human is that most humans are conscious of their existence over time, and have desires and purposes that extend into the future—see, for instance, M. Tooley, "Abortion and Infanticide," *Philosophy and Public Affairs*, vol. 2, no. 1 (1972). Of course, if one took this view one would have to hold—as Tooley does—that killing a human infant or mental defective is not in itself wrong, and is less serious than killing certain higher mammals that probably do have a sense of their own existence over time.

9. Ruth Harrison, *Animal Machines* (Stuart, London, 1964). This book provides an eye-opening account of intensive farming methods for those unfamiliar with the subject.

Conservatives Consider the Crushing Cost of Environmental Extremism
Robert W. Lee*

There is certainly nothing wrong with environmentalism, but there is a great deal wrong with the sort of "environmentalism" to which our nation has been subjected in recent years. It is one thing to strive to be good stewards of the land, air, and water through the application of sensible, cost-effective policies based on marketplace and common-law incentives for polluters to "clean up their act." It is quite another to impose on industry and individuals the sort of draconian, often counterproductive, schemes which have become a hallmark of federal intervention in the field of environmentalism since 1970.

There is substantial doubt whether federal policies have resulted in a net improvement in the quality of the national environment, but there is no question at all that they have led to a massive increase in the size and expense of government and its control of the private sector, while seriously encroaching on the personal freedom of individual Americans. Some observers believe such results were the primary objectives from the start, with scare stories about environment being cranked up as an excuse to achieve them.

Gary Allen reported in *American Opinion* for May 1970, more than thirteen years ago: "Through the use of highly emotional rhetoric, and by playing upon fears of impending social and environmental chaos, the Left is hoping to convert sincere and legitimate concern over the quality of our environment into acceptance of government control of that environment. . . . The objective is federal control of the environment in which we all must live." Which might explain why, no matter what the immediate ecological grievance has been, private property and individual enterprise have always been branded the culprits while more government was offered as the solution. Every new regulation has in some way controlled and manipulated one or more aspects of our social and economic life while decreasing our individual freedom. Gary Allen was, alas, right on target.

The average American has paid for all of this government regulation as a *taxpayer* (to finance the bureaucracy itself) and as a *consumer* (since the cost of regulations imposed by the bureaucracy boosted the price of nearly every commodity). In addition, there have been such less-obvious costs as those suffered when plans to build factories and other important projects were delayed or abandoned, along with the jobs they would have created, after government red tape made such endeavors unbearably frustrating and financially unrewarding.

While it is impossible to settle an exact figure for the total financial burden which American industry has suffered from overzealous, often malicious, environmentalism during the past decade, the direct cost undoubtedly exceeds half a trillion dollars, while the indirect cost may be three or four times that amount. One study released in the late Seventies concluded that pollution controls alone had already cost our country approximately ten percent of its industrial capacity. Another study by a prominent accounting firm, evaluating the impact of regulation on forty-eight major companies during 1977, had discovered: "The complexities and volume of EPA [*Environmental Protection Agency*] regulations made it necessary for [*the 48*] companies to incur $36 million [*in expenses*] . . . solely to maintain internal environmental programs and to keep current with existing regulations and practices and to prepare for new regulations." Needless to say, those millions of dollars were *not* devoted to increased economic productivity, job creation, new plants and equipment.

In 1980, direct environmental controls added approximately $400 to the annual expenses of a family of four. That figure is predicted to reach $638 within five years. The Council on Environmental Quality speculates that the cost of administering the Clean Air Act will total $300 billion for the period 1979 through 1988. And, no less a "Liberal" than the late Nelson Rockefeller estimated the cost of implementing the Water Pollution Control Act at *three trillion dollars*. And each new car is saddled with close to $700 in antipollution paraphernalia, while homes cost two to three thousand dollars more due to direct federal, state, and local environmental regulations.

The increased cost of local utilities is also attributable in large part to regulatory excesses, as indicated by this "Dear Customer" explanation sent to those serviced by Utah Power and Light Company in the spring of 1978: "Through 1977, we spent a total of $140,000,000 for pollution control equipment. In the next five years, we'll spend $190,000,000! More in five years than in all the other years we've been in business! About 25 percent of all of the dollars in our generating plant construction program go for this purpose." The situation is typical for utilities nationwide.

And, a key factor helping to bring our steel industry to its knees has been the enormous cost of meeting pristine environmental standards. For instance, it may be relatively cost-effective to remove, say, 95 percent of pollutants from industrial exhaust, but it costs billions to remove each percentage point thereafter. One study commissioned by the E.P.A. itself revealed that it costs twenty-six cents per kilogram to eliminate ninety percent of the pollutants from making carbon steel, but $4.98 to remove ninety-seven percent and $32.20 to get rid of ninety-nine percent. On one occasion, the E.P.A. approved regulations prohibiting steel plants from emitting "any visible emissions" whatsoever, despite the fact that it cost $1200 per pound per hour to remove the first 99 percent of such visible emissions, and a mind-boggling $400,000 per pound per hour to remove that last one percent.

Scores of similar statistics, from dozens of other industries, could be cited. And remember, we are considering only the cost of *environmental* regulation, which is but a fraction of the total regulatory burden that is estimated to exceed $135 billion annually. In many (perhaps most) cases, the cost of fighting pollution the federal way exceeds the cost of the damage supposedly inflicted by the pollution being fought.

It is important to keep some sort of perspective regarding the extent of man-made pollution. For instance, during all of his earthly existence, man has yet to equal the particulate and noxious-gas levels of the combined volcanic eruptions on Krakatoa, Indonesia (1883), Katmai, Alaska (1912), and Hekla, Iceland (1947). Indeed, nature contributes approximately 60 percent of all particulates in the atmosphere, 65 percent of the sulfur dioxide, 70 percent of the hydrocarbons, 93 percent of the carbon monoxide, 90 percent of the ozone, and 99 percent of the nitrogen oxides. While environmentalists become frenzied about the ten million tons of man-made pollutants injected into the atmosphere by Americans each year, they largely ignore the 1.6 *billion* tons of methane gas emitted each year by swamps, and the 170 million tons of hydrocarbons released annually by forests and other forms of vegetation. On one occasion, officials of a major city on the West Coast became agitated about the extent to which the disposal of human waste might be "polluting" the Pacific Ocean, oblivious to the fact that similar waste from gray whales, or even schools of anchovies, far exceed any such contribution which residents of the city could conceivably make.

Although trees and other greeneries contribute some 3.5 billion tons of carbon monoxide to the atmosphere each year, compared to mankind's 270 million tons, environmentalists continually attack the automobile as a deadly polluter. Professor E. J. Mishan of the London School of Economics, for instance, once described the private automobile as a disaster for the human race which pollutes air, clogs streets, destroys natural beauty, etc., etc. Which is verbal pollution of the worst sort. As Professor Hans Sennholz has noted in rebuttal, "The automobile has meant high standards of living, great individual mobility and productivity, and access to the countryside for recreation and enjoyment. In rural America it is the only means of transportation that assures employment and income. Without it, the countryside would surely be depopulated and our cities far more congested than now."

A balanced perspective of the pollution picture could lead to reasonable, cost-effective programs to moderate man-made pollution. Unfortunately, the environmental field is today dominated by special interests and advocates of big government who willfully distort and exaggerate the problem in order to justify their efforts to undermine the Free Market economic system and increase government control over our lives.

Consider, for instance, the National Environmental Policy Act of 1969, and how it came about. On January 28, 1969, a Union Oil Company well on a lease in the Santa Barbara Channel blew out. Within ten days, it discharged 235,000 gallons of oil into the Pacific Ocean, fouled thirty miles of beach, and damaged some boats and wildlife. Environmentalist organizations and radical politicians, bolstered by the "Liberal" news media, labeled the event an ecological catastrophe. *Life* magazine reported that the Channel was "a sea gone dead." And news commentators routinely referred to the "hundreds of thousands" of birds killed by the blowout. Yet, it was subsequently established that only "an estimated 600 birds were affected by the oil." (*Energy Crisis In America;* Washington, *Congressional Quarterly,* 1973) And, when all the facts were in, there had been no increase in mortality among whales or seals and no long-lasting ill effects on other animal or vegetable life. Nature accomplished most of the cleanup (and man the rest) in short order.

Yet, in the wake of the Santa Barbara oil spill, and the wildly exaggerated reports about the damage it had supposedly inflicted on the environment, our fickle Congress approved the National Environmental Policy Act in December of that year.

The new law contained a number of loosely worded provisions which sounded humanitarian and harmless to most observers. But it gave environmental activists the legal foothold they needed to make court challenges against business activities nationwide. Indeed, this new law defined "environment" in such vague terms that the courts had virtually unlimited authority to nullify or modify at whim various laws passed by Congress, actions by Executive agencies, etc. During the previous 182 years of our history (from 1789 to 1971), the Supreme Court had heard only four cases relating to the environment, all of which had been brought by state governments. But, by the end of 1971, more than 160 cases based on the 1969 Act were pending in federal courts, nearly all of which were filed by activist lawyers representing radical environmentalist groups. As author Dan Smoot noted in his best-selling book *The Business End of Government* (Boston, Western Islands, 1973): "Within eighteen months that law had been responsible for stopping the building of nuclear power plants; for preventing oil exploration on the outer-continental shelf; for sharply curtailing oil production in off-shore fields already explored and tapped; for prohibiting the building of the Alaska pipeline; for preventing the leasing of oil-shale lands; and for reducing the production of coal."

The impact of the 1969 law on construction of the Alaska pipeline is especially revealing as an example of the high price we pay for environmental extremism. On September 11, 1969, Alaska auctioned off $900 million worth of oil leases to a consortium of oil companies anxious to develop an 800-mile pipeline to tap the rich oil-reserves (estimated at ten billion barrels) of the Prudhoe Bay area of Alaska's North Slope. Originally, the consortium planned to spend $1 billion and have perhaps two million barrels of oil flowing daily within three years. But the National Environmental Policy Act was used as the basis for years of legal harassment which delayed the project for more than four years, assuring (among other things) that no Alaska oil was available when the energy crunch of 1973–1974 was inflicted on the nation.

It was in the midst of that "energy crisis" (November 13, 1973) that Congress, at long last, put an end to the obstruction by approving the pipeline project and banning further lawsuits on environmental grounds. The projected cost of the pipeline had been swollen by all of this to around $4 billion. Harassed every foot of the way, the project was completed within four years and oil began to flow on June 20, 1977.

Note that, had the pipeline been completed within a forty-three month time span following its instigation in 1969, it would have been carrying oil by the spring of 1973, in plenty of time to blunt the fuel shortage. The environmentalist "victory" in delaying the pipeline not only gave the American people memorably long gas lines and the many other inconveniences associated with the shortage, but forced us to pay an additional $25 billion to $30 billion in inflated oil prices to the bandits of O.P.E.C. as well. And, when all was said and done, *none* of the horror stories predicted for Alaska's flora and fauna which had been concocted to justify the delays (such as the claim that hot oil flowing through the pipeline would melt the permafrost) came to pass. The horror claims were an outright fraud.

The momentum ignited by the Santa Barbara oil spill eventually led to the first so-called Earth Day, an event organized by the radical and anticapitalist student activists associated with the ecology movement, as a mass protest against "destruction of the world's life-giving resources."

It was less than three months after Earth Day (July 9, 1970) that President Richard Nixon transmitted his "reorganization Plan Number 3" to Congress, announcing that he would create the Environmental Protection Agency as an umbrella agency to consolidate and administer federal antipollution programs. Congress concurred in the plan on October 2, 1970, and—following a sixty-day planning period—the E.P.A. formally began operating on December 2, 1970, with a Budget of $303 million and staff of 3860. My how Topsy has grown! For Fiscal Year 1983, the agency's budget was $3.7 *billion* and its staff equivalent to 10,925 full-time employees.

According to the American Legislative Exchange Council, the E.P.A. has spawned an average of ninety regulations each year since its inception. In some instances, the heavy-handed manner in which those edicts have been administered has itself discouraged advances in pollution control. As explained by Richard L. Stroup and John A. Baden of the Center for Political Economy and Natural Resources at Montana State University:

"An industry that develops a new technique for reducing harmful discharges may be unwilling to use it because it may lead to a tightening of emission standards for the entire industry. For example, the EPA discovered that cement plants were capable of filtering out significant levels of harmful particulate emissions. As a result, the agency imposed emission levels for cement plants that were more stringent than emission levels for electric power plants. In other words, electric power plants were allowed to pollute more. Angered by the supposed inequities sanctioned by the EPA, a Portland cement plant challenged the agency's rate structure in court. In denying the challenge, the court argued that if an industry can more effectively control emissions, it should be required to do so. Because of such cases, many critics accuse the EPA of penalizing innovation, leading to continued rather than reduced pollution levels." (*Natural Resources: Bureaucratic Myths and Environmental Management,* San Francisco, Pacific Institute for Public Policy Research, 1983)

There is simply no way to do justice here to the havoc wrought by E.P.A.'s edicts. A few randomly selected samples must suffice.

Consider, for instance, the so-called "significant deterioration" clean-air standard which demands that the "significant deterioration" of air quality will not be allowed in an area *even when the new level of air quality remains above federal standards.* That draconian standard is nowhere to be found in the Clean Air Act of 1970. It was promulgated by a federal court, incorporated into E.P.A. guidelines, and upheld by the Supreme Court in June of 1973. The antigrowth implications of the standard are obvious, and ominous, as noted by syndicated columnist M. Stanton Evans in *Human Events* for August 28, 1976: "The impact of this ultra-purist ruling is felt mainly in rural areas that are planning any kind of economic development—industry, shopping centers, a housing complex. It is an obvious barrier to growth and economic progress, mandating that any area now consisting of sylvan glades or open fields remain that way. It is a de facto 'no growth' policy for America, a form of backdoor land control."

Another area of regulatory overkill is that of pesticides. In 1975, E.P.A. officials alleged that hundreds of thousands of farm workers were injured each year by pesticides and that hundreds had died. When pressed for specifics, the agency eventually admitted that its claims were baseless. An E.P.A. spokesman confessed: "We used these statistics in good faith, thinking they were accurate, and they turned out not to be accurate. They cannot possibly be substantiated."

The E.P.A.'s ban on DDT (except in "extreme emergencies," as defined by the bureaucrats, not the actual circumstances of the case) enabled Tussock moths to defoliate nearly seven hundred thousand acres of forest land in Washington, Oregon, and northern Idaho a decade ago. It was the only pesticide proven effective against the destructive creatures. The E.P.A.'s own Hearing Examiner had reported in early 1972 (following eighty-one days of Hearings, involving 125 witnesses, and ten thousand pages of testimony) that "DDT as offered under the registrations involved herein is not misbranded. DDT is not a carcinogenic hazard to man. The uses of DDT under the registrations involved here do not have a deleterious effect on freshwater fish, estuarine organisms, wild birds or other wildlife. . . . in my opinion, the evidence in this proceeding supports the conclusion that there is a present need for the essential uses of DDT."

Yet, six months later, then-E.P.A. Administrator William Ruckelshaus banned the pesticide except for emergencies, and his successor (Russell Train) refused to grant an emergency exception so it could be used in time to save those Western forests from the ravages of the Tussock moth.

Similar environmental extremism, this time at the state level, seriously exaggerated the threat posed to fruit and vegetable crops in California by the Mediterranean fruit fly during 1980 and 1981. The Medflies, which were first discovered in the state in June of 1980, were quickly eradicated in the Los Angeles area, but proved to be tenacious in the north. Plans to spray infested areas from the air with the effective pesticide malathion were brought to a halt when environmental groups, bolstered by support from then-Governor Jerry Brown, instigated a storm of protest that such aerial spraying would be "death from the sky." This despite the fact that the substance had long been used safely to spray mosquitos on the East Coast; had been found noncarcinogenic by two separate National Cancer Institute studies; and, had been found by California's own Health Service Department to be the "least toxic of the organo-phosphate pesticides" which "degrades and disappears relatively rapidly after application."

Governor Brown refused to take effective action as the Medfly infestation spread, until at last the Reagan Agriculture Department (on July 10, 1981) threatened a statewide quarantine of California produce unless aerial spraying was begun. The infestation, you see, was on the verge of moving beyond California and threatening the long-term production of more than two hundred varieties of fruits and vegetables nationwide. Governor Brown reluctantly backed down and allowed the aerial spraying to begin on July fourteenth. Within one month, the infestation was under control, and total victory over the Medfly was formally declared on September twenty-third. Nevertheless, the damage to crops from the environmentalist delay totaled approximately $100 million.

The E.P.A. should be abolished. It cannot be adequately moderated. President Reagan initially appointed Anne Burford to administer the agency under a mandate which could be summarized as: Stop the war against private industry and try to persuade companies to improve their record, reserving federal coercion for the recalcitrant few which refuse to cooperate. Mrs. Burford worked admirably to abide by that humane and reasonable guideline. For her efforts, she was brutally savaged by environmental extremists within Congress and the "Liberal" press until, at last, she felt compelled to resign.

The Burford mandate has apparently been abandoned even by President Reagan himself, who selected as her successor William Ruckelshaus, the original E.P.A. Administrator who banned D.D.T. and otherwise set the agency rolling along its destructive course. On April 6, 1983, the post-Burford E.P.A. returned to form by proposing a truly asinine national emission standard for radionuclides. As explained by Representative John T. Myers (R.-Indiana): "Both the National Commission on Radiation Protection and the International Commission on Radiological Protection have proposed and support a maximum radiation exposure limit for the public of 500 millirems per year annual dose equivalent to the whole body, gonads, or bone marrow, and 1,500 millirems per year to other organs. EPA would reduce the $^{500}/_{1500}$ millirem exposure limit to 10 millirems per year to the whole body, gonads, or bone marrow and thirty millirems to other organs—a reduction of 98 percent. . . . The absurd stringency of this proposed standard is most apparent when one considers that the average radiation exposure to all of us in the United States from environmental sources is 100 to 200 millirems per year and that the dose from only one round-trip intercontinental flight can exceed a ten millirem whole body limit. Implementation of these standards will result in the unnecessary expenditure of hundreds of millions of tax and industry dollars, will seriously impair vital national defense activities, and will provide no benefits to the health or safety of the American public."

So it is again business as usual at the E.P.A., and so it will likely remain until the American people recognize the extent to which this outrageous regulatory monster is ripping them off as taxpayers, consumers, and free citizens.

Consumer Affairs

Interview with Richard Grant

Each of the applied ethics sections of this text (Parts 2–5) includes an interview with a key figure who is prominent in his/her field. The purpose of these interviews is to bridge the gap between theory and practice and offer the student an exposure to how people in the "real world" confront practical, ethical issues.

Dr. Richard Grant is chief of Orthopedic Surgery at Howard University Medical School. Dr. Grant is a graduate of Stanford University and Howard University Medical School.

Q: *What do you think are the most pressing ethical problems in Consumer Affairs, relating to Health Care, today?*

A: Some of the basic ethical problems would include the following:

1. All people, regardless of need or financial status, deserve the best possible health care.
2. As a nation, we cannot, or somehow will not, be able to afford to finance the issues raised in point number one.
3. Some type of compromise is necessary.
4. Who do you think receives the bottom end of the stick when we start compromising on issues of health care distribution? This brings into play the reality of racism, sexism, and the general tendency in a capitalistic system to let the bottom 12% of the economic tier hang by themselves.
5. The end result of a system that is based upon economic privilege is that the health-care marketplace ends up as being translated as follows: "The more things change, the more they stay the same." One would have to be a bit naive to think that the upper half of the nation's economic system will substantially sacrifice in order to provide health care entitlements for the bottom half. In this respect, we have a long way to go toward evolving an equitable distribution of health-care benefits to the entire nation and of realizing the principles of the Clinton "credit card" for universal health care coverage.

Most thoughtful physicians are aware that health spending has increased at approximately 10% per year, which is certainly out of line with the economy, and is now estimated to be increasing at a rate which is 2.5 times the documented U.S. inflation rate. We are experiencing an increase in the number of "working poor" American consumers and immigrants who are seeking health care and have no health-care insurance. This number has evidently increased by about two million through the end of 1993. Currently, it is estimated that we have about 39 million people who do not have recognizable health-care insurance. Supposedly about $1/4$ of this group of 39 million people are children.

The National Medical Association, which represents a significant percentage of practicing African-American physicians in the United States came out in favor of a "single payer" system (similar to the Canadian system). This is different from the Clinton Plan. However, there are other competing plans as well, such as the Chaffee Plan, the Cooper Plan, the Gramm Plan and the Michel Plan. It is difficult to say which would garner the most votes among minority physicians. . .

As I look at Clinton's health care credit card, I wonder if we are not moving into a situation where we are adding to the national debt. Universal health-care coverage and comprehensive health-care benefits translate into some significant tax increase, either a national sales tax or an inventory tax on health care providers and allied health care concerns. Ultimately, our future personal income tax and health-care costs will be forever joined at the hip. . .

There is some concern among most physicians, and I am certain there is some concern among African-American physicians, about the heavy handed techniques of the government as it seeks to control $1/7$ of the nation's economy represented by today's health-care industry and its allied concerns. Health-care reform, or health-care refinancing, or health-care rationing, or managed care competition, essentially translate into a more stringent control of all components of the health industry.

In order to control this $1/7$th of the economy, Clinton has proposed byzantine tiers of bureaucracy and supporting rhetoric. If we consider possibilities for payment of the Clinton universal health-care card, 80% of the money supposedly is going to come from Medicare and Medicaid savings, by reducing payments to health care providers, hospitals, and nursing homes—and by reducing the amount of funding for post graduate education (i.e., internships, fellowships, residencies, and subspecialty training). In the past, the reduced payments to the health-care industry have usually translated into passing the costs on to consumers with the deeper pockets, such as small businesses, large corporate concerns, and families with decent incomes. In the past we have seen this translate into a succession of higher annual premiums.

However, in order to counteract cost shifting, the proposals by the Clinton Plan indicate that there may be state level budget caps. For instance, if the state exceeds its health care budget ceiling, it won't be able to pass on those costs to the available deeper pockets in the health care marketplace. Alternatively, states may have to resort to raising taxes on health-care providers or to raising health insurance premiums paid by businesses.

I am sure that if the government agencies see a pattern of reaching the cost ceilings, prematurely, then the identifiable "perpetrators" will be taxed to resolve the difference. As the atmosphere for cost containment becomes a matter of economic survival, all health care players will continue to run scared, enforcing health care industry discipline in the interests of their own business survival.

Finally, one of the greatest concerns facing most health care providers, especially health care providers in urban areas and minority providers, is the concept of tort reform. Medicine's stormy relationship with the legal system has been treated by all of the health care revisionists with a "whisper." The general attitude seems to be "physician, cure thyself"—weed out all of the physicians who are repetitively sued or are practicing bad medicine.

The relationship between the health-care community and the legal profession must be improved. It is not uncommon for physicians practicing in the surgical subspecialties to have their annual malpractice insurance rise by $10,000 to $20,000 per year! It would seem to me that one of the major propositions of health-care reforms should be true and universal tort reform. Some control will have to be exerted over the specialized legal interests in malpractice settlements. It is a fact that generally a huge portion of a malpractice award does not go to the victim, but rather to the lawyer who wins the case. Neither the consumer nor the medical community learns anything from this process aside from the alarming intricacies of the legal system.

I believe that an equitable arbitration system would be a more moral approach to a patient's right for swift and fair compensation. In such an arbitration system, physical injury is identified and compensated without expensive lawyers as "middle men." The standard should be "physiological improvement" and not "strict liability" (which does not take moral/professional culpability into account).

Q: *What other solutions would you propose?*

A: Do you want a fairy tale, or some version of reality?

Q: *I am the author of fiction and love it dearly, but I suppose we must resign ourselves, in this context, to reality.*

A: The names change, but the problems are the same: racism, indifference to poverty, and a prevalence of plutomania. These rule the day. These factors continue to provoke the social pathologies of our civilization. You can play all you want with this or that, but we all know that "those who have, will not give up what they have to those who have not"—especially if the have nots are young Black, Hispanic, Asian, or any identifiable persons of color or ethnicity.

These are the real dynamics of our American culture. Let's face facts. The career plan for a typical middle class white adolescent allows that he or she can attend high school and achieve a bit, experiment with life, underachieve at times, and still get into a decent college. Then, with parental influence, he or she gets a high-paying job and pats him or herself on the back on how he or she really "earned" everything that came to them. This is the contradiction and tyranny of privilege which becomes part and parcel of being born into a predominant ethnic group.

By comparison, the career tract for a typical young African American is this: if you have a business sense and no apparent legitimate financial opportunities, then you start your own business—dealing drugs (who is going to make you a loan to establish a legitimate franchise?).

You want to have a job, but you must consider that there is 35% unemployment facing you in a decaying urban center. No unemployment if you are a willing "entrepreneur." Fatal choice. Bang, you are incarcerated. Labeled a felon. Receive a mandatory sentence (usually twice the sentence your white counterpart in the suburbs faces—remember parental influence fighting for the suburban child while society's welfare policies have removed much parental influence from urban African-American families).

Minorities are provided a high school post graduate program of incarceration. At least $22,000 to $26,000 per year is spent by taxpayers in order to provide for the salaries of the prison guards and the cost of housing prisoners. No real education is provided—not even relevant trade skills—during the years of imprisonment. This allows mainstream society to look away and contain invisible men in invisible prisons. Once paroled, the felon cannot vote and is, therefore, devoid of any politically recognizable power. Often, I wonder what would happen if the absentee vote were suddenly granted to incarcerated or paroled felons. How would mainstream politicians change their campaign tactics in order to respond to such an enormous voting block?

However, consider this: if you put a promissory note in front of a responsible minority mother or father and said, "Look, I got up to $30,000 a year provided for your son or daughter to go to college if they are ready for it." If you then went around to the poor and disadvantaged and made them this kind of offer, I promise you this current drug problem would be greatly diminished. Responsibility for neighborhoods and responsibility for cities come about through jobs, home ownership, education and a resilient sense of optimism.

Q: *And yet many would blame those groups in poverty for not "transcending their lot."*

A: I saw a movie recently called "Schindler's List." At one point during the movie, one could see that the Jewish community was stripped of family, property, resources, and contacts: they were literally torn from mainstream German society overnight. As that process continued inextricably, six million lives were lost in the Holocaust.

I often compare this to the "sixty million and more" that Tony Morrison talks about in the preface of her book, *Beloved*. Her sixty million in the book's dedication reminds us of those who were lost during the slave trade between Africa and the Americas. Returning to the extrication of the Jewish population from Germany, and their incarceration in the ghetto, one would wonder how the Germans would look upon the Jews, who had been violently reduced to an inhuman existence?

Would the European oppressors ask the Jewish community to raise themselves up by the boot straps? If you can consider the irony of this stance, one will see that the acts of oppression correctly identify the dimensions of the oppressor. Great irony prevails in the relations between America and the African-American community.

Ultimately, what African Americans seek is hope. One wonders if that is just too much in America. There has to be an alternate plan for young African-American males and females that is not associated with a premature violent death or chemically induced self destruction.

Q: *Is hope possible?*

A: Yes, but not instantaneously since racism is probably as old as any civilization around Mesopotamia. It is as old as prostitution or soldiering. But should that stop us? Jesus said, "The poor you will have with you always." Yet he also favored justice over sacrifice and praised those who brought healing and peace.

We must not allow the complexity of the matter to be an excuse for writing off a whole segment of our population.

Q: *Do you see the problems of poverty and health care as linked?*

A: Inextricably. But to pretend that some system of layered bureaucracy will somehow bring health equity in a society devoid of social equity is an empty theory.

The heart of the matter is this: the government is not really concerned about the poor who cannot afford health-care coverage. Elected government officials must respond to money and power (both of which are lacking among the disenfranchised).

Business, on the other hand, predictably presses for a favorable and stable business environment (marketplace) so that business can make the fiscal projections that favor profit and encourage reinvestment.

The ideal situation is to let physicians make the kinds of decisions they are trained to make. Let physicians advocate the parameters and definitions of "best care" for their patients.

This may prove to be too expensive for the political priorities of the United States, but I would contend that we could counter this expense with a concentrated push to alleviate poverty by offering job training to everyone and to provide jobs once one completes his or her training. Day care must be provided for children, as the majority of families are faced with the need for two incomes.

Drug and alcohol abuse must be combated by an honest "no holds barred" education process. Primary care should focus upon the promotion of healthy lifestyles. This should begin on the first day of kindergarten.

Q: *What are the trade-offs between having business or government run the health care system?*

A: Good question. The former must be obsessed with efficiency and profit in order to survive. The latter pretends to recognize human dignity. However, I've had considerable experience with the federal government as a health-care provider (through Medicare and Medicaid) and the reality is much different. The government has no moral center. It is merely an institution which responds to whichever power forces happen to be pressuring it at the moment.

At least the business community is up front about their self-absorbed focus upon profits.

Q: *What would be examples of macro and micro cases?*

A: The macro case would involve the decisions that the health care network administrator would have to make. These would include the acceptability of various medical/surgical procedures for the participants in his or her health-care network. At times this type of trade off can be very difficult to negotiate, suggesting the stringency of rationing with all of its implications of societal denial and/or withholding.

On the micro side, I would give you a fairly common case today. That is the Emergency Room Physician: the new "gate keeper." In this case this physician is caring for an indigent patient coming through the emergency room doors. Now the policy for most hospitals—except for "charity" hospitals—is that one is expected to stabilize the patient's condition and either retain the patient for admission or transfer to a hospital designated as a "charity hospital" or "county/public" medical center.

The problem is this: what if the treatment available to the patient (because of some specialized condition or critical emergency) at the charity hospital will not adequately fulfill the patient's needs? In this case, some emergency room doctors are forced to make a very difficult decision. If they admit the patient, they will most likely have to respond to the administrators who are looking at the potential fiscal loss to the hospital. Too many instances of accepting charitable cases or "non-compensable" cases may put his future employment in question. The doctors are trained to alleviate suffering and to help people to get well. Are you helping someone to become better and recover by sending him or her to "St. Elsewhere" where the patient may or may not get adequate treatment?

Q: *If you were put in charge of everything, what would you do to reform the system?*

A: First, I would consider limiting physician's salaries. This must be done with the input of all the parties involved: consumers' groups, insurance companies, and the government. Second, I would institute tort reform (as discussed earlier). Third, we must take care of the social situation which creates a counter culture of underprivileged people. No matter what we do, we will not have adequate urban health care until young African-American males and females realize a career path which provides educational change and advancement.

America's social patterns have to change but they will never change until we confront these uncomfortable truths that weigh on the neck of the greater society which controls the portals of entry into mainstream society. If we do not confront these inequities and inequalities, these truths will do more than weigh on our necks—they will become a millstone.

▼ Writing the Report

Assessing Embedded Levels

Our goal in this series of exercises is to be able to write a report that evaluates a business case. Your evaluation should include an examination of cost issues and ethical issues. In the last section we discussed how to analyze the case into these categories. In this section we will work on comparing the two types of issues. There are multiple ways this can be accomplished, but the one offered here invokes a technique which rates cost and ethical issues as having three levels of complexity: Surface, Medium, and Deep. The level of interaction allows you to see at a glance how the competing areas of cost issues and ethical issues conflict.

One needs a model of some sort to evaluate the strength of the cost issues and ethical issues that may come into conflict. It is not the case that whenever ethical issues and cost issues conflict, that one *automatically* chooses either. Some ethical problems are easily remedied and do not require forgoing the dictates of the cost issues. At other times an ethical dilemma is so entrenched that it will override any cost issue advantages.

What is needed is a methodology for comparison. The "embedded concept" model is one such methodology. I will illustrate how this works with a couple of examples. In the examples, I employ a spreadsheet to further clarify the ways embedded concepts interact. You, also, may want to use this technology if you have access to one of the popular spreadsheet computer programs. However, use of a spreadsheet here is not necessary. A more conventional approach would simply be to discuss these differences through narrative description.

The spreadsheet is no substitute for solid narrative description, but at the very least it simplifies and makes visual the model I want to put forward.

Let us begin with another example. **Case 2:** An airport is expanding. At public hearings it is found that the new landing approach sequence will have an impact on residents who live below these approaches. They are upset because of the impact of the noise and the potential lowering of their property values. There is another approach sequence that is less convenient and will cause little to no impact on residents. To change the approach sequence will require new permit and development costs that will have to be borne by the airport authority. Also, the alternate route is a little less convenient to airlines and will require slightly more fuel on their part. Should the airport authority accept the alternate landing approach?

If you take the point of view of the airport authority you can create a list of ethical issues and cost issues using the model discussed in Part 2. Such a list might look like the following:

Cost Issues
Inconvenience of new route
Extra fuel experienced by airlines
New permit and development costs

Ethical Issues
The rights of people not to have their
    basic well-being disturbed
Property rights

At this point we need to compare the two lists. This requires us to take the report one step further. In the spreadsheet approach we can set out the cost and ethical issues under the headings of embeddedness. For simplicity I have chosen three categories: Surface, Medium, and Deep. I then assess where each issue falls. It is important to be able to logically argue for your choice here to justify the level of embeddedness chosen.

Analysis of Landing Patterns

	Surface	Medium	Deep
Cost Issues			
Inconvenience of new route	x		
Extra fuel experienced by airlines	x		
New permit and development costs		x	
Ethical Issues			
The rights of people not to have their basic well-being disturbed			x
Property rights		x	

In this simple case the ethical issues are more deeply imbedded into the problem than the prudential issues. That means they are "easier" to take care of. When this is the case one should alter the factors which are less imbedded. This means that in the airport landing example, the alternate route should be chosen. The additional expenses and other cost issues are not as imbedded as the ethical impact of the proposed route. Therefore, the alternate route ought to be the choice over the proposed route.

In our next situation it is not so simple. **Case 3:** The ABC plant is one of the few remaining asbestos fabrication plants in the country. This plant is located in rural Kentucky in a town which has no other manufacturing industry. Ten years ago the only other manufacturer, American Motors, closed its "Gremlin" facilities there. The closure of the ABC plant will probably put many people into poverty.

Federal regulations have varied drastically over the last twenty years concerning asbestos. As testing has become more exact it has been demonstrated that increasingly smaller amounts of asbestos have proved to be "safe." However, the industrial use of asbestos as a gasket, for example, has no peer.

The ABC plant is an old manufacturing facility still producing asbestos gaskets. When considering employee safety, it seems that they should consider altering their production methods to a "dustless" underwater fabrication process. However, this has negative side effects: 1) There is a great cost involved in converting machinery to a new manufacturing process. 2) The federal regulation climate is unpredictable. 3) The waste water, though conforming to current U.S. standards, might not be treatable in other regulatory environments. 4) Maybe asbestos is harmful at any dosage. 5) Virtually all of the competition has left the marketplace. This leaves the avenue open to you to operate a venture which has very high profit margins since your only competition (a synthetic plastic gasket) is inferior in performance and double your price. 6) Perhaps you will not be able to operate your plant forever, but at present you are making good money for your stockholders, and after all, they own the company. 7) The time frame for which this process will pay off completely is within the five-year capital depreciation period stipulated by the IRS (in other words, as long as you can squeeze five years out of the regulatory climate, your stockholders will win financially). The probability of heading off a regulatory shutdown for at least five years is good.

Analysis of Asbestos Manufacturing

	Surface	Medium	Deep
Cost Issues			
Converting plant			x
Possible early obsolescence due to scientific findings			x
Very profitable venture			x
Ethical Issues			
You may be killing your workers			x
You may be killing the public at large			x
Local Area depends upon plant for jobs			x

This situation is different. The cost and ethical issues are both deeply embedded. There is not a "simple" solution as there was in the earlier case. At this point, the spreadsheet analysis *shows* us that we have a difficult choice. The law says we may continue. But the recent trend of scientific evidence suggests that asbestos is harmful to people's health.

How does one make a decision? One way is to create complimentary logical arguments which can be compared at their most controversial premises. By comparing the strongest arguments for each you should be able to arrive at an answer. The mechanics of this method are detailed in the next section.

Here the main concern is the ability to assess the levels of embeddedness. Some of the common problems that my students have had doing this are:

1. **Not having detailed enough cost and ethical issues lists.** Remember, whether you assess embeddedness via a spreadsheet or through discursive paragraphs, you are working from your original analysis of the problem. If you haven't uncovered all the important facets, this will show in your depiction of embeddedness. You will notice "gaps" and the feeling that something is missing. Go back over the issues lists. One approach is to re-write the case in your own words. Expand or recast the case in some way. By

doing this you become the author and are forced to recognize key elements in the case as presented.

2. **A tendency to see everything at the same level of embeddedness.** The concept of embeddedness does not help if everything is always at the same level. You need to view embeddedness as a way of describing how close an issue is to the essential structure of the cost or ethical issue. The more "accidental" or "incidental" the issue, the more it should be classed as "surface." To get a better fix on what is the essential structure of a cost or ethical issue, try and create short descriptions justifying your choice of that element as an issue in the case. As you set out your description think about the element in its relation to the whole. If that relation couldn't be otherwise without seriously altering the whole, then it is essential. If you can find other substitutes which would work just as well, then it is incidental.

3. **Having too many cost and ethical issues listed.** This is the flip side to #1 above. Often the student who has too much detail is either going off on too many tangents away from the case at hand, or he or she is renaming the same issue in a number of different ways. In either event, setting out an essential description of your elements (as in #2 above) can help you shorten your issues lists to only those items requisite for your evaluation.

Good solid work on these preliminary steps generally creates a more satisfactory result in your argumentative stage. This is where you may finally apply your ethical theory to your annotated issues sheets.

Macro and Micro Cases

The cases section of this book are divided into two categories: macro and micro. Each type of case employs a different point of view.

Macro Case.   The macro case takes large institutional entities as its focus. For example one might examine Beechnut and the apple juice case or BCCI as a multinational banking concern. The purpose of the macro case is to get you thinking about how corporations should act in their environment. You will take the perspective of a high level official and make judgments which will affect many thousands.

Micro Case.   The micro case takes individuals working within business as its focus. For example, one might look at a mid-level manager's approach to end of the year sales reports, or an engineer's decision to be a "whistle blower." The attraction of these cases is that you can project yourself realistically into these cases. It is probable that you will be in positions similar to the micro case descriptions (whereas only a fraction of people will ever really be a macro case decision maker).

Case Development. The word 'case' is used in different ways by different people. This book will suggest one form of case response. The method for preparing and developing these cases is suggested in the essays entitled: "Writing the Report" which can be found at the end of each section in the book. Your professor may also have specific guidelines of his/her own.

For those who wish to use it, this approach offers a bridge between various traditional approaches to case studies, taught in business schools, with a philosophical method that emphasizes essay development. The intention throughout is that you expand your mind with the general essays and develop a practical skill in applying an ethical theory to thorny moral/cost conflicts through writing a business report that defends a particular course of action.

Please note that though most of the cases presented here have fictional venues, they are based upon composites of real Corporate America.

 # acro Cases

Case 2.1—Transplants vs. Pre-natal Care

You are the head of the managed care board at an insurance company. Your company has instituted an HMO network that seeks to gain significant market share in the states of Maryland, Virginia, D.C., Delaware, Pennsylvania, New Jersey and New York. The problem confronting you is controlling costs. You are faced with the following proposition:

1. Organ transplants are very expensive and the number of people needing them continues to grow. In your sample space and estimated population you would have had thirty transplant cases. At an average of $400,000 per transplant, that costs $12,000,000.
2. Complications in pregnancy are of two varieties: (a) those that could have been prevented by proper medical care and (b) those that will occur despite proper preventative care. In the first category you estimate that the company could save $5,000,000 and countless deaths that occur each year in your sample population if you had an aggressive, free pre-natal program.
3. Childhood illness and infant medical complications are also areas of potential savings if an aggressive, free childhood wellness program were adopted. The extent of these savings is at least $1,000,000.
4. The cost for instituting the programs in #2 & #3 would be $18,000,000. The savings amount to $6,000,000. The net cost is $12,000,000. This

happens to equal the amount presently being spent on transplants plus the projected health savings that the programs will produce.

5. Therefore, it is recommended to the board that it not include transplants in its covered medical expenses and instead initiate the programs described in #2 & #3 above.

Pro: The number of people hurt by this proposal is around 30 annually. These people will not get transplants when they need them and will die (unless they are lucky enough to be able to afford the transplants separately). The number of people helped by the proposal would be around 40,000. These are people whose pregnancies would have otherwise ended in miscarriage or stillbirth. Thousands of babies' lives can be saved if we can only find the money to fund the programs necessary to save them.

In addition, the spread of diseases among children, and medical complications associated with infants, is on the rise. Thousands of these young lives can be enhanced by this program and the public health in general can be improved. It has also been shown that instances of child abuse increase among continually crying babies. Babies cry uncontrollably not because they are bad, but because they are sick. This program will literally save these children. We must act.

It is unfortunate that some people will have to die. But we do not have the money to treat everyone with the highest degree of care. It's simply too expensive. Therefore, we must make this trade off.

Con: It all sounds so good to talk about saving babies and children at the expense of a few hundred people who need organ transplants. That is until you are the one needing the transplant.

We now have the technological means of saving lives that otherwise would have been lost. How can a physician look his patient in the eye and say, "We have the means to save your life through an operation that has been highly perfected, but we cannot do so because it's too expensive"? This is entirely against everything that medicine stands for.

If this proposal goes forward only the rich will be able to have full, quality health care. We will be saying, "If you are wealthy, then you'll be able to take advantage of all the advances of modern medicine, but if you aren't then 'tough luck.'"

I am not in favor of this proposal which would establish a two tier health system in this country. It's wrong. You can't quantify human life. The trade offs of numbers are all wrong. To a physician each human life is precious. We must act as advocates to do all we can to save life. We must reject this proposal.

Using an Ethical Theory as your guide, write your opinion whether or not to adopt the proposal.

Case 2.2—The Selling of T–Man Action Toys

We all know about T–Man and T–Woman, the animated characters who top the charts of Saturday morning cartoon television. The unique sounds they make when they fight super criminals and their deadly laser guns make them a hit among the pre-adolescent set.

You work for the Bellevue Advertising Agency on Madison Avenue. Mactold Toys has approached you about the campaign to sell T–Man and T–Woman. What Mactold is interested in is a campaign that links right into the cartoon adventures themselves. "If it is seamless," said Sally Ware, the marketing VP for Mactold, "the children will think they are still within the scenario of the morning's adventure. They will feel as if they must have their own set of T–toys in order to fully appreciate the show. With twenty million viewers, that's a ton of money."

You listen to Ms. Ware tell you what Mactold has in mind and you promise to come up with a marketing plan in two weeks. However, the more you think about it, the more you are troubled. You are not sure that a "seamless" television commercial for children is really such a good thing to do. You decide to ask for a staff meeting.

Two of your top people, Ms. Black and Mr. White take opposite views.

MS. BLACK: We need the Mactold account, but the plan for a "seamless" advertisement program is not the way to do it. The FCC has been very tight about children's advertising, because children are more easily manipulated than adults.

Seamless advertising blurs the distinction between fact and fiction. Children must know when someone is making a pitch to them instead of confusing TV show and commercial. I know I wouldn't want my child exposed to those sorts of commercials.

Instead, let's make a point of making it very separate. We can use live child actors who are playing with the toys and having a grand time. By moving from animation to real people we will be letting the children know that there is a break in the show and that now we are in reality.

I think Mactold will get better results with my idea.

MR. WHITE: I think Ms. Black is making something of nothing. Children are smarter than you think. We shouldn't treat them like moldable clay. If they can't figure out that a commercial is going on when we tell them the price of the toy and that accessories are sold extra—not to mention "batteries not included," then those children need remedial attention.

I was a kid once and I hated it when TV commercials "dumbed down" to me. Look, the plain truth is that kids like the animation. They are attracted to it. If we don't make our commercial so irresistible that they like it as much as the show, then we will lose them to the donut bag in the kitchen.

> The FCC regs are no problem to "work around." I say, "Give the client what she wants. If she wants seamless advertising, then seamless advertising it is."

You are undecided. The company has been hurting lately due to some large accounts cutting back. You can really use the business. On the other hand you want to do what's "best"—whatever that means.

What does it mean? What should be your decision, and why?

Case 2.3—Green Zippers?

You have been given the responsibility of designing an entire line of young women's clothes. You are after a "natural" and "environmentally friendly" ambiance in your line of clothes. Even the name of the line, "Green Wear" takes its name from the European environmental movement.

Many of your T–shirts have eco–slogans on them. Now you are creating pants and you discover that the zippers are metal plated. Your uncle used to work in the metal plating business so you know that this industry discards waste water that is extremely toxic to streams and lakes.

On the chance that the industry might have changed since your uncle's time, you do some investigation of your own. You discover that though some measures of recapturing the poisons and heavy metals used in the process have been implemented by the vendors you are considering, still there is considerable discharge.

"They are well within Federal regulations," says the president after you approach him with your concerns.

"But the guidelines are too lax. Damage is being done. It's hardly in line with the philosophy of 'Green Wear.'"

"There's no alternative. Everyone makes zippers this way. What are you going to do? Start your own zipper plant?"

"What about buttons?"

"Buttons, snaps they're all the same. Everyone uses electroplating. You're tilting at windmills. Nobody thinks about this sort of thing anyway. Even you wouldn't have known about it if your relative hadn't been involved once. Give it up and let's get that line finished."

You leave and do more investigation and find a tribe of Native Americans who have a factory that makes custom buttons. They are "all natural" and you could have a buttoned fly instead of a zippered fly on the pants.

The problem is that buttons are more expensive to buy and (because they are handmade) they will be more expensive to sew on. (The slight variations that all hand made products possess make it hard to use with precision tooled machines. The buttons will require a larger labor component in assembly. Therefore a greater cost.)

The bottom line is that the new buttons will add $2 to a pair of pants that sells for $50. It is a very competitive industry. $2 can be a lot. What do you do? Either way your boss expects a report to justify your decision. Weigh practical issues and ethical considerations to come up with your decision.

Case 2.4—The Gun Adapter Kit

Patriot Fire Arms has always been a struggling company. It was formed forty years ago by Arnold Pinkas as a company specializing in hunting rifles. Over the years the firm has entered certain niche markets when it found it could not compete with large manufacturers like Winchester.

One niche market that kept the company afloat in the late 60s was a line of replica guns from the Revolutionary War time onwards. These guns actually fire. The bullets and powder to operate these weapons is also manufactured by Patriot.

Then came the downturn of the late 70s and Patriot continued its "History Series" with "Guns from Vietnam." The problem was that automatic weapons were illegal. But what Patriot did was create a weapon that looked authentic, but only fired a single shot at a time. At the same time it created a Rifle Customizing Kit that could turn your single shot rifle into an automatic. In order to make it clear that you weren't singling out your Vietnam Rifle, you made the materials in the kit sufficiently generic that it could turn virtually any rifle into an automatic.

Sales went through the roof. The company was never so popular. Patriot even stopped advertising. It wasn't necessary. Everyone wanted the Rifle Customizing Kit. Sales of the kit were more than double the sales of all other lines in the company combined.

Here's where you come in. You have just inherited Uncle Harold's 1/3 voting share in the company. This makes you the second largest stockholder. The other two are Patsy Pinkas who holds 45% and Brad Benson (also known as "Bubba") who holds 22%.

You have studied the Rifle Customizing Kit and have called a meeting of the other two stockholders to discuss it. You say, "I have some grave reservations about whether we should continue manufacturing this product. It can be used to create machine guns and these are used all too frequently in our cities as a part of organized crime and drug deals."

Patsy says, "It's clear that you are new to this business. My father, who started this business, found quickly enough that the only way we could survive was to find a specialty area. We showed off our fine workmanship to produce replica guns from every period in American History. This line is what keeps us in business."

You respond, "But it's not the replica line that I have trouble with, it's the Rifle Customizing Kit. This kit can be used to modify an Uzi or another rifle to an automatic weapon delivering two-hundred rounds per minute. What possible use could that be except to promote crime?"

Then Bubba cuts in, "Lookee here, now. We're free and in the clear. Our lawyers tell us we're clean, and believe me, we pay them enough that they've got to be right. We don't promote crime. We promote gun collecting. Antique gun collecting. What better way to teach your kids about American History?

"Anyway, if some fools out there want to twist our intention (which, by the way, is printed in bold letters right on the box) and create automatic weapons to commit crimes, then I'm sorry. I say make the penalties higher for people committing crimes with guns. That will stop the crooks if anything will. In the meantime, why penalize law abiding Americans who have the Constitutional right to "bear arms"? It's crazy.

"We're legal. We print our intentions on the box. We in no way encourage illegal usage of our product. Almost every product can have an illegal usage if someone is sick enough to try it. Why you could make a bomb in a Crisco can! Does that mean that Crisco should stop manufacturing their product?"

Patsy adds, "We're not unreasonable. We'd like to hear all you have to say, pro or con on this subject. That way no one can accuse us of being narrow minded on the subject. If you can convince us we're wrong, we're willing to change our position. Why don't you think this out—keeping in mind some of the things we've been talking about. Then see where you stand on this."

You agree. You decide to write a report weighing the ethical and practical issues in order to come up with recommendations that you might be able to put forward.

 icro Cases

Case 2.5—Angioplasty for John Doe

You work in the emergency room of a private hospital in a large urban city associated with a prominent university. You have had surgical training and have a sub-specialty in cardiology. You are an African American. You know the hospital's policy concerning admissions: "Charity patients who need treatment and do not have insurance, must be stabilized and then transferred to the public hospital which has a mission of caring for charity patients." Simple. Period. The end.

Then there is the history. Margaret Johnson ignored the policy. She's gone. Then there was Frank Thomas and Aser Bilgrami. The same story. They didn't follow the policy and now they are unemployed. (When you are 'let go' from one group in a metropolitan area, it is difficult to find comparable work in the same area.)

This is what has happened to you. An African-American male has come into the ER at your hospital complaining of chest pains. You determine that he has had a mild cardiac event, but that it is probable (based upon other factors in the profile) that he has a clogged artery. A procedure, angioplasty, can significantly aid this case. Angioplasty is a medical intervention in which a small "balloon" is inserted to clear clogged arteries. This is the standard procedure for someone in this situation.

The problem is this. The public hospital has a very weak cardiac unit. They get very poor compensation for what they do. Consequently, if a patient could go anywhere else, he would. The public hospital has lagged behind in materials, equipment and personnel. You know that fatalities run significantly higher at the charity hospital.

To further complicate this, it should be mentioned that you take that portion of the Hippocratic oath which enjoins you "to do no harm." Sending this patient, John Doe, to the public hospital would not be in the best medical interests of the patient.

Maybe you could get Medicaid (a government program for the indigent) to cover this patient, but Medicaid pays pennies on the dollar. You also realize that if the hospital took in all the patients that it could handle better than the public hospital, then it would go out of business in less than a year. This would serve nobody's purposes.

Still, the fact remains that you have a fellow human being in front of you that has a good chance to live a meaningful existence if the angioplasty is done at your hospital, and a poor chance to survive if you send him to the public hospital.

What do you do? And why?

Case 2.6—Black Boxes at Radio Hut

You work at Radio Hut, a large national retail store that specializes in items electronic: radios, computers, and various gadgets and accessories. You are a graduate student in English literature at the University of Washington in Seattle. You are under a deadline of sorts in your program. It is November and you have to get in a draft of your dissertation by February 1st or you will miss the deadline for finishing up your Ph.D. this year. You have to finish up this year because your dissertation director, Ms. Take, is going on a three year leave of absence to finish up her opus magnum. With your director effectively gone, you'd be back at square one and it could mean another year or two under a different director.

You are thirty years old and ready to get on in your life. The last thing you want is to waste another two years. (Besides your wife has just finished her doctorate and is on the "job market" in economics, and you'd like to be living in the same city as your wife.) The trouble is that you owe the university money and you need to put together two jobs in order to possibly pay the interest on your debts and finish your degree.

This job at Radio Hut is very important to you. It is not the only job in town, but the local economy is very tight and a job like this—that pays a good salary and has commissions on top of that—is hard to find in the present job market. This is the Christmas season and you figure that you can earn enough to have your arrears paid to the university by next month.

The problem is this. Radio Hut sells a black box that is called a Message Scrambler. The Message Scrambler works with a satellite dish to provide the owner with free, undetected television access to virtually any television station (this includes 'cable' channels). But this circumvents the cable TV services. No fee is paid to them. This is obviously an infringement upon their copyright. This bothers you. As a student of literature, you are acutely aware of the need to protect the creative "rights" of authors and their sponsors (publishers, impresarios, et al.).

Obviously this illegal usage of the Message Scrambler cannot be advertised or printed by the company in any documentation. Radio Hut would be criminally liable if they did. But still, they want the capabilities of the device to be communicated to the customers. The only way that can happen is for the sales people to verbally discuss this with customers "on the sly."

Your supervisor has told you to explain to potential customers the value of the black box. You are supposed to alert them as to how this machinery will help them escape the monthly fees of full service cable TV.

But you don't want to do this. You feel that you could, in good conscience, tell customers how they could use the scrambler to aid in reconstruction of their video tapes and public television signals, but you feel like you are a criminal accessory when you advise customers to break the law.

On the other hand, your supervisor is the one telling you to do this. He has mentioned this to you time and time again. Several fellow employees have been present during your talks with your supervisor so that you could (perhaps) document his directives—if it came to that.

You need this job. Times are tough. Lots of people cheat the cable networks. Your supervisor says only suckers pay full fare. You don't agree, but you don't want to be canned. And your supervisor has made it clear that if you aren't a "team player" that you will not finish out the week.

Set out your mental dialogue considering ethical and practical considerations.

Case 2.7—The "Girl" in the Bikini

"We've always used a girl in a bikini to sell our men's cologne. It works. The men really go for those near naked girls." The speaker was Fred Newman, your boss. He is an advertising exec from "the old school." He even chomps on a cigar (generally unlit due to new non-smoking regulations).

You are looking at photos of nearly-naked women in provocative poses. You are supposed to design three ads. Fred has given you the photos and the copy, "Bull Cologne: It brings out the animal."

You looked at the photos and went to Fred questioning whether you had to have the models so suggestively dressed (or rather undressed) next to a man in a tuxedo. You feel that the overall impression is rather degrading to women. The man is clearly a sophisticated "man of the world" and the woman is a one-dimensional sex object. The classic "bimbo" pose. This offends you. Your own sister was sexually assaulted two years ago so that the depiction of women in this way is especially important to you.

Your job is to layout the ads. There is no one else who can do this task. Therefore, you went to Fred to see whether there was any way to alter the visual image that you were sending out.

"No way. Our readers like skin. Big breasts and lots of skin. That grabs their attention."

"So grabbing their attention is all that we're aiming at?"

"When did you fall off the boat?" said Fred with a deprecating laugh. He put his cigar back into his mouth, turned, and walked away.

You do a mock–up, but are uncomfortable with it. The lighting and printing of the ad accentuates your displeasure over what you're doing. Then it comes to you. You could re-print the photo in black and white as a negative reverse: the black would become white and the white would become black. Further, you could scan the result into your CAD unit and use small 'x's' to create all the shading.

The result changes a picture that looked like a Playboy centerfold into something like an Andy Warhol parody. Now the focus is not sensual, but intellectually removed. Your attention is drawn to the weirdness of the composition rather than to the "power man" over "poor submissive little bimbo." It has moved into a realm that invites the audience to rethink the entire composition.

You love it. No longer are you putting down women, but you have created a commentary on ads that do. The problem is your boss, Fred. Fred has never liked you. He may hit the ceiling. He may fire you. He may do any number of bad things to you in retaliation. In this business being "black-balled" can be fatal.

But the ad does grab the reader's attention. And that is what Fred said he wanted. But you know that's probably not what he meant. Fred often is unable to articulate exactly what he means.

Is that your problem? Fred's the boss. You've had problems before. This could be it. You set both layouts before you. On the left is the woman in the bikini. On your right is your Warhol-like rendition. Same picture. Same text. Radically different presentation.

Which should you bring forward to your boss? Which will you bring? Can you really afford to be true to your inner convictions?

Case 2.8—The Empty Wastepaper Basket or The Empty Gesture

You have always been environmentally conscious. From your younger days in scouting to the present, you love the outdoors and believe in conservation. When you were promoted to the position of office manager in the consulting firm, one of the first things you did was to instigate recycling bins for paper and for bottles and cans. Your city has a voluntary recycling program. Every Tuesday you have to take your recyclables to the rear of the building and throw them into specially marked bins.

There is no cost to the company. The recyclables are taken down by the custodian whose services are already sub–contracted for. The problem is this. The employees of the company aren't using the system.

You thought that you would have to go through a "retraining" period in which you would have to educate the employees to use the recycling containers. You even typed out a two-page memo on the subject. But the memo found its way into the general trash container.

Six months went by and you have been chiding the workers to do their part. At first the secretaries recycled, but just as quickly, they took their cues from their bosses. If the bosses thought it was a joke, then so did the secretaries. The recyclable cans were largely empty.

There are two sorts of responses that people make to you: 1. It is a bother to have to think about which of three cans to throw refuse. This is a high pressure job. No one has time to sort garbage into three categories. 2. It doesn't do much good to put a few pieces of paper from one office into some experimental program that will probably fold anyway. 3. The company has much better things to do than to concentrate upon how to throw away a piece of paper. If this is a major issue to the office manager, then perhaps the office manager has too little to do and is being paid too much.

The consensus generally is to eliminate the three-can system.

Your difficulty is that you believe that there is a moral responsibility to be environmentally conscious. This three-can system may not be much, but it is something. And though it may be a bother to think about where one is throwing away her or his trash, it is nonetheless an important consideration. To integrate environmental consciousness into everyday life is a positive action. This you believe.

On the other hand, the system isn't working. Should you continue in your efforts? Is it worth antagonizing other employees (most of whom outrank you)? Might you be doing more harm than good if you are causing negative feelings about environmental issues? Are you really doing anything, or is it merely an empty gesture?

Go through your mental calculations on this issue.

Government Issues

CHAPTER 13

Regulation

The Impact of Regulation

Donna J. Wood

Many managers think of the impact of regulation on businesses and society in terms of polar trade-offs—higher costs versus protection of "the public interest." There's some truth in this view, but in fact the impacts of regulation are much broader and further-reaching than the dollars expended on compliance. Regulation has significant effects—positive and negative—on every sector of the business environment.

Forcing Social Change

For better or worse, regulation does bring about social change. The equal opportunity and affirmative action rules of the 1960s, for example, required companies to give equal consideration and special assistance to minorities and women in employment practices. Years later, these groups have not made all the gains they have sought, but they are now represented in every employment category and rank and are increasingly accepted as professionals and managers. Given the extent of prejudices and discrimination that have existed in society, these gains are a major social change, with serious impacts on labor market composition, consumer preferences, and employer policies and procedures. Such advances probably would not have been made without the push of law and regulation.

Donna J. Wood. *Business & Society* (Glenview, Illinois: Scott, Foresman & Co., 1990), pp. 363–377.

Encouraging Knowledge Production

An often-overlooked social effect of regulation is that it encourages the production of scientific knowledge. Regulatory decisions may be made on the basis of argument, belief, emotion, political influence, and other nonrational grounds. But regulatory activity often encourages additional study of issues and events, thus providing a useful service for society.

In the 1970s, for example, some scientists and environmental protection advocates pressed the Environmental Protection Agency to ban the use of chlorofluorocarbons (CFCs) because of alleged negative effects on the earth's protective ozone layer. The EPA instituted a ban on CFCs in aerosol products in 1978, then backed off from further controls at the urging of chemical manufacturers and settled for five years to study the effects of CFCs on atmospheric ozone. (CFCs are also used in refrigerants, foam insulation, and solvents.) Studies made during this period indicate that atmospheric ozone is being depleted, thus allowing "more ultraviolet radiation to reach the earth, causing additional skin cancer, damaging crops, destroying plastics, and altering the climate."[1] A major long-term study at the University of Illinois found that from 1979 to 1986, ozone levels declined by five percent, a much sharper drop than anyone had expected.[2] With such solid evidence, both domestic regulation and international agreements were more easily supported. In Montreal in September 1987, thirty-one nations agreed to limit the use of CFCs and other atmosphere-damaging chemicals. The U.S. Senate ratified this treaty by a vote of 83–0 on March 14, 1988.[3]

Having Real and Symbolic Public Interest Effects

Finally, two important social effects of regulation have to do with "the public interest" and how this interest may be served. First, regulation may have *real* effects on "the public interest." Regulation may protect such interests, for example, by requiring more and better information, by reducing product and employment hazards, by improving air and water quality, and by ensuring equal employment opportunity. These interests may be harmed if regulation introduces prohibitive costs that reduce business's ability to compete in world markets and thus result in layoffs, plant closings, and community decline.[4]

Second, the existence and nature of regulation sends *symbolic* messages to the public. It can reassure the public by giving a sign that its "interests" are being protected, whether or not this is actually the case. Or, if a regulation is seen as too lax, too weak, or targeted to business's interests, it can lead to charges that government is ignoring "the public interest."[5]

Economic Impacts

Some of the economic impacts of regulation, such as its effects on costs and prices and on the public interest, have been studied a great deal. Other economic effects of regulation, including its role in setting behavioral limits for managers, bringing about social change, and encouraging knowledge production, are less well known.

Extra Costs and Higher Prices

Cost and price increases are the outcomes that come immediately to mind when we think of the economic impacts of regulation. Murray Weidenbaum has estimated that for each dollar spent on a regulatory agency budget, twenty dollars are spent by businesses in extra costs such as purchasing and installing equipment, training workers, and adding staff to manage regulatory compliance and reporting.[6] The costs of litigation, liability insurance and liability payouts, and fines for noncompliance must be added. If companies cannot bear these extra costs and go out of business, workers, communities, suppliers, stockholders, and customers can be negatively affected.

Critics suggest that regulatory compliance costs have become excessive and are not balanced by equal or greater benefits. Sam Peltzman, for example, has analyzed the costs and benefits of the 1962 amendments to the Food, Drug, and Cosmetics Act of 1938—the law requiring all new drugs to be tested for efficacy as well as safety. He maintains that it would have been less expensive for the United States to bear the cost of 18,000 thalidomide babies than to delay the introduction of penicillin by one year.[7] Lester B. Lave claims that the "social" regulations of the 1960s and 1970s—environmental protection, worker and product safety, equal employment opportunity—have resulted in smaller gains than their costs would warrant.[8] Murray Weidenbaum criticizes consumer advocacy groups for completely ignoring business interests: "They expect business firms to listen carefully to and respond rapidly to their 'demands,' but they cavalierly dismiss the points made by any business official as mere self-serving apologetics."[9]

Regulatory compliance creates substantial outlays for companies. Eli Lilly & Company says that fifty cents out of the cost of the average prescription is spent on compliance. R. J. Reynolds' 1977 compliance costs were about $29 million. Dow Chemical Company claims its compliance costs are over $400 million per year. Members of the American Hospital Association spent $800 million in 1976 on regulatory matters. And General Motors estimates its annual compliance costs at over $1 billion.[10] Fines for noncompliance should not be ignored, though companies bring these costs upon themselves. Compliance costs are passed on to consumers in higher prices. Federally required pollution control devices on motor vehicles, for example, cost consumers an estimated $300 million in 1968, but added $18 billion in extra costs in 1984.[11]

There is another side to the story. Some analysts suggest that economists have focused too heavily on the readily quantifiable costs and benefits of regulation, and that compliance costs may be more than balanced by unexamined economic, social, and psychological benefits. Wood has criticized Peltzman's cost-benefit analysis of drug regulation for making unwarranted assumptions and for ignoring many of the costs associated with the thalidomide scandal.[12] Mescon and Vozikis report:

> An air-quality study commissioned by the EPA concluded that home buyers place a monetary value on environmental considerations in the house selection process. This conclusion was bolstered by a report of the California Association of Realtors that concluded that . . . "the price of suburban homes in smog covered areas had risen 112 percent in the decade of the 1970s, while the price of the same house in a smog free area had risen 340 percent in the same time period."[13]

Other studies provide similar support for regulatory efforts. Sanford Rose suggests that environmental protection costs do not exceed benefits, and shows how the recreational value of an unpolluted river or the property damage caused by air pollution—some of the factors generally thought to be "intangible"—can be quantified in dollars.[14] A Massachusetts Institute of Technology research team reported, among others, the following benefits of health, safety, and environmental regulations.[15]

- Public health benefits from regulating automobile pollution are worth $2.5 to $10 billion a year.
- OSHA inspections have prevented accidents conceivably resulting in 40,000 to 60,000 lost workdays and up to 350 deaths.
- Automotive safety standards have resulted in a 15 to 30 percent reduction in deaths and serious injuries.
- Crib safety standards may have resulted in reducing crib deaths by as much as 44 percent since 1974.

Balancing regulatory costs and benefits is no small task. The message for managers is that the costs to businesses alone do not tell the whole story.

More Paperwork and Red Tape

Paperwork imposes direct costs, opportunity costs, and psychological costs such as irritation and anxiety. The numbers are staggering: "The Commission on Federal Paperwork estimates that the government cranks out enough documents each year to fill 51 major-league baseball stadiums. . . . In the course of a year, the private sector fills out approximately 4000 different federal forms, requiring almost 150 million man-hours and costing the private sector $25 billion per year."[16] In 1980, Congress attempted to stem the growth of required paper by passing the Federal Paperwork Reduction Act, "to reduce paperwork and enhance the economy and efficiency of the government and the private sector by improving federal information policymaking."[17] No manager to date, however, has been heard to say that the act has made any difference in the volume of required paperwork.

The red tape aspects of regulatory reporting may be even more significant than the sheer volume. Surprisingly, there is a positive side to red tape: It is sometimes the only barrier a regulator can erect to prevent business from taking actions harmful to workers, consumers, or others. Frances Kelsey of the Food and Drug Administration was forced to use "red tape" when she actively sought to delay U.S. approval of thalidomide by insisting over a period of many months that the U.S. licensee, the Richardson-Merrill Company, fill out more papers and fill them out more thoroughly, conduct more studies, provide more information. This "benefit" of red tape is only such by default; it would not exist if agencies had appropriate enforcement mechanisms at their disposal.

On the negative side, and perhaps more significant, red tape connotes unnecessary delay, picky bureaucratism, and lack of understanding of business's need to act fast to seize opportunities. It therefore feeds adversarial relations between business and government and results in bad feelings all around.

Reduced Consumer Choice

Some regulation is designed to protect free-market functioning by enhancing the quality of consumer choice—providing better information, for example. Ironically, however, a great deal of regulation seems to reduce the choices available to consumers, thus artificially limiting the market's ability to respond to demand. Before the breakup of AT&T, the phone company was a regulated monopoly; consumers had no choice but to use its services if they wanted telephones. Regulation that erects barriers to entry in certain industries (such as steel or autos) eliminates the possibility of consumers choosing the products of small, new firms. Tariffs and import quotas reduce consumers' ability to choose imported goods. Peter Temin has complained that the regulatory approval process for new drugs prevents consumers from choosing unapproved products.[18] In recent years, terminally ill patients have traveled to other nations to obtain drugs approved abroad but still entangled in the approval process in the United States and thus not available at home. And products that are banned by the government (such as Tris-treated children's sleepwear, certain pesticides, and food additives) cannot be chosen in the marketplace.

Free-market and public choice economists maintain that consumers should be entirely free to purchase harmful or suspect products if they wish to do so. Information is always imperfect, and there is no necessary reason to expect the government to have better information than consumers. Further, even if there is no doubt that a product is hazardous, people, they argue, have a right to injure themselves.

Regulatory advocates counter with a three-pronged argument: (1) without regulation, companies have no incentive to provide adequate or accurate information, thus distorting the value of consumer choice; (2) the government has a duty to protect people as much as possible from making bad decisions; and (3) the negative effects of harming oneself do not end with the chooser. Someone must pay the costs of medical treatment, disability maintenance, and assistance to families who lose their breadwinners; others may suffer or be injured by one person's "bad" choice.

Conclusion

Regulation, despite business complaints about its extent and costs, is a legitimate way for society to enforce its value choices. Regulation is often difficult for managers to understand because it seems to have so many different rationales and to address so many competing interests. The truth is simple. Regulation *does* address competing interests and derives from various rationales; there is no single "plan" or pattern that can explain all regulatory activity.

The growth of regulation (and its current magnitude) has been one of the most striking phenomena of this century. However, regulation does not expand "just because"; it grows because there are needs to be met and demands made of the government. Some of those demands have come from consumers, some from investors, some from workers, and some from managers and business owners.

Even though the regulatory growth of the past two decades may have been stemmed, the "fourth branch of government" is not going to disappear. Regulatory oversight of business activities has grown to the point where government must be considered a working partner—sometimes cooperative, sometimes hostile—of any business.

Notes

1. Richard Hoppe, "Ozone: Industry Is Getting Its Head Out of the Clouds," *Business Week* (Oct. 13, 1986): 114.
2. James Gleick, "Sharp Ozone Drop Found Worldwide in 8-Year Period," *New York Times* (Jan. 1, 1988): 1, 37.
3. Philip Shabecoff, "Treaty on Ozone Is Backed in Senate," *New York Times* (March 15, 1988): C-2.
4. See Susan B. Garland, "Congress Is Closing In on a Plant-Closing Law," *Business Week* (July 27, 1987): 35.
5. See Murray Edelman, *The Symbolic Uses of Politics* (Urbana, IL: University of Illinois Press, 1964), and *Politics as Symbolic Action: Mass Arousal and Quiescence* (New York: Academic Press, 1971).
6. Murray Weidenbaum, *Business, Government and the Public,* 2nd ed. (Englewood Cliffs, NJ: Prentice-Hall, 1981).
7. Sam Peltzman, *Regulation of Pharmaceutical Innovation: The 1962 Amendments* (Washington, DC: American Enterprise Institute, 1974).
8. Lester B. Lave, *The Strategy of Social Regulation* (Washington, DC: The Brookings Institute, 1981).
9. Murray L. Weidenbaum, *The Future of Business Regulation: Private Action and Public Demand* (New York: AMACOM, 1979), p. 145.
10. Timothy S. Mescon and George S. Vozikis, "Federal Regulation—What Are the Costs?" *Business* (Jan.-March 1982): 35.
11. Frederick G. Kappler and Gary L. Rutledge, "Expenditures for Abating Pollutant Emissions from Motor Vehicles, 1968–1984," *Survey of Current Business* 65:7 (July 1985): 29–35.

12. Donna J. Wood, *Strategic Uses of Public Policy: Business and Government in the Progressive Era* (Boston: Ballinger, 1986).

13. Mescon and Vozikis, p. 36. See also *Federal Regulatory Directory, 1979–80* (Washington, DC: Congressional Quarterly, Inc.), pp. 41–42; and Douglas M. Costle, "Dollars and Sense," *Environment* (October 1979): 27.

14. Sanford Rose, "The Economics of Environmental Quality," *Fortune* 81:2 (Feb. 1970): 120–123, 184–186.

15. "Last Line," *Technology Review* (April 1981): 93; and Mescon and Vozikis, p. 36.

16. Mescon and Vozikis, p. 35.

17. From the preface of the Paperwork Reduction Act of 1980, Public Law 96–511.

18. Peter Temin, *Taking Your Medicine: Drug Regulation in the United States* (Cambridge, MA: Harvard University Press, 1980).

Criteria for Government Regulations

Norman E. Bowie

In a penetrating analysis of law (*The Morality of Law*), Lon Fuller identified eight conditions that any legal system must fulfill if it is to be considered a good legal system.[1] These eight conditions include (1) laws must be general (laws are not made to apply to one individual), (2) laws must be publicized, (3) laws cannot be made retroactively, (4) laws must be understandable, (5) the set of laws should not contain rules that are contradictory, (6) laws must be within the power of citizens to obey them, (7) laws must maintain a certain stability through time, and (8) laws as announced must be in agreement with their actual administration.

Fuller's eight conditions for a good legal system have such a ring of self-evidence about them that explanatory comments can be kept to a minimum. However, in the course of supplying some explanatory comment, the extent to which government regulation violates these eight conditions for good law will become obvious. The condition of generality is clearly related to the analyses of justice and the universalizability required by Kant's categorical imperative. Rules are not directed toward a single person but rather are to apply to a class of persons. Relevantly similar persons are to be treated similarly. What is a reason in one case must be a reason in all similar cases.

Despite this requirement of generality, much regulatory law proceeds in an opposite direction. Fuller says,

> In recent history perhaps the most notable failure to achieve general rules has been that of certain of our regulatory agencies, particularly those charged with allocative functions. . . . [T]hey were embarked on their careers in the belief that by proceeding at first case by case they would gradually gain an insight which would enable them to develop general standards of decision. In

Adapted from Norman E. Bowie, *Business Ethics,* © 1982, pp. 118–124. Reprinted by permission of Prentice-Hall, Inc., Englewood Cliffs, NJ.

some cases this hope has been almost completely disappointed; this is notably so in the case of the Civil Aeronautics Board and the Federal Communications Commission.[2]

If general rules are essential to good regulatory law as has been argued, then the case-by-case method is inadequate. If the government takes a position regarding water pollution from one of Bethlehem Steel's plants, the president of Bethlehem Steel should be able to conclude that the government will take a similar position on similar conditions at all Bethlehem's plants. Moreover, the president of Bethlehem Steel should be able to conclude that the same position will be taken when the same situation exists at other competing steel plants. If Fuller's description is right, the state of regulatory law is such that the president of Bethlehem Steel could *not* conclude that a similar position would be taken and hence much regulatory law is seriously deficient.

The second condition is that the laws be publicized. This condition goes hand in hand with the conditions of generality and stability. One cannot obey the law if one does not know what the law is. Regulatory law does conform— on the whole—to this condition. The regulations do appear in federal documents such as the *Federal Register*. However, any academic researcher who has worked with government documents knows that finding a rule or regulation is often no easy task. Large corporations have legal teams to assist them in knowing what the law is. However, as government regulations grow, the small business houses suffer a distinct handicap in their capability to know the law. To the extent the regulations change rapidly over time, the publicity requirement becomes harder and harder to meet.

Third, laws should not be made retroactively, and generally they are not. The reason for this requirement is clear. Laws are designed to guide behavior. A retroactive law violates the fundamental purpose of laws since it obviously cannot guide conduct. It punishes behavior that was legal at the time it was done. Business leaders complain that government regulators at least approach violating this condition when they threaten firms with penalties for environmental damage when there is no way for the firm to have known that some of its activities were causing environmental damage. A company should not be penalized for damage it caused to the earth's ozone layer when it produced fluorocarbons in the 1960s.

The fourth requirement of clarity is, to many business executives, the condition that government regulations most often violate. Loaded with jargon and bad grammar, these regulations often present a nightmare for highly trained corporate legal staffs and an impossible situation for small companies. An example to illustrate the point:

212.75 Crude Oil Produced and Sold from Unitized Properties.

(b) Definitions. For purposes of this section—"Current unit cumulative deficiency" means (1) for months prior to June 1, 1979, the total number of barrels by which production and sale of crude oil from the unitized property was less than the unit base production control level subsequent to the first month (following the establishment of a unit base production control level for that unitized property) in which any crude oil produced and sold from that unit was eligible to be classified as actual new crude oil (without regard to whether the amount of actual new crude oil was exceeded by the amount of imputed new crude oil), minus the total number of barrels of domestic crude oil produced and sold in each prior month from that unitized property (following the establishment of a unit base production control level for that unitized property) which was in excess of the unit base production control level for that month, but which was not eligible to be classified as actual new crude oil because of this requirement to reduce the amount of actual new crude oil in each month by the amount of the current unit cumulative deficiency.[3]

Fifth, a system of laws that contains laws contradicting one another is inadequate because a situation covered by the contradictory laws requires the impossible. Fuller focuses on the federal Food, Drug, and Cosmetic Act.

> Section 704 of that act defines the conditions under which an inspector may enter a factory; one of these conditions is that he first obtain the permission of the owner. Section 331 makes it a crime for the owner of the factory to refuse "to permit entry or inspection as authorized by section 704." The Act seems, then, to say that the inspector has a right to enter the factory but that the owner has a right to keep him out by refusing permission.[4]

Actually, the instances of contradiction cited by businesspersons are not so obvious as those in the case given. Most contradictions in laws governing business practice result from two sources: (1) from contradictory rules issued by independent agencies responsible for the same area and (2) from contradictory rules issued by independent agencies on separate matters but when applied in a specific case lead to contradiction.

To illustrate just how complex the issue of the contradictory nature of law can become, consider, for example, the recent Sears suit against a number of federal agencies or officers, including the Attorney General, the Secretary of Labor, the chairman of the Equal Opportunity Commission (EOC), and seven other cabinet officers and federal agencies. The issue of contention is antidiscrimination statutes. Employers like Sears are not to discriminate on the basis of race, sex, age, or physical and mental handicaps. Yet the employer is required to give preference to veterans. But since veterans are overwhelmingly male, the required preference for veterans is in contradiction with the requirement that no preference be given to sex. Preferences for veterans ipso facto give preference to males. It is reported that

> The Company [Sears] asked the court to grant an injunction requiring the defendants "to coordinate the employment of anti-discrimination statutes" and to issue uniform guidelines that would tell employers "how to resolve existing conflicts between affirmative-action requirements based on race and sex and those based on veterans' status, age, and physical or mental handicaps."[5]

Without judging either Sears' motives for the suit or its behavior with respect to nondiscrimination, the Sears request for consistency is warranted in point of logic and good regulation.

Sixth, laws requiring the impossible violate the fundamental purpose of law—the guidance of human conduct. This point seems so obvious that it hardly needs comment. Yet a tradition is growing in legal circles that clearly violates this principle. Strict liability holds a person or corporation liable for an act even when they are not responsible for it. Fuller points out the absurdity of allowing strict liability to expand so that it covers all activities.

> If strict liability were to attend, not certain specified forms of activity, but all activities, the conception of a causal connection between the act and the resulting injury would be lost. A poet writes a sad poem. A rejected lover reads it and is so depressed that he commits suicide. Who "caused" the loss of his life? Was it the poet, or the lady who jilted the deceased, or perhaps the teacher who aroused his interest in poetry? A man in a drunken rage shoots his wife. Who among those concerned with this event share the responsibility for its occurrence—the killer himself, the man who lent the gun to him, the liquor dealer who provided the gin, or was it perhaps the friend who dissuaded him from securing a divorce that would have ended an unhappy alliance?[6]

Hence, to conform to this requirement of good law, the government regulations of business must rest on an adequate theory that delineates a class of undesirable acts that can result from business activity and then assesses the extent to which business must be shown to be responsible for their acts before being held liable. It may well be, for example, that some activities (blasting) are so dangerous that strict liability should be invoked to discourage the activity in question. However, in many cases strict liability is not the appropriate legal category and business people are quite right in being concerned about its ever-growing application.

Another condition that seems constantly violated in the government regulation of business is Fuller's seventh requirement of constancy through time. Government regulations are in a constant state of flux. One political party replaces another in the White House and the rules of the game change. Let there be a change in the leadership of a major congressional committee and the rules change again.

During the early years of the environmental crisis, companies were forced or encouraged to abandon coal because it tended to be a highly polluting fuel. Now that the energy crisis is here, companies are being encouraged or forced to return to coal to save precious oil. The expenses involved in these transitions are staggering. Something must be done to control the anarchic flux so characteristic of the government regulation of business.

Finally, there should be agreement between the law and the way it is administered. It is one thing to discover what the law is. It is quite another to have the law enforced as written. Business people argue that the federal and state regulatory bureaucracies are filled with petty individuals whose only means of gaining self-respect is by blocking the legitimate plans or aims of business. The time and effort involved in fighting these people discourages the growth of small business and encourages large businesses to provide either a psychic or monetary bribe to clear the roadblocks. There has been much talk about protecting employee rights within the firm. Devices must also be found to protect the legitimate interests of individual businesses from the government bureaucracy.

To balance this criticism, the reader should know that Fuller's eight conditions for good law represent an ideal for a legal system. The reader should also realize that Fuller's ideal works best for statutes; it works somewhat less well for administrative decisions. No legal system can conform completely to Fuller's ideals. Take the condition that the law must be stable through time. Change, including change in the conditions that produced the law in the first place, requires changes in the law as well. Before OPEC and the oil crisis, cleaning up the atmosphere required regulations that discouraged the burning of coal. The oil embargo changed all that. Strategic considerations required encouragement for the use of coal. This shift in policy was expensive, but, given the changes in the world situation, the shift was necessary.

Fuller would agree here. Indeed, that is why he refers to his eight conditions as constituting a morality of the ideal rather than a morality of duty. However, Fuller is right in indicating that departures from these eight conditions do have costs, including the cost of undermining the law itself.

Others might argue that regulatory law is something of a misnomer. Regulatory "law" has less in common with law than it does with judicial decisions or executive decisions. What constitutes the disanalogy, Fuller's critics believe, is that judicial decisions or executive decisions are geared to specific situations and hence have less of the characteristic of generality than do statutes. Fuller might concede much of this point yet insist, correctly I believe, that his eight conditions still serve as an ideal for judicial and executive decisions as well. After all, Supreme Court *decisions* are viewed by everyone as establishing precedents. Perhaps the rule for the pricing of gas at the pumps need not be clear to everyone, but it should at least be clear to the oil companies, shouldn't it?

With these cautions in mind, Fuller's eight conditions for good law are fundamentally sound. Even when Fuller's eight conditions are recognized as an ideal, the fact that so much government regulatory policy stands in violation of them points out a serious inadequacy in the use of government regulation for achieving ethical corporate behavior. After all, government through its judicial system and through some regulation is, as we have seen, a requirement for a stable business environment. Both the law and business are rule-governed activities. When the rules that apply to business or that sustain and protect business violate the conditions for good law, business is harmed. Laws that are not stable do adversely affect incentives and efficiency. Laws that are not clear or that require the impossible, or that apply retroactively, or that are contradictory are unreasonable and unworkable. Both the business community and the public at large have every right to insist that the laws regulating business should conform to the criteria for good law.

Notes

1. Lon Fuller, *The Morality of Law,* rev. ed. (New Haven, CT: Yale University Press, 1964), p. 39.
2. *Ibid.,* p. 46.
3. *Federal Register,* Vol. 44, no. 69, April 9, 1979.
4. Fuller, *The Morality of Law,* p. 67.
5. "Sears Turns the Tables," *Newsweek,* February 5, 1979, pp. 86–87.
6. Fuller, *The Morality of Law,* p. 76.

R.I.P.: The Good Corporation

Robert J. Samuelson

IBM's fall from grace is more than a big business story. It also represents last rites for the "good corporation." This was our ideal of what all American companies might become. They would marry profit-making and social responsibility, economic efficiency and enlightened labor relations. IBM was the model. It seemed to do everything right, and its present troubles (including its first layoffs) have shattered the vision with unmistakable finality.

The resulting psychic void explains much of today's sense of economic insecurity. The spread of the "good corporation" was supposed to provide stable jobs and generous fringe benefits—health insurance and pensions—for more and more Americans. Instead, the process is sliding into reverse. As companies strive to stay competitive, they are shedding workers, encouraging early retirement and cutting fringe benefits. Consider:

In 1979, 55 percent of full-time male workers had employer-paid pensions. By 1988, that had dropped to 49 percent, according to the Labor Department.

Health insurance coverage is eroding, and workers must pay more of the premiums. A study by Foster Higgins, a consulting firm, finds that nearly four-fifths of companies now require employees to pay an average of $107 a month for family coverage, up from $69 in 1989.

Companies are also trimming—or eliminating—health insurance for retirees. In 1992, about half of workers in companies with more than 200 employees were promised retiree benefits, down from two-thirds in 1983, reports the consulting firm KPMG Peat Marwick.

The once-imagined vision of universal benefits and secure jobs is fading. It is not that executive suites have suddenly been hijacked by mean-spirited monsters who have replaced the previous compassionate saints. Both images are obviously overdrawn. Countless companies still make ample profits while

Washington Post, Wednesday, June 30, 1993.

treating their workers well, as a recent book ("The 100 Best Companies to Work for in America") shows.

There's 3M, which allows many employees to devote 15 percent of their time to projects of their own choosing. One recent payoff: Post-It note pads. There's Merck, which has pioneered major drugs and has such a good reputation that it receives 150,000 job applications a year. There's Motorola, which has invested massively in worker training.

Nor is it true that stable jobs have vanished. Among men, the typical worker between the ages of 45 and 54 has been with his present employer 12 years. About a third have been there 20 years or more. As more women pursue careers, their job tenure is actually increasing. Still, something has changed. What's gone is a sense of confidence, a faith that jobs—or careers—are permanent. The anxiety may exaggerate the reality, but it is keenly felt.

The idea of the "good corporation" assumed that superior American management could easily blend two roles: the company as a fierce economic competitor and the company as a welfare state for its workers. There seemed to be no conflict. Stable jobs and ample fringe benefits would make workers loyal, and loyal workers would make companies prosper. IBM is hardly the first company to disappoint the ideal. The unraveling really started in the 1970s with troubles at firms like Penn Central and Chrysler.

But IBM's downfall has special meaning, because it seemed the best of the best. No company, regardless of how prosperous, now seems permanently safe from upheaval. We overestimated the prowess of U.S. management and underestimated the disruptive power of market changes, from new technologies to foreign competitors. We also found that corporate generosity does not automatically create corporate competence. Companies where life became too cushy often lapsed into overconfident mediocrity.

In some ways, these changes have been healthy. The new insecurity—more realistic than the old complacency—often motivates managers and workers to keep their companies viable. But in another sense, the changes have left us adrift. We now lack a clear concept of what "good management" means. It used to be benevolent shrewdness. Does it now include necessary cruelty: axing one-third of the company to save the other two-thirds?

What also has been wounded is our idea of the welfare state. Since World War II this has always been an unofficial blend of private and government benefits. As more firms became "good companies," we thought, more workers would receive welfare benefits (health insurance, pensions). Government would protect only the poor, disabled and aged. Companies had become spontaneous instruments of social policy; for a citizenry suspicious of government, this seemed just fine.

There were always some groups that didn't fit easily into this welfare system, as Mary E. O'Connell of Northeastern University writes in *The American Prospect* magazine. These included workers in low-paying industries with high labor turnover and women who moved between the home and paid work. But these excluded groups are now increasingly joined by full-time career workers, whose companies either aren't offering comprehensive benefits or are cutting back. Gaps in the social safety net widen.

What to do? The impending health care debate is partially a product of this breakdown. People increasingly fear losing health insurance, so government may mandate—or provide directly—the coverage. Parental-leave legislation (requiring time off for new parents) reflected the same impulse. If companies don't do the right thing, then government will make them. But, of course, it isn't that simple.

Governments that saddle companies with more labor costs ultimately discourage companies from hiring. And mandated benefits, whether paid by government with payroll taxes or simply imposed on business by regulation, are higher labor costs. The effect is the same as an increase in the minimum wage: If the wage rises too high, companies won't hire workers who seem worth less. Europe has drifted disastrously down this path. In 1970, its unemployment was 2.6 percent; now it is about 11 percent.

So the death of the "good corporation" poses hard issues. There are many good companies, but many don't reach our ideal, and some that now do won't in the future. We are discovering the world as it is, not as we wished it to be.

New Patterns in Government Regulation of Business

George A. Steiner*

A new wave of government regulation of business began in 1962. The purpose of this article is primarily to illustrate the dimensions of this new wave and their significance to individual businesses and the evolution of the business institution. These dimensions are not presented in any particular order of importance. They are not mutually exclusive. All are interrelated.

Not only has the volume of regulation growth dramatically during the past sixteen years but also, when aggregated with past governmental regulations, the result is an extraordinary total body of federal regulations affecting business.[1] So huge is this body of regulation that one executive lamented, and probably correctly: "The volume of laws and regulations is such that no one can comply faithfully with all rules. No large organization can effectively police all its employees."[2]

It is not easy to portray the sheer volume of regulations to which business is subject. One dimension, of course, is federal expenditure for regulatory

Excerpted from "New Patterns in Government Regulation of Business," published in *MSU Business Topics*, Autumn 1978. Reprinted by permission of publisher.
*Kunin Professor of Business and Society, and Professor of Management Emeritus, University of California/Los Angeles.

activities, most of which goes to pay employees to regulate business. From 1974 to 1978, federal expenditures (for consumer safety and health; job safety and other working conditions; energy; financial reporting and other financial controls; and industry-specific regulation) increased 85 percent, from $2.030 billion to $3.764 billion.[3]

In 1975 there appeared in the *Federal Register* 177 proposed rules and 2865 proposed amendments to existing rules. During the same period, the *Federal Register* printed 309 final rules and 7305 final rule amendments. In 1975, therefore, federal agencies had under consideration more than 10,000 regulations. This was an increase of 14 percent over 1974. The number of pages in the *Federal Register* rose from more than 20,000 in 1970 to more than 60,000 in 1975, an increase of more than 200 percent.[4]

As late as the mid-1950s, the federal government assumed major regulatory responsibility in only four areas: antitrust, financial institutions, transportation, and communications. In 1976, eighty-three federal agencies were involved in regulating private business activity. Of these, thirty-four had been created after 1960.[5] Included in the former group are agencies such as the Interstate Commerce Commission, Civil Aeronautics Board, Federal Trade Commission, Federal Communications Commission, Federal Reserve Board, and Securities and Exchange Commission. In the latter group are the newer agencies, such as the Environmental Protection Agency, Equal Employment Opportunity Commission, Consumer Product Safety Commission, and Occupational Safety and Health Administration.

The Growing Costs of Regulation

Federal expenditures for regulatory employees, noted above, are merely the tip of the iceberg of the total cost of these regulations. There is, of course, no reliable single measure of cost; a number of types of cost must be considered.

In 1975 the Ford administration made an official estimate that the annual cost to consumers of unnecessary and wasteful regulatory policies was $2000 per family. The total cost, therefore, was estimated to be $130 billion. The Center for the Study of American Business, Washington University, St. Louis, Missouri, calculated that in fiscal 1979 the aggregate cost of government regulation would be $102.7 billion. By comparison, the total costs in fiscal 1977 were $79.1 billion.[6] While these numbers cannot, of course, be exact, they do reveal the magnitude of the cost.

Old and New Regulation

It is important to observe that there are major differences between the old and new models of regulation. The new model might be called *functional social* regulation in contrast to the older *industrial* regulation. All regulation, of course, is social in that it is ultimately concerned with social welfare, but there are basic distinctions between the models.

The old style of regulation was concerned with one industry, such as railroads, airlines, drugs, and so on. The focus was on such matters as markets, rates, and obligations to serve the public. There were regulations that cut across industry lines but the main focus was on industrial segments. In contrast, the newer functional regulations cut across industrial lines. They are broader in scope and are concerned with one function in an organization, not the entirety of the organization. As a result, of course, the newer regulations affect far more industries and companies than older regulations and, therefore, more customers.

Newer regulations have different purposes and apply different policies and methods. There are several aspects of this dimension. First, in a simplistic way, the purposes of the new legislation differ from the older regulatory agencies. For example, the older independent regulatory agencies, such as the Civil Aeronautics Board, the Federal Trade Commission, and so on, were designed to prevent monopoly; increase competition; save free enterprise from big business; establish uniform standards of safety, security, communications, and financial practice; and prevent abuses of managerial practices.

The newer regulations are the results of pressures to improve the quality of life. The purposes of the newer regulations are to clean up the environment, employ minorities, assure greater safety and health of workers, provide more information to consumers, protect consumers from shoddy products, and so on.

Second, in the achievement of their purposes the newer agencies do not establish policy to guide private industry in its operations, but specify in detail what shall be done. The National Highway Traffic Safety Administration, which now administers the Motor Vehicle Safety Standards Act of 1966, is very specific about safety features which automobiles must have. This is what Charles Schultze calls a "command and control" method of regulation. He points out that once a decision is made to intervene in the market, the current pattern of regulation is not to seek to alter incentives in the marketplace, modify information flows, or change institutional structures. Rather, direct intervention, the command and control technique, is almost always chosen. Seldom do we try other alternatives, "regardless of whether that mode of response fits the problem."[7]

A third dimension of the new regulations is that legislation is lengthy and specific. Government regulatory legislation in the past established broad policies, with comparatively little specific guidance, and gave the regulatory agency wide powers to set detailed regulations in conformance with the public interest and the policy guidelines drawn by the Congress. Today's legislation tends to be lengthy and detailed. The EPA, for example, administers statutes that run into hundreds of pages of detailed specifications. The Clean Air Act sets specific pollution-reduction targets and timetables and leaves the EPA little discretion.

Two significant results ensue. First, government today is an active managerial partner with business executives. This partnership extends all the way from the governance of corporations to the specific ways in which products are produced and distributed. Many business managers today are in fact acting as agents of the government without being under contract.[8] Second, government is losing the power of motivated individuals in the decentralized market process. As Schultze has put it:

> Regardless of the circumstances . . . new social intervention has almost always been output-oriented, giving short shrift to the process-oriented alternative. And this has proven a costly bias. It has, with no offsetting gain, forfeited the strategic advantages of market-like arrangements. It has led to ineffective and inefficient solutions to important social problems. It has taxed, well beyond its limit, the ability of government to make complex output decisions. And it has stretched thin the delicate fabric of political consensus by unnecessarily widening the scope of activities it must cover.[9]

Nonsense Regulations

One significant dimension of federal regulation is the growth of nonsense regulations.[10] OSHA regulates trivia in exquisite detail, as the following examples from the *Code of Federal Regulations* of 1 July 1975 reveal:

> Section 1910.35(b): Exit access is that portion of a means of egress which leads to the entrance to an exit.
>
> Section 1910.25(d)(vii): [out of 21 pages of fine print devoted to ladders] when ascending or descending, the user should face the ladder; . . . (d)(2)(xx): The bracing on the back leg of step ladders is designed solely for increasing stability and not for climbing.
>
> Section 1910.244(a)(2)(vii): Jacks which are out of order shall be tagged accordingly, and shall not be used until repairs are made.

Such trivia has little to do with the important causes of industrial accidents and worker illness. Many silly rules on worker safety have been eliminated or modified, but many remain.[11]

Nonsense regulations are not, of course, confined to OSHA. Other regulatory agencies are just as guilty of this shortcoming.

Conflicts Among Regulations

There have always been conflicts among government regulations, but the number, intensity, and incidence have been mounting. Cases have arisen in which the EPA has demanded that a plant convert from coal to oil to reduce atmospheric pollution. At the same time, power plants have been ordered to convert from oil to coal by the Department of Energy to reduce oil consumption. Antipollution requirements have forced some companies to abandon marginal plants, a policy which conflicts with federal goals of reduced unemployment.[12]

New Technological Issues

The new policy regulations are raising significant and controversial technological issues. For example, we all want clean air, clean water, less noise, and protection of workers from carcinogens. In dealing with such matters the question of standards arises. Generally speaking, the costs of eliminating 90 percent of hazardous effluent from a belching smokestack are not great in light of total costs of production. Each additional percentage point of air purification, however, can be achieved only by accelerating costs, until the last few percentage points become prohibitively expensive.

Extremely sensitive issues arise with respect to equating statistical loss of life with costs of controls. Sam Peltzman, for instance, concluded that Federal Drug Administration regulations which delay the introduction of new drugs on the market save fewer lives than would a quicker introduction of the drugs.[13] Of course, different lives are involved. How should the cost-benefit equation be balanced?

With growing scientific knowledge, more and more hazards to life are becoming apparent. Decisions about technical matters, such as whether to put fluorocarbons or another substance in spray-propelled fluids, no longer are being left to private industry. No one knows in all cases what a rational decision is or how it should be made.

New biological, chemical, and other findings are continuously raising difficult technical questions. They reflect, of course, a growing awareness of hazards to human life and a national policy to reduce them. The policy is not a question here, but the fact is that new regulations do become embroiled in controversial technical issues undreamed of in the past.

Bureaucratic Imperialism

Bureaucrats tend to be arbitrary, authoritarian, arrogant, and uncompromising in making and applying rules. Furthermore, a certain antipathy toward business exists in the U.S. federal bureaucracy, and in recent years this tendency seems to have increased. Irving Kristol, who has been observing the scene for some time, has concluded:

> Here we must be candid as well as careful. Though officialdom will deny it—sometimes naively, sometimes not—it is a fact that most of those holding career jobs in EPA, OSHA, and other newer regulatory agencies have an ideological animus against the private economic sector. . . . They are not in those jobs because they could not find any others. Most of them, in truth, are sufficiently educated and intelligent to find better-paying jobs in the world of business. But they are not much interested in money. They are idealistic—that is, they are concerned with exercising power so as to create "a better world."[14]

Another characteristic of some officials is a reluctance, if not lack of interest, to consider the cost of their regulations. Weidenbaum quotes a member of the CPSC: "When it involves a product that is unsafe, I don't care how much it costs the company to correct the problem."[15] Such an attitude can lead not only to ignoring alternative solutions to a problem but also to severe injury to the regulated. Weidenbaum cites the example of an offending company that had not pasted a label on its product bearing the correct statement required by a regulation ("cannot be made nonpoisonous"). The company was forced to destroy the contents. "If you do not care about costs," noted Weidenbaum, "apparently you do not think about such economical solutions as pasting a new label on the can."[16]

A more serious illustration of the unfortunate results of such an attitude concerns the Marlin Toy Products Company of Horicon, Wisconsin. The CPSC mistakenly put the company's toy on its ban list. When the error was called to its attention, the agency refused to issue a retraction, and the company was forced out of business.[17]

Regulations that are trivial, seemingly contrary to common sense, arbitrarily imposed and administered, and difficult to understand tend to erode respect for the law and willingness to comply with it.

Conflicts Among Economic, Legal, and Political Rationality

A major pattern in federal regulation is the significant shift which has taken place from market to political-legal decisions. More and more governmental regulatory decisions are supplanting market decisions, and less reliance is being placed on the market mechanism in achieving the objectives of society.

Associated with this phenomenon is the conflict which often occurs among economic, political, and legal rationality. What is politically rational may not be, and frequently is not, economically rational. The obvious result, therefore, is the injection of more and more irrationality into the private market mechanism. A theme discussed by Schultze is the tendency of government to intervene in resource allocation decisions in order to achieve equity and income distribution goals.[18] The failure to disentangle the two may lead to irrational economic decisions because of what politicians see as politically rational actions. The problem in devising an energy program is a case in point.

As implementation and adjudication of regulations move into courts of law, a further potential conflict with economic rationality arises. Courts have their own rationality rooted, of course, in the law. Rationality concerns adherence to legal precedents, seeking a balance among many competing values and interests, and a bias toward exploration of all matters in a case with equal thoroughness and diligence, irrespective of their relative importance in economic life.[19] It is not at all surprising, therefore, that many legal decisions may not square with the logic of the economic market mechanism.

Within a particular government regulatory agency with rationality of politics and law may collide with economic rationality. A former U.S. tariff commissioner, a trained economist, has lamented the difficulties in behaving like an economist in a government agency.[20]

The Regulatory Cost-Benefit Equation

Regulations have protected and subsidized business interests as well as consumer and general public interests. Regulation has helped society achieve economic and social goals. It has helped to improve the position of minorities, achieve cleaner air, hold business accountable, prevent abuses of the market mechanism, prevent monopoly, reduce industrial accidents, and so on. The list of pluses of government regulation is long.

On the other hand, there are substantial costs of regulation, using cost in a broad sense. Many, but by no means all, have been discussed here.

In the aggregate, the costs of today's government regulations seem greater than the benefits. Twenty-five years ago the power scale between business and government was balanced reasonably well.[21] Five years ago, the balance seemed to be reasonable.[22] Today, the overall balance is significantly upset in favor of government.

Notes

1. It is recognized, of course, that there is a vast and growing volume of state and local regulation of business. Limited space forces me to deal only with federal controls.
2. Eleanore Carruth, "The 'Legal Explosion' Has Left Business Shell-Shocked" *Fortune* 87 (April 1973): 65.
3. Murray L. Weidenbaum, "A Fundamental Reform of Government Regulation," in George A. Steiner, ed., *Business and Its Changing Environment* (Los Angeles: UCLA Graduate School of Management, 1978), p. 189.
4. William Lilley III and James C. Miller III, "The New Social Regulation," *Public Interest* 45 (Spring 1977): 5–51.
5. Charles L. Schultze, The *Public Use of Private Interest* (Washington, D.C.: The Brookings Institution, 1977), p. 7.
6. Reported in the *New York Times,* 13 April 1978.
7. Schultze, *Public Use of Private Interest,* p. 13.
8. Weidenbaum, "Business, Government, and the Public."
9. Schultze, *Public Use of Private Interest.*
10. *Ibid.*
11. "Interview with Eula Bingham, Head of the Occupational Safety and Health Administration," *U.S. News & World Report,* 16 January 1978, p. 65.
12. Murray L. Weidenbaum, "The Costs of Government Regulation," Publication No. 12, Center for the Study of American Business, Washington University (St. Louis: February 1977).
13. Sam Peltzman, "An Evaluation of Consumer Protection Legislation: The 1962 Drug Amendments," *Journal of Political Economy* 81 (September/October 1973): 1049–91.
14. Irving Kristol, "A Regulated Society?" *Regulation* 1 (July/August 1977): 13.
15. Murray L. Weidenbaum, "The Case for Economizing on Government Controls," *Journal of Economic Issues* 11 (June 1975): 207.
16. *Ibid.*
17. Comptroller General of the United States, *Banning of Two Toys and Certain Aerosol Spray Adhesives,* MWD-75-65 (Washington, D.C.: U.S. General Accounting Office, 1975).
18. Schultze, *Public Use of Private Interest.*
19. Norman Kangun and R. Charles Moyer, "The Failings of Regulation," *MSU Business Topics* 24 (Spring 1976): 5–14.
20. Penelope Hartland-Thunberg, "Tales of a One-time Tariff Commissioner," *Challenge* 19 (July-August 1977): 6–12.

21. George A. Steiner, *Government's Role in Economic Life* (New York: John Wiley & Sons, 1953).
22. George A. Steiner, *Business and Society,* 1st ed. (New York: Random House, 1971).

Government Regulation: The Vision Thing

Jane Uebelhoer

Government regulation is a topic of central importance in business ethics. As the other authors in this section have explained in detail, the requirements of governments are a major determinant in the operations of most businesses. Government interventions have the potential to do great harm and great good for business' many stakeholders.

My main interest in this article is with deficiencies in our analyses of government regulation, rather than with deficiencies in the regulations themselves. I will discuss these deficiencies and propose an alternative approach.

Tellingly, people often react with strong emotion to the topic of government regulation of business. Consider what the well-known economist Milton Friedman has to say: He asks, what does a drastic slowdown in economic growth in the United States have to do with a "veritable explosion in government regulatory activity"?

> The answer is that whatever the announced objectives, all of the movements in the past two decades—the consumer movement, the ecology movement, the back-to-the-land movement, the protect-the-wilderness movement, the zero-population growth movement, the "small is beautiful movement", the antinuclear movement—have had one thing in common. All have been anti-growth. They have been opposed to new developments, to industrial innovation, to the increased use of natural resources. Agencies established in response to these movements have imposed heavy costs on industry after industry to meet increasingly detailed and extensive government requirements.[1]

On the opposite side of the political spectrum, we can find government regulation being denounced with similar passion. According to socialist political scientist Michael Parenti,

> The political appointees who preside over the various administrative units of government are usually so tightly bound to private interests that it is often difficult to tell the regulators from the regulated. . . . In a capitalist society the special interests are the *systemic interest,* controlling the economic life of the society. . . . And when meeting the system on its own terms, regulation becomes a way to rig prices at artificially high levels, control markets for the benefits of large producers, secure high profits, and allow private corporations more direct and covert access to public authority.[2]

Jane Uebelhoer. "Government Regulation: The Vision Thing." Original essay.

How is it that Friedman and Parenti can both condemn regulation, but for precisely opposite reasons? How can regulation seem to Friedman to be a drag on business, hamstringing enterprise and sapping its vitality, while Parenti sees regulation as a boondoggle orchestrated by the rich for the rich?

The explanation is due in part to the fact that Parenti and Friedman take as their main examples different types of regulation. Friedman's main, but not exclusive, targets are social regulations like those coming out of the Food and Drug Administration (FDA) and the Environmental Protection Agency (EPA).

In contrast, Parenti's chief complaints are against industry regulation like that issued by the Federal Communications Commission (FCC), Interstate Commerce Commission (ICC) or the Nuclear Regulatory Commission (NRC). Parenti claims that this type of regulation "limits entry into a market, subsidizes select industries, sets production standards that only big companies can meet, weakens small competitors, and encourages monopoly pricing."[3]

But this difference in emphasis between Parenti and Friedman is only part of the story. I believe that the conventional understandings of business, and government, and government regulation of business, are too ideological to be useful. When partisans like Parenti and Friedman battle over regulation, they are struggling ultimately over larger questions about who should control political and economic systems.

Government Regulation: The Standard View

Most analyses of government regulation of business, including the essays which appear in this volume (Wood, Bowie, and Steiner) take mainstream microeconomic theory as a background assumption. This theory depicts economic exchange as taking place in markets which are, ideally, perfectly competitive and free. Such markets exhibit the following characteristics:

1. There are numerous buyers and sellers, none of whom has a substantial share of the market.
2. All buyers and sellers can freely and immediately enter or leave the market.
3. Every buyer and seller has full and perfect knowledge of what every other buyer and seller is doing, including knowledge of the prices, quantities, and qualities of all goods being bought and sold.
4. The goods being sold in the market are so similar to each other that no one cares from whom each buys or sells.
5. The costs and benefits of producing or using the goods being exchanged are borne entirely by those buying or selling the goods and not by any other external parties.
6. All buyers and sellers are utility maximizers: each tries to get as much as possible for as little as possible.
7. No external parties (such as the government) regulate the price, quantity, or quality of any of the goods being bought and sold in the market.[4]

It is commonly argued[5] that perfectly competitive, free markets are morally good. Utilitarians claim that such markets will maximize utility because they are efficient. Justice is served because everyone receives both benefits and burdens exactly in proportion as they contribute. And negative rights are respected because everyone will enjoy more liberty than could be obtained under any other system.

No market exhibits all seven of these characteristics. Some markets have only one or a few sellers (e.g., electric power); some markets impose barriers to entry (e.g., licenses to practice medicine); participants in some markets have imperfect knowledge (e.g., consumers purchasing pesticides); some goods in a market are dissimilar to other goods in that market (e.g., when consumers are loyal to a brand); some costs are borne by people outside the market (e.g., people who live downstream of a polluting factory); some buyers are not utility maximizers (e.g., a shopkeeper who sets prices altruistically); and some markets are regulated by external parties (e.g., imports which are subject to tariffs).

Within this analysis, the object of any morally defensible regulation of business by government would be to make a real market more like the ideal market. That is, legitimate regulation aims to correct market defects.

So, on this analysis, moral assessment of government regulation is a straightforward matter. First, we give a strong weight to not interfering in people's exchanges because we value liberty and choice for their own sake. Holding this value constant, does a regulatory intervention bring markets much closer to the ideal? Does the intervention correct a significant market defect better than any alternative intervention, and much better than no intervention at all? It is permissible for the regulator to act only if the answers are "yes"?

Problems with the Standard View

If we start from the ideal of perfectly competitive free markets, it is glaringly obvious that all markets will always be extremely defective. We noted above that no market exhibits all seven of the features of the ideal, but on closer inspection we will find that very few markets exhibit any of them. A quick run through the list will make the point.

1. There are numerous buyers and sellers, none of whom has a substantial share of the market. (*Virtually all markets in the United States today are highly concentrated.*[6])

2. All buyers and sellers can freely and immediately enter or leave the market. (*Substantial barriers are common.*)

3. Every buyer and seller has full and perfect knowledge of what every other buyer and seller is doing, including knowledge of the prices, quantities, and qualities of all goods being bought and sold. (*Far from the truth.*)

4. The goods being sold in the market are so similar to each other that no one cares from whom each buys or sells. (*Real difference in quality, and perceptions of differences created by marketing, are the rule.*)

5. The costs and benefits of producing or using the goods being exchanged are borne entirely by those buying or selling the goods and not by any other external parties. (*Everything we do pollutes, depletes resources, takes a toll on workers' health, etc.*)
6. All buyers and sellers are utility maximizers: each tries to get as much as possible for as little as possible. (*This is the "economic man" assumption about which much will be said later.*)
7. No external parties (such as the government) regulate the price, quantity, or quality of any of the goods being bought and sold in the market. (*See the articles above by Steiner and Wood.*)

It is remarkable on inspection how very fanciful these characteristics are. "The issue is not why abstractions should be employed in pursuing general economic questions—the nature of the inquiry makes this inevitable—but why would one choose an assumption which one believed to be not merely inaccurate in detail but fundamentally mistaken?"[7]

In sum, the promising framework for assessing government intervention—good regulations correct market defects—turns out to be much less useful than we had hoped.[8] Since no amount of intervention could even in principle transform a market into the ideal, what's to be done? What's to be avoided?

The Feminist Vision

There are many feminisms. One form, liberal feminism, is consistent with the standard analysis sketched above. The concern of liberal feminists is equality of opportunity. Liberals believe that a person's talents, and the demand for those talents in the market, should determine status and income.[9]

Liberal feminists claim that job markets are flawed to the extent that women are the victims of discrimination. Discrimination is a barrier against entry by women into the labor market, and such barriers are market defects that should be corrected. Decisions with regard to hiring, training, promotion and retention should be made without regard to the gender of the candidate. To the extent that government intervention can create gender blindness, without producing more harm and disruption in the process, government may intervene.

For our purposes here, I will contrast liberal feminists with critical feminists, a large, extremely diverse group. Critical feminists share a commitment to unmasking structures of domination and subordination in society. Critical feminists contend that the race, class and gender of a subject necessarily influences the subject's beliefs and experiences.[10]

A feminist would begin this project by noticing that public policy has always been and continues to be the domain of middle class white males. Public policy bears the stamp of its creators, it promotes their interests, and mistakes their experiences for the human experience.

To illustrate, let's begin to unmask the standard analysis of government regulation. Why, in the first place, should the regulation of business be considered a problem? Why think in dichotomous terms about "business" and "government"?

The standard analysis draws upon John Locke's view of rights and property. Locke is credited with framing modern political debate by asking the question, "When is the government justified in limiting the liberty of citizens?" This question assumes that people are atomistic individuals and that negative rights, the rights to be left alone to do as one pleases, are of the first importance. Further, Locke developed a moral justification for private property,[11] and argued for a natural moral right to hold and use property that was legitimately acquired. Locke's theory of the social contract encourages us to think of human beings as having skills and interests which predate our membership in a society. It should not surprise us that the figures which emerge from the state of nature to enter into the social contract have the distinctive values and interests of white, middle class, English men.

Locke helps us set the stage for economic man—a view of people as freestanding individuals who are exclusively self-interested and completely rational. As we learned above, ideal markets are ones peopled by economic men. This world is one in which rational self-interested individuals perpetually busy themselves with maximizing their own wealth. It is economic men who go into business, and markets emerge at the intersection of their self-interested activities. Because each is concerned to get the most for the least at all times, it is guaranteed that every resource will be put to its most efficient use. Economic man wants nothing more than to be left alone to enrich himself, and it is most fortunate, even if paradoxical that, as Adam Smith claims, the unrestrained pursuit of self-interest is the ideal means to achieve the common good.

Ipso facto, government regulation of business is wrong except to correct market defects. Government's function is to codify the law of nature, and to judge and punish those who break the law. It is our moral duty to engage in economic activity, a duty which follows from our moral obligation to preserve our lives. Government must stand clear of legitimate economic activities.

Who is comprehended under the term "economic man"? Not children or old people or sick people with nothing to sell in the market. A mainstream economist would have to admit that gestation and lactation are economic activities; through these activities women give birth to and suckle human capital. But birthing and rearing children are not activities which would be pursued by rational utility maximizers. Something is wrong with women or something is wrong with the model. We might share the amazement of economist Rebecca Blank:

> Too often, during a seminar or conversation with a colleague, I've suddenly realized with surprise, "He really *believes* all of this stuff about individuals constantly making fully informed and rational choices accounting for all expected lifetime costs and benefits." . . . The analytical cleanliness

and mathematical manipulability of the economic model, while enormously attractive intellectually, was never convincing enough to overcome my intuitive reaction: "This model should never be confused with reality."[12]

In the standard model, there are self-made men. Like the man in Locke's story, these men happen upon land which was previously unclaimed by anyone, including indigenous peoples. They clear the land, plant it, harvest the fruits, and thereby acquire rights of ownership over as much of the produce of the land as they can use before it spoils.

What's wrong with this picture? Very few contemporary people have been the first to claim land. And why should we assume at the outset that land is the sort of thing one can rightfully own, and rightfully exclude others from using? Perhaps land is always on loan. And whatever plausibility this story might have had for real sodbusters and homesteaders, it seems to lack all connection to the CEO of a Fortune 500 firm.

A more realistic picture of the entrepreneur's relation to the group has the businessperson using countless public resources. Businesses use air, water, minerals, plants, and soil. Businesses draw upon infrastructure like roads, telephone cables, electrical power, water, and sewers. They employ workers raised by their parents, educated in public schools, born in public hospitals, and perhaps buried at public expense. The enterprise relies on know-how accumulated by human communities for aeons. The businessperson is alive and well by the generosity of his or her parents, grandparents, teachers, priests, and neighbors. The police and military protect the business and the businessperson from foreign and domestic aggressors. They also protect air traffic, shipping, ownership of and access to natural resources, and access to foreign markets. The environment is fouled at many stages of the process. And the businessperson's very success dictates the conditions of life for countless others. Will we ride in cars or on trains? Will we make a living wage or not?

No, there are no self-made men. And given that the community supports and enables the activities of the businessperson at every step, ought not the community determine the direction of the enterprise?

Assume instead with some feminist theorists a model of being human suggested by the expression the "body politic." Each of us is an interdependent member of a human community, and these communities are interdependent parts of the biosphere. Each of us shapes and is shaped by others. We are a system of connected selves, and we will necessarily prosper or fail together.

Perhaps greed and self-interest are neither necessary nor ideal. Perhaps we should valorize instead the perspective which the Buddhist takes on work:

> The Buddist point of view takes the function of work to be at least three fold: to give a man a chance to utilize and develop his faculties; to enable him to overcome his egocenteredness by joining with other people in a common task; and to bring forth the goods and services needed for a becoming existence.[13]

In short, we would have a richer, more powerful explanatory scheme if we embedded the model of economic man in a larger descriptive framework; that is, we should see "economic man" as an example of a how people sometimes approach economic activities.

In this broader model it would be easier to pursue alternative values. Examples include resource conservation; social justice; affordable quality day care; progressive income tax; public support for the arts; long vacations for everyone; decentralization of economic and political decision making; and workplace democracy.

Feminist Theory and Government Regulation

In this broader model inspired by feminism, how would we assess government regulation? A specific, instructive example is supplied by Donald McCloskey. He argues that if we were to look at the economy through feminine eyes we would place a much higher monetary value on a human life than we do now.

> . . . individual self-valuation is only part of the value of a life. In a society with solidarity a life is technically speaking a public good, to be valued by summed values that the citizenry places on it. . . . The upshot is that the value of life calculated on the assumption of *vir economicus* is probably a small fraction of the correct, conjective value . . . interfering more with the devil-may-care-attitude of males, especially young ones . . . Consequently, though a feminine economy would need spontaneously less interference, the interference that did take place would be more thorough—one might say, more motherly.[14]

If McCloskey's arguments hold, we would find lawmakers and regulators operating on the feminist model being more conservative about the risks businesspeople would be able to impose on nonconsenting workers, consumers and third parties.

Economic and political decision making would be decentralized, participatory and inclusive. Regulation which we morally approve of must both be arrived at through a just process, and must bring about desirable consequences. To arrive at morally defensible regulation it is necessary to "include the perspectives of those historically excluded from the construction of economic knowledge into the critical dialogues of the field."[15] We must take seriously the fact that each of us speaks out a "sociologically specific, explicitly gendered, and practically engaged situation"[16] by including all parties at the table when policies are formulated and adopted.[17]

When operating in the feminist model we would still value liberty and economic efficiency—we want to get everyone's needs met and have time for leisure. So although we need not be apologetic about imposing requirements on business activities, we will do so carefully and thoughtfully.

Conclusion

The standard analysis of government regulation of business is highly ideological. It assumes individualism, and it masks gender and other power relations in politics and the economy. By throwing the topic open to reconceptualization from a feminist perspective, we have begun to sketch a new set of criteria for the moral assessment of government interventions in business. In the process we have also hinted at new ideals for businesspersons and new social expectations for business.

Notes

1. Milton and Rose Friedman, *Free to Choose: A Personal Statement* (New York: 1990), 191.
2. Michael Parenti, *Democracy for the Few, 5th ed.* (New York: 1988), 268–269.
3. Parenti, 272–273.
4. Manuel G. Velasquez, *Business Ethics: Concepts and Cases* (3rd) (Englewood Cliffs, 1992) 175.
5. See for example Douglas S. Sherwin, "The Ethical Roots of the Business System", in A Pablo Iannone (ed.) *Contemporary Moral Controversies in Business* (New York, 1989), 35–43; Richard T. DeGeorge, *Business Ethics (3rd)* (New York, 1990) 122–123; John R. Boatright, *Ethics and the Conduct of Business* (Englewood Cliffs, 1993), 91–120; Velasquez, 180–184.
6. Roger N. Waud, *Microeconomics, 5th ed.* (New York: 1992) 298–301.
7. Amartya K. Sen, "Rational Fools: A Critique of the Behavioral Assumptions of Economic Theory," in *Beyond Self-Interest,* Jane J. Mansbridge, ed. (Chicago: 1990), 25.
8. The standard analysis is useful as a general rationale. We can appeal to this model of economic exchange in an attempt to justify a move to internalize costs, or provide information to consumers, or punish price fixing. These initiatives could be justified on other grounds as well.
9. Alison M. Jaggar and Paula Rothenberg Struhl, *Feminist Frameworks* (New York: 1979) 82.
10. Or as Nancy Fraser puts it, critical social theory would "employ categories and explanatory models which revealed rather than occluded relations of male dominance and female subordination. And it would demystify as ideological any rival approaches that obfuscated or rationalized those relations." *Unruly Practices: Power, Discourse and Gender in Contemporary Social Theory,* (Minneapolis: 1989) 113.
11. John Locke, *The Second Treatise of Government* (Indianapolis, 1952) 16–13.
12. Rebecca M. Blank "What Should Mainstream Economists Learn from Feminist Theory?" in Marianne A. Ferber and Julie A. Nelson (eds.) *Beyond Economic Man: Feminist Theory and Economics* (Chicago, 1993) 133.
13. E. F. Schumacher, *Small Is Beautiful: Economics as if People Mattered.* (New York: 1973), 54–55.
14. Donald N. McCloskey, "Some Consequences of a Conjective Economics" in Ferber and Nelson, 80.
15. Helen E. Longino, "Economics for Whom?" in Ferber and Nelson, 168.
16. Fraser, 7.
17. These are akin to the proposals advanced by Osborne and Gaebler in their book which has been so popular with the Clinton Administration, *Reinventing Government,* (New York, 1993). Government decision making, they say, must be pushed out to the periphery, to the many public employees working in public institutions.

CHAPTER 14

The Government's Role in Economic Justice

Interpretations of the Second Principle

John Rawls

The Liberal Interpretation

The principle of efficiency can be applied to the basic structure by reference to the expectations of representative men.[1] Thus we can say that an arrangement of rights and duties in the basic structure is efficient if and only if it is impossible to change the rules, to redefine the scheme of rights and duties, so as to raise the expectations of any representative man (at least one) without at the same time lowering the expectations of some (at least one) other representative man. Of course, these alterations must be consistent with the other principles. That is, in changing the basic structure we are not permitted to violate the principle of equal liberty or the requirement of open positions. What can be altered is the distribution of income and wealth and the way in which organizational powers, and various other forms of authority, regulate cooperative activities. Consistent with the constraints of liberty and accessibility, the allocation of these primary goods may be adjusted to modify the expectations of representative individuals. An arrangement of the basic structure is efficient when there is no way to change this distribution so as to raise the prospects of some without lowering the prospects of others.

There are, I shall assume, many efficient arrangements of the basic structure. Each of these specifies a particular division of advantages from social

John Rawls, *A Theory of Justice* (Cambridge, MA: Harvard U. Press, 1971). "A Liberal Social Order."

cooperation. The problem is to choose between them, to find a conception of justice that singles out one of these efficient distributions as also just. If we succeed in this, we shall have gone beyond mere efficiency yet in a way compatible with it. Now it is natural to try out the idea that as long as the social system is efficient there is no reason to be concerned with distribution. All efficient arrangements are in this case declared equally just. Of course, this suggestion would be outlandish for the allocation of particular goods to known individuals. No one would suppose that it is a matter of indifference from the standpoint of justice whether any one of a number of men happens to have everything. But the suggestion seems equally unreasonable for the basic structure. Thus it may be that under certain conditions serfdom cannot be significantly reformed without lowering the expectations of some representative man, say that of landowners, in which case serfdom is efficient. Yet it may also happen under the same conditions that a system of free labor cannot be changed without lowering the expectations of some representative man, say that of free laborers, so this arrangement is likewise efficient. More generally, whenever a society is relevantly divided into a number of classes, it is possible, let us suppose, to maximize with respect to each one of its representative men at a time. These maxima give at least this many efficient positions, for none of them can be departed from to raise the expectations of any one representative man without lowering those of another, namely, the representative man with respect to whom the maximum is defined. Thus each of these extremes is efficient but they surely cannot be all just, and equally so. These remarks simply parallel for social systems the situation in distributing particular goods to given individuals where the distributions in which a single person has everything is efficient.

Now these reflections show only what we knew all along, that is, that the principle of efficiency cannot serve alone as a conception of justice.[2] Therefore it must be supplemented in some way. Now in the system of natural liberty the principle of efficiency is constrained by certain background institutions; when these constraints are satisfied, any resulting efficient distribution is accepted as just. The system of natural liberty selects an efficient distribution roughly as follows. Let us suppose that we know from economic theory that under the standard assumptions defining a competitive market economy, income and wealth will be distributed in an efficient way, and that the particular efficient distribution which results in any period of time is determined by the initial distribution of assets, that is, by the initial distribution of income and wealth, and of natural talents and abilities. With each initial distribution, a definite efficient outcome is arrived at. Thus it turns out that if we are to accept the outcome as just, and not merely as efficient, we must accept the basis upon which over time the initial distribution of assets is determined.

In the system of natural liberty the initial distribution is regulated by the arrangements implicit in the conception of careers open to talents (as earlier defined). These arrangements presuppose a background of equal liberty (as specified by the first principle) and a free market economy. They require a formal equality of opportunity in that all have at least the same legal rights of access to all advantaged social positions. But since there is no effort to preserve an equality, or similarity, of social conditions, except insofar as this is necessary to preserve the requisite background institutions, the initial distribution of assets for any period of time is strongly influenced by natural and social contingencies. The existing distribution of income and wealth, say, is the cumulative effect of prior distributions of natural assets—that is, natural talents and abilities—as these have been developed or left unrealized, and their use favored or disfavored over time by social circumstances and such chance contingencies as accident and good fortune. Intuitively, the most obvious injustice of the system of natural liberty is that it permits distributive shares to be improperly influenced by these factors so arbitrary from a moral point of view.

The liberal interpretation, as I shall refer to it, tries to correct for this by adding to the requirement of careers open to talents the further condition of the principle of fair equality of opportunity. The thought here is that positions are to be not only open in a formal sense, but that all should have a fair chance to attain them. Offhand it is not clear what is meant, but we might say that those with similar abilities and skills should have similar life chances. More specifically, assuming that there is a distribution of natural assets, those who are at the same level of talent and ability, and have the same willingness to use them, should have the same prospects of success regardless of their initial place in the social system, that is, irrespective of the income class into which they are born. In all sectors of society there should be roughly equal prospects of culture and achievement for everyone similarly motivated and endowed. The expectations of those with the same abilities and aspirations should not be affected by their social class.[3]

The liberal interpretation of the two principles seeks, then, to mitigate the influence of social contingencies and natural fortune on distributive shares. To accomplish this end it is necessary to impose further basic structural conditions on the social system. Free market arrangements must be set within a framework of political and legal institutions which regulates the overall trends of economic events and preserves the social conditions necessary for fair equality of opportunity. The elements of this framework are familiar enough, though it may be worthwhile to recall the importance of preventing excessive accumulations of property and wealth and of maintaining equal opportunities of education for all. Chances to acquire cultural knowledge and skills should not depend upon one's class position, and so also the school system, whether public or private, should be designed to even out class barriers.

Notes

1. For the application of the Pareto criterion to systems of public rules, see J. M. Buchanan, "The Relevance of Pareto Optimality," *Journal of Conflict Resolution,* vol. 6 (1962), as well as his book with Gordon Tullock, *The Calculus of Consent* (Ann Arbor, The University of Michigan Press, 1962). In applying this and other principles to institutions I follow one of the points of "Two Concepts of Rules," *Philosophical Review,* vol. 64 (1955).

Doing this has the advantage, among other things, of constraining the employment of principles by publicity effects. See §23, note 8.

2. This fact is generally recognized in welfare economics, as when it is said that efficiency is to be balanced against equity. See for example Tibor Scitovsky, *Welfare and Competition* (London, George Allen and Unwin, 1952), pp. 60–69 and I. M. D. Little, *A Critique of Welfare Economics,* 2nd ed. (Oxford, The Clarendon Press, 1957), ch. VI, esp. pp. 112–116. See Sen's remarks on the limitations of the principle of efficiency, *Collective Choice and Social Welfare,* pp. 22, 24–26, 83–86.

3. This definition follows Sidgwick's suggestion in *The Methods of Ethics,* p. 285n. See also R. H. Tawney, *Equality* (London, George Allen and Unwin, 1931), ch. II, sec. ii; and B. A. O. Williams, "The Idea of Equality," in *Philosophy, Politics, and Society,* ed. Peter Laslett and W. G. Runciman (Oxford, Basil Blackwell, 1962), pp. 125f.

The Principles of a Liberal Social Order

Friedrich A. von Hayek

1. By 'liberalism' I shall understand here the conception of a desirable political order which in the first instance was developed in England from the time of the Old Whigs in the later part of the seventeenth century to that of Gladstone at the end of the nineteenth. David Hume, Adam Smith, Edmund Burke, T. B. Macaulay and Lord Acton may be regarded as its typical representatives in England. It was this conception of individual liberty under the law which in the first instance inspired the liberal movements on the Continent and which became the basis of the American political tradition. A few of the leading political thinkers in those countries like B. Constant and A. de Tocqueville in France, Immanuel Kant, Friedrich von Schiller and Wilhelm von Humboldt in Germany, and James Madison, John Marshall and Daniel Webster in the United States belong wholly to it.

2. This liberalism must be clearly distinguished from another, originally Continental European tradition, also called 'liberalism' of which what now claims this name in the United States is a direct descendant. This latter view, though beginning with an attempt to imitate the first tradition, interpreted it in the spirit of a constructivist rationalism prevalent in France and thereby made of it something very different, and in the end, instead of advocating limitations on the powers of government, ended up with the ideal of the unlimited powers of the majority. This is the tradition of Voltaire, Rousseau, Condorcet and the French Revolution which became the ancestor of modern socialism. English utilitarianism has taken over much of this Continental tradition and the late-nineteenth-century British liberal party, resulting from a

Published in *Il Politico,* 1966. Reprinted in *Studies in Philosophy, Politics and Economics,* ed. Friedrich A. von Hayek, by permission of the University of Chicago Press. © 1967 by F. A. von Hayek. All rights reserved. Reprinted by permission of the editors of *Il Politico.*

fusion of the liberal Whigs and the utilitarian Radicals, was also a product of this mixture.

3. Liberalism and democracy, although compatible, are not the same. The first is concerned with the extent of governmental power, the second with who holds the power. The difference is best seen if we consider their opposites: the opposite of liberalism is totalitarianism, while the opposite of democracy is authoritarianism. In consequence, it is at least possible in principle that a democratic government may be totalitarian and that an authoritarian government may act on liberal principles. The second kind of 'liberalism' mentioned before has in effect become democratism rather than liberalism and, demanding *unlimited* power of the majority, has become essentially anti-liberal. . . .

6. Liberalism . . . derives from the discovery of a self-generating or spontaneous order in social affairs (the same discovery which led to the recognition that there existed an object for theoretical social sciences), an order which made it possible to utilize the knowledge and skill of all members of society to a much greater extent than would be possible in any order created by central direction, and the consequent desire to make as full use of these powerful spontaneous ordering forces as possible.

7. It was thus in their efforts to make explicit the principles of an order already existing but only in an imperfect form that Adam Smith and his followers developed the basic principles of liberalism in order to demonstrate the desirability of their general application. In doing this they were able to presuppose familiarity with the common law conception of justice and with the ideals of the rule of law and of government under the law which were little understood outside the Anglo-Saxon world; with the result that not only were their ideas not fully understood outside the English-speaking countries, but that they ceased to be fully understood even in England when Bentham and his followers replaced the English legal tradition by a constructivist utilitarianism derived more from Continental rationalism than from the evolutionary conception of the English tradition.

8. The central concept of liberalism is that under the enforcement of universal rules of just conduct, protecting a recognizable private domain of individuals, a spontaneous order of human activities of much greater complexity will form itself than could ever be produced by deliberate arrangement, and that in consequence the coercive activities of government should be limited to the enforcement of such rules, whatever other services government may at the same time render by administering those particular resources which have been placed at its disposal for those purposes.

9. The distinction between a *spontaneous order* based on abstract rules which leave individuals free to use their own knowledge for their own purposes, and an *organization or arrangement* based on commands, is of central importance for the understanding of the principles of a free society and must in the following paragraphs be explained in some detail, especially as the spontaneous order of a free society will contain many organizations (including the biggest organization, government), but the two principles of order cannot be mixed in any manner we may wish.

10. The first peculiarity of a spontaneous order is that by using its ordering forces (the regularity of the conduct of its members) we can achieve an order of a much more complex set of facts than we could ever achieve by deliberate arrangement, but that, while availing ourselves of this possibility of inducing an order of much greater extent than we otherwise could, we at the same time limit our power over the details of that order. We shall say that when using the former principle we shall have power only over the abstract character but not over the concrete detail of that order.

11. No less important is the fact that, in contrast to an organization, neither has a spontaneous order a purpose nor need there be agreement on the concrete results it will produce in order to agree on the desirability of such an order, because, being independent of any particular purpose, it can be used for, and will assist in the pursuit of, a great many different, divergent and even conflicting individual purposes. Thus the order of the market, in particular, rests not on common purposes but on reciprocity, that is on the reconciliation of different purposes for the mutual benefit of the participants. . . .

16. The spontaneous order of the market resulting from the interaction of many . . . economics is something so fundamentally different from an economy proper that it must be regarded as a great misfortune that it has ever been called by the same name. I have become convinced that this practice so constantly misleads people that it is necessary to invent a new technical term for it. I propose that we call this spontaneous order of the market a *catallaxy* in analogy to the term 'catallactics', which has often been proposed as a substitute for the term 'economics'. (Both 'catallaxy' and 'catallactics' derive from the ancient Greek verb *katallattein* which, significantly, means not only 'to barter' and 'to exchange' but also 'to admit into the community' and 'to turn from enemy into friend'.)

17. The chief point about the catallaxy is that, as a spontaneous order, its orderliness does *not* rest on its orientation on a single hierarchy of ends, and that, therefore, it will *not* secure that for it as a whole the more important comes before the less important. This is the chief cause of its condemnation by its opponents, and it could be said that most of the socialist demands amount to nothing less than that the catallaxy should be turned into an economy proper (i.e., the purposeless spontaneous order into a purpose-oriented organization) in order to assure that the more important be never sacrificed to the less important. The defence of the free society must therefore show that it is due to the fact that we do not enforce a unitary scale of concrete ends, nor attempt to secure that some particular view about what is more and what is less important governs the whole of society, that the members of such a free society have as good a chance successfully to use their individual knowledge for the achievement of their individual purposes as they in fact have.

18. The extension of an order of peace beyond the small purpose-oriented organization became thus possible by the extension of purpose-independent ('formal') rules of just conduct to the relations with other men who did not pursue the same concrete ends or hold the same values except

those abstract rules—which did not impose obligations for particular actions (which always presuppose a concrete end) but consisted solely in prohibitions from infringing the protected domain of each which these rules enable us to determine. Liberalism is therefore inseparable from the institution of private property which is the name we usually give to the material part of this protected individual domain. . . .

20. Liberalism recognizes that there are certain other services which for various reasons the spontaneous forces of the market may not produce or may not produce adequately, and that for this reason it is desirable to put at the disposal of government a clearly circumscribed body of resources with which it can render such services to the citizens in general. This requires a sharp distinction between the coercive powers of government, in which its actions are strictly limited to the enforcement of rules of just conduct and in the exercise of which all discretion is excluded, and the provision of services by government, for which it can use only the resources put at its disposal for this purpose, has no coercive power or monopoly, but in the use of which resources it enjoys wide discretion. . . .

22. Liberalism has indeed inherited from the theories of the common law and from the older (pre-rationalist) theories of the law of nature, and also presupposes, a conception of justice which allows us to distinguish between such rules of just individual conduct as are implied in the conception of the 'rule of law' and are required for the formation of a spontaneous order on the one hand, and all the particular commands issued by authority for the purpose of organization on the other. This essential distinction has been made explicit in the legal theories of two of the greater philosophers of modern times, David Hume and Immanuel Kant, but has not been adequately restated since and is wholly uncongenial to the governing legal theories of our day.

23. The essential points of this conception of justice are (a) that justice can be meaningfully attributed only to human action and not to any state of affairs as such without reference to the question whether it has been, or could have been, deliberately brought about by somebody; (b) that the rules of justice have essentially the nature of prohibitions, or, in other words, that injustice is really the primary concept and the aim of rules of just conduct is to prevent unjust action; (c) that the injustice to be prevented is the infringement of the protected domain of one's fellow men, a domain which is to be ascertained by means of these rules of justice; and (d) that these rules of just conduct which are in themselves negative can be developed by consistently applying to whatever such rules a society has inherited the equally negative test of universal applicability—a test which, in the last resort, is nothing else than the self-consistency of the actions which these rules allow if applied to the circumstances of the real world. These four crucial points must be developed further in the following paragraphs.

24. *Ad (a):* Rules of just conduct can require the individual to take into account in his decisions only such consequences of his actions as he himself can foresee. The concrete results of the catallaxy for particular people are, however,

essentially unpredictable; and since they are not the effect of anyone's design or intentions, it is meaningless to describe the manner in which the market distributed the good things of this world among particular people as just or unjust. This, however, is what the so-called 'social' or 'distributive' justice aims at in the name of which the liberal order of law is progressively destroyed. We shall later see that no test or criteria have been found or can be found by which such rules of 'social justice' can be assessed, and that, in consequence, and in contrast to the rules of just conduct, they would have to be determined by the arbitrary will of the holders of power.

25. *Ad (b):* No particular human action is fully determined without a concrete purpose it is meant to achieve. Free men who are to be allowed to use their own means and their own knowledge for their own purposes must therefore not be subject to rules which tell them what they must positively do, but only to rules which tell them what they must not do; except for the discharge of obligations an individual has voluntarily incurred, the rules of just conduct thus merely delimit the range of permissible actions but do not determine the particular actions a man must take at a particular moment. (There are certain rare exceptions to this, like actions to save or protect life, prevent catastrophes, and the like, whether either rules of justice actually do require, or would at least generally be accepted as just rules if they required, some positive action. It would lead far to discuss here the position of such rules in the system.) The generally negative character of the rules of just conduct, and the corresponding primacy of the injustice which is prohibited, has often been noticed but scarcely ever been thought through to its logical consequences.

26. *Ad (c):* The injustice which is prohibited by rules of just conduct is any encroachment on the protected domain of other individuals, and they must therefore enable us to ascertain what is the protected sphere of others. Since the time of John Locke it is customary to describe this protected domain as property (which Locke himself had defined as 'the life, liberty, and possessions of a man'). This term suggests, however, a much too narrow and purely material conception of the protected domain which includes not only material goods but also various claims on others and certain expectations. If the concept of property is, however, (with Locke) interpreted in this wide sense, it is true that law, in the sense of rules of justice, and the institution of property are inseparable.

27. *Ad (d):* It is impossible to decide about the justice of any one particular rule of just conduct except within the framework of a whole system of such rules, most of which must for this purpose be regarded as unquestioned: values can always be tested only in terms of other values. The test of the justice of a rule is usually (since Kant) described as that of its 'universalizability', i.e., of the possibility of willing that the rules should be applied to all instances that correspond to the conditions stated in it (the 'categorical imperative'). What this amounts to is that in applying it to any concrete circumstances it will not conflict with any other accepted rules. The test is thus in the last resort one of the compatibility or non-contradictoriness of the whole system of rules,

not merely in a logical sense but in the sense that the system of actions which the rules permit will not lead to conflict.

28. It will be noticed that only purpose-independent ('formal') rules pass this test because, as rules which have originally been developed in small, purpose-connected groups ('organizations') are progressively extended to larger and larger groups and finally universalized to apply to the relations between any members of an Open Society who have no concrete purposes in common and merely submit to the same abstract rules, they will in this process have to shed all references to particular purposes.

29. The growth from the tribal organization, all of whose members served common purposes, to the spontaneous order of the Open Society in which people are allowed to pursue their own purposes in peace, may thus be said to have commenced when for the first time a savage placed some goods at the boundary of his tribe in the hope that some member of another tribe would find them and leave in turn behind some other goods to secure the repetition of the offer. From the first establishment of such a practice which served reciprocal but not common purposes, a process has been going on for millennia which, by making rules of conduct independent of the particular purposes of those concerned, made it possible to extend these rules to ever wider circles of undetermined persons and eventually might make possible a universal peaceful order of the world. . . .

32. The progressive displacement of the rules of conduct of private and criminal law by a conception derived from public law is the process by which existing liberal societies are progressively transformed into totalitarian societies. This tendency has been most explicitly seen and supported by Adolf Hitler's 'crown jurist' Carl Schmitt who consistently advocated the replacement of the 'normative' thinking of liberal law by a conception of law which regards as its purpose the 'concrete order formation' *(konkretes Ordnungs-denken)*. . . .

34. If it was the nature of the constitutional arrangements prevailing in all Western democracies which made this development possible, the driving force which guided it in the particular direction was the growing recognition that the application of uniform or equal rules to the conduct of individuals who were in fact very different in many respects, inevitably produced very different results for the different individuals; and that in order to bring about by government action a reduction in these unintended but inevitable differences in the material position of different people, it would be necessary to treat them not according to the same but according to different rules. This gave rise to a new and altogether different conception of justice, namely that usually described as 'social' or 'distributive' justice, a conception of justice which did not confine itself to rules of conduct for the individual but aimed at particular results for particular people, and which therefore could be achieved only in a purpose-governed organization but not in a purpose-independent spontaneous order.

35. The concepts of a 'just price', a 'just remuneration' or a 'just distribution of incomes' are of course very old; it deserves notice, however, that in the course of the efforts of two thousand years in which philosophers have speculated about the meaning of these concepts, not a single rule has been discovered which would allow us to determine what is in this sense just in a market order. Indeed the one group of scholars which have most persistently pursued the question, the schoolmen of the later middle ages and early modern times, were finally driven to define the just price or wage as that price or wage which would form itself on a market in the absence of fraud, violence or privilege—thus referring back to the rules of just conduct and accepting as a just result whatever was brought about by the just conduct of all individuals concerned. This negative conclusion of all the speculations about 'social' or 'distributive' justice was, as we shall see, inevitable, because a just remuneration or distribution has meaning only within an organization whose members act under command in the service of a common system of ends, but can have no meaning whatever in a catallaxy or spontaneous order which can have no such common system of ends.

36. A state of affairs as such, as we have seen, cannot be just or unjust as a mere fact. Only in so far as it has been brought about designedly or could be so brought about does it make sense to call just or unjust the actions of those who have created it or permitted it to arise. In the catallaxy, the spontaneous order of the market, nobody can foresee, however, what each participant will get, and the results for particular people are not determined by anyone's intentions; nor is anyone responsible for particular people getting particular things. We might therefore question whether a deliberate choice of the market order as the method for guiding economic activities, with the unpredictable and in a great measure chance incidence of its benefits, is a just decision, but certainly not whether, once we have decided to avail ourselves of the catallaxy for that purpose, the particular results it produces for particular people are just or unjust.

37. That the concept of justice is nevertheless so commonly and readily applied to the distribution of incomes is entirely the effect of an erroneous anthropomorphic interpretation of society as an organization rather than as a spontaneous order. The term 'distribution' is in this sense quite as misleading as the term 'economy', since it also suggests that something is the result of deliberate action which in fact is the result of spontaneous ordering forces. Nobody distributes income in a market order (as would have to be done in an organization) and to speak, with respect to the former, of a just or unjust distribution is therefore simple nonsense. It would be less misleading to speak in this respect of a 'dispersion' rather than a 'distribution' of incomes.

38. All endeavours to secure a 'just' distribution must thus be directed towards turning the spontaneous order of the market into an organization or, in other words, into a totalitarian order. It was this striving after a new conception of justice which produced the various steps by which rules of

organization ('public law'), which were designed to make people aim at particular results, came to supersede the purpose-independent rules of just individual conduct, and which thereby gradually destroyed the foundation on which a spontaneous order must rest.

39. The ideal of using the coercive powers of government to achieve 'positive' (i.e., social or distributive) justice leads, however, not only necessarily to the destruction of individual freedom, which some might not think too high a price, but it also proves on examination a mirage or an illusion which cannot be achieved in any circumstances, because it presupposes an agreement on the relative importance of the different concrete ends which cannot exist in a great society whose members do not know each other or the same particular facts. It is sometimes believed that the fact that most people today desire social justice demonstrates that this ideal has a determinable content. But it is unfortunately only too possible to chase a mirage, and the consequence of this is always that the result of one's striving will be utterly different from what one had intended.

40. There can be no rules which determine how much everybody 'ought' to have unless we make some unitary conception of relative 'merits' or 'needs' of the different individuals, for which there exists no objective measure, the basis of a central allocation of all goods and services—which would make it necessary that each individual, instead of using *his* knowledge for *his* purposes, were made to fulfil a duty imposed upon him by somebody else, and were remunerated according to how well he has, in the opinion of others, performed this duty. This is the method of remuneration appropriate to a closed organization, such as an army, but irreconcilable with the forces which maintain a spontaneous order.

41. It ought to be freely admitted that the market order does not bring about any close correspondence between subjective merit or individual needs and rewards. It operates on the principle of a combined game of skill and chance in which the results for each individual may be as much determined by circumstances wholly beyond his control as by his skill or effort. Each is remunerated according to the value his particular services have to the particular people to whom he renders them, and this value of his services stands in no necessary relation to anything which we could appropriately call his merits and still less to his needs.

42. It deserves special emphasis that, strictly speaking, it is meaningless to speak of a value 'to society' when what is in question is the value of some services to certain people, services which may be of no interest to anybody else. A violin virtuoso presumably renders services to entirely different people from those whom a football star entertains, and the maker of pipes altogether different people from the maker of perfumes. The whole conception of a 'value to society' is in a free order as illegitimate an anthropomorphic term as its description as 'one economy' in the strict sense, as an entity which 'treats' people justly or unjustly, or 'distributes' among them. The results of the market process for particular individuals are neither the result of anybody's will that

they should have so much, nor even foreseeable by those who have decided upon or support the maintenance of this kind of order. . . .

45. The aim of economic policy of a free society can therefore never be to assure particular results to particular people, and its success cannot be measured by any attempt at adding up the value of such particular results. In this respect the aim of what is called 'welfare economics' is fundamentally mistaken, not only because no meaningful sum can be formed of the satisfactions provided for different people, but because its basic idea of a maximum of need-fulfilment (or a maximum social product) is appropriate only to an economy proper which serves a single hierarchy of ends, but not to the spontaneous order of a catallaxy which has no common concrete ends.

46. Though it is widely believed that the conception of an optimal economic policy (or any judgment whether one economic policy is better than another) presupposes such a conception of maximizing aggregate real social income (which is possible only in value terms and therefore implies an illegitimate comparison of the utility to different persons), this is in fact not so. An optimal policy in a catallaxy may aim, and ought to aim, at increasing the chances of any member of society taken at random of having a high income, or, what amounts to the same thing, the chance that, whatever his share in total income may be, the real equivalent of this share will be as large as we know how to make it.

47. This condition will be approached as closely as we can manage, irrespective of the dispersion of incomes, if everything which is produced is being produced by persons or organizations who can produce it more cheaply than (or at least as cheaply as) anybody who does not produce it, and is sold at a price lower than that at which it would be possible to offer it for anybody who does not in fact so offer it. (This allows for persons or organizations to whom the costs of producing one commodity or service are lower than they are for those who actually produce it and who still produce something else instead, because their comparative advantage in that other production is still greater; in this case the total costs of their producing the first commodity would have to include the loss of the one which is not produced.)

48. It will be noticed that this optimum does not presuppose what economic theory calls 'perfect competition' but only that there are no obstacles to the entry into each trade and that the market functions adequately in spreading information and opportunities. It should also be specially observed that this modest and achievable goal has never yet been fully achieved because at all times and everywhere governments have both restricted access to some occupations and tolerated persons and organizations deterring others from entering occupations when this would have been to the advantage of the latter.

49. This optimum position means that as much will be produced of whatever combination of products and services is in fact produced as can be produced by any method that we know, because we can through such a use of the market mechanism bring more of the dispersed knowledge of the members of society into play than by any other. But it will be achieved only if we leave

the share in the total, which each member will get, to be determined by the market mechanism and all its accidents, because it is only through the market determination of incomes that each is led to do what this result requires.

50. We owe, in other words, our chances that our unpredictable share in the total product of society represents as large an aggregate of goods and services as it does to the fact that thousands of others constantly submit to the adjustments which the market forces on them; and it is consequently also our duty to accept the same kind of changes in our income and position, even if it means a decline in our accustomed position and is due to circumstances we could not have foreseen and for which we are not responsible. The conception that we have 'earned' (in the sense of morally deserved) the income we had when we were more fortunate, and that we are therefore entitled to it so long as we strive as honestly as before and had no warning to turn elsewhere, is wholly mistaken. Everybody, rich or poor, owes his income to the outcome of a mixed game of skill and chance, the aggregate results of which and the shares in which are as high as they are only because we have agreed to play that game. And once we have agreed to play the game and profited from its results, it is a moral obligation on us to abide by the results even if they turn against us. . . .

61. In conclusion, the basic principles of a liberal society may be summed up by saying that in such a society all coercive functions of government must be guided by the overruling importance of what I like to call THE THREE GREAT NEGATIVES: PEACE, JUSTICE AND LIBERTY. Their achievement requires that in its coercive functions government shall be confined to the enforcement of such prohibitions (stated as abstract rules) as can be equally applied to all, and to exacting under the same uniform rules from all a share of the costs of the other, noncoercive services it may decide to render to the citizens with the material and personal means thereby placed at its disposal.

Economic Justice

Milton Fisk

Defenders of the capitalist form of society do not defend a right to economic equality. Economic inequality is, they argue, to everyone's advantage. Yet some of these defenders of capitalism are also supporters of liberal democracy. They must then recognize limits to economic inequality beyond which even capitalism should not go. Vast concentrations of economic wealth are sources of political power that strangle the basic liberties of a democratic society. But many defenders of capitalist society maintain that in the US at least these limits to economic inequality have not been reached.

From Milton Fisk, *Ethics and Society* 1980, pp. 224–235. Reprinted by permission of The Harvester Press, Ltd. and New York University Press.

The purpose of this [paper] is to show that the arguments justifying the existing high degree of economic inequality fall apart. To show this it will not be necessary to defend, or to reject, the right to complete economic equality. Nonetheless, this [paper] points in an egalitarian direction. For it shows also that the degree of economic inequality inevitable within even a reformed capitalist society cannot be justified from the perspective of working-class morality.

1 Economic Inequality

According to many writers on US society, the stage of widespread affluence has been reached within the US. There is, on the one hand, a reduced level of economic inequality, and there is, on the other hand, an elimination of the lower classes as a majority in favour of a large and prosperous middle class. The misery and inequality that characterized nineteenth- and early twentieth-century capitalism have been redeemed with the arrival of the "affluent society." This picture, however, conceals the urgent problem of economic inequality within the US. As Gabriel Kolko notes in his pathbreaking dissenting work on income distribution, "The predominantly middle-class society is only an image in the minds of isolated academicians."[1]

First let us look at the distribution of before-tax personal, as opposed to corporate, income during the period 1910–70 to get some idea as to whether there has been a significant trend toward equality. To do this we can consider families as broken up into five groups of equal size, ranging from those with the highest to those with the lowest income. (People living in families make up roughly 90 per cent of the US population.) *In the sixty-year period considered, families in the highest fifth received between 40 and 45 per cent of all family income.* That is, they received at least two times more than they would have if every family received the same income. Despite variations from year to year, there is no overall trend in this period toward a significantly smaller share of the national income for the richest fifth. The middle fifth has received between 15 and 18 per cent of all family income. This means that it received over the entire sixty-year period less than it would have if income were egalitarian. For this group the trend, within these narrow limits, has been for a slight rise in its share of income, but after World War II that rise stopped completely. Finally, what about the families in the poorest quintile? That group has received between 4 and 6 per cent of the national personal income, which runs up to five times less than it would receive under equality. The overall trend has been for families in this bottom group to get proportionately the same during the sixty-year period. As regards income in the US, then, there is significant and continuing inequality.[2] The top fifth as a whole takes six to ten times more of the national family income than does the bottom fifth. (Data for non-family persons shows even greater inequality.)

Our data has so far been taken on before-tax income. Will not taxation make the picture one of greater equality? It does change the picture as regards equality but only in an insignificant way. Many taxes are regressive: they are a larger fraction of lower than of higher incomes. Social security taxes, property taxes, and sales taxes are all regressive. It cannot be expected that these would provide a shift toward equality. But even the federal income tax, which is progressive, has failed to do more than decrease by two per cent the share of national income of the top fifth. The increase in the share of the bottom fifth resulting from federal income taxes has remained a fraction of a per cent. Moreover, the percentage of all taxes coming from the non-owning classes has been rising steadily since World War II. Taxes have, then, failed to equalize income significantly.[3]

We are dealing with a society in which private ownership of the means of production is a fundamental feature. Some personal income comes from ownership, to be sure, but one cannot say exactly how wealth is distributed simply on the basis of knowing how income is distributed. For one thing, a significant but variable share of returns from ownership is invested in new means of production and does not appear as dividend income. Nonetheless, in a capitalist society we can predict that wealth, like income, is unevenly distributed. It is highly concentrated in the hands of a very few owners: they own the plants, the trucks, the warehouses, the mines, the office buildings, the large estates, and the objects of art. The poor are often net holders of "negative wealth" because of their debts. *Between 1810 and 1969, the concentration of wealth has remained remarkably constant; the top one per cent as regards wealth has held between 20 and 30 per cent of all the wealth in the US.* In 1962 the poorest 20 per cent held less than one-half of one per cent of the nation's wealth.[4]

Nonetheless, some currency has been given to the view that corporate ownership has become widespread and that workers are now significant owners. Stock ownership is, indeed, more widespread, but this has not seriously affected the high degree of concentration of stock ownership in the hands of the wealthiest.

By 1962, the wealthiest one percent of the population still held 72 percent of the nation's corporate stock. In that year, the wealthiest one percent also held 48 percent of the nation's bonds, 24 percent of the loans, and 16 percent of the real estate.[5] Clearly then wealth is even less equitably distributed than income in the US, and the inequality has been one of long duration. Pensions for workers account for nearly ten percent of corporate stock. This may provide workers with security after retirement, but it does not give them the power of wealth holders. The reason is that they have no control over these pension funds, which merely add power to the financial institutions that manage them. . . .

A large prosperous middle class has by no means replaced the struggling lower classes as the majority class. With more than half of the people living below the modest but adequate budget of the BLS, the underbelly of US capitalist society is a deprived majority, just as it was fifty years ago. "In advanced capitalist societies, the costs of staying out of poverty (i.e., of satisfying invariant subsistence needs) grows as the economy grows. Consequently, there is no long-term tendency in advanced capitalist societies for the incidence of poverty to decrease significantly as the economy grows."[6] The economic inequality of US society is not just relative inequality, for it is an inequality that means deprivation for a sizeable chunk of the society.

2 Ownership and Productivity

There are several strategies used by spokespersons of the ruling class to defend the situation of inequality described above. The first defence rests on the rights of ownership. The second rests on the need for inequality in order to increase productivity. In the next section, a third strategy will be discussed: it rests on the notion of a fair wage.

According to the *first defence* of inequality, those who have put their hard-earned money into a business enterprise have the right to appropriate the fruits of that enterprise and divide them according to their own decisions. Thus the product that workers have made is controlled by owners and not by the workers. Owners are within their rights to divide the product in such a way that inequality is great and poverty widespread. An entire web of ideology has been woven on this basic frame of the rights of ownership. Part of that web is the system of law, backed by police force, entitling the owner to the fruits of the worker. From the perspective of members of the working class, there are several holes in this defence. These holes show that what is built on the frame of ownership rights is indeed only ideology.

On the one hand, if ownership rights lead to continued inequality and poverty, then from a working-class perspective there simply are no such rights. The attitude that ownership of the means of production is sacred merely protects the owners at the expense of those who suffer the resulting inequality. A right is more than such an attitude; it must be justified and indeed justified from a class standpoint. Economic inequality can be justified by ownership rights only if there are such rights. There may well be such rights from the perspective of the ruling class. Yet the continued inequality and poverty resulting from ownership are evidence favouring the view that relative to the working class owners have no legitimate right to the fruits of enterprise.

On the other hand, the basis given for the justification of the owner's right to the fruits of enterprise is not adequate. That basis was the hard work of the investor. Investment, however, is an on-going process in a viable firm. The initial investment is followed by many subsequent investments. Let us grant that the owner has worked hard—whether in the form of the honest toil of the self-employed person or in the form of the forcible plunder of the syndicated criminal—to accumulate the initial investment. But when the plant is rebuilt or expanded, the new investment will be possible only because of the hard work of the workers. Once new investment has been made, there is no longer the same basis for saying that the original owner has the right to control the entire product of the new investment. The logic of "hard work" applies here to. If the owner worked hard to accumulate the initial investment, it is equally true that the workers worked hard to make the new investment possible. Thus, in a viable firm, the workers should, on the logic of hard work, have a right to appropriate an ever increasing share of the product. The capitalist's own logic backfires! . . .

According to the *second defence* of inequality, significant inequality with poverty at the bottom is a necessary condition for making the society as affluent as it is. In a widely published newspaper article entitled "Morality and the Pursuit of Wealth" appearing in July 1974, the President of the US Chamber of Commerce, Arch Booth, said the realization of equality by the transfer of wealth from the haves to the have-nots would lessen the "work incentive of the most productive members of society" and endanger "the ability of the economic system to accumulate capital for new productive facilities." Booth's solution is to let the rich keep on investing in productive facilities thereby increasing the share the poor get through better wages and higher employment.

There is one glaring fallacy in this argument. It is the logical fallacy of an "incomplete disjunction." The disjunction Booth offers us is that *either* we have a forced redistribution of income within capitalism *or* we let the income of the non-owners rise naturally by increasing investment. But the disjunction needs to be expanded to include at least one more alternative: beyond capitalism, it is possible to expand productive facilities through the investment of collective rather than of private capital. In one form of collective ownership, workers would manage the investment of collective capital in order to advance their interests. In this case, the inequality in both wealth and income needed for growth under private capitalism becomes unnecessary. Without significant inequality, private capitalism would lack the centres of economic power needed to put large amounts of labour to work in order to produce a surplus for growth. The model here for a system of collective ownership of the means of production is not that of nationalized industry run by a bunch of officials who are not controlled by workers. This would be the bureaucratic model found in places like the USSR which are no longer private capitalist societies. Rather, the model is that of a workers' democracy in which democracy extends down to the workplace and in which workplaces are coordinated by a council of representatives from each. This socialist alternative is sufficient to make Booth's disjunction incomplete. . . .

3 A Fair Wage

A *third strategy* for defending the inequality and the poverty that is to be found today in the US introduces the concept of compensation for work. The defence is that labour is sold on the free market and, on the whole, the free market determines a *just* price for things. Thus, since inequality and poverty are, in part, a result of the free market for labour, there is no *right* to economic equality or even to a "modest budget." A free market must not involve the use of power by those who exchange their goods and services within it to coerce those with whom they exchange.

This argument seems to leave open the possibility that wages should mount and thus that the worker should come closer to the owner in economic status. But in fact this possibility is not open. As pointed out in Section I, the range of inequality and the degree of poverty in the US have remained remarkably constant. The majority of the people are at or below the level of existence provided by the modest budget. Because of the greater power and organization of the owning class, the wages and salaries of workers remain at a level that allows them merely to perform their jobs well and to raise a new generation of workers. (Differences between the wages of, say, industrial and clerical workers need to be viewed against the background of a general pull toward this subsistence level.) To perform well and to reproduce themselves they have been forced to purchase the ever more elaborate and hence more expensive means of satisfying survival needs and the needs specific to their jobs. Short-term variations in the supply of and demand for labour are only part of this long-term pattern of compensating workers at a subsistence level. At this level, there is nothing much left over for savings and investments that might narrow the gap between them and the owning class. . . .

What, then, is a fair wage from the perspective of the working class? Suppose we are calves who face the prospect of going to slaughter as one-year olds. The farmers who send us to slaughter find that this is the age at which to realize a maximum profit on us. So one year is the 'fair' time, from the perspective of the farmers, for calves to enjoy themselves before slaughter. An inquisitive calf poses the question, "What is the true 'fair' time for cattle to live before slaughter? Is it two years, or even three?" A selfish calf who has no regard for the farmer and the future of cattle farming generally shouts, "Stop quibbling; we should demand a moratorium on beef eating. An end to the slaughter of cattle!" Similarly, Marx said that the slogan, "A fair day's wage for a fair day's work!" should be replaced by the slogan, "An end to the wage system!"[7] Instead of the wage system, work should be done in such a way that the workers' compensation is not just a function of the greater power of a non-working ruling class.

The wage system is a system that in advanced industrial countries has been central to the domination of lower classes by a ruling class. Through that system people are set to work in order to preserve or increase the control of wealth by and, thus, the power of a minority class. They are thus given from what they produce only what is needed to reproduce their labour. When part of the product of workers is used in this way to perpetuate and strengthen the domination of a non-working class, workers are properly said to be "exploited." Acceptance of the wage system and plans to reform it from within do not face up to the key role wages play in domination. When workers themselves decide how they are to be compensated out of what they produce, the wage system has ceased to exist and along with it exploitation. . . .

The struggle for higher income begins the organization of people for the collective action that is needed to abolish the wage system itself. This long-term perspective has for some time been forgotten by trade unions everywhere. Their leaders advocate accommodation with the existing system of domination of working people. These leaders talk about a fair wage but they mean only the wages and benefits they think they can wheedle out of the owners. Their conception of fairness and of rights is no longer a class conception. A class conception makes overthrowing the wage system a right of working people.

4 A Just Distribution

Let us leave defences of present economic inequality and take up a proposal for limiting inequality. If capitalist arguments justifying present inequality fail, then where is the line to be drawn for an acceptable degree of inequality? Our problem is how to distribute a product that has come about through the combined efforts of people in different roles. Since isolated producers are the exception, we cannot start with the assumption that there is a product to which an individual producer is "entitled" because he or she is "responsible" for that product.[8] In deciding on a principle of just distribution there are two factors to be considered.

On the one hand, there is the average amount of goods per individual in the population, and, on the other hand, there is the degree of inequality with which goods are actually parceled out to individuals. Increasing the average amount of goods per individual might increase the inequality of distribution, whereas decreasing the inequality in distribution might decrease the average per individual. In capitalism we saw that inequality of wealth is a condition of economic growth. Also, inequality of income within the working class weakens solidarity, making possible a greater surplus and hence greater growth. If strict equality means poverty all around, we might recoil from strict equality and look for a balance between a large average amount and considerable equality. But so far we have no clue as to where to strike this balance.

John Rawls has recently proposed an interesting way of balancing a high average amount of goods with a low degree of inequality.[9] The idea is that we are to avoid demanding such a low degree of inequality that the worst off are penalized by getting less than they would with a higher degree of inequality. We are to avoid only those high degrees of inequality that are arrived at by preventing the worst off from getting the most they could get.

Rawls formulated this in his Principle of Difference which tells us to "maximize the expectations of the least favoured position". . . .

[But] Rawls talks about distribution without relating it to production. He assumes wrongly that the validity of his principle is absolute, rather than relative to circumstances within production. One thing is certain: In capitalist society there is not the least chance that the Rawlsian scheme could be put into practice. The reason is simply that the organization of production in a capitalist society centres around increasing productive facilities through the making of profits. The class of owners would not advance the interests characteristic of their class by agreeing to maximize the expectations of the least favoured. Given its power, this class would block the realization of the scheme.

Suppose, though, that some mode of production would allow for distribution in accordance with the Principle of Difference. Should not one simply choose to bring about such a mode of production? Certainly—if the Principle of Difference is valid. But its validity is relative to production in the following way. Validity in general is relative to classes, and classes are essential roles in a given mode of production. One should, then, choose to realize the principle only if it is valid relative to one's class. Nonetheless, that class might have to change the existing mode of production in order to realize the new distribution. Even though the capitalist mode of production excludes the application of the Principle of Difference, it may be a valid principle for one of the lower classes within capitalism.

A distributional plan is not just because it is elegant or intuitive but because it answers to needs arising in production. Not only the actual but also the just distribution is dependent on production.

Notes

1. Gabriel Kolko, *Wealth and Power in America* (Praeger, New York, 1962), p. 108.
2. These data are based on tables in Kolko, *Wealth and Power in America,* p. 14, and in Frank Ackerman and Andrew Zimbalist, "Capitalism and Inequality in the United States," in *The Capitalist System,* 2nd ed., p. 298.
3. Kolko, *Wealth and Power in America,* Ch. II, and Ackerman and Zimbalist "Capitalism and Inequality in the United States," in *The Capitalist System,* 2nd ed., p. 303. In Sweden, by contrast, taxes change the ratio of the bottom third to that of the top third from 38 to 48 percent.
4. Lititia Upton and Nancy Lyons, *Basic Facts: Distribution of Personal Income and Wealth in the United States* (Cambridge Institute, 1878 Massachusetts Ave., Cambridge, Mass., 1972), p. 6, and Ackerman and Zimbalist, "Capitalism and Inequality in the United States," in *The Capitalist System,* 2nd ed., p. 301.
5. Upton and Lyons, *Basic Facts,* p. 31.
6. Bernard Gendron, "Capitalism and Poverty," *Radical Philosophers' Newsjournal,* 4, January 1975, p. 13. This essay appears as Ch. XII of Gendron's *Technology and the Human Condition* (St. Martin's Press, New York, 1977).
7. Karl Marx, *Wages, Price, and Profit* (1865) (Foreign Language Press, Peking, 1970), Ch. XIV.
8. On entitlement, see Robert Nozick, *Anarchy, State, and Utopia* (Basic Books, New York, 1974), Ch. VII.
9. Rawls, *A Theory of Justice,* pp. 78–80.

A Libertarian View of Justice

Robert Nozick

The Entitlement Theory

The subject of justice in holdings consists of three major topics. The **first** is the *original acquisition of holdings,* the appropriation of unheld things. This

Robert Nozick, *Anarchy, State & Utopia* (NY: BasicBooks, 1974), pp. 150–153.

includes the issues of how unheld things may come to be held, the process, or processes, by which unheld things may come to be held, the things that may come to be held by these processes, the extent of what comes to be held by a particular process, and so on. We shall refer to the complicated truth about this topic, which we shall not formulate here, as the principle of justice in acquisition. The **second** topic concerns the *transfer of holdings* from one person to another. By what processes may a person transfer holdings to another? How may a person acquire a holding from another who holds it? Under this topic come general descriptions of voluntary exchange, and gift and (on the other hand) fraud, as well as reference to particular conventional details fixed upon in a given society. The complicated truth about this subject (with placeholders for conventional details) we shall call the principle of justice in transfer. (And we shall suppose it also includes principles governing how a person may divest himself of a holding, passing it into an unheld state.)

If the world were wholly just, the following inductive definition would exhaustively cover the subject of justice in holdings.

1. A person who acquires a holding in accordance with the principle of justice in acquisition is entitled to that holding.
2. A person who acquires a holding in accordance with the principle of justice in transfer, from someone else entitled to the holding, is entitled to the holding.
3. No one is entitled to a holding except by (repeated) applications of 1 and 2.

The complete principle of distributive justice would say simply that a distribution is just if everyone is entitled to the holdings they possess under the distribution.

A distribution is just if it arises from another just distribution by legitimate means. The legitimate means of moving from one distribution to another are specified by the principle of justice in transfer. The legitimate first "moves" are specified by the principle of justice in acquisition.[1] Whatever arises from a just situation by just steps is itself just. The means of change specified by the principle of justice in transfer preserve justice. As correct rules of inference are truth-preserving, and any conclusion deduced via repeated application of such rules from only true premises is itself true, so the means of transition from one situation to another specified by the principle of justice in transfer are justice-preserving, and any situation actually arising from repeated transitions in accordance with the principle from a just situation is itself just. The parallel between justice-preserving transformations and truth-preserving transformations illuminates where it fails as well as where it holds. That a conclusion could have been deduced by truth-preserving transformations illuminates where it fails as well as where it holds. That a conclusion could have been deduced by truth-preserving means from premises that are true suffices to show its truth. That from a just situation a situation *could* have arisen via justice-preserving means does *not* suffice to show its justice. The fact that a thief's victims voluntarily *could* have presented him with gifts does not entitle the thief to his ill-gotten gains. Justice in holdings is historical; it depends upon what actually has happened. We shall return to this point later.

Not all actual situations are generated in accordance with the two principles of justice in holdings: the principle of justice in acquisition and the principle of justice in transfer. Some people steal from others, or defraud them, or enslave them, seizing their product and preventing them from living as they choose, or forcibly exclude others from competing in exchanges. None of these are permissible modes of transition from one situation to another. And some persons acquire holdings by means not sanctioned by the principle of justice in acquisition. The existence of past injustice (previous violations of the first two principles of justice in holdings) raises the **third** major topic under justice in holdings: the rectification of injustice in holdings. If past injustice has shaped present holdings in various ways, some identifiable and some not, what now, if anything, ought to be done to rectify these injustices? What obligations do the performers of injustice have toward those whose position is worse than it would have been had the injustice not been done? Or, than it would have been had compensation been paid promptly? How, if at all, do things change if the beneficiaries and those made worse off are not the direct parties in the act of injustice, but, for example, their descendants? Is an injustice done to someone whose holding was itself based upon an unrectified injustice? How far back must one go in wiping clean the historical slate of injustices? What may victims of injustice permissibly do in order to rectify the injustices being done to them, including the many injustices done by persons acting through their government? I do not know of a thorough or theoretically sophisticated treatment of such issues.[2] Idealizing greatly, let us suppose theoretical investigation will produce a principle of rectification. This principle uses historical information about previous situations and injustices done in them (as defined by the first two principles of justice and rights against interference), and information about the actual course of events that flowed from these injustices, until the present, and it yields a description (or descriptions) of holdings in the society. The principle of rectification presumably will make use of its best estimate of subjunctive information about what would have occurred (or a probability distribution over what might have occurred, using the expected value) if the injustice had not taken place. If the actual description of holdings turns out not to be one of the descriptions yielded by the principle, then one of the descriptions yielded must be realized.[3]

The general outlines of the theory of justice in holdings are that the holdings of a person are just if he is entitled to them by the principles of justice in acquisition and transfer, or by the principle of rectification of injustice (as specified by the first two principles). If each person's holdings are just, then the total set (distribution) of holdings is just. To turn these general outlines into a specific theory we would have to specify the details of each of the three principles of justice in holdings: the principle of acquisition of holdings, the principle of transfer of holdings, and the principle of rectification of violations of the first two principles. I shall not attempt that task here.

Notes

1. Applications of the principle of justice in acquisition may also occur as part of the move from one distribution to another. You may find an unheld thing now and appropriate it. Acquisitions also are to be understood as included when, to simplify, I speak only of transitions by transfers.
2. Bernard Williams, "The Idea of Equality," in *Philosophy, Politics, and Society,* 2nd series, eds. Peter Laslett and W. G. Runciman (Oxford: Blackwell, 1962), pp. 110–131.
3. If the principle of rectification of violations of the first two principles yields more than one description of holdings, then some choice must be made as to which of these is to be realized. Perhaps the sort of considerations about distributive justice and equality that I argue against play a legitimate role in *this* subsidiary choice. Similarly, there may be room for such considerations in deciding which otherwise arbitrary features a statute will embody, when such features are unavoidable because other considerations do not specify a precise line; yet a line must be drawn.

Distributing Goods according to Moral Ground Rules

Alan Gewirth

In the static phase of the *PGC's** instrumental justification of social rules, it is assumed that to begin with persons are occurrently equal in their effective possession of rights at least to basic goods in that they mutually refrain from seriously harmful actions, so that the rules of the criminal law are required simply to protect these rights and to redress the balance when it is disturbed. In the dynamic phase, on the other hand, it is recognized that there is a dispositional inequality of effective rights to well-being. Many persons may lack adequate food, housing, necessary medical care, and other basic goods, and they may also lack the capacities to assure that they will continue to have these goods as needed; they may be subjected to degrading conditions of dependence, danger, and disease in their situations of life and work; they may also not have the means to increase their capabilities of purpose-fulfilling action, such as adequate education and income. Insofar as persons who labor under such economic and other handicaps and privations cannot remedy these lacks through their own efforts and are not provided with the means of remedy by others, they do not have effective rights to well-being. In their case, by comparison with persons who have such effective rights, the *PGC's* requirement of the equality of generic rights is violated. This violation is at least potentially transactional. Even if the inferior position of those who lack effective rights to well-being is not directly the result of exploitative and other harmful actions by other persons, their position makes them vulnerable to such actions. Their life chances are sharply reduced by the social environment that maintains this unequal distribution of well-being. Such maintenance operates at least by permitting different persons to have drastically unequal starts in life because of

Alan Gewirth, *Reason & Morality* (Chicago, Illinois: U of Chicago Press, 1978), pp. 312–317.
*For an explanation of the Principle of Generic Consistency, PGC, see chapter 4.

the economic status into which they are born. Although, as was noted above, persons are not simply the passive products of external forces, their capacities for self-development require an initial basis in familial and societal nurturing. If the appropriate background is absent, children born into poverty generally face serious disadvantages with regard to well-being.

Social rules are dynamically-instrumentally justified when they serve to remove or at least reduce this inequality of effective rights. In their bearing on the distribution of wealth, the aim of these rules is for the most part meliorative rather than conservative or revolutionary. As such, they fall between two extremes. A certain libertarian extreme would defend the existing distribution of wealth insofar as it has resulted from voluntary or contractual arrangements that ensue on an initial, presumably just acquisition. The other, egalitarian extreme proposes a drastic redistribution to be guided solely by the aim of maximally benefiting those who are least advantaged. The former extreme does not recognize the independent right to well-being, including additive goods, on the part of those whose initial position in life subjects them to serious disadvantages. The latter extreme does not recognize the independent right to freedom as applied in the production of valued commodities and the consequent earning of income. Thus the two extremes overlook, respectively, the claims of severe economic need and the claims of desert as based on voluntary effort and accomplishment. The retort that all effort is a product of forces beyond the agent's control ignores that persons with similar advantaged socioeconomic backgrounds may differ drastically in the ways they voluntarily marshal the resources available to them. On the other hand, the retort that voluntary exchanges and autonomous effort provide sufficient justifications for all distributions of wealth ignores the extent to which unfavorable familial and social backgrounds severely handicap both the exertion of effort and the possibility of successful agency.

In contrast to these extremes, the *PGC* recognizes the claims of both freedom and well-being. The aim of the social rules it justifies dynamically-instrumentally is neither to distribute or redistribute wealth with no regard for contribution or effort nor to maintain the existing distribution unchanged while ignoring the disadvantages that unfavorable economic and social backgrounds impose on persons' capabilities for attaining additive and even basic well-being. Rather, the aim of the *PGC's* social rules, in their bearing on economic distribution, is the double one of permitting the free exertion of productive effort to reap its rewards and of providing compensating goods to those who are disadvantaged in the ways indicated above. The point of this latter aim, in keeping with the *PGC's* concern for the conditions of agency, is not to reinforce or increase dependence but rather to give support that enables persons to attain the conditions whereby they can control their own lives and effectively pursue and sustain their own purposes without being subjected to domination and harms from others. Thereby they will have their generic rights respected while respecting the generic rights of others, and they will be able to make their own contribution by productive work. It must be recognized, however, that such moderately equalizing and hence redistributive conditions must often include political as well as economic changes whereby productive work is made available. It is a matter not only of developing personal skills and other additive goods but also of fostering an economic environment in which there are sufficient employment opportunities for utilizing these skills. The possibilities of such fostering are, of course, limited by the resources actually available in a given society; but when possible and needed, there must be help from other societies.

The rules that serve this equalizing function must have three kinds of contents. First, they must provide for supplying basic goods, such as food and housing, to those persons who cannot obtain them by their own efforts. Second, they must try to rectify inequalities of additive well-being by improving the capabilities for productive work of persons who are deficient in this respect. Education is a prime means of such improvement, but also important is whatever strengthens family life and enables parents to give constructive, intelligent, loving nurture to their children. The wider diffusion of such means is a prime component of increasing equality of opportunity. Third, the rules must provide for various public goods that, while helping all the members of the society, serve to increase the opportunities for productive employment.

These contents of the rules are recognizably derivative from the *PGC's* equality of generic rights. The rules are to be instrumental toward promoting equality of well-being in the internal, conceptual sense of 'instrumental' discussed above in connection with the criminal law for the rules themselves embody the egalitarianism of the end. Thus there can be no question of such utilitarian instrumentalism as would allow the enslavement or impoverishment of some persons in order to maximize freedom or well-being overall.

There still remains the question of how the equalizing rules are to be applied and made effective. This is a question of external instrumentalities, of the causal factors that are most likely to bring it about that the rules achieve their equalizing ends. Since this is an empirical causal question, the answer must be in terms of various probabilities. There are two chief alternatives: the effectuating agency may be either the voluntary activity of individuals or groups or the coercive activity of the state. The latter alternative is more likely to achieve the desired end. Thus the duty to make the arrangements for applying the equalizing rules should pertain in the first instance to the state when members of the whole society governed by it have the required resources or means. The social rules in question should be democratically enacted laws of the state prescribing to state officials, who are ultimately responsible to the democratic electorate, that they make the necessary arrangements, and also prescribing to individual citizens that they contribute to these arrangements by paying taxes in proportion to their ability.

Social rules are required here because, the need for such arrangements is recurrent and affects sizable numbers of persons. The *PGC's* prescription that persons suffering from economic deprivation be helped hence cannot be addressed simply to individual agents; an association of persons is required for this purpose. This association, moreover, is to be the political one of the state with its coercive laws. Like the problems that evoke the criminal law, if the needs in question are recurrent and pressing they should not be left to the vicissitudes of private charity. Voluntary associations for providing needed food and other basic goods, unlike voluntary associations for punishing criminals, would indeed be helpful; the nonuniformity of the resulting provisions above a certain minimum, being ameliorative rather than punitive, would not violate the recipients' rights to well-being. But it is plausible to hold that the primary responsibility must rest with the state, because only the state has the ability to assure that three required aspects of these arrangements are forthcoming. First, as was already mentioned, the arrangements must be securely provided as needed; hence, if they are left only to the optional decisions of willing private persons, sufficient funds may not be given. Second, the benefits of these arrangements must be equitably and impartially distributed to the persons who need them, without discrimination based on the variable preferences of potential providers. Third, the duty to contribute to such arrangements through taxes must also be equitably distributed to all the persons who have the required economic resources, in proportion to their ability. To leave the fulfillment of this duty solely to voluntary associations would allow many persons to shirk their duty. In this way, the state has a further moral basis as being instrumental to the redistributive justice required by the *PGC*.

There are traditional objections, many of which go back at least to Herbert Spencer, against making the supplying of food and other components of well-being a legally prescribed duty. These objections are to be dealt with in ways similar to those presented above in connection with the duty to rescue. The present sociopolitical context also makes it possible to give a further related reply. Persons are not treated as mere means, nor is their rationally justifiable freedom violated, when they are taxed in order to help other persons who are starving or otherwise suffering from economic privation. For the principle underlying the taxation of the affluent to help the needy is concerned with protecting equally the rights of all persons, including the affluent. The *PGC's* requirement that agents act in accord with the rights of their recipients entails that all prospective purposive agents must refrain from harming one another and that in certain circumstances they must help one another if they can. Hence, limitations on their freedom to abstain from such help are rationally justified. The facts that only some persons may actually be threatened with harm or need help at a particular time, and that only some other persons may be in a position to inflict harm or to give help, do not alter the universality of the *PGC's* provision for the protection of rights. Such protection is not only occurrent but also dispositional and a matter of principle; it manifests an impartial concern for any and all persons whose rights may need protection. Hence, the *PGC's* requirement for taxing the affluent involves treating all persons as ends, not merely as means.

This point also bears on the objection that the above economic and social rights, including the right to be given food and the other goods needed for alleviating severe economic handicaps, cannot be "human" rights because they do not meet the test of universality. According to this test, for a moral right to be a human one it must be a right of all persons against all persons: all persons must have the strict duty of acting in accord with the right, and all persons must have the strict right to be treated in the appropriate way. Thus all persons must be both the agents and the recipients of the modes of action required by the right. This test is passed by the rights to life and to freedom of movement: everyone has the duty to refrain from killing other persons and from interfering with their movements, and everyone has the right to have his life and his freedom of movement respected by other persons. But in the case of the right to be relieved from starvation or severe economic deprivation, it is objected that only some persons have the right: those who are threatened by starvation or deprivation; and only some persons have the duty: those who are able to prevent or relieve this starvation or deprivation by giving aid.

The answer to this objection need not concede that this right, like other economic and social rights, is universal only in a "weaker" sense, in that while all persons have the right to be rescued from starvation or deprivation, only some persons have the correlative duty. Within the limits of practicability, all persons have the right and all have the duty. For all persons come under the protection and the requirements of the *PGC* insofar as they are prospective purposive agents. Hence, all the generic rights upheld by the *PGC* have the universality required for being human rights.

It is, indeed, logically impossible that each person be at the same time both the rescuer and the rescued, both the affluent provider and the deprived pauper. Nevertheless, the fact that some prospective purposive agent may not at some time need to be rescued from deprivation or be able to rescue others from deprivation does not remove the facts that he has the right to be rescued when he has the need and that he has the duty to rescue when he has the ability and when other relevant conditions are met. As we have seen, this duty stems, in the way indicated earlier, from the claim he necessarily makes or accepts that he has the generic rights by virtue of being a prospective purposive agent. The universality of a right is not a matter of everyone's actually having the related need, nor is it a matter of everyone's actually fulfilling the correlative duty, let alone of his doing so at all times. Nor is it even a matter of everyone's always being able to fulfill the duty. It is rather a matter of everyone's always having, as a matter of principle, the right to be treated in the appropriate way when he has the need, and the duty to act in accord with the right when the circumstances arise that require such action and when he then has the ability to do so, this ability including consideration of cost to himself.

When it is said that the right to be relieved from economic deprivation and the correlative duty pertain to all persons insofar as they are prospective purposive agents, this does not violate the condition that for human rights to be had one must only be human, as against fulfilling some more restrictive description. As was indicated earlier, all normal humans are prospective purposive agents; the point of introducing this description is only to call attention to the aspect of being human that most directly generates the rights to freedom and well-being. In this regard the right in question differs from rights that pertain to persons not simply by virtue of being prospective purposive agents but only in some more restricted capacity, such as being teachers as against students, umpires as against batters, or judges as against defendants. The universality of human rights derives from their direct connection with the necessary conditions of action, as against the more restrictive objects with which nongeneric rights are connected. And since both the affluent and the economically deprived are prospective purposive agents, the latter's right to be helped by the former is a human right.

Business and Government

▶ *Interview with Linda Chavez.*

Each of the applied ethics sections of this text (Parts 2–5) includes an interview with a key figure who is prominent in his/her field. The purpose of these interviews is to bridge the gap between theory and practice and offer the student an exposure to how people in the "real world" confront practical, ethical issues.

Linda Chavez is the former executive director of the U.S. Commission on Civil Rights. She is the author of *Out of the Barrio: Toward a New Politics of Hispanic Assimilation,* published by Basic Books in 1991. Currently, she is a senior fellow at the Manhattan Institute and director of The Center for the New American Community.

Q: *What do you think are the most pressing ethical problems in Government-Business Issues today from both a micro and a macro perspective?*

A: Let me begin by describing two phenomena that characterize our society today and which represent changes from earlier times. First, you have a situation in which the value structure of society as a whole has fragmented. There is not a single recognized value system which all people can plug into in order to regulate their lives. In times past this function was carried on by organized religion. The major religions in this country all subscribed to a similar moral ethic which they taught to the people who attended their congregations. Moral discourse was possible between people of different faiths because there was always this fundamental bedrock of agreement.

Having a common value structure is important for society as a whole (macro picture). This is because the large institutions had to square themselves to this common value structure. It gave a single frame of reference by which moral judgments could be rendered. When this structure began to decay, the ability to hold meaningful moral discussion also decayed. This led to people "talking at" each other and not "with" each other.

An example of this decay and the effect upon society can be found in the writings of Dostoevsky. We all know the famous "Grand Inquisitor" passage in the *Brothers Karamazov*. In that case the utility for society from organized religion as an institution is described (whether or not the truths of religion are correct). In a slightly different fashion you have the causal mechanism of how this operates in the character of Raskolnikov *(Crime and Punishment)*. He contemplates whether or not to murder. The flaw in his reasoning which leads him on is the lack of restraint. Raskolnikov pictures himself as a "superman" who is above the institutional restraints of the "herd morality" which is represented in organized religion. Thus it is that when Raskolnikov "frees" himself of these constraints, he commits murder.

In the macro picture this is what happens to society. When the collective masses cease to be restrained by a common set of moral dictums, only individual license reigns.

Second, from the micro perspective, I would say that the consequence of this trend is a lack of individuals taking personal responsibility for their actions. If there is not a clear code that prescribes behavior along with foreseeable consequences, then every evil that befalls a person can be depicted as coming from without. Since it comes from without, remedy can be sought from without. Thus, people look to sue for any and everything. Someone is to blame besides themselves. Nothing is their fault.

Obviously, this is an erosion of a personal morality that effects business people at every level. A defensive mentality sets in where manipulation of power to address any dislike and irritation replaces individual scrutiny of the "right" or "wrong" of action—which will have decided consequences.

Even more frightening to me is that this abdication of responsibility undercuts our whole notion of free will. And once we jettison that, we have no morality.

Q: *How do you feel these trends you identify will affect our country and the relationship of Business to Government?*

A: I think we can take it as a given that business cannot operate in an environment that is totally without rules. I know that some economists like Milton Friedman and political libertarians may take a view like that, but I disagree. We need some regulation of business by government. The question is where to draw the line?

Let's examine some extremes. With no regulation there is the potential of exploitation as everyone pursues his own interest. However, with excessive regulation (which is present in many industries today) we exacerbate problems that are already there. We have all seen what a mess government regulation has made of the country's welfare system. We have encouraged the break-up of families and have worsened the problem of poverty rather than alleviated it.

Or again, there are the so-called "protected" industries. We wanted to remain competitive in some area—say dairy farming—and the result is that the government programs have actually made us less competitive in those industries. We have to accept that some industries might fail. This is a consequence of the free market. By over regulating industries we create a drag on the economy. And though the subsidies may have been instituted with the best intentions in mind, they have had the opposite effect.

Secondly, over regulation encourages people to disregard the law. We set up so many rules and so much paperwork that it almost takes a moral zealot to follow them all. In reality what happens is that people begin picking and choosing which rules they will choose to follow based upon their personal convenience. And after they have disregarded government regulation once, you can bet that they will be more likely to disregard it again in the future.

Thus, seen from this perspective, excessive regulation which is enacted out of the intention to bring a dose of morality and fairness into business, actually has the opposite effect: it encourages immorality. People disobey what they perceive to be inane rules with no positive purpose. And once on the slippery slope of civil disobedience, they are much more likely to continue in increasingly greater infractions.

Q: *What direction would you prefer be taken?*

A: As I noted above, both the extremes of no regulation and over regulation are to be avoided. But there is no single rule that dictates what is too much. If I were to formulate some principle I suppose it would be that government must not be seen as our first recourse to address problems. The government must trust its citizens to take responsibility themselves. Let's see if a problem works itself out before we ask government to step in.

Q: *What about the role of government to ensure economic justice?*

A: We cannot let people starve. We do need a safety net for those incapable of caring for themselves. Government does have a role, but it has over stepped its role so often that it exacerbates the very issues it has set out to eradicate (as I mentioned with welfare, earlier). Certainly, government has a role, but government acts best when it does not try to take on the entire role itself.

Q: *What concrete cases can you cite that support the position you are taking?*

A: On the macro level I would point to the atomic energy industry. Here you have an entire industry that has been regulated into extinction. Sure there are problems with atomic wastes, but on balance the health risks are far less than coal-produced electricity, for example. Yet, in spite of this, we have watched the government increase its regulations until it smothered the industry.

On the micro level I would cite the case of suits against smoking companies by people who have been life-long smokers. We have had warnings on cigarettes for thirty years. It is inconceivable that people smoked cigarettes and did not know that it was bad for their health.

Now, when they are dying because of the effects of their habit, they refuse to take responsibility for their actions and look to someone else, the tobacco companies, to blame. If people aren't going to accept responsibility for reading the health warnings on cigarette packages, then why have we gone to the trouble and expense to have these warnings printed?

Q: *If the situation exists in which the value structure is fragmented, and individuals are abdicating their moral responsibility, then what is the hope for morality?*

A: I think it would have to be to return to the sources of our moral strength as a nation. These have been found in the traditional religions. People need values. But when they turn away from religion they turn to government instead to provide these values. But government cannot deliver. This is because government has no values. It is an arena of power. I think that we have been looking to government for something it is incapable of delivering: moral value. Instead, I believe we must turn again to the sources of our moral virtue which have fortified us since the founding of our country.

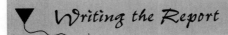

▼ Writing the Report

Applying Ethical Issues

We are finally at the last stage of the process of assessing ethical cases. By this point we have: 1. Chosen an ethical theory (whose point of view we will adopt); 2. Set out cost issues and ethical issues lists; and 3. Annotated the issues lists by examining how embedded each issue is to the essential nature of the case at hand. What remains is the ability to come to an action decision once everything is set out for us. [After these steps are completed the conclusions must be set out in a report.]

To do this we must enter an argumentative phase. In this phase I suggest that you create brainstorming sheets headed by the possible courses of action open to you. On each sheet you will construct an argument that supports that particular course of action utilizing the annotated issues sheets you have already created.

Then compare what you believe to be the pivotal issues that drive each argument. Use your chosen ethical theory to decide which issue is most compelling. Be prepared to defend your outcomes recommendation.

Let us return to the case of the asbestos fabrication plant. As you may recall, the case went like this: **Case 3:** The ABC plant is one of the few remaining asbestos fabrication plants in the country. This plant is located in rural Kentucky in a town which has no other manufacturing industry. Ten years ago the only other manufacturer, American Motors, closed its

"Gremlin" facilities there. The closure of this plant will probably put many people into poverty.

Federal regulations have varied drastically over the last twenty years concerning asbestos. As testing has become more exact it has been demonstrated that increasingly smaller amounts of asbestos have proved to be "safe." However, the industrial use of asbestos as a gasket, for example, has no peer.

The ABC plant is an old manufacturing facility still producing asbestos gaskets. When considering employee safety, it seems that they should consider altering their production methods to a "dustless" underwater fabrication process. However, this has negative side effects: 1) There is a great cost involved in converting machinery to a new manufacturing process. 2) The federal regulation climate is unpredictable. 3) The waste water, though conforming to current U.S. standards, might not be treatable in other regulatory environments. 4) Maybe asbestos is harmful at any dosage. 5) Virtually all of the competition has left the marketplace. This leaves the avenue open to you to operate a venture which has very high profit margins since your only competition (a synthetic plastic gasket) is inferior in performance and double your price). 6) Perhaps you will not be able to operate your plant forever, but at present you are making good money for your stockholders, and after all, they own the company. 7) The time frame for which this process will pay-off completely is within the five-year capital depreciation period stipulated by the IRS (in other words, as long as you can squeeze five years out of the regulatory climate, your stockholders will win financially). The probability of heading off a regulatory shutdown for at least five years is good.

In the case, it will be remembered that the cost and the ethical issues were both deeply embedded. This creates an intractable conflict. There is no simple way to satisfy one against the other.

What is necessary is to "know one's own mind" on the issue. How does one do this? Obviously, there is no single solution to this, but one approach is to emphasize the conflict on the key premises of the arguments which support each. What do I mean by the key premises of the arguments?* Well, this goes into the nature of argument. In any argument there is a conclusion. If you want to contrast two arguments, you must begin by contrasting two conclusions.

Conclusions are supported by premises which (logically) cause the acceptance of the conclusion. Therefore, what you must do is to create at least two arguments which entail different conclusions.

What this means is this. You must create brainstorming lists on the *key issue(s)* involved in the disputation. The key issue(s) of the disputation is that

*For a more detailed exposition of the use of structured, informal argument see my book, *The Process of Argument* (Englewood Cliffs, NJ: Prentice Hall, 1988, rpt. 1994 by University Press of America). See particularly the sections on the mechanics of argument and how to turn your argument into an essay.

concept that "makes all the difference." In the case at hand we have a number of key issues. Let's try to construct both "pro" and "con" arguments which seek to make their points.

▼ ## Sample "Pro" Brainstorming Sheet

Position to be supported: Continue fabricating asbestos gaskets.

Key thoughts on the subject:

1. There is a danger in everything. No manufacturing process is completely safe.
2. Once set in the form of sealed gaskets there has never been a proven health hazard to consumers.
3. All health awareness is directed towards our own employees.
4. It is expensive (though not excessive) to keep modifying our existing plant to meet present government guidelines, but government guidelines have changed radically over twenty years.
5. Government guidelines are often behind the scientific "health problems" curve.
6. The only way to protect employees is to convert to a "dustless" underwater fabrication process.
7. Trailings in the waste water (though meeting current standards) might be subjecting the rural area in which you live to environmental hazards.
8. The rural area in which you live needs these jobs. Who cares is a few "so-called" environmental "wish list" proposals fall by the wayside? People need jobs to live!
9. *This is a very profitable venture.*

Argument:

1. The stockholders own this company and deserve the best return on their dollar—Fact
2. The A.B.C. company is in a unique position to garner (at least for the time being) a very lucrative profit—Fact
3. Conversion of the plant to UNDERWATER FABRICATION will meet all existing government regulations—Fact
4. The time frame for which this process will pay-off completely is within the five-year capital depreciation period stipulated by the IRS—Fact
5. The probability of heading off a regulatory shutdown for at least five years is good.
6. It is probable that the company can make money by converting to the underwater fabrication process—2–5

7. One ought to act in the stockholder's best interests—Fact
8. The A.B.C. company ought to approve the underwater fabrication process—1, 6, 7.

▼ ## Sample "Con" Brainstorming Sheet

Position to be supported: Stop fabricating asbestos gaskets.

Key thoughts on the subject:

1. Asbestos is an antiquated, dangerous substance which will soon be banned by the government.
2. The underwater process only protects employees under current governmental regulations. But these are likely to change (given the pattern over the past twenty years). It is possible that even with the new process you are killing your workers. This is not right even if the workers enter into the job knowing there are risks.
3. The environmental waste will significantly harm the environment.
4. Even though the locals might not complain about this pollution (because they so value their jobs), this amounts to exploitation. They will "sell out" their own health and future generations for the short term benefit of a few jobs now.
5. The "best interests" of the stockholders does not mean getting all the money it can possibly garner. It must also abide by ethical issues of personal concern for the employees and the environment at large [tenet of one version of Kant's categorical imperative].

Argument:

1. The company can continue to make money fabricating these gaskets in the short term—Fact
2. The company has an obligation to act in the "best interests" of the stockholders—Fact
3. The "best interests" of the stockholders include acting in an ethically responsible way—Assertion
4. Continuing to manufacture asbestos gaskets—even with the underwater fabrication process—will harm the health of both employees and the environment at large—Assertion
5. Harming the health of employees and the environment at large, just for the sake of money, is to exploit both one's employees and host community—Assertion
6. Exploitation is unethical—Assertion (set out your own moral theory here for a justification)

7. To continue manufacturing asbestos gaskets with or without the underwater process *is unethical—4–6*

8. Though the company can make money by continuing to manufacture asbestos gaskets, it should get out of the business—7, 1–3

Once you have set out arguments both "pro" and "con" for the action issue [to continue or cease manufacture of asbestos gaskets] it is up to you to assess which argument is stronger. This requires creating a "key issues" comparison sheet. Take the most pivotal issue(s) in each argument and set them side-by-side. Then employ your own business decision making model (including your chosen ethical theory) to arrive at your decision. It is important that you include an ethical component in your argument—whichever conclusion you reach.

Sample "Key Issues" Comparison Sheet

Pro=# 2. The A.B.C. company is in a unique position to garner (at least for the time being) a very lucrative profit—-Fact

7. One ought to act in the stockholder's best interests—Fact
   Con=# 4. Continuing to manufacture asbestos gaskets—even with the underwater fabrication process—will harm the health of both employees and the environment at large—Assertion

5. Harming the health of employees and the environment at large just for the sake of money is to exploit both one's employees and host community—Assertion

6. Exploitation is unethical—Assertion (set out your own moral theory here for a justification)

   Assessment: Though the fabrication of asbestos gaskets in this marketplace offers a good financial opportunity for stockholders, and though the company will be doing nothing *illegal* in continuing in this line of business, it would be unethical to do so. Questions about possible health hazards to employees and environment outweigh financial gains. There are no adequate safeguards. Therefore, the company should get out of the asbestos fabrication business and do whatever it can for the town and its employees regarding replacement to other parts of the company (if possible) or job placement (if no internal jobs are available elsewhere).

   You are now ready to write your report.

Macro and Micro Cases

The cases section of this book are divided into two categories: macro and micro. Each type of case employs a different point of view.

Macro Case. The macro case takes large institutional entities as its focus. For example one might examine Beechnut and the apple juice Case or BCCI as a multi-national banking concern. The purpose of the Macro Case is to get you thinking about how corporations should act in their environment. You will take the perspective of a high level official and make judgments which will affect many thousands.

Micro Case. The micro case takes individuals working within business as its focus. For example, one might look at a mid-level manager's approach to end of the year sales reports, or an engineer's decision to be a "whistle blower." The attraction of these cases is that you can project yourself realistically into these cases. It is probable that you will be in positions similar to the Micro Case descriptions (whereas only a fraction of people will ever really be a Macro Case decision maker).

Case Development. The word "case" is used in different ways by different people. This book will suggest one form of case response. The method for preparing and developing these cases is suggested in the essays entitled: "Writing the Report" which can be found at the end of each section in the book. Your professor may also have specific guidelines of his/her own.

For those who wish to use it, this approach offers a bridge between various traditional approaches to case studies, taught in business schools, with a philosophical method that emphasizes essay development. The intention throughout is that you expand your mind with the general essays and develop a practical skill in applying an ethical theory to thorny moral/cost conflicts through writing a business report that defends a particular course of action.

Please note that though most of the cases presented here have fictional venues, they are based upon composites of real Corporate America.

 acro Cases

Case 3.1—Nuclear Power Plant in California

You sit on the regulation board of the Atomic Energy Commission. You have noted that there have not been any applications set before you in California since the Diablo Canyon project that was submitted over two decades ago.

You now have to review plans for a new nuclear power plant in California (just south of San Francisco). The plant would replace current power plants which emit hydro-carbons into the atmosphere at 7x the present allowable standard (and 17x the prospective standard in the year 2000).

The opponents of the project point to three factors in their opposition to the power plant.

1. There is no clear method for disposing of nuclear wastes. Nobody wants it: it is *hostis humani generis* (an enemy of the human race). If the waste cannot be disposed of, then it will end up in the San Francisco area and create a potential health hazard.
2. The potential for a nuclear accident is always present. Though there have not been any other "Three Mile Island" incidents in the United States, still the potential is there for a major accident. The winds in the Bay area could exacerbate such a situation.
3. California is an earthquake waiting to happen. The existence of a nuclear power facility so near to the San Andreas Fault could trigger an accident of catastrophic proportions.

The supporters of the power plant make the following arguments.

1. The present power plants pollute the air and are killing people every day. This is not a 'maybe" or a 'might happen' but an actual fact. Nuclear power does not create air pollution. Air pollution is a major problem in California.
2. The only accident in the United States (the Three Mile Island incident) was extremely minor compared to what is happening every day in conventional power plants, which *actually* harm the atmosphere.
3. America's energy needs continue to grow. Either we create conventional plants that burn coal or other fossil fuels that are destroying the environment, or we must cut back on our energy demands. This would mean giving up our standard of living and our pre-eminent place as a world superpower. For most Americans this would be unacceptable. Therefore, an alternate energy source is needed for fuel. Solar, geothermal and other such technologies have proven impractical. As it stands, it's nuclear or conventional. Both have problems, but the energy need is there. A choice has to be made. Nuclear energy is the better alternative.

To further complicate the issue the public utility company is insisting on a change in the regulatory process which would make it impossible to stop the project once it has been approved. Opponents of nuclear power, they contend, have used the process of appeal to slow down construction so that plants can never be built on time and end up costing customers exorbitantly for overrun expenditures. The higher utility costs not only come from ordinary people's pockets, but contribute to an emerging image of California as a hostile place to do business. Thus, the effect of higher utility costs would be to drive business out of an area already hurt by the downsizing of the computer industry.

The proposal before you is: (a) Whether or not to approve the proposal to build a nuclear power plant in the San Francisco area; and (b) If the request is approved, then whether to simplify the current rules that allow for injunctions to halt construction whenever there is suspicion that the public welfare is in jeopardy.

The Atomic Energy Commission is deadlocked. As chair you will cast the deciding vote and must write a report that justifies your action.

Case 3.2—Regulation of the Airlines Industry

You sit on the board of the FAA which is holding hearings about whether Congress should "re-regulate" the airlines industry. You listen to two witnesses. The first is from United Airlines and the second is from the fictional East-West Airlines. The question before you is whether the airline companies of the United States ought to be subject to strict fare regulation or not.

United Airlines. Speaking for United Airlines I can say that the climate of deregulation that has prevailed since the Reagan Administration is "an accident waiting to happen." Let me clarify these thoughts. First, let's review the past. In the 1960s and the 1970s when air travel really "took off" (excuse the pun), the United States market was tightly regulated. Tight regulations mean that organizations that "play by the rules" are rewarded by being paid a fair tariff for air travel.

In such an environment we were able to offer grades of 'stand-by' fares to students, servicemen, and other needy individuals who wanted to fly, but did not have the money for full fare.

When there was government regulation, the rules were simpler. A standard rate structure existed (which could be deviated from in a limited number of ways). The airlines were locked in to a fixed rate and could compete in the areas that counted most: customer service, timely departures/arrivals, prompt baggage handling.

What has happened in the climate of deregulation, is that smaller companies, who do not have the overhead of a full service carrier, slash their prices and only compete on profitable routes. What would happen if the U.S. Postal Service allowed competition in the delivery of mail. I'll tell you what: small, non-unionized companies would emerge which would offer to deliver mail in only the high density population areas, viz. the areas in which they could make money. You wouldn't find any start-up companies competing for the "RFD" routes. The rural areas would be left with nothing.

The same is true with the airline industry. When you allow the small carriers to merely enter the profitable routes, then you are undercutting the basic fabric of full service, unionized operations. We are not ashamed to be a union carrier, but many of these new companies, who want to compete in limited markets, are not. They may not give their workers the guarantees that only result from cooperative bargaining.

For these reasons, and more, we ask the committee to re-instate regulated air fares.

East-West Airlines. The United States was built upon a simple principle: fair and open competition. We believe that it is essential the committee re-member this principle as it deliberates about re-instating regulated air fares.

Let us begin at the beginning. The airline industry is not very old. Organized air travel began in the late 1920s but didn't really catch hold until the 1950s. It was still very common for travelers in the 1970s to be sitting next to an adult who had never flown in an airplane. This is an infant industry, still.

What is the best climate for an infant industry to grow to maturity? Is it one in which the government randomly selects rates that contain layers of fat in order to guarantee that no matter what the airlines will turn a profit? This is the logic of the failed regimes of the planned government economies of Eastern Europe and Russia.

In the United States things are different. Here a business must satisfy the public or die a deserved death. We need government off of our backs. Pencil pushers never had to hustle for business. What do they know about regulating a "real business"?

If we can offer a better deal for air travel, then let the public decide which carrier to choose. If the fat cats of the industry cry about servicing unprofitable routes, let them get out of those markets. Capitalism suggests that if you cannot pay the freight, then get out of line. It is very possible that some areas of the country which currently enjoy international air connections will have to take a train or a bus to the nearest hub that will satisfy their travel needs. These are facts.

As to our non-union status I could note that in all categories of labor in our organization, we are paying our non-union employees more than our competitors. No union could ever get a foothold here. This is because we have established a company on the principles of "the American way."

The vote is sure to be tight. As chair you must submit a report of your opinion that the other members of the committee must accept, reject or modify. Make your report.

Case 3.3—Taxation Policy

You sit on the House Ways and Means Committee. There is a mandate from the president to reconsider the way we tax our citizens. You must choose between two alternatives: income taxes and consumption taxes. The thrust of the president's directive is to discover which method leads to the most equitable and efficient method for raising revenue in the country.

One proponent from each side will speak.

Income Taxes. Those who can afford to pay, should pay. That is, and has always been, the argument for income taxes. It is only with income taxes that we can ascertain who has "gotten" *what* in order to determine who will "give" *what*.

Now there are some who will argue that the rich can maneuver around paying taxes and it is the rich (or the relatively rich) who are the targets of progressive income taxation. If this is true, then it would create a situation in which a false scenario is presented to the American public that such-and-such rules exist for the betterment of all. But (under this argument) if the rich *do not* pay their fair share, then this facade is but a cruel hoax.

What the advocates of this proposal contend is that there should exist an income tax with the minimum number of exemptions. Such a tax system would not allow people to "slip through" loopholes in the tax system. If a person has means above another, then that person should pay more. It is that simple.

Therefore, what we propose is that revenues be derived by a graduated income tax system in which there are few deferments and in which the "upper half" of the income curve are held accountable for what they make. After all, they did not accumulate their wealth without the sweat of the lower half. This is true even of salaried employees who can often shield their consciences by the fact that they pull a paycheck and do not "own their business." This give a false sense of being a "working man." Such cardboard, proletariat want-ta-bees should stop and reflect where they fit into the scheme of things and consider that their existence in the upper half means that there is someone who is suffering in the lower half.

There is no other way to redress this wrong save progressive income taxation.

Consumption Taxes. Our taxation system is a joke. Sure progressive income taxes make sense—if you are an idealist or some college student thinking about the way the world ought to be. But face facts. There is a tremendous underground economy. This economy pays no taxes. Cash is the name of the game. Starting with sales of illegal drugs to "independent contractors" working in the trades the message is clear: lots of business gets done by cash or barter.

Now does the United States government get its rightful piece of this commerce? No way. Only if the government focuses its tax policy upon consumption can it regain what is rightfully its own. If you buy a Mercedes, there is no way that you can avoid the sales taxes. This is because retail businesses are easy to control. Much easier that Sam or Sally drywaller working somewhere for cash—or Bill or Belinda drug dealer scoring crack for thousands of hidden dollars.

Consumption. That is where it is at. Easy to monitor. Easy to collect. What could be fairer? Oh, I know that some say that the consumption tax affects the poor more heavily than the rich. If the poor are taxed on the bread they buy, then that dollar takes more out of their pocket than it does for a more affluent person.

But what is the alternative? Give more tax breaks to the rich? Get real. The tax codes are made by rich people for rich people. There is an illusion of fairness, but with all the loopholes the actual monies paid are a smaller percentage than is paid by the working class person. This could change by instituting a "progressive" consumption tax. Low taxes on food and simple utilities and greater taxes on goods that people could live without. In this way we can bring equity back to the American tax system.

You must now write your recommendation to the president. What system will you advocate and why?

Case 3.4—The Safety Net

The budget is tight. You are the Under Secretary of Health and Human Services. The Secretary has directed you to report on the state of our present set of entitlement programs that are designed to help the poor. In thirty days you will have to submit a report to your boss. What will you say?

Present System. The present welfare system was created in the 1930s in order to help the United States deal with the devastating effects of the Great Depression. It made the assumption that every able-bodied person would seek work, but that there were not enough jobs to go around. To alleviate mass starvation and human misery, a set of programs were established one-by-one.

By 1970 these programs had expanded to include many basic human needs: food, clothing, shelter, and medical care. By going through proper channels a person could obtain food stamps to pay for minimal food. Cash grants took care of clothing, and vouchers paid the rent. Medicaid looked after medical payments in cooperation with the states.

Critics of the present welfare system come from the right and the left. From the right it is often contended that able-bodied people are encouraged to shirk work, to cheat, and get a "free ride." From the left it is contended that there are not enough programs to provide job skills that would permanently allow those on welfare a place in the American economy.

Proposals.

1. Government/Business partnership. Business provides the jobs. The government realizes that businesses that hire people who have been out of the labor force may incur higher costs. Therefore, it is the place of government to offer generous incentives (including outright grants) to business to hire, train and create new consumers and taxpayers. The cost of this plan would be modest because the tax credits to business would be

offset by the additional taxes which would be levied upon the new workers in the labor force.

2. The government must take the lead in creating a comprehensive new welfare system. Safeguards can be set up to eliminate fraud. The government would guarantee work to all Americans (in make-shift jobs, if necessary). Mothers would be given free child care and everyone (including disabled Americans) would pull his/her weight and share in the dignity that only an earned paycheck can provide.

   This program would be expensive. Business would be asked to bear the brunt of this added cost.

3. Cut welfare to the bone. Let people "sink or swim." Those who can't cut it can move to another country, get a job, or starve to death.

4. Keep the present system.

Your Report. In your report you must not only argue for one of the proposals, but you must make clear what the relative roles of business and government should be in establishing economic justice in our country.

icro Cases

Case 3.5—Product Liability and Acme Tobacco

You are sitting on a jury. The case before you is Smith vs. Acme Tobacco. The suit alleges that Acme Tobacco knowingly sold a product, cigarettes, that cause cancer. Mrs. Smith was a pack-and-a-half smoker for forty years. Now she has terminal lung cancer. She is suing for medical and punitive damages amounting to ten million dollars.

The Argument for Mrs. Smith. Mrs. Smith says that any company that knowingly manufactures and sells a product that is dangerous must be accountable for any and all damages that might result. Even though the packages have warnings, Mrs. Smith assumed that any product that is legally sold has the sanction of the company and/or the United States government. Poison, for example, would not knowingly be sold to people as a consumer foodstuff.

The same holds true for tobacco. Big business has an inherently paternalistic responsibility to its customers. It must always think of their best interests. This drives the creation of all sorts of safety regulations and advances in packaging, etc.

Why should tobacco be any different? The company knows it is poison and yet continues to market it aggressively—even using advertising to entice people to use their product. This is reckless and tobacco companies should be made to pay.

The Argument for the Tobacco Company. Though there seems to be great evidence that the excessive use of tobacco can cause health problems, this has never been proven beyond a shadow of a doubt. If one examines health risks to moderate users of tobacco, the link is even more tenuous. Why should a company be responsible for consumers who use their products irresponsibly? Do we hold knife makers liable when some one uses the knife to stab someone?

If Mrs. Smith had smoked one or two cigarettes a day instead of a pack and a half, then she would probably be fine today. But even if we concede the health point (just for the sake of argument), how can we be held accountable for health risks when each and every package of cigarettes and each and every advertisement carries a health warning to all potential users of our product? This product labeling is expensive, but we willingly comply because we want to be good citizens. We warn potential users of potential health problems. They are adults. Can't they make up their own minds about how they are to live their lives?

Autonomy is a basic principle of freedom. We don't tell people they cannot go skydiving, bungie jumping or engage in other dangerous activities. This is America. People can do as they please. We don't need Big Brother telling us how to live. If Mrs. Smith wanted to smoke, that was her right. The cigarette packages and advertisements both contained health warnings. The choice was hers and she made it. Now she wants to say that someone else should be blamed for her own choice. The only way to accept such a conclusion would be to eschew the principles of liberty upon which this country was founded. In America you make your choices and you must live with them.

The Jury Decision. The judge has instructed you to consider paternalism and autonomy (among other issues) when you decide how far a company should be held responsible for the deleterious effects of its products.

Case 3.6—Jones vs. The Flaming Pit Restaurant

You are sitting on the jury of this civil trial.* The plaintiff, Tom Jones, was a promising pre-med college student at Marquette University in Milwaukee, Wisconsin. Tom is suing The Flaming Pit Restaurant, a popular family restaurant, for three million dollars.

The Facts. The Flaming Pit Restaurant is a family restaurant that sells 95% food and 5% alcohol. The hours of operation are T–F 11:00 am–11:00 pm; Saturday 11:00 am–12 midnight; Sunday 1:00 pm–9:00 pm. They are closed

---

*This is based on a real case. The names have been changed, but the facts have been kept essentially as they were.

Mondays. There is no live music or dancing. The average client is 25–90 with a strong German, family theme prevalent. The restaurant has been in business for 70 years. It has been profitable, but in today's competitive climate, profit margins of the fifties and sixties have thinned dramatically. This is so acute that over the past few years the management has seriously considered closing its doors. It has not done so partly because the present owners respect the traditions of their grandparents who built the restaurant and because they employ graduates from an alternative high school for dropouts. This restaurant provides jobs for those who otherwise might become criminals. This civic mission is important to the present owners.

On April 4th of last year Tom Jones was coming home from studying in the library. It was a Sunday. It was eleven o'clock in the evening. The restaurant was closed. There were no cars in the parking lot. Tom cut across the parking lot on the way to his apartment.

Then it happened. A souped up "hot rod" came roaring into the parking lot from the street. The driver was wild. Tom tried to run, but he was slowed by all the books he was carrying. The car hit Tom. Tom screamed. The hot rod sped away without stopping. A pedestrian came to Tom's aid and remembered three numbers of the car's license plate.

Tom was rushed to the hospital. Unfortunately, it was too late. Tom suffered a neck injury as he fell and is paralyzed forever.

Thanks to the well lit parking lot, the good samaritan who helped Tom was able to get enough information so that the police made an arrest within fourteen hours. The driver showed signs of elevated cocaine levels that indicated he was out of control of his vehicle. He had several previous arrests. Unfortunately, he had no insurance on the automobile he had been driving.

The only entity that had insurance was The Flaming Pit. The restaurant had been closed. The restaurant's parking lot conformed to all the safety codes of the city–and then some. But the fact remains that the accident occurred on the restaurant's parking lot.

Pro Plaintiff. The plaintiff, Tom Jones, was a promising student who wanted to become a doctor. He could have made over ten million dollars in lifetime salary (assuming low inflation). The plaintiff is not suing for lost salary, but merely for the expensive medical and custodial expenses that will be necessary to keep him alive until his natural death. The plaintiff is the son of a single parent mother, who makes a very modest salary. Tom was a scholarship student. Tom's mother cannot afford to provide care for him. It is not the restaurant's fault that the accident occurred on their property, but nevertheless, they are the only ones with insurance money enough to foot the bill.

Pro Defendant. Money does not grow on trees. Life isn't fair. These are two truisms we all must accept.

The defendant in this case has been a model citizen of the community. It is a tragedy that Mr. Jones will have his promising life diminished by a reprehensible criminal (he was sentenced for twenty years). This is a terrible loss both to Mr. Jones and the community he was intending to serve as a physician.

However, we must distinguish sadness and responsibility. The Flaming Pit Restaurant has been a fixture of this community for years. They have hung on even when economic conditions dictated closing their doors. How are they being rewarded for their loyalty to the community?

What will happen if this suit is successful? The Flaming Pit will close. They have gotten estimates from their insurance carrier of how much their premiums will rise as the result of this suit and the new amount will put them out of business. This will be a loss to the community. Jobs will be lost. A program for troubled youth will now be without its largest sponsor. A healthy family establishment will become a part of the past. And why? Is it because the restaurant did anything wrong? Did they violate any safety regulations or keep an unsafe parking lot? No. It was a model parking lot. In fact, the lighting was so far beyond code that it enabled the person that aided Mr. Jones to identify the criminal's car. How ironic that the very fact that they were so consciousness is a potential factor in their downfall. Can we let this happen? It is up to you men and women of the jury.

Your report. What should be the judgment? Consider the interests of both parties. Then consider the wider question of whether business is/should be concerned in the well being of society even when no fault has been assigned to them. It is a thorny question. Employ an ethical theory to justify your decision.

Case 3.7—Homeowners Insurance and the Boxer Insurance Agency

You are Loretta Boxer. You own an insurance agency that features one of the national companies. The problem is this: You are located in Rogers Park in Chicago. Most of your business is in this affluent area or in even more affluent areas in the northern suburbs (Evanston, Kennilworth, and Winetka).

Background. Homeowners insurance is an alliance between groups of homeowner, condo owners, and renters who share their common risks so that they might be able to take care of each other when disaster strikes. In mutual companies, when the "luck" is good, then all the policy holders benefit. When times are bad, then all suffer together.

The Risks. Houses over forty years old have fires at eight times the rate that new houses do. Therefore, it is often the case that insurance companies create special requirements for these types of houses. Unfortunately, houses in the inner cities are almost always over forty years old.

Crime is another problem, but this seems not to be an unmanageable risk (vis-à-vis inner city and other insurance risks).

Fraud is a significant problem. Statistically, people who have nowhere else to turn, look to the Federal Government and large corporations as final refuges when all else fails. So when you need a buck—file a claim. Claims of this sort are high in poverty areas (particularly during hard economic times).

Definitions. "Redlining" is a term that refers to an unethical (and illegal) practice of "skimming" only the best business and leaving the rest to the federally-funded programs. In redlining, an insurance company may use insurance underwriting criteria that go beyond normal risk assessment and enter into the realm of irrational prejudice. In these cases, insurance companies refuse to provide insurance to perfectly sound, sober risks just because they happen to belong to a group which the head underwriter thinks is "shifty" or "not our kind of people." Obviously, this is a gross abuse of the principle of insurance which (at its core) is a communal system of risk distribution.

The Problem. Your situation is this: One of your producers lives on the south side of Chicago in a predominantly poor, African-American community. This producer, Leon, has been coming up with a number of home-owner leads in his community. You have sent them into the company according to the printed criteria. But the head underwriter at the company wants you to kill the applications from the zip code areas from which Leon is writing policies.

You mention that your claims experience has been good in these areas, but the head underwriter reminds you that you must sell three-hundred $300 policies to make up for one $90,000 loss. And that losses in that area are just waiting to happen.

You disagree. The head underwriter says that if you make waves, then every policy—of any type—that you try to write will be held up so long that the customers will go elsewhere.

Options.

1. Give in and quash the application along with Leon.
2. Take it up with someone higher up in the insurance company.
3. Bring the situation to the attention of the agents' association in the hopes that some meaningful, internal reform might result.
4. Go to the newspaper so that it might catch the attention of lawmakers who will come down with new legislative guidelines.

What should you do and why?

Cases 3.8—Desert Storm and Chronic Fatigue Syndrome

You are the home appliances manager in a department store in Cincinnati. One of your employees, Sam Horn, has not been performing well of late. He has been lackadaisical and not responsive to customers. This is not like Sam. At one time he was the hub in what was one of the best home appliances departments in the city.

What happened to Sam was this. In 1991 he served in Desert Storm. Though there was no documented chemical attacks in the war, a number of veterans have noted various combat maladies. Some of these have resulted in chronic fatigue syndrome. This disease affects different people variously, but it often leads to a loss of the ability to work efficiently.

Sam's doctor has diagnosed him as having this condition and has recommended that Sam take time off from work. The problem is that Sam has taken time off from work. It has done him no good. Sam's condition continues to worsen.

The department store carries no disability insurance on its employees. Therefore, if Sam cannot do the work, Sam will be fired. But before Desert Storm—for ten years—Sam was one of the best and hardest workers in the whole store. You feel bad about firing Sam. After all, it wasn't his fault that his reserve unit was called up for war. He served his country and he served his store (for ten years).

In addition Sam's wife, Rosa, has a pre-existing health condition of her own. If you fire Sam both he and his wife will be unable to obtain health insurance.

You consider taking the situation to your boss. But you know what your boss will say: "This company is not a welfare agency. When Sam produced for us we paid him a fair wage. He was well compensated for the work he did for us. Now, however, he is unable to uphold his end of the bargain. He has moved from the best employee to one of the worst. This cannot go on without hurting the company. You have no choice but to let him go. After all, it is the government's and not industry's job to see to the welfare of its citizens."

You know that there are no government programs to help Sam. The V.A. does not recognize Sam's ailment as coming from the war. Perhaps Sam could get some dollars if he were put up against the wall. But is that the proper move to make?

You are Sam's manager. What should you do, and why?

International Issues

- ▶ **Bribery**
- ▶ **Multi-National Corporations**

CHAPTER 15

Bribery

What's Wrong with Bribery

Scott Turow*

The question on the floor is what is wrong with bribery? I am not a philosopher and thus my answer to that question may be less systematic than others, but it is certainly no less deeply felt. As a federal prosecutor I have worked for a number of years now in the area of public corruption. Over that course of time, perhaps out of instincts of self-justification, or, so it seems, sharpened moral insights, I have come to develop an abiding belief that bribery is deeply immoral.

We all know that bribery is unlawful and I believe that the legal concepts in this area are in fact grounded in widely accepted moral intuitions. Bribery as defined by the state of Illinois and construed by the United States Court of Appeals for the Seventh Circuit in the case of *United States v. Isaacs,* in which the former Governor of Illinois, Otto Kerner, was convicted for bribery, may be said to take place in these instances: Bribery occurs when property or personal advantage is offered, without the authority of law, to a public official with the intent that the public official act favorably to the offeror at any time or fashion in execution of the public official's duties.

Under this definition of bribery, the crime consists solely of an unlawful offer, made or accepted with a prohibited state of mind. No particular act need be specified; and the result is immaterial.

Found in *Journal of Business Ethics,* Vol. 4, No. 4 (1985), pp. 249–251. Copyright © 1985 by D. Reidel Publishing Company. Reprinted by permission of Kluwer Academic Publishers.
*Deputy Chief at the Criminal Receiving and Appellate Division of the U.S. Attorney's office and author of *One L* and *Presumed Innocent.*

This is merely a matter of definition. Oddly the moral underpinnings of bribery are clearer in the context of another statute—the criminal law against mail fraud. Federal law has no bribery statute of general application; it is unlawful of course to bribe federal officials, to engage in a pattern of bribery, or to engage in bribery in certain other specified contexts, e.g., to influence the outcome of a sporting contest. But unlike the states, the Congress, for jurisdictional reasons, has never passed a general bribery statute, criminalizing *all* instances of bribery. Thus, over time the federal mail fraud statute has come to be utilized as the vehicle for some bribery prosecutions. The theory, adopted by the courts, goes to illustrate what lawyers have thought is wrong with bribery.

Mail fraud/bribery is predicated on the theory that someone—the bribee's governmental or private employer—is deprived, by a bribe, of the recipient's undivided loyalties. The bribee comes to serve two masters and as such is an'unfaithful servant.' This breach of fiduciary duty, when combined with active efforts at concealment becomes actionable under the mail fraud law, assuming certain other jurisdictional requisites are met. Concealment, as noted, is another essential element of the crime. An employee who makes no secret of his dual service cannot be called to task; presumably his employer is thought to have authorized and accepted the divided loyalties. For this reason, the examples of maitre d's accepting payments from customers cannot be regarded as fully analogous to instances of bribery which depend on persons operating under false pretenses, a claimed loyalty that has in truth been undermined.

Some of the stricter outlines of what constitutes bribery, in the legal view, can be demonstrated by example. Among the bribery prosecutions with which I have spent the most time is a series of mail fraud/bribery cases arising out of corruption at the Cook County Board of Appeals. The Board of Appeals is a local administrative agency, vested with the authority to review and revise local real estate property tax assessments. After a lengthy grand jury investigation, it became clear that the Board of Appeals was a virtual cesspool, where it was commonplace for lawyers practicing before the Board to make regular cash payments to some decisionmakers. The persons accused of bribery at the Board generally relied on two defenses. Lawyers and tax consultants who made the payments often contended that the payments were, in a fashion, a necessity; the Board was so busy, so overcome by paperwork, and so many other people were paying, that the only way to be sure cases would be examined was to have an 'in' with an official whom payments had made friendly. The first argument also suggests the second: that the payments, whatever their nature, had accomplished nothing untoward, and that any tax reduction petition granted by the bribed official actually deserved the reduction it received.

Neither contention is legally sufficient to remove the payments from the category of bribery. Under the definition above, any effort to cause favorable action constitutes bribery, regardless of the supposedly provocative circumstances. And in practice juries had great difficulty accepting the idea that the lawyers involved had been 'coerced' into making the boxcar incomes—sometimes $300,000 to $400,000 a year—that many of the bribers earned. Nor is the merits of the cases involved a defense, under the above definitions. Again, in practical terms, juries seemed reluctant to believe that lawyers would be passing the Board's deputy commissioners cash under the table if they were really convinced of their cases' merits. But whatever the accuracy of that observation, it is clear that the law prohibits a payment, even to achieve a deserved result.

The moral rationale for these rules of law seems clear to me. Fundamentally, I believe that any payment to a governmental official for corrupt purposes is immoral. The obligation of government to deal with like cases alike is a principal of procedural fairness which is well recognized. But this principal is more than a matter of procedure; it has a deep moral base. We recognize that the equality of humans, their fundamental dignity as beings, demands that each stand as an equal before the government they have joined to create, that each, as Ronald Dworkin has put, has a claim to government's equal concern and respect. Bribery asks that that principal be violated, that some persons be allowed to stand ahead of others, that like cases not be treated alike, and that some persons be preferred. This I find morally repugnant.

Moreover, for this reason, I cannot accept the idea that bribery, which is wrong here, is somehow more tolerable abroad. Asking foreign officials to act in violation of moral principles must, as an abstract matter, be no less improper than asking that of members of our own government; it even smacks of imperialist attitudes. Furthermore, even dealing with the question on this level assumes that there are societies which unequivocally declare that governmental officials may properly deal with the citizenry in a random and unequal fashion. I doubt, in fact, whether any such sophisticated society exists; more than likely, bribery offends the norms and mores of the foreign country as well.

Not only does bribery violate fundamental notions of equality, but it also endangers the vitality of the institution affected. Most bribery centers on persons in discretionary or decision-making positions. Much as we want to believe that bribery invites gross deviations in duty, a prosecutor's experience is that in many cases there are no objectively correct decisions for the bribed official to make. We discovered that this was the case in the Board of Appeals prosecutions where a variety of competing theories of real estate valuation guaranteed that there was almost always some justification, albeit often thin, for what had been done. But it misses the point to look solely at the ultimate actions of the bribed official. Once the promise of payment is accepted, the public official is no longer the impartial decision-maker he is supposed to be. Whatever claims he might make, it is difficult to conceive of a public official who could convince anyone that he entirely disregarded a secret 'gift' from a person affected by his judgments.

Indeed, part of the evil of bribery inheres in the often indetectable nature of some of its results. Once revealed, the presence of bribery thus robs persons affected of a belief in the integrity of *all* prior decisions. In the absolute case, bribery goes to dissolve the social dependencies that require discretionary decision-making at certain junctions in our social scheme. Bribery, then, is a crime against trust; and to the extent that trust, a belief in the good faith of discretionary decision-makers, is essential to certain bureaucratic and governmental structures, bribery is deeply corrosive.

Because of its costs, the law usually deems bribery to be without acceptable justification. Again, I think this is in line with moral intuitions. Interestingly, the law does not regard extortion and bribery as mutually exclusive; extortion requires an apprehension of harm, bribery desire to influence. Often, in fact, the two are coincident. Morally—and legally, perhaps—it would seem that bribery can be justified only if the bribe-giver is truly without alternatives, including the alternative of refusing payment and going to the authorities. Moreover, the briber should be able to show not merely that it was convenient or profitable to pay the bribe, but that the situation presented a choice of evils in which the bribe somehow avoided a greater peril. The popular example in our discussions has been bribing a Nazi camp guard in order to spare concentration camp internees.

Ethics and the Foreign Corrupt Practices Act

Mark Pastin* and Michael Hooker[†]

Not long ago it was feared that as a fallout of Watergate, government officials would be hamstrung by artificially inflated moral standards. Recent events, however, suggest that the scapegoat of post-Watergate morality may have become American business rather than government officials.

One aspect of the recent attention paid to corporate morality is the controversy surrounding payments made by American corporations to foreign officials for the purpose of securing business abroad. Like any law or system of laws, the Foreign Corrupt Practices Act (FCPA), designed to control or eliminate such payments, should be grounded in morality, and should therefore be judged from an ethical perspective. Unfortunately, neither the law nor the question of its repeal has been adequately addressed from that perspective.

Excerpted from "Ethics and the Foreign Corrupt Practices Act" by Mark Pastin and Michael Hooker, in *Business Horizons* (December 1980). *Business Horizons:* Copyright © 1980, by the Foundation for the School of Business at Indiana University. Reprinted by permission.
*Director, Lincoln Center for Ethics, Arizona State University.
[†]President, University of Maryland, Baltimore.

History of the FCPA

On December 20, 1977 President Carter signed into law S.305, the Foreign Corrupt Practices Act (FCPA), which makes it a crime for American corporations to offer or provide payments to officials of foreign governments for the purpose of obtaining or retaining business. The FCPA also establishes record keeping requirements for publicly held corporations to make it difficult to conceal political payments proscribed by the Act. Violators of the FCPA, both corporations and managers, face severe penalties. A company may be fined up to $1 million, while its officers who directly participated in violations of the Act or had reason to know of such violations, face up to five years in prison and/or $10,000 in fines. The Act also prohibits corporations from indemnifying fines imposed on their directors, officers, employees, or agents. The Act does not prohibit "grease" payments to foreign government employees whose duties are primarily ministerial or clerical, since such payments are sometimes required to persuade the recipients to perform their normal duties.

At the time of this writing, the precise consequences of the FCPA for American business are unclear, mainly because of confusion surrounding the government's enforcement intentions. Vigorous objections have been raised against the Act by corporate attorneys and recently by a few government officials. Among the latter is Frank A. Weil, former Assistant Secretary of Commerce, who has stated, "The questionable payments problem may turn out to be one of the most serious impediments to doing business in the rest of the world."[1]

The potentially severe economic impact of the FCPA was highlighted by the fall 1978 report of the Export Disincentives Task Force, which was created by the White House to recommend ways of improving our balance of trade. The Task Force identified the FCPA as contributing significantly to economic and political losses in the United States. Economic losses come from constricting the ability of American corporations to do business abroad, and political losses come from the creation of a holier-than-thou image.

The Task Force made three recommendations in regard to the FCPA:

- The Justice Department should issue guidelines on its enforcement policies and establish procedures by which corporations could get advance government reaction to anticipated payments to foreign officials.
- The FCPA should be amended to remove enforcement from the SEC, which now shares enforcement responsibility with the Department of Justice.
- The administration should periodically report to Congress and the public on export losses caused by the FCPA.

In response to the Task Force's report, the Justice Department, over SEC objections, drew up guidelines to enable corporations to check any proposed action possibly in violation of the FCPA. In response to such an inquiry, the Justice Department would inform the corporation of its enforcement intentions. The purpose of such an arrangement is in part to circumvent the intent of the law. As of this writing, the SEC appears to have been successful in blocking publication of the guidelines, although Justice recently reaffirmed its intention to publish guidelines. Being more responsive to political winds, Justice may be less inclined than the SEC to rigidly enforce the Act.

Particular concern has been expressed about the way in which bookkeeping requirements of the Act will be enforced by the SEC. The Act requires that company records will "accurately and fairly reflect the transactions and dispositions of the assets of the issuer." What is at question is the interpretation the SEC will give to the requirement and the degree of accuracy and detail it will demand. The SEC's post-Watergate behavior suggests that it will be rigid in requiring the disclosure of all information that bears on financial relationships between the company and any foreign or domestic public official. This level of accountability in record keeping, to which auditors and corporate attorneys have strongly objected, goes far beyond previous SEC requirements that records display only facts material to the financial position of the company.

Since the potential consequences of the FCPA for American businesses and business managers are very serious, it is important that the Act have a rationale capable of bearing close scrutiny. In looking at the foundation of the FCPA, it should be noted that its passage followed in the wake of intense newspaper coverage of the financial dealings of corporations. Such media attention was engendered by the dramatic disclosure of corporate slush funds during the Watergate hearings and by a voluntary disclosure program established shortly thereafter by the SEC. As a result of the SEC program, more than 400 corporations, including 117 of the Fortune 500, admitted to making more than $300 million in foreign political payments in less than ten years.

Throughout the period of media coverage leading up to passage of the FCPA, and especially during the hearings on the Act, there was in all public discussions of the issue a tone of righteous moral indignation at the idea of American companies making foreign political payments. Such payments were ubiquitously termed "bribes," although many of these could more accurately be called extortions, while others were more akin to brokers' fees or sales commissions.

American business can be faulted for its reluctance during this period to bring to public attention the fact that in a very large number of countries, payments to foreign officials are virtually required for doing business. Part of that reluctance, no doubt, comes from the awkwardly difficult position of attempting to excuse bribery or something closely resembling it. There is a popular abhorrence in this country of bribery directed at domestic government officials, and that abhorrence transfers itself to payments directed toward foreign officials as well.

Since its passage, the FCPA has been subjected to considerable critical analysis, and many practical arguments have been advanced in favor of its repeal.[2] However, there is always lurking in back of such analyses the uneasy feeling that no matter how strongly considerations of practicality and economics may count against this law, the fact remains that the law protects morality in forbidding bribery. For example, Gerald McLaughlin, professor of law at Fordham, has shown persuasively that where the legal system of a foreign country affords inadequate protection against the arbitrary exercise of power to the disadvantage of American corporations, payments to foreign officials may be required to provide a compensating mechanism against the use of such arbitrary power. McLaughlin observes, however, that "this does not mean that taking advantage of the compensating mechanism would necessarily make the payment moral."[3]

The FCPA, and questions regarding its enforcement or repeal, will not be addressed adequately until an effort has been made to come to terms with the Act's foundation in morality. While it may be very difficult, or even impossible, to legislate morality (that is, to change the moral character and sentiments of people by passing laws that regulate their behavior), the existing laws undoubtedly still reflect the moral beliefs we hold. Passage of the FCPA in Congress was eased by the simple connection most Congressmen made between bribery, seen as morally repugnant, and the Act, which is designed to prevent bribery.

Given the importance of the FCPA to American business and labor, it is imperative that attention be given to the question of whether there is adequate moral justification for the law.

Ethical Analysis of the FCPA

The question we will address is not whether each payment prohibited by the FCPA is moral or immoral, but rather whether the FCPA, given all its consequences and ramifications, is itself moral. It is well known that morally sound laws and institutions may tolerate some immoral acts. The First Amendment's guarantee of freedom of speech allows individuals to utter racial slurs. And immoral laws and institutions may have some beneficial consequences, for example, segregationist legislation bringing deep-seated racism into the national limelight. But our concern is with the overall morality of the FCPA.

The ethical tradition has two distinct ways of assessing social institutions, including laws: *End-Point Assessment* and *Rule Assessment*. Since there is no consensus as to which approach is correct, we will apply both types of assessment of the FCPA.

The End-Point approach assesses a law in terms of its contribution to general social well-being. The ethical theory underlying End-Point Assessment is utilitarianism. According to utilitarianism, a law is morally sound if and only if the law promotes the well-being of those affected by the law to the greatest extent practically achievable. To satisfy the utilitarian principle, a law must promote the well-being of those affected by it at least as well as any alternative law that we might propose, and better than no law at all. A conclusive End-Point Assessment of a law requires specification of what constitutes the welfare of those affected by the law, which the liberal tradition generally sidesteps by identifying an individual's welfare with what he takes to be in his interests.

Considerations raised earlier in the paper suggest that the FCPA does not pass the End-Point test. The argument is not the too facile one that we could propose a better law. (Amendments to the FCPA are now being considered.[4]) The argument is that it may be better to have *no* such law than to have the FCPA. The main domestic consequences of the FCPA seem to include an adverse effect on the balance of payments, a loss of business and jobs, and another opportunity for the SEC and the Justice Department to compete. These negative effects must be weighed against possible gains in the conduct of American business within the United States. From the perspective of foreign countries in which American firms do business, the main consequence of the FCPA seems to be that certain officials now accept bribes and influence from non-American businesses. It is hard to see that who pays the bribes makes much difference to these nations.

Rule Assessment of the morality of laws is often favored by those who find that End-Point Assessment is too lax in supporting their moral codes. According to the Rule Assessment approach: A law is morally sound if and only if the law accords with a code embodying correct ethical rules. This approach has no content until the rules are stated, and different rules will lead to different ethical assessments. Fortunately, what we have to say about Rule Assessment of the FCPA does not depend on the details of a particular ethical code.

Those who regard the FCPA as a worthwhile expression of morality, despite the adverse effects on American business and labor, clearly subscribe to a rule stating that it is unethical to bribe. Even if it is conceded that the payments proscribed by the FCPA warrant classifications as bribes, citing a rule prohibiting bribery does not suffice to justify the FCPA.

Most of the rules in an ethical code are not *categorical* rules; they are *prima facie* rules. A categorical rule does not allow exceptions, whereas a prima facie rule does. The ethical rule that a person ought to keep promises is an example of a prima facie rule. If I promise to loan you a book on nuclear energy and later find out that you are a terrorist building a private atomic bomb, I am ethically obligated not to keep my promise. The rule that one ought to keep promises is "overridden" by the rule that one ought to prevent harm to others.

A rule prohibiting bribery is a prima facie rule. There are cases in which morality requires that a bribe be paid. If the only way to get essential medical care for a dying child is to bribe a doctor, morality requires one to bribe the doctor. So adopting an ethical code which includes a rule prohibiting the payment of bribes does not guarantee that a Rule Assessment of the FCPA will be favorable to it.

The fact that the FCPA imposes a cost on American business and labor weighs against the prima facie obligation not to bribe. If we suppose that American corporations have obligations, tantamount to promises, to promote the job security of their employees and the investments of shareholders, these obligations will also weigh against the obligation not to bribe. Again, if government legislative and enforcement bodies have an obligation to secure the welfare of American business and workers, the FCPA may force them to violate their public obligations.

The FCPA's moral status appears even more dubious if we note that many of the payments prohibited by the Act are neither bribes nor share features that make bribes morally reprehensible. Bribes are generally held to be malefic if they persuade one to act against his good judgement, and consequently purchase an inferior product. But the payments at issue in the FCPA are usually extorted *from the seller*. Further it is arguable that not paying the bribe is more likely to lead to purchase of an inferior product than paying the bribe. Finally, bribes paid to foreign officials may not involve deception when they accord with recognized local practices.

In conclusion, neither End-Point nor Rule Assessment uncovers a sound moral basis for the FCPA. It is shocking to find that a law prohibiting bribery has no clear moral basis, and may even be an immoral law. However, this is precisely what examination of the FCPA from a moral perspective reveals. This is symptomatic of the fact that moral conceptions which were appropriate to a simpler world are not adequate to the complex world in which contemporary business functions. Failure to appreciate this point often leads to righteous condemnation of business, when it should lead to careful reflection on one's own moral preconceptions.

Notes

1. *National Journal,* June 3, 1978: 880.
2. David C. Gustman, "The Foreign Corrupt Practices Act of 1977," *The Journal of International Law and Economics,* Vol. 13, 1979; 367–401, and Walter S. Surrey, "The Foreign Corrupt Practices Act: Let the Punishment Fit the Crime," *Harvard International Law Journal,* Spring 1979: 203–303.
3. Gerald T. McLaughlin, "The Criminalization of Questionable Foreign Payments by Corporations," *Fordham Law Review,* Vol. 46: 1095.
4. "Foreign Bribery Law Amendments Drafted," *American Bar Association Journal,* February 1980: 135.

Bribery and Ethics: A Reply to Pastin and Hooker

Robert E. Frederick*

In their article on the Foreign Corrupt Practices Act, Mark Pastin and Michael Hooker used both "end-point assessment" and "rule assessment" to evaluate the FCPA from a moral point of view.[1] They argue that neither method of assessment supports the FCPA and hence that it "has no clear moral basis, and may even be an immoral law."[2] It seems to me, however, that Pastin and Hooker's arguments are not compelling and that there is a sense in which the FCPA does have a sound moral basis. Thus in the remainder of this paper I will give reasons why I think Pastin and Hooker are mistaken. I will begin with their end-point assessment of the FCPA and then turn to the rule assessment. In the final section I will have some brief comments about extortion and the FCPA.

I

End-point assessment is based on the moral theory of utilitarianism. If we use end-point assessment to evaluate a law, then according to Pastin and Hooker it is a morally sound law "if and only if the law promotes the well-being of those affected by the law to the greatest extent practically achievable."[3] They argue that the FCPA has not promoted the well-being of those affected by the law to the greatest extent practically achievable, since it has led to a loss of business and jobs, it has unfavorably affected the balance of payments, and it is a source of discord between government agencies.[4] Hence, they suggest that the FCPA does not pass the end-point test of moral soundness.

It is difficult to judge the strength of this argument against the FCPA, since it is very difficult to find and evaluate objective empirical evidence that either confirms or disconfirms the economic harm allegedly caused by the FCPA. There is anecdotal evidence that the FCPA has caused some firms a loss of business.[5] In a 1983 study of the data, however, John L. Graham finds that "the FCPA has not had a negative effect on U.S. trade," and in a 1987 analysis of U.S. trade in the Mideast, Kate Gillespie concludes that "The FCPA potential to hurt U.S. exports remains unproved."[6] These studies do not show that the FCPA has promoted the well-being of those affected by it to the greatest extent practically achievable, so they do not show that the FCPA passes the end-point assessment test of moral soundness. Perhaps the best we can say about the studies is that they seem to show, not that we are economically any better off for having the FCPA on the books, but rather that we are not any worse off.

Let us suppose, however, that there is good evidence that the FCPA has caused a loss of U.S. exports and a loss of jobs in U.S. export-related industries. Would this show that the FCPA does not pass the end-point assessment? It seems to me it would not. One of the central tenets of utilitarianism is that the well-being of any one person or group of persons is not to count more or be of more moral weight than the well-being of some other person or group of persons. Thus the well-being of people in the United States does not count more than the well-being of people in France or Uganda or China. Now, if the FCPA causes a U.S. firm to lose an export contract, then some foreign competitor must have gotten that contract. Thus it could be that a loss of exports and jobs in the United States would be offset by an increase in exports and jobs in some foreign country. Assuming the people receiving the goods are as well off with either vendor, and since the well-being of people in the United States does not count more than the well-being of people in the country that got the contract, the net effect of the FCPA on economic well-being once we consider *everyone* affected by it, might be entirely neutral.

If this argument is correct, it shows that from a utilitarian point of view the FCPA is morally neutral. It neither harms nor enhances total economic well-being. Thus, as long as we consider only economic well-being, end-point assessment does not provide moral grounds for either favoring or opposing the law. Of course, it is possible that the FCPA affects well-being in non-economic ways. For example, one might argue that insofar as the FCPA discourages the corrupt practice of bribery, people both in the United States and abroad are better off. But it seems to me that considerations of well-being, although important, do not address the central moral issues raised by the FCPA. For that we have to turn to rule assessment.

II

Pastin and Hooker claim that a law passes the rule assessment test of moral soundness "if and only if the law accords with a code embodying correct moral rules."[7] They then try to show that the FCPA does not pass the rule assessment test regardless of the actual content of the moral code. This may seem a little extreme, since it may be that the correct moral code contains a rule such as "under no circumstances is bribery morally permissible." But Pastin and Hooker circumvent this problem by claiming that the rule against bribery is always a prima facie rule, i.e., it can be overridden by other moral considerations in appropriate circumstances. They then seem to claim that in the arena of international competition other moral considerations frequently override the rule. And since the FCPA makes no allowance for such instances—it prohibits bribes even in cases where it is morally permissible to offer a bribe—it does not accord with the moral code and does not pass the end-point assessment.

But is the rule against bribery a prima facie rule? And even if it is, are there moral considerations that frequently override it? I will try to show that for certain types of bribery the moral rule against bribery is not a prima facie rule and that in other cases the considerations Pastin and Hooker mention are not overriding. I will begin with a brief description of what I take to be a central case of bribery, and then, using that case as a focal point for discussion, I will say something about why I think bribery is morally wrong.

Suppose you find yourself in the following situation: You are taking a difficult course required for your major. You work hard, go to class, do all the homework, and are well satisfied with the B you received for a final grade. You happen to find out, however, that an acquaintance of yours made an A in the course even though he missed most of the classes, didn't do the homework, and didn't even show up for the final exam. You know this person is no genius, so you wonder how he did it. You are so curious, in fact, that you decide to ask him. "Well," he replies, "let's just say I know how to spread some money around where it will do the most good."

You are outraged, since the clear implication is that your acquaintance bribed the professor to give him an A. But exactly why are you outraged? Exactly what is wrong with bribery?

The best way to begin to answer that question is to get as clear as we can about the main characteristics of a central case of bribery, such as the one just described. The first thing to note is that the above situation is a kind of social practice which is governed in all essential respects by an agreement or understanding between the participants. This understanding, parts of which may be explicit and parts implicit, is voluntary, at least in the sense that no one is threatened with unjustifiable harm if they do not take the class, and the understanding does not require that any of the participants engage in morally impermissible behavior. In addition, the agreement defines the role, position, or function of each participant in the practice and delineates the kinds of behaviors that are acceptable or unacceptable for each role or position in certain circumstances. For example, even though it may never be explicitly stated, it is a part of the understanding, and undoubtedly a part of your expectations for the course, that all students will be graded solely on the amount and quality of work that they do.

The understanding can be broken in a number of ways, some of which are innocuous and do not involve immoral behavior. But the case of bribery in question is not innocuous. It is an attempt by one student to gain an unfair advantage over the other students by offering the professor something of value in return for the professor violating the understanding by giving the student special treatment. It is, in effect, an attempt by one of the participants to subvert the original understanding by entering into a new one with terms that are incompatible with the terms of the original.

If we put all these things together we can give a complete, although somewhat complex, characterization of central cases of bribery:

> In central cases bribery is a violation of an understanding or agreement which defines a social practice. It is an attempt by one person(s) X to secure an unfair advantage over another person(s) Y by giving a third person(s) Z something of value in exchange for Z giving favorable treatment to X by violating some prima facie duty Z has in virtue of Z's position, role, or function in a morally permissible understanding in which X, Y, and Z are all voluntary participants.

Thus, if my analysis is correct, central cases of bribery always involve social practices in which there are voluntary and morally permissible agreements or understandings, always involve a three-term relationship, and are always attempts to gain an unfair advantage. Noncentral cases of bribery deviate from central cases in that they apparently either do not involve morally permissible agreements, or voluntary agreements, or there is no three-term relationship, or they are not attempts to gain an unfair advantage.

We are finally in a position to say something about what is wrong with central cases of bribery. To give someone an unfair advantage is to give them special treatment that others do not receive, treatment that cannot be justified under the terms of the original understanding, and treatment that the other parties of the understanding would not acquiesce to if they were to know about it. And to give someone such an advantage is, it seems reasonable to say, morally wrong. To paraphrase Aristotle, it is not to treat equals equally. Hence to *accept* a bribe is morally wrong. This does not explain why *offering* a bribe is morally wrong. But I suggest, as a general moral principle, that if one person attempts to get another person to do something morally wrong, then the attempt is also morally wrong. Hence, if I attempt to bribe you to do something that is morally wrong, my attempt to bribe you is morally wrong regardless of whether you accept the bribe or not.

If the rule against bribery is a prima facie rule, then, even for central cases of bribery, there must be some possible circumstances in which it can be overridden. But what circumstances might those be? Under what conditions is it morally permissible to give someone an unfair advantage over others? It seems to me there are no such conditions. It is never morally permissible to give someone an unfair advantage, nor is it morally permissible to induce someone to provide an unfair advantage. Hence, for central cases, the rule against bribery is not a prima facie rule. Thus, the FCPA does have a clear moral basis since it prohibits a type of bribery that is always morally wrong.

III

There are two ways that Pastin and Hooker might respond. We concede, they might say, that central cases of bribery are always wrong. Given your characterization of central cases it could hardly be otherwise. Yet in foreign competition such cases hardly ever occur. Noncentral cases are much more common, and in these cases the rule against bribery is prima facie. Their second response would probably be to point out, as they do in their article, that many of the payments prohibited by the FCPA are not bribes at all, but extortions. And, they might continue, since the FCPA as it is presently formulated prohibits noncentral cases of bribery, and since it prohibits most types of extortion, it lacks a completely sound moral basis. The reason is that in many instances it is morally permissible to pay bribes in noncentral cases, or to make extortion payments. Thus, the FCPA does not pass the rule assessment test after all, since the FCPA is not in *complete* accord with the correct moral code.

To some extent I am sympathetic with these responses. They do show, I believe, that there are considerations in favor of *revising* the law.[8] This is not too surprising, since there are many laws that could be improved. But it is important to see that, as long as the FCPA is on the books in its present form, the responses I have attributed to Pastin and Hooker give no justification whatever for violating the law by offering a bribe. Let me explain.

Suppose for a moment that we have not made the distinction between central and noncentral cases of bribery, and suppose Pastin and Hooker are correct about the rule against bribery always being a prima facie rule. If it is, then if one has other moral obligations that override the obligation not to bribe, it is morally permissible to offer a bribe. So, in order to determine whether it is permissible, we need to know something about what kinds of obligations might override the rule against bribery.

It is beyond the scope of this article to examine all the different obligations that might override the rule against bribery, but Pastin and Hooker do mention one that deserves discussion. It is the obligation businesspeople have to protect the financial interests of corporate investors. Pastin and Hooker seem to say that in order to protect these interests businesspeople must sometimes offer bribes. I believe, however, that this mistakes the obligations businesspeople actually have. Except in very unusual circumstances they are only obligated to protect the interests of investors *within* the limits established by law. They simply have no obligation to protect those interests by breaking the law. Thus, investors can have no *moral* complaint against a businessperson if they suffer a financial loss because the businessperson refused to break a law.

There are occasions on which it is morally permissible or obligatory to break the law. If the law is flagrantly unjust, or if following the law is likely to cause severe and irremediable harm, then our moral obligations may outweigh our legal ones. But it has not been established that the FCPA is flagrantly unjust or that following it is likely to cause severe and irremediable harm. Hence, there is no justification for concluding that businesspeople are morally required to violate the FCPA by offering bribes, even assuming the rule against bribery is always prima facie.[9]

IV

One aspect of the FCPA that I have only touched on is the prohibition of most types of extortion payments. Typically extortion is an attempt by one person(s) X to gain from another person(s) Y something of value to which X has no rightful claim by an actual or implied threat to harm unjustifiably Y's legitimate interests unless Y yields the thing of value to X. For example, if your professor makes it known to you that she will not grade your work fairly unless you give her $100, then she is attempting extortion.

Although there are clear differences between extortion and central cases of bribery, extortion and noncentral cases of bribery are often confused. For example, an illustration Pastin and Hooker use—"bribing" a doctor to get essential medical treatment for a child—seems to me a form of extortion instead of bribery.[10]

It is important to distinguish carefully between extortion and bribery, since the moral relationships in extortion are quite different from the moral relationships in bribery. For example, in extortion, but not in bribery, there is a threat to vital interests. And since, I believe, it is always morally wrong to threaten unjustifiably vital interests, demanding extortion is always morally wrong. But it is sometimes morally permissible to make an extortion payment provided that no other reasonable alternative is available to protect threatened vital interests. Paying the doctor to treat the child is a good example. Thus, there is a sense, absent in cases of bribery, in which someone making an extortion payment is a victim of morally improper behavior.

Pastin and Hooker appear to argue that since it is at least sometimes morally permissible to make extortion payments, and since the FCPA prohibits most types of extortion payments, the FCPA is defective from a moral point of view. But I suggest that we look at the FCPA in a different light. Businesspeople who are forced to make extortion payments to protect threatened interests are victims of a corrupt and immoral practice. We do have moral obligations to protect people from such victimization. How should we do it? It is unlikely that businesspeople acting individually would be able to prevent extortion. What is needed is concerted action, and one effective way to achieve concerted action is through regulation and law.[11] If the FCPA prohibition of extortion payments is strictly enforced, then U.S. firms will not do business in countries where extortion is common. And if we can encourage other countries strictly to enforce laws against extortion, or to pass such laws if they do not have them, then businesspeople in those countries will respond similarly. This will eventually bring pressure on the remaining countries where extortion is common, since it will close them off from products and services that are needed for their economies. And this, in turn, should make them much more likely to enforce laws against demanding extortion. Thus, instead of the FCPA being morally defective, if it is strictly enforced, and if other countries enforce similar laws, the FCPA can advance a worthwhile moral purpose by helping stop the victimization imposed by extortion.

It would be naive to think that extortion can be completely eliminated via the sort of concerted action I have proposed, but I believe it is morally unacceptable to take no action against it at all. Enforcing the FCPA and similar laws is one way to help the international business community avoid falling victim to extortionists' demands. Hence, in my view the FCPA should not be revised to permit extortion payments. If anything, the prohibition of such payments should be strengthened.

There is one misunderstanding I would like to forestall. It might be suggested that prohibiting extortion payments is *imposing* morality. As long as we are concerned with a rule assessment of the FCPA, this is a completely mistaken view. The correct moral code, on which rule assessment is based, is a moral code that applies to everyone at all times. It exempts no one. Thus if a practice is a violation of the code, as I have claimed demanding extortion always is, to refuse to pay extortion is not in any sense imposing morality. It is refusing to participate in and make possible behavior prohibited by the moral code, behavior that is immoral for anyone in any country.

In conclusion I would like to emphasize that my analysis and discussion of bribery and extortion is by no means complete. I have not tried to address many issues that could be raised, and with many others I have undoubtedly raised more questions than I have answered. But I do think I have shown that Pastin and Hooker are incorrect in claiming that the FCPA does not pass either end-point or rule assessment tests of moral soundness. The FCPA may not be a perfect law, but it is not entirely without moral justification.[12]

Notes

1. Mark Pastin and Michael Hooker, "Ethics and the Foreign Corrupt Practices Act," in *Business Ethics: Readings and Cases in Corporate Morality,* ed. W. Michael Hoffman and Jennifer Mills Moore, 2d ed. (New York: McGraw-Hill Book Company, 1989), p. 551.
2. *Ibid.,* p. 555.
3. *Ibid.,* p. 553.
4. It is beyond my expertise to say whether, in this case, discord between agencies is a good thing or a bad one, so I will not comment on it.
5. Suk H. Kim, "On Repealing the Foreign Corrupt Practices Act: Survey and Assessment," *Columbia Journal of World Business,* Fall 1981, pp. 16–20. Also see Justin G. Longenecker, Joseph A. McKinney, and Carlos W. Moore, "The Ethical Issue of International Bribery: A Survey of Attitudes among U.S. Business Professionals," *Journal of Business Ethics,* vol. 7, no. 5, May 1988, pp. 341–346.
6. John L. Graham, "Foreign Corrupt Practices: A Manager's Guide," *Columbia Journal of World Business,* Fall 1983, p. 89. Kate Gillespie, "Middle East Response to the Foreign Corrupt Practices Act," *California Management Review,* vol. 29, no. 4, Summer 1987, p. 28.
7. Pastin and Hooker, p. 554.
8. I will argue later that the FCPA prohibition of extortion payments should not be revised.
9. The same sort of argument applies against making extortion payments. However, extortion is more complex, since in some cases severe harm may be caused by refusing to make an extortion payment. The FCPA makes provision for some of these cases. In the final section I will suggest one way such harm might be avoided.
10. There are a number of more difficult cases. For example, it is often said that in some countries bribery is a common practice. But are payments made in such countries bribes or extortion payments? Can bribery be a common practice, or after a certain point does it become institutionalized extortion?
11. Longenecker, McKinney, and Moore, p. 346.
12. My thanks to W. Michael Hoffman and Jennifer Mills Moore for their comments on an earlier draft of this paper.

Foreign Corrupt Practices Act: A Legal and Moral Analysis

Bill Shaw

1. Introduction

Bribery of foreign public officials is common throughout the world today. Since the passage of the Foreign Corrupt Practices Act in 1977,[1] American businesses operating abroad are well advised to behave ethically and avoid the practice of bribing foreign public officials.

Journal of Business Ethics 7 (1988), 789–795, © 1988 by Kluwer Academic Publishers.

Even though many American businessmen claim that this law is harming our country's interests abroad,[2] the United States is not the only country to have passed such a law. Sweden has also enacted criminal legislation dealing specifically with the bribery of foreign officials.[3]

In light of this act, it is extremely important for managers to develop a system that will communicate to their employees the fact that a company will not tolerate bribery of foreign officials. Penalties for single violation include the possibility of a $1,000,000 fine for business firms and a $10,000 fine coupled with five years imprisonment for individuals (officers, directors, employees of the firm).[4] In addition, individuals who are fined cannot be reimbursed by the business that they work for.[5]

SEC v. Ashland Oil

A recent example will show how serious a violation of the Foreign Corrupt Practices Act of 1977 can be and the type of situation that is likely to produce a violation of this act. One such case is *SEC v. Ashland Oil, Inc.,* which was filed in the United States District Court for the District of Columbia in 1986.[6]

According to the SEC complaint, Ashland Oil and its then CEO Orin Atkins agreed to pay an entity controlled by an Omani government official approximately $29 million for a majority interest in Midlands Chrome, Inc., a price which was far more than it was worth, allegedly for the purpose of obtaining crude oil at a highly favorable price.[7] When Atkins proposed the acquisition of Midlands Chrome to the Ashland board of directors, he allegedly told the board that while the acquisition was a high risk project, it "had the potential for being more than offset by a potential crude oil contract."[8]

Even though the mining claims owned by Midlands Chrome did not prove profitable, Ashland was awarded a crude oil contract by the Omani government for 20,000 barrels of oil a day for one year at a $3 per barrel discount from the regular selling price.[9] Ashland claimed that the discount was in consideration of technical services rendered by it to Oman.[10] Solely through this contract Ashland could have profited by more than $40 million over the life of the contract simply by taking the oil it received at a discount and immediately selling it on the spot market.[11] The case was settled with Ashland Oil, Inc. and Atkins agreeing to an injunction against future violations.[12]

The SEC action against Ashland is only the third such suit to be brought under the Foreign Corrupt Practices Act of 1977 and the first against a major corporation.[13] The Ashland case was also the first to involve an ostensibly legitimate business transaction.[14] It gives evidence that the SEC is willing to look at the substance of the transaction even if the transaction is done in a proper form.

While the SEC has not brought a large number of actions under the Foreign Corrupt Practices Act of 1977, this does not mean that it is totally apathetic. As the Ashland case vividly shows, managers cannot afford to ignore this act and do so only at great peril.

The next section of this paper will examine the conduct that the Foreign Corrupt Practices Act prohibits. In addition, the reach and types of prohibited acts will be examined in light of the ethical constructs of utility, justice and rights. It is hoped that by performing this analysis, we can determine whether or not the Foreign Corrupt Practices Act promotes ethical business conduct. If it does in fact promote ethical conduct, or if in some ways it falls short of that objective, we will be better able to judge whether it needs fine tuning, a major over-haul, or no modification at all.

2. Foreign Corrupt Practices Act: Prohibited Conduct in Light of Ethical Considerations

The Foreign Corrupt Practices Act attempts to eliminate bribery of foreign officials by U.S. corporate officials and their agents through both an anti-bribery and an accounting provision. The antibribery provision prohibits certain issuers, domestic concerns, or their agents from being involved directly or indirectly in making specified payments to foreign officials, officials of foreign political parties, or candidates for foreign political office for the purpose of obtaining or retaining business.[15] The accounting provision requires each reporting entity to keep books and records that accurately reflect the entity's transactions and to devise and maintain an adequate system of internal controls to assure that the entity's assets are used for proper corporate purposes.[16]

In order to determine whether the Foreign Corrupt Practices Act goes as far as ethical standards would demand, we will first examine the types or categories of bribes. Then we must determine whether or not the Foreign Corrupt Practices Act prohibits the classes of bribes we conclude are unethical.

W. Michael Reisman has broken bribes into three different classes based upon the purpose and effect of the transaction.[17] Reisman's categories are as follows: transaction bribes, variance bribes, and outright purchases.[18] A transaction bribe, more commonly identified as a grease payment, is a payment that is routinely and impersonally made to a public official to secure or accelerate the performance of his official function.[19] A variance bribe occurs where the briber pays an official to secure the suspension or nonapplication of a legal norm in an instance where its application would be appropriate.[20] The third of Reisman's groups, outright purchase, is where payment is made in order to secure the favor of a foreign employee who remains in place in an organization to which he appears to pay full loyalty while actually favoring the briber's conflicting interest.[21]

A determination of whether each of these types of payments are ethical or not can be made by examining them under a utilitarian, moral rights, and social justice framework. The answer to this inquiry will assist us in deciding whether the Foreign Corrupt Practices Act and its costs of administration are a sufficient means of inducing, or compelling, ethical behavior from U.S. business firms.

A. Utility

The utilitarian framework holds that ethical conduct is that which produces the greatest net benefits for society as a whole, i.e., the greatest good for the greatest number.[22] This principle assumes that all benefits and costs of an action can be measured on a common scale and then added to or subtracted from one another.[23]

In examining whether transaction bribes, variance bribes, and outright purchases are ethical, the utilitarian framework is not a great deal of help. This is because the utilitarian system of analysis is case specific with each instance being judged on its own unique facts.[24] Therefore, a bribe will be ethical or not in a particular situation based on the societal benefits and costs of making the bribe. In looking at the benefits of the bribe, one would have to include the increase in business that would not have resulted but for the bribe of a foreign official. Some of the costs of bribery include the actual monetary payment, and damage to the reputation of the company and to American business in the eyes of foreign nationals. Therefore, because utilitarianism is situation specific and the fact that quantification of the benefits and costs may be difficult if not impossible, one cannot say that foreign bribery is unethical in all instances.

B. Moral Rights

A right is an individual's entitlement to something.[25] It is a morally justifiable claim to some good or to protection from harm.[26] A person has a right when that person is entitled to act in a certain way or is entitled to have others act in a certain way toward him or her.[27]

It will be helpful to look at each type of bribe under the rights analysis to determine whether there are any grounds upon which they may be supported. Basically, conduct that does not interfere with another's rights, and does not coerce another party is judged to be moral under a rights analysis.[28]

The first type of bribe, the transaction bribe, speeds action by foreign officials that they would otherwise take. This type of bribe clearly does not coerce an official to take action he would not otherwise take but it may interfere with other rights. By getting a foreign official to expedite your request, you are causing other people's interests to be put on the back burner. Every party has the right to equal treatment. By bribing a foreign official to get speedier service, you are violating the rights of other people to equal treatment.

On the other hand, such a system can be justified where such payments are above-board and each party has the ability to get speedier treatment. As long as this type of system is the regular method of doing business and all parties know about it, all competitors are on an equal footing. The crux of the matter here is whether the payments are in fact bribes and therefore unethical because all parties do not have equal rights, or whether the payments are governmentally "approved" and made in the normal course of business.

The variance bribe on the other hand is unethical because it violates competitors' rights to equal treatment. Beyond that it is a contract for the performance of an illegal act. In a like manner, the outright purchase or the procurement of a company man is unethical because it binds the employee to perform illegal and disloyal acts, i.e., acting against the interests of his employer to further the ends of some other party. Such an arrangement is often maintained by coercion or duress and thus violates the rights of the employee as well. This coercion or duress is the result of the ability of the briber to threaten to reveal the relationship between the briber and the employee if the employee does not continue to cooperate.

C. Social Justice

The last ethical framework for examining these three types of bribes is justice or fairness. It is the nature of these concepts to demand that comparative, balanced, and even-handed treatment be given to the members of a group when benefits and burdens are distributed, when rules and laws are administered, when members of a group cooperate or compete with each other, and when people are punished for the wrongs they have done or compensated for the wrongs they have suffered.[29]

The transaction bribe under the fairness criteria will be unethical if companies that are similar in all respects relevant to the kind of treatment in question are not given similar benefits, even if they are dissimilar in other irrelevant respects.[30] The question then becomes whether companies that do not bribe receive the same treatment as those that do bribe. With a transaction bribe all companies get the same service but the company that pays a bribe gets it faster. One could conclude that slower service is not the same service at all and thus the companies are not treated equally because one company paid a bribe. The two companies are not treated equally, thus the bribe is unethical. The decision whether this treatment is ethical or not turns on the conclusion whether the services each receives is the same or different, and if different, on whether unequal treatment that has been induced by the bribe can be justified.

The variance bribe is unethical based on fairness principles because some companies can avoid the imposition of a law by the payment of a bribe. Such payment should not have any influence on whether or not a law is enforced in a particular instance. Thus one company is receiving favored treatment based on something that should not affect the enforcement of a law.

Outright purchases are unethical under a fairness analysis. The employee is not giving his benefits to the employer as he should be, but is instead giving his benefits to someone else because of the payments of bribes. The payment of bribes should not be made to affect an employee's loyalty; he should render all the benefits to the entity that is employing him, not to the one bribing him.

The above ethical analysis shows us that under a rights and fairness analysis, transaction bribes may or may not be ethical while variance and outright purchase bribes are unethical. Utilitarian analysis cannot be used effectively to decide which of these three types of bribes is unethical.

The Foreign Corrupt Practices Act outlaws variance and outright purchase bribes, but allows transaction or grease bribes.[31] By contrast, each of these types of bribes are expressly prohibited in domestic U.S. situations;[32] transaction bribes are outlawed in many countries.[33] This would seem to support the analysis that above transaction bribes are in fact unethical.

On the basis of this inquiry, one must conclude that the Foreign Corrupt Practices Act does not cover as much ground as ethical behavior would demand. Thus if a company behaves ethically, it will not only satisfy the minimum standard of the Foreign Corrupt Practices Act but also go beyond that which is legally required.

In the next section of this paper, the focus will be on two of the major problem areas of the Act. Businessmen claim that it is these ambiguities that are effectively hampering their operations overseas.

3. Problems with Foreign Corrupt Practices Act

The Senate Report on S.708 asserts that "as a result of unnecessary interpretive problems, U.S. business has lost legitimate export opportunities and has incurred unreasonable costs in attempts to comply with the Foreign Corrupt Practices Act provisions."[34] Senator Dixon claims that the Act in its "present form acts as an export disincentive."[35]

There are two ambiguities in particular that are considered by the business community to be major stumbling blocks. These two problems are questions about the "reason to know" language[36] of the Act and its accounting provisions.[37]

A. "Reason to Know"

Under the Foreign Corrupt Practices Act, the individuals that can be held liable for bribery are not only those who directly or indirectly bribe a foreign official but, also those who *know or have reason to know* that a bribe is being given.[38] The reason to know standard has been criticized because it is vague and ambiguous.[39]

While it is relatively certain that this language covers payments made to agents for the purpose of being passed along as bribes to foreign officials, it is uncertain what other areas are covered.[40] Adding to the question of the coverage of this statute is the fact that the Act itself gives no guidelines explaining the meaning of the reason to know standard and there have not been enough cases under the Foreign Corrupt Practices Act to flesh out the full extent of its meaning.

Without effective court pronouncements on what constitutes a reason to know, it is difficult to assess whether this standard mandates (1) a regular system of procedures designed to detect corruption, (2) due diligence type reviews of company records, (3) board of director liability for the behavior of employees solely because the board has managerial review power. The best we can do is examine what commentators and governmental bodies have said.

It has been asserted that "the effect of the reason to know language is to create a standard of negligence that imposes a duty on corporate management to inquire about possible improper or illegal payments."[41] It is thus hoped that the anti-bribery provision would produce accountability, and that to avoid criminal accountability, "self-enforcing, preventive mechanisms" would be introduced at the corporate level.[42]

Two recent SEC suits, both of which were settled by consent decrees, make the SEC opinion about the reach of the reason to know language clear. Based on the SEC's complaints in *SEC v. Katy Industries*[43] and *SEC v. Oil Refining Corp.*[44] it is obvious that the SEC believes that if a party has *any reason to suspect* that a payment will be used to influence public officials, then that party could be liable under the Foreign Corrupt Practices Act.[45]

If the Act needs to be amended to eliminate ambiguities because it is acting as an "export inhibitor," presumably due to the uncertainty of how to comply with its provisions,[46] such amendment should wait the day that a decline in exports can be persuasively, if not conclusively, attributed to the Act rather than to interest rates, strength of the dollar, price, quality and the like. A number of times in the recent past bills have been proposed in Congress to eliminate this language, but as of this writing all have failed because the equation, "F.C.P.A. causes a decline in exports," is too simplistic to carry the day.

Even though the "reason to know" language has drawn fire and may at some stage be due for revision, it is not the only controversial provision of the Foreign Corrupt Practices Act. This act also contains accounting provisions that have caused a certain amount of trouble for American businesses.

B. Accounting Provisions

The Foreign Corrupt Practices Act accounting provisions, set forth in 15 U.S.C. sec. 78m, require that every issuer, "make and keep books, records, and accounts, which in reasonable detail, accurately and fairly reflect the transactions and dispositions of the assets of the issuer." In addition, this section requires issuers to "devise and maintain a system of internal accounting controls sufficient to provide reasonable assurances that transactions are executed in accordance with management's authorization;" recorded in a way that will "permit the preparation of financial statements in conformity with generally accepted accounting principles;" and permit the disbursement of assets "only in accordance with management's general or specific authorization."[47] Finally, the recorded assets should be "compared with existing assets at reasonable intervals" with "appropriate action" being taken when differences are found.[48]

It is important to note that the accounting restrictions do not apply just to illegal foreign payments but to the everyday operations of the business as well. By requiring more in-depth accounting disclosure, it will be much more difficult, if not impossible, for businesses to hide foreign bribes in their accounting records and financial statements.

While it is a good idea for Congress to make it more difficult to cover up illegal bribes through stricter accounting rules, it is not clear that the Foreign Corrupt Practices Act has succeeded in this regard. The reason for this is that many businessmen and accountants feel that the accounting requirements are not giving them sufficient guidance and are leading them into a no-win situation.[49]

These companies fear that failing to live up to uncertain standards will expose companies to criminal penalties,[50] therefore businesses are keeping more and better records than is necessary under the Act or good business practice.[51] The end result is that the cost of complying with the act has greatly increased the costs of doing business.[52] It is therefore not surprising that in a recent Harris Poll, 68% of businessmen favored a reduction in the amount of required record keeping under the Foreign Corrupt Practices Act.[53]

Further, and most significantly, no concrete standard has been set forth to determine what information must be reported in accounting records. Two differing possibilities exist, *reasonableness* and *materiality*. The SEC claims that only reasonable detail of transactions must be recorded.[54] The American Bar Association, on the other hand, claims that only material information need be disclosed.[55]

In order to help businesses get a firm handle on what is required of them, one of these two standards, or some other, needs to be chosen. While reasonableness is a commonly used legal standard, materiality is the preferable standard because it is one that accountants and businessmen are most familiar with and one that will effectively advance the purpose of the Act.

In accounting, materiality has been defined as "the magnitude of an omission or misstatement of accounting information that, *in the light of surrounding circumstances,* makes it probable that the judgement of a reasonable person relying on the information would have been changed or influenced by the omission or misstatement."[56] This means that if the omission or inclusion of an amount would not change or influence the decision of a rational decision maker, it is immaterial.[57]

Under this standard, information about all foreign bribes would have to be reported. This is the type of information that would influence the judgement of a rational decision maker since it reflects on the legal and moral tone of a company. At the same time, business would not have to keep track of trivial expenses that would not influence the decision of a rational decision maker. Therefore, all foreign bribes would be reported because they are material. Expenses that are not material would only be reported if the benefit of recording them outweighed the cost of collecting and recording them.[58]

Thus the materiality standard will reduce management uncertainty about what items need to be reported and reduce some of the burdensome expenses businesses are now incurring by going too far in their reporting efforts. Since managers and accountants have a firm grasp of the concept, it can produce the desired results in accounting records in minimum time. Such a system taken as a whole would reasonably meet the statute's specified objectives and would satisfy its requirements.

4. Conclusion

The Foreign Corrupt Practices Act of 1977, while scarcely litigated, has had a significant impact on operations of U.S. business firms at home and abroad. In fact, it demands no more than that companies and their employees behave ethically.

Despite this goal, ambiguities in the statute have reduced its effectiveness. A genuine export crisis—one that is distinctly tied to the operation of the Act—may bring about some future adjustment to the reason to know standard. For the time being, however, clarity in the accounting requirement, which can be easily introduced, is the more pressing issue. With a vigorous enforcement effort, the Act can restore the reputation for fair and honest dealings that has long characterized U.S. business firms in the international marketplace.

Notes

1. The Foreign Corrupt Practices Act of 1977, 15 U.S.C. 78a, 78m, 78dd-1, -2, 78ff.
2. *Business Accounting and Foreign Trade Simplification Act: Hearings on S.708 Before the Subcommittee on Securities and the Subcommittee on International Finance and Monetary Policy of the Senate Committee on Banking, Housing and Urban Affairs,* 97 Cong., first session 1–2 (1981) (statement of Senator D'Amato).
3. Swedish Penal Code, SFS 1977: 103 (Jan. 1, 1978).
4. The Foreign Corrupt Practices Act of 1977, 15 U.S.C. 78dd-2.
5. *Id.*
6. *Oil Company, Former CEO Settle Foreign Corrupt Payment Charges,* 18 Sec. Reg. & L. Rep. (BNA) 1006 (July 11, 1986).
7. *Id.*
8. *Id.*
9. *Id.*
10. *Id.*
11. *Id.*
12. The Wall Street Journal, July 10, 1986, at 54.
13. *Oil Company, Former CEO Settle Foreign Corrupt Payment Charges,* 18 Sec. Reg. & L. Rep. (BNA) 1006 (July 11, 1986).
14. *Id.*
15. Porrata-Doria, *Amending the Foreign Corrupt Practices Act of 1977: Repeating the Mistakes of the Past,* 38 Rutgers L.R. 29, 30 (1985).
16. *Id.* at 31.

17. W. Michael Reisman, *Folded Lies* (1979).

18. *Id.* at 69.

19. *Id.*

20. *Id.* at 75.

21. *Id.* at 88–89.

22. M. Velasquez, *Business Ethics: Concepts and Cases,* 46 (1982).

23. *Id.* at 47.

24. *Id.* at 36. The case-specific utilitarianism discussed in the text is known as *act utilitarianism*. A variation of this, known as *rule utilitarianism,* focuses not on the specific, unique facts of a case, but on the long-term and seeks to determine which rule of conduct, bribery or non-bribery, will produce the most consistent long-term guidance with the least loss of utility. In other words, rule utilitarianism will not quite maximize utility on a case-by-case basis, but it will, on the positive side, make up for that by providing stability and consistency. However, both versions of utilitarianism demand too much in terms of seeing into the future and quantifying the results to be of value to this analysis.

25. *Id.* at 59.

26. Des Jardins, "An Employee's Right to Privacy," in *Contemporary Issues in Business Ethics,* 223 (J. Des Jardins and J. McCall, eds.) 1985.

27. M. Velasquez, *Business Ethics: Concepts and Cases,* 59 (1982).

28. *Id.* at 65.

29. *Id.* at 75.

30. *Id.* at 77.

31. Porrata-Doria, *supra* Note 15 at 36.

32. 18 U.S.C. sec. 201(g) (1982).

33. See Note, *The Foreign Corrupt Practices Act of 1977: A Solution or a Problem 11 Cal. W. Int'l L. J.* 111, 128–134 (1981).

34. Bader and Shaw, *Amendment of the Foreign Corrupt Practices Act* 15 N.Y.U.J. INT'L L. & Pol.627, 634 (1983).

35. 127 Cong. Rec. S. 13975 (daily ed. Nov. 23, 1981).

36. 15 U.S.C. 78dd-1, dd-2 (1977).

37. 15 U.S.C. 78m (1977).

38. 15 U.S.C. 78dd-1, dd-2 (1977).

39. Porrata-Doria, *supra* Note 15 at 37.

40. *Id.*

41. Bader and Shaw, *supra* Note 34 at 631.

42. S. Rep. No. 114, 95th Cong., 1st Session 4 at 10 (1977).

43. [July–Dec] Sec. Reg. & L. Rep. (BNA) No. 469 at A-1 (N.D.Ill. Aug. 30, 1978) (settled by consent decree).

44. [July–Dec] Sec. Reg. & L. Rep. (BNA) No. 513 at A-23 (D.D.C. July 19, 1979) (settled by consent decree).

45. Porrata-Doria, *supra* Note 15 at 42.

46. *Business Accounting and Foreign Trade Simplification Act: Joint Hearing on S.414 Before the Subcommittees on International Finance and Monetary Policy and Securities of the Senate Committee on Banking, Housing, and Urban Affairs, 98th Congress,* 1st Session 25 (1983) (statement of William E. Brock, United States Trade Representative) at 50.

47. 15 U.S.C. sec. 78m (1977).

48. *Id.*

49. Statement of William E. Brock, United States Trade Representative, *supra* Note 46.

50. *Id.* at 26.

51. Porrata-Doria, *supra* Note 15 at 45.

52. Statement of William E. Brock, United States Trade Representative, *supra* Note 46 at 26.

53. Business Week, *The Antibribery Act Splits Executives,* Sept. 19, 1983, at 15.

54. S.E.C. Release No. 34–17, 500, 3 Fed. Sec. L. Rep. (CCH) paragraph 23, 632H at 17, 233–5 (Jan. 29, 1981).
55. ABA Committee on Corporate Law and Accounting, *A Guide to the New Section 13(b)(2) Accounting Requirements of the Securities Exchange Act of 1934,* 33 Bus. Law 307, 315 (1978).
56. Financial Accounting Standards Board, *FASB Concepts Statement 2,* May 1980 (emphasis supplied).
57. Welsch, Newman, and Zlatkovich, *Intermediate Accounting 7th ed.,* (1986) at 22.
58. Financial Accounting Standards Board, *supra* Note 56.

Graduate School of Business,
University of Texas at Austin,
Austin, TX 78712-1175,
U.S.A.

Multi-National Corporations

Global Distributive Justice

Thomas Donaldson

Rights

Rights establish minimum levels of morally acceptable behavior. One well-known definition of a "right" construes it as a "trump" over a collective good, which is to say that the assertion of one's right to something, such as free speech, takes precedence over all but the most compelling collective goals, and overrides, for example, the state's interest in civil harmony or moral consensus.

Rights are at the rock bottom of modern moral deliberation: Maurice Cranston writes that the litmus test for whether something is a right or not is whether it protects something of "paramount importance." If I have a right to physical security, then you should, at a minimum, refrain from depriving me of physical security (at least without a rights-regarding and overriding reason). It would be nice, of course, if you did more: if you treated me charitably and with love. But you must *at a minimum* respect my rights. Hence, it will help to conceive the problem of assigning minimal responsibilities to multinational corporations through the question, "What specific rights should multinationals respect?"

Notice that the flip side of a right typically is a duty. This, in part, is what gives aptness to Joel Feinberg's well-known definition of a right as a "justified entitlement *to* something *from* someone." It is the "from someone"

The Ethics of International Business, T. Donaldson, (Oxford: Oxford University Press, 1989), 66–73, 81–94.

part of the definition that reflects the assumption of a duty, for without a correlative obligation that attaches to some moral agent or group of agents, a right is weakened—if not beyond the status of a right entirely, then significantly. If we cannot say that a multinational corporation has a duty to keep the levels of arsenic low in the workplace, then the worker's right not to be poisoned means little.

In wrestling with the problem of which rights deserve international standing, James Nickel recommends that rights that possess international scope be viewed as occupying an intermediary zone between abstract moral principles such as liberty or fairness on the one hand, and national specifications of rights on the other. International rights must be more specific than abstract principles if they are to facilitate practical application, but less specific than the entries on lists of rights whose duties fall on national governments if they are to preserve cosmopolitan relevance. Nickel says little about which criteria should distinguish rights appropriate at the national level from rights appropriate at the international level, except to mention the relevance of a given nation's "historical era." But the difference he has in mind seems obvious: one nation's particular social capacities or social traditions may favor the recognition of certain rights that are inappropriate to other nations. Citizens of a rich, technologically advanced nation, for example, but not of a poor, developing one may be viewed as possessing a right to a certain technological level of health care. A citizen of the United States may have the right to kidney dialysis; a citizen of Bangladesh may not.

As a first approximation, then, let us interpret a multinational's obligations by asking which *international rights* it should respect. We understand international rights to be the sort of moral precepts that lie in a zone between abstract moral principles and national rights specifications. Multinationals, we shall assume, should respect the international rights of those whom they affect, especially when those rights are of the most fundamental sort.

But whose list of fundamental rights shall we choose? Libertarians sometimes endorse well-pruned lists of liberty-centered rights, ones that resemble the first ten amendments to the U.S. Constitution (the Bill of Rights) without the subsequent historical additions. Welfare liberals sometimes endorse lush, intertwined structures that include entitlements as well as freedoms. Who is to say that a given person's list, or a given country's list for that matter, is preferable to another's?

One list receiving significant international attention, a list bearing the signatures of most of the world's nations, is the Universal Declaration of Human Rights. However, it and the subsequent International Covenant on Social, Economic and Cultural Rights, have spawned controversy despite the fact that the Universal Declaration of Human Rights was endorsed by virtually all of the important post-World War II nations in 1948 as part of the affirmation of the U.N. Charter. What distinguishes these lists from their predecessors, and what serves also as the focus of controversy, is their inclusion of rights that have come to be called "social," "economic," "positive," or "welfare" rights.

Many have balked when confronted with such lists, arguing that no one can have a right to a specific supply of an economic good. Can anyone be said to have a "right," for example, to 128 hours of sleep and leisure each week? And, in the same spirit, some international documents have simply refused to adopt the welfare-affirming blueprint established in the Universal Declaration. For example, the "European Convention of Human Rights" omits mention of welfare rights, preferring instead to create an auxiliary document ("The European Social Charter of 1961") which includes many of what earlier had been treated as rights as "goals." Similar objections underlie the bifurcated covenants drawn up in an attempt to implement the Universal Declaration: one such covenant, entitled the "Covenant on Civil and Political Rights," was drawn up for all signers, including those who objected to welfare rights, and a companion document, entitled the "Covenant on Economic, Social and Cultural Rights," was drawn up for welfare rights defenders. Of course, many countries signed both; but some signed only the former.

A number of philosophers have offered eloquent defenses of welfare rights, and have used them to analyze the obligations of developed to less developed countries. James Sterba argues that "distant peoples" (for example, people in developing countries) enjoy welfare rights which members of the developed countries are obliged to respect. Welfare rights are defined as rights to whatever is necessary to satisfy "basic needs," needs "which must be satisfied in order not to seriously endanger a person's health and sanity." It is Sterba's principal thesis that the welfare rights of distant peoples and future generations may be justified by the concept of a right of all persons to life and fair treatment. The thesis means—to take only one application—that multinationals are obliged to avoid work place hazards that seriously endanger workers' health.

Henry Shue advances a similar notion, but does so in a far more detailed and comprehensive manner, in his book *Basic Rights*. His analysis has special relevance for our purposes. Shue asserts that his principal purpose is to "try to rescue from systematic neglect within wealthy North Atlantic nations a kind of right that . . . deserves as much priority as any right: rights to subsistence." The substance of a basic right is "something the deprivation of which is one standard threat to rights generally," and basic rights include welfare rights. They include, in particular, the right to subsistence, which Shue defines as a right to "minimal economic security," entailing, in turn, a right to, for example, "unpolluted air, unpolluted water, adequate food, adequate clothing, adequate shelter, and minimal preventative public health care."

The chief examples of basic rights other than a right to subsistence, for Shue, are the rights of freedom of physical movement, security, and political participation. The right to freedom of physical movement is a right to not have "arbitrary constraints upon parts of one's body, such as ropes, chains, . . . and the absence of arbitrary constraints upon the movement from place to place of one's whole body, such as . . . pass laws (as in South Africa)." The right to security is a right not to be subjected to "murder, torture, mayhem, rape, or assault"; and the right to political participation is the right to have "genuine influence upon the fundamental choices among the societal institutions and the societal policies that control security and subsistence and, where the person is directly affected, genuine influence upon the operation of institutions and the implementation of policy. This later concept underlies the cherished idea in the United States, defended from the Revolutionary War to the present, that everyone has a right to affect his or her national destiny.

For Shue, the essence of a basic right is its status as a prerequisite for the enjoyment of other rights. Thus, being secure from beatings is a prerequisite for the enjoyment of, for example, the right to freedom of assembly, since one's freedom to hold political meetings is dependent upon one's freedom from the fear of beatings in the event one chooses to assemble. Shue insists correctly that benevolent despotism cannot ensure such basic rights. One's rights are not protected even by the most enlightened despot in the absence of social institutions that guarantee that basic rights will be preserved in the event such benevolence turns to malevolence. Illusions, as the saying goes, are not liberties.

Accordingly, Shue considers it a "minimal demand" that "no individuals or institutions, including corporations, may ignore the universal duty to avoid depriving persons of their basic rights."

Shue is no doubt correct in thinking that the seeming "strangeness" of welfare rights reflects a blind spot in Western liberalism for severe economic need. Notably, nowhere does U.S. law affecting foreign policy mention subsistence rights, and though the State Department is required by law to note formally human rights violations, it resists listing the nonfulfillment of vital needs as rights violations. Shue's analysis, moreover, provides a formidable argument on behalf of such rights.

His strategy is successful in part because it unpacks the sense in which it is contradictory to support any list of rights without at the same time supporting any specific right upon whose preservation the list can be shown to depend. It is a strategy with direct application to the controversy between defenders and critics of welfare rights, for if he is correct, even a list of *non*welfare rights ultimately depends upon certain basic rights, at least a few of which are welfare rights. His argument utilizes the following, simple propositions:

1. Everyone has a right to something.
2. Some other things are necessary for enjoying the first thing as a right, whatever the first right is.
3. Therefore, every one also has rights to the other things that are necessary for enjoying the first thing as a right.

We can grasp Shue's point more easily by considering on the one hand a standard objection to welfare rights, and on the other, a response afforded by Shue's theory. Many who criticize welfare rights utilize a traditional philosophical distinction between so-called negative and positive rights. A "positive" right is said to be one that requires persons to act positively to *do* something; a "negative" right requires only that people not deprive directly. Hence, the right to liberty is said to be a "negative" right, whereas the right to enough food is said to be a "positive" one. With this distinction in hand, it is common to proceed to make the point that no one can be bound to improve the welfare of another (unless, say, that person has entered into an agreement to do so); rather, at most they can be bound to *refrain* from damaging the welfare of another.

Shue's argument, however, reveals the implausibility of the very distinction between negative and positive rights. Perhaps the most-celebrated and best-accepted example of a "negative" right is the right to freedom. Yet the meaningful preservation of freedom requires a variety of positive actions: for example, on the part of the government it requires the establishment and maintenance of a police force, courts, and the military, and on the part of the citizenry it requires ongoing cooperation and diligent (not merely passive) forbearance. And the protection of another so-called negative right, the right to physical security, necessitates "police forces; criminal rights; penitentiaries; schools for training police, lawyers, and guards; and taxes to support an enormous system for the prevention, detention, and punishment of violations of personal security."

This is compelling. The maintenance and preservation of many nonwelfare rights (where, again, such maintenance and preservation is the key to a right's status as "basic") requires the support of certain basic welfare rights. For example, certain liberties depend upon the enjoyment of subsistence, just as subsistence sometimes depends upon the enjoyment of some liberties. One's freedom to speak freely is meaningless if one is weakened by hunger to the point of silence.

Although it establishes the legitimacy of some welfare rights, Shue's argument is nonetheless flawed. In the first place, from the standpoint of moral logic, his methodology appears to justify the more important in terms of the less important. That is to say, insofar as a basic right is defined as one whose preservation is necessary for the preservation of all rights generally, the determination of what counts as "basic" will occur by a process which takes as fundamental all rights, including nonbasic ones, and then asks which among those rights are rights such that their absence would constitute a threat to the others. Not only does this fail to say anything about the moral grounding of rights in general, it also hinges the status of the basic rights on their ability to support all rights, including nonbasic rights, and this appears to place the justificatory cart before the horse. This problem enlarges when we notice that many of the so-called nonbasic rights such as freedom of speech at least appear to be of equal importance to some so-called basic rights. One is left wondering why a few of the world's most important rights, such as the rights to property, free speech, religious freedom, and education, are regarded as "nonbasic."

Shue himself acknowledges that status as a basic right does not guarantee that the right in question is more important. At one point, while contrasting a nonbasic right, such as the right to education, to a basic right, such as the right to security, he writes, "I do not mean by this to deny that the enjoyment of the right to education is much greater and richer—more distinctively human, perhaps—than merely going through life without ever being assaulted." But he next asserts the practical priority of basic rights by saying, "I mean only that, if the choice must be made, the prevention of assault ought to supersede the provision of education." So while denying that basic rights are necessarily more important than nonbasic ones in all respects, he grants that they are more important in the sense that probably matters most: they are given priority in decisions in which a choice must be made between defending one right and defending another. He concludes, "Therefore, if a right is basic, other, nonbasic rights may be sacrificed, if necessary, in order to secure the basic right."

But what Shue leaves obscure is the matter of which rights *other* than basic rights are deserving of emphasis. For Shue, every right must occupy one of two positions on the rights hierarchy: it is either basic or not. But then how are individuals, governments, and corporations to know which rights should be honored in a crunch? Shue clearly believes that individuals, governments, and corporations must honor *basic* rights, but what of the remaining nonbasic rights? What of the right of freedom of speech, to property, or to a minimal education? And if they are to be recognized as significant, then why? Surely, Shue will agree that all *nation-states* must honor the right to freedom of speech, but is the same true of all individuals and corporations? Does it follow that corporations must tolerate all speech affecting the workplace and never penalize offending workers, even when the speech is maliciously motivated and severely damages profitability? And are all *states* responsible for defending *all* other nonbasic rights?

We may seek help in a different direction, this time an attempt to wrestle with the status of international rights made by James Nickel. Nickel helps alleviate the problems arising from Shue's formulas by moving beyond Shue's simple specification of basic rights to the establishment of four conditions that *any* would-be international right must pass:

1. The right must protect something of very great importance.
2. The right must be subject to substantial and recurrent threats.
3. Evidence must be provided that observance of a political right is required for an adequate response to the threats in number 2.
4. The obligations or burdens imposed by the right must be affordable in relation to resources, other obligations, and fairness in the distribution of burdens.

The first condition recognizes that if claims are made to things which have little or only moderate importance, then even if those claims happen to be valid, they cannot aspire to the status of "rights." Again, rights lay down minimal, not maximal, conditions upon the behavior of others, and are allowed to trump even collective social goods. Hence, they refer to goods of critical importance and impose duties that are not to be taken lightly.

Fundamental International Rights

We are now prepared to identify some of the items that should appear on a list of fundamental international rights, as well as to lay the groundwork for interpreting their application to multinational corporations. To review quickly: we have defined a fundamental international right as satisfying the three conditions that emerged from a revision of Nickel's original list, and which must be respected by all international actors, including nation-states, individuals, and corporations. (We may abbreviate the expression "fundamental international right" to "fundamental right.") The first and second of these conditions concern the need for the right to protect something of great importance, and to be subject to substantial and recurrent threats. The third condition establishes limitations upon the duties associated with the prospective right. We have interpreted this third, "fairness-affordability" condition to mean that for a proposed right to qualify as a genuine right, all moral agents must be able under ordinary circumstances, and after having received any charitable aid due them, to assume the various burdens and duties that fairly fall upon them in honoring the right, and, further, that some "fair" arrangement exists for sharing the duties and costs among the various agents who must honor the right. This arrangement, moreover, must allow the possibility (although not necessarily the probability) that the right will be enjoyed by most people in most instances. In addition a "compatibility proviso" serves to eliminate the need to establish a rights pecking order.

Though probably not complete, the following list contains items that appear to satisfy the three conditions and hence to qualify as fundamental international rights:

1. The right to freedom of physical movement
2. The right to ownership of property
3. The right to freedom from torture
4. The right to a fair trial
5. The right to nondiscriminatory treatment (freedom from discrimination on the basis of such characteristics as race or sex.)
6. The right to physical security
7. The right to freedom of speech and association
8. The right to minimal education
9. The right to political participation
10. The right to subsistence

This is a minimal list. Some will wish to add entries such as the right to employment, to social security, or to a certain standard of living (say, as might be prescribed by Rawls' well-known "difference" principle). Disputes also may arise about the wording or overlapping features of some rights: for example, is not the right to freedom from torture included in the right to physical security, at least when the latter is properly interpreted? We shall not attempt to resolve such controversies here. Rather, the list as presented aims to suggest, albeit incompletely, a description of a *minimal* set of rights and to serve as a beginning consensus for evaluating international conduct. If I am correct, many would wish to add entries, but few would wish to subtract them.

It would be unfair, not to mention unreasonable, to hold corporations to the same standards of charity and love as human individuals. Nor can they be held to the same standards to which we hold civil governments for enhancing social welfare—since many governments are formally dedicated to enhancing the welfare of, and actively preserving the liberties of, their citizens. The profit-making corporation, in contrast, is designed to achieve an economic mission and as a moral actor possesses an exceedingly narrow personality. It is an undemocratic institution, furthermore, which is ill-suited to the broader task of distributing society's goods in accordance with a conception of general welfare. The corporation is an economic animal; although its responsibilities extend beyond maximizing return on investment for shareholders, they are informed directly by its economic mission.

The "minimal/maximal" distinction mirrors the application of the "fairness-affordability" criterion; both imply that duties of the third class, to aid the deprived, do not fall upon for-profit corporations except, of course, in instances in which a corporation itself has done the depriving. Barring highly unusual circumstances,[1] both distinctions imply that whatever duties corporations may have to aid the deprived are "maximal," not "minimal," duties. They are duties whose performance is not required as a condition of honoring fundamental rights or of preserving the corporation's moral right to exist.

The same considerations are relevant when sorting out the specific correlative duties of for-profit corporations according to the fairness-affordability criterion as when distinguishing between minimal and maximal duties. For example, it would be strikingly generous for multinationals to sacrifice some of their profits to buy milk, grain, and shelter for people in poor countries, yet it seems difficult to view this as one of their minimal moral requirements, since if anyone has such minimal obligations, it is the peoples' respective governments or, perhaps, better-off individuals. This is another way of saying that it is an unfair arrangement—and hence would conflict with the fairness-affordability criterion—to demand that multinational corporations, rather than national governments, shoulder such burdens. These are maximal, not minimal, duties, and a given corporation's failure to observe maximal duties does not deprive that corporation of its moral right to exist. Furthermore, from our analysis of rights—in which we noted that rights impose demands of minimal conduct—it follows that when a corporation fails to discharge a maximal duty to aid the deprived, the failure does not necessarily constitute a violation of someone's *rights*. A corporation's failure to help provide housing for the urban poor of a host country is not a *rights* violation.

The same, however, is not true of the second class of duties, to protect from deprivation. These duties, like those in the third class, are also usually the province of government, but it sometimes happens that the rights to which they correlate are ones whose protection is a direct outcome of ordinary corporate activities. For example, the duties associated with protecting a worker from the physical threats of other workers may fall not only upon the local police, but also to some extent upon the employer. These duties, in turn, are properly viewed as correlative duties of the right—in this instance, the worker's right—to personal security.

*   *   *

What the list of rights and correlative corporate duties establishes is that multinational corporations frequently do have obligations derived from rights when such obligations extend beyond simply abstaining from depriving directly to actively protecting from deprivation. It implies, in other words, that the relevant factors for analyzing a difficult issue, such as hunger or high-technology agriculture, include not only the degree of factual correlation existing between multinational policy and hunger, but also the recognition of the existence of a right to subsistence along with a specification of the corporate correlative duties entailed.

I have argued that the ten rights identified in this chapter constitute minimal and bedrock moral considerations for multinational corporations operating abroad. Though the list may be incomplete, the human claims that it honors, and the interests those claims represent, are globally relevant. The existence of fundamental international rights implies that no corporation can wholly neglect considerations of racism, hunger, political oppression, or freedom through appeal to its "commercial" mission. These rights are, rather, moral considerations for every international moral agent, although, as we have seen, different moral agents possess different correlative obligations. The specification of the precise correlative duties associated with such rights for corporations is an ongoing task that this chapter has left incomplete. Yet the existence of the rights themselves, including the imposition of duties upon corporations to protect—as well as to refrain from directly violating—such rights, seems beyond reasonable doubts.

Notes

1. Extraordinary conditions are capable of creating exceptions to the principle. For example, suppose that an earthquake devastates a host country and that thousands of local residents are dying for want of blood. Suppose further that the branch of a multinational corporation happens to possess the means to provide blood on a short-term basis and hence save thousands of lives, while the local government does not. In such an instance, the company may have a minimal duty to aid in the rescue; that is, it may have a correlative duty (correlative to the right of persons to physical security) to aid the deprived. Such exceptions have analogues in the realm of individual action. For example, normally we do not consider helping a particular person in distress a "perfect" duty—a duty that one must perform. Although we may regard helping people in distress a duty, we allow considerable discretion as to when and how the helping occurs. But if one happens to be walking on a lonely mountain trail and discovers a hiker who has slipped and clings precariously to a ledge, it becomes a perfect duty to help short of risking one's own personal security.

Global Distributive Justice and the Corporate Duty to Aid

Kevin T. Jackson

Recently, Thomas Donaldson has made a formidable contribution to our thinking about the global responsibilities of business by demonstrating that, in general, basic international human rights impose correlative duties not only on individuals and nations, but also on multinational corporations (Donaldson, 1989). However, Donaldson denys that the corporate duty to render aid to those deprived of basic human rights is a minimal moral mandate, except in certain special circumstances, detailed *infra*. In a separate discussion of international ethics D. A. J. Richards (1982, p. 275) has persuasively shown how a Rawlsian-based conception of a global "difference principle" leads us to see the duty to aid as a fundamental requirement of international justice—not a Kantian imperfect charitable obligation (Kant, 1964) for saints and heros only—at least as regards individuals and nations *qua*, moral agents. I think Richards' position is largely correct; and due to current disparities in distributions of wealth and resources worldwide, I maintain that a robust basic duty to aid applies naturally to the activities of **all** resource-holding international actors and institutions. Accordingly, I am led to question the special rationale Donaldson provides for treating the *corporate* duty to render aid so differently. To put the matter bluntly, I seriously doubt that a globalized conception of justice-as-fairness licenses multinational businesses to avoid the duty of aid by hiding behind convenient self-serving proclamations of "limited economic missions," at least without incurring a charge of unjust ideological maneuvering on this point. I will begin with an examination of Donaldson's argument for truncating corporate duties to aid (type III duties).

Truncating Type III Duties for Corporations

Unlike individuals and nations, multinational corporations, Donaldson asserts, do not as a general rule have base-line moral duties to aid those deprived of basic human rights, except in two kinds of cases: (i) those in which the corporation itself has caused the rights deprivation, and (ii) those in which "exceptional circumstances" exist. In support of this contention, Donaldson argues (a) that corporations, unlike nation-states and individuals, are "economic animals" which have "limited economic missions;" (b) that considerations of "fairness" and "affordability" dictate that governments—and not corporations—bear responsibility for aiding those deprived of fundamental rights; and (c) that to the extent that corporations do have duties to aid the deprived, they represent "maximal" not "minimal" obligations. A minimal duty is construed as one which, if not honored, results in the loss of a corporation's "moral right to exist."

Journal of Business Ethics **12**: 547–551, 1993.

The "Limited Economic Mission" Rationale

What arguments might be advanced against the grounds Donaldson offers for attenuating duties to aid with respect to corporations? It is not clear that corporations really are, in the relevant moral sense, limited economic agents with limited economic objectives. Thus, contrary to the now waning view that the corporation is merely an economic entity, a widely respected article has emphasized the appropriateness of analogizing, for purposes of responsibility-ascription, the corporation to the individual in the sense that corporations evince both rationality and respect in their goal-setting and decision-making capacities (Goodpaster and Matthews, 1982). Moreover, in addition to supporting numerous charitable and humanitarian causes, many corporations routinely contribute to election campaigns, form political action committees (PACs), provide honoraria to members of Congress and so on (Weidenhaum, 1990). As such, they clearly assume significant noneconomic, *i.e.* political, legal and moral roles as well as economic ones. A critic may retort that such non-economic roles are ultimately taken on to advance a corporation's special and paramount economic objectives, such as generating profits for shareholders and investors, creating jobs for employees, and providing goods and services for consumers. However, this sort of charge could analogously be leveled at the frequently obsessive life goals of many materialistic people who seek to amass obscene personal fortunes. Surely it does not follow that upper-crust "yuppies" have managed to shed basic humanitarian responsibility for aiding others in virtue of their choice for a distorted priority of values.

The "Fairness-Affordability" Rationale

Saying that considerations of fairness and affordability militate against holding corporations responsible for duties to aid does not serve to resolve the deeper—and key—moral question of what one may objectively claim to be fair and affordable in particular cases in which one considers whether a corporate duty to aid exists. Donaldson states flat out that:

> [W]hile it would be strikingly generous for multinationals to sacrifice some of their profits to buy milk, grain, and shelter for persons in poor countries, it seems difficult to consider this one of their minimal moral requirements, since if anyone has such minimal obligations, it is the people's respective governments, or perhaps, better-off individuals. This is another way of saying that it is an unfair arrangement—and hence would conflict with the fairness-affordability criteria to demand that multinational corporations, rather than national governments, shoulder such [type III] burdens. (Donaldson, 1989, p. 85; this volume, p. 537.)

There are some underlying problems connected with the notions of fairness and affordability involved here that must be highlighted. Saying, for instance, that a multinational corporation cannot "afford" to help shelter the homeless, feed the hungry or perhaps simply encourage its legal department to handle *pro bono* cases for indigents in a country that systematically deprives human rights (as many firms have done on behalf of *apartheid* resistors in South Africa), or saying that it is "unfair" to ask them to undertake these sorts of actions, amount to controversial assertions. And yet Donaldson's general exemption of corporations from shouldering type III duties amounts to a shorthand way of collectively rendering conclusory judgments in advance of the kind of reflective casuistical deliberations that are needed to support meaningful decisions in many particularly hard and debatable cases. Thus, there is something artificial and arbitrary, not to say disingenuous, about Donaldson's general disclaimer that obligations to render aid to the poor in the developing world are not fair and affordable for multinational enterprises as a class (absent causal involvement in rights deprivations and/or out-of-the-ordinary circumstances).

I should say at this point that I concur with George Brenkert's observation in a recent criticism of another argument from Donaldson's book that the concept of affordability ought to be replaced by a broader concept of capability that would encompass not only a corporation's financial resources but other non-monetary resources at its disposal as well. (Brenkert, 1992.) Once this substitution is in place, the question in the present context arises: how much assistance can we reasonably expect a corporation to provide to those deprived of basic rights? Most would agree it is highly dubious to assert that a corporation alone must bear full responsibility for aiding the deprived. We expect governments and wealthy individuals to share that responsibility. Yet in many run-of-the-mill situations a poor host country's government (and similarly poor neighboring nation-states) are incapable of providing enough much needed aid, making corporations which profit from operations in the country or region plausible candidates for rendering assistance. I emphasize that these circumstances are today all-too-ordinary and do not reflect the sort of "exceptional circumstances" Donaldson's model appears to contemplate. Of course, corporations cannot reasonably be expected to discharge duties of aid to the extent that they would manifestly lose a competitive advantage in their markets or be led into outright bankruptcy. (Obviously, we don't expect nation-states to go belly-up from giving humanitarian assistance either.) And I would caution that the claim that corporations have duties to aid should not be overblown into the much less plausible assertion that corporations must be blamed for not completely elevating all individuals deprived of basic rights to a completely deprivation-free existence. But all of this is not to say (as Donaldson does) that corporations do not have the type III duties in question. Instead, it is to allow that we would rightly excuse the corporation for not being capable of absolutely discharging those duties, given the host of other obligations owed to other stakeholders (shareholders, employees, customers, and so on) that it must satisfy as well.

In fact, this is precisely where the Rawls-Richards approach becomes useful, as it provides a yardstick for the fairness-affordability criterion calibrated in terms of the background dimension of international distributive justice passed over by Donaldson's approach.

Modifying Rawls' specifications of the original position (Rawls, 1972), for present purposes, we may imagine individuals situated under an internationally encompassing veil of ignorance. That is, individuals do not know what nation they belong to; they do not know whether they are an employee in a maquiladora in Juarez, a CEO of a multinational corporation in Manhattan, or whether they are unemployed and without means of subsistence, perhaps even starving to death in Lima. Nor do they know the relative affluence or impoverishment of the country in which they live. The crucial point here is that they need to reach an agreement (under the supposition that they will make a rational choice in the face of uncertainty) on the principles that will govern the social, political, and economic relationships between individuals, nations, and other globally-active institutions—including multinational corporations.

Importantly, the principles of justice thus derived need not be conceived of as dependent upon the presence of either conventional business practices or extant schemes of cooperation, centrality of operations, and sustained reciprocity among international agents—even though the latter clearly exist to a limited degree amongst both governments and multinational firms. One may reasonably suppose that individuals in an international original position would accept a modification of Rawl's own version of the difference principle addressed not only (as Richards holds) to nations, but also to productive organizations that have reasonable capacities for distributing resources to less developed countries which would reduce human suffering. I would venture to postulate that the sort of vast economic inequalities obtaining as between, say, the holdings of a highly profitable business enterprise and the abject poverty of the inhabitants of a host under-developed country are justified only if they are reasonably expected to work to the advantage of the least advantaged. My argument is that a robust conception of the corporations' duty to aid the deprived as a *prima facie* obligation of distributive justice flows from the modified circumstances of the original position. As a *prima facie* obligation it may well be that in particular cases, considerations of cost will render it unfair to expect that a corporation will respect it. But one need not suppose beforehand that, as a general rule, considerations of cost and affordability necessarily would always be dispositive of the corporation's obligation to render humanitarian assistance from the perspective of contractors in the original position.

The Minimal-Maximal Distinction

In saying that I take the corporate duty to aid as a *prima facie* obligation of global distributive justice I must hasten to add that I do not intend to attribute (as Donaldson does) the special senses of "minimal" and "maximal" moral duties to the obligation to aid. The reason is simple: the idea of a corporation forfeiting its "moral right to exist" is insufficiently cogent to support drawing a bright line between minimal and maximal corporate moral obligations. (And frankly, if this kind of normative corporate "death" were to be the transcendental sanction for malfeasances of minimal moral duties, the modern corporation would either be extinct or else on the endangered species list in the noumenal world!) I take it that, like the concept of a "social contract for business," the notion that a corporation failing to discharge minimum moral obligations loses its moral right to exist is at bottom a heuristic device. So construed, I fail to see why we are not free, within reason, to redraw virtually any proposed line dividing a minimal duty from a maximal duty—with equal, or even more enlightened, heuristic value—in the interest of redistributing basic resources to those who are deprived of them and who could be assisted at comparatively slight cost and effort to the corporate moral agent.[1]

Is Poverty and Unmitigated Suffering in Developing Nations an "Exceptional Circumstance"?

Given the widespread poverty, chronic malnutrition and lack of access to health care throughout the hundreds of developing countries in which multinational business chart their markets, I doubt the cogency of the "exceptional circumstances" proviso for third class corporate duties. If unusually dire circumstances (Donaldson's example of earthquake victims) genuinely warrant the ascription of a corporate duty to aid as an exception to a general rule, all I can say is that regrettably, throughout most of the developing nations today the situation is the reverse. The Donaldsonian exception ought therefore to be the rule.

Moreover, Donaldson's analysis of the "exceptional circumstances" prong of corporate third-class duties confuses the broad notion of a duty to aid the deprived with the much narrower sub-concept of a duty to rescue those temporarily in distress. This latter aspect of my argument can best be elaborated with the help of Henry Shue's distinctions between different categories of type III duties. According to Shue, type III duties include, first, obligations to aid those deprived of basic rights where the moral agent stands in a certain role or special relationship to the victim (*e.g.,* a nurse or lifeguard). These are called type III-1 duties. Second, there are obligations to aid stemming from the failure of social institutions to aid, termed type III-2 duties. Finally, Shue distinguishes obligations to aid those deprived of basic rights as a consequence of disasters, labeled type III-3 duties. (Shue, 1980.)

Thus, typical rescue situations involve a person or group of persons suddenly falling away from a *status quo*. A cyclone hits a village; a baby falls into a swimming pool. Normally, such situations give rise to the type III-3 duties due to the out-of-ordinary "act of God" or accident scenario. But whereas the rescue situation involves some antecedent enjoyment of a basic right which is deprived by a perilous occurrence, duties to aid the deprived also arise in circumstances in which a person or group of persons may have never had a prior enjoyment of the basic right. Again, these latter situations give rise to type III-1 duties (in which the duty to aid is tied to particular roles or relationships) and type III-2 duties (in which aid is needed due to deprivations resulting from social failures to perform type I and type II duties). What

Donaldson's framework does not provide, however, is an acceptable principled basis for drawing the bottom line for corporate duties to aid at type III-3 duties to the exclusion of type III-1 and type III-2 duties unless the narrowly drawn exceptions exist.

Conclusion

A couple of possible criticisms need to be considered at this point. First, some may object that it's just contrary to our common sense intuitions about the conventional roles of business to blame the profit-driven corporate entity for not giving up some of its revenues or resources for "charitable" purposes. Such critics ought to bear in mind not only the sobering fact that our common sense in moral matters is fallible and often in need of enlightened revision, but, in addition, that the corporate duty of aid is often a background norm intimately bound up with and presupposed by familiar direct legal duties of the corporation which are themselves widely accepted in the business community. This helps to explain why we would be especially justified in blaming the multinational corporation for unlawfully evading its fair share of taxes imposed on it by the government of a developing host country. The host government will have *pro tanto* less revenue available to assist its own indigent citizens in need of aid as a consequence of the corporation's delict.

Second, I expect that the aspect of my analysis most likely to upset those affiliated with international business enterprises is its apparent ideological bent in favor of the interests of the poor in developing countries at the expense of corporate wealth held in developed countries. In response I would refer opponents to a salient underlying feature of the internationalized original position: the hypothetical model directs one toward an honest and unbiased reflection on how one would opt to be treated were one's own social and economic circumstances to be reversed with, for instance, an inhabitant of a less developed host country confronted with scarcity, malnutrition, poverty, and so on. Thus, the goal here is to approach the philosophical ideals of political neutrality and moral universalizability rather than sanctifying the corporate quest for maximizing profits, power and advantage.

Note

1. It should be noted that in many civil law systems it is an actionable offense (for individuals) to fail to assist those in need of aid—even strangers—unless rendering aid would imperil one's own life or well-being, or would demand unreasonable cost or effort (Feinberg.) And some have argued that the common law reluctance to legislate such a natural duty of aid is unwarranted and at odds with a principle of benevolence that undergrids common-law patterns found in, for instance, the law of contract. (Weinrib, 1980.)

References

Brenkert, G.: 1992, "Can We Afford International Human Rights?," *Journal of Business Ethics* **11**, 515–521.

Donaldson, T.: 1989, *The Ethics of International Business* (Oxford University Press, New York).

Feinberg, J.: "The Legal and Moral Responsibility of the Bad Samaritan," in J. Feinberg and H. Gross, *Philosophy of Law* (Wadsworth Publishing Co., Belknop, CA).

Goodpaster, K. and Matthews, J.: 1982, "Can a Corporation Have a Conscience?," *Harvard Business Review*, January–February.

Kant, I.: 1964, *The Metaphysical Principles of Virtue* (M. Gregor, trans.).

Rawls, J.: 1971, *A Theory of Justice* (Harvard University Press, Cambridge, MA).

Richards, D. A. J.: 1982, "International Distributive Justice," in J. Pennock and J. Chapman (eds), *Ethics, Economics, and the Law* (New York University Press, New York).

Shue, H.: 1980, *Basic Rights: Subsistence, Affluence, and U.S. Foreign Policy* (Princeton University Press, Princeton, N.J.).

Weidenbaum, M.: 1990, *Business, Government, and the Public*, pp. 423–27.

Weinrib, E.: 1980, "The Case for a Duty to Rescue," *The Yale Law Journal*, Vol. 90.

Fordham University,
Graduate School of Business Administration,
New York, NY 10023,
U.S.A.

The Perils of Corporate Largess: A Reply to Professor Jackson
Thomas Donaldson

Professor Kevin Jackson raises a critical challenge.[1] Not lightly, and not without deep reflection, should we let rich and powerful global corporations off the moral hook. Not lightly should we excuse the Sonys and General Motors of the world from the burdens of remedying global rights abuses. And this is the nub of the issue between Professor Jackson and me; for even though I have written that corporations should bear heavy and often unacknowledged duties in honoring human rights, I have also stipulated that these duties (unless "exceptional" circumstances obtain) should fall *only* in two classes, namely:

1. Refraining from depriving people of the object of a right.
2. Protecting (in some instances) the right from being deprived.

And I have explicitly excluded the final class of duties (which I do argue fall on nation states, individuals, and certain other groups), i.e.:

3. Restoring to people whose rights have been violated the object of the right. But why, Professor Jackson writes, should we excuse corporations from the duty of correcting rights abuses? Why should they not shoulder, just as individuals and nation states do, the obligations to restore food to the poor, shelter to the homeless, civil liberties to the politically abused, property to the dispossessed, and education to the illiterate? So, he wishes to argue that it is a responsibility of for-profit corporations to correct human rights

Thomas Donaldson. "The Perils of Corporate Largess: A Reply to Professor Jackson," Georgetown University, 1994. Original essay.

abuses, while I do not. As it happens, we both agree that for-profit corporations must never *take,* say, bread from the hungry and that it must frequently play a role in *protecting* people from being hungry. Yet, again, we disagree over whether as a matter of normal practice they must *provide* bread to the hungry.

My answer to Professor Jackson is that for-profit corporations are simply not fit for such duties. Although they are richer and taller than most of us, they have exceedingly narrow personalities. Indeed, they inhabit a marketplace that tends to further warp their moral character. But we should not be distressed about this fact, for profit-making corporations would make lousy custodians of duties of the kind we have in mind. We are, in turn, wise to entrust most of these duties to democratic nation states and better-off individuals.

Before getting down to details, it is important to note that the differences between my views and Professor Jackson's are less dramatic than might first be supposed. As he grants, I do not deny all obligations of for-profit corporations to restore to deprived people the objects of rights, since I require corporations to restore them when *they* did the depriving or when "exceptional" circumstances obtain (Professor Jackson even seems to believe that exceptional circumstances are quite common in Third World countries today).[2] Nor does Professor Jackson himself assert that for-profit corporations *always* have such obligations, for as he remarks, "Of course, corporations cannot reasonably be expected to discharge duties of aid to the extent that they would manifestly lose a competitive advantage in their markets. . . ." Later, he adds that "we would rightly excuse the corporation for not being capable of absolutely discharging those duties, given the host of other obligations owed to other stakeholders (shareholders, employees, customers, and so on) that it must satisfy as well." So the difference between us is more a matter of degree than of kind.

To understand why I disagree with Professor Jackson, it is important to see how very different the question "What responsibilities does a *for-profit corporation* have?" is from the question "What responsibilities does a *person* have?" We assume that a generic answer exists for the second in a way that we do not for the first. We assume that *if* persons have the duty to help the starving, then they have this duty no matter who they are, where they live, or what time period they inhabit. Ancient Romans, modern Laotians, and seventeenth-century Elizabethans are all assumed to have an obligation to help the starving—at least within reasonable limits reflecting their ability and other commitments. This is because we assume that there is something *morally the same* about people. This fact is reflected in virtually every ethical theory throughout history, but most recently has been explicitly emphasized in the efforts of Ronald Dworkin and Amartya Sen.[3] But we never make the same assumptions about organizations, and for very good reason. There is little or nothing morally the same about the Acme Laundry bowling team, the Soviet Army, a jury in a murder trial, a bridge club, and the EEC. These organizations have little in common except being organizations. Their obligations and rights vary widely and it would be ludicrous to assign the same generic obligations to all. All people may have the duty of charity, i.e., of giving at least some money or material possessions to the poor, but same could hardly be said of a neighborhood car pool, the Red Cross (which is itself a charity), the Sting Fan Club, or the Presidential Commission on Aging. The individual members of these organizations no doubt have duties of charity, but the organizations themselves are designed for specific purposes that make hoisting upon them the duty of charity awkward to say the least.

This is not to deny that there are shared obligations of for-profit corporations. Yet it stands to reason that these will be very different from other organizations, such as not-for-profit corporations (say, the Red Cross), sports teams, and governments. Indeed, because corporations are artifacts, which is to say that we *make* them what they are rather than *finding* them in nature, it follows different nation states and cultures may choose to define corporations' obligations in different ways.[4] One society might impose heavy obligations even as another imposes lighter ones. The United States, through its elected congress, might, for example, give large tax breaks to U.S. corporations under the express agreement that corporations shoulder broad responsibilities for training the hard core unemployed. Yet another country might tax corporations heavily and use the tax money to establish training programs for the unemployed.

Since, then, the obligations of for-profit corporations can be shaped to some extent by society, we should think seriously about *which* obligations we assign them. The issue at hand is whether we should assign them in a way that *includes* or *excludes* the obligation of correcting rights abuses as a normal part of their business activities. Even though, as I have written elsewhere, it makes sense to impose a number of significant obligations upon corporations,[5] it makes little sense to impose on them rights-abuse correcting obligations. Two reasons are decisive.

First, corporations are not democratic entities, and hence lack the authority to dispense societies resources, even for good causes. On the occasions when corporations have attempted to use their resources politically, the results have frequently been unsavory. ITT's notorious anti-democratic activities in Chile a few decades ago, or United Fruit's efforts in Central America to overthrow a democratically elected president, are cases in point. The CEOs of General Motors or Nissan are not representatives of the people, they take no oath of office, and they lack the moral authority to distribute society's scarce resources. Nor should there be any doubt that distributing society's resources is what the current debate is about. If corporations were to assume general responsibility for correcting rights abuses, the price tag would be astronomical. Restoring physical security, property, and civil liberties, not to mention providing food and shelter to the homeless, is an awesome task that manages even to outstrip the coffers of most nation states. Were for-profit corporations to take on these duties, there is only one place from where the money could come, namely, revenues derived from customer sales. Assuming good luck, all competitors in an industry would add to the prices they charge in a manner sufficient to cover the cost of correcting rights abuses. But who would pay? An ongoing supply of revenue could come from only one place, namely, customers. Thus, we would witness the spectacle of consumer goods costing dramatic multiples of current prices, with the surplus collected by corporations and then distributed for "the good of society" by corporate executives. It is, frankly, not a pretty picture.

I said all competitors in an industry would raise prices "assuming good luck." If good luck did not prevail (which almost certainly would happen) some competitors would raise prices and use the proceeds to correct rights abuses while others would attempt to "free ride" by keeping prices the same and sticking to business. This, then, raises the even worse spectacle of ethically upstanding companies (ones who are sincerely attempting to fulfill their duty of correcting rights abuses by restoring the objects of rights to people) being driven out of business by unscrupulous competition. The market, history teaches, is an unsympathetic taskmaster. It works to the advantage of society when it is used to pit companies against one another in a struggle to satisfy our commercial needs. But it was never designed to serve the function of distributing wealth for the good of society.

One may have followed my logic so far, and still have a nagging doubt. Did not Professor Jackson also offer a *positive* argument on behalf of corporations restoring rights abuses? Did he not argue that no less than John Rawls's theory of justice implied that corporations should take on rights-restoring obligations? He writes,

> I would venture to postulate that the sort of vast economic inequalities obtaining as between, say, the holdings of a highly profitable business enterprise and the abject poverty of the inhabitants of a host underdeveloped country are justified only if they are reasonably expected to work to the advantage of the least advantaged. My argument is that a robust conception of the corporation's duty to aid the deprived as a *prima facie* obligation of distributive justice flows from the modified circumstances of the original position.

This is a misuse of Rawls's theory. Rawls never intended for his famous "difference" principle to apply to *specific* cases of inequality such as between "a highly profitable business enterprise" and "the inhabitants of a host underdeveloped country." Rather he meant it to apply to *systemic* inequalities brought about by structural inequalities. In fact, his theory is usually construed as a *justification* for the dramatic difference in wealth between, say, a highly profitable businessperson and a very poor person, since the modified free market structure that allows the profitable businessperson to obtain her wealth also works ultimately to promote the "advantage of all, including that of the least well off." Rawls also explicitly denies the application of his theory beyond national borders and hence excludes the cross-national comparison Jackson envisions from the scope of his theory.[6]

In summary, even though multinational corporations have an important role to play in *protecting* against human rights abuses, it would be a grave error to assign them the generic responsibility of *correcting* human rights abuses. Multinational corporations have many strengths, but serving as a dispassionate custodian and distributor of society's money is not one of them.

Notes

1. Kevin T. Jackson, "Distributive Justice and the Corporate Duty to Aid," *Journal of Business Ethics* 12, 1993: 547–551. Professor Jackson's paper is largely a criticism of a key argument in my book, *The Ethics of International Business* (Oxford University Press, 1989).

2. I also do not mean to deny the importance or legitimacy of the common practice (more often followed in the U.S. than other developed countries) of a corporations' giving a small percentage of its pre-tax profits to charitable causes.

3. See Amartya Sen, *Inequality Reexamined*. (Cambridge: Harvard University Press, 1992); and Dworkin, Ronald, *Taking Rights Seriously*. (Cambridge: Harvard University Press, 1979).

4. See Thomas Donaldson and Thomas W. Dunfee, "Toward a Unified Conception of Business Ethics: Integrative Social Contracts Theory," *Academy of Management Review,* 19, 1994; and also "Integrative Social Contracts Theory: A Communitarian Conception of Economic Ethics," forthcoming in *Economics and Philosophy.*

5. As I argued in an earlier work, one of the key obligations society should impose upon corporations is that of producing goods well and efficiently and in a way that enhances employee and customer welfare. They also must shoulder the obligation of respecting all valid rights and, what is closely connected to this, observing principles of social justice (see Thomas Donaldson, *Corporations and Morality,* Prentice-Hall, 1982, especially Chapter 3.)

6. On this point, however, there is room to question Rawls, as I did in "The Ethics of Conditionality in International Debt," in *Millennium: Journal of International Studies* Vol. 20, 2 (Summer, 1991), pp. 155–169.

Ethics and the Gender Equality Dilemma for U.S. Multinationals

Don Mayer and Anita Cava

> We hold these truths to be self-evident: that all men are created equal, and endowed by their creator with certain rights—life, liberty, and the pursuit of happiness.
>
> U.S. Declaration of Independence, 1776

> All human beings are born free and equal in dignity and rights.
>
> United Nations Universal
> Declaration of Human Rights, 1948

Judging from the U.S. Declaration of Independence, gender equality was not self-evident in 1776. By 1948, however, the Universal Declaration of Human Rights took care not to exclude women from the ambit of declared rights. Since then, while gender equality has come a long way in the United States, many difficult and divisive issues remain unresolved. After completing a global

Journal of Business Ethics **12**: 701–708, 1993.

inventory of attitudes on gender equality, Rhoodie (1989) concluded that many nations give only "lip service" to the goals of gender equality articulated in international conventions and declarations such as the U.N. Declaration of Human Rights (1948). Given the uneven progress of gender and racial equality in the world, it is inevitable that multinational enterprises (MNEs) encounter uneven ethical terrain.

Recently, the U.S. Congress and the Supreme Court have differed markedly over how the principles of non-discrimination in Title VII of the Civil Rights Act of 1964 (Title VII) should be applied by U.S. MNEs in their overseas activities. Both Congress and the Court recognized that U.S. non-discrimination laws may create difficulties for U.S. companies doing business in host countries where racial and/or gender discrimination is a way of life. But Congress, having the last word, decided in the Civil Rights Act of 1991 that Title VII protects U.S. citizens from employment discrimination by U.S. MNEs in their overseas operations.[1]

In so doing, Congress effectively reversed the Supreme Court, which only a few months earlier had decided that Title VII did not apply "extra-territorially" (E.E.O.C. v. Aramco, 1991).[2] According to the Court, to apply U.S. laws abroad might cause "unintended clashes between our laws and those of other nations which could result in international discord." The majority of the Court wanted Congress to be entirely clear about its intent before imposing the ethical values inherent in Title VII on the activities of a U.S. company in a foreign country.

This reluctance is understandable. It seems logical to assume that companies would prefer not to have two personnel policies, one for U.S. citizens and one for host country nationals and others. Human resource directors indicate a preference for following the laws and customs of the host country while doing business there, but a concern for furthering human rights values of the U.S.[3] Such a preference corresponds to other observed realities, since the recent history of law and business ethics shows that a number of U.S. MNEs would engage in bribery in foreign countries, if that should be the custom, in order to remain "competitive." Similarly, many U.S. MNEs were willing to acquiesce to *apartheid* in South Africa, despite the fact that such behavior would not be tolerated in the United States.

The multinational that adopts such a policy of moral neutrality follows what Bowie (1977) has identified as moral relativism. The approach of a moral relativism is characterized as—"When in Rome, do as the Romans do." This prescription has its arresting aspects. If Rome existed today as a commercial power, would U.S. corporate executives entertain one another by watching slaves battle to the death, attending Bacchanalian orgies, or cheering while faithful but hapless Christians were being mauled by lions? While such practices do not have overt current counterparts, there are nonetheless substantial differences among cultures in matters of gender equality (Rhoodie, 1989).

How does the MNE deal ethically with such contrasts? Bowie suggests that while ethical relativism cannot support business ethics in the global economy, neither can we afford to be "ethnocentric" and assume that "our" way is the one "right way." Bowie uses the term "ethnocentric" to describe a view that "when in Rome, or anywhere else, do as you would at home," (Bowie, 1988; Wicks, 1990). Essentially, it was this concern that animated the Supreme Court's decision in *Aramco,* which explicitly worried about "unintended clashes" between U.S. law and Saudi Arabian law. Further, it is this concern about "ethnocentrism" that fuels speculation that applying Title VII's equal opportunity provisions in countries like Japan is a recipe for corporate non-competitiveness and perhaps even a form of cultural imperialism.

This article explores some of the difficulties faced by U.S. multinationals in complying with Title VII as applied abroad and examines the ethical arguments surrounding achieving the goal of gender equality. Part I discusses the current dilemma for international human resource managers and their employees, as well for citizens of host countries. We focus on Japan as a model of a country in transition and consider the extreme situation of the Islamic countries as a counterpoint in the analysis. The emphasis is on practical and legal considerations. Part II returns to the issues of ethical relativism and cultural imperialism, and suggests that U.S. multinationals should not opt for moral relativism by deferring entirely to cultural traditions in countries such as Japan, traditions that may be contrary to declared international standards for gender and racial equality and contrary to apparent global trends.

I. Perspectives on the Current Dilemma

Human resource managers, employees, and host country nationals will have varying perspectives on the application of U.S. civil rights statutes for the promotion of gender equality in the foreign workplace. Each merits consideration in order to understand the framework within which an ethical analysis can be applied.

A. The MNE Managerial Perspective

For a MNE whose operations cover the U.S., Europe, Asia, and the Middle East, the differing cultural norms with respect to equal opportunity in the workplace are a bit unreal. Despite strong movements for gender equality in the Scandinavian countries and, to a lesser extent, in the U.S. and Europe, the basic condition of women worldwide is largely "poor, pregnant, and powerless" (Rhoodie, 1989). The differences among various nations span a continuum from cultures with a strong commitment to gender equality in the workplace to those with strong commitments to keeping women out of the workplace entirely (Mayer, 1991).

For the MNE trying to "do the right thing," the situation suggests a kind of ethical surrealism, where reality retreats before an unreal mix of elements—social, cultural, legal, and philosophical. It seems natural that companies doing business abroad would want to follow host country laws and customs. Obviously, following U.S. law only for U.S. employees poses a dual dilemma. First, assuming that gender discrimination is culturally accepted and legally tolerated in many foreign countries, what should be the MNE personnel policy? The MNE has the option of designing a single non-discriminatory policy for all workers or creating a two-track system, protecting the legal rights of U.S. nationals while accommodating the host country's norms for their nationals and others. Second, where the MNE has adopted a Code of Ethics for global application and the Code specifically refers to equal opportunity, can the MNE honor its commitment in a principled way?

Strict compliance with an ethical position would suggest a simple solution to this conundrum: Adopt an equal opportunity program, educate all employees, and enforce it consistent with Title VII's mandates across the board. Admittedly, however, following U.S. law worldwide, for all employees, is surely "ethnocentric" and may also be unworkable. In some host countries, such as Saudi Arabia, the legal conflicts may be pronounced. In others, such as Japan, the cultural conflicts may undermine consistent enforcement of Title VII-oriented policies throughout the workforce.

Taking Japan as an example, the U.S. MNE doing business in Tokyo is confronted with a patriarchal society in which women are expected to manage household work while men dominate the other forms of work (Lebra, 1984). Although men and women receive comparable educations through the high school level, women are expected to marry by age 25. Employment after that age is generally discouraged (Prater, 1981). There is seldom, if ever, a managerial track for Japanese women: if employed by a major Japanese company, they are often given positions largely designed to make the office environment more comfortable (such as by serving tea and appearing 'decorative'), and are not taken seriously as career office workers (Seymour, 1991).

For a U.S. MNE to announce a policy of equal opportunity for Japanese operations, tie that policy to Title VII enforcement, and expect no negative results would require a supposition that the overwhelmingly male population of Japanese customers, suppliers, and government officials would treat U.S. women and Japanese women equally. But, in fact, the sensitivity of Japanese males to sexual harassment issues is only dawning (Ford, 1992; Lan, 1991), and some other forms of overt discrimination are likely. Assuming, as seems warranted, that the MNEs female employees will be adversely affected to some degree by prevailing male attitudes in Japan, how would the company find that balanced approach that yields the least friction and the best results?

Such a question suggests that a utilitarian analysis, or some pragmatism, may be entirely appropriate here. It is well beyond the scope of this paper to suggest how absolute adherence to Title VII and equal opportunity principles should be tempered to achieve greater harmony with the host country culture, but a few observations are in order. First, Title VII's dictates may need to be culturally adjusted. An "appropriate" response to repeated incidents of Japanese males looking up female employees' skirts may be more educational than admonitory, at least for the first transgressions. Second, companies should be wary of any utilitarian or pragmatic approaches that predict a "non-competitive" result unless business hews to some perceived cultural norms. This point needs further elaboration.

In a country such as Saudi Arabia, the cultural norms and the sacred law, of *Shari'a,* are fairly congruent. The winds of change are not, seemingly, as strong as in other parts of the world. Japan, on the other hand, has demonstrated its willingness to adopt some "Western ways" in order to be part of the global economy, and there is considerable evidence that Japanese pragmatism has already created some new opportunities for women in the workplace (Prater, 1991). Moreover, legislation exists which purports to promote gender equality in the workplace, though some critics have questioned its efficacy (Edwards, 1988). In short, the "downside" of promoting equal opportunity in Japan because of cultural norms may easily be overstated; while Japanese males are not as sensitive to sexual harassment issues, for example, there are signs that they are becoming so (Lan, 1991).

For a host country culture that is less in flux, and whose culture and laws present a unified force against social change, the ethical issues change somewhat. This is because Title VII expressly allows discrimination in certain instances through the *bona fide* occupational qualification (BFOQ)[4] exception. The BFOQ exception provides that it will **not** be illegal to discriminate "on the basis of . . . religion, sex, or national origin in those certain instances where religion, sex, or national origin is a *bona fide* occupational qualification reasonably necessary to the normal operation of that particular business or enterprise."

In *Kern v. Dynalectron,*[5] for example, a company in the business of flying planes into the holy city of Mecca advised potential employees that Saudi Arabian law prohibited the entry of non-Moslems into the holy area under penalty of death. One pilot took instruction in the Moslem religion, but was Baptist at heart, and rescinded his "conversion." Returning to the U.S., he sued under Title VII for employment discrimination based on religion. The federal appeals court ultimately determined that Title VII applied but that being Moslem was, in this situation, a *"bona fide* occupational qualification" and not discriminatory.

It remains to be seen how gender qualifications may be raised and litigated for alleged discrimination overseas. But if those qualifications have the force of law, and are not the result of cultural preferences only, the most serious ethical dilemma is whether or not to do business in that country at all. To take an example based on racial classification, if South African law prohibited blacks from being hired by MNEs, the MNEs' only ethical choices would be to (1) do business in South Africa and comply with the law, (2) refuse to do business in South Africa, or (3) do business there and hire blacks anyway.

How are these three options analyzed from a perspective of ethics and the law? Option (3) may certainly be seen as an ethical policy, though probably of the "ethnocentric" variety, yet few ethicists and even fewer business executives would counsel such a course. Option (1) is well within the mainstream of ethical relativism, and, we would argue, is less ethical than choosing option (2). But again, **cultural** conflicts do not create such choices; legal mandates do. And countries whose cultural values are colliding with the values of "outsiders" may choose, at least temporarily, to preserve their culture through legal mandates. Saudi Arabia has laws which prohibit women from travelling alone, working with men, working with non-Muslim foreigners, and these laws apply to foreign women as well as host country women (Moghadam, 1988).

Even without such explicit laws of prohibition, MNEs and their human resource managers may hesitate to violate unwritten or cultural laws, and taking moral relativism's approach to the problem of gender equality in other countries may seem prudent. But such an approach seems to depend on a rather sketchy kind of utilitarian analysis: Engaging in overt equal opportunity policies will result in cultural condemnation, loss of customer and client contacts, and eventual unprofitability of the entire overseas enterprise. But in host countries whose culture is tied to the mainstream of world business, long-held attitudes will be difficult to maintain, and the negative impact of "doing things differently" should not be overestimated, nor should the definite benefits and opportunities of pursuing gender quality be overlooked (Lansing and Ready, 1988).

In this context, a comment about the employee's perspective seems appropriate. It might be difficult to generalize here because individual perspective often differs, depending upon personal ideology, situation, and career opportunities. However, from the viewpoint of a female manager in a U.S. MNE, we will assume that the greatest good would be a business world safe for gender equality and supportive of same. Adler and others have noted the difficulty of persuading MNEs that women managers can succeed in many countries whose cultures actively promote gender inequality (Adler, 1984). Certainly, a U.S. female manager's inability to obtain first-hand experience in dealing with Japanese businesses comes close to being a career handicap, and for Japanese women, the existence of opportunities outside the home may safely be regarded as benefits.

Ultimately, most American citizen employees of MNEs will test any policy by asking whether or not they are personally adversely affected. Companies that take care to structure career advancement opportunities such that experience in countries hostile to a protected class may find themselves with few employee complaints. However, MNEs not able to finesse the mandate of Title VII and the reality of certain foreign cultures will find themselves facing a similar set of choices described above with respect to apartheid. Now, however, a decision to accommodate host country norms must be accompanied by a fund out of which to pay judgments in Title VII litigation.

B. The Host Country's Perspective

From the overall Japanese societal perspective, the changes contemplated by a mandate of gender equality may indeed be troubling. The social structure that has built up over centuries, which has "worked" to achieve stability and a degree of consensus and comfort, could crumble if more and more women leave household work to obtain work in the "business world." Who will do the careful packing of lunches, the guidance for "cram courses" after school, tending to the children and dinner and bedtime while spouse is engaged in the obligatory socializing with office mates after hours? While Japanese men may now be undertaking more domestic duties, the differences are still staggering. One recent estimate suggested that Japanese women put in four to five hours of domestic work daily, while their husbands put in eight minutes (Watanabe, 1992).

Any change in the prescribed social order is bound to seem disruptive, and, therefore, negative. As one Islamic man declared to a National Public Radio correspondent during the Persian Gulf war, if women are allowed in the workplace, the forces of social decay would soon send the divorce and crime rates skyrocketing. This argument, a kind of utilitarian "parade of horribles,"[6] overtly trades on fear of change, is not empirically rigorous, and assumes that changes in the U.S. over a fifty year period represent the ultimate result of mindless social tampering. For the Islamic, this particular proponent of gender inequality in the workplace has a back-up argument, the *Qur'an*.

By appeal to divine, or infinite wisdom, we find an argument more akin to natural law or universalism. The argument may even suppose that not only Islamic society, but all other societies, would be well advised to follow this divinely decreed social ordering. What is manifest to the Islamic mind is contrary, it would seem, to "Western" notions of gender equality. This conflict pits two "objective" or "universal" truths against one another: the "truth" of the *Qur'an* and the "truth" of the Universal Declaration of Human Rights. Is the moral relativist right, after all?

II. Ethical Relativism and Ethical Ethnocentrism: A Synthesis for Overseas Gender Discrimination Issues

In general terms, the theory of moral relativism holds that different moral standards are "equally valid or equally invalid," and there are no "objective standards of right and wrong or good and evil that transcend the opinions of different individuals or different societies."[7] At the opposite extreme of the continuum is the objective approach, which is premised on the notion that there are "transcultural" norms that are universally valid.

Bowie (1988) suggests that the proper view is a point closer to the latter position. Although he stops short of embracing universalism, Bowie believes there are minimum ethical principles that are universally evident such as "do not commit murder" and "do not torture." These principles, clearly, can be enforced without imposing ethnocentric (or imperialistic) views upon a host country. To these minimum universal principles, Bowie adds the "morals of the marketplace," which are required to support transactions in the business world. These include honesty and trust. The combination of these two strands of quasi-universalism is as far as Bowie will go in staking his claim on the continuum.

Consider again the dilemmas faced by a U.S. MNE doing business in Japan, trying to integrate a tradition and practice of equal opportunity into a tradition and practice of unequal opportunity. One strategy for "blending in" with the Japanese market might be to adopt a thoroughly Japanese outlook and approach. That would include differing pay scales for men and women, actively discouraging women past the age of 25 from working with the company, and pointedly not inviting women employees to the after-five work/social functions that seem to play such an important part in an employee's successful corporate bonding.

Other than outright moral relativism, the social contract approach would appear to be the most likely proponent of such assimilation. Social contract theory examines the ethical foundations of societies by the relationships that exist within and between people, organizations, and groups. In an article on "extant social contracts," Dunfee (1991) explains and defends this communitarian approach to ethics, which appears grounded in relativism, but he also appears to offer an escape clause by way of a "filtering" device using utilitarian or deontological approaches. Dunfee would apparently recognize that racial discrimination is more widely condemned, and that gender discrimination is more widely tolerated, and conclude that perpetuating gender discrimination is less unethical than perpetuating racial discrimination. In a subsequent article, Dunfee and Donaldson (1991) retreat somewhat from the relativism approach and appear to suggest some dimensions of gender equality qualify as a "hypernorm," that is, a norm "recognized as core or foundational by most humans, regardless of culture." The example they give, however, is that of Saudi Arabia prohibiting women from driving, a rule that violates hypernorms of freedom of movement and rights of self-realization. Obviously, this issue does not approach the complexity posed by the international application of gender equality in the workplace.

In essence, what seems problematic for social contract theory is the substantial variance between the almost universally professed ideals of gender equality and the globally pervasive policies of gender inequality. If one looks to social practice for guidance as to what is ethical, gender inequality becomes relatively more ethical; yet if one looks to professed ideals and principles of equality, many existing forms of gender inequality (dowry deaths, female infanticide, widow-burning, and abortion based on male preference) (Howe, 1991) seem inexcusable. Ethical guidelines, apart from legal obligations, seem to require more explicit direction.

Bowie rejects relativism and argues for recognition of minimum universal principles and morals of the marketplace, an essentially deontological approach. He suggests that the latter may even control over the former where completely foreign agents meet to do business. Bowie draws upon democratic theory, torture and genocide, and examples based on bribery, apartheid, and political-economic values to make his point. He is, however, silent on gender discrimination. One wonders whether Bowie would view this issue as primarily social or as a political-economic priority on a plane with his other examples.

We take the position that neither relativism nor extant social contract theory are much help to MNEs in a host country whose values run counter to the company's ethical code or the laws and traditions of its country of origin. Instead, the concepts of minimum universal principles and morals of the marketplace legitimately can be broadened to embrace gender equality. Support for this position is evident in the increasingly international consensus on this point.

For example, as Frederick (1991) has pointed out, the United Nations Universal Declaration of Human Rights, the OECD Guidelines for Multinational Enterprises, and the International Labor Office Tripartite Declaration all give support to "nondiscriminatory employment policies" and the concept of "equal pay for equal work." Note that neither of these policies is widespread in Japan. In The United Nations Convention on the Elimination of All Forms of Discrimination Against Women (1979) was ratified by a large number of nations, both industrialized and developing. The European Community has passed a number of Council directives aimed at promoting gender equality in employment (Weiner, 1990).

We believe that by following policies which generally promote gender equality, without slavish adherence to all U.S. judicial opinions on Title VII and with good faith adjustments where cultural conditions require, a U.S. MNE in Japan can maintain its own code of ethics without the "inevitable" loss of "competitiveness." Moreover, it can do so without being "ethnocentric" or "imperialist," and by doing so it can avoid a kind of ethical balkanization that adherence to moral relativism would require. After all, a dozen different HRM policies, each geared to the host country's dominant yet often changing traditions.

This does not mean that resort to more universal declarations of principle are based on a need for Wicks' "metaphysical comfort." We agree with Wicks that our grasp of certain principles in some sense depends on our own experience and what "works." Did the social movement toward greater gender and racial equality in the United States come about because of *a priori* arguments on the ethical treatment of women and blacks, or because there was already equality in some areas and a perception that things "were not working"? There is no way to know with certainty, but there need be no need to identify either "ideal principles" or "real experience" as the mother lode for ethical discoveries.

Values, to be shared, must be mutually discovered. Universal standards, such as those proposed by the United Nations, come out of experience, and do not just emerge *a priori* (Frederick, 1991). Even without "metaphysical comfort," a MNE can be satisfied that there is an emerging consensus on gender equality. In going to a traditional culture where gender inequality is the norm, the MNE must be aware that there is another community emerging, one whose shape is as yet dimly perceived, but a community where goods, services, and information are traded with ever-increasing speed. Included in the information exchange in the communication of different values, and while these values are not being passed along in traditional ways, their transmission is inevitable. In this exchange of values and ideas, the ideals of equality are manifest in many ways. Any MNE, whatever the cultural norms it confronts in a particular country, would be wise to pay attention.

Notes

1. Civil Rights Restoration Act of 1991, P. L. 102–166, Nov. 21, 1991, 105 Stat. 1071. For the purposes of this discussion, a U.S. MNE is an enterprise with operations in one or more foreign countries.
2. *E.E.O.C. v. Aramco, Boureslan v. Aramco,* 111 S. Ct. 1227 (1991).
3. The authors mailed a survey entitled "Use of U.S. Employment Discrimination Law Abroad" to human resource directors of 120 companies identified as multinational enterprises. In part, the questionnaire solicited information about whether or not the company felt it wise to apply Title VII abroad. The eight responses that were received provide anecdotal, as opposed to statistically significant, information. Six respondents indicated it would be "unwise" to attempt to apply Title VII to U.S. citizens working abroad. The reasons given appear predictable: it would be "difficult"; it is the "local manager's responsibility"; we "do not attempt" to impose our norms on others. Two respondents believed it would be wise to implement such a policy despite the obstacles discussed in this paper. Nonetheless, all respondents indicated that the policy is appropriately enforced in the U.S. and two believed it would be wise to do so abroad as well.
4. 42 U.S.C. § 2000e-1 (1988).
5. 577 F. Supp. 1196, *affirmed* 746 F.2d 810 (1984).
6. George Christie, of Duke University Law School, coined this phrase in reference to attorneys, who learn to see the dark possibilities issuing from any proposed action and are prone to recite a "parade of horribles" to their clients.
7. Van Wyk, *Introduction to Ethics,* St. Martin's Press, New York (1990), p. 15.

References

Adachi, K.: 1989, "Problems and Prospects of Management Development of Female Employees in Japan," *Journal of Management Development* **8**(4), 32–40.

Alder, N.: 1984, "Women in International Management: Where are They?," *California Management Review* **26**, 78–89.

Bassiry, G. R.: 1990, "Business Ethics and the United Nations: A Code of Conduct," *SAM Advanced Management Journal* (Autumn), pp. 38–41.

Bellace, J.: 1991, "The International Dimension of Title VII," *Cornell International Law Journal* **24**, 1–24.

Bowie, N.: 1988, "The Moral Obligations of Multinational Corporations," in Luper-Fay (ed.), *Problems of International Justice* (Westview Press, New York), pp. 97–113.

Bowie, N.: 1977, "A Taxonomy for Discussing the Conflicting Responsibilities of a Multinational Corporation," in *Responsibilities of Multinational Corporations to Society* (Arlington, Va.: Council of Better Business Bureau), pp. 21–43.

Carney, L. and O'Kelly: 1987, "Barriers and Constraints to the Recruitment and Mobility of Female Managers in the Japanese Labor Force," *Human Resource Management* **26**(2), 193–216.

Daimon, S.: 1991, "'Karoshi' Phenomenon Spreading to Female Workforce," *Japan Times Weekly* (Intl. Ed.), Sept. 30–Oct. 6, p. 7.

Donaldson, T. and T. Dunfee: 1991, "Social Contracts in Economic Life: A Theory," No. 91–156 (revised) Working Paper Series, Department of Legal Studies, The Wharton School, University of Pennsylvania, pp. 27–32.

Dunfee, T.: 1991, "Extant Social Contracts," *Business Ethics Quarterly* **1**, 22–37.

Edwards, L.: 1988, "Equal Employment Opportunity in Japan: A View from the West," *Industrial and Labor Relations Review* **41**(2), 240–250.

Ford, J.: 1992, "Sexual Harassment Taken for Granted," *Japan Times Weekly* (Intl. Ed.), Feb. 10–16, p. 4.

Frederick, W.: 1991, "The Moral Authority of Transnational Corporate Codes," *Journal of Business Ethics* **10**, 165–177.

Gundling, E.: 1991, "Ethics and Working with the Japanese: The Entrepreneur and the Elite Course," *California Management Review* **33**(3), 25–39.

Howe, M.: 1991, "Sex Discrimination Persists, According to a U.N. Study," *New York Times* June 16, p. A4, col. 1.

Lan, S.: 1991, "Japanese Businessman Produces Video to Prevent Lawsuits," *Japan Times Weekly* (Intl. Ed.), Nov. 11–17, p. 8.

Lansing, P. and K. Ready: 1988, "Hiring Women Managers in Japan: An Alternative for Foreign Employers," *California Management Review* **30**(3), 112–121.

Lebra, D.: 1984, *Japanese Women: Constraint and Fulfillment* (University of Hawaii Press, Honolulu).

Mayer, D.: 1991, "Sex Discrimination Policies for U.S. Companies Abroad," in Sanders, W. (ed.), *Proceedings of the Council on Employee Responsibilities and Rights* (forthcoming).

Moghadam, V.: 1988, "Women, Work, and Ideology in the Islamic Republic," *International Journal of Middle East Studies* **20**, 221–243.

Neff, R.: 1991, "When in Japan, Recruit as the Japanese Do—Aggressively," *Business Week* June 24, p. 58.

Prater, C.: 1991, "Women Try on New Roles; But Hopes Can Still Collide With Tradition," *Detroit Free Press* November 27, p. 1 (5th in a series, later published in the *New York Times*).

Rhoodie, E.: 1989, *Discrimination Against Women: A Global Survey of the Economic, Educational, Social and Political Status of Women* (London, U.K., McFarland and Company).

Seymour, C.: 1991, "The Ad-business: Talented Women Need Not Apply," *Japan Times Weekly* (Intl. Ed.), Dec. 9–15, p. 7.

Simon, H. and F. Brown: 1990/91, "International Enforcement of Title VII: A Small World After All?," *Employee Relations Law Journal* **16**(3), 281–300.

United Nations: 1979, *Convention of the Elimination of All Forms of Discrimination Against Women*, U.N. Doc. A/34/36 (Dec. 18, 1979).

Watanabe, T.: 1992, "In Japan, a 'Goat Man' or No Man; Women are Gaining More Clout in Relationships," *Los Angeles Times* Jan. 6, A1, col. 1.

Weiner, M.: 1990, "Fundamental Misconceptions About Fundamental Rights: The Changing Nature of Women's Rights in the EEC and Their Application in the United Kingdom," *Harvard International Law Journal* **31**(2), 565–574.

Wicks, A.: 1990, "Norman Bowie and Richard Rorty on Multinationals: Does Business Ethics Need 'Metaphysical Comfort'?," *Journal of Business Ethics* **9**, 191–200.

*Management Department,
School of Business Administration,
Oakland University,
Rochester, Michigan,
U.S.A.*

*Business Law Department,
School of Business Administration,
University of Miami,
Coral Gables, Fl 33124,
U.S.A.*

Ethical Dilemmas for Multinational Enterprise: A Philosophical Overview

Richard T. De George*

First World multinational corporations (MNCs) are both the hope of the Third World and the scourge of the Third World. The working out of this paradox poses moral dilemmas for many MNCs. I shall focus on some of the moral dilemmas that many American MNCs face.

Third World countries frequently seek to attract American multinationals for the jobs they provide and for the technological transfers they promise. Yet when American MNCs locate in Third World countries, many Americans condemn them for exploiting the resources and workers of the Third World. While MNCs are a means for improving the standard of living of the underdeveloped countries, MNCs are blamed for the poverty and starvation such countries suffer. Although MNCs provide jobs in the Third World, many criticize them for transferring these jobs from the United States. American MNCs usually pay at least as high wages as local industries, yet critics blame them for paying the workers in underdeveloped countries less than they pay American workers for comparable work. When American MNCs pay higher than local wages, local companies criticize them for skimming off all the best workers and for creating an internal brain-drain. Multinationals are presently the most effective vehicle available for the development of the Third World. At the same time, critics complain that the MNCs are destroying the local cultures and substituting for them the tinsel of American life and the worst aspects of its culture. American MNCs seek to protect the interests of their shareholders by locating in an environment in which their enterprise will be safe from destruction by revolutions and confiscation by socialist regimes. When they do so, critics complain that the MNCs thrive in countries with strong, often right-wing, governments.[1]

The dilemmas the American MNCs face arise from conflicting demands made from opposing, often ideologically based, points of view. Not all of the demands that lead to these dilemmas are equally justifiable, nor are they all morally mandatory. We can separate the MNCs that behave immorally and reprehensibly from those that do not by clarifying the true moral responsibility of MNCs in the Third World. To help do so, I shall state and briefly defend five theses.

Thesis 1: Many of the moral dilemmas MNCs face are false dilemmas which arise from equating United States standards with morally necessary standards. Many American critics argue that American multinationals

From *Ethics and the Multinational Enterprise,* edited by W. Michael Hoffman, Ann E. Lange and David A. Fedo (Lanham, MD: University Press of America, 1986).
*Distinguished Professor of Philosophy, University of Kansas.

should live up to and implement the same standards abroad that they do in the United States and that United States mandated norms should be followed.[2] This broad claim confuses morally necessary ways of conducting a firm with United States government regulations. The FDA sets high standards that may be admirable. But they are not necessarily morally required. OSHA specifies a large number of rules which in general have as their aim the protection of the worker. However, these should not be equated with morally mandatory rules. United States wages are the highest in the world. These also should not be thought to be the morally necessary norms for the whole world or for United States firms abroad. Morally mandatory standards that no corporation—United States or other—should violate, and moral minima below which no firm can morally go, should not be confused either with standards appropriate to the United States or with standards set by the United States government. Some of the dilemmas of United States multinationals come from critics making such false equations.

This is true with respect to drugs and FDA standards, with respect to hazardous occupations and OSHA standards, with respect to pay, with respect to internalizing the costs of externalities, and with respect to foreign corrupt practices. By using United States standards as moral standards, critics pose false dilemmas for American MNCs. These false dilemmas in turn obfuscate the real moral responsibilities of MNCs.

Thesis 2: Despite differences among nations in culture and values, which should be respected, there are moral norms that can be applied to multinationals.   I shall suggest seven moral guidelines that apply in general to any multinational operating in Third World countries and that can be used in morally evaluating the actions of MNCs. MNCs that respect these moral norms would escape the legitimate criticisms contained in the dilemmas they are said to face.

1. *MNCs should do no intentional direct harm.*
   This injunction is clearly not peculiar to multinational corporations. Yet it is a basic norm that can be usefully applied in evaluating the conduct of MNCs. Any company that does produce intentional direct harm clearly violates a basic moral norm.
2. *MNCs should produce more good than bad for the host country.*
   This is an implementation of a general utilitarian principle. But this norm restricts the extent of that principle by the corollary that, in general, more good will be done by helping those in most need, rather than by helping those in less need at the expense of those in greater need. Thus the utilitarian analysis in this case does not consider that more harm than good might justifiably be done to the host country if the harm is offset by greater benefits to others in developed countries. MNCs will do more good only if they help the host country more than they harm it.

3. *MNCs should contribute by their activities to the host country's development.*
   If the presence of an MNC does not help the host country's development, the MNC can be correctly charged with exploitation, or using the host country for its own purposes at the expense of the host country.

4. *MNCs should respect the human rights of its employees.*
   MNCs should do so whether or not local companies respect those rights. This injunction will preclude gross exploitation of workers, set minimum standards for pay, and prescribe minimum standards for health and safety measures.

5. *MNCs should pay their fair share of taxes.*
   Transfer pricing has as its aim taking advantage of different tax laws in different countries. To the extent that it involves deception, it is itself immoral. To the extent that it is engaged in to avoid legitimate taxes, it exploits the host country, and the MNC does not bear its fair share of the burden of operating in that country.

6. *To the extent that local culture does not violate moral norms, MNCs should respect the local culture and work with it, not against it.*
   MNCs cannot help but produce some changes in the cultures in which they operate. Yet, rather than simply transferring American ways into other lands, they can consider changes in operating procedures, plant planning, and the like, which take into account local needs and customs.

7. *MNCs should cooperate with the local government in the development and enforcement of just background institutions.*
   Instead of fighting a tax system that aims at appropriate redistribution of incomes, instead of preventing the organization of labor, and instead of resisting attempts at improving the health and safety standards of the host country, MNCs should be supportive of such measures.

Thesis 3: Wholesale attacks on multinationals are most often overgeneralizations. Valid moral evaluations can be best made by using the above moral criteria for context-and-corporation-specific studies and analysis. Broadside claims, such that all multinationals exploit underdeveloped countries or destroy their culture, are too vague to determine their accuracy. United States multinationals have in the past engaged—and some continue to engage—in immoral practices. A case by case study is the fairest way to make moral assessments. Yet we can distinguish five types of business operations that raise very different sorts of moral issues: 1) banks and financial institutions; 2) agricultural enterprises; 3) drug companies and hazardous industries; 4) extractive industries; and 5) other manufacturing and service industries.

If we were to apply our seven general criteria in each type of case, we would see some of the differences among them. Financial institutions do not generally employ many people. Their function is to provide loans for various types of development. In the case of South Africa they do not do much—if anything—to undermine apartheid, and by lending to the government they usually strengthen the government's policy of apartheid. In this case, an argument can be made that they do more harm than good—an argument that several banks have seen to be valid, causing them to discontinue their South African operations even before it became financially dangerous to continue lending money to that government. Financial institutions can help and have helped development tremendously. Yet the servicing of debts that many Third World countries face condemns them to impoverishment for the foreseeable future. The role of financial institutions in this situation is crucial and raises special and difficult moral problems, if not dilemmas.

Agricultural enterprises face other demands. If agricultural multinationals buy the best lands and use them for export crops while insufficient arable land is left for the local population to grow enough to feed itself, then MNCs do more harm than good to the host country—a violation of one of the norms I suggested above.

Drug companies and dangerous industries pose different and special problems. I have suggested that FDA standards are not morally mandatory standards. This should not be taken to mean that drug companies are bound only by local laws, for the local laws may require less than morality requires in the way of supplying adequate information and of not producing intentional, direct harm.[3] The same type of observation applies to hazardous industries. While an asbestos company will probably not be morally required to take all the measures mandated by OSHA regulations, it cannot morally leave its workers completely unprotected.[4]

Extractive industries, such as mining, which remove minerals from a country, are correctly open to the charge of exploitation unless they can show that they do more good than harm to the host country and that they do not benefit only either themselves or a repressive elite in the host country.

Other manufacturing industries vary greatly, but as a group they have come in for sustained charges of exploitation of workers and the undermining of the host country's culture. The above guidelines can serve as a means of sifting the valid from the invalid charges.

Thesis 4: On the international level and on the national level in many Third World countries the lack of adequate just background institutions makes the use of clear moral norms all the more necessary.   American multinational corporations operating in Germany and Japan, and German and Japanese multinational corporations operating in the United States, pose no special moral problems. Nor do the operations of Brazilian multinational corporations in the United States or Germany. Yet First World multinationals operating in Third World countries have come in for serious and sustained moral criticism. Why?

A major reason is that in the Third World the First World's MNCs operate without the types of constraints and in societies that do not have the same kinds of redistributive mechanisms as in the developed countries. There is no special difficulty in United States multinationals operating in other First World countries because in general these countries *do* have appropriate background institutions.[5]

More and more Third World countries are developing controls on multinationals that insure the companies do more good for the country than harm.[6] Authoritarian regimes that care more for their own wealth than for the good of their people pose difficult moral conditions under which to operate. In such instances, the guidelines above may prove helpful.

Just as in the nations of the developed, industrial world the labor movement serves as a counter to the dominance of big business, consumerism serves as a watchdog on practices harmful to the consumer, and big government serves as a restraint on each of the vested interest groups, so international structures are necessary to provide the proper background constraints on international corporations.

The existence of MNCs is a step forward in the unification of mankind and in the formation of a global community. They provide the economic base and substructure on which true international cooperation can be built. Because of their special position and the special opportunities they enjoy, they have a special responsibility to promote the cooperation that only they are able to accomplish in the present world.

Just background institutions would preclude any company's gaining a competitive advantage by engaging in immoral practices. This suggests that MNCs have more to gain than to lose by helping formulate voluntary, UN (such as the code governing infant formulae),[7] and similar codes governing the conduct of all multinationals. A case can also be made that they have the moral obligation to do so.

Thesis 5: The moral burden of MNCs do not exonerate local governments from responsibility for what happens in and to their country. Since responsibility is linked to ownership, governments that insist on part or majority ownership incur part or majority responsibility. The attempts by many underdeveloped countries to limit multinationals have shown that at least some governments have come to see that they can use multinationals to their own advantage. This may be done by restricting entry to those companies that produce only for local consumption, or that bring desired technology transfers with them. Some countries demand majority control and restrict the export of money from the country. Nonetheless, many MNCs have found it profitable to engage in production under the terms specified by the host country.

What host countries cannot expect is that they can demand control without accepting correlative responsibility. In general, majority control implies majority responsibility. An American MNC, such as Union Carbide, which had majority ownership of its Indian Bhopal plant, should have had primary control of the plant. Union Carbide, Inc. can be held liable for the damage the

Bhopal plant caused because Union Carbide, Inc. did have majority owner-ship.[8] If Union Carbide did not have effective control, it is not relieved of its responsibility. If it could not exercise the control that its responsibility de-manded, it should have withdrawn or sold off part of its holdings in that plant. If India had had majority ownerhip, then it would have had primary respon-sibility for the safe operation of the plant.

This is compatible with maintaining that if a company builds a hazardous plant, it has an obligation to make sure that the plant is safe and that those who run it are properly trained to run it safely. MNCs cannot simply transfer dangerous technologies without consideration of the people who will run them, the local culture, and similar factors. Unless MNCs can be reasonably sure that the plants they build will be run safely, they cannot morally build them. To do so would be to will intentional, direct harm.

The theses and guidelines that I have proposed are not a panacea. But they suggest how moral norms can be brought to bear on the dilemmas Amer-ican multinationals face and they suggest ways out of apparent or false dilem-mas. If MNCs observed those norms, they could properly avoid the moral sting of their critics' charges, even if their critics continued to level charges against them.

Notes

1. The literature attacking American MNCs is extensive. Many of the charges mentioned in this paper are found in Richard J. Barnet and Ronald E. Muller, *Global Reach: The Power of the Multinational Corporations,* New York: Simon & Schuster, 1974, and in Pierre Jalee, *The Pillage of the Third World,* translated from the French by Mary Klopper, New York and London: Modern Reader Paperbacks, 1968.

2. The position I advocate does not entail moral relativism, as my third thesis shows. The point is that although moral norms apply uniformly across cultures, U.S. standards are not the same as moral standards, should themselves be morally evaluated, and are relative to American conditions, standard of living, interests, and history.

3. For a fuller discussion of multinational drug companies see Richard T. De George, *Business Ethics,* 2nd ed., New York: Macmillan, 1986, pp. 363–367.

4. For a more detailed analysis of the morality of exporting hazardous industries, see my *Business Ethics,* 367–372.

5. This position is consistent with that developed by John Rawls in his *A Theory of Justice,* Cambridge, Mass.: Harvard University Press, 1971, even though Rawls does not extend his analysis to the international realm. The thesis does not deny that United States, Ger-man, or Japanese policies on trade restrictions, tariff levels, and the like can be morally evaluated.

6. See, for example, Theodore H. Moran, "Multinational Corporations: A Survey of Ten Years' Evidence," Georgetown School of Foreign Service, 1984.

7. For a general discussion of UN codes, see Wolfgang Fikentscher, "United Nations Codes of Conduct: New Paths in International Law," *The American Journal of Comparative Law,* 30 (1980), pp. 577–604.

8. The official Indian Government report on the Bhopal tragedy has not yet appeared. The Union Carbide report was partially reprinted in the *New York Times,* March 21, 1985, p. 48. The major *New York Times* reports appeared on December 9, 1984, January 28, 30, and 31, and February 3, 1985.

▼ International Issues

▶ *Interview with S. Janakiram*

Each of the applied ethics sections of this text (Parts II–V) includes an interview with a key figure who is prominent in his/her field. The purpose of these interviews is to bridge the gap between theory and practice and offer the student an exposure to how people in the "real world" confront practical, ethical issues.

Mr. S. Janakiram has been working for the World Bank for the past fifteen years in over fifty developing countries in Africa, Asia, and Latin America, specializing mostly in agricultural and industrial sectors. Presently he has been spearheading projects in The Russian Federation.

Q: *What are the most pressing ethical problems facing business in the international sphere?*

A: Ethical problems facing business in the international sphere need to be viewed in a relative perspective. It is important, first to determine whether a clearly defined ethos exists within the international arena where moral issues could be raised, discussed, and adjudicated. Given the complex nature of various systems around the world, it is difficult for such a common platform to exist, although various attempts are being made to achieve this.

But this is not an easy matter. For example, it is often asserted that the realm of morals exists only within individual countries. Each supports its own culture which defines and justifies its own morality. According to this point of view, in the realm of "inter-national" affairs there is only a Hobbsian "state of nature." In such a state of nature "anything goes."

While this is a common attitude, it need not be the case. It may be *descriptively* true of the interactions of many of the world's regions today, it does not have to be this way.

Prescriptively, I believe these attitudes stand in the way of the developing world economy. If we are to have a global marketplace, then there should be a single morality which governs behavior. Before this can become the case, the international community must come to grips with the descriptive reality that, at present, there are a plurality of countries who exhibit various social and business practices. It is within this sphere that international business must now operate.

Q: *How would such a commonly recognized morality develop?*

A: In a world where vast differences exist in the standards of living and economic well being (the disparity between the rich and poor nations continues to increase as well as within the countries themselves), it is indeed difficult to achieve a commonly recognized morality. This is not to say that we should not strive to achieve one such common platform, but we should keep in mind the harsh realities we are operating under.

From the standpoint of business, I would say that at present there are two large forces acting in the international economy: (a) the interests of the countries involved and (b) the interests of the Multinational Corporations. What would be in the interests of the country's relationships, need not necessarily be in the interests of the operating business (whose primary objective to maximize profit).

Let us take an example of a business proposal by a large U.S. based company to build a finished textile goods factory in China. At least two factors influence its decision, first is the production of a high quality, salable, exportable product at competitive prices. The low price will be largely due to low labor costs. Labor prices in China are much lower than they are in the U.S. Therefore, market factors dictate moving production operations to China.

The second factor is the overall stability of the country. This can be measured in terms of political leadership and macro-economic factors. While this may be a good business proposition, it can run into bilateral/multilateral conflict from the country's relationships (national interests) and ethical issues.

Continuing with our example, you may have been reading in the newspapers that China's policies on the use of human labor (prisoners are pressed into duty for pennies a day) and associated human rights violations are in direct conflict with policies pursued by the United States. Therefore, if a country's relationships are taken into account, and ethical issues were given the highest priority, then such a project should not go ahead, and even if the business were to go ahead, the U.S. Government could enforce its will through high tariffs which would make the imports of the finished textile products prohibitively expensive, and thereby negating the effects of low production costs.

Q: *So the bilateral/multilateral policies can sabotage the efforts of international institutions.*

A: It is quite possible that on occasions, depending on whose interests are going to be affected, that such situations could occur. If the leadership of the country is strong and is governed by strong ethical standards, such conflicts could be avoided, or at least resolved in a satisfactory manner.

Q: *That sounds a lot like an evolution from the international "state of nature" scenario you brought up earlier.*

A: Yes. But all too often it is the "state of nature" model which prevails.

Q: *How do multinational corporations fit into this picture?*

A: With the rapid globalization in trade and communication links, the interdependence between nations is on the increase. Companies can no longer operate in a total vacuum. They increasingly need to consider opportunities being presented in various parts of the world. With more and more large corporations strategizing along these lines, there is increasing competition, and those who can effectively combine their company's plans with the host country's own perspectives and thinking would benefit the most. In this regard, the multinationals can play an important role in bringing good business practices to the developing countries, similar to the ones they are pursuing in their home countries.

Q: *How can multinational companies play a role in evolving the industries of a country?*

A: By creating value-added industries that will enhance future industries within a country. This will create a series of linkage effects. For example, consider the role of MNC's (multinational corporations) in Africa. For many years they relied on several African countries for raw material supply for their industrial plants, which were mostly located in developed countries.

While this practice did stimulate industrial development in a few countries, much more could have been achieved if additional investments were also made to process these raw materials further and create additional employment and a wide variety of high value added products.

Q: *What about the threat of nationalization of industries when all phases of production occur in one country?*

A: Of course this is a risk faced by almost all multinationals, but through experience over several years of operations, they have to a large extent, learned how to cope with these situations and accordingly take measures to mitigate the inherent risks involved with such events. However, it depends on how good the working relationships are between the multinational companies and the developing countries and how deeply involved they are in promoting development and well being within the countries in which they operate.

Q: *What about a micro case in international business?*

A: I believe that many people justify unethical behavior because they have a "when in Rome, do as the Romans do" attitude. This is wrong. First the basis of morality is more universal than is often thought to be the case. In the five largest and most influential religions of the world, viz., Christianity, Islam, Hinduism, Buddhism and Judaism, there is general agreement that lying, cheating, and stealing are all wrong. Each asserts the existence of certain universal principles. Since most people in the world accept one of these religions, there should be general agreement about the foundations of ethics.

Obviously, there can be a gap between what should be the grounds for common agreement and the way things are. However, the recognition of this common philosophical/religious base is an important start.

Our companies are better served if we take personal responsibility for the actions that we take. One ought not be afraid to do what one believes is the right thing to do. This is true even if, in the short run, it may have a negative impact upon the company. The management of any good company should recognize this. They should support employees who dare to act out of integrity.

In the long run such ethical behavior is always the best thing—not just for yourself—but for the entire world community.

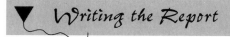

Structuring the Essay

In previous sections we have moved from adopting an ethical theory to weighing and assessing the merits of deeply embedded cost issues and ethical issues conflicts. The method works like this: 1) Chose an ethical theory (whose point of view you will adopt). 2) Set out cost issues and ethical issues lists. 3) Annotate the issues lists by examining how embedded each issue is to the essential nature of the case at hand. 4) Create a brainstorming list which includes both key thoughts on the subject and "pro" and "con" arguments on the possible courses of action. 5) Compare pivotal premises in those arguments using ethical considerations as part of the decision making matrix. 6) Make a judgment on which course of action ought to be taken (given the conflicts expressed in #4 & #5). 7) Set out your ideas in a written report. This report is your recommendation to management about what to do in this situation.

We are now up to point seven in this process. If we continue to follow case 3, the essay might look something like this:

Sample Skeleton Structure of Essay

Executive Summary.   Though the fabrication of asbestos gaskets in this marketplace offers a good financial opportunity for stockholders, and though the company will be doing nothing *illegal* in continuing in this line of business, it would be unethical to do so. Questions about possible health hazards to employees and environment outweigh financial gains. There are no adequate safeguards. Therefore, the company should get out of the asbestos fabrication business and do whatever it can for the town and its employees regarding job relocation to other parts of the company (if possible) and/or local job placement (if no internal jobs are available elsewhere).

This report will support the policy conclusions outlined above. In doing so it will examine the strongest positions pro and con regarding continuation of asbestos fabrication by the A.B.C. company.

The Pro Position.   The A.B.C. Company should continue fabricating asbestos gaskets.

[Transfer the material below to narrative description including additional development of your thoughts.]

Key Thoughts on the Subject:

1. There is a danger in everything. No manufacturing process is completely safe.
2. Once set in the form of sealed gaskets there has never been a proven health hazard to consumers.
3. All health awareness is directed towards our own employees.
4. It is expensive (though not excessive) to keep modifying our existing plant to meet present government guidelines, but government guidelines have changed radically over twenty years.
5. Government guidelines are often behind the scientific "health problems" curve.
6. The only way to protect employees is to convert to a "dustless" underwater fabrication process.
7. Trailings in the waste water (though meeting current standards) might be subjecting the rural area in which you live to environmental hazards.
8. The rural area in which you live needs these jobs. Who cares if a few "so-called" environmental "wish list" proposals fall by the wayside? People need jobs to live!
9. *This is a very profitable venture.*

Argument:

1. The stockholders own this company and deserve the best return on their dollar—Fact
2. The A.B.C. company is in a unique position to garner (at least for the time being) a very lucrative profit—Fact
3. Conversion of the plant to UNDERWATER FABRICATION will meet all existing government regulations—Fact
4. The time frame for which this process will pay-off completely is within the five-year capital depreciation period stipulated by the IRS—Fact
5. The probability of heading off a regulatory shutdown for at least five years is good.
6. It is probable that the company can make money by converting to the underwater fabrication process—2–5
7. *One ought to act in the stockholder's best interests—Fact*
8. The A.B.C. company ought to approve the underwater fabrication process—1,6,7.

The Con Position.   A.B.C. should stop fabricating asbestos gaskets.

[Transfer the material below to narrative description including additional development of your thoughts.]

Key Thoughts on the Subject:

1. Asbestos is an antiquated substance which will soon be banned by the government.
2. The underwater process only protects employees under current governmental regulations. But these are likely to change (given the pattern over the past twenty years). It is possible that even with the new process you are killing your workers. This is not right even if the workers enter into the job knowing there are risks.
3. The environmental waste will significantly harm the environment.
4. Even though the locals might not complain about this pollution (because they so value their jobs), this amounts to exploitation. They will "sell out" their own health and future generations for the short term benefit of a few jobs now.
5. The "best interests" of the stockholders does not mean getting all the money it can possibly garner. It must also abide by ethical issues of personal concern for the employees and the environment at large [tenet of one version of Kant's categorical imperative].

Argument:

1. The company can continue to make money fabricating these gaskets in the short term—Fact
2. The company has an obligation to act in the "best interests" of the stockholders—Fact
3. The "best interests" of the stockholders includes acting in an ethically responsible way—Assertion
4. Continuing to manufacture asbestos gaskets—even with the underwater fabrication process—will harm the health of both employees and the environment at large—Assertion
5. Harming the health of employees and the environment at large just for the sake of money is to exploit both one's employees and host community—Assertion
6. Exploitation is unethical—Assertion (set out your own moral theory here for a justification)
7. To continue manufacturing asbestos gaskets with or without the underwater process *is unethical*—4–6
8. Though the company can make money by continuing to manufacture asbestos gaskets, it should get out of the business—7, 1–3

(Insert any concluding remarks here.)

The above represents the briefest skeleton of an outcomes recommendation. The length can vary as well as any supporting data (charts, etc.) which can bolster your position. Depending upon your instructor, you may be asked to present an outcomes recommendation to the entire class. When this is the assignment, it is important to remember that the same principles that go into any group presentation also apply here—including slides, handouts, and any other visual aids that will engage your audience. It is essential to include your audience in your argument as it develops.

Whether it is a written report or a group presentation, the methodology presented ought to give you a chance to logically assess and respond to business problems which contain moral dimensions.

I will conclude with a few general questions which some of my students in the past have raised about writing the ethical outcomes recommendation.

What if I cannot see the other side? This is a common complaint among students. They see everything as black or white/true or false. But truth is never advanced by prejudice. It is important as rational humans to take every argument at its face value and to: 1. Determine what it says; 2. Determine the objections to the key premises; 3. Determine what is the strongest form of the thesis; 4. Assess the best arguments **for** and **against** the thesis.

What is the best way to reach my assessment of the best alternative? The basic strategy of the essay is to take the best two arguments which you have selected to support the conflicting alternatives and then to focus upon that single premise which seems to be at odds with the other argument. At this point you must ask yourself: "Why would someone believe in either argument-one or argument-two?" If you don't know, you don't deserve to offer an opinion—yet.

The rational person seeks to inform his/herself by "getting into the skin" of each party. You must understand why a thinking person might think *that* way.

If you deprecate either side, you lessen yourself because you decrease your chances to make your best judgment.

The rational individual seeks the truth. You don't wish to burden your psyche with illogical beliefs. Therefore, you will go to great lengths to find the truth of the "key premises" that you wish to examine.

In your final essay you will focus upon one of the argument's premises and find that:

A. The demonstrated truth of the conclusion depends upon the premises that support it.
B. If those supporting premises are false, then the conclusion is not proven.
C. Since we have assumed that the premises are all necessary to get us to the conclusion, if we refute one premise, we have refuted the conclusion.

What if I place cost issues or ethical issues too highly in my assessment of the outcome?   The purpose of presenting embedded issues analysis is to force you to see that not all ethical issues lie at the heart of the problem. Some can be satisfied rather easily. If this is the case, then you should do so. When it is possible to let the cost issues determine the outcome without sacrificing ethical standards, then it is your responsibility to do so. There are clearly some ethical principles that cannot be sacrificed no matter what the cost. It is *your* responsibility to determine just what these cases are and just *which* moral principles are "show stoppers."

Are ethical values the only values an individual should consider?   Each person has a number of personal values which are important to him or to her. These must be taken into account in real situations. Often they may mean that though *you* can't perform such and such an act, it is not requisite that the company forego doing whatever the cost issues dictate in that situation. For example, you may be asked to perform a task on an important religious holy day. Since your religion is important to you, you can't work on that day, but that does not mean you will recommend the company abandon the task which another person could perform (who did not believe in that religion, for example).

What happens when you get the cost issues and ethical issues confused?   This happens often among managers at all levels. The problem is that one set of issues is neglected or it is too quickly assigned to being of surface embeddedness. Stop. Go through the method again step-by-step. It may restore your perspective.

Macro and Micro Cases

The cases section of this book are divided into two categories: macro and micro. Each type of case employs a different point of view.

Macro Case.   The macro case takes large institutional entities as its focus. For example one might examine Beechnut and the apple juice case or BCCI as a multinational banking concern. The purpose of the Macro Case is to get you thinking about how corporations should act in their environment. You will take the perspective of a high level official and make judgments which will affect many thousands.

Micro Case.   The micro case takes individuals working within business as its focus. For example, one might look at a mid-level manager's approach to end of the year sales reports, or an engineer's decision to be a "whistle blower." The attraction of these cases is that you can project yourself realistically into these cases. It is probable that you will be in positions similar to the Micro Case descriptions (whereas only a fraction of people will ever really be a Macro Case decision maker).

Case Development.   The word 'case' is used in different ways by different people. This book will suggest one form of case response. The method for preparing and developing these cases is suggested in the essays entitled: "Writing the Report" which can be found at the end of each section in the book. Your professor may also have specific guidelines of his/her own.

For those who wish to use it, this approach offers a bridge between various traditional approaches to case studies, taught in business schools, with a philosophical method that emphasizes essay development. The intention throughout is that you expand your mind with the general essays and develop a practical skill in applying an ethical theory to thorny moral/cost conflicts through writing a business report that defends a particular course of action.

Please note that though most of the cases presented here have fictional venues, they are based upon composites of real Corporate America.

acro Cases

Case 4.1—Mining in Africa

You are the president of Zandec, a multinational mining company with its international headquarters in New York City. Your development team has discovered one of the richest iron deposits in the world in Nubia, a sub-Sahara African nation.

The Board of Directors has requested that you create a marketing plan for your operations in Nubia. To do this you are considering several factors.

The History.   First you must consider the history of Nubia. It was a former French colony and won its independence in 1962. From that time onward, Nubia has had various dictators who have consolidated the nation's tribes/clans into a power base intended to insure the continued influence and wealth of the dictator. The people live largely in an agrarian setting. Others work as miners in the old tin and copper mines. There is little industry. It is estimated that poverty is so acute that three of ten children are brain damaged by the age of twelve due to lack of adequate nutrition.

In addition, AIDS has been a major killer of young people in the country.

Aside from an initial nationalization of foreign/colonial industry at independence, there has not been any subsequent action taken against foreign investment. However, if a coup d'etat were to occur, there is no certainty that the new dictator would continue this pro-foreign investment attitude.

The work force is largely unskilled and the literacy rate is only 15%. The religious mix is 10% Moslem; 8% Christian; 62% native religions; 20% no religion. The per capita income is $40 per year.

The Proposal. Zandec has already purchased options to mine any minerals they discover at a fixed price (a percentage of the three month rolling average price of the mineral on three commodities indices). No new negotiation on that score is necessary. The president of Zandec was only too happy to strike a deal (any deal) so long as he got hard currency. (Rumor has it that the money is resting in a numbered Swiss bank account.) In today's market it was a very good deal for Zandec. The negotiators were empowered to go up to 50 percent higher than they did.

Your development team was not in accord about how to proceed with operations in Nubia. There were three options defended.

Option One. Nubia is a land-locked country. Therefore, the most efficient procedure would be to mine and slurry at the proposed site. Two exit routes from the country should be considered in case the exit route from one direction is closed due to war or other civil insurrection. This will mean either aiding in the repair of rail lines or improving existing roadways for truck shipping.

Local people would be hired to mine. A village could be established near the mine with a school and hospital. Meals would be served at noon, and wages kept low so that order might be maintained. After all, the workers will have free food, shelter, medical care and schooling. What do they need money for? It will only get them into trouble.

Option Two. I propose to mine, refine and create finished steel in Nubia. We own a steel mill in Germany which would be used in option one. What I want to do is to create another mill in Nubia. The costs of production would be those shown in the table on the top of page 576.

As you can see—even with the costs of the new mill—which would be depreciated over twenty years—it makes economic sense to run our entire production out of Nubia.

What other advantages are there? Well, for one, we would be helping the Nubian economy more. This makes for a stable Nubia and a stable Nubia is good for Zandec. Second, we would require more manpower and could integrate Nubians into our operations at more levels. This is especially important because instead of selling our steel in the European marketplace as Option One envisions, we would be selling in the African marketplace. Thus it would be necessary to have African executives in our operation.

This also makes sense to me because it involves our company more fully into the Nubian economy. If another government should emerge, we

A Comparison of Options One and Two

[Per unit costs]

	Option One	Option Two
Mining	$1.00	$1.00
Shipping	$0.25	$0.00
Refining/steel production	$0.55	$0.25
Capital depreciation	$0.00	$0.25
Total cost of finished steel	$1.80	$1.50
Fulfillment	$0.30	$0.65
Administration/Sales	$0.11	$0.02
Total cost of sales	$2.21	$2.17
Regional market price	$4.95	$5.25
Adjusted market price*	$4.95	$4.93
Net Profit per unit	$2.74	$2.76

*Adjustments for unstable currency and market conditions

would be in a much sounder position if we have woven ourselves into the fabric of the country than we would if we were always perceived as a foreign entity which only took and never gave.

Option Three. This is similar to option two except I would like to go one step further. I would like to convince a partner to join us in our Nubian venture. This partner would take our finished steel and make durable goods. This would lower our costs of fulfillment and make us more profitable. Further, it would go one more step toward making Nubia a developing economy.

The Issues. The proponent for option one believes that options two and three are too risky. After all, this is a developing nation. "We are not risking our own money, you know. This money belongs to stockholders. It is their pensions and futures we are playing with. The only conservative move is to minimize our downside as much as possible. If AIDS or a coup d'etat were to rock the country significantly, we could be sitting on a big financial loss. Those little figures you show, only work if the operation lasts twenty years. You cannot make that assumption in Nubia."

The proponents for options two and three repeated their basic argument adding further, "It isn't right to come into a country and only use what you want and then run away. If that country has something that we want, then we must be prepared to enter into a long term, mutually beneficial relationship with them. Any other approach is simply wrong."

You have some of the arguments before you. Prepare your report to the Board keeping in mind the practical and moral dimensions. Recommend one of the three options.

Case 4.2—*The Bounty Seed Company*

The Bounty Seed Company Ltd. is headquartered in London, UK. You have been assigned as Chief Operations Officer of the Bounty Seed Company division in India. You are now confronted with a serious problem. You must write a report immediately in response to a home office memo you received this morning demanding an explanation and course of action vis-a-vis your foray into hybrid seeds.

The Problem.

A. Why hybrid seeds? Seed companies cannot copyright seeds unless they are new. Old, traditional seeds are in the "public domain." Thus, if a seed company wants to retain control of its product, it must create hybrid seeds.

   Hybrid seeds seek to solve particular problems resident in traditional sub-species. For example, susceptibility to insects, yield, color and robustness can all be improved through the hybrid process.

   Hybrid seeds can thus "out perform" traditional seeds.

B. In India (a largely vegetarian country), grain harvests are important. Hybrid seeds can markedly improve productivity. This can aid an important part of the diet and lessen starvation and improve the quality of life.

C. Hybrid seeds are created from traditional seeds. The traditional seeds are ancient. They are as diverse as the regions themselves. Hybrid seeds will standardize (to some extent) the genetic grain populations.

Critics Note.

1. A standardized genetic population is less evolutionary fit than a more diverse genetic population. Thus, hybrid seeds may be setting up the Indian grain "gene pool" for disaster. This would occur if there were a change in environment (due, for example, to global warming or to trace levels of some chemical in the air) which the new standardized genetic population could not handle. When there was diversity in the population, changes in environment would merely alter the numbers of some genetic combinations over others. The species, as a whole, would have a much better chance of survival.

2. There is something that smacks of exploitation in the process of hybridization. A foreign company comes in and takes ancient Indian genetic material that has come down from thousands of years of Indian farmers. This genetic material is recombined into a new amalgam and sold back to the same farmers. It is copyrighted and now belongs to the company. Thus, the company has appropriated genetic material that goes deep into India's past and makes a profit from it.

   If the original genetic material was owned by the Indian people, then perhaps a royalty should be paid to the farmers who had nurtured the genetic heritage.

3. The new hybrids are threatening to put local Indian seed companies out of business. This means Bounty Ltd. is put in the position of appearing to hurt the economy even as it is helping it. If the net result is that more money is going out of the country than is entering, it makes Bounty Ltd. look like an extension of British Colonial India.

D. As a result of the critics noted above, there have been several instances of sabotage at Bounty's storehouses. If these continue, the cost of doing business in India could become too great. It is believed that Dharva Seeds is responsible for the violence. A local politician is sympathetic to Dharva. (It should be also noted that it appears that the local politician is a silent partner in a firm that owns 30% of Dharva's stock.)

E. The hybrid seed market in India is very lucrative. After being in business there for only four years, Bounty Ltd. has garnered a 35% market share and is the largest overseas affiliate with the parent company.

Possible Solutions. The following solutions have been offered to you by your staff. You can consider these and others in making your recommendations to the home office.

A. Expose the local politician and his stake in Dharva. This would make him unpopular and might stop the violence.

B. Enlist national help in added police and protection.

C. Bribe the local politician. The man is obviously dishonest. Pay him off and stop the violence.

D. Create a private security force and use lethal force (if necessary) to protect your property.

E. Buy the local seed companies and create a monopoly.

F. Hire more locals in leadership roles so that the company appears to be more of an "Indian" company.

G. Pull out and go home.

Keeping in mind these options and others, create an action plan which you can recommend to the home office in response to their memo.

Case 4.3—Integration, Separation, or Exclusion?

You work for a Dutch chemical company that has just built a plant in northeast Turkey. The plant is perfectly situated near sources of rare natural elements which you need to make fertilizers and pesticides. The plant is also perfectly positioned to serve the emerging agricultural demands of the Middle East.

The problem is this. You noticed during the construction of the facility that there was quite a bit of tension among three ethnic groups in the region: Turks, Arabs, and Kurds. None likes the others. There were several deaths during construction which were alleged to have been caused by this enmity.

You do not want to have an operation that is constantly being slowed down (and/or sabotaged) because your labor force cannot work as a team.

You call together your management group and three solutions are put forth.

Solution One. Work at integrating the labor force in a way that they are not integrated in society. The theory here is that most people hate each other only because they don't know each other as individual people. They are merely known as being of a particular group. Those groups are given "group characteristics" and thus the enemy is seen as a monolithic, impersonal entity.

By putting your employees into intimate work relations they will recognize the humanity of their neighbors. Through careful pre-employment training, you can set the ground rules and a tone of cooperation that might make your company—not only profitable—but a positive force for social change.

Solution Two. Solution one is too idealistic. Do you really think that one company is really going to change attitudes that have existed for a thousand years in a one- or two-day training session? What do you propose—that they all hug each other? If they do that, someone is going to stick a knife in the other's back.

We have to deal with reality as it is, not a reality which we all might wish for. That reality says that these groups hate each other. There are deep historical reasons for these feuds. We have to accept that they exist and do our best to separate each ethnic type. Never let them interact with each other. Let them all have separate toilets and eating facilities. Stagger the working hours so that they don't even see each other coming or going. No favoritism must be shown to any group. We will have to market this hard. All treated equal.

It will only be by a program of comprehensive segregation that we can avoid the jealousy of one group against the other and the ensuing labor strife that this would cause.

Solution Three. I agree with "two" that there is nothing we can do about this social enmity. What I disagree about is the way to handle it. There is no way to keep the groups separate. If they work in one facility they will always be fighting. No matter what we try to do to prevent it, discord will occur. Therefore, we must select one group of people and hire only them. The obvious choice would be the Turks. After all, it is their country. The central government could help us with soldiers to make a show of force in case the Arabs or Kurds try any 'funny business.'

We can import workers, if necessary, from other parts of the country. This would have the social effect of making the region more homogeneous and perhaps more peaceful for the Turks. We end up as heroes on two fronts: a. Our plant runs efficiently because we only have one ethnic group working there; and b. The region becomes calmer because the Arabs and Kurds will be driven back into Iraq.

You take the opinions of your management team into account and then think about whether there are any other possibilities. Finally, you must write your report to company headquarters justifying the decision you have made.

Case 4.4—I.U.D. and Third World Markets

Your company specializes in creating modifications of existing products and then selling them to the same markets at lower costs. The product you have modified is an inter-uterine device that resembles the ill fated Dalcon Shield. You believe that you have solved the difficulties that faced the Dalcon Shield. The U.S. market is impossible for this product since the bad publicity over the Dalcon Shield makes inter-uterine birth control sales very speculative and full of legal liability.

But the Third World markets are a different story. The number one problem in developing countries is overpopulation. Birth control is difficult in many areas because pills are too expensive and require a type of habitual use that is not culturally ingrained. Besides, resupply is a continual problem. Condoms are not in full supply and make women dependent upon the man's careful and responsible use. The i.u.d. is an obvious answer to these problems.

It can be inserted once and need not be reinserted or checked for months at a time. This is a perfect solution for areas that have limited access to doctors. i.u.d.s are inexpensive and seem to fit the needs of developing countries.

The problem is that some people are contending that your product does not protect its users from pelvic inflammatory disease. This infection can cause the user to become sterile. It is generally not life threatening.

Now in the United States or European markets this charge would be a problem. You would have to go through extensive and expensive tests to verify the safety of your product. The time and expense of these tests would make your product too expensive to sell.

In the Third World there is not a clamoring for tests. The U.N. World Health Organization has decided to let each country decide whether it wants to import the i.u.d.s.

The question is whether you should go ahead with the product. You must make the decision. Within your organization there are two camps.

Con. We should not go forward with this product. Just because the governments of developing nations put birth control—at any price—above individual safety, does not mean we should. There is a real question whether our product is safe. Until we know for sure, we cannot put women around the world at risk.

I say test the product or if that is too expensive, then we should move on to another line. You know that we wouldn't even be having this conversation if it were a developed country we were talking about. You cannot have two standards for your products. Humans are humans. And no matter where they live they deserve the respect of being sold safe and effective goods.

Pro. Might I remind you that we have sunk considerable money into this product already. The prototype was not cheap. We cannot be so facile about canceling a product which is set for mass manufacturing and world wide marketing.

You say that the product may be unsafe. Well, you will never satisfy everyone. We seem to be able to satisfy the leaders of the countries we are approaching. We have written agreements which will allow us to sell them our birth control device. The price is set. We cannot raise it for two years (which added tests would require us to do).

Further, safety is my concern, too. Even in the worst case scenario we are only talking about three or four women per hundred who *might* contract pelvic inflammatory disease. And what will happen to them if they do? They will become sterile. Is that so bad in countries in which food is so scarce? It might be a favor to many women.

Then think of the alternative: more and more babies. The food supply cannot keep pace. What would you prefer—many children starving to death or a few sterile women?

We live in an imperfect world. I wish there were a risk-free way to combat this thing. There isn't. But we have a chance to make money and help solve a global problem at the same time. I say we market it.

The ultimate decision is yours. Justify your decision making reference to practical and ethical concerns.

icro Cases

Case 4.5—Filing Taxes in a Foreign Country

You are an American accountant who works for CHIPS, an American software company. You work in the newly opened French office in Paris. Your company has been making inroads into the previously protected French software market. Your company is doing quite well. During its first ten months of operations it has already garnered 11% market share and keeps climbing.

The problem is this. Phyllis Sims, a VP and your boss, has told you to prepare the company's French tax return according to "French" standards. This means underreporting earnings by 15%. "They expect it," she says. "That is why they make their rates as high as they do."

"But I have not been trained to underreport earnings," you say. "It's my name that goes at the bottom of the tax form as 'preparer.'"

"Don't worry. Nothing is going to happen. And even if it did, the company would stand by you."

"I don't know. I'm having some trouble with this."

"What's the trouble? You want to send in an 'American-style' return which you see as entirely factually correct. Well, we have our little 'tricks,' too. These may seem a bit shady to people from other countries. Professional standards are relative to the professional climate in which one is practicing. This is France. You have to abide by their standards. Check up on this if you don't believe me.

"At any rate, I want a draft of our returns on my desk in ten days."

You know a couple French accountants and are able to verify that what your boss has told you is essentially correct. Still, it bothers you to file what you consider to be a false return. Sitting on the metro, as you travel home to your apartment, you jot a few notes down on a piece of paper.

Options:

1. Follow the French way and do just what your boss says.
2. Ask your boss to put her request to you in writing so that you can pro-tect yourself should you need to. (Though she probably wouldn't do it.)
3. Prepare the return the French way, but indicate enough in your notes to protect yourself.
4. Take the matter over the head of your boss to the home office.
5. Request a transfer back to the United States. (But that may damage your career.)
6. Quit.

There may be other options. In the morning you promise yourself that you will make a decision about what to do. You will set your thoughts down in writing weighing the practical and ethical considerations.

Case 4.6—"Babes" in Thailand

You are the Director of Human Resources (personnel manager) at an American Bank with a branch in Bangkok, Thailand. It is your job to hire lower level jobs and maintain personnel policies.

The company has given you considerable latitude in framing employee work rules that you feel are proper for your Thailand operation. (Anything too outrageous, of course, would have to be cleared with your bosses.)

You have hired both men and women tellers and loan officers. Herein lies the problem. The traditional Thai culture is predominantly male controlled. Women have a low place in society. They are treated as objects that exist merely for the pleasure of men.

You have noticed this attitude in the workplace. Sexual harassment is rampant. The women are called "babes"—and that's the best of the offensive appellations used. Inappropriate touching and degrading attitudes abound.

Something has to be done. You bring up your concerns to your boss, Martin Boardman. He tells you that you cannot change an entire culture. This is the way of the world, he says. Besides, the women in the office don't seem to mind. He hasn't seen any of them complaining. Some even giggle when they are tapped on the buttocks or "brushed against." Perhaps, he suggests, you are the only one who has a problem with all of this. Perhaps it is merely your Americanized attitudes that are offended.

But, after all, they have hired *you* to be in charge of these things. If you don't like the way the men are acting toward the women, then Mr. Boardman suggests firing all the women. Then there would be no problem.

In any event, Mr. Boardman wants a report outlining your solution to the problem on his desk Monday morning.

Women are oppressed in Thailand. Female babies are considered to be virtually worthless except as they can be sold into prostitution at ages as young as nine or ten. The prostitution industry is so large in Thailand that it is the single largest employer of women in the country. Here women work for men in a kind of slavery in which they make their "masters" rich while they earn next to nothing.

If you fired the women in your bank as a solution to your problem, then you could be relegating them to such a life. You could not do this.

If you fired all the men in your bank, then you might hurt the bank's position. In this society it is probable that customers would not trust a bank staffed only with women. If the bank's revenues fall and they close the branch, then the same net effect occurs with the women employees put onto the street.

A third alternative would be to institute rigid work rules which you enforce. This will ensure a more fair work environment. The question is whether the male employees will accept it. If they don't, then they might: (a) quit, (b) engage in a work slowdown which will hurt the bank, (c) mutiny and challenge your authority.

Situations (a) and (b) would clearly hurt the bank. Your actions could be tied to them and it could hurt your career. Situation (c) would force a showdown. You are not confident that Mr. Boardman would back you in a power struggle. You could lose your job.

A fourth possibility would be to do nothing. Maybe you are just over sensitive to women's rights because you are an American. You don't think so, but perhaps you could try watching passively. If it got too bad, you could transfer home. But that, also, would be a bad career move.

You feel lost. You decide to put it down until tomorrow. Then you will write your report and place it on Mr. Boardman's desk—ahead of schedule.

Case 4.7—Living Among the Dying in Bangladesh

You are an American engineer for the World Bank living for two years in Bangladesh while you supervise the building of a dam that is largely being financed by money supplied by the World Bank.

You are paid a good salary that in the United States would make you upper middle class in Washington, D.C., where you normally live. But in Bangladesh you live in luxury. The house you are renting is twice the size of your American house and you have a dozen servants. (In America you don't even employ a cleaning person.)

No one in the family has to shop for food or cook or clean the house. Everything is done by the servants. This makes you feel as if you were "to the manor born." Your children go to a school for foreigners and the whole social situation has a kind of "clubby" atmosphere.

You are of two minds about this. On the one hand it is very comfortable to have so many luxuries. It is a kind of fantasy fulfillment. You are living in a dream land. On the other hand the poverty about you is striking. People are continually starving to death. Even a bowl of rice regularly is the Bangladeshi's definition of middle class. This disparity between what *you* have and what *they* have disturbs you.

You try to tell yourself that you are in no way taking money away from these people. After all, you are there on a mission to help them. The new dam will do much to control the flooding in the delta region that often kills thousands. The money that is paying your salary is not being paid by the government but from the World Bank. Their money comes from its member nations, the large industrial countries of the world. Thus, you tell yourself, your relative affluence is a separate event from these people's poverty.

You tell yourself this, but still, something jars you about the relative disparity.

One day a child of one of your servants comes by for his mother. You notice that the child is very thin and looks hungry so you offer the child some bread to eat. The child takes the bread and goes home.

The next day when your servant is about to leave her whole family meets her at the gate. This comprises a husband, the husband's father and brother and four children. They all carry empty bowls. The look in their faces shows that they want something to eat. You give them some soup and a loaf of bread. It isn't much, you say to yourself. Besides, you want to be able to do what you can.

The next day at the same time there is a crowd of nearly one hundred people at your gate. They are all carrying bowls. "They are my clan," says your servant. "But I don't have enough food for them all. You work in my kitchen. You should know that."

"They are my clan," she repeats.

"I don't mind feeding your child, or even your family," you say. "But I'm not equipped to feed your clan."

"They are my clan," she replies.

"Wait here," you say. Then you go into the house. You call a friend of yours and go through the situation.

"Your first mistake was to give food to the child," was your friend's reply.

"I couldn't just let him go hungry."

"Well, you now see the consequence of your actions. They will become angry if you don't feed them and could attack your family. You can't feed only some or they will fight among themselves. You can't feed all of them or you'll have a thousand on your doorstep tomorrow. I'm afraid the only thing to do is to fire the servant and call for the police. If they see you aren't afraid to knock their skulls in, then they will leave you alone."

"But I'm not a 'knock-their-skulls-in' kind of person."

"It's them or you. What's it going to be?"

You get off the phone. You look out the window. When you were in the United States you didn't have to look at this. You could sit back in your chair and read a good book and nobody would bother you. But now there seems to be no escape.

You are not keen on your friend's suggestion, but what are the alternatives? Write out a list of possible courses of action and detail the practical and ethical implications of each. Then choose one of those action plans and develop it more fully.

Case 4.8—Juan Gonzales and the Blue Water

You are a floor supervisor in a textile mill run in Chile. Your company owns several mills of this type around the world. Each is part of a distribution network that is regionally based. This strategy is to protect the corporation from the effects of local politics or regional conflicts. Your distribution network comprises two mills in Chile and an assembly plant in Honduras. Your mill produces cloth that will go into "look alike" custom clothes that are sold in the United States and Europe. The cloth is "assembled" in Honduras and then shipped to New York, London, Paris and Rome.

You have a problem with one of your workers, Juan Gonzales. Juan runs one of your large carding machines. These machines are important in the production process. When they are mismanaged or are broken, the whole assembly process stops. And the only way to be profitable is for the machines to keep working.

Juan has not been doing the kind of job on his machine that you know he can do. You decide to have a talk with Juan about it. Juan tells you that his boy had been playing near the mill over the weekend and noticed that the runoff tanks overflowed. It had been raining the day before. So on Monday after the rain he went again and he saw the same result. The blue water ran into the stream which is the town's water supply. The water was blue in color because of the dyes and chemicals used in the plant and even Juan's child knew that people should not be drinking blue water.

"But the water isn't blue by the time it gets to the village," you say. "All the color goes away."

"But do the bad things inside the water go away? We have the runoff tank for a reason. That reason is that the blue water is poison."

"And that's the reason you've been doing so poorly at your job?"

"My mind is on that blue water. I get to thinking that I may be poisoning the people of my village."

"You do too much thinking, Juan," you say. "Go back to your machine."

"Will you look into the blue water?"

You nod your head. At the next rain you have your dye chemist take samples of water at two points along the stream and then in the well water in town. His findings support Juan Gonzales' point. The water contains high levels of toxic chemicals.

This puts you in a difficult position. First, you know that a serious problem exists. Second, your boss is so "production" minded that he will not be sympathetic to shutting down the plant to make the necessary repairs (not to mention the added cost involved). Third, the government has given you carte blanche to operate as you have to. There are no legal regulations that you are violating. The government wants people to be employed not unemployed. People with jobs do not start revolutions.

So, you ask yourself, what's the problem?

1. I'm completely within the law.
2. If I make a big deal about this, I'll probably lose my job and nothing will happen anyway;
3. Even the home office probably doesn't care about this.

But then there is Juan Gonzales. He knows. The chemist knows. And you are responsible for morale among your workers. You are the floor manager.

What do you do? Do you fire Juan Gonzales for poor work? Do you get the chemist transferred? Do you try to address the pollution problem? If so, how? If not, then how do you contain the problem?

For your own peace of mind set out an action plan addressing the practical and ethical issues involved.

COPYRIGHTS AND ACKNOWLEDGEMENTS

The author is indebted to the following for permission to reprint from copyrighted material:

Oxford University Press. For the excerpts from *Nicomachean Ethics* by Aristotle, translated by W. D. Ross. Copyright © 1925 by Oxford University Press. Reprinted by permission of publisher.

A. C. Pegis Estate. For the excerpts from *Summa Theologica* by St. Thomas Aquinas, translated by Anton Pegis. Reprinted by permission of estate.

University of Notre Dame Press. For the excerpts from *After Virtue* by Alasdair MacIntyre. Copyright © 1984 (second edition) by University of Notre Dame Press. Used by permission of publisher.

Foundation for the School of Business at Indiana University. For "A Different Look at Codes of Ethics" by Robin, Giallourakis, David, and Moritz. Reprinted from *Business Horizons,* January/February 1989. Copyright © 1989 by the Foundation for the School of Business at Indiana University. Used with permission.

Oxford University Press. For the excerpts from *The Right and the Good* by W. D. Ross. Copyright © 1930 by Oxford University Press. Reprinted by permission of publisher.

President and Fellows of Harvard College. Reprinted by permission of Harvard Business Review. "Is Business Bluffing Legal?" by Albert Z. Carr, (January/February 1968). Copyright © 1967 by the President and Fellows of Harvard College; all rights reserved.

Blackwell Publishers. For "The Interpretation of the Moral Philosophy of J. S. Mill" by J. O. Urmson. Reprinted from *Philosophical Quarterly,* volume 3. Copyright © 1953 by Blackwell Publishers. Used with permission.

Blackwell Publishers. For "Extreme and Restricted Utilitarianism" by J. J. C. Smart. Reprinted from *Philosophical Quarterly,* volume 6. Copyright © 1956 by Blackwell Publishers. Used with permission.

Random Century Group. For the excerpt from *Groundwork for the Metaphysics of Mortals* by Immanuel Kant. Translated by H. J. Paton and published by Hutchinson Publishers. Reprinted by permission of the author's estate and Random Century Group, 20 Vauxhall Bridge Road, London.

The University of Chicago Press. For the excerpts from *Reason and Morality* by Alan Gewirth. Copyright © 1978 by the University of Chicago Press. Reprinted by permission of publisher and author.

Pastin and Hooker, "Ethics and the Foreign Corrupt Practices Act." Reprinted from *Business Horizons,* December 1980. Copyright © 1980 by the Foundation for the School of Business at Indiana University. Used with permission.

Robert E. Frederick. For "Bribery and Ethics: A Reply to Pastin and Hooker" from *Business Ethics,* Second Edition. Reprinted by permission of the author.

Kluwer Academic Publishers. For "Foreign Corrupt Practices Act: A Legal and Moral Analysis" by William Shaw. Reprinted from *Journal of Business Ethics,* volume 7. Copyright © 1988 Kluwer Academic Publishers. Reprinted by permission of publisher.

Kluwer Academic Publishers. For "An Empirical Investigation of International Marketing Ethics: Problems Encountered by Australian Firms" by Robert W. Armstrong. Reprinted from *Journal of Business Ethics,* volume 11. Copyright © 1992 Kluwer Academic Publishers. Reprinted by permission of publisher.

Oxford University Press. For the excerpts from *The Ethics of International Business* by Thomas Donaldson. Copyright © 1989 by Oxford University Press. Reprinted by permission of publisher.

Kluwer Academic Publishers. For "Global Distributive Justice and the Corporate Duty to Aid" by Kevin T. Jackson. Reprinted from *Journal of Business Ethics,* volume 12. Copyright © 1993 Kluwer Academic Publishers. Reprinted by permission of publisher.

Kluwer Academic Publishers. For "Ethics and the Gender Equality Dilemma for U.S. Multinationals" by M. S. Singer and A. E. Singer. Reprinted from *Journal of Business Ethics,* volume 12. Copyright © 1993 Kluwer Academic Publishers. Reprinted by permission of publisher.

University Press of America. For "Ethical Dilemmas for Multinational Enterprise: A Philosophical Overview" by Richard T. De George from *Ethics and the Multinational Enterprise,* eds. Hoffman, Lange, and Fedo. Copyright © 1986 University Press of America. Reprinted by permission.

Healthcare Financial Management Association. For "Alternatives to Federal Regulatory Realignment of Health Care" by Christopher J. Kalkhof. Reprinted with permission from the January 1994 issue of *Healthcare Financial Management.* Copyright © 1994 Healthcare Financial Management Association.

The Hastings Center. For "The Oregon Priority-Setting Exercise" by David C. Hadorn. Copyright © 1991 The Hastings Center. Reprinted by permission.

The Hastings Center. For "Oregon's Denial" by Paul T. Menzel. Copyright © 1992 The Hastings Center. Reprinted by permission.

Thomas Donaldson. For "The Perils of Corporate Largess: A Reply to Professor Jackson." Copyright © 1994 Thomas Donaldson. Reprinted by permission of the author.

DATE DUE

DEMCO 38-297